UNEQUAL CHANCES
Ethnic Minorities in Western Labour Markets

PROCEEDINGS OF THE BRITISH ACADEMY · 137

UNEQUAL CHANCES
Ethnic Minorities in Western Labour Markets

Edited by
ANTHONY F. HEATH & SIN YI CHEUNG
with
SHAWNA N. SMITH

Published for THE BRITISH ACADEMY
by OXFORD UNIVERSITY PRESS

Oxford University Press, Great Clarendon Street, Oxford OX2 6DP

Oxford New York
Auckland Cape Town Dar es Salaam Hong Kong Karachi
Kuala Lumpur Madrid Melbourne Mexico City Nairobi
New Delhi Shanghai Taipei Toronto

With offices in
Argentina Austria Brazil Chile Czech Republic France Greece
Guatemala Hungary Italy Japan Poland Portugal Singapore
South Korea Switzerland Thailand Turkey Ukraine Vietnam

Published in the United States
by Oxford University Press Inc., New York

© The British Academy 2007
Database right The British Academy (maker)

First published 2007

All rights reserved. No part of this publication may be reproduced,
stored in a retrieval system, or transmitted, in any form or by any means,
without the prior permission in writing of the British Academy,
or as expressly permitted by law, or under terms agreed with the appropriate
reprographics rights organization. Enquiries concerning reproduction
outside the scope of the above should be sent to the Publications Department,
The British Academy, 10 Carlton House Terrace, London SW1Y 5AH

You must not circulate this book in any other binding or cover
and you must impose this same condition on any acquirer

British Library Cataloguing in Publication Data
Data available

Library of Congress Cataloging in Publication Data
Data available

Typeset by J&L Composition, Filey, North Yorkshire
Printed in Great Britain
on acid-free paper by
The Cromwell Press Limited
Trowbridge, Wilts

ISBN 978–0–19–726386–0

ISSN 0068–1202

Contents

Notes on Contributors	vii
Preface	xv

1. The Comparative Study of Ethnic Minority Disadvantage   1
   ANTHONY HEATH & SIN YI CHEUNG

2. Diversity and Mobility in Australia   45
   CHRISTINE INGLIS & SUZANNE MODEL

3. Continuing Ethnic Segmentation in Austria   103
   IRENA KOGAN

4. Down and Out: The Children of Migrant Workers in the Belgian Labour Market   143
   KAREN PHALET

5. Inclusion for all but Aboriginals in Canada   181
   SOOJIN YU & ANTHONY HEATH

6. Is French Society Truly Assimilative? Immigrant Parents and Offspring on the French Labour Market   221
   ROXANE SILBERMAN & IRENE FOURNIER

7. Educational Hurdles on the Way to Structural Assimilation in Germany   271
   FRANK KALTER & NADIA GRANATO

8. Instant Absorption of Immigrants and Persistent Exclusion of Arab Citizens in Israel   321
   YOSSI SHAVIT, NOAH LEWIN-EPSTEIN & IRIT ADLER

9. Equal Opportunities or Social Closure in the Netherlands?   359
   PAUL TESSER & JAAP DRONKERS

10. The Legacy of *Apartheid*: Racial Inequalities in the New South Africa   403
    DONALD J. TREIMAN

11. The Farther They Come, the Harder They Fall? First- and Second-Generation Immigrants in the Swedish Labour Market — 451
    JAN O. JONSSON

12. Nice Work if You can Get it: Ethnic Penalties in Great Britain — 507
    SIN YI CHEUNG & ANTHONY HEATH

13. Progress in Reducing Catholic Disadvantage in Northern Ireland — 551
    YAOJUN LI & RICHARD O'LEARY

14. The New Second Generation at the Turn of the New Century: Europeans and non-Europeans in the US labour market — 591
    SUZANNE MODEL & GENE A. FISHER

15. Crossnational Patterns and Processes of Ethnic Disadvantage — 639
    ANTHONY HEATH

Author Index — 697
Subject Index — 703

Notes on Contributors

Irit Adler received her Ph.D. in Sociology from Tel-Aviv University in 2004. She is a researcher in B. I. and Lucille Cohen Institute for Public Opinion Research in Tel Aviv University, and currently teaches at Tel-Aviv University and the Tel-Aviv-Yaffo Academic College. Her main areas of interest are social stratification and housing inequality. Her recent publications include a chapter on inequality in home ownership in Israel, co-authored with Noah Lewin-Epstein and Moshe Semyonov, in *Home Ownership and Social Inequality in Comparative Perspective* (edited by Karin Kurz and Hans-Peter Blossfeld, 2004) and a paper on social inequality and place of residence, co-authored with Noah Lewin-Epstein and Yossi Shavit, in *Research in Stratification and Social Mobility* (2005).

Sin Yi Cheung is Senior Lecturer at the Department of Sociology, University of Birmingham. Previously she was a Principal Lecturer teaching sociology at Oxford Brookes University since obtaining her D.Phil. at St Antony's College, Oxford in 1998. Her research interests are sociology of education, work and employment and ethnic minorities. Recently she has completed a research project (with Anthony Heath) commissioned by the Department for Work and Pensions on ethnic penalties and employment sector in Britain. Her current work includes a study on the changing inequalities in higher education in Britain. She continues her research in horizontal stratification in education and ethnic minorities in the labour market. She has also published in areas of women and work and on socially disadvantaged groups such as lone parents and children in care.

Jaap Dronkers is Professor of Social Stratification and Inequality at the European University Institute in San Domenico di Fiesole, Italy. He has published extensively on the causes and consequences of unequal educational and occupational attainment, on changes in educational opportunities, on differences between public and religious schools, the education of elites, the relations between school and the labour market, the causes and consequences of growth of educational participation and on the effect of parental divorce on their children. Recent examples of his non-Dutch articles are: 'Do Public and Religious Schools Really Differ? Assessing the European Evidence' in *Educating Citizens. International Perspectives on Civic Values and School Choice* (edited by P. J. Wolf and S. Macedo, 2004); 'Recruitment of members of Dutch noble and high-bourgeois families to elite positions in the 20th century', *Social Science Information* (2004) (with H. Schijf and J van den Broeke-George); 'Family Policies and Children's School Achievement in Single- Versus Two-Parent Families', *Journal of Marriage and Family* (2003) (with S.-I. Pong and G. Hampden-Thompson).

Gene Fisher is Professor Emeritus of Sociology at the University of Massachusetts, Amherst. His chief interests are statistics and quantitative methods. His most recent publication, co-authored with Anthony Harris, Stephen Thomas and David Hirsch, is 'Murder and medicine: the lethality of criminal assault 1960–1999', *Homicide Studies* (2002). He is also working with Gordon Sutton on estimating Hispanic under-representation in federal jury selection.

Irène Fournier entered the CNRS (National Center for Scientific Research) in 1967 as a research assistant and joined the LASMAS (Laboratoire d'analyse secondaire et de méthodes appliquées à la sociologie) in 1986 where she was in charge of the Public Statistics Data Sets Archives for Social Sciences. Her main interest is in statistics for social sciences and she has worked in the fields of education, labour employment and immigration. She has published in the latter field with Roxane Silberman including 'Les secondes générations sur le marché du travail en France: une pénalité qui persiste. Contribution à la discussion sur l'assimilation segmentée', *Revue Française de Sociologie* (2006).

Nadia Granato works at the Institute for Employment Research (IAB) of the German Federal Employment Agency. She studied Sociology at the University of Mannheim and received her doctorate from the University of Giessen, where she wrote a dissertation on ethnic inequality in the labour market. Her current work addresses labour market participation and unemployment with a special emphasis on regional aspects. Her publications include *Ethnische Ungleichheit auf dem deutschen Arbeitsmarkt* (2003), 'Demographic Change, Educational Expansion, and Structural Assimilation of Immigrants: The case of Germany' (with Frank Kalter), *European Sociological Review* (2002), and 'Die Persistenz ethnischer Ungleichheit auf dem deutschen

Arbeitsmarkt' (with Frank Kalter), *Kölner Zeitschrift für Soziologie und Sozialpsychologie* (2001).

Anthony Heath is Professor of Sociology at the University of Oxford, a Fellow of Nuffield College and co-director of CREST (the Centre for Research into Elections and Social Trends). He was elected a Fellow of the British Academy in 1992. His main research interests are social stratification, political sociology and ethnicity. His recent publications include *Understanding Social Change* (edited with Duncan Gallie and John Ermisch, 2005) and *The Rise of New Labour* (with Roger Jowell and John Curtice, 2001). He contributed to the recent Cabinet Office report on ethnic minority disadvantage in Britain and, with Sin Yi Cheung, to a report for the Department for Work and Pensions on ethnic penalties in the labour market.

Christine Inglis is Director of the Multicultural and Migration Research Centre at the University of Sydney. She has a long-standing interest in issues of migration and settlement in Australia and internationally, especially Asian migration and on the relationship between research and policy. Current research projects focus on the transnational experiences of Turkish, Hong Kong and Chinese in Australia; the role of middle-class and professional migrants, especially those from China and the United Kingdom, and education planning for diversity. Major publications include '*Making Something of Myself ...' Educational Attainment and Social and Economic Mobility of Turkish Young People in Australia*; *Asians in Australia: The Dynamics of Migration and Settlement*; *Teachers in the Sun: The Impact of Immigrant Teachers on the Labour Force*; and *Multiculturalism: New Policy Responses to Diversity* (1996).

Jan O. Jonsson is Professor of Sociology at the Swedish Institute for Social Research, Stockholm University. His research interests are social stratification, especially educational inequality and social mobility; sociology of the family; and life-course studies. He is director of the Swedish Level of Living Surveys and is also responsible for a series of surveys on the living conditions of 10–18 year-olds. His publications include *Can Education be Equalized?* (edited with Robert Erikson, 1996), *Cradle to Grave: Life Course Change in Modern Sweden* (edited with Colin Mills, 2001), and, with Richard Breen, 'Inequality of opportunity in comparative perspective: Recent research on educational attainment and social mobility', *Annual Review of Sociology* (2005).

Frank Kalter has been Professor for Sociology at the Institute for Sociology at the University of Leipzig, Germany, since 2004. He studied Sociology and Mathematics at the University of Cologne, and earned his doctorate as well as his habilitation at the University of Mannheim. His major research areas include rational choice theory, research methods, sociology of the family, as well as migration and integration of ethnic minorities. In the latter field he has, amongst others, published two books (both in German: *Wohnortwechsel in Deutschland*, 1997; *Chancen, Fouls und Abseitsfallen*, 2003) and several articles in sociological journals. Currently his research focus is on the empirical relevance of mechanisms impeding intergenerational structural assimilation, based on a general resource-theoretical perspective. He is also conducting a research project on the role of networks in Polish-German migration processes.

Irena Kogan is a senior research fellow at the Mannheim Centre for European Social Research (MZES), University of Mannheim. Born in the Ukraine, she received her MA in sociology from Tel-Aviv University (Israel) and her Ph.D. from the University of Mannheim (Germany). Her main research interests include immigration, social stratification and inequality in cross-national perspective. She is the author of a recent book *Working through barriers: Host country institutions and immigrant labour market performance in Europe* and a number of articles dealing with immigrant labour market integration in various journals including *European Sociological Review*, *Social Forces*, and *International Migration Review*.

Noah Lewin-Epstein is Professor of Sociology at Tel-Aviv University. He is past president of the Israeli Sociological Society (2000–3) and he currently serves at Tel-Aviv University. His areas of interest include social inequality, ethnic stratification, and comparative survey research. His recent journal publications address a variety of topics including social justice and the welfare state (in *Social Justice Research*); comparative integration of immigrants from the former Soviet Union in Canada and Israel (in *International Migration Review*); and welfare regimes and women's part time employment (in *American Journal of Sociology*). He is also co-editor with Moshe Semyonov of *Stratification in Israel: Class, Ethnicity and Gender* (2004).

Yaojun Li is Professor of Sociology at Manchester University, UK. His research interests are in social stratification, social capital and labour market situation of minority ethnic groups. Recent publications have appeared in *British Journal of Political Sciences*, *European Sociological Review*, *British Journal of Sociology*, *Sociology*, *Work, Employment and Society*, *Sociological Review*, *International Journal of Sociology* and *Sociological Research Online*. He also has various book chapters and consultation papers for the British government organisations. He has conducted several research projects funded by the ESRC and other organisations. He is on the Editorial Board of *Sociology* and the Advisory Board for the Joseph Rowntree Foundation. He is a reviewer for *American Journal of Sociology*, *American Sociological Review*, *Social Forces*, *Political Studies*, *British Journal of Sociology*, *European Sociological Review*, *Sociology*, *Sociological Review*, *Sociological Review Online* and *Health*. He is also a reviewer for British and Irish government research agencies.

Suzanne Model is Professor and Director of Undergraduate Studies in the Department of Sociology at the University of Massachusetts in Amherst. Most of her research entails cross-national comparisons of the socio-economic attainment of immigrants, particularly Black Caribbeans and Chinese. Her most recent publication is 'Nonwhite origins, Anglo destinations: immigrants in the USA and Britain', in *Ethnicity, Social Mobility, and Social Policy: Comparing the USA and the UK* (edited by Glenn Loury, Tariq Modood and Steven Teles, 2005).

Richard O'Leary is a lecturer in the School of Sociology, Queen's University, Belfast, Northern Ireland. He has published widely on comparative studies of minority–majority relations and intermarriage in journals such as the *European Sociological Review*, *Sociology*, and *British Journal of Sociology* and edited *Patterns and Processes of Religious Change in Modern Industrial Societies* (2004). He is currently researching religious change in China.

Karen Phalet is Professor at the Department of Psychology, University of Leuven. Her main interest is in comparative research on migration, ethnic minority disadvantage, discrimination and prejudice. She has published extensively on issues of immigrant integration, ethnic and religious identity, the second generation, and educational inequality in Europe. Recent publications have appeared in international journals such as *British Journal of Educational Psychology* (2005), *Journal of Ethnic and Migration Studies* (2004), *Studi Emigrazione* (2003), *Ethnicities* (2002), and *Journal of Comparative Family Studies* (2001). With Antal Orkeny she edited *Ethnic Minorities and Interethnic Relations in Context*

(2001) and she contributes regularly to international volumes such as the *Cambridge Handbook of Acculturation*. She is Associate Editor of the *Journal of Cross-Cultural Psychology*.

Yossi Shavit is Professor of Sociology at Tel Aviv University. His main areas of interest are social stratification and sociology of education. He has led several internationally comparative research projects on educational and occupational stratification including *Persistent Inequality* (with H.-P. Blossfeld, Westview Press, 1993), and *From School to Work* (with W. Müller, Clarendon Press, 1998). With Richard Arum and Adam Gamoran, and research teams in fifteen countries, he recently completed a comparative study on *Stratification in Higher Education: A Comparative Study* (Stanford University Press, 2007). In addition, he has studied processes of educational and occupational stratification in Israel, Italy and the United States. Yossi Shavit is a former secretary of the Research Committee on Stratification of the International Sociological Association (RC28). He chaired the Social and Political Science Department at the European University Institute in Florence, as well as the Sociology & Anthropology Department at Tel Aviv University. Currently, he heads the B. I. and Lucille Cohen Institute for Public Opinion Research at Tel Aviv.

Roxane Silberman is senior researcher at the CNRS (National Center for Scientific Research). She studied sociology at the Ecole Normale Supérieure in Paris and entered the CNRS in 1986. Recent publications on immigration focus on second generation attaintments and include 'Les secondes générations sur le marché du travail en France: une pénalité qui persiste. Contribution à la discussion sur l'assimilation segmentée', *Revue Française de Sociologie* (2006), co-authored with Irene Fournier, 'The immigration aftermath of decolonization: the case of second generation North Africans in France', *International Migration Review* (2002) and 'Segmented assimilation in France? Discrimination in the labor market against the second generation' in *Ethnic and Racial Studies*, both co-authored with Richard Alba. She also has played a major role in the founding of national Data Archives for data sets in France and is currently in charge of the National Data Committee for Human and Social Sciences.

Paul Tesser completed his doctoral thesis in 1986 on social factors in the school careers of pupils in secondary education. He then worked at the Institute for Applied Sociology at the University of Nijmegen. From 1992 to 2002 he was senior researcher at the Social and Cultural Planning

Bureau of the Dutch government and author of the annual report on ethnic minorities in the Netherlands. Since 2002 he has been senior adviser to the Dutch Minister of Immigration and Integration.

Donald J. Treiman is Distinguished Professor of Sociology at the University of California, Los Angeles and Director of the California Center for Population Research. His earlier work focused on cross-national comparisons of occupational prestige hierarchies, resulting in *Occupational Prestige in Comparative Perspective* (1977). He continues to focus on social inequality, but from an increasingly demographic perspective. For many years he has been engaged, with a Dutch colleague, Harry Ganzeboom, in a large-scale cross-national comparison of patterns in status attainment, which draws upon some 300 surveys conducted in nearly 50 nations throughout the twentieth century. He also has conducted national probability sample surveys in South Africa, six Eastern European nations, and China. Currently he is developing a new project on internal migration in China.

Soojin Yu is a senior policy research officer at the Department of Citizenship and Immigration in Canada. She is currently working on the reform of Canada's asylum system. She holds a doctorate degree in sociology from Oxford University, where she compared native-born ethnic groups' economic and socio-cultural integration patterns in Canada and Britain. Her research interests include ethnic groups, integration, international migration and cross-national comparison.

Preface

We must begin by expressing our great appreciation for the labours of our international colleagues who have contributed to this volume. As well as the great care and efforts that they have devoted to the individual country chapters and the great patience with which they have tolerated our shortcomings as editors, they have been a stimulating source of intellectual ideas and debate and we count ourselves fortunate to have made so many new friendships.

Our collaboration has been made possible by generous financial help that enabled us to arrange a series of meetings of the team to discuss the general strategy for the project and the initial drafts of the chapters. We are particularly indebted to the British Academy which funded a Symposium on ethnic minority disadvantage, and we also received substantial help from Oxford Brookes University and Nuffield College, Oxford. A further meeting was held in conjunction with Research Committee 28 of the ISA and we are very grateful to our colleagues in RC28 for their intellectual support. Shawna Smith, Colin Baldwin and Jane Greig were indispensable during the editorial process and made light of the mammoth task we gave them.

We are also very aware of the intellectual debt that we owe to Yossi Shavit and Hans-Peter Blossfeld whose path-breaking volume on *Persistent Inequality* was the inspiration for our own cross-national research and which has provided us with a model of how this kind of collaborative research should be carried out.

We are acutely aware of the limitations of our own research, but we hope that we have been able to contribute to debates about one of the major issues in contemporary western societies.

Oxford, January 2006
Anthony Heath
Sin Yi Cheung

1

The Comparative Study of Ethnic Minority Disadvantage

ANTHONY HEATH & SIN YI CHEUNG

Introduction

ETHNIC MINORITY DISADVANTAGE IN THE LABOUR market has been a matter of growing concern in many developed countries in recent years. There is substantial evidence of ethnic stratification, or a vertical mosaic as Porter (1965) memorably described Canada, with white groups from the charter populations[1] occupying the top of the hierarchy and visible minorities the bottom. With the increasing migration from less-developed to developed countries in recent decades, the ethnic mix of developed countries is set to grow considerably.

Insofar as this ethnic stratification is caused by discrimination, whether direct or indirect, then it is a source of major public concern. Discrimination on the basis of ascriptive factors, such as social origins or ethnicity, is generally regarded to be a source of economic inefficiency and waste. More importantly, it is a source of social injustice and, in the literal sense, of social exclusion. It provides a major challenge to normative principles of equality of opportunity that are espoused by virtually all developed countries. It may also be a source of social disorder and conflict. Accordingly ethnic inequalities have been the focus of many policy interventions and continue to be of great concern to governments.

Our focus in this volume is on ethnic inequalities in the labour market, particularly with respect to access to jobs. There are of course many other areas of inequality that could be investigated, such as

---

[1] By charter population we refer to the population that drew up the state's constitution or its equivalent. These are the politically dominant groups at the time of the modern state's foundation. In many cases these are of course quite different groups from the indigenous peoples who were incorporated by force into the modern state.

inequalities in education, housing, health or political influence but in order to keep our task manageable we focus on the labour market, which happens to have been one of the major areas of policy intervention. Our key question is whether ethnic minorities compete on equal terms in the labour market with equally qualified members of the charter populations. Have developed countries extended the principles of meritocracy and equality of opportunity to ethnic minorities, enabling them to gain access to advantaged positions within the social structure on the same terms as the politically dominant groups? Or are there processes of social closure, operating either through direct discrimination or legal restrictions as in the case of apartheid, or more subtly through social exclusion from the networks and social relations that are important for economic advancement, that subvert principles of meritocracy and might tend to perpetuate ethnic stratification?

The early evidence from the classical countries of immigration such as the USA, Canada and Australia suggested that, while the migrant generation experienced substantial disadvantages, in succeeding generations minorities gradually assimilated both socially and economically and were able to compete on equal terms with the charter population (Jones 1988; Card *et al.* 2000; Perlmann and Waldinger 1999). As Model and Fisher note in their chapter, the optimists anticipate that a similar process will occur for the newer migrant groups too. The pessimists, however, argue that this pattern of gradual assimilation across generations did not apply equally to all groups even in the earlier period but only really held for groups of European ancestry. African Americans in particular continued to be disadvantaged even after many generations in the USA (Lieberson 1980). Gradual assimilation, therefore, may well not apply to the new, non-European migrants or their descendants. Some pessimists point to the continuing prejudice and discrimination that members of the receiving countries exhibit towards 'visible' minorities and to the legacy of past discrimination; others point to the continuing cultural and social legacies that will be passed on to newer generations by their parents and which may tend to inhibit economic success.

To explore these questions we need to compare the experience of different generations. There has already been a great deal of work carried out on migrants, whom we term the 'first generation', documenting the often substantial disadvantages that they experience (see for example Reitz 1998; Hirschman *et al.* 1999; Van Tubergen 2006; Kesler 2006; Kogan 2007). However, migrants will often be at a disadvantage because the process of migration in itself tends to be disruptive. Immigrants' problems may also include lack of fluency in the language of the charter population, foreign educational credentials and foreign work experience. Their disadvantages in the labour market may not necessarily be indicative of inequality of opportunity but may reflect their lack of resources.[2] For both optimists and pessimists the key question is what happens to the second and succeeding generations who have acquired linguistic fluency, domestic qualifications and domestic work experience.

Much of the previous research on intergenerational differences has focused on the classical countries of immigration—Australia, Canada and the USA—which have been built by migrants from their modern foundation as states (albeit with important indigenous populations). The last decades of the twentieth century, however, have seen new waves of migration both to these classical countries of immigration and to many other developed countries, notably in Western Europe which shifted after the middle of the twentieth century from being immigrant-sending to immigrant-receiving countries. The majority of these migrants have been labour migrants, attracted by economic opportunities but taking up relatively low-paid jobs in the countries of destination. Others have been refugees fleeing persecution or civil war, while there have also been some highly skilled groups moving directly into professional or managerial posts.

The reasons for these recent migrations have many similarities with the earlier migrations from Europe to the new world but there have been important differences in the patterns of the sending and receiving countries (Castles and Miller 2003). Whereas Europe was a major origin of the earlier migrations, it is now an important destination and the countries of origin now tend to include many less-developed countries (in many but by no means all cases the former colonial dependencies of the great European empires). This raises important questions about whether the new migrants and their descendants will follow the same trajectories as the earlier migrants in the first half of the twentieth century and before.

---

[2] The notion of equality of opportunity is a notoriously slippery one. In the Western liberal tradition the notion of equality of opportunity initially referred to the absence of the legal barriers that prevented some groups, such as Catholics in eighteenth-century England, from obtaining government employment. Sociologists have often used the term more broadly to include the absence of *de facto* barriers as well as *de iure* barriers; for example the abolition of school fees for secondary education was seen as part of a programme of ensuring equality of educational opportunity for working-class children in Britain. Other sociologists use the term even more broadly to include any inequality of outcome. It seems to us more useful to retain the notion of some kind of external barrier. See for example Rawls (1972: 107) and the references cited there.

We might also expect there to be important differences between these immigrant-receiving countries in the fortunes of migrants and their descendants. There are major national differences in the 'warmth of the welcome' (to use Reitz's phrase). Countries vary in their governmental policies towards migrants and their descendants, in the attitudes of their publics towards visible minorities, and in their general levels of meritocracy.[3] It will be of considerable interest to see whether these national differences are reflected in any measurable differences in the degree of ethnic stratification that prevails.

In order to address these questions we have carried out standardised analyses using nationally representative samples, standardised coding of the variables, and standardised statistical models in a range of developed countries. In this respect we are modelling our work on the cross-national studies of Shavit and Blossfeld (1993) and of Shavit and Müller (1998) which have been landmarks of rigorous cross-national research. In addition to the classic immigration countries of Australia, Canada, Israel and the US, we cover the major new immigration countries of Western Europe—Austria, Belgium, France, Germany, the Netherlands, Sweden and the United Kingdom of Great Britain and Northern Ireland. We also include South Africa, originally a 'settler' society in many ways like Australia, Canada, and the USA, but also one whose system of apartheid marks it out as an extreme case of institutionalised ethnic disadvantage.

Generational differences

As we have suggested, there are a number of reasons why migrants may have difficulties in the labour markets of the developed countries to which they have emigrated. In particular they may be lacking the 'human capital' necessary for economic success in these markets. The simplest model of labour-market success, initially developed by economists such as Becker (1964) and Mincer (1974), postulates that an individual's human capital or skills (which are usually assumed to reflect their education and work experience) and not economically irrelevant ascribed characteristics

---

[3] Meritocracy is as slippery a concept as inequality of opportunity with varying usages in ordinary language and in technical sociology. We use it here in the most usual sociological sense of a system where occupational attainment depends on achieved criteria such as education and competence on the job rather than on the basis of ascribed characteristics such as race or social class origins. For a detailed discussion of the concept and its use in sociology see Goldthorpe (1996).

such as social class origins or ethnicity will determine economic success, since rational profit-maximising firms will pay each individual according to his or her marginal productivity. On this account it is irrational to discriminate against a member of an ethnic minority solely on the grounds of, say, the irrelevant criterion of skin colour, because that would imply hiring a white worker with lower productivity and hence failing to maximise profit. It follows that workers with equal human capital will, in a perfect market, have the same chances of being employed, and will receive the same wages, irrespective of their ethnicity.[4]

This very simple model suggests a number of reasons why immigrants might fare badly in the labour market and why their descendants, the second generation, might have more success. First of all, the first (immigrant) generation will often lack the kinds and levels of human capital that are relevant in the country of destination. Labour migrants from less-developed countries in particular will often have relatively low levels of education and other forms of human capital since they are typically coming from countries where educational provision is much more limited than in the destination countries. On this account alone, they would be expected to fill relatively low-level jobs on arrival. Secondly, migrants may lack fluency in the language of the destination country. Even if they are highly educated, lack of fluency will effectively reduce their potential productivity in many jobs where communication skills are important and may tend to restrict them to less-skilled manual labour (or to work with co-ethnics with whom there are no language barriers) (Carliner 2000; Chiswick 2002).

Additionally, the qualifications that migrants obtained in their countries of origin may not have the same value on the labour market in their country of destination. This may be because employers are unable to evaluate foreign qualifications and therefore prefer domestic qualifications with known relations to skill and productivity to foreign ones with unknown implications for productivity. Or it may be because of various restrictive practices or regulations, as in the case of many professions where foreign qualifications are not recognised and foreign professionals are simply not allowed to practice until they have acquired the appropriate

---

[4] A standard extension of this basic model allows for information difficulties, on the part of employers. Thus there may be what economists term 'statistical discrimination': employers may have found from experience that members of a particular ethnic group may have higher (or lower) productivity than other workers with similar qualifications. They therefore may come to use ethnicity as a signal for higher (or lower productivity) and hire accordingly. (See, for example, Arrow 1972.)

domestic qualifications. (This of course is a major departure from the assumption of a perfect market that underpins the standard economic theory.) In similar fashion foreign work experience may not be easily transferable to the destination labour market (Friedberg 2000).

We might generally expect these kinds of factors to lead migrants from less-developed countries, with their lack of educational provision and more rural economies that have perhaps less relevance to work in developed post-industrial economies, to have less favourable outcomes on the labour market. Hence we might expect on these grounds to find an ethnic hierarchy with the charter population at the top, migrants from developed countries coming next, and migrants from less-developed countries coming at the bottom.

The standard economists' model, then, suggests a number of reasons why the characteristics of many migrant groups might tend to lead them to fare badly in the labour market of the destination country. On these accounts, it is the migrants' lack of human capital, and the employers' difficulties in evaluating the human capital that they do have, which explains their lack of success. However, there may also be some counterbalancing assets that migrants have. Migration is a costly experience (both financially and psychologically), and hence migrants may be expected to be 'positively selected'. That is, they may have greater qualities of drive and ambition than would be normal among their compatriots with the same formal levels of qualification. Economists tend to assume that migrants who have come further will (other things being equal), be more positively selected. The extent to which such positive selection outweighs the disadvantages outlined above is impossible to ascertain a priori, but it raises the possibility that 'positive selection' might mask the disadvantages normally associated with migration.[5]

In addition to these elements of the standard economist's models, there are various social processes that have been suggested and that may hamper migrants. In particular sociologists such as Granovetter (1973) and Lin (1999) have drawn attention to networks as channels of information about job opportunities. Migrants may have limited social networks involving members of the charter population and may thus have

---

[5] Economists such as Borjas (1987) have also suggested that there may be 'negative selection' and in particular that migrants from relatively unequal societies will be negatively selected and will tend to be drawn from the less successful members of their society (since more successful ones in an unequal society will have less to gain by moving to a more equal society). While theoretically ingenious, there is little empirical support for this claim.

limited information about some job openings, particularly those where recruitment follows informal lines. To be sure they may have advantages in gaining access to co-ethnic networks and to employment in so-called ethnic enclaves, but these opportunities are unlikely to be as well paid as those in the dominant labour market. (For a recent review see Waldinger 2005.)

There may also be relevant socio-cultural differences—as Kalter and Granato suggest in their chapter in this volume, the first-generation migrants may have a 'sojourner' orientation to their country of destination, expecting to return 'home' after acquiring financial assets from their stay abroad. (See also Dustmann 1993.) Such a sojourner orientation may lead them to invest less time and effort in acquiring skills or contacts that would help them in the destination labour market. Or they may lead migrants to make different trade-offs from members of the charter population when looking for work. For example, they may seek high monetary returns in the short run (for example by working anti-social hours) rather than taking jobs that offer better medium-term prospects but lower current monetary returns (Heath and Ridge 1983). Social networks linking migrants to their families and communities of origin may also influence migrants' orientations, since migrants may be expected to send remittances home to support their relatives. Remittances home are well documented and are a major source of finance to many less-developed countries such as Morocco, Algeria, Tunisia and Turkey (Castles and Miller 2003: 126–7). These expectations may be another factor leading migrants to be particularly hard-working, thus reinforcing the economists' positive selection arguments.

Finally sociologists have emphasised aspects of prejudice and discrimination that may affect migrants, perhaps especially those from culturally dissimilar backgrounds from the destination society or those who are particularly 'visible' (Burstein 1994). An important distinction is between direct discrimination, where employers exhibit a conscious preference for members of one ethnic group over another even when their expected productivity is the same, and indirect discrimination where the 'colour-blind' application of existing rules nonetheless tends to disadvantage particular ethnic groups.[6] Direct discrimination may be expected to be more prevalent when the labour market is slack or where there

---

[6] A classic example of indirect discrimination is that of the allocation of social housing through a points system that gave preference to long-term residents over recent arrivals. See Rex and Moore (1967).

are major imperfections in the labour market such as barriers to entry and/or monopoly power.[7] (A monopolist can indulge a taste for discrimination without major economic repercussions from competitors and consumers.) Direct discrimination can also be enshrined in law, as for example in the South African system of apartheid.

We will in this volume give considerable attention to the first generation, but our primary interest is in the second and later generations. By the 'second generation' we mean the children of migrants who have themselves grown up and been educated in the countries of destination. While migrants may make some advance over the course of the lifecycle and may gradually improve their position the longer they have lived in the destination country, our expectation is that a great deal of progress will be intergenerational in character. There are some powerful theoretical grounds for believing that the second generation will have more favourable outcomes in the labour market than the first. In particular, we would expect the great majority of the second generation to have increased their levels of human capital, for example by obtaining fluency in the language of the charter population, learning a language generally being easier at school age rather than in late adulthood (Lippi-Green 1997), and to have taken some advantage of the greater educational opportunities available in a developed country than in a less-developed country. In this respect, then, we expect to find major advancements in their human capital. We also expect their human capital to be more comparable with that of the charter population and thus to have similar pay-offs in the labour market. For example, they will now have western qualifications that are known to employers rather than unknown foreign ones, and they will have domestic rather than foreign labour-market experience.

We expect these intergenerational differences to increase access to the more privileged professional and managerial jobs of what can be termed the salariat. These are jobs for which educational qualifications and communication skills are especially important and which would therefore have been largely closed to the first generation from less-developed countries if they were lacking in these skills. On the other hand, the positive selection that was assumed to be present in the first generation may not

---

[7] Dual labour-market theory with its distinction between primary and secondary labour markets and the hypothesised difficulty of ethnic minorities gaining access to the primary labour market depends essentially on the existence of market imperfections and direct or indirect discrimination. See for example Doeringer and Piore (1971).

exist to quite the same extent in the second. There could then be some 'regression to the mean': groups that outperformed the charter population in the first generation may not be so distinctive in the second generation.

Some of the sociological factors that affected the first generation may also be less in evidence in the second generation. It would be surprising if a sojourner orientation were to persist to the same extent as in the first generation, although some refugee groups may perhaps continue to aspire to return to their countries of origin should the political situation there change. But in general we would expect there to be greater similarity between the orientations of the second generation and the charter population than there was in the first generation. This acculturation might be particularly noticeable among women, whose expectations about marriage, equality within the family, fertility levels and economic activity may come to approximate more closely to those of their contemporaries in the charter population. Again, we would expect these kinds of changes to take an intergenerational rather than an intragenerational character on the usual sociological lines of socialisation theory. Orientations may also shift from the country of origin in the parents' generation to the country of destination in the children's generation and the role of remittances is likely to be reduced, since the parental generation will typically now be resident in the country of destination and hence in receipt of state pensions and the like.[8] 'Home' has now become the country of destination not the country of their parents' origin.

However, these generational changes may not always lead to improved outcomes for the second generation. As Portes and Zhou have argued, while the migrant generation may have been willing to undertake the menial jobs that natives prefer to shun, the second generation will have acquired the same wage and consumption standards as their peers in the charter population (Portes and Zhou 1993). This could lead to higher rates of unemployment in the second generation if the native-born minorities have higher 'reservation wages' than the foreign-born migrant generation.

Social networks may also change character across generations as young people have more opportunities to meet members of other ethnic groups and in particular members of the charter population at school or university. This, and associated patterns of intermarriage,

---

[8] However, transnational communities may slow this process down and make continued orientations towards co-ethnics overseas a major force.

are likely to be highly dependent on structural factors such as the proportion of co-ethnics resident in one's area (Model and Fisher 2002).

Another key issue is whether prejudice and discrimination decline against the second generation. Again, a generational theory of change may be appropriate, but this time applied to the members of the charter population. In particular, following the 'contact hypothesis' (Allport 1954; Brown *et al.* 1999) we might expect that younger generations within the charter population who have greater social contact with ethnic minorities might feel less prejudiced towards them.

However, while sociological accounts of generational change anticipate reduced disadvantages, other aspects of sociological accounts anticipate that disadvantage may persist across generations, even if gradually reducing. Firstly, we might expect the general processes of social reproduction that have been well documented by sociologists for charter populations to apply to populations of immigrant ancestry. It is one of the truisms of the sociology of education and of social mobility that disadvantaged social class origins in the parents' generation lead to poorer educational attainment and, both directly and indirectly, lower occupational attainment in the children's generation (Duncan 1968; Erikson and Jonsson 1996; Heath and McMahon 2005; Hout 2005). Hence if the migrant generation has low education and disadvantaged occupational positions, then this alone would lead one to expect their children to continue to be disadvantaged both educationally and occupationally. Hence we expect to find some degree of intergenerational continuity in patterns of gross disadvantage, even if the extent of disadvantage is gradually ameliorated from generation to generation.[9]

In addition there can be expected to be a process of cultural as well as of social reproduction. The parents of the second generation may not speak the host country language or not speak it fluently; leading to greater disadvantages in the educational system than experienced by peers from the charter population. The second generation may lack access to the heritage culture of the charter population that Bourdieu has argued is crucial for educational success. Parents' lack of familiarity with the

---

[9] However, we would do well to remember Duncan's own conclusions that the disadvantaged position of Blacks in American society were only in part a consequence of their disadvantaged social origins and that 'until we summon up the courage to distinguish between the problems of poverty and the problems of race, we shall have to reckon with the consequences of our lack of candor' (Duncan 1968, p. 109).

education system may lead to less-informed educational choices (Kristen 2005).

This may be compounded by group processes or what economists call 'human capital externalities' (Borjas 1995). Thus an individual may be affected not only by his or her own social origins but also by those of his peers. If ethnic minorities live in neighbourhoods predominantly composed of other low-income families, then this will tend to reduce his or her own attainment (perhaps through a process of lowering expectations or perhaps because of the poorer quality schooling that poor neighbourhoods tend to have). On these grounds, therefore, we would expect to see some continuity of ethnic disadvantage across generations. The ethnic hierarchy established in the first generation might therefore be continued in the second generation. However, this process might not happen equally for all groups. Portes and Zhou (1993) have suggested various ways in which minorities might be able to escape this process of social reproduction. Thus some groups, such as Indian Sikhs, may have strong family and community resources that promote upwards mobility and strong boundaries that might prevent their children from adopting the low aspirations of their socially disadvantaged peers in the charter population.

While the second generation can be expected to fare rather better than the first, albeit often still remaining at an overall disadvantage, the experience of third and later generations seems to be more problematic and there appears to be no guarantee of continuing generational progress. While many groups of European ancestry have effectively assimilated into the charter populations, visible minorities may remain disadvantaged after many generations. Borjas (1992, 1995) suggests that the human capital externalities mentioned earlier may prevent the attainment of parity indefinitely. As Ogbu (1978, 1987) has suggested, involuntary migrants may develop an oppositional culture that does not promote labour-market success. The same process may apply to those who have experienced persistent discrimination and feel excluded from the destination society. Wilson (1987) has memorably described the problems faced by African Americans when work disappears. The legacy of structural disadvantage and social exclusion may thus persist indefinitely.

We are not able to present a great deal of evidence in this volume on the third or later generations, although our chapter authors are able to look at a small number of third-generation groups in Australia, Canada and the USA. Our general expectation is that groups of European ancestry will gradually merge with the charter populations, ethnic boundaries gradually blurring and disappearing with ethnicity coming to have more and more a purely symbolic character (Gans 1979; Alba 2005). The blurring of ethnic boundaries removes many of the sociological bases for unequal labour-market experiences. Whether this process will apply equally to minorities of non-European ancestry is an open question, with the experience of African Americans suggesting a negative answer.

We are also able, in a number of countries, to look at the experience of indigenous minorities such as aboriginals in Australia, native Americans in the US and Canada, Palestinians in Israel, Catholics in Northern Ireland and Blacks in South Africa. Like African Americans these can be thought of as involuntary minorities.[10] Perhaps even more than with the voluntary groups of migrants and their descendants, the treatment of involuntary minorities presents a challenge to dominant ideologies of equality of opportunity in developed countries. While the apartheid system of South Africa is the most notorious example of institutionalised discrimination and closure against involuntary minorities, institutionalised political and economic exclusion have also historically been practised against indigenous peoples in Australia, Canada and the USA, against Irish Catholics in Northern Ireland and against Palestinians in Israel.

The experience of involuntary minorities is of considerable theoretical interest. Do they exhibit, perhaps in more extreme form, the same kinds of disadvantage experienced by voluntary minorities from less-developed countries? Or is their current situation qualitatively different, reflecting their historical experience of social, economic and political exclusion from full membership of the dominant nation-state?[11]

---

[10] Of course, one could argue that the second and later generations are themselves involuntary and that only the first generation count as voluntary. In turn one might begin to wonder how many of the first generation were truly voluntary: it is becoming more widely recognised that forced migration includes more than the narrow legal definition of a refugee. But at heart the issue is not so much a conceptual one as an empirical one: do the original circumstances of the migration, such as slavery, conquest or forcible transportation as convicts, lead to lasting legacies that impinge on their descendants' experiences in school and the labour market? For further discussion see Gibson 1997.

[11] For example Inglis and Model report in their chapter that Australian indigenes were not given full citizenship until 1967.

Crossnational differences

The arguments we have reviewed above are of a rather general character and might be expected to apply in a similar fashion (although not necessarily in similar magnitude) across most developed countries. However, there might also be reason to expect systematic differences between the countries of destination in the extent to which they facilitate ethnic minorities' economic advancement. In this context it may be useful to begin by distinguishing, on the one hand, general features of societies, such as their degree of meritocracy or 'openness' and, on the other hand, specific features oriented to ethnic minorities such as the levels of racial prejudice directed against visible minorities or the effectiveness of anti-discrimination legislation.

First of all, we might expect prejudice against ethnic minorities and racial discrimination to vary between societies. Eurobarometer data has suggested that there are considerable differences between European societies in self-rated prejudice.[12] According to the Eurobarometer, for example, Belgian public opinion comes out as more prejudiced and xenophobic than that in Sweden or the Netherlands. There is also electoral evidence of considerable recent support for Far Right parties in a number of European countries, notably Austria, France, Belgium (more particularly Flanders) and the Netherlands, as well as in Australia. While the explanation of Far Right support is not entirely straightforward and should not be assumed solely to reflect the extent of xenophobia in the country, the strength of the Far Right tells us something about the context of reception that immigrants and their descendants face.[13] Prejudice and the active hostility of the Far Right might be expected to lead to defensive reactions on the part of ethnic minorities, especially visible minorities from non-European origins that are the particular targets of racism. This could for example take the form of community closure and greater residential segregation, with consequences for human capital externalities as discussed in the previous section.

Exclusionary attitudes might also be related to the dominant conceptions of nationhood in each society, and these in turn might have

---

[12] Europa <ec.europa.eu/public_opinion/archives/ebs/ebs_138_tech.pdf>.
[13] Kitschelt (1995) argues persuasively that support for the Far Right will reflect the relationship between the political opportunity structure and the distribution of xenophobic attitudes in the white electorate. Thus a country such as Britain may exhibit very low support for Far Right parties because mainstream parties have adopted exclusionary policies towards immigration thus occupying part of the political territory that Far Right parties would normally hope to colonise.

important practical consequences for immigrants and their descendants. Thus it would not be surprising if societies that had more 'ethnic' conceptions of the nation were to show higher levels of exclusionary attitudes towards migrants and their descendants than did societies with more 'civic' conceptions of citizenship.[14] The classic literature suggests that countries such as Germany will have an ethnic conception while France and the USA have more civic conceptions. In the ethnic conception of the nation, membership depends more on the ascriptive character of one's ancestry than on residence or other achieved characteristics. In the civic conception, in contrast, membership of the nation can be acquired through acceptance of the customs and practices of the society. The ease of acquiring citizenship and the criteria for doing so will be a key consequence of these different conceptions, *ius sanguinis* typically being associated with an ethnic conception and *ius soli* with a civic conception. In Germany for example, the law of return gives citizenship automatically to ethnic Germans but naturalisation processes for non-Germans have historically been difficult and rarely used.[15] In the classic settler societies such as Australia, Canada and the USA, on the other hand, we have tended to find civic conceptions of national identity and relatively accessible mechanisms for acquiring citizenship. In Australia, for example, as Inglis and Model note in their chapter, citizenship can be obtained after only two years legal residence.

The ease of gaining citizenship may also have important practical consequences, particularly for employment in the public sector. In many countries, non-nationals are not permitted to work in the civil service and, since the public sector can be a major vehicle for ethnic advancement (Waldinger 1996; Lim 2001; Heath and Cheung 2006), reduced opportunities for public sector employment for ethnic minorities may be a more important constraint than its numerical importance might suggest.

The prohibition of non-nationals from civil service jobs in the public sector, coupled with restrictive citizenship laws, is an example of what we have termed indirect discrimination, and is likely to vary considerably across countries. Direct discrimination by employers is also likely to vary across countries and may reflect the nature of a society's legislative framework and its implementation as well as more general attitudes of racial

---

[14] Brubaker (1992) is the classic treatment of this distinction between ethnic and civic conceptions of the nation.
[15] However, as Kalter and Granato note in their chapter, naturalisation processes in Germany became more liberal in 2000.

prejudice and tastes for discrimination. Some societies such as the US and Northern Ireland have affirmative action legislation, others such as Britain have legislation outlawing racial discrimination in employment (and have some enforcement procedures although not perhaps as effective as the US ones),[16] while many European countries have had no legislation in this area until very recently. At the other extreme, South Africa of course had legislation excluding non-whites until democratisation in 1994.

We suggest that these aspects of racial prejudice, lack of effective anti-discrimination legislation, difficulties in accessing citizenship, and ethnic conceptions of the nation are likely to form a general syndrome, with civic conceptions of the nation being associated with the opposite syndrome. One broad hypothesis, then, would be that disadvantage would tend to increase as one moves towards the ethnic end of the spectrum.[17]

A second, conceptually very different spectrum may be suggested when we turn to consider the more general features of a society and their patterns of social reproduction. As we suggested earlier, some degree of social reproduction is present in all the societies under study, but the extent of reproduction varies considerably from one country to another. It has already been demonstrated in the case of social mobility that some countries, such as Israel, Netherlands, Sweden and Australia, are more open or fluid than typical European countries such as Britain and France, whereas Germany is significantly less open (Grusky and Hauser 1984; Ganzeboom, Luijkx and Treiman 1989; Erikson and Goldthorpe 1992; Breen 2004).[18] In effect this means that in Sweden (Germany) the ascribed characteristic of class origins has a smaller (larger) association with occupational outcomes than it does in other European countries.

The nature of the mechanisms that generate these cross-national variations in social fluidity are not well understood. Erikson and Goldthorpe (1992), Grusky and Hauser (1984) and Breen (2004) suggest that social democratic policies by left-leaning governments may be an important

---

[16] See for example MacEwen 1995.

[17] It would be a major research project in its own right to determine how consistent this spectrum was, whether it was unipolar or bipolar, and where particular countries fell on it. For the beginnings of such a study see Jones and Smith (2001), Hjerm (1998).

[18] There are a very large number of technical issues involved in this literature which we cannot address here. However, it is important to note the well-known distinction between absolute and relative mobility rates. The concept of fluidity or openness is generally taken to refer to relative mobility rates, usually measured by odds ratios. Increased fluidity does not necessarily mean that a higher proportion of the population has experienced social mobility. See Breen (2004) for a lucid discussion of the measurement issues.

source of social fluidity, although Erikson and Goldthorpe are at pains to point out that it is not simply the fact of a social democratic party in power that is important but the extent to which such a government has succeeded in pushing through egalitarian programmes of reform. These egalitarian policies can take a variety of forms; most notably in Scandinavian countries they have been oriented towards reducing actual inequalities of condition between classes through programmes of progressive taxation and redistribution.[19]

At any rate, whatever the specific mechanisms involved, a society's actual level of openness will have some straightforward implications for continuity of ethnic disadvantage insofar as ethnic minorities have been channelled into disadvantaged social class positions in the first generation. If class origins have a stronger relationship with occupational destinations in certain countries, then we would expect to find greater intergenerational continuity for ethnic minorities too. (Of course, for ethnic minorities which were advantaged occupationally in the first generation, this would also mean greater success in the second generation.) We would expect greater intergenerational ethnic continuity of advantage or disadvantage in a country such as Germany where class reproduction is stronger than in a country like Sweden where it tends to be weaker.

It is also conceivable that a country which displays greater openness and places less weight on the ascribed characteristic of social origins will also place less weight on the ascribed characteristic of ethnic origins. Left-leaning governments, for example, might be expected to be more active in pursuing programmes of anti-discrimination legislation or active policies of assistance for ethnic minority integration. To be sure, the vigorous American programme of affirmative action indicates that this is not a prerogative of European social democratic parties in the same way that redistributive programmes are.

However, we should not assume that the only mechanisms that tend to reduce the weight placed on ascribed characteristics are policies enacted by left-leaning governments. Modernisation has been suggested as an important driver of a shift from ascription to achievement (e.g. Blau and Duncan 1967; Treiman 1970) and has been advanced as a possible explanation for the trend towards increasing openness over time found in a number of countries. Modernisation might be associated with a greater

---

[19] While Erikson and Goldthorpe (1992, p. 388) did find some relationship between economic equality and fluidity in their cross-national comparison, Breen's more recent analysis has failed to replicate their finding on contemporary data.

reliance on formal criteria of selection and a reduced reliance on more particularistic criteria based on friendship networks, patronage or contacts. This could for example arise partly through the spread of large-scale bureaucratic organisations in the process of modernisation, or it might reflect a more general change in society, in response to the challenges of a more competitive global economy. Either way, these processes might tend to assist ethnic minorities if they lack access to the social networks and primary group affiliations of the dominant groups within the society (cf. Gordon 1964).

These remarks are necessarily somewhat tentative given the lack of understanding why (some would argue whether) modernisation has tended to increase social fluidity. It would nevertheless be of considerable interest to see whether the higher levels of class fluidity observed in some societies are also associated with higher levels of ethnic equality with the charter populations. Interestingly, this would tend to be a rather different cross-national pattern from that anticipated from the civic–ethnic argument (France for example being a relatively rigid society with respect to social mobility but highly civic in its conception of the nation) although there would be some overlap.

A third possible dimension is the economic. Economic conditions could well be important for the extent of ethnic minority disadvantage. For example, there is some evidence that ethnic minority unemployment rates are hyper-cyclical, that is when unemployment rates increase generally, those for ethnic minorities increase even more rapidly. Our suggestion here is that the rate of change of demand for labour (and for different skill levels of labour) may impact on ethnic minority disadvantage. When there is a shortage of labour, employers are unlikely to indulge any tastes for discrimination.

The scope for employers to discriminate may also depend upon the general nature of the economy as well as on the state of the business cycle. The classic economic theory suggests that discrimination is irrational in a perfect market and, while we have some scepticism about the extent to which any real-world economy approximates the economists' ideal type of perfect market, political economists have recently made a good case for distinguishing between the more liberal and flexible market economies of the US and Britain and the more regulated economies of Continental Europe (Soskice 1999; see also Ebbinghaus and Manow 2001; Hall and Soskice 2001). De-regulated economies might be expected to be more competitive and hence to exhibit less discrimination. On somewhat similar lines Kogan has argued that 'the degree of labor market flexibility in a given country might influence employers' decision making when hiring workers, particularly immigrants, since in highly protected labor markets employers are faced with potentially higher firing costs' (Kogan 2005, pp. 4–5). In these labour markets, employers may more readily resort to statistical discrimination in order to minimize their risks when hiring labour.

In practice we shall find that civic conceptions of the nation, social fluidity and deregulated labour markets are empirically correlated. With the limited number of countries available for our analysis, therefore, it will clearly not be possible to distinguish precisely between the validity of the different hypotheses. This is of course the classic 'small N' problem (Lieberson 1991). However, even with a much larger N, problems of determining the causal relations involved are impossible to solve. The monitoring of natural experiments is likely to be more instructive. For example, did the introduction of affirmative action legislation in Northern Ireland reduce the disadvantages experienced by Catholics? Did Britain's shift from a highly regulated economy to a decentralised liberal market economy following Margaret Thatcher's reforms indirectly improve the competitive situation of Britain's ethnic minorities? Will Germany's shift towards increasing access to citizenship reduce ethnic disadvantage there?

The countries included in the study

Our focus in this volume is on the developed countries that have seen large influxes of immigrants in the second half of the twentieth century. To be sure, ethnic inequalities are of great importance in many other countries too, but in order to keep the scope of the enquiry manageable, we limit ourselves to a study of developed countries that have been a major destination of migrants.[20] There are of course many other countries that could also have been included in such a volume as ours. There

---

[20] With the exception of South Africa, our countries all come towards the top of UNDP's rankings on the Index of Human Development. In 2003 their ranking was as follows: Australia 3rd, Canada 5th, Sweden 6th, Belgium 9th, USA 10th, Netherlands 12th, UK 15th, France 16th, Austria 17th, Germany 20th and Israel 23rd. South Africa was ranked 120th, although it was the highest-ranked of all the Sub-Saharan countries. However, we should note, as Don Treiman points out in his chapter, that whites in South Africa almost certainly enjoy standards of living (and no doubt the other aspects of the HDI) on a par with those enjoyed by the charter populations in our other twelve countries.

are other Western European countries that have been receiving labour migrants and refugees in recent decades, although the ones we have selected are broadly those that have received the largest numbers (and have the largest second-generation populations). It would also have been good to include New Zealand, another 'new' society with a large indigenous population of Maoris while Japan with its large Korean minority and indigenous population of Burakamin would also have been interesting. Many of the newly developed countries of East Asia are ethnically divided too and would make interesting studies in their own right but they must await a further study.

Firstly, then, we have a group of developed countries in Western Europe: Austria, Belgium, France, Germany, the Netherlands, Sweden and the United Kingdom (where we distinguish between Great Britain and the very different experience of Northern Ireland). These are countries which until the last fifty years were to a large extent ethnically homogeneous with a dominant national-cum-ethnic group (although we should not forget the history of minorities such as Jews and Roma throughout Western Europe and the multinational character of Britain, composed of English, Welsh and Scots, and of Belgium, composed of Flemish and Walloons). As the individual chapters in this volume document, these countries have seen recent influxes of migrants from the less-developed world, with large numbers of labour migrants and of refugees, as well as greater internal mobility from one European country to another following European integration.

As Table 1.1 shows, the second generation is still relatively small in these countries, with between 1% and 5% of the working-age population identifiably having a distinctive ancestry from that of the charter population, although it is set to grow given the larger number of first-generation migrants now resident in these countries. (See the later section of this chapter for a discussion of the problems of definition and measurement of ethnicity and ancestry.)

Within this Western European group there are some important differences in the national sources of migration. On the one hand Germany and Austria have received considerable labour migration from Turkey and Eastern Europe as well as many refugees from the former Yugoslavia. Britain and France on the other hand have experienced much more migration from their former overseas colonies in Africa and the Caribbean (and in Britain's case from South Asia). Sweden is different again with a substantial amount of migration from Nordic countries and with relatively little from less-developed countries.

Table 1.1. Cross-national differences in the size of the charter and ethnic minority populations (percentage of adult population of working age[a]).

	Charter population[b]	First generation[c]	Second generation	Third or later generations	Indigenous groups
Australia	39.8	25.8	19.0	15.0	0.4 (Aboriginal plus Oceanic)
Austria	90.7	7.7	1.6		
Belgium	87.9	7.8	4.3		
Canada	46.8	20.7	9.4	21.5	1.6 (Aboriginal)
France	76.5	8.6	15.0		
Germany (West)[d]	92.4	6.4	1.2		
Israel	9.0	29.1	40.3		19.9 (Palestinian)
Netherlands	82.5	9.0	8.5		
South Africa	11.6	2.3		13.1 (Coloured, Asian etc)	72.9 (Black)
Sweden	84.9	11.2	3.9		
UK—GB	91.0	6.5	2.5		
UK—NI	56.3				43.7 (Catholic)
USA	64.9	12.3	4.7	17.3	0.7 (American Indian)

Source: Chapters in this volume except for Netherlands, where figures were specially provided by Paul Tesser.

[a] The figures show the percentages of the working-age population, which is defined as those aged 18–59 (except for Sweden where it is 25–49, Belgium where it is 18–49, and Israel where it is 21–59).

[b] In the case of Australia the charter population is defined as people of 3rd or later generation Australian or Anglo-Celtic ancestry. In the case of Canada they are people of 3rd generation French, British or Canadian ancestry. In Israel they are people of 3rd generation Jewish ancestry; in South Africa they are defined as Whites including both English and Afrikaans speakers. In Northern Ireland they are Protestant and others. In the USA they are Non-Hispanic whites. These definitions of the charter populations are not always the same as the reference groups used in the statistical analyses.

[c] For definitions of generation see Table 1.4 below.

[d] For Germany the figures refer only to the former West Germany and exclude the areas of the former GDR.

Secondly we have the 'new' or perhaps more accurately 'settler' societies of Australia, Canada and the USA, which have acquired the majority of their populations in the form of migrants from overseas over the course of the last few centuries although each also has its own important, long-standing but now much outnumbered, indigenous population—Aboriginals in Australia and Canada, and American Indians in the USA. While these three states were all founded (in the modern era) on white migrations from Europe, they too have seen recent large influxes of labour migrants and refugees from less-developed countries as well as some migration from other developed countries. As we can see from Table 1.1, all three have larger percentages of both first and second generation immigrants than do the Western European countries.

In the USA this recent migration has been largely from Latin America, particularly from Mexico. In Canada the pattern of origins is more akin to that of Great Britain, reflecting their historical ties, with large groups from the Caribbean but also from the Far East. Australia is different again with a particularly large number of arrivals from China and relatively few from the less-developed countries of Africa, the Caribbean or South and West Asia.

We also include Israel, Northern Ireland and South Africa. These are also settler societies built on migration although they have some distinctive features that set them apart from the other countries treated in this volume. Israel can be regarded as another 'new' society in many ways akin to Australia, Canada and the US although more recently founded. Like the other new societies it has an important indigenous population consisting of Palestinians, and like them it has also seen large recent influxes from less-developed countries as well as from developed ones. Israel is of course distinct in the fact that the recent migration waves are wholly Jewish and do not consist of labour migrants in the conventional sense. Whereas recent influxes to the other migration-receiving countries of Western Europe, North America and Australia have brought large numbers of migrants with religions different from those of the (culturally Christian) charter populations, Israel's inflow has been solely of co-religionists of the dominant group. This may have implications for the warmth of the welcome.

South Africa also has much in common with the three classic settler societies of Australia, Canada and the US. Like them it was founded by colonists from Western Europe nearly four centuries ago, and like Canada its colonists were ethnically and nationally divided between descendants of the original Dutch and of later British settlers. And like them it has a large indigenous population, although numerically its indigenous population is the majority rather than the small minorities now found in the other countries. South Africa of course is also distinct in its history of apartheid. It is thus in many respects an outlier, but nonetheless provides something of an extreme by which we can perhaps calibrate the inequalities found elsewhere. As Treiman argues in his chapter, South Africa is of unusual sociological interest because it was until 1994 the only remaining state whose political system and state institutions were explicitly designed to secure the advantage of one ethnic group at the expense of the remainder of the population. The data for South Africa come from 1996, shortly after the transition to a multiracial democracy and thus documents the racial inequalities left as a legacy of the *apartheid* system of racial domination in place from 1948 through 1994. It will be of particular interest to see if the patterns of inequality found in South Africa are qualitatively different from those in our other countries, or are simply more extreme versions of the same kind of inequality found elsewhere.

Finally we include Northern Ireland, partly because it is part of the UK, along with Great Britain, and partly because it was the first of Britain's 'overseas' colonies with Protestant British settlers migrating to a largely Catholic Ireland. Like South Africa it has a legacy of institutionalised ethnic inequalities designed to secure the advantage of Protestants over the indigenous Catholic population. However, efforts to dismantle the system of oppression and exclusion have a longer history than in South Africa and have perhaps had time to demonstrate some results. In their chapter, Li and O'Leary look at the progress that has been achieved over the last two decades in securing equality of treatment for the two main ethno-religious groups.

While South Africa and Northern Ireland are thus in many ways very different from the other countries included in this volume, there is a major point of comparison with Australia, Canada, Israel and the US in the relations between the dominant group of white European settlers and the indigenous minorities.

Table 1.2 brings out clearly the differing origins of migrants and their descendants in the countries under consideration. Apart from strong similarities between Austria and Germany, almost every other country is *sui generis*. Only a few ethnic groups (notably Turks and Italians) are present in large numbers in several countries. Many groups are present in large numbers only in a single country (as for example Mexicans in the USA or Pakistanis in Britain).

It should be recognised from the outset that this will make it well-nigh impossible to make any categorical judgements about which countries exhibit more equal treatment of ethnic minorities. However, what we can do is to examine the experience of some specific groups, such as the Turks and Italians, in a range of different countries, and we can also begin to look for patterns in the experience of broader groupings, such as indigenous minorities or minorities originating from less-developed countries. As far as cross-national comparisons are concerned, therefore, our objectives must be limited and exploratory.

The chapters in this volume will nonetheless enable us to begin a preliminary exploration of some of the ideas sketched out in the previous

Table 1.2. Cross-national differences in the nature of the main ethnic minority groups (all generations combined) (percentage of adult population of working age).

	Largest ethnic minority groups				
Australia	Chinese 3.3	Italian 3.0	Greek 1.9	SE European 1.8	German 1.5
Austria	Yugoslavian 3.4	Developed origins (mainly German) 2.1	Turkish 1.7	East European 1.4	
Belgium	Italian 1.9	Moroccan 1.1	French 1.0	Dutch 0.8	Turkish 0.6
Canada	British 21.8	French 14.3	Chinese 3.0	Italian 2.7	German 2.4
France	South European 6.5	Maghrebin 4.4	Sub-Saharan African 1.9	East European 1.4	Near Eastern 0.9
Germany (West)	Turkish 2.5	Yugoslavian 1.2	Italian 0.7	Greek 0.5	
Israel	East European 28.8	Palestinian 21.4	Middle Eastern 15.8	North African 15.1	West European 4.6
Netherlands	Turkish 1.9	Moroccan 1.6	Antillean 1	Surinamese 1	
South Africa	Black 74.5 (Zulu 22.0, Xhosa 16.4)	Coloured 9.3 (Afrikaans speakers 7.4)	White Afrikaans speakers 7.1	White English speakers 4.8	Asian 3.0 (Hindu 1.5, Moslem 0.7)
Sweden	Finnish 4.9	Norwegian/Danish 2.0	Middle Eastern 1.6	West European 1.0	East European 1.0
UK: GB	Irish 1.5	Indian 1.5	Caribbean 1.5	Pakistani/Bangladeshi 1.0	West European 1.0
UK: NI	Protestant 53.1	Catholic 43.7			
USA	Black 12.0	Mexican 6.3	Puerto Rican 0.9	American Indian 0.7	Filipino 0.7

Source: Chapters in this volume

section about the societal conditions and policies that may be more or less conducive to the equal treatment of ethnic minorities. Our first hypothesis is that the classic immigration countries of Australia, the US and Canada, with civic conceptions of citizenship and tougher anti-discrimination legislation, greater social fluidity and more flexible economies may provide warmer welcomes and more equal treatment for migrants and their descendants. Israel might also be expected to fit into this first group, at least as far as Jewish migrants and their descendants are concerned although we might expect larger disadvantages in Israel for the indigenous population of Palestinians. On the other hand, Continental European countries such as Austria and Germany with ethnic conceptions of citizenship, weak anti-discrimination legislation, greater social rigidity and more regulated labour markets may provide more difficult environments for ethnic minorities. Britain, France, the

Netherlands and Sweden will be interesting theoretically as they do not fit so neatly into either pattern.

Methods of analysis

In considering ethnic minority disadvantage in the labour market it is important to distinguish between three distinct concepts, namely

- Gross disadvantage
- Net disadvantage (which we term 'ethnic penalty') after controlling for human capital and other individual characteristics
- Differential returns to human capital.

By the gross disadvantage we refer to overall differences between ethnic groups and the charter population in, for example, their rates of unemployment or in their rates of access to the relatively secure and privileged professional and managerial jobs that make up the salariat. For example, in the case of Austria we find that the unemployment rate of second-generation Turkish men is 8.9%, more than double that of native Austrians, for whom it was only 3.7% in the period covered by the Austrian data. Similarly, only 3.9% of second-generation Turkish men had jobs in the salariat compared with the figure of 23.7% for native Austrians. The differences between these percentages for the charter population and ethnic group give us measures of the gross disadvantages experienced by second-generation men in Austria.

Gross disadvantages are important in giving us an idea about the character and extent of ethnic stratification. However, they do not necessarily tell us much about equality of opportunity in the labour market, since much of the gross disadvantage may be explained by factors prior to entering the labour market, such as the level of education acquired at school or university. It is also important to recognise that some highly educated groups may appear relatively successful in gross terms but nonetheless experience considerable disadvantage in the labour market once their high qualifications are taken into account. For example, in Britain 37% of first-generation African men have jobs in the salariat compared with 35% of the charter population. This apparent parity is however misleading since fully one third of Africans have tertiary qualifications while less than one in seven of the charter population do. After controlling for education, it emerges that Africans experience considerable disadvantages in the British labour market.

We therefore look at the net disadvantages that groups experience in the labour market after taking account of their age and education. These net differences tell us, for example, whether members of a particular ethnic group have higher risks of unemployment than do members of the charter population of the same age and qualifications. Any disadvantage that remains can be termed an 'ethnic penalty' (Heath and McMahon 1997; Berthoud 2000; Carmichael and Woods 2000).

In research on social stratification it has been customary to display the process of stratification in diagrammatic form showing the links between origins (O), Education (E) and Destination (D). (See for example Erikson and Jonsson 1996.) A particular interest in this stratification research concerns the OD link, that is, the direct effect of origins on destinations, controlling for educational level. The typical finding is that, even in developed liberal societies such as the ones under consideration in this volume, there is still a positive association between advantaged social origins and advantaged class destinations, even after controlling for education. The existence of a significant OD link is often taken to be evidence of a lack of meritocracy or lack of equality of opportunity in the society (although as we noted earlier these two concepts are notoriously slippery and contested).

We can also put our own research into this framework but with ethnic origin replacing social origin in Figure 1.1. We expect to find that, analogously to the social stratification research, there is a significant OD link, with members of ethnic minorities from less-developed countries having lower-class destinations, even after controlling for education, than do members of the charter population. This OD link, if present, would indicate an ethnic penalty (or ethnic premium if the association were to be a positive rather than a negative one). A particular focus of this volume, therefore, is on the magnitude of this OD link in the different countries and on the nature of the ethnic minorities to which it applies.

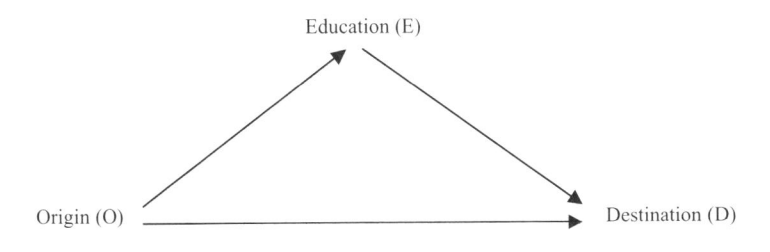

Figure 1.1. The Origin–Education–Destination linkages.

Figure 1.1 assumes that the nature of the ED link is the same for the different ethnic groups as for the charter population, but this assumption may not be correct. Therefore as well as investigating whether, and for which groups, there is a significant ethnic penalty, we also need to consider whether the nature of the ED link is the same for the ethnic minorities as it is for the charter population (technically whether there is an interaction between ED and O). Another way of putting this is to ask whether ethnic minorities receive lower returns on their educational investments than do members of the charter population or, which amounts to the same thing, whether ethnic penalties are greater (or smaller) at higher levels of education than they are at lower levels.

As we noted earlier, there is substantial evidence that foreign qualifications may not bring the same payoffs in the labour market as do domestic qualifications. For the first generation with foreign qualifications, then, we expect to find that the ED link is weaker than it is for the charter population. It will be of considerable interest to see whether this also applies to the second generation. If the explanation for the differential returns to education is the foreign qualifications of the first generation, then we would not expect to find differential returns in the second generation.

On the other hand, stratification research has found that, in the case of social class origins, there is indeed an interaction but of a rather different pattern: people from more advantaged social backgrounds seem able to access salariat jobs even without having high educational levels, whereas for people from less advantaged backgrounds, high educational levels are essential for gaining entry into the salariat (Hout 1988). Analogous processes might be at work in the case of ethnic origins. High levels of education might be essential for ethnic minorities if they are to access the salariat whereas members of the charter population might be able to access these jobs even in the absence of high qualifications. In effect, then, members of the charter population might have lower returns to their educational investments since they might be able to obtain prestigious jobs even with low education. We might expect this phenomenon to be more apparent in societies such as South Africa, which were historically organised so as to maintain the privileged positions of the charter population.

In the chapters that follow, therefore, our contributors report, first, the gross disadvantages, giving straightforward cross-tabulations of labour-market outcomes by ethnic origin without any controls. We also show cross-tabulations of educational level and economic activity by ancestry. The economic activity cross-tabulations are particularly important as they indicate whether there may be selection biases that need to be remembered when interpreting the patterns of ethnic penalties in the labour market. For example, we might find some groups where a relatively large proportion of the men are neither in education and training nor in the labour market looking for work. These might be 'discouraged workers'. Their absence from the labour market may mean that our subsequent analysis of labour-market outcomes underestimates the true extent of ethnic minority disadvantage. Similarly, among women we will find that some groups have rather low rates of economic activity, perhaps reflecting traditional values or early marriage and child-rearing. The women from these groups who do work may well be 'positively selected' with important consequences for our interpretation of the size of any ethnic penalties that they experience in the labour market.

The second stage is a multivariate analysis of unemployment, restricting the analysis to the sample members who are economically active. Our response variable is the relative chances of being in employment as opposed to being unemployed. In other words we model the avoidance of unemployment. Our predictors are age and age squared, educational level, marital status and ethnicity. We include a term for age squared since age tends to have a curvilinear relationship with unemployment. Unemployment tends to be relatively high among young people, declines somewhat at older ages but then rises again as people move towards retirement age. Marital status is also included as a control variable since it has frequently been shown that married men have lower rates of unemployment than single men while married women have lower rates of labour-market participation. Education is included as our principal measure of human capital. We use the CASMIN schema (Shavit and Müller 1998), distinguishing five levels, which we treat as a categorical rather than a continuous variable when it is included in the model as a main effect:

- Full tertiary qualifications, primarily university degrees (CASMIN 3b)
- Lower tertiary, covering post-school qualifications such as non-degree teacher training or nursing qualifications (CASMIN 3a)
- Full secondary, covering maturity certificates such as the German Abitur, French Baccalaureat, or British A levels (CASMIN 2c)
- Lower secondary qualifications, covering academic or vocational training that falls short of full secondary (CASMIN 1c, 2ab).
- Social minimum, generally corresponding to the minimum level of compulsory schooling (CASMIN 1ab).

We should note that our contributors were not always able to distinguish all these five levels in their datasets, and so in some cases only four levels are distinguished.

Finally we have our measure of ethnicity (or more strictly ancestry). We take the appropriate charter population as the reference category and then distinguish a number of ethnic group and generation combinations. For example, in the British case we have:

- Native-born of British ancestry
- First generation from Sub-Saharan Africa
- First-generation Caribbeans
- First-generation Indians
- First-generation Irish
- First-generation Pakistanis and Bangladeshis
- First generation from other Western European countries
- Second-generation Caribbeans
- Second-generation Indians
- Second-generation Irish
- Second-generation Pakistanis and Bangladeshis.

We leave it to our country specialists to decide, on the basis of their local knowledge and data availability, which ethnic/generation groups can be distinguished and how to combine smaller groups into meaningful larger ones (for example in the British case combining Pakistanis and Bangladeshis in order to obtain an adequate sample size). In general we exclude groups where there are fewer than 100 respondents in the sample since estimation of parameters becomes unreliable. In some cases such as Australia, Canada and the USA some third (or later) generation groups can also be distinguished, as can indigenous peoples.

The parameter estimates associated with the different ethnic/generation groups are our measures of 'ethnic penalties'. An alternative strategy might have been to fit separate variables for generation and ethnicity, but there are a number of technical difficulties with this strategy.[21] It is also important to note that the first generation should not be regarded as the parents of the second generation. The first-generation

---

[21] One difficulty with including separate terms for generation and ethnicity is that there may be structural zeros, i.e. there may not be any first-generation members of the charter population (or if there are, they may be a rather unusual group). It makes more sense to use a generation variable in analyses of the ethnic minorities on their own, excluding the charter population. Another difficulty is that there will often be interactions between generation and ethnicity, making a single estimate of a 'generation effect' misleading.

Irish in Britain, for example, includes some young people who have only recently arrived in Britain as well as older people who arrived many years ago. Our strategy instead allows us to make direct comparisons between the outcomes for the second-generation groups and the charter population instead of a possibly misleading comparison between generations. Only in the case of France can we make a direct comparison between parental and filial generations.

Our basic model therefore takes the form:

$$\text{Ln}(P/1-P) = B_0 + B_1(\text{Age}) + B_2(\text{Age})^2 + \Sigma B_j(\text{Marital Status}) + \Sigma B_k(\text{Education}) + \Sigma B_l(\text{Ethnic/generational group})$$

We then add an additional model in which we include interactions between ethnic/generational group and education in order to investigate whether ethnic minorities receive lower (or higher) returns on their educational investments than the charter population. In order to provide a parsimonious model, we treat education as a continuous variable (scored 2, 1, 0, -1, -2) in the interaction term while continuing to treat education as categorical when it appears as a main effect. This means that we have one interaction term (rather than four) for each ethnic group. This can be written as follows:

$$\text{Ln}(P/1-P) = B_0 + B_1(\text{Age}) + B_2(\text{Age})^2 + \Sigma B_j(\text{Marital Status}) + \Sigma B_k(\text{Education}) + \Sigma B_l(\text{Ethnic/generational group}) + \Sigma B_m(\text{Ethnic/generational group*scale})$$

Following the analysis of unemployment, we then turn to people in employment and look at occupational class. We use a shortened version of the Erikson/Goldthorpe classification of occupational class that has been widely used in comparative research (Erikson and Goldthorpe 1992; Breen 2004). We distinguish five main classes:

- The salariat—professionals, managers and administrators (Classes I and II in the Erikson/Goldthorpe classification).
- The routine non-manual class—clerical and other routine non-manual employees in administration and commerce (Class IIIa)
- The petty bourgeoisie—small proprietors and artisans with or without employees, and self-employed farmers (Classes IVa, b, c).
- The skilled manual class—skilled workers, technicians and supervisors of manual workers (Classes V and VI)
- The semi- and unskilled class—less-skilled workers in manual, service and agricultural work (Classes IIIb, VIIa, VIIb).

Our particular interest is in the access of the second generation to the relatively secure and privileged professional and managerial work of the salariat and their avoidance of semi- and unskilled work, which was the typical destination for many migrant workers in the first generation. Entry into the petty bourgeoisie is also of considerable interest as some ethnic groups (although by no means all) appear to use self-employment as one way of escaping unemployment.

In the case of occupational class, we employ multinomial logistic regression but in all other respects the model is the same as that for unemployment. As with unemployment we also fit interaction terms between education and ethnicity (again treating education as a continuous variable in the interaction).

We carry out separate analyses for men and women. Even in the case of the charter populations, the process of stratification does not always work in exactly the same way for women as for men; in particular in many countries women do not experience the same gains in occupational attainment over the life cycle that men do. (As we shall see in the later analyses, in almost every country the effect of age on entry into the salariat is much smaller for women than for men.) Moreover, as we shall see, there are often important differences between men and women within a particular ethnic group in their economic outcomes. Rather than fitting complex models with numerous interactions between gender and the other variables, we have preferred to show separate analyses for men and women.

In some countries we also look at earnings, but this outcome is not available in all the datasets available to our contributors. It is, however, a valuable addition where it is available. One problem with the use of such broad occupational categories as the salariat is that the salariat includes a considerable range of occupations and it may well be that ethnic minorities, when they gain access to the salariat, are largely restricted to its lower levels. Similarly self-employment may not be nearly as advantageous to ethnic minorities as it typically is for members of the charter population. By exploring ethnic minority earnings within each class (as we can in the case of Australia, the Netherlands, the USA and Britain), we can test whether this is in fact the case.

We do not pretend that the models we fit to the data are comprehensive. We have chosen to fit rather basic models for which appropriate data can be found in a range of developed countries. Our models should be conceived as essentially descriptive in purpose, telling us whether ethnic minorities obtain similar labour-market outcomes to members of the charter population with the same qualifications and of the same age and marital status. They tell us *whether* there are ethnic penalties, not *why* those penalties occur. In this respect, our work is analogous to work in social stratification which shows that there are direct effects of social origins on occupational destinations, after controlling for educational level, but does not tell us what the mechanisms generating the direct effects are. We include age and marital status in our analyses as these are potentially 'confounding' variables that might affect our estimation of the ethnic penalties.[22] We do not, however, attempt to include 'mediating' variables that might help us explain why certain groups experience ethnic penalties.

It would of course be desirable to go beyond this descriptive work and to attempt an explanation of the ethnic penalties. In the case of the first generation one might include mediating variables measuring fluency in the language of the charter population, how long the respondent has been resident in the country of destination, whether he or she has domestic or foreign qualifications, and so on. In the case of the second generation it would be desirable, inter alia, to have measures of social class origins and levels of social and geographical segregation, but none of our countries had these variables available in their data sources.[23]

However, it is important to emphasise that even more comprehensive models would still not enable us to infer that any remaining disadvantage was caused by discrimination. There is always the possibility that unmeasured positive or negative selection effects rather than discrimination could account for the disadvantage. Statistical analysis of the sort we carry out is not well-suited to the analysis of discrimination, for which more direct methods, such as field experiments, are needed. (For an excellent review see Darity and Mason 1998.) Quite aside from being utterly

---

[22] Age is a confounding variable as there is a strong relationship between age and our dependent variables and some (but not all) of our second-generation ethnic minorities are younger on average than the charter population. Moreover age cannot be regarded as a mediating variable since it would be absurd to suggest that ethnicity had any causal impact on one's age. It would also be desirable in many countries to include region as another potentially confounding variable and in some cases this has therefore been included. Perhaps the most surprising thing is that the standard literature on occupational attainment does not control for these confounding effects.

[23] Social class origins are likely to be particularly important in explaining the educational attainments of the second generation but are likely to have more modest effects on the estimated ethnic penalties net of education. In the British case we can in fact control for social class origins and, as reported in the final chapter, inclusion of class origins as a control variable fails to explain much of the ethnic disadvantage.

impractical in the present context, a 'fully-specified' statistical model of ethnic disadvantage is an inappropriate ideal.[24]

Our objective, therefore, is a more limited one. We do not attempt comprehensive explanatory models (which in any case would be futile given the limited nature of the data sources, hardly any of which measure key variables such as language fluency). Nor, for the same reason, do we formally model the various selection biases. Instead we have opted for relatively simple models that can readily be replicated in the different countries given available data resources and that have a straightforward, albeit largely descriptive, interpretation.

Data sources

The contributors to this volume have carried out the analyses on the most authoritative datasets available for their respective countries. Investigation of the labour-market fortunes of the second generation imposes quite serious demands on data sources. In particular we need very large datasets since, as we could see from Table 1.1, the proportions of the labour force that are made up of second-generation ethnic minorities are still relatively small in most of our countries. Our contributors have therefore tended to use data sources such as public use samples from the census, micro-censuses or large-scale government-sponsored surveys of the labour force, and in one case special studies of ethnic minorities (the Netherlands). Table 1.3 shows the data sources used for the thirteen countries that are considered here.

For broad descriptive purposes these are the most authoritative datasets available. In general they have high response rates, substantially higher than those used in most sociological research. (For technical details on each survey see the individual chapters.) They are conducted by national statistical offices to the highest standards of survey or census research. There are some variations in coverage, with the Dutch surveys being rather distinct from all the others. The data sources also vary in size, affecting the number of ethnic minorities that can be distinguished and the size of the standard errors.

---

[24] Here we follow the canons of evidence-based medicine which hold that properly conducted randomised experiments, which is what field experiments essentially are, are superior to the statistical analysis of cross-sectional data, if the goal is to test causal hypotheses. While sophisticated econometric models which use procedures for tackling issues of selection bias and so on may have some role to play, they are essentially second best to field experiments.

Table 1.3. Data sources.

	Data source	Years	Agency responsible	N (after selections)	Comments
Australia	Australian Census, 1% sample (CURFs)	2001	Australian Bureau of Statistics	99,253	Excludes temporary visitors and overseas students resident for less than 12 months
Austria	Austrian Microcensus. Respondents surveyed in March of each year	1995, 1997, 1999, 2001	Austrian Central Statistical Office	128,274	
Belgium	Sample of anonymised records from Belgian Census; 10% of respondents of Belgian origin, 50% of immigrant population	1991	National Institute of Statistics	535,219	
Canada	2.7% sample (PUMF) from the Canadian Census	2001	Statistics Canada	452,578	
France	Formation Qualification Professionnelle survey	2003	INSEE	35,065	
Germany	Public use sample (70%) from the Microcensus (1% sample of all private households)	1993 and 1996		476,127	Because of the panel design of the Microcensus, 1 in 8 respondents may appear twice in the dataset
Israel	Labour Force Surveys	1992–2000	Central Bureau of Statistics	68,639	Age range 25–59 for 1992–4 and 21–59 for 1995–2000
Netherlands	SPVA datasets: samples of private households from four ethnic groups with comparison group of the indigenous population in the same municipalities	1988, 1991, 1994 and 1998	Social and Cultural Planning Office	31,292	
South Africa	10% public use sample from the 1996 Census	1996	Statistics South Africa	1,864,017	

Table 1.3. Data sources. (cont.)

	Data source	Years	Agency responsible	N (after selections)	Comments
Sweden	Census linked with register information	1990	Statistics Sweden	2,824,652	Analysis restricted to residents of Sweden born between 1941 and 1964. Recent arrivals excluded
UK: Great Britain	General Household Surveys	1991–6, 1998, 2000–01	Office for National Statistics	99,553	
UK: NI	Continuous Household Surveys	1985/6 and 2002/3	Northern Ireland Statistical Research Agency	15,563	
USA	Current Population Survey, March Supplement	1995, 1997, 1999, 2001	US Bureau of the Census	306,608	

Our data sources also differ in their measurement of our key variables, reflecting different national traditions for collecting information on occupation and education. However, we are reasonably confident that these measures are broadly comparable as regards our simplified five-category measures of education and occupation (or at least are no worse in this respect than most other cross-national enquiries). However, they do differ in very important ways in their measurement of ethnicity, and it is to this that we now turn.

Measurement and definition of ethnicity

A particular problem in the cross-national study of ethnic minority disadvantage is the measurement of ethnicity. In essence, ethnicity is a subjective concept depending on shared self-conceptions of members of the groups concerned. Max Weber, for example, wrote: 'We shall call "ethnic groups" those human groups that entertain a subjective belief in their common descent because of similarities of physical type or of customs or both, or because of memories of colonization and migration' (Weber [1922] 1978, p. 389). In essence, this defines the concept that we are endeavouring to measure in this volume. However, we need to recognise that these subjective conceptions tend to be place and time-specific and are subject to processes of change resulting from interactions with the host community and with other ethnic groups. Many writers have suggested that across generations there may be a gradual blurring of ethnic boundaries as groups become more or less assimilated and, while theories of assimilation have been the subject of heated debates, it is clear that ethnic groups vary across time and space in their extent of group formation and identity. In Alba's evocative phrase, there may be bright or blurred boundaries (Alba 2005). These variations are particularly evident in the use of the ethnic language or in intermarriage rates with the charter population. We are not, therefore, dealing with homogeneous or static social formations.

There are also major measurement issues. In practice, we find that there are several different national traditions for measuring something that approximates, more or less closely, to sociological conceptions of ethnicity. First, there are countries such as Australia and Canada that ask respondents about their ancestry. These are self-report measures that rely on subjective beliefs about common descent. Secondly, there are countries such as Sweden and France which do not ask about ethnicity at all but do, in some data sources, include questions on the respondents' own and parents' countries of birth, from which measures of national origin can be established. Third, there are countries such as Austria and Germany where the standard sources include questions on nationality (which will approximate more or less closely to national origins). Table 1.4 shows how we have measured ethnicity and generation in the thirteen countries under consideration.

There are to be sure, major problems with all three methods. Self-report measures of ancestry may involve selection biases. For example, some ancestries may be stigmatised and respondents may not be willing to report, for example, indigenous ancestries. Alternatively individuals who are less assimilated may be more willing to offer a distinct ethnic ancestry while more assimilated individuals may, for example, prefer to report an Australian or Canadian ancestry and will thus become invisible in the dataset. Such selection biases may tend to exaggerate the extent of ethnic disadvantage. There may also be important cross-national variations in the treatment of mixed origins. In the USA, for example, people of mixed origin may report themselves simply as African American whereas in Canada the nature of the question wording used in the Census may encourage them to report themselves as having multiple ancestries.

Nationality clearly has the drawback that naturalised citizens from a particular national origin cannot be identified. This tends to be less of a

Table 1.4. Measures of ethnicity and generation.

	Reference group	Ethnic groups	First generation	Second generation	Third generation
Australia	Native-born respondents with both parents born in Australia and reporting Australian ancestry only	Self-reported ancestry	Foreign-born respondents	Native-born respondents who had one or both of their parents foreign-born	Native-born respondents with both parents born in Australia and reporting a non-Australian ancestry
Austria	Respondents of Austrian nationality born in Austria	Nationality and country of birth	Foreign-born respondents who arrived in Austria after age six	Foreign nationals born in Austria plus foreign-born respondents who arrived in Austria at or before age six	Cannot be distinguished
Belgium	Respondents of Belgian nationality	Nationality and country of birth	Foreign nationals who arrived in Belgium after age six	Foreign nationals born in Belgium or who arrived in Belgium at or before age six	Cannot be distinguished
Canada	Respondents of British ancestry born in Canada and with both parents born in Canada	Self-reported ancestry	Foreign-born respondents who arrived in Canada after age four	Native-born respondents (plus those who arrived before age five) who had both parents foreign-born	Native-born respondents with native-born parents reporting a non-British ancestry
France	Native-born respondents with French nationality at birth and neither parent born overseas	Country of birth and parents' country of birth and nationality at birth	Foreign-born respondents who arrived after age five	Native-born respondents (plus those who arrived before age six) who had one or both parents foreign-born	Cannot be distinguished
Germany	Respondents of Germany nationality	Nationality	Foreign nationals born abroad who arrived in Germany after age six	Foreign nationals born in Germany plus those who arrived in Germany at or before age six	Cannot be distinguished

Country					
Israel	Jews born in Israel with parents born in Israel	Religion together with own and parents' country of birth	Foreign-born respondents who arrived in Israel after age six	Native-born respondents (plus those who arrived at or before age six) whose parents were foreign-born	Jews born in Israel with parents born in Israel (the reference group)
Netherlands	Respondents born in the Netherlands both of whose parents were born in the Netherlands	Own and parents' country of birth	Foreign-born respondents	Native-born respondents with at least one of the parents foreign-born	Cannot be distinguished
South Africa	English-speaking whites	Racial group			Native-born classified on the basis of Census racial group and home language
Sweden	Respondents born in Sweden both of whose parents were born in Sweden	Own and parents' country of birth	Foreign-born respondents who arrived in Sweden after age seven	Native-born respondents (plus those who arrived at or before age seven) both of whose parents were foreign-born	Cannot be distinguished
UK: GB	Respondents born in the UK both of whose parents were born in the UK	Own and parents' country of birth	Foreign-born respondents who arrived in the UK after age six	Native-born respondents (plus those who arrived before age seven) both of whose parents were born in the same foreign country	Cannot be distinguished
UK: NI	Protestants	Religion			Not applicable
USA	Native-born non-Hispanic whites	Own and parents' country of birth for 1st and 2nd generation. Self-reported race for 3rd generation	Foreign-born respondents who arrived in the USA after age six	Native-born respondents (plus those who arrived at or before age six) both of whose parents were born in the same foreign country	Native-born with native-born parents who, on the basis of replies to questions on race and descent were either non-white, Hispanic or both

problem for the first generation (who can in any event often be identified from country of birth), but in the case of the second generation in Germany and Austria there is a particular difficulty in the case of, for example, people of Turkish ancestry who have naturalised and taken German or Austrian citizenship. They will not be identifiable as second-generation Turks but will be included within the charter population. Our country experts discuss in detail the magnitude of the problems that arise from this and are able to make some estimates of its likely impact on the reported results.

The use of parental country of birth is also far from unproblematic. In particular many migrant-sending countries were themselves ethnically diverse. India is a striking example. It is perhaps the most ethnically diverse society in the world, with hundreds of different linguistic and religious groups. To treat these as all equally Indian, as we are forced to do by data limitations, is clearly a gross over-simplification. This will not necessarily hold true for all origin countries but we need to be aware of the limitations to our analysis generated by this problem. It will be a particular concern for cross-national research if different ethnic groups from within a particular origin country migrate to different destination countries. This means that we will no longer be comparing like with like and that apparent host-country differences in labour-market experiences may actually be generated by unmeasured ethnic differences within the origin country.

There are also problems when the two parents come from different countries of origin. These should not be assumed automatically to indicate individuals of mixed origin. For example individuals born in the west may marry recent arrivals who were born in the country of origin or, where there are traditions of arranged marriages, may find a partner still living in the country of origin. Our general strategy, therefore, has not been to attempt to identify mixed groups but to define a particular origin group as one where both parents were born in the same country of origin.[25]

We are not aware of any straightforward solutions to these problems. In some cases our authors have been able to carry out checks or to replicate their results using other measures. And we have asked our contributors to draw attention to the major measurement problems in the

---

[25] In the case of the Netherlands and France, the mixed nature of ethnicity in some of the origin countries was felt not to make this an appropriate strategy.

individual country chapters. We feel it is important to be explicit about the nature of the measures used and their limitations and not to sweep them under the carpet. In general, however, we suspect that these problems will increase with the number of generations. In later generations, the proportions acquiring citizenship or intermarrying will be larger, and hence the blurring of boundaries and the scope for selective processes of self-identification will be greater too. Comparisons of third or later generation groups should therefore be treated with greater caution than comparisons of the second generation.

The definition of generation also involves some practical problems. We define the first generation as those born abroad or who arrived after the start of compulsory schooling (generally taken to be age six) while the second generation are defined as those who arrived at or before the start of compulsory schooling or who were born in the country of destination. The rationale for this is that individuals who arrive at or before the start of compulsory schooling will have received the whole of their education in the country of destination and are therefore likely to speak the host language fluently and to have domestic rather than foreign qualifications. The precise age at which full-time schooling starts does, however, vary somewhat between our countries, and there are also some limitations on the measurement of age at arrival. It would also have been useful to distinguish a 'one and a half' generation whose members arrived during the period of full-time schooling and would therefore typically have domestic qualifications. However sample size limitations meant that this was not feasible as a general strategy.

In some cases we can also distinguish the third generation and indigenous populations. This is done essentially by supplementing our measures based on own and parents' country of birth with questions on self-reported ancestry since none of our datasets have information on grandparents' countries of origin. However, as we noted above, these comparisons may be particularly problematic since these self-report measures of ancestry may be the product of a variety of social processes. As Glazer (2005) argues 'the amount of mixture among groups, through marriage, is today such that the answers to the ancestry question, if one is not an immigrant or the child of an immigrant with a clear sense of ancestry, are not very helpful in distinguishing an ethnic group much beyond the second generation. The answers then become so variable, so dependent on cues from the census itself . . . as to be hardly meaningful' (Glazer 2005, p. 59). While Glazer's claim makes considerable sense in Australia or Canada and may be especially applicable to groups of

European ancestry, it may not apply to quite the same extent to African Americans (where intermarriage rates are very much lower) and probably even less true of our groups in South Africa where intermarriage was explicitly forbidden by law.

While we hope that our work will be improved upon by later scholars with access to properly harmonised datasets, we believe that our results will give some powerful pointers to the extent to which ethnic minorities experience disadvantage in the labour market. While we shall not be able to give definitive answers to our research questions, our findings will, we believe, present a major challenge both to other social scientists interested in explaining inequalities of opportunity and to policy-makers and governments who have responsibility for ensuring equal treatment for all their citizens.

References

Alba, R. (2005), 'Bright versus blurred boundaries: second-generation assimilation and exclusion in France, Germany and the United States'. *Ethnic and Racial Studies* 28, 20–49.

Allport, G. W. (1954), *The Nature of Prejudice* (Reading, MA: Addison-Wesley).

Arrow, K. (1972), 'Some mathematical models of race discrimination in the labour market'. In A. Pascal (ed.), *Racial Discrimination in Economic Life* (Lexington, DC: Heath), pp. 187–203.

Becker, G. S. (1964), *Human Capital: a theoretical and empirical analysis, with special reference to education* (New York: National Bureau of Economic Research).

Berthoud, R. (2000), 'Ethnic employment penalties in Britain', *Journal of Ethnic and Migration Studies*, 26, 389–416.

Blau, P. M. and Duncan, O. D. (1967), *The American Occupational Structure* (New York: Wiley & Sons).

Borjas, G. J. (1987), 'Self-selection and the earnings of immigrants', *The American Economic Review*, 77, 531–53.

Borjas, G. J. (1992), 'Ethnic capital and intergenerational mobility', *Quarterly Journal of Economics*, 107, 123–50.

Borjas, G. J. (1995), 'Ethnicity, neighbourhoods and human capital externalities', *American Economic Review*, 85, 365–90.

Breen, Richard (ed.) (2004), *Social Mobility in Europe* (Oxford: Oxford University Press).

Brown, R., Vivian, J., and Hewstone, M. (1999), 'Changing attitudes through intergroup contact: the effects of group membership salience', *European Journal of Social Psychology*, 29, 741–64.

Brubaker, R. (1992), *Citizenship and Nationhood in France and Germany* (Cambridge, MA: Harvard University Press).

Burstein, P. (ed.) (1994), *Equal Employment Opportunity* (New York: Aldine).

Card, D., Dinardo, J., and Estes, E. (2000), 'The more things change: immigrants and the children of immigrants in the 1940s, 1970s, and 1990s'. In George J. Borjas (ed.), *Issues in the Economics of Immigration* (Chicago: University of Chicago Press), pp. 227–71.

Carmichael, F. and Woods, R. (2000), 'Ethnic penalties in unemployment and occupational attainment: evidence for Britain', *International Review of Applied Economics*, 14, 71–98.

Carliner, G. (2000), 'The language ability of US immigrants: assimilation and cohort effects, *International Migration Review*, 34, 158–82.

Castles, S. and Miller, M. J. (2003), *The Age of Migration: International Population Movements in the Modern World* (New York: The Guilford Press).

Chiswick, B. R. (2002), 'Immigrant earnings: language skills, linguistic concentrations and the business cycle', *Journal of Population Economics*, 15, 31–57.

Darity, W. A. Jr. and Mason, P. L. (1998), 'Evidence on discrimination in employment: codes of color, codes of gender', *Journal of Economic Perspectives*, 12, 63–90.

Doeringer, P. B. and Piore, M. J. (1971), *Internal Labour Markets and Manpower Analysis* (Lexington, MA: Heath Lexington Books).

Duncan, O. D. (1968), 'Inheritance of poverty or inheritance of race'. In Daniel P. Moynihan (ed.), *On Understanding Poverty: perspectives from the social sciences* (New York: Basic Books), pp. 85–110.

Dustmann, C. (1993), 'Earnings adjustments of temporary migrants', *Journal of Population Economics*, 6, 153–8.

Ebbinghaus, B. and Manow, P. (eds.) (2001), *Comparing Welfare Capitalism: Social Policy and Political Economy in Europe, Japan and the USA* (London: Routledge).

Erikson, R. and Goldthorpe, J. H. (1992), *The Constant Flux* (Oxford: Oxford University Press).

Erikson, R. and Jonsson, J. (1996), *Can Education be Equalized? The Swedish case in comparative perspective* (Boulder, CO: Westview Press).

Friedberg, R. M. (2000), 'You can't take it with you: Immigrant assimilation and the portability of human capital', *Journal of Labor Economics*, 18, 221–51.

Gans, H. J. (1979), 'Symbolic ethnicity: the future of ethnic groups and cultures in America', *Ethnic and Racial Studies*, 2, 1–20.

Ganzeboom, H. B. G., Luijkx, R., and Treiman, D. J. (1989), 'Intergenerational class mobility in comparative perspective', *Research in Social Stratification and Mobility*, 8, 3–84.

Gibson, M. (1997), 'Ethnicity and school performance: complicating the immigrant/involuntary minority typology'. *Anthropology and Education Quarterly*, 28, 431–54.

Glazer, N. (2005), 'American diversity and the 2000 census'. In Glenn C. Loury, Tariq Modood and Steven M. Teles (eds.), *Ethnicity, Social Mobility and Public Policy* (Cambridge: Cambridge University Press), pp. 50–66.

Goldthorpe, J. H. (1996), 'Problems of "meritocracy"'. In Robert Erikson and Jan O. Jonsson (eds.), *Can Education be Equalized?* (Boulder, CO: Westview Press), pp. 255–87.

Gordon, M. (1964), *Assimilation in American Life: The Role of Race, Religion and National Origin* (New York: Oxford University Press).

Granovetter, Mark S. (1973), 'The strength of weak ties', *American Journal of Sociology*, 78, 1361–80.

Grusky, D. B. and Hauser, R. M. (1984), 'Comparative social mobility revisited: models of convergence and divergence in 16 countries', *American Sociological Review*, 49, 19–38.

Hall, P. A. and Soskice, D. (eds.) (2001), *Varieties of Capitalism: The Institutional Foundations of Comparative Advantage* (New York: Oxford University Press).

Heath, A. F. and Cheung, S. Y. (2006), 'Ethnic penalties in the public and private sectors'. Report to the Department of Work and Pensions.

Heath, A. F. and McMahon, D. (1997), 'Education and occupational attainments: the impact of ethnic origins'. In V. Karn (ed.), *Ethnicity in the 1991 Census, vol 4: Education, Employment and Housing* (London: HMSO), pp. 91–113.

Heath, A. F. and McMahon, D. (2005), 'Social mobility of ethnic minorities'. In Glenn C. Loury, Tariq Modood and Steven M. Teles (eds.), *Ethnicity, Social Mobility and Public Policy* (Cambridge: Cambridge University Press), pp. 393–413.

Heath, A. F. and Ridge, J. M. (1983), 'Social mobility of ethnic minorities'. In K. Kirkwood, M. A. Herbetson and A. S. Parkes (eds.), *Biosocial Aspects of Ethnic minorities, Journal of Biosocial Science*, Suppl. No. 8, pp. 169–84.

Hirschman, C., Kasinitz, P., and DeWing, J. (eds.) (1999), *The Handbook of International Migration: The American experience* (New York: Russell Sage Foundation).

Hjerm, M. (1998), 'National identities, national pride and xenophobia: a comparison of four Western countries', *Acta Sociologica*, 41, 335–47.

Hout, M. (1988), 'More universalism, less structural mobility—the American occupational structure in the 1980s', *American Journal of Sociology*, 93, 1358–1400.

Hout, M. (2005), 'Educational progress for African-Americans and Latinos in the United States from the 1950s to the 1990s: the interaction of ancestry and class'. In Glenn C. Loury, Tariq Modood and Steven M. Teles (eds.), *Ethnicity, Social Mobility and Public Policy* (Cambridge: Cambridge University Press), pp. 262–87.

Jones, F. L. (1988), *The Recent Employment and Unemployment Experiences of First, Second and Later Generations of Immigrants in Australia* (Canberra: Office of Multicultural Affairs).

Jones, F. L. and Smith, P. (2001), 'Individual and societal bases of national identity: a comparative multi-level analysis'. *European Sociological Review*, 17, 103–18.

Kesler, C. (2006), 'Social Policy and Immigrant Joblessness in Britain, Germany and Sweden', *Social Forces*, 85, 743–70.

Kitschelt, H. (1995), *The Radical Right in Western Europe: A Comparative Analysis* (Ann Arbor: University of Michigan Press).

Kogan, I. (2005), 'Unemployment among recent immigrants in Europe: the role of host-countries' labor-market characteristics (Unpublished paper, MZES, Mannheim).

Kogan, I. (2007), *Working Through Barriers: Host community institutions and immigrant labour market performance in Europe* (Dordrecht: Springer).

Kristen, C. (2005), *School Choice and Ethnic School Segregation: primary school selection in Germany* (Munster: Waxmann).

Lieberson, S. (1980), *A Piece of the Pie: Blacks and White Immigrants since 1880* (Berkeley: University of California Press).
Lieberson, S. (1991), 'Small Ns and big conclusions: an examination of the reasoning in comparative studies based on a small number of cases', *Social Forces*, 70, 307–20.
Lim, N. (2001), 'On the back of blacks? Immigrants and the fortunes of African Americans'. In R. Waldinger (ed.), *Strangers at the Gates: New Immigrants in Urban America* (Berkeley, CA: University of California Press), pp. 186–227.
Lin, N. (1999), 'Social networks and status attainment', *Annual Review of Sociology*, 25, 467–87.
Lippi-Green, R. (1997), *English with an Accent* (New York: Routledge).
MacEwen, M. (1995), *Tackling Racism in Europe: An examination of anti-discrimination law in practice* (Oxford: Berg).
Mincer, J. (1974), *Schooling, Experience and Earnings* (New York: Columbia University Press).
Model, S. and Fisher, G. (2002), 'Unions between blacks and whites: England and the US compared', *Ethnic and Racial Studies*, 25, 728–54.
Ogbu, J. U. (1978), *Minority Education and Caste: The American System in Cross-Cultural Perspective* (New York: Academic Press).
Ogbu, J. U. (1987), 'Variability in minority responses to schooling: non-immigrants vs. immigrants. *Anthropology and Education Quarterly*, 18, 312–34.
Perlmann, J. and Waldinger, R. (1999), 'Immigrants, past and present: a reconsideration. In C. Hirschman, P. Kasinitz and J. DeWind (eds.), *The Handbook of International Migration: The American Experience* (New York; Russell Sage Foundation), pp. 223–38.
Porter, John (1965), *The Vertical Mosaic: An Analysis of Social Class and Power in Canada* (Toronto: University of Toronto Press).
Portes, A. and Zhou, M. (1993), 'The new second generation: segmented assimilation and its variants'. *Annals of the American Academy of Political and Social Science*, 530, 74–96.
Rawls, J. (1972), *A Theory of Justice* (Oxford: Clarendon Press).
Reitz, J. G. (1998), *Warmth of the Welcome: The Social Causes of Economic Success for Immigrants in Different Nations and Cities* (Boulder, CO: Westview Press).
Rex, J. and Moore, R. S. (1967), *Race, Community and Conflict* (Oxford: Oxford University Press for the Institute of Race Relations).
Shavit, Y. and Müller, W. (eds.) (1998), *From School to Work: A Comparative Study of Educational Qualifications and Occupational Destinations* (Oxford: Oxford University Press).
Shavit, Y. and Blossfeld, H.-P. (eds.) (1993), *Persistent Inequality: Changing Educational Attainment in Thirteen Countries* (Boulder, CO: Westview Press).
Soskice, D. (1999), 'Divergent production regimes: coordinated and uncoordinated market economies in the 1980s and 1990s'. In H. Kitschelt, P. Lange, G. Marks and J. D. Stephens (eds.), *Continuity and Change in Contemporary Capitalism* (Cambridge: Cambridge University Press), pp. 101–34.
Treiman, D. J. (1970), 'Industrialization and social stratification'. In E. O. Laumann (ed.), *Social Stratification: Research and Theory for the 1970s* (Indianapolis: Bobbs-Merril), pp. 207–34.

Van Tubergen, F. (2006), *Immigrant Integration: A Cross-National Study* (New York: LFB Scholarly Publishing).

Waldinger, R. (1996), *Still the Promised city? African-Americans and New Immigrants in Postindustrial New York* (Cambridge, MA: Harvard University Press).

Waldinger, R. (2005), 'Networks and niches: the continuing significance of ethnic connections'. In Glenn C. Loury, Tariq Modood and Steven M. Teles (eds.), *Ethnicity, Social Mobility and Public Policy* (Cambridge: Cambridge University Press), pp. 342–62.

Weber, Max ([1922] 1978), 'Ethnic groups'. In G. Roth and C. Wittich (eds.), *Economy and Society: An Outline of Interpretive Sociology*, Vol. 1, Part II (Berkeley, CA: University of California Press), pp. 385–98.

Wilson, W. (1987), *The Truly Disadvantaged: the inner city, the underclass, and public policy* (Chicago: University of Chicago Press).

2

Diversity and Mobility in Australia

CHRISTINE INGLIS & SUZANNE MODEL

Summary. The Australian story of ethnic relations has, in its short history, been very much a story of two groups: the Indigenes and the migrants. One of the major themes evident in this analysis of the Australian ancestry data from the 2001 Census is that, 100 years after the founding of Australia, the same pattern still characterises relations between the non-Indigenes and the Australian-born Aboriginal and Torres Strait Islander population. On all the measures that have been examined here, they are the ethnic group which is most clearly marginalised and characterised by ethnic penalties. Over three decades after the 1967 referendum granting Indigenes full citizenship, the general picture is of continuing economic and social disadvantage in spite of, or some would argue because of, a variety of targeted programmes, among an Indigenous population which has a far wider range of geographical and social circumstances than any other Australian ethnic group. In contrast to the ongoing evidence of Indigenous disadvantage in Australia, the experience of immigrant groups provides a far more positive picture of the ability of migrants from a diverse range of European and non-European backgrounds to be incorporated into the Australian labour market. While there are clear variations within the first generation, by the second and later generations, 'ethnic penalties' suggestive of disadvantage and discrimination have substantially disappeared. Significantly this applies as much to a physically distinctive group such as the Chinese as it does to those from ancestries more similar in physical appearance to the predominantly Anglo-Celtic Australian benchmark norm. This positive effect is, if anything, more evident among women than men. The greater homogeneity in women's labour-market experiences coexists with the continuing tendency for women's labour-market attainments to be, in general, lower than those for men. The high levels of intermarriage evident by the second generation results in a large number of individuals being from mixed ancestries and so not included in our analysis except in general groupings such as 'Australian-Other' or 'Other'. However, this intermarriage is a further pointer to a pattern of non-economic incorporation in Australia which involves limited discrimination and extensive integration.

Introduction

SINCE THE COMMENCEMENT OF EUROPEAN SETTLEMENT in 1788, immigration has been central to Australian population growth and economic development. The last two centuries have witnessed significant changes in the patterns of immigration and the origins and characteristics of the migrants. By 2001, nearly a quarter of Australia's population was overseas born while another one in five had at least one parent born overseas. In a population of 19 million the absolute numbers of immigrants (4.1 million first-generation, overseas-born and another 3.4 million second-generation with one or both parents born in Australia) is less than in countries such as the United States or Canada. Nevertheless, the much higher proportion of immigrants in Australian society (23.2%), compared with Canada (18.4%) and the US (11%), makes it an extremely significant case when considering factors affecting the socio-economic mobility of immigrants and their descendants.

Changing patterns of migration

While the origins of European settlement of Australia as a British penal colony are well known, less widely appreciated is that the state has played a continuing and highly significant role in promoting and controlling immigration.[1] Throughout the nineteenth century the British administration of the six Australian colonies was actively involved not only in sending convicts, but also, in attracting free settlers with inducements of travel

---

[1] A major source of information on both Australian immigration and its ethnic diversity is contained in J. Jupp (ed.), *The Australian People: an encyclopedia of the nation, its people and their origins* (Oakleigh: Cambridge University Press, 2001).

expenses and land to settle in what was a distant and unknown part of the world. Not until the first commercial discovery of gold in 1851 was there a surge of independent migration as fortune hunters from Europe, the Americas and China responded to news of the potential for wealth in Australia's gold fields. This new influx of immigrants, coming from many countries, greatly increased the diversity of Australia's immigrant population which had hitherto been drawn primarily from Britain and Ireland.

Those gold seekers who remained after the gold rushes ended helped compensate for the loss of convict labour after Britain finally ceased sending prisoners to Western Australia in 1868. However, significant sections of the population, including the trade union movement, became alarmed at the possibility that non-European, and particularly Chinese, labour would undermine the hard-earned economic gains of Australian workers. Accordingly, the Australian colonies adopted a variety of measures similar to those in North America to restrict Asian migration and settlement (Price 1974). When the Australian colonies gained their independence in 1901 and federated to form the Commonwealth of Australia, one of the first actions of the new nation was to enact legislation to restrict the entry of non-Europeans. In fact, the numbers of Chinese in Australia in 1901 had already declined from the decade previously as they, and other migrants affected by the severe economic depression of the 1890s, left to seek better economic opportunities elsewhere.

When Australia federated in 1901, nearly one quarter of the non-indigenous population were overseas born (see Table 2.1). This level of immigrants in the Australian population was not, however, reached again for another ninety years. In the first half of the twentieth century a variety of events discouraged both independent and government sponsored

Table 2.1. Australia's Migrant Population 1901–2001 (column percentages).

	1901	1911	1947	1961	1971	1981	1991	2001
First Generation	22.93	17.67	9.82	16.93	20.22	20.88	22.79	23.15
Second Generation	77.07	82.33	90.18	83.07	19.22	20.43	20.14	19.33
Third + Generation					60.55	58.69	57.18	57.52
Total Population	3,773,801	4,455,005	7,579,358	10,508,186	12,755,638	14,576,330	16,850,533	18,972,354

Source: Australian Bureau of Statistics Population Census.
Note: Prior to 1971, the Census did not include the full-blood aboriginal population.

immigrants. During the First and Second World Wars the disruption of shipping meant that transport was not available to bring immigrants who, in any case, may have been reluctant to undertake a long and potentially dangerous sea voyage. In addition, Australia was particularly badly affected by the world economic depression of the 1930s with very high levels of unemployment. The government response was to cut out immigrant assistance programmes and discourage new migrants, who were seen as potentially adding to the existing high levels of unemployed. This policy of discouraging and reducing immigration at times of economic recession is a long-standing strategy of the Australian state intended to reduce the potential for economic competition and conflict between existing residents and new arrivals. The overall impact of these developments on migration was that by 1947, just after the end of the Second World War, the overseas-born population was at the all time low of less than 10%. Of these 10%, three quarters were from Britain and Ireland, with the other major immigrant groups being born in Italy, New Zealand, Germany, Greece, British India and Ceylon, Poland and China.

Even before the end of the Second World War the Australian government had developed a major plan to develop national infrastructure and restructure the economy, for the war had highlighted major inadequacies in these areas. Manpower was viewed as vital to achieving these objectives as well as to overcoming perceptions that Australia was an unpopulated country open to invasion. The slogan 'Populate or Perish' enjoyed wide currency in this period and was important in legitimating extensive immigration. As in earlier periods, the government concern to attract permanent settlers led to an emphasis on family migration. The immigrant families were important not only in providing the workers but also the consumers for the expanded manufacturing sector viewed as an important part of Australian economic restructuring. When the government announced its ambitious plan to increase Australia's population by 1% a year through immigration, much emphasis was placed on the positive contribution the 'new Australians', as they were called, would make to Australia. There was also considerable emphasis placed on the way in which the newcomers would reflect the British dominance in the population.

Over the next two decades, as the state became involved in paying the transportation and settlement costs of large numbers of immigrants, the preference for British immigrants was increasingly honoured in the breech. Indeed, over the last half century, there have been significant changes in the origins of Australian immigrants. The first groups of post-war immigrants were from the United Kingdom and East European refugees. As the British government became more reluctant for its population to emigrate and the numbers of refugees available for resettlement declined, Australia turned to countries in Northern Europe (the Netherlands and Germany) and, then, to Southern and Southeastern Europe: Greece, Italy, Malta and Yugoslavia. With economic opportunities improving in Western Europe, Australia then looked further afield, signing a bilateral agreement with Turkey in 1967 to assist Turkish immigrants. After 1966, economic and political unrest and civil war in Lebanon saw large numbers of predominantly Christian Lebanese migrate to Australia following in the footsteps of late nineteenth-century arrivals who were at that time described as 'Syrians'. After 1976 as the country descended into civil war, an increasing number of Muslim Lebanese began to arrive. While few received government assistance to immigrate, their arrival was facilitated by the Australian government granting them quasi-refugee status under the humanitarian entry program. The extension of the bilateral arrangements favouring immigration from the Mediterranean and Middle East countries was driven by the need for predominantly unskilled and semi-skilled labour. Arrivals from these countries tended to be less well-educated than the immediate post-war arrivals from Eastern Europe and Northwestern Europe. They also frequently lacked knowledge of English, which was a major handicap in predominantly English-speaking Australia.

Over this same period the White Australia Policy to exclude non-European immigrants was also being substantially modified, not least because of diplomatic pressures from newly independent Asian countries. By 1973, the policy was formally abolished and Australia adopted a non-discriminatory selection policy based on the Canadian points system. At the same time, preferential treatment for British citizens was abolished and the criterion for gaining Australian citizenship, two years permanent residence, was applied to all immigrants. The three main criteria established for immigrant selection then became family reunion, economic contribution and refugee or humanitarian considerations. The actual number of visas for each of these categories of entrants is set on an annual basis after community consultation, and changes have regularly taken place in the specific criteria relevant to the economic or skilled migration programme. In accord with the non-discriminatory nature of the policy, there are no quotas for other criteria such as nationality, birthplace or ethnicity, except in the case of groups from time to time identified for acceptance under humanitarian entry. The outcome of each year's migration programme reflects the influence of a variety of stakeholders including migrant communities, business and humanitarian groupings.

While Australia's strong commitment to family migration as a means of encouraging permanent settlement is supported by migrant groups keen to ensure that opportunities for family reunion continue, economic and humanitarian migration has played a significant role in initiating new migration streams. Thus, in the aftermath of the Vietnam war, large numbers of Indo-Chinese entered Australia as refugees, thereby laying the bases for subsequent growth through family reunion migration. Similarly, by the 1980s, Australia was again undertaking a major restructure of its economy intended to cope with the impact of globalisation and economic change, particularly in Asia. Whereas in the immediate post-World War Two period the labour market was seen as needing unskilled and semi-skilled migrant manpower, now the emphasis changed to seeking highly skilled workers able to contribute towards the development of the tertiary sector of the economy and knowledge-based industries. No longer was family reunion migration sufficient to ensure the supply of such skilled labour and so greater emphasis was placed on selecting skilled migrants. This shift coincided with economic growth in Europe which meant that emigration to Australia was now much less attractive than in the immediate post-war period. Thus, a largely unanticipated outcome of this growing emphasis on skilled migration was the entry of highly educated and skilled migrants from Asia, many of them ethnic Chinese, particularly those who had fluency in English as this played a major part in the selection criteria of skilled (but not family reunion or humanitarian) immigrants. By the late 1980s, political change in Eastern Europe with the fall of communism was also associated with growing numbers of humanitarian migrants including from the former Yugoslavia. Likewise, special provisions were made to grant temporary and then permanent residence status to students from the People's Republic of China in the aftermath of the Tiananmen Square incident. They were then able to introduce their relatives through the family reunion programme. The effect of these and similar changes was the growth of new immigrant groups in the Australian population.

Since the mid 1990s, largely in response to business lobbying, Australia has moved significantly from its earlier firm stance against temporary labour migration. A variety of policy changes have made it easier for companies to bring in highly skilled workers for initial periods of up to four years and, also, for international students studying in Australian universities to convert from temporary to permanent residence status at the end of their studies. By the end of the 1990s such long term temporary migrants entering Australia were actually outnumbering those admitted as permanent residents. The effect of their presence in the resident population, as reflected in the 2001 Census, is to increase the trend in permanent migrant selection towards migrants (both permanent and temporary) from middle class backgrounds in their own countries (Inglis, 1999). This contrasts with the immediate post-war period when the majority of immigrants had lower levels of skills and education.

Settlement policies and incorporation

As a nation with an extensive state commitment to immigration and also to state intervention in various areas of daily life including economic regulation and education, Australia has had a long history of extensive state involvement in both the settlement and the incorporation of immigrants. One of the earliest expressions of this was the assistance given to the nineteenth-century free settlers to obtain land. This assistance extended in the post-war period to providing fares and housing on arrival to assisted passage immigrants, but is now only provided to refugees and humanitarian arrivals. Other services offered include English language classes for both adults and children. Especially important has been the emphasis on granting citizenship which, since the 1970s, has meant that after two years as a permanent resident, individuals can apply for Australian citizenship. This provides opportunities to vote as well as eligibility for permanent status in the public service and defence forces. A more general change which occurred in the 1970s was the abandonment of assimilation as the overarching ideological and policy framework for the incorporation of immigrants. This approach assumed that all immigrants should, and would, become indistinguishable from the dominant Anglo-Celtic population. But, even more significantly, its practical policy implication was that no special government programmes or services were necessary or should be offered to migrants to facilitate their incorporation apart perhaps from some assistance with learning English.

By the 1960s migrant and non-migrant lobby groups were highlighting the difficulties confronting immigrants seeking to incorporate into Australian society in an equitable fashion. At the same time, there was also questioning of the necessity, and feasibility, of immigrants abandoning their own cultural heritage, and discussion of the possibility that difficulties in incorporation had the potential to lead to a retreat into isolated and marginal communities. Together this questioning of the practicality and desirability of assimilation as a policy framework for incorporation led to the gradual development of the alternative policy strategy of multiculturalism (Martin 1978). In Australia this has always involved a focus on addressing issues related to both equity and cultural maintenance as a means for redressing social and economic disadvantage (Inglis 1996). Significantly, multiculturalism has been promoted not simply as a policy for immigrants and their children but, rather, as a policy for all Australians (Office of Multicultural Affairs 1989). Multiculturalism has impinged on a wide range of key Australian institutions ranging from schools, to hospitals, the legal system and the workplace. While it is certainly possible to question how far-reaching have been the moves towards making Australian institutions more responsive to diversity, the last three decades have involved changes which are clearly visible to the migrant parents of today's second-generation Australians.

The experiences of the second generation

The expansion of Australian immigration after the Second World War was accompanied by extensive research on the immigration experience, covering such topics as relations with home societies, extent of assimilation, patterns of ethnic concentration and settlement, ethnic identity and, by the late 1960s, the second-generation children of migrants who had either been born in Australia or who had arrived when young and grown up in Australia (Inglis 1975). One outcome of this research was to highlight the patterns of ethnic disadvantage and labour-market inequality characterising particularly those more recent migrants who had come from Southern European countries such as Greece, Italy and Malta. With agreement about the existence of disadvantage, debate focused on the reasons, which ranged from institutional, neo-Marxist explanations to neo-liberal individualistic ones, referring to the human capital and resources of the different immigrant groups (see for example Wooden, Holton *et al.* 1994). Given the ideological emphasis on assimilation and the commitment to its associated settlement policy which denied the need for active policy initiatives to facilitate settlement, the experiences and outcomes for the children of immigrants became an important theoretical as well as political focus (Martin 1978). Their experiences were directly relevant to debates about the potential for social mobility and whether Australia was developing into a society which, with increasing ethnic diversity, was one where assumed earlier opportunities for advancement among predominantly Anglo-Celtic immigrants would continue to be achievable for more recent migrants from diverse backgrounds and, significantly, for those who lacked English language skills.

The theoretical and research interest in the second generation's educational experiences and outcomes coincided with a national focus on educational inequality. When the Australian Labor Party took office in 1972 after two decades of conservative rule, education was one of the issues it immediately addressed by the establishment of a committee of inquiry and subsequent policy responses addressing inequality in educational outcomes related to gender, class background, rural residence, migrant and Indigenous background and disability. Research evidence during the 1970s and 1980s on educational attainment by migrants and their children highlighted the complex picture which existed, especially among the second generation. The absence of a national data base made it difficult to come to definitive conclusions about the extent of inequalities in educational outcomes and scholastic attainment (Jakubowicz 1985). Making comparisons between ethnic groups extremely difficult were the varying methodologies, measures of attainment/disadvantage and the focus on different groups. However, the studies did highlight the very extensive diversity in educational attainment and disadvantage among ethnic groups. Among educators and the general public there was also a growing perception that students from certain ethnic backgrounds, including Greeks and Asians, especially Chinese, were achieving even better than Australian-born children of Anglo-Celtic origins. While studies of educational attainment never settled definitively the relative importance of 'class' as against 'ethnicity', or, indeed, gender, there was already growing evidence that educational disadvantage among ethnic minorities, including those from non-English speaking backgrounds (NESB),[2] was not inevitably continuing into the second generation (Poole 1981; Sturman 1985). As many of the second generation were from families with limited pre-migration levels of education and socio-economic capital, cultural factors increasingly became an important element in explanations.

---

[2] The distinction between those from English and non-English speaking backgrounds (ESB and NESB) has been the major policy distinction in Australia since the mid 1970s. Comparable to the use made in, for example, Canada between 'visible minorities' and others it reflects the view that disadvantage was potentially significantly linked to lack of English fluency as well as reflecting different cultural patterns from those of the Anglo-Celtic majority. Its adoption in the mid-1970s was also linked to the search for a term which encompassed the potential for disadvantage to extend beyond the first-generation migrants.

In particular, attention was given to the importance which these groups placed on education as a means of social mobility motivating their emigration and, also, their aspirations for their children in Australia.

By comparison with education, there has been less research on how the second generation translate their educational attainment into occupational success. Reviewing the work which had been done up to the late 1980s, Jones noted that studies showed fairly general agreement that there was no empirical evidence that the children of immigrants suffer any inequity in their access to high status jobs and pay (Jones 1988, p. 22). This conclusion was also largely supported by more detailed reviews from the early 1990s (Wooden, Holton *et al.* 1994). Over the last decade there have been major changes in the structures of the Australian labour market and social policies, as well as in the patterns of immigration which indicate that now is an appropriate time to revisit the issue of second-generation labour-market disadvantage. Up until the early 1970s, Australia experienced virtually full employment with levels of unemployment about 2%. As in many other industrialised countries, the next three decades were associated with far higher levels of unemployment, which have only recently begun to return to a situation where there is discussion of 'full-employment' (albeit at levels of 5% of the population). There is widespread acknowledgement of especially high levels of unemployment among particular immigrant groups and in the Indigenous population, even while there is some indication of bipolar patterns of occupational attainment within particular ethnic groups. The economic restructuring begun in the 1980s has seen the demise of employment opportunities in labour-intensive manufacturing but, at the same time, there has been an increase of both skilled and unskilled employment in the services sector. How these changes have affected not only immigrants, but also their children is an important question. Exploring it is now more feasible given the larger numbers of second-generation immigrants from non-Anglo-Celtic background.[3]

Many studies, especially by labour-market researchers, have relied on the use of aggregate data which only distinguishes between those of English and non-English speaking backgrounds (Wooden, Holton *et al.*

---

[3] Using data from the 1985 and 1987 National Social Science Survey, Jones reported that small sample sizes were a key factor precluding an adequate exploration of the impact of education on occupational outcomes for Aborigines and Southern Europeans. F. L. Jones, 'The Transition from School to Work in Australia', in Y. Shavit and W. Müller (eds.), *From School to Work: a comparative study of educational qualifications and occupational destinations* (Oxford: Clarendon Press, 1997), pp. 49–70.

1994). However, given the diversity among immigrant groups, Australian sociological researchers have favoured analyses which take into account the diversity even among groups from similar geographical and cultural regions and with similar migration patterns and post-arrival labour-market experiences. To explore this diversity, researchers have tended to rely on qualitative and quantitative data sources which are not amenable to the use of multiple regression analyses. One noteworthy exception is the study undertaken by Jones using ancestry data from the 1986 Census to analyse in considerable detail the outcomes for individuals of Chinese ancestry. This study was based on the unit-record census data (Final Unit Record File) which gives more detail on age, period of residence, age left school and year of highest qualification, compared to the public use sample (Jones 1992). In terms of socio-economic status Jones reported that second-generation Chinese women do as well as Anglo-Celts while Chinese men fare marginally better (Jones 1992). However, the pattern is complex and potentially affected by factors including involvement in full-time or part-time work. There is also an indication that the educational attainment of third-generation Chinese reverts to the levels of educational attainment characteristic of the majority Anglo-Celtic group (Jones 1992). Three other studies have also used multiple regression analysis to explore more generally the experiences of the second generation. Using 1981 Census sample data Evans and Kelley (1991) found little support for economic discrimination affecting second-generation men from Anglophone, Mediterranean or other migrant backgrounds. However, this lack of economic discrimination did coexist with evidence of more general 'exclusionary' discrimination which involves employers expressing prejudice against hiring particular ethnic groups. Flatau and Hemmings (1991) examined the incidence of unemployment, wage levels and educational attainments of a sample of 16- to 22-year-olds from the 1985 Australian Longitudinal Survey. They concluded that the second generation experienced less disadvantage than the first generation and often were indistinguishable from the third and higher generations. A slightly more complex picture in terms of birthplace was reported by Brooks (1997) who used the 1% sample from the 1991 Census. He concluded that birthplace of parents had little overall influence on the likelihood of experiencing unemployment or of not participating in the labour force for the second generation.

A major recent study by Khoo and her colleagues (Khoo, McDonald *et al.* 2002) has used the 1996 Census material to explore in considerable detail the outcomes for different second-generation groups from major countries of emigration. Although based on cross-tabulations by birthplace, an important feature of this study is that it makes use of cohort analysis to explore the implications of the migration wave in which individuals entered Australia. It also distinguishes between the NESB groups on the basis of the very different levels of English proficiency which characterise migration from particular countries. Thus, while the majority of immigrants from Singapore have high levels of English proficiency related to the shift of that country's education system towards English, the same is not the case for often equally well-educated individuals from Taiwan. While this should not affect the children of these immigrants directly, it is nevertheless an important potential factor in their home environment. Other such influences may include the time of arrival in Australia as it affects economic opportunities and the expectations and support for incorporation.

Key findings from the Khoo study are that, for the younger second-generation group aged 15 to 24 years who are in transition from education to work, the second generation have higher levels of educational enrolment than do the third generation. This educational difference is most evident among the second generation from middle or low income suburbs. Among those in the workforce, the levels of unemployment are higher for the second than the third generation. As Khoo and her colleagues note, those in the second generation aged 25 to 44 years have completed their education and are established in their working lives. They conclude that:

> The 1996 census data confirm the findings of earlier studies that the second generation who are mostly of Southern or Eastern European origins have better educational and occupational outcomes than those of UK or Western European origins. Although small in number, the second generation of parents born in Malaysia or China has the highest proportion with university qualifications and in professional occupations. The second generation of Eastern European or Asian origins who are in managerial or professional occupations also have higher incomes. (Khoo, McDonald *et al.* 2002, p. viii)

More generally they note that 'while it is possible to draw conclusions about the socio-economic outcomes of the second generation of European origins whose parents immigrated during the 1950s and 1960s, it is still premature to assess the socioeconomic outcomes of the second generation of non-European origins whose parents immigrated after 1975' (Khoo, McDonald *et al.* 2002, p. x) On the basis of the small non-European numbers there is evidence of their high levels of university level qualifications but there is considerable variation in the ethnic and socio-economic backgrounds of this group. They conclude by noting that:

> Although there are clear indications that these second generation youth are remaining in the education system longer than their peers who are at least third generation, it will be another five to ten years before their socio-economic outcomes will be fully known. (Khoo, McDonald *et al.* 2002, p. x)

In contrast to the research on the educational and occupational circumstances of recent immigrants, the evidence on the educational and labour-market experiences of the Indigenous population,[4] as well as on other key indicators of social welfare including health and levels of imprisonment, provides a picture of an established ethnic minority experiencing ongoing disadvantage (Altman 2001). However, within the Indigenous population there is an amazing diversity of economic and social circumstances unrivalled in the general population. While the majority (73%) live in major urban areas and towns, and are involved in the market economy, 27% live in remote and isolated parts of Australia, on pastoral stations, Indigenous communities and camps where they rely to some extent on a more traditional, non-market economy (Altman 2001). A further feature of the Indigenous population is its almost fourfold growth from 116,000 in 1971 to 410,000 in 2001. While high fertility and increased accuracy of enumeration are important in this growth, also very significant is the increased willingness by individuals to identify their Indigenous origins.

Australian ethnic minorities

In the present research, the importance of undertaking analysis which overcomes the simplification associated with using composite categories such as NESB was a major consideration. However, while the use of detailed population data is very useful, it is not generally available in Australia in a form which allows regression and similar forms of analysis to test the influence of key factors on economic outcomes. Data which allows such analysis is only provided in the confidential unit record files (CURFs) which are based on a 1% sample of the census population. While the use of this data for the present study facilitates comparison with the data from other countries contained in this book, a limitation is that the 1% sample size is often too small to explore the experiences of

---

[4] The term 'Indigenous' is used to refer to the two main groups living in Australia at the time of European settlement. These are the Aborigines and the less numerous but nevertheless distinct Torres Strait Islanders. Both experienced European colonisation.

certain groups. In particular, it has not been possible to examine the outcomes for the second generation of many of the more recently arrived immigrant groups such as the predominantly refugee Vietnamese, the Turkish and highly educated Indians since their numbers in the CURF 1% sample are too small to allow for meaningful analysis.

Recent Australian censuses contain a variety of measures which can be used as indicators of ethnic origins: birthplace of individuals and their parents, language spoken at home, religion and, in 2001, 'ancestry'. Previously an ancestry question had been included in the 1986 Census which took place just prior to the bicentenary of European settlement. There had also been questions in earlier censuses asking for individuals' 'race'. Individuals are also asked to indicate if they are of Aboriginal or Torres Strait Islander origin. As the 2001 Census coincided with the centenary of Australian Federation and nationhood, it again included a question on ancestry to gain a more detailed understanding of Australian society on this important anniversary. The important quality of ancestry for the present study is that, in conjunction with information on parents' birthplaces, it is possible to identify both second- and third-generation ancestry.[5]

Table 2.2. Australian population (aged 18–59) from different origins (table percentages).

	First generation	Second generation	Third generation	N
Australian	0.05	1.78	24.84	26.67
Anglo-Celtic	7.16	3.96	14.93	26.03
Dutch	0.45	0.53	0.05	1.03
German	0.45	0.37	0.63	1.45
Italian	0.89	1.90	0.22	3.02
Maltese	0.28	0.34	0.02	0.64
Greek	0.65	1.13	0.07	1.86
Lebanese	0.50	0.31	0.02	0.83
Chinese	3.02	0.23	0.03	3.28
Southeast European	1.15	0.59	0.02	1.76
Central & East European	0.79	0.53	0.06	1.39
Australia-Other	0.10	3.28	5.34	8.72
Oceanic/Aboriginal, Indigenous	0.60	0.04	0.36	1.01
Other	9.74	4.00	8.57	22.31
Total percent	25.83	19.00	55.17	100.00
Total N	25,634	18,858	54,761	99,253

[5] For more detailed information on the ancestry question and how it has been used to construct the ancestries analysed in this study see Appendix 1.

Table 2.2 is based on the 1% CURF sample and shows the ancestry and generation for those ancestry groups whose size warrants their inclusion in this study. The effects of the different migration flows described above are clearly evident in the generational 'depth' of the various ancestry groupings. On the census, individuals were able to provide more than one ancestry. Indeed, 22.1% of the population did so (Kunz and Costello 2003). However, for purposes of our analysis, unless otherwise indicated, the single 'ancestries' identified in Table 2.2 are based on individuals aged 18 to 59 years old who gave only one ancestry or, in the case of regionally based ancestries, such as Anglo-Celtic or Southeast European where both their coded ancestries were from the same region, on multiple ancestries. Included in the category of Anglo-Celtic are individuals who identified themselves as having ancestries linked to various parts of the United Kingdom: English, Scots and Welsh as well as Irish. The term 'Anglo-Celtic', rather than the census terminology of United Kingdom and Ireland, is used in this analysis since it captures the way in which the earlier very strong class and religious divisions which separated nineteenth-century arrivals from England, Scotland and Ireland have largely dissipated since the Second World War with the arrival of newer, more diverse, immigrant groups.[6]

The first point to note is that the two largest ancestry groups are Australians and Anglo-Celts. But, whereas those who cite themselves as having purely Australian ancestry are concentrated in the third generation, those with an Anglo-Celtic ancestry are located across all three generations. Analysis of the 1986 ancestry data showed that, of the 20% who identified as Australians, most were English speaking, third generation from Anglo-Celtic backgrounds (Khoo and Lucas 2004). By 2001, 35.5% of the population gave Australian as at least one of their ancestries but these people remained predominantly at least third-generation individuals who spoke only English in their homes, even if their actual ethnic origins were becoming more diverse. Included among the Australians were, for example, some two-thirds of the 410,000 people (2.2% of the total

---

[6] Ancestry Data from the 1986 census shows that those of Irish ancestry had similar, or even slightly higher, levels of education, workforce participation, occupations and income than did those of British ancestry of the same generation in Australia. F. L. Jones, *Ancestry Groups in Australia: a descriptive overview* (Canberra: The Office of Multicultural Affairs and Centre for Multicultural Studies, 1991).

population) who elsewhere on the census indicated that they were of Indigenous, Aboriginal or Torres Strait Islander, background.[7]

Following the Australian and Anglo-Celtic groups in numerical prominence is the very heterogeneous group we call 'Other'. These are individuals who report either an ancestry, such as South African, New Zealander or Vietnamese, too small for separate analysis in this study, or two different ancestries (neither of which is 'Australian'). In addition to the 22.3% of working age in our study who are categorised as 'Other' there are another 8.7% who report their ancestry as being 'Australian' and another ancestry. The fact that more than one-fifth of the population report such mixed ancestries is an important feature of Australian society and highlights the extent of ethnic mixing and intermarriage in the first as well as later generations. However, precisely because of the diversity of the 'Other' group in terms of generation and ancestry, it is difficult to draw any clear conclusions about their educational and economic performance.

While extensive Chinese migration to Australia goes back to the nineteenth century, the recent arrival of large numbers of Chinese since the ending of the White Australia policy in the early 1970s is reflected in their prominence among the 18- to 59-year-olds who are the focus of this study. These Chinese actually come from many parts of the Chinese diaspora: Southeast Asia as well as Hong Kong, Taiwan and the People's Republic of China. As a result there is considerable diversity in their background, migration history and experiences in Australia (Jones 1992; Inglis 1998). Other more recent ancestry groups are the Lebanese, although the existence of a nineteenth-century migration of individuals, who at that time were called 'Syrians', is reflected in the small number of third-generation Lebanese in the sample. Two geographically grouped sets of ancestries are also more prominent among the first generation. Included among those from Central and Eastern Europe are a significant number of Hungarians, many of whom arrived after the Hungarian uprising in 1956, and Polish individuals some of whom (like a number from the Baltic states) came as refugees after the Second World War. However, also included is another group of more recent Polish-born arrivals, often

---

[7] A Census Paper identifies that methodological differences in collecting Census Data from identified Indigenous communities which are normally isolated and remote were a major factor associated with most individuals from these areas selecting an Indigenous rather than 'Australian' ancestry (Kunz and Costello 2003).

highly educated, who arrived after the Solidarity-led changes in Poland. Among the Southeastern Europeans are a substantial number of individuals from parts of the former Republic of Yugoslavia including Croatians, Serbians and Bosnians. While the more recent arrivals have come as refugees, the migration history of the earlier arrivals from these groups is similar to that of many post-war Greeks and Italians.

The longer-established nature of the Dutch, Italian, Greek and Maltese communities, resulting from migrants who arrived in the 1950s and 1960s, is evident from the way the majority are concentrated in the second generation. The first-generation Dutch are widely perceived to have a rather different background and settlement experience from the Greek, Italian and Maltese who tended to be less educated and from rural areas, often working as unskilled labour in manufacturing. While many Germans also came to Australia soon after the Second World War, the existence of an established German population, originating from German Lutheran migration to South Australia in the nineteenth century, also contributes to the way those of German ancestry are most likely to be third generation. The final ancestry group is described as 'Oceania' Aboriginal, Indigenous. While it is not a homogeneous group, the first generation consists almost entirely of Melanesians, Micronesians and Polynesians, including New Zealand Maoris, from the South Pacific, while the third generation includes Aborigines, Torres Strait Islanders and descendants of the South Sea Islanders (Kanakas) who were brought to Australia in the nineteenth century to work in the Queensland cane fields. This third-generation group is thus the group in the analysis which can be equated with Australia's Indigenous population, especially those living in isolated and remote rural communities with limited educational, occupational and social opportunities (Kunz and Costello 2003).

Educational qualifications

Responsibility for schooling and education in Australia rests with the eight individual states and territories although, through its control of funding, the Federal government has contributed towards the growing homogeneity of the national education system. School attendance is compulsory up to at least the age of 15 years but the final end of year examinations which determine students' eligibility to attend university are normally completed at 18 years old. In addition to the university system Australia has an extensive system of technical and further education

(TAFE) colleges which originally provided training for apprentices in the trade areas, of which only hairdressing was available to women. In recent years the TAFE courses have expanded into other vocational areas and the certificates and diplomas for successful completion of TAFE courses are increasingly recognised for credit towards relevant university degrees. A major feature of Australian education over recent decades has been the growing participation rates at all levels of education. Two major periods of educational expansion have occurred since the Second World War. In the 1960s and 1970s, 85% of students completed Year 10, while 34% continued to Year 12. By the early 1990s, retention to Year 10 was universal and by 1992, 75% of students completed Year 12. Women were by then more likely to complete Year 12 than men, in part reflecting the wider opportunities for men to enter TAFE training before completing secondary school (Marginson 1997). Although the retention rate to Year 12 plateaued in the later 1990s in conjunction with lower levels of unemployment, by 2001 the apparent retention rate[8] to Year 12 was again increasing to 68.1% for men and 79.1% for women. Reflecting the continuing educational divide between the Indigenous and non-Indigenous student population, the comparable figures for the Indigenous (i.e. Aboriginal and Torres Strait Islander), school populations was 74.5% for non-Indigenous and 35.7% for Indigenous students (Australian Bureau of Statistics 2004). The growing numbers of students completing Year 12 was closely linked to the expansion of enrolments in universities with 23.6% of 19-year-olds enrolled in higher education in 1992. But this was only part of the story since, at that time, four in five 15- to 19-year-olds were participating in some form of formal education. Apart from the growing participation of women in tertiary education where, by 1993, they constituted 53.5% of all university enrolments, another trend was the increasing involvement of students aged over 30 in higher education and TAFE. Often these individuals were upgrading their qualifications as in the case of those undertaking MBA degrees or post-graduate diplomas.

While the increasing levels of educational participation are not unique to Australia, they need to be taken into account when considering the educational qualifications of those from different ancestries and genera-

---

[8] The term 'apparent retention rate' refers to the percentage of the student cohort enrolled in the first year of secondary education who then continue to Year 12. As it does not correct for student repetition, emigration and other changes to the school population, it is an estimate of overall school retention.

tion. Since the focus for this analysis of educational qualifications is on those aged 18 to 59, it is important to note that many individuals in our sample will still be continuing with their education to the extent that they are studying for post-secondary qualifications. Furthermore, among the Australian-born, the younger age groups in general will have higher levels of educational attainment than their older peers. Hence, to the extent that certain ancestry groups have relatively young second-generation populations, this may affect their levels of reported educational qualifications in an often somewhat contradictory fashion. Finally, it must be born in mind that the Australian data include among the first generation all individuals born overseas regardless of whether they had all or some of their education in Australia.

Nearly one-third of all the men in the sample have incomplete secondary schooling while a similar figure have gained post-secondary vocational qualifications (see Table 2.3A). Taking the third-generation Australian men as a benchmark, it is evident that similar high levels of incomplete secondary schooling exist for all the third-generation groups, although extremely high levels of educational disadvantage among the Indigenous, Aboriginal and Torres Strait Islander group are clear from the way 83% report only incomplete secondary schooling. Even allowing for the fact that this ancestry group does not contain the many Indigenes who identified themselves as Australian, perhaps because of their mixed ancestry, the finding is consistent with what is known about Indigenous disadvantage in Australia and the continuing poor retention rates noted above. Among the second-generation Australian-born, who may also be somewhat younger, none have the high levels of incomplete secondary schooling noted in the benchmark group. However, the disparity is most marked among the non-Australian and non-Anglo-Celtic groups. This is consistent with findings from earlier research that families from a non-English speaking background place particular importance on their children gaining a good education as a means to social mobility. The story among the first-generation migrants is more varied although the high levels of incomplete secondary schooling for those from Southeastern Europe, Italy, Greece, Malta and Oceania is also consistent with what is known of the levels of educational attainment among those who arrived in Australia after the completion of their education overseas. The lowest levels of incomplete secondary schooling are recorded among the two groups of most recent migrants whose arrival in Australia coincided with immigrant selection policies favouring the more highly educated, the Chinese and the Central and Eastern Europeans. It should also be noted

Table 2.3A. Highest educational qualification, by ancestry and generation: Men (row percentages).

	Incomplete secondary	Completed secondary	Post-secondary vocational	Tertiary	Sample N
Third-generation					
Australian	36.9	17.9	33.2	12.1	11,781
First generation					
Anglo-Celtic	26.5	16.2	39.8	17.5	3,663
German	22.4	11.2	45.3	21.1	232
Italian	47.3	10.9	34.1	7.8	461
Dutch	28.7	13.9	43.5	13.9	231
Maltese	60.2	9.0	27.8	3.0	133
Greek	55.0	12.6	24.2	8.3	302
Lebanese	46.7	20.4	25.4	7.5	240
Chinese	19.8	31.3	17.9	31.0	1,274
Southeast European	39.2	20.7	28.7	11.4	536
C and E European	18.2	189.0	37.4	25.4	374
Oceanic	48.9	24.3	21.4	5.4	276
Second generation					
Australian	32.9	25.8	29.0	12.3	872
Anglo-Celtic	32.7	21.6	32.9	12.8	1,951
German	22.1	14.4	45.3	18.2	181
Italian	27.7	22.1	35.1	15.1	953
Dutch	28.7	15.5	42.2	13.6	265
Maltese	30.4	16.4	45.0	8.2	171
Greek	19.4	29.4	32.1	19.1	571
Lebanese	23.4	39.0	28.4	9.2	141
Chinese	5.3	44.7	10.6	39.3	94
Southeast European	18.2	29.1	34.9	17.8	292
C and E European	19.5	19.8	33.1	27.6	257
Australia-Other	25.5	24.45	33.20	12.86	1,509
Third generation					
Anglo-Celtic	35.5	16.6	34.7	13.2	7,468
German	44.2	15.7	30.8	9.3	344
Italian	36.6	21.4	33.9	8.0	112
Aboriginal, Indigenous	83.0	9.1	6.3	1.7	176
Australia-Other	30.0	18.8	34.4	16.8	2,439
Other	25.7	24.0	30.1	20.3	12,382
Total	31.4	20.2	32.6	15.8	49,680

that they, too, would have potentially benefited from the recent expansion of education in their own countries of origin.

Complementing the picture from examining those with the lowest level of educational qualifications is the picture obtained when those with the highest level of education, tertiary degrees and post-graduate qualifications are considered. Not surprisingly, the Aboriginal and Indigenous group have extremely low levels of tertiary qualifications, less that 2%. When we look at the second generation, the tendency is repeated for those from non-Australian and non-Anglo-Celtic backgrounds to be better qualified. The exceptions are the Maltese and Lebanese men. This pattern of relative underachievement by comparison not only with the Australians, but also with those who arrived with similar backgrounds and migration histories from Italy and, in particular, Greece is consistent with other research findings on these groups. What is particularly striking are the high levels of tertiary qualifications among the Chinese, 39.3% of whom have completed tertiary studies, and the Central and Eastern European group, where 27.6% of the men have tertiary degrees compared with the third-generation Australian men's figure of 12.1%. Among the first generation the Chinese and Central and Eastern European men also have outstandingly high levels of tertiary education which may reflect the recent selection policies favouring highly skilled immigration. As among the second generation, the levels of tertiary qualifications among the Maltese men are also lower than for the Greek, Italian, Southeastern European and Lebanese men. This suggests that whereas those Maltese who arrived as young children and had their schooling in Australia have not continued on to tertiary studies, the same is not true for the Greek, Italian as well as Lebanese men who also had a significant part of their education in Australia.

An examination of the educational qualifications for women replicates many of the intergenerational and ancestry differences noted among their menfolk (see Table 2.3B). However, in part because of their lower levels of post-secondary vocational qualifications, women, display a more bipolar pattern of educational qualifications. They are slightly more likely to have tertiary degrees than men (18% compared with 15.8%) but they are also more likely not to have completed secondary schooling (40.2% compared with 31.4%).

Again, Aboriginal and Indigenous women have the lowest level of educational qualifications of all groups. In the second generation, except for the Maltese women, the non-Australian and non-Anglo-Celtic groups are less likely to have only incomplete secondary schooling as their highest qualification. When we turn to the first generation there is, again, the same pattern of over-representation of women from Lebanese (61.1%) Italian (67.5%), Greek (73.7%) and Maltese ancestry (76.7%) among those with incomplete secondary schooling although the percentages with this limited level of education is higher than among their menfolk.

Table 2.3B. Highest educational qualification, by ancestry and generation: Women (row percentages).

	Incomplete secondary	Completed secondary	Post-secondary vocational	Tertiary	Sample N
Third-generation Australian	47.7	19.7	18.2	14.4	12,041
First generation					
Anglo-Celtic	41.4	20.7	21.1	16.9	3,281
German	33.8	18.9	27.9	19.4	201
Italian	67.5	11.8	13.4	7.3	397
Dutch	46.6	19.7	21.2	12.4	208
Maltese	76.7	12.4	8.5	2.3	129
Greek	73.7	13.9	6.3	6.0	316
Lebanese	61.1	24.9	8.3	5.7	229
Chinese	21.5	32.6	17.6	28.3	1,501
Southeast European	42.4	26.6	21.3	9.7	545
C and E European	25.8	20.7	26.8	26.8	392
Oceanic	45.5	34.3	14.4	5.8	277
Second generation					
Australian	44.4	27.5	15.1	12.9	806
Anglo-Celtic	41.5	22.4	20.5	15.6	1,865
German	40.2	18.5	20.1	21.2	184
Italian	33.5	25.7	24.7	16.2	884
Dutch	41.4	21.1	19.9	17.5	251
Maltese	44.7	22.0	21.4	11.9	251
Greek	20.1	27.8	26.8	25.3	507
Lebanese	27.9	32.4	27.9	11.8	136
Chinese	11.2	43.9	6.5	38.3	107
Southeast European	23.1	34.9	24.6	17.4	264
C and E European	29.9	19.5	22.3	28.3	251
Australia-Other	31.5	27.8	18.9	21.8	1,671
Third generation					
Anglo-Celtic	47.6	18.9	19.3	14.2	6,901
German	46.1	21.4	20.8	11.7	267
Italian	39.2	28.9	16.5	15.5	97
Aboriginal, Indigenous	83.2	6.2	9.3	1.2	161
Australia-Other	36.8	20.7	21.0	21.5	2,742
Other	32.3	24.4	20.3	23.0	14,012
Total	40.2	22.3	19.5	18.0	50,782

When we consider those women with tertiary qualifications, the same general levels of participation are noted as among the men. The exception is that, whereas among the first-generation women they are less likely to have tertiary qualifications than their menfolk, among the majority of the second and third-generation ancestry groups the women have typically higher levels of tertiary qualifications than the men. Among third-generation Australian women, for example, 14.4% have tertiary education compared with only 12.1% for their menfolk. Although the differences are often small, they suggest that women have actively pursued education as a means of empowerment and social mobility even where they are from backgrounds where women have traditionally not been encouraged to gain extensive education. The groups with fewer women than men reporting tertiary qualifications are the Aboriginal and Indigenous group and the second-generation Chinese, Southeastern European and the Central and Eastern Europeans.

Economic activity and study

As Australian students normally only begin tertiary studies at about the age of 18, the potential exists for many of the individuals in the sample to be still continuing their studies on a full-time basis at the tertiary or post secondary vocational level. Among the benchmark third-generation Australians, 3.2% report they are studying full-time (Table 2.4A). In the third generation the only group which reports a higher involvement are the small number of Italians. Among the first-generation immigrants slightly higher levels of study are reported by those from Oceania, Southeastern Europe, Central and Eastern Europe and, most prominently the Chinese (19.0%). While the Chinese figure is not entirely surprising given their high levels of tertiary qualifications noted above, it must also be taken into account that some of these Chinese students may actually be international students who have come to Australia to pursue full-time educational studies extending for periods longer than one year. However, among the second-generation Chinese, who are not international students, nearly one third also report they are studying full-time, which is consistent with the high level of second-generation Chinese with tertiary qualifications and the relative youth of the second-generation Chinese ancestry group.

The Australian data does not allow us to determine the reasons why individuals may not be participating in the labour market. However, as it is possible for individuals to gain access to their superannuation benefits from the age of 55 years and the government-funded age pension at 65, it may be that a number of the men in the sample have taken voluntary, or involuntary, retirement. Older men in particular who have lost their jobs may find it difficult to re-enter the labour market and so decide to withdraw from it. Another reason for reporting they are no

Table 2.4A. Economic activity, by ancestry and generation: Men (row percentages).

	Active	Other	Full-time student	Sample N
Third-generation Australian	87.0	9.7	3.2	12,118
First generation				
Anglo-Celtic	88.4	10.5	1.1	3,731
German	81.3	17.0	1.7	235
Italian	82.9	16.5	0.6	473
Dutch	84.3	13.6	2.1	235
Maltese	73.9	26.1	0.0	138
Greek	74.4	24.4	1.3	316
Lebanese	72.6	24.6	2.8	252
Chinese	72.7	8.3	19.0	1,367
Southeast European	76.8	18.0	5.2	555
C and E European	81.7	14.9	3.4	383
Oceanic	80.4	14.6	5.0	301
Second generation				
Australian	83.7	11.3	5.1	906
Anglo-Celtic	88.3	8.4	3.3	2,002
German	94.5	3.8	1.6	183
Italian	92.3	4.3	3.8	975
Dutch	92.9	4.1	3.0	268
Maltese	92.1	7.4	0.6	176
Greek	89.3	6.5	4.2	589
Lebanese	75.3	13.6	11.0	154
Chinese	68.5	0.0	31.5	111
Southeast European	89.1	5.6	5.3	302
C and E European	87.5	8.7	3.8	264
Australia-Other	88.2	6.9	4.9	1,538
Third generation				
Anglo-Celtic	87.3	10.3	2.5	7,661
German	90.6	7.4	2.0	352
Italian	86.6	5.9	7.6	119
Aboriginal, Indigenous	62.8	33.5	3.7	191
Australia-Other	88.4	8.0	3.6	2,474
Other	83.9	9.5	6.7	12,836
Total	85.7	9.9	4.4	51,205

longer economically active may be that they have suffered work-related injuries which have necessitated their retirement. The highest percentage of those reporting they are not economically active are the Aborigines and Indigenous group who are more than three times likely than the third-generation Australians to be outside the labour market and not studying full-time. Apart from illness, many of these men may also be living in remote and isolated communities where there is little opportunity for them to become involved in economic activities. Among the first-generation migrants, except for the Anglo-Celtic men, there are also high levels of economic inactivity which may reflect the way many of these men worked initially in heavy industry where they were at particular risk of industrial accidents, and also long-term redundancy. This is because the restructuring of the Australian economy, which began in the 1980s, has involved the closure of many of the manufacturing industries which provided work opportunities for those with fewer skills or poorer knowledge of English. The second-generation men are generally less likely to be economically inactive than the benchmark third-generation Australians. The major exception are the Lebanese men 13.6% of whom report they are not economically active. Since they are not a particularly old population, the reasons for their absence from the workforce are less clear but suggest they have been able to access welfare or disability benefits. At the same time, it is noteworthy that the second-generation Lebanese men have more than double the levels of participation in full-time education compared with other second-generation groups, apart from the Chinese, who tend to be younger, with nearly half aged between 18 and 24, the major age group likely to be continuing in full-time education.

The major difference in the patterns of economic activity and study among the men and women is that the women are more than twice as likely not to be involved in economic activity (Table 2.4B). A major reason is clearly involvement in full-time domestic duties. Absence from the labour market is most evident among the first, and to a lesser extent, the second, generation Lebanese women, who report the highest levels in both generations. One explanation for this is that those born in Lebanon typically have above average numbers of children and this may carry through from the first to the second generation. Alongside this non-participation in the labour market, both first- and second-generation Lebanese women are the group who, after the Chinese, are most likely to be still undertaking full-time study. Another noteworthy feature of women's educational participation is that Australian and Anglo-Celtic women are more likely than their men folk in the same generation to be continuing with full-time study. By the third generation this pattern of greater involvement in full-time study is typical of all the third-generation women apart from the small number of those with Italian ancestry. Although high levels of non-participation are also evident among first-generation Italian, Maltese and Greek women, these patterns are not continued into the second generation. While generation-linked cultural change is a potential explanation, first-generation women from these backgrounds when they first arrived in Australia were also employed extensively in manufacturing with the potential for exposure to industrial accidents as well as redundancy. Indeed, data from the 1950s and 1960s shows that these women, even when married, had higher levels of labour-force participation than did Australian-born women (Richmond 1974). Chinese women, like the Chinese men, are very much involved in full-time study, although in the first generation the numbers outside the labour market are not dissimilar to the German and Anglo-Celtic women. While Aboriginal and Indigenous women report high levels of non-participation in the labour market, the disparity is slightly less marked than among their menfolk.

Table 2.4B. Economic activity, by ancestry and generation: Women (row percentages).

	Active	Other	Full-time student	Sample N
Third-generation Australian	71.4	24.4	4.2	12,397
First generation				
Anglo-Celtic	71.7	25.4	2.9	3,340
German	70.6	25.0	4.4	204
Italian	58.8	40.0	1.2	408
Dutch	66.2	31.9	1.9	210
Maltese	51.5	48.5	0.0	132
Greek	49.4	48.5	2.2	326
Lebanese	32.1	61.5	6.4	234
Chinese	57.0	23.1	19.9	1,608
Southeast European	61.0	32.8	6.3	571
C and East European	65.9	29.6	4.5	399
Oceanic	59.6	33.1	7.3	287
Second generation				
Australian	67.7	24.7	7.6	852
Anglo-Celtic	71.9	24.3	3.8	1,906
German	73.3	25.5	3.2	187
Italian	77.4	20.2	2.4	907
Dutch	73.2	24.0	2.8	254
Maltese	77.7	21.7	0.6	166
Greek	80.5	15.8	3.8	527
Lebanese	59.9	31.6	8.6	152
Chinese	69.2	8.6	22.2	117
Southeast European	76.1	19.1	4.9	284
C and E European	74.4	21.0	4.6	262
Australia-Other	72.4	20.8	6.8	1,713
Third generation				
Anglo-Celtic	72.0	24.6	3.4	7,068
German	71.6	25.0	3.4	268
Italian	82.5	12.6	4.9	103
Aboriginal, Indigenous	49.4	46.4	4.2	166
Australia-Other	72.8	22.5	4.7	2,804
Other	69.0	24.0	7.0	14,449
Total	69.9	24.7	5.4	52,301

They also report slightly higher levels of participation in full-time education than the men, with the same participation rate as the third-generation Australian benchmark group.

Occupational class

In Australia, the salariat is now the most important occupational grouping for men, with one-third working as professionals or managers (Table 2.5A). At the other end of the occupational hierarchy are semi- and unskilled occupations involving one-fifth of the male labour force. In 2001, just under 13% were part of the petty bourgeoisie.

One of the most interesting findings is that by the third generation there is little deviation among the ancestry groups from the overall pattern of employment. The notable exceptions are the Aboriginal and Indigenous workers who are nearly three times more likely to be working in the unskilled and semi-skilled occupations, twice as likely to be unemployed and with less than one-third of the normal participation in the salariat. This pattern of limited participation in the higher status occupations far exceeds that evident among the third-generation Italian men.

The limited occupational distinctions between third-generation ancestry groups is all the more interesting as it stands in marked contrast to the heterogeneity evident among the first-generation migrant workers. Taking the salariat as the benchmark, there is very widespread diversity among the migrant groups. Chinese, Central and Eastern Europeans, Anglo-Celts, Germans and Dutch are far more likely to be employed in the salariat than the benchmark third-generation Australians, who resemble the Greeks and Italians in their participation, which in turn far exceeds that of the Lebanese, Maltese, Southeast Europeans and groups from Oceania. The effects of the recent policy preference for selecting highly skilled permanent as well as short-term or temporary migrants is evident in the involvement of the Chinese, Central and Eastern Europeans, as well as Anglo-Celts. The latter, together with the early German and Dutch post-war migrants also tended to have trade or other skills which set them apart from the Greek, Italian, Lebanese, Maltese and Southeastern Europeans, who entered Australia predominantly from unskilled and semi-skilled occupational backgrounds, even if their foreign born children who grew up in Australia did gain higher levels of education and qualifications. This has certainly happened among some of the foreign-born sons from Greek, Italian and Lebanese ancestries.

Table 2.5A. Current occupation, by ancestry and generation: Men (row percentages).

	Salariat	Routine non-manual	Petty bourgeoisie	Skilled manual	Semi- and unskilled	Unemployed	N
Third-generation							
Australian	30.3	7.7	13.3	16.0	24.9	7.8	10,379
First generation							
Anglo-Celtic	40.5	9.2	12.5	13.5	18.1	6.3	3,246
German	38.8	5.9	11.2	14.4	20.2	9.6	188
Italian	28.8	7.8	24.1	11.9	22.5	4.9	386
Dutch	35.5	8.6	22.8	11.7	15.7	5.6	197
Maltese	18.8	7.9	14.9	9.9	40.6	7.9	101
Greek	28.2	7.1	22.0	12.3	23.8	6.6	227
Lebanese	22.4	1.1	24.0	11.2	22.4	19.0	179
Chinese	44.8	7.3	11.5	8.5	18.4	9.5	972
Southeast European	18.4	4.4	16.2	15.3	36.3	9.4	413
C and E European	36.4	6.5	15.3	14.0	19.5	8.4	308
Oceanic	13.2	4.6	6.6	14.1	48.4	13.2	242
Second generation							
Australian	27.8	8.9	9.1	16.6	27.4	10.3	746
Anglo-Celtic	31.8	8.6	11.8	17.3	22.3	8.2	1,737
German	34.7	5.9	14.7	17.7	21.2	5.9	170
Italian	30.8	10.3	20.5	16.1	18.6	3.7	891
Dutch	35.4	3.3	15.5	17.1	22.8	6.1	246
Maltese	24.2	8.3	14.0	25.5	23.6	4.5	157
Greek	38.7	9.9	12.7	13.0	17.3	8.4	514
Lebanese	30.7	7.0	14.9	12.3	19.3	15.8	114
Chinese	57.3	14.7	4.0	8.0	10.7	5.3	75
Southeast European	34.6	4.6	8.1	18.5	23.1	11.2	260
C and East European	47.6	8.9	8.0	13.3	11.6	10.7	225
Australia-Other	35.2	8.7	9.6	16.9	22.9	6.8	1,339
Third generation							
Anglo-Celtic	32.2	8.4	14.9	14.5	22.7	7.2	6,575
German	34.5	8.5	13.6	15.8	23.1	4.4	316
Italian	26.5	8.8	10.8	15.7	35.3	2.9	102
Aboriginal, Indigenous	10.8	5.4	3.6	6.3	59.5	14.4	111
Australia-Other	36.0	8.6	13.6	14.4	21.1	6.2	2,162
Other	35.9	8.5	11.3	13.1	21.8	9.4	10,576
Total	33.6	8.2	13.0	14.5	22.7	8.0	43,154

Among the first-generation men, the group with the lowest occupational status consists of those from Oceanian ancestries which include New Zealand Maoris and those from elsewhere in Oceania. Where these individuals have New Zealand citizenship they have freedom to move and work in Australia comparable to the conditions that now operate in the European Union for nationals of member states. As such, even the recent arrivals have not been affected by the policy preference to select highly qualified workers. With the Maltese and Southeastern European men they constitute a significant part of the unskilled and semi-skilled labour force, and have unemployment levels approaching those of first-generation Lebanese men. The lower occupational status of Maltese, Southeastern European and Oceanian migrants is not necessarily associated with a higher level of participation in the petty bourgeoisie. Self-employment is far more common among those from Italian, Greek, Lebanese and Dutch backgrounds. The first Lebanese arrivals in the late nineteenth century established an economic niche for themselves as traders and hawkers, a pattern noted in other parts of the Lebanese diaspora. Subsequently, Italian and Greek migrants also established economic niches in small food-related businesses including groceries, green-groceries, fish-shops and restaurants. Among the Dutch migrants, their involvement as petty bourgeoisie is linked not so much to classic migrant small retail businesses as to businesses involving trade and agricultural skills. Significantly, although Chinese migrants also operated their own niche businesses as market gardeners and in other food-related areas before World War Two, the data from 2001 show that self-employment is now less important for them than salariat occupations, a pattern that continues into the second generation.

One of the most interesting features of the occupational patterns of the second-generation ancestry groups is that, apart from the Maltese and the Australians, all are more likely to have moved into the salariat than the benchmark third-generation Australians. The potential existence of a bipolar pattern of labour-market participation is most evident among the Lebanese second-generation men who report a level of unemployment only slightly lower than among their first-generation peers. Among the Maltese second-generation men, with their low level of unemployment, there has been some intergenerational occupational mobility, with a quarter now working in skilled manual occupations rather than in unskilled and semi-skilled occupations. In contrast to the immigrant first generation, in all except those of German ancestry there has been a reduced involvement in the labour market as petty bourgeoisie. Clearly, the salariat has been a major occupational destination and one which accords with the aspirations frequently noted among parents for whom a better life involves working in a high status, white-collar occupation with expectations of good levels of earnings.

Gender based differences in occupational patterns are evident when comparing women's with men's occupations. Women are far more likely to be employed in routine non-manual occupations and, conversely, to have lower rates of employment in all other areas with the notable exception of the salariat, where women in Australia are increasingly

Table 2.5B. Current occupation, by ancestry and generation: Women (row percentages).

	Salariat	Routine non-manual	Petty bourgeoisie	Skilled manual	Semi- and unskilled	Unemployed	N
Third-generation Australian	32.9	31.4	6.9	2.0	20.8	6.0	8,739
First generation							
Anglo-Celtic	39.0	30.4	7.8	1.9	15.7	5.2	2,359
German	37.5	26.4	9.0	2.8	16.7	7.6	144
Italian	21.9	27.5	13.3	2.6	30.5	4.3	233
Dutch	36.0	25.0	16.2	1.5	14.7	6.6	136
Maltese	24.2	27.3	9.1	3.0	34.9	1.5	66
Greek	25.2	19.5	17.6	2.5	31.5	3.8	159
Lebanese	28.8	20.6	12.3	1.4	24.7	12.3	73
Chinese	36.2	21.1	7.7	3.5	20.1	11.5	897
Southeast European	22.6	17.9	8.2	4.1	39.0	8.2	341
C and E European	36.9	25.4	9.2	1.2	18.9	8.5	260
Oceanic	20.1	27.4	2.4	2.4	34.8	12.8	164
Second generation							
Australian	28.4	27.8	6.9	1.9	26.1	9.0	568
Anglo-Celtic	34.7	31.8	6.2	1.9	18.7	6.8	1,345
German	38.8	30.6	7.5	0	14.9	8.2	134
Italian	27.9	36.1	6.8	4.3	20.1	4.9	693
Dutch	35.0	31.2	9.8	3.3	16.4	4.4	183
Maltese	25.8	45.3	3.9	2.3	21.9	0.8	128
Greek	39.2	28.9	6.7	1.7	17.1	6.5	416
Lebanese	40.9	22.7	6.8	2.3	14.8	12.5	82
Chinese	45.0	28.8	3.8	1.3	15.0	6.3	80
Southeast European	32.2	34.1	4.7	2.8	19.0	7.1	211
C and E European	42.1	33.7	3.7	3.2	11.6	5.8	190
Australia-Other	38.3	27.7	4.9	3.0	19.5	6.5	1,224
Third generation							
Anglo-Celtic	33.9	31.5	8.0	2.1	19.3	5.2	5,010
German	31.3	27.6	9.9	2.6	22.9	5.7	192
Italian	27.4	33.3	7.1	1.2	27.4	3.6	84
Aboriginal, Indigenous	25.0	22.4	2.6	2.6	30.3	17.1	76
Australia-Other	40.3	29.8	6.0	2.1	15.6	6.2	2,022
Other	38.0	27.4	6.4	2.1	18.2	7.9	9,813
Total	35.3	29.5	7.0	2.2	19.4	6.7	36,028

prominent as a result of their growing involvement in professional, if not managerial, occupations (see Table 2.5B).

Among third-generation women, there is, as in the case of men, a shift towards greater homogeneity in occupations. This is most strikingly evident in the much higher levels of participation in the salariat by Aboriginal and Indigenous women, who are not far behind Italian women in their participation. However, this is part of a bipolar pattern since, as among their menfolk, they are also over-represented among the unemployed and those working in semi- and unskilled occupations.

Among the first-generation, migrant women, the same groups are over-represented in the salariat as among the men, although the disparity between the highest participation (by the Chinese and Central and Eastern European groups) and the lowest (those from Oceanic backgrounds) is far less than in the case of the men. There is also remarkable similarity to the patterns found among men in the relative importance of other occupations across the groups. One exception, however, is that the Chinese women report a level of unemployment only slightly below that of the Lebanese women. This is not, however, found among the second generation.

Among the second-generation women, except among the Anglo-Celtic and Dutch, there is a higher participation in the salariat by the different ancestry groups, even those such as the Italian, Maltese and Southeastern European, who still are below the participation of the benchmark third-generation Australian group. The move of the Greek and the Lebanese second-generation women into the salariat is particularly notable, although in the case of the Lebanese the sample size is small, not least, as was noted above, because of their high level of non-participation in the labour market. Another dimension of the somewhat bipolar pattern within the Lebanese group is that among the second-generation women there continues to be the same high level of unemployment found among the first-generation immigrants. The disparities in the involvement of second generation in the various occupations are much less than among their menfolk, which replicates the finding for the first generation. That is women from different ancestry groups differ less in their occupations than do their menfolk. Whether this reflects the narrower range of occupations 'open' to women than men is an issue to keep in mind.

Avoidance of unemployment

Unemployment is widely seen as the clearest indication of exclusion from the labour market. The regression results presented in Table 2.6 provide evidence of the extent to which particular groups are able to avoid such exclusion and, conversely, which groups are more prone to unemployment, as indicated by a negative score. Beginning with the table's lower panel, observe that the effect of such factors as age, education and marital status operate in the generally expected fashion. The effect of age is curvilinear with unemployment initially declining with age and then increasing as individuals become older. Married people or those in de facto relationships are less likely to be unemployed, although divorced women experience higher levels of unemployment. Increased education is associated with higher chances of employment, thereby coinciding with the views of many immigrant parents that education is the road to social and economic mobility in Australia.

The extent to which certain ancestry groups experience an 'ethnic penalty', with significantly higher levels of unemployment after controlling for their age, level of education and marital status, varies across groups and, to a lesser extent, generations. Among men, significantly higher levels of unemployment by comparison with the third-generation Australian benchmark group are found among first-generation migrants of Oceanic, Chinese, Lebanese Southeastern and Central and Eastern European ancestries as well, perhaps surprisingly, as Germans and the diverse, multi-generational Other group. In the second generation, the effects of an ethnic penalty are less evident, with unemployment being significantly higher only among Lebanese and Central and Eastern

Table 2.6. Logistic regression of employment and unemployment (parameter estimates: contrasts with unemployment).

	Men				Women			
	Model A		Model B		Model A		Model B	
Intercept	−2.25	(0.07)	−2.31	(0.07)	−2.76	(0.09)	−2.81	(0.09)
Ancestry								
Australian 3	0		0		0		0	
Anglo-Celtic 1	−0.08	(0.08)	−0.08	(0.09)	−0.18	(0.11)	−0.17	(0.11)
German 1	**−0.64**	(0.26)	**−0.62**	(0.28)	**−0.82**	(0.32)	**−0.86**	(0.33)
Italian 1	0.21	(0.24)	0.31	(0.29)	−0.06	(0.33)	−0.21	(0.36)
Dutch 1	−0.07	(0.32)	−0.12	(0.32)	−0.56	(0.35)	−0.51	(0.39)
Maltese 1	−0.15	(0.38)	0.01	(0.48)	1.00	(1.01)	–	–
Greek 1	−0.02	(0.27)	−0.05	(0.29)	0.21	(0.42)	−0.57	(0.82)
Lebanese 1	**−1.28**	(0.20)	**−1.29**	(0.20)	**−1.05**	(0.37)	−0.68	(0.51)
Chinese 1	**−0.59**	(0.12)	**−0.58**	(0.13)	**−1.11**	(0.12)	**−1.04**	(0.14)
Southeast European 1	**−0.52**	(0.18)	**−0.58**	(0.18)	**−0.61**	(0.21)	**−0.63**	(0.21)
C and E European 1	**−0.50**	(0.21)	−0.37	(0.25)	**−0.91**	(0.23)	**−0.66**	(0.30)
Oceanic 1	**−0.64**	(0.20)	−0.36	(0.27)	**−0.79**	(0.24)	**−0.81**	(0.27)
Australian 2	−0.10	(0.13)	−0.14	(0.13)	−0.21	(0.16)	−0.12	(0.18)
Anglo-Celtic 2	−0.03	(0.10)	−0.06	(0.10)	−0.12	(0.12)	−0.14	(0.12)
German 2	0.09	(0.33)	0.41	(0.42)	−0.55	(0.33)	−0.55	(0.33)
Italian 2	**0.68**	(0.18)	**0.65**	(0.19)	0.17	(0.18)	0.14	(0.19)
Dutch 2	0.04	(0.27)	0.06	(0.29)	0.27	(0.37)	0.23	(0.37)
Maltese 2	0.59	(0.39)	0.53	(0.39)	**2.25**	(1.01)	–	–
Greek 2	−0.14	(0.17)	−0.18	(0.17)	−0.14	(0.21)	−0.22	(0.22)

	Model 1		Model 2		Model 3		Model 4	
Lebanese 2	**−0.63**	(0.27)	**−0.62**	(0.29)	**−0.67**	(0.33)	−0.28	(0.43)
Chinese 2	0.35	(0.52)	0.60	(0.73)	0.02	(0.47)	1.27	(1.01)
Southeast European 2	−0.40	(0.21)	**−0.42**	(0.21)	−0.09	(0.28)	−0.24	(0.28)
C and E European 2	**−0.56**	(0.23)	**−0.69**	(0.23)	−0.25	(0.32)	−0.23	(0.34)
Australian-Other 2	0.19	(0.12)	0.21	(0.12)	−0.06	(0.13)	−0.08	(0.13)
Anglo-Celtic 3	0.04	(0.06)	0.06	(0.06)	0.07	(0.08)	0.10	(0.08)
German 3	**0.58**	(0.28)	0.55	(0.30)	−0.10	(0.32)	−0.11	(0.32)
Italian 3	**1.28**	(0.59)			0.86	(0.59)	0.83	(0.64)
Aboriginal, Indigene 3	−0.33	(0.28)	**−1.00**	(0.32)	**−0.98**	(0.32)	**−1.21**	(0.38)
Australian-Other 3	0.10	(0.10)	0.08	(0.10)	−0.14	(0.10)	−0.16	(0.11)
Other	**−0.31**	(0.05)	**−0.33**	(0.05)	**−0.44**	(0.06)	**−0.42**	(0.06)
Age	**0.01**	(0.00)	**0.01**	(0.00)	**0.03**	(0.00)	**0.03**	(0.00)
Age-squared	**−0.01**	(0.00)	**−0.001**	(0.00)	**−0.001**	(0.00)	**−0.001**	(0.00)
Qualifications								
Incomplete secondary	**−0.67**	(0.05)	**−0.76**	(0.06)	**−0.65**	(0.06)	**−0.73**	(0.07)
Completed secondary	0		0		0		0	
Post-secondary vocational	**0.16**	(0.05)	**0.15**	(0.07)	0.01	(0.01)	0.06	(0.08)
Tertiary	**0.65**	(0.08)	**0.75**	(0.11)	**0.70**	(0.08)	**0.91**	(0.13)
Marital Status								
Single	0		0		0		0	
Married	**1.06**	(0.05)	**1.07**	(0.05)	**0.84**	(0.06)	**0.83**	(0.06)
Divorced	0.10	(0.07)	0.10	(0.07)	**−0.27**	(0.08)	**−0.29**	(0.08)
Significant Interactions with Education								
Aboriginal 3			**−0.98**	(0.32)	Greek 2		**0.69**	(0.26)
Australia, other 2			**0.29**	(0.13)	Chinese 1		**−0.26**	(0.11)
Anglo-Celtic 1			**−0.17**	(0.08)	C and E European 1		**−0.55**	(0.22)
Chinese 1			**−0.21**	(0.11)	Other		**−0.19**	(0.06)
Chi-square (d.f.)	1871.2 (36)		1914.89 (65)		1335.52 (36)		1368.35 (65)	
N	43,154		42,315		36,028		35,192	

Notes: Emboldened coefficients indicate significance at the 0.05 level or better; standard errors are given in parentheses.

Europeans. Conversely, second- and third-generation Italian men stand out with lower than anticipated levels of unemployment. These figures suggest that, other things being equal, generational time in Australia has the ability to overcome barriers to participation in the labour market. Nevertheless, the experience of groups such as the Lebanese highlights the need to explore further the role of discrimination and cultural factors in unemployment.

The precise nature of barriers to employment can be difficult to determine. In Australia it is widely believed that fluency in English, and also period of residence, alongside contextual factors such as the economic environment on their arrival and the existence of institutional discrimination are all factors affecting employment outcomes. The present data allows us to explore whether education interacts in a complex manner with unemployment outcomes. This was tested in the second model (Model B) which examined whether increased levels of education was associated with the expected reduced risk of unemployment. While there was in general support for this interpretation, in the case of first-generation Anglo-Celtic, Chinese, and those of Aboriginal and Indigenous ancestry more education did not result in lower levels of unemployment. The latter finding was particularly interesting since the initial analysis suggested that, in general, Aboriginal and Indigenous men, 83% of whom had never completed secondary school, fared no worse in the labour market than other men of comparable background. The finding on educational qualifications indicates that better-educated Aboriginal and Indigenous men were, however, more likely to experience unemployment. Whether the better-educated men are more likely to be competing for employment in the general, rather than a regional or niche, job market and hence are more likely to suffer various forms of discrimination is one possibility. In contrast to the Aboriginal and Indigenous group, the first-generation Chinese are the best-educated of all the first-generation ancestry groups, reporting very high levels of tertiary education. However, the findings from this analysis indicate that those among them with more education are actually more likely to experience unemployment. Among the reasons for this may be that they lack fluency in spoken and written English, and also their tertiary qualifications may not be recognised, formally or informally, as being of the same standard of those individuals educated in Australia or British-oriented education systems. Another possibility is that the better-educated men may be pursuing a strategy in which unemployment is seen as preferable to working in jobs where they are underemployed and their skills and experience are not recognised.

The final columns of Table 2.6 indicate that similar patterns of ethnic penalty characterise women as men from the same ethnic backgrounds. In the first generation, unemployment is significantly more likely among Oceanic, Chinese, Lebanese, Southeastern and Central and Eastern

European women as well, again somewhat surprisingly, as Germans and the very diverse and multi-generational Other group. In the second generation, the effects of an ethnic penalty are less evident, with unemployment being significantly higher only among Lebanese. Conversely, Maltese women show markedly lower levels of unemployment. This data suggests that second-generation women are more likely than men to avoid unemployment, which may relate to the tendencies noted in earlier tables for second-generation women to be very similar, or even outperform, the third-generation Australian women. However, another possibility to note is that women may avoid unemployment by leaving the labour market. For women this can be a socially more acceptable option than for men, who we noted above were much less likely to be economically inactive than comparable women. The major contrast with male unemployment patterns actually is the case of Aboriginal and Indigenous women who were significantly more likely to experience unemployment than other comparable women. However, when it comes to examining the effects of education on unemployment, the more highly educated Aboriginal and Indigenous women do not experience the higher levels of unemployment noted among better-educated Aboriginal and Indigenous men. Both the first-generation Chinese women as well as those of Central and Eastern European ancestry were, like Chinese men, finding that those with higher levels of education are not so likely to be protected from unemployment. The reasons for this may be similar to those among men and involve their fluency in English, and also educational qualifications obtained in a non-British educational system. Within the Greek community, considerable importance is attached to educational success which results in higher levels of educational attainment (Martin and Meade 1979). In line with this perception is the present finding which shows that, among second-generation Greek women, more extensive education is linked to lower levels of unemployment.

Occupational attainment

Gaining employment is an important first step towards incorporation in society. The equally important next step is to obtain a job commensurate with an individual's skill and experience, and here again, there is the potential for ethnic penalties to come into play. Regression analysis of the Australian data follows that used for other countries in this study and focuses on comparing employment in the salariat and the petty bourgeoisie with the likelihood of being employed in unskilled manual occupations, with the Australian third generation being the comparison group. Starting again with the lowest panel, Table 2.7A shows that education is an important factor in avoiding employment in unskilled manual occupations. Just as those men who have gained post-secondary and tertiary qualifications are significantly more likely than their counterparts to be employed in the salariat and the petty bourgeoisie, so too are married men more likely to hold desirable occupations than are single men. In the case of the petty bourgeoisie, divorced men are also more likely to be among the petty bourgeoisie than single men. Age, as found in other countries, is also generally associated with avoiding employment in unskilled jobs.

When considering participation in the salariat it is evident that the tendency is for first-generation men to be less likely to gain employment there than their third-generation Australian counterparts. The underrepresentation is significantly marked for Maltese, Southeastern and Central and Eastern European men and those from Oceania. The one group who are markedly over-represented are Anglo-Celtic men. This is not entirely surprising since in recent years they have constituted the major group of highly skilled migrants admitted on long term temporary

Table 2.7A. Logistic regression of occupational class: Men (parameter estimates; contrasts with semi- and unskilled class).

	Salariat		Routine non-manual		Petty bourgeoisie		Skilled manual	
Intercept	−0.04	(0.06)	**−0.84**	(0.07)	**−1.17**	(0.07)	**−1.47**	(0.07)
Ancestry								
Australian 3	0		0		0		0	
Anglo-Celtic 1	**0.23**	(0.06)	**0.35**	(0.08)	−0.13	(0.08)	0.09	(0.07)
German 1	−0.21	(0.23)	−0.33	(0.35)	**−0.61**	(0.28)	−0.13	(0.27)
Italian 1	−0.06	(0.16)	0.14	(0.22)	0.24	(0.16)	−0.05	(0.19)
Dutch 1	0.13	(0.24)	0.40	(0.31)	0.38	(0.24)	0.01	(0.29)
Maltese 1	**−0.89**	(0.30)	−0.35	(0.39)	**−0.81**	(0.31)	**−0.76**	(0.37)
Greek 1	−0.07	(0.20)	−0.01	(0.29)	0.26	(0.20)	0.13	(0.24)
Lebanese 1	−0.21	(0.25)	**−1.87**	(0.72)	**0.60**	(0.23)	−0.10	(0.29)
Chinese 1	−0.04	(0.11)	−0.06	(0.15)	−0.07	(0.13)	−0.08	(0.14)
Southeast European 1	**−1.40**	(0.17)	**−1.13**	(0.26)	**−0.57**	(0.16)	−0.29	(0.16)
C and E European 1	**−0.46**	(0.19)	−0.25	(0.27)	−0.16	(0.21)	0.02	(0.21)
Oceanic 1	**−1.46**	(0.22)	**−1.25**	(0.32)	**−1.38**	(0.27)	**−0.63**	(0.21)
Australian 2	0.02	(0.12)	0.08	(0.15)	−0.12	(0.15)	−0.04	(0.12)
Anglo-Celtic 2	**0.20**	(0.08)	**0.21**	(0.11)	0.09	(0.10)	**0.20**	(0.09)
German 2	−.06	(0.24)	−0.27	(0.36)	0.12	(0.28)	0.01	(0.26)

Italian 2	0.20	(0.11)	**0.48**	(0.14)	**0.79**	(0.12)	0.23	(0.12)
Dutch 2	0.11	(0.19)	**−0.87**	(0.38)	0.11	(0.22)	0.01	(0.22)
Maltese 2	−0.04	(0.26)	0.12	(0.33)	0.24	(0.29)	0.32	(0.24)
Greek 2	**0.47**	(0.15)	**0.46**	(0.18)	**0.53**	(0.17)	0.06	(0.17)
Lebanese 2	**0.68**	(0.30)	0.17	(0.42)	**1.07**	(0.34)	−0.15	(0.36)
Chinese 2	**1.24**	(0.43)	**1.30**	(0.47)	0.36	(0.70)	0.34	(0.55)
Southeast European 2	0.08	(0.19)	−0.58	(0.32)	−0.16	(0.27)	0.06	(0.21)
C and E European 2	**0.69**	(0.24)	**0.67**	(0.30)	0.10	(0.32)	**0.58**	(0.28)
Australian-Other 2	**0.21**	(0.09)	0.15	(0.12)	−0.01	(0.12)	0.02	(0.10)
Anglo-Celtic 3	0.09	(0.05)	**0.17**	(0.06)	**0.12**	(0.06)	−0.01	(0.05)
German 3	**0.37**	(0.17)	0.25	(0.23)	0.02	(0.20)	0.21	(0.19)
Italian 3	−0.14	(0.29)	−0.12	(0.38)	−0.21	(0.36)	−0.46	(0.32)
Aboriginal, Indigene 3	**−1.13**	(0.34)	**−0.93**	(0.43)	**−1.78**	(0.52)	**−1.30**	(0.41)
Australian-Other 3	**0.16**	(0.07)	**0.21**	(0.10)	0.12	(0.09)	−0.02	(0.08)
Other	0.02	(0.04)	0.10	(0.06)	−0.06	(0.05)	−0.09	(0.05)
Age	**0.03**	(0.00)	**0.01**	(0.00)	**0.05**	(0.00)	**−0.02**	(0.00)
Age-squared	**−0.002**	(0.00)	**−0.001**	(0.00)	**−0.002**	(0.00)	**0.001**	(0.00)
Qualifications								
Incomplete secondary	**−1.22**	(0.04)	**−0.88**	(0.05)	**−0.26**	(0.05)	0.01	(0.05)
Completed secondary	0		0		0		0	
Post-secondary vocational	**0.44**	(0.04)	0.01	(0.05)	**0.96**	(0.05)	**1.84**	(0.05)
Tertiary	**2.82**	(0.07)	**1.16**	(0.08)	**1.10**	(0.09)	**0.37**	(0.12)
Marital Status								
Single	0		0		0		0	
Married	**0.61**	(0.04)	**0.23**	(0.05)	**0.76**	(0.05)	**0.28**	(0.05)
Divorced	0.11	(0.07)	0.04	(0.09)	**0.23**	(0.08)	0.12	(0.08)
Chi-square (d.f.)			16471.32 (144)					
N			39,723					

Notes: Reference category is unskilled manual work. Emboldened coefficients indicate significance at the 0.05 level or better; standard errors are given in parentheses.

entry visas whose migration is directly linked to their employment in the salariat. Although both first-generation Chinese and Lebanese men were significantly more likely to be unemployed, this pattern is not replicated in employment in the salariat and points to the existence of a bipolar pattern of economic activity for both ethnic groups. The importance of the migration experience as a key factor associated with under-participation in the salariat is reinforced by the experiences of the second- and third-generation men, many of whom are actually over-represented in the salariat by comparison with the third-generation Australians. The exceptions to this trend are, again, the Aboriginal and Indigenous men who are significantly under-represented in the salariat and, indeed, in all others apart from the unskilled manual occupations.

Among those in the petty bourgeoisie a similar pattern of initial under-representation in the first generation is followed by over-representation in the second generation. The over-representation of the first- and second-generation Lebanese in the petty bourgeoisie can be seen as following a tradition which began in the early years of Lebanese immigration when they gained a reputation as hawkers and traders. Traditionally both Italians and Greeks had a reputation for their involvement in the food industry particularly as owners of greengrocers, fish and chip shops and restaurants. While this tradition of business ownership is not significantly present among the first generation, it may explain the preference evident among the second generation. The absence of Chinese as prominent participants in the petty bourgeoisie is somewhat unexpected given the emphasis attributed by themselves and others to their pursuing this route in the countries to which they have emigrated. The Australian data suggests that what is sometimes asserted to be a cultural preference is overlooked in situations where opportunities for participation in the salariat are available.[9]

Among women, a similar pattern of incorporation in the labour market is as evident as among men (see Table 2.7B). The more educated and the married are more likely to be employed in the salariat and the petty bourgeoisie than the less educated and the single. The higher involvement of divorced as compared to single women, as well as men, in the petty bourgeoisie is an interesting finding which raises questions as to whether such occupations have particular appeal for single parents who can balance child care responsibilities by working in their own business. Although interesting questions, ultimately they cannot be answered from our present analysis.

Again, as with their menfolk, the same patterns of participation in the salariat exist with the first-generation women tending to be under-represented although the groups affected in this way also include the Greek, Chinese and Italian women. By the second and third generation the employment of all women is very similar to that of the third-

[9] It should be noted that as defined in this study the petty bourgeosie includes both large and small enterprises. It thus may confound two somewhat different outcomes: on the one hand, the use of self-employment as a means for avoiding economic discrimination; on the other, the gaining of significant power and influence from operating a large and profitable enterprise.

Table 2.7B. Logistic regression of occupational class: Women (parameter estimates; contrast with semi- and unskilled class).

	Salariat		Routine non-manual		Petty bourgeoisie		Skilled manual	
Intercept	**0.62**	(0.07)	**0.84**	(0.06)	**−1.87**	(0.12)	**−2.79**	(0.16)
Ancestry								
Australian 3	0		0		0		0	
Anglo-Celtic 1	0.13	(0.08)	0.12	(0.07)	0.02	(0.10)	0.24	(0.18)
German 1	−0.22	(0.27)	−0.18	(0.27)	−0.12	(0.35)	0.53	(0.55)
Italian 1	**−0.92**	(0.21)	**−0.58**	(0.18)	−0.27	(0.22)	0.10	(0.44)
Dutch 1	0.23	(0.29)	0.01	(0.29)	**0.67**	(0.32)	0.17	(0.75)
Maltese 1	−0.56	(0.35)	**−0.62**	(0.32)	−0.75	(0.46)	0.25	(0.75)
Greek 1	**−0.53**	(0.24)	**−0.89**	(0.23)	0.12	(0.24)	0.19	(0.53)
Lebanese 1	−0.21	(0.35)	**−0.69**	(0.35)	0.14	(0.42)	−0.53	(1.04)
Chinese 1	**−0.79**	(0.11)	**−0.65**	(0.11)	−0.19	(0.15)	**0.52**	(0.21)
Southeast European 1	**−1.34**	(0.17)	**−1.39**	(0.16)	**−0.86**	(0.22)	0.01	(0.30)
C and E European 1	**−0.71**	(0.21)	**−0.39**	(0.20)	−0.18	(0.26)	−0.62	(0.60)
Oceanic 1	**−0.84**	(0.24)	**−0.71**	(0.20)	**−1.57**	(0.52)	−0.29	(0.53)
Australian 2	−0.19	(0.14)	**−0.27**	(0.12)	0.12	(0.19)	−0.27	(0.32)
Anglo-Celtic 2	0.17	(0.10)	0.11	(0.09)	0.10	(0.14)	−0.02	(0.22)
German 2	0.24	(0.30)	0.19	(0.28)	0.27	(0.40)	—	
Italian 2	**−0.38**	(0.13)	0.03	(0.11)	0.01	(0.18)	**0.62**	(0.22)
Dutch 2	0.08	(0.25)	0.14	(0.23)	0.57	(0.31)	0.69	(0.46)
Maltese 2	−0.19	(0.29)	0.32	(0.24)	−0.32	(0.50)	−0.03	(0.62)
Greek 2	−0.13	(0.16)	−0.11	(0.16)	0.30	(0.24)	−0.33	(0.41)
Lebanese 2	0.67	(0.36)	−0.04	(0.36)	0.88	(0.51)	0.09	(0.77)
Chinese 2	0.37	(0.39)	0.32	(0.36)	0.54	(0.68)	−0.04	(1.05)
Southeast European 2	0.03	(0.22)	0.08	(0.20)	0.16	(0.37)	0.26	(0.45)
C and E European 2	0.30	(0.27)	0.49	(0.25)	−0.26	(0.44)	**0.96**	(0.47)
Australian-Other 2	0.11	(0.10)	−0.06	(0.09)	−0.01	(0.16)	0.38	(0.20)
Anglo-Celtic 3	0.04	(0.06)	0.05	(0.05)	0.13	(0.08)	0.12	(0.13)
German 3	−0.22	(0.23)	−0.30	(0.21)	0.07	(0.29)	0.12	(0.48)
Italian 3	−0.26	(0.35)	−0.10	(0.29)	0.34	(0.48)	−1.85	(1.03)
Aboriginal, Indigene 3	0.04	(0.34)	−0.56	(0.33)	−1.28	(0.75)	0.03	(0.74)
Australian-Other 3	**0.26**	(0.08)	**0.18**	(0.08)	0.14	(0.12)	0.24	(0.18)
Other	**−0.15**	(0.05)	**−0.12**	(0.04)	−0.01	(0.07)	0.06	(0.11)
Age	**0.04**	(0.00)	**0.01**	(0.00)	**0.06**	(0.00)	**−0.02**	(0.00)
Age-squared	**−0.003**	(0.00)	**−0.002**	(0.00)	**−0.003**	(0.00)	−0.001	(0.00)
Qualifications								
Incomplete secondary	**−1.11**	(0.05)	**−0.52**	(0.04)	**−0.32**	(0.07)	0.07	(0.11)
Completed secondary	0		0		0		0	

Table 2.7B. Logistic regression of occupational class: Women (parameter estimates; contrast with semi- and unskilled class). (*cont.*)

	Salariat		Routine non-manual		Petty bourgeoisie		Skilled manual	
Post-secondary vocational	**0.95**	(0.05)	**0.50**	(0.05)	**0.74**	(0.08)	**1.63**	(0.11)
Tertiary	**2.85**	(0.07)	**0.58**	(0.07)	**0.85**	(0.11)	**0.51**	(0.20)
Marital Status								
Single	0		0		0		0	
Married	**0.15**	(0.05)	0.04	(0.05)	**1.38**	(0.10)	0.09	(0.11)
Divorced	−0.02	(0.07)	−0.01	(0.06)	**0.29**	(0.13)	0.16	(0.16)
Chi-square (d.f.)				12361.63 (144)				
N				33633				

Notes: Reference category is unskilled manual work. Emboldened coefficients indicate significance at the 0.05 level or better; standard errors are given in parentheses.

generation Australian women, with only the second-generation Italian women being markedly under-represented. Particularly striking is the similarity of Aboriginal and Indigenous women's participation in the salariat to that of other women. Given the greater likelihood that this group is also unemployed, and is most unlikely to actually be participating in the labour market, it appears that there is a bipolar pattern of labour-market activity among the Aboriginal and Indigenous women.

Among women there is little evidence of the petty bourgeoisie being a preferred occupation for specific ethnic groups. Among the Dutch, Central and Eastern European and Oceanic first-generation migrant women, there is actually an under-representation relative to the benchmark, third-generation Australian group. One of the most striking features among the employment patterns of working women is how closely they follow the patterns evident among the third-generation Australian women. The major departure is with the first-generation migrants generally being under-represented in the routine non-manual occupations and this disappears by the second generation. The data in fact suggests that, instead of the existence of ethnic penalties determining the occupations of women in Australia, shared gender-based influences may play a role in the employment patterns of all the women.

Data on the differential returns to education for both men and women are contained in Table 2.8A and Table 2.8B which list only the groups for which a significant interaction was recorded. Among the men in particular it is difficult to discern any clear pattern emerging with regard to employment in the salariat or the petty bourgeoisie. Given the number of ethnic groups being studied and, hence, the number of interactions being tested, it may be that some of the significant results actually reflect the operation of chance. One of the most interesting features of women's occupational involvement is that, for those in the salariat, groups ethnically 'closer' to the third-generation Australian benchmark, such as those of Anglo-Celtic or mixed Australian and Other ancestry, tend to get significantly poorer returns for their education. How much this is a reflection of numerous tests for interaction effects producing chance results is difficult to determine. Otherwise, it may point to a tendency for women from

Table 2.8A. Occupational class and differential returns to education: Men (parameter estimates; contrasts with semi- and unskilled manual class).

	Salariat		Routine non-manual		Petty bourgeoisie		Skilled manual	
Main effects of Ancestry								
Australian-Other 3	0.07	(0.08)	0.19	(0.10)	0.12	(0.09)	0.01	(0.09)
Australian 2	0.07	(0.12)	0.06	(0.16)	−0.28	(0.17)	0.01	(0.13)
Italian 2	0.20	(0.12)	**0.38**	(0.14)	**0.78**	(0.12)	0.20	(0.13)
Greek 2	**0.43**	(0.16)	0.32	(0.20)	**0.53**	(0.18)	0.11	(0.18)
Lebanese 2	**0.80**	(0.32)	0.23	(0.45)	**0.97**	(0.39)	0.01	(0.38)
Australian-Other 2	0.14	(0.10)	0.08	(0.12)	−0.08	(0.12)	0.07	(0.10)
Anglo-Celtic 1	**0.25**	(0.07)	**0.33**	(0.08)	−0.18	(0.08)	0.06	(0.08)
German 1	−0.18	(0.26)	−1.08	(0.59)	−0.59	(0.31)	−0.81	(0.50)
Chinese 1	−0.07	(0.12)	−0.19	(0.17)	−0.10	(0.13)	−0.02	(0.14)
Other	0.01	(0.05)	0.02	(0.06)	−0.08	(0.05)	−0.06	(0.05)
Significant interactions								
Australian-Other 3	0.04	(0.08)	0.03	(0.11)	−0.15	(0.09)	**−0.18**	(0.09)
Australia 2	−0.12	(0.13)	0.14	(0.17)	**0.34**	(0.17)	−0.16	(0.14)
Italian 2	−0.20	(0.12)	0.10	(0.15)	**−0.28**	(0.12)	−0.16	(0.14)
Greek 2	−0.18	(0.17)	0.07	(0.21)	−0.36	(0.19)	**−0.39**	(0.19)
Lebanese 2	**−0.86**	(0.32)	**−1.32**	(0.56)	−0.30	(0.39)	−0.80	(0.42)
Australian-Other 2	−0.01	(0.10)	0.12	(0.13)	0.02	(0.13)	**−0.29**	(0.11)
Anglo-Celtic 1	**−0.17**	(0.07)	−0.08	(0.09)	−0.06	(0.08)	−0.12	(0.08)
German 1	0.21	(0.26)	**1.13**	(0.47)	0.08	(0.31)	0.89	(0.48)
Chinese 1	−0.10	(0.11)	0.14	(0.15)	−0.12	(0.13)	**−0.45**	(0.15)
Other	**−0.14**	(0.05)	0.08	(0.06)	**−0.15**	(0.05)	**−0.27**	(0.05)
Chi-square (d.f.)			16420.43 (260)					
N			39,000					

Notes: Reference category is unskilled manual work. Emboldened coefficients indicate significance at the 0.05 level or better; standard errors are given in parentheses.

Table 2.8B. Occupational class and differential returns to education: Women (parameter estimates; contrasts with semi- and unskilled class).

	Salariat		Routine non-manual		Petty bourgeoisie		Skilled manual	
Main effects of Ancestry								
Australian-Other 3	**0.24**	(0.09)	0.14	(0.08)	0.08	(0.12)	0.19	(0.18)
Anglo-Celtic 2	0.11	(0.10)	0.04	(0.09)	0.03	(0.14)	−0.09	(0.22)
Italian 2	**−0.44**	(0.14)	−0.01	(0.11)	−0.07	(0.18)	**0.53**	(0.23)
Australian-Other 2	0.10	(0.10)	−0.13	(0.09)	−0.10	(0.16)	0.28	(0.20)
Anglo-Celtic 1	0.12	(0.08)	0.06	(0.08)	−0.05	(0.11)	0.13	(0.19)
Chinese 1	**−0.82**	(0.14)	**−0.90**	(0.12)	−0.28	(0.16)	**0.53**	(0.22)
Other	**−0.15**	(0.05)	**−0.18**	(0.05)	−0.07	(0.07)	−0.01	(0.11)
Significant Interactions								
Australian-Other 3	**−0.18**	(0.09)	−0.12	(0.09)	−0.15	(0.12)	−0.19	(0.20)
Anglo-Celtic 2	**−0.21**	(0.10)	−0.18	(0.10)	−0.19	(0.14)	−0.20	(0.24)
Italian 2	−0.25	(0.13)	**−0.27**	(0.12)	−0.19	(0.18)	−0.08	(0.24)
Australian-Other 2	**−0.41**	(0.10)	**−0.30**	(0.10)	**−0.32**	(0.15)	−0.34	(0.22)
Anglo-Celtic 1	**−0.20**	(0.08)	−0.11	(0.08)	−0.15	(0.11)	0.13	(0.19)
Chinese 1	−0.03	(0.12)	**0.33**	(0.12)	−0.15	(0.16)	−0.12	(0.23)
Other	**−0.24**	(0.05)	−0.10	(0.06)	**−0.24**	(0.07)	−0.10	(0.12)
Chi-square (d.f.)			12149.30 (260)					
N			32,887					

Notes: Reference category is unskilled manual work. Emboldened coefficients indicate significance at the 0.05 level or better; standard errors are given in parentheses.

these backgrounds to be less oriented to upward mobility and to be content with underemployment in lower status occupations, albeit ones in which they have lesser responsibilities and work-related pressures.

Income

In contrast to occupation, which provides an indicator of social class linked primarily to status rather than economic position or power, income constitutes a direct measure of the material rewards individuals have attained in the labour market and whether they are experiencing material disadvantage. Furthermore, it can point to the existence of glass ceilings or similar barriers which transfer discrimination from hiring to promotion practices. It also directly affects life chances and opportunities for consumption related to participation in diverse cultural and status oriented groups. We therefore carry out a regression analysis of income differences within each of our five broad social classes in order to see whether ethnic minorities secure the same levels of income as the members of the charter population within the class in question.

This regression analysis examining the extent to which income levels indicate the operation of ethnic penalties for individuals from diverse ancestries and generational backgrounds has been expanded to include, in addition to education and marital status, two additional types of variable, which are often suggested as directly affecting income potential. The first is knowledge and fluency in English since, in Australia's very diverse society, it is rare to find self-contained ethnic niche economies where individuals can advance significantly without using English in their day to day work. In the analysis presented in Tables 2.9A and 2.9B, two measures of English proficiency are used. The first compares individuals who only speak English in their homes (84.6%) thus approximating a measure of 'native speaker', with individuals who speak languages other than English in their homes and report they either speak 'no English' or 'do not speak it well'. The second measure compares those who speak languages other than English in the home, and also indicate they speak English either 'well', or 'very well' with the same comparison group as those who have either limited or no English.

The second type of variable which is used in analysing the income data is geographical residence. This allows us to explore the potential influence on income of differences related to the operation of regional labour markets. Australia's population is concentrated in a small number of major cities the largest of which are Sydney and Melbourne with populations in 2001 of respectively 4 million and 3.4 million or 21% and 18% of the total population. These are also the two cities which have the largest numbers of individuals speaking a language other than English in the home. Using non-urban residence as the comparison, the analysis examines the effects of living respectively in Sydney, Melbourne and other urban areas.

The effect of age and education on the income levels of Australian men conforms to the normal patterns with older workers typically having higher levels of income—although with a curvilinear effect. The exception is among the petty bourgeoisie. Our regression analysis also indicates that increasing educational levels are associated with higher income levels. Given the close relationship between post-secondary vocational education as the entry point to skilled manual work and related petty bourgeoisie enterprises, it is not surprising to find that possession of this

Table 2.9A. Regression of Income within Occupational Classes: Men (parameter estimates).

	Salariat		Routine non-manual		Petty Bourgeoisie		Skilled manual		Unskilled manual	
Intercept	**2.40**	(0.07)	**2.55**	(0.10)	**2.42**	(0.10)	**2.69**	(0.06)	**2.59**	(0.04)
Ancestry										
Australian 3	0		0		0		0		0	
Anglo-Celtic 1	**0.05**	(0.02)	0.00	(0.03)	**0.13**	(0.04)	0.01	(0.02)	0.03	(0.02)
German 1	0.04	(0.07)	**0.27**	(0.14)	0.15	(0.16)	−0.01	(0.09)	−0.06	(0.08)
Italian 1	−0.05	(0.05)	−0.10	(0.08)	**0.18**	(0.09)	−0.03	(0.07)	0.10	(0.06)
Lebanese 1	**−0.32**	(0.09)	**−0.66**	(0.43)	−0.13	(0.13)	−0.18	(0.10)	−0.04	(0.08)
Chinese 1	**−0.07**	(0.03)	−0.10	(0.06)	**−0.27**	(0.09)	−0.04	(0.06)	0.00	(0.04)
SE European 1	0.01	(0.06)	−0.02	(0.11)	**0.31**	(0.10)	0.01	(0.06)	0.04	(0.05)
Australian 2	0.04	(0.04)	0.04	(0.06)	**0.19**	(0.09)	−0.04	(0.04)	−0.03	(0.04)
Greek 2	−0.04	(0.04)	**0.15**	(0.07)	0.03	(0.10)	−0.07	(0.06)	0.00	(0.06)
Lebanese 2	0.18	(0.10)	**0.33**	(0.15)	−0.11	(0.18)	−0.04	(0.13)	−0.03	(0.11)
CE European 2	0.01	(0.05)	−0.15	(0.10)	**0.37**	(0.17)	0.12	(0.09)	0.11	(0.10)
Australian-Other 2	0.02	(0.03)	0.07	(0.04)	0.09	(0.07)	−0.01	(0.03)	**0.07**	(0.03)
Aboriginal, Indigenous 3	**−0.38**	(0.16)	−0.34	(0.19)	−0.18	(0.42)	**−0.42**	(0.16)	**−0.34**	(0.06)
Age/10	**0.11**	(0.00)	**0.10**	(0.00)	−0.01	(0.00)	**0.11**	(0.00)	**0.08**	(0.00)
$(Age/10)^2$	**−0.07**	(0.01)	**−0.07**	(0.01)	0.00	(0.01)	**−0.10**	(0.01)	**−0.07**	(0.00)
Qualifications										
Incomplete sec	**−0.20**	(0.02)	**−0.10**	(0.02)	−0.01	(0.03)	**−0.06**	(0.02)	**−0.04**	(0.01)
Complete sec	0		0		0		0		0	
Post-sec vocational	−0.01	(0.01)	−0.01	(0.02)	**0.11**	(0.03)	**0.14**	(0.02)	0.02	(0.02)
Tertiary	**0.27**	(0.01)	**0.14**	(0.03)	**0.30**	(0.05)	**0.29**	(0.04)	0.03	(0.03)
Marital status										
Single	0		0		0		0		0	
Married	**0.12**	(0.01)	**0.10**	(0.02)	0.02	(0.03)	**0.14**	(0.02)	**0.10**	(0.01)
Divorced/separated	**0.05**	(0.02)	**0.08**	(0.03)	**0.20**	(0.05)	**0.07**	(0.03)	**0.04**	(0.02)
English-speaking										
English at home	**0.60**	(0.07)	**0.37**	(0.09)	0.13	(0.09)	0.08	(0.05)	**0.16**	(0.04)
Different language at home, English spoken well	**0.51**	(0.07)	**0.32**	(0.09)	−0.03	(0.09)	0.02	(0.05)	**0.14**	(0.04)
Different language at home, English not spoken well	0		0		0		0		0	
Residence										
Non-urban	0		0		0		0		0	
Other large city	**−0.03**	(0.01)	**−0.04**	(0.02)	**−0.14**	(0.03)	−0.02	(0.01)	**−0.02**	(0.01)
Sydney	**0.14**	(0.01)	**0.07**	(0.02)	**0.20**	(0.03)	**0.06**	(0.02)	**0.05**	(0.01)
Melbourne	0.02	(0.02)	−0.01	(0.02)	−0.05	(0.03)	−0.02	(0.02)	0.01	(0.02)
Adjusted R-squared	0.159		0.163		0.046		0.276		0.102	
N	13,498		3,240		4,973		5,745		8,815	

Notes: Emboldened coefficients indicate significance at the 0.05 level or better; standard errors are given in parentheses.

Table 2.9B. Regression of Income within occupational classes: Women (parameter estimates).

	Salariat		Routine non-manual		Petty Bourgeoisie		Skilled manual		Unskilled manual	
Intercept	**2.59**	(0.10)	**2.58**	(0.10)	**2.29**	(0.20)	**2.34**	(0.17)	**2.73**	(0.06)
Ancestry										
Australian 3	0		0		0		0		0	
Lebanese 1	−0.08	(0.13)	0.05	(0.14)	−0.24	(0.37)	**1.64**	(0.50)	−0.03	(0.13)
Italian 2	0.04	(0.04)	−0.03	(0.04)	**0.33**	(0.16)	0.04	(0.11)	−0.06	(0.05)
Greek 2	0.08	(0.05)	**0.11**	(0.05)	0.01	(0.20)	−0.04	(0.20)	**−0.16**	(0.07)
Aboriginal, Indigenous 3	**−0.37**	(0.14)	−0.25	(0.13)	1.26	(0.94)	0.39	(0.35)	−0.20	(0.12)
Australia-Other 3	0.04	(0.02)	0.02	(0.02)	−0.03	(0.10)	0.02	(0.09)	**0.07**	(0.04)
Age/10	**0.10**	(0.01)	0.01	(0.01)	0.00	(0.03)	**0.08**	(0.02)	**0.05**	(0.01)
$(Age/10)^2$	**−0.08**	(0.00)	**0.08**	(0.01)	0.03	(0.02)	**−0.10**	(0.02)	**−0.09**	(0.01)
Qualifications										
Incomplete sec	**−0.17**	(0.02)	−0.02	(0.01)	−0.03	(0.06)	−0.09	(0.06)	−0.01	(0.02)
Completed sec	0		0		0		0		0	
Post-sec vocational	**0.04**	(0.02)	**0.02**	(0.01)	−0.10	(0.06)	0.03	(0.05)	**0.06**	(0.02)
Tertiary	**0.27**	(0.01)	**0.15**	(0.02)	**0.18**	(0.09)	0.17	(0.10)	**0.12**	(0.04)
Marital status										
Single	0		0		0		0		0	
Married	0.01	(0.01)	**0.05**	(0.01)	0.14	(0.10)	0.10	(0.05)	−0.03	(0.02)
Divorced/separated	**0.08**	(0.02)	**0.16**	(0.02)	0.13	(0.12)	**0.41**	(0.08)	**0.21**	(0.03)
English-speaking										
English at home	**0.35**	(0.10)	**0.23**	(0.09)	**0.36**	(0.16)	**0.35**	(0.15)	0.03	(0.05)
Different language at home, English spoken well	**0.30**	(0.10)	0.18	(0.09)	0.08	(0.16)	0.23	(0.14)	0.05	(0.05)
Different language at home, English not spoken well	0		0		0		0		0	
Residence										
Non-urban	0		0		0		0		0	
Other large city	**−0.04**	(0.01)	0.01	(0.01)	−0.09	(0.05)	−0.04	(0.05)	−0.01	(0.02)
Sydney	**0.12**	(0.01)	**0.09**	(0.01)	0.11	(0.07)	**0.17**	(0.06)	−0.04	(0.02)
Melbourne	0.02	(0.02)	−0.01	(0.02)	−0.10	(0.07)	−0.02	(0.06)	0.01	(0.02)
Adjusted R-squared	0.126		0.078		0.028		0.185		0.078	
N	11,655		9,773		2,124		713		6,356	

Notes: Emboldened coefficients indicate significance at the 0.05 level or better; standard errors are given in parentheses.

level of educational qualification is significantly related only to those two types of occupations. Married, and divorced or separated men are also more likely to have higher incomes than single men. When examining location, the significant advantage of higher incomes is evident for those living in Sydney, Australia's major contender for global city status, when compared with those in non-urban areas. Those living in cities other than Sydney or Melbourne have significantly lower incomes than those in non-urban areas which may reflect how such areas do include a certain proportion of very highly paid workers in the mining and other resource industries. Population data from the 2001 Census indicated that the median individual income reported in both Sydney and Melbourne was $400–499 dollars a week, the same figure as for the Northern Territory, where, in addition to the less wealthy Indigenous population, there is also a significant population working in the mining and resource sector.

Perhaps one of the most striking features of the analysis is the limited extent to which ancestry or generation is significantly related to income. (For simplicity we report only the significant parameter estimates for ancestry.) In the case of the salariat, ethnic penalties are only evident for the first-generation Lebanese and Chinese and the Aborigines and Indigenes. The first-generation Anglo-Celtic members of the salariat are the only ancestry group to have significantly higher incomes than other members of the salariat, which may reflect their prominence among those recruited as temporary migrants to work in this rapidly growing area of the labour market. Membership in the petty bourgeoisie is sometimes suggested as a strategy whereby minority groups seek to avoid discrimination in other sectors of the labour market. In the case of the first-generation Anglo-Celtic, Italian and Southeast European and the second-generation Australian and Central and Eastern European men, employment in the petty bourgeoisie has contributed to them having significantly higher levels of income than the benchmark third-generation Australians. The only group for whom membership of the petty bourgeoisie has not resulted in such gains are the first-generation Chinese. However, it may still be providing them with a means of avoiding the unemployment which faces many other first-generation Chinese men. The ancestry group which experiences the most significant income disadvantage is the Aboriginal and Indigenous group. The most straightforward interpretation of this result is discrimination.

The income patterns among working women are similar to those for men although there is less evidence of significant deviations from the third-generation Australian benchmark. This replicates earlier sections of the analysis which suggest that women are far more homogeneous than are men in their labour-market experiences; a finding which points to the potential role of gender as a key factor which 'trumps' other characteristics. In the case of education it is really only those with tertiary education who benefit significantly. The finding that it is divorced or separated women who are most likely to have income significantly above the benchmark may have a number of explanations including that these women work for longer hours than those who are married. Women who only speak English at home are certainly more likely to report higher incomes, but for those speaking languages other than English in the home it is only women employed in the salariat and who speak English well who are similarly advantaged.

When considering the role of ancestry in determining women's incomes there is very little evidence of significant variation. Aboriginal and Indigenous women in the salariat have lower incomes, which may reflect the way they are concentrated in less well paid areas of the salariat such as education and health. However first-generation Chinese and Lebanese women do not experience the disadvantages reported by their menfolk in the salariat or other areas. In the case of the petty bourgeoisie only second-generation Italian women differ significantly with higher incomes. That among women so few ancestry groups report significantly above-average incomes certainly suggests the greater homogeneity, and potentially, common barriers facing working women. One strategy which women may pursue in responding to occupational opportunities which would be linked to significantly lower incomes is to withdraw from the labour market and this may partially account for the few groups with significantly lower than average incomes.

Conclusion

The Australian story of ethnic relations has, in its short history, been very much a story of two groups: the Indigenes and the migrants. Since first European settlement in 1788 there have coexisted two separate sets of institutional structures affecting ethnic relations (Inglis 1994). One, involving the Indigenous and European settlers, was similar to that found in white settler colonies throughout the 'new' world. The other, also typical of many such colonies, was based on free, voluntary migration. While the latter form of inter-ethnic relations has been widely associated in both discourse and theory with patterns of incorporation based on extensive assimilation, the former has been historically linked with major patterns of marginalisation and discrimination.

One of the major themes evident in this analysis of the Australian ancestry data from the 2001 Census is that, 100 years after the founding of Australia, this same pattern still characterises the Australian-born Aboriginal and Torres Strait Islander population. On all the measures that have been examined here, they are the ethnic group which is most clearly marginalised and characterised by ethnic penalties. Those in our sample are also known to live mainly in isolated communities where the educational and occupational opportunities are, to say the least, limited. While their situation of marginalisation and disadvantage may be worse than that of the majority of the Indigenes with mixed ancestry living in Australia's cities, other research cautions against assuming that the majority of the Indigenous population experience fewer ethnic penalties. Over three decades after the 1967 referendum granting Indigenes full citizenship, the general picture is of continuing economic and social disadvantage in spite of, or some would argue because of, a variety of targeted programmes, among an Indigenous population which has a far wider range of geographical and social circumstances than any other Australian ethnic group. Against this background, one of the most interesting findings to emerge from our analysis is of the variations which do exist and which, in particular, speak to the somewhat different experiences of Indigenous men and women. While equally poorly educated, the women have a slightly higher likelihood of continuing in full-time education. Although less likely to be working, those who are in paid work are twice as likely as their menfolk to have occupations in the salariat. Indigenous women are certainly more likely to be unemployed than comparably educated third-generation Australian and other women, yet, among those who are employed, they do not have the same experience as their menfolk of experiencing ethnic penalties. This suggests that there is a bipolar tendency whereby a relatively small group with education have entered the salariat unlike other Indigenous women and men. This pattern links to the not uncommon observation that the impact of European settlement has been most negatively experienced by Indigenous men, who have become involved in a self-destructive round of practices such as drunkenness and domestic violence, which all too frequently result in arrest and even suicide in police custody. In these circumstances it is the women who take on the major role of providing stability in the family and community.

In contrast to the ongoing evidence of Indigenous disadvantage in Australia, the experience of immigrant groups provides a far more positive picture of the ability of migrants from a diverse range of European and non-European backgrounds to be incorporated into the labour market. While a limitation of the present analysis is that it does not allow us to explore the impact on the immigrant generation of length of residence, age of arrival or whether their educational qualifications were obtained in Australia or not, it certainly precludes the easy assumption that

Australians and Anglo-Celtic peoples necessarily dominate the labour market. It is true that there are ancestry groups such as the Maltese and the more recent Lebanese migrants whose overall profile is characterised by limited entry into the ranks of the highly educated and the salariat. But even among these groups there is considerable variation. Whereas the Maltese tend to be incorporated in the lower levels of the labour market, among the Lebanese population there is much greater diversity suggestive of a bipolar pattern. On the one hand there are those unemployed or outside the labour market. There is also a much smaller group who are participating on a comparable basis to the Australian-born third generation and many of their ethnic minority peers. A similar bipolar picture characterises the highly diverse Chinese immigrant group which includes on the one hand many individuals fluent in English and with recognised qualifications through their education in Australia or English-speaking former colonies such as Hong Kong, Malaysia and Singapore. On the other hand there are the substantial numbers of Chinese from the People's Republic of China and Taiwan who are often handicapped in the labour market by their limited English and foreign educational qualifications. It is this latter group of Chinese which are most likely to experience unemployment and lower occupational status (Model and Inglis 2004).

While there are clear variations within the first generation, by the second and later generations 'ethnic penalties' suggestive of disadvantage and discrimination have substantially disappeared. Significantly this applies as much to a physically distinctive group such as the Chinese as it does to those from ancestries more similar in physical appearance to the predominantly Anglo-Celtic Australian benchmark norm. This positive effect is, if anything, more evident among women than men. The greater homogeneity in women's labour-market experiences coexists with the continuing tendency for women's labour-market attainments to be, in general, lower than those for men. The high levels of intermarriage evident by the second generation results in a large number of individuals being from mixed ancestries and so not included in our analysis except in general groupings such as 'Australian-Other' or 'Other'. However, this intermarriage is a further pointer to a pattern of non-economic incorporation in Australia which involves limited discrimination and extensive integration.

Pleasing though this outcome may be, the question remains of how to explain it. Will the factors associated with it apply to the children of newer immigrants, and also those who are yet to arrive in Australia? Indeed, even the many second-generation young people who in our sample are still continuing with their education, will they too be able to realise the same levels of attainment? In terms of educational qualifications there is certainly evidence of continuing achievement. Major second-generation groups which are just entering the labour market in significant numbers include the children of middle-class Indian professionals as well as those of Indo-Chinese, particularly Vietnamese, refugees. The first-generation Indians are typical of many of the recently arrived middle class achieving outstanding success in the labour market for reasons related to their educational and cultural capital (Inglis and Wu 1992). Like the Chinese they place considerable emphasis on the importance of education for their children and there is considerable anecdotal evidence from examination results and university enrolments that their children are succeeding educationally. A similar emphasis is also evident among Vietnamese migrant parents despite their more limited educational capital and occupational attainment. Likewise another immigrant group which, in the 1970s, shared the distinction with the Vietnamese of routinely being identified as severely disadvantaged, are the Turkish. By the 1980s, there was already an indication that the emphasis which they, too, placed on education was achieving results involving rapidly improving educational levels that were already beginning to translate into movement into the salariat (Inglis *et al.* 1992). Nevertheless the translation of educational attainment into economic outcomes cannot be assumed, especially in an environment of credential inflation and rapidly increasing levels of educational attainment among all groups.

Apart from citing general observations which suggest that the economic outcomes continue, overall, to be positive, two comparative studies of the economic outcomes for migrants to Australia, Canada and the United States provide a basis for suggesting a reasonably encouraging prognosis. Despite the way in which the United States continues still to dominate thinking and imagination as *the* land of opportunity for immigrants, both Borjas (1990) and Reitz (1998) demonstrate using 1980 and 1981 census data for the three countries that immigrants to Canada, and particularly Australia, do far better than those who have immigrated to the US. While they agree on these findings, their explanations vary. Borjas primarily emphasises the importance of the move by both Australia and Canada to more selective immigration policies emphasising economic criteria. Reitz, however, demonstrates the importance of additional institutional factors in each nation including the labour market, the nature of social welfare and, most importantly, education. More specifically, he argues that it is the limited gap in the educational attainments of the Australian-born population and recent immigrants, which has been a key factor in the comparative absence of economic disadvantage among Australian immigrants.

In the two decades since the studies by Borjas and Reitz, there has been an increasing emphasis on the selection of highly skilled immigrants and, in more recent years, an increase in the levels of immigration. Even among those migrating to Australia on the basis of family rather than economic criteria, there has been an increasing level of educational and occupational attainment. As noted above, many immigrant groups, even those where parents have low levels of educational attainment, have emphasised the importance of education and tertiary study for their children. As a result, even groups such as the Turkish are gradually closing the gap with the third-generation Australian population (Jones 1988). Regrettably, despite some improvements, the gap between the Indigenous and non-Indigenous population still remains substantial. In the last twenty years there has also been a major restructuring of the Australian economy. This has involved both macro and micro changes in the operation of the economy and the regulation of the labour market. One consequence has been the growth of the salariat, and, in particular, of professional occupations. As entry to the professions is closely tied to educational qualifications, it is not perhaps surprising to find that ethnic minorities and women have moved in increasing numbers into the professions. However, over the same time, there has not been a comparable increase in their proportions in the managerial occupations which constitute part of the salariat. This may reflect the greater potential for subjectivity and 'glass ceilings' to operate in employment in managerial occupations. It also highlights how, when using broad occupational categories such as 'salariat' or 'petty bourgeoisie', some of the complexity of the labour market, and the potential of what Evans and Kelley (1991) referred to as 'exclusionary' discrimination may be overlooked. However, given close links between education and access to the professions, the growth of professional occupations in Australia is a positive indicator that opportunities for continuing economic access by the second generation will continue. Even in ethnic groups with only small numbers participating in the salariat, those who are there provide role models for younger members of the ethnic community and show that the aspirations of many immigrant parents for their children to enter this area can be translated into reality.

Alongside these more positive indicators for the future there have been a series of less encouraging developments. While unemployment levels in Australia have declined, there has been a growing economic inequality which coincides with the deregulation of the economy, the disbanding of the arbitration system, which played a major national role in setting wages and work conditions, and the decline of trade unions. At the same time, there has been a shift away from a community-oriented welfare system to one emphasising that individuals should pay for a range of support services, including tertiary education. How these changes will affect migrants and their children it is yet too early to say, although social welfare advocates argue that these changes will have the greatest impact on those most materially and culturally disadvantaged in Australian society. As they coincide with a reduced government commitment to actively promoting multiculturalism and tolerance, the potential exists for 'exclusionary' discrimination to become more significant in determining economic outcomes. The groups most likely to be affected are those cast as threatening to society which, in the present political climate of concerns about terrorism, are Muslims. Australian Muslims have come from many different countries in Asia, the Middle East and Africa. As one of the newest groups of immigrants, the experiences of them and their children in the labour market will provide an important test of the factors affecting economic access and mobility in Australia and its continuity.

APPENDIX 1
Sources and measures

Source

The source is the 1% Confidentialised Unit Record Files (CURF) from the 2001 Australian Census. This sample is based on self-reported data from the resident population of 18.9 million persons on Census night which was the 7 August 2001. The only exception is data collected by interview in predominantly Indigenous settlements in remote and isolated areas. For the purposes of the present analysis, the individuals who were temporary visitors residing in Australia for less than one year were excluded. Thus the present analysis potentially includes overseas students studying in Australia for degrees and other courses longer than one year. The majority of these students are from Asia, many of them ethnic Chinese. The version of the CURF used in this analysis is the Basic dataset rather than the more detailed RADL Expanded version which would have allowed examination of a wider range of ancestry groups.

However, the sample size of the additional ancestry groups identifiable in the RADL Expanded dataset is typically less than 100 for the second-generation males and females in the target age range of 18 to 59 years. Their inclusion hence would have created a problem of statistical reliability in this analysis.

Measures[10]

Ancestry

The measure of ancestry used in this analysis is based on answers to the question: 'What is the person's ancestry? Provide more than one ancestry as necessary.' A note on the form added that: 'When answering this question, consider and mark the ancestries with which you identify most closely. Count your ancestry back as far as three generations if known e.g. consider your parents, grand-parents and great-grandparents.'

In order to meet the minimum requirements of 100 cases for males and females in the second generation using the Basic dataset it was still necessary to combine some ancestries. As coding was provided for the first two ancestries identified by individuals this was taken into account in constructing specific individual ancestries. Where individuals gave only one ancestry as their first and, in some cases, second response, this was taken as their ancestry. These ancestries were 'Australian', United Kingdom/Ireland which, following current usage, is called 'Anglo-Celtic', Dutch, German, Italian, Maltese, Greek, Lebanese and Chinese. Where individuals reported Australian and another ancestry they were classified as 'Australian-Other'. Geographic names are used for countries and regions where it was necessary to combine groups for purposes of analysis. 'Southeastern European' includes those such as Albanians, Bosnians, Croatians, Macedonians, Romanians and Serbians, while 'Central and Eastern European' includes Czechs, Hungarians, Poles, Ukrainians and Russians. The 'Oceania/Aboriginal/Indigenous' category includes Indigenous ancestries from Australia and the Pacific. The final category, 'Other' includes a heterogeneous group of individuals including New Zealanders, Other Europeans and individuals from the Middle East, Africa and the Americas as well as individuals with non-Australian mixed ancestries.

---

[10] For more detailed information on the measures in the 2001 Census see Australian Bureau of Statistics, *2001 Census Directory* (Canberra: Australian Bureau of Statistics, 2001).

Generation

This was based on whether the individual was born overseas. Those who were born abroad and whose birthplace was stated were classified as first generation if their parents were also born overseas. Second generation were those persons born in Australia who had one or both of their parents born overseas. Note that the census did not ask for country of parents' birth where they were born outside Australia. The third generation were those born in Australia with both their parents also born in Australia.

Age

Up to 24 years, age was based on single years but after that only five-year age groupings were available.

Marital Status

This measure was constructed from responses to replies concerning legally registered marital status and social marital status. Persons were coded as married if they described themselves as in a 'registered' or in a 'de facto' marriage. Persons describing themselves as divorced, separated and widowed were coded as formerly married.

Highest Educational Qualification

This measure was obtained by combining responses to 'highest level of primary or secondary schooling completed' and the question asking 'highest level of qualification obtained' which includes post-secondary qualifications. The lowest level of education available was for those who did not complete secondary school by gaining a formal end of school certificate.

Economic Activity

This measure was obtained by combining information from the variable on student status, which reported whether the individual was a full-time student, with the reply to the question concerning labour-market status. The latter did not collect information to distinguish between those who are not economically active because they are retired, involved only in looking after the home or some other reason.

Unemployment

Persons who reported that they were unemployed and looking either for full-time or part-time work.

Occupation

This was based on the answers to two questions. The first was the main job held in the last week coded as one of the nine major categories of the Australian Standard Classification of Occupations, second edition. The second question asked about labour-force status, distinguishing employees, employers, own account workers and family workers. In order to approximate the Goldthorpe occupational class measure used in other chapters, the following variables were constructed:

> Salariat consists of 'Professionals' and 'Associate Professionals' in all four labour force statuses as well as those 'Managers and Administrators' who are employees.
> Petty Bourgeoisie consists of all those in the remaining occupational groupings who are not employees being either employers, own account workers or contributing family workers.
> Routine Non-Manual are 'Advanced Clerical and Service Workers' as well as 'Intermediate Clerical, Sales and Service Workers' who are employees
> Skilled Manual are 'Tradespersons and Related Workers' who are employees.
> Semi- and Unskilled are 'Intermediate Production and Transport Workers', 'Elementary Clerical, Sales and Service Workers' and 'Labourers and Related Workers' who are employees.

Income

The variable used in the analysis is the log of hourly income. This measure is constructed from the gross weekly income (including pensions and allowances) which the individual usually receives each week from all sources and the usual hours the individual worked each week. The CURFs code weekly income as belonging to one of fourteen intervals, the first two of which are, respectively, negative or none. Time worked is also coded occasionally as intervals. Thus, the first task was to assign all values coded as intervals to their respective midpoints. Next, respondents' hourly earnings were defined; this number is the quotient of estimated weekly income divided by estimated weekly hours. Finally, the natural log of this quotient was obtained. Note that this procedure renders meaningless the income of persons without jobs.

References

Altman, J. (2001), 'The Economic Status of Indigenous Australians'. In J. Jupp (ed.), *The Australian People: an encyclopedia of the nation, its people and their origins* (Oakleigh: Cambridge University Press), pp. 135–41.

Australian Bureau of Statistics (2001), *2001 Census Directory* (Canberra: Australian Bureau of Statistics).

Australian Bureau of Statistics (2004), *Australia: Social Trends 2004* (Canberra: Australian Bureau of Statistics).

Borjas, G. (1990), *Friends or Strangers: the impact of immigrants on the US economy* (New York: Basic Books).

Brooks, C. (1997), *Labour Market outcomes of Second Generation Australians* (Canberra: AGPS).

Evans, M. and Kelley, J. (1991), 'Prejudice, Discrimination and the Labor Market: attainment of immigrants in Australia'. *American Journal of Sociology*, 97(3): 721–59.

Flatau, P. and Hemmings, P. (1991), *Labour Market Experience, Education and Training of Young Immigrants in Australia: an intergenerational study* (Canberra: AGPS).

Inglis, C. (1975), 'Some Recent Australian Writing on Immigration and Assimilation', *International Migration Review*, 9, 335–44.

Inglis, C. (1994), 'Race and ethnic relations in Australia: theory, methods and substance'. In P. Ratcliffe (ed.), *Race, Ethnicity and Nation: International perspectives on social conflict* (London: University of London Press), pp. 68–90.

Inglis, C. (1996), *Multiculturalism: New Policy Responses to Diversity* (Paris: UNESCO).

Inglis, C. (1998), 'Communities: Australia'. In L. Pan (ed.), *The Encyclopedia of the Chinese Overseas* (Cambridge, Mass.: Harvard University Press), pp. 274–85.

Inglis, C. (1999), 'Middle Class Migration: new considerations in research and policy'. In G. Hage and R. Couch (eds.), *The Future of Multiculturalism* (Sydney, Research Institute for Humanities and the Social Sciences), pp. 45–64.

Inglis, C., Elley, J., and Manderson, L. (1992), *Making Something of Myself . . . educational attainment and social and economic mobility of Turkish-Australian young people* (Canberra: Office of Multicultural Affairs).

Inglis, C. and Wu, C.-T. (1992), 'The "New" Migration of Asian Skills and Capital to Australia'. In C. Inglis, S. Gunasekeran, G. Sullivan and C.-T. Wu (eds.), *Asians in Australia: the Dynamics of Migration and Settlement* (Singapore: Institute of Southeast Asian Studies), pp. 193–230.

Jakubowicz, A. (1985), *Education and Ethnic Minorities: issues of participation and equity*, Discussion Paper no. 1 (Canberra: National Advisory and Coordinating Committee on Multicultural Education).

Jones, F. L. (1988), *The Recent Employment and Unemployment Experiences of First, Second and Later Generations of Immigrants in Australia* (Canberra: Office of Multicultural Affairs).

Jones, F. L. (1991), *Ancestry Groups in Australia: a descriptive overview* (Canberra: The Office of Multicultural Affairs and Centre for Multicultural Studies).

Jones, F. L. (1992), 'Labour Market Outcomes Among the Chinese at the 1986 Census'. In C. Inglis, S. Gunasekaran, G. Sullivan and C.-T. Wu (eds.), *Asians in Australia: the dynamics of migration and settlement* (Singapore: Institute of Southeast Asian Studies), pp. 117–56.

Jones, F. L. (1997), 'The Transition from School to Work in Australia'. In Y. Shavit and W. Müller (eds.), *From School to Work: a comparative study of educational qualifications and occupational destinations* (Oxford: Clarendon Press), pp. 49–70.

Jupp, J. (2001) (ed.), *The Australian People: an encyclopedia of the nation, its people and their origins* (Oakleigh: Cambridge University Press).

Khoo, S.-E. and Lucas, D. (2004), *Australians' Ancestries 2001* (Canberra: Australian Bureau of Statistics).

Khoo, S.-E., McDonald, P., Giorgas, D., and Birrell, B. (2002), *Second Generation Australians* (Canberra: Australian Centre for Population Research & the Department of Immigration and Multicultural and Indigenous Affairs).

Kunz, C. and Costello, L. (2003), '2001 Census: Ancestry: Detailed Paper' (Census Paper no. 03/01b), *Population Census Evaluation* (Canberra: Australian Bureau of Statistics).

Marginson, S. (1997), *Educating Australia: government, economy and citizen since 1960* (Oakleigh: Cambridge University Press).

Martin, J. (1978), *The Migrant Presence* (Sydney: Allen & Unwin).

Martin, J. I. and Meade, P. (1979), *The Educational Experiences of Sydney High School Students: Report No. 1* (Canberra: Australian Government Publishing Service).

Model, S. and Inglis, C. (2004), *Chinese Immigrants in America and Australia: the effects of birthplace and host society on labor market success* (Paper presented at the American Sociological Association Conference, San Francisco).

Office of Multicultural Affairs (1989), *National Agenda for a Multicultural Australia* (Canberra: Australian Government Publishing Service).

Poole, M. E. (1981), 'Educational Opportunities for Minority Groups: Australian research reviewed'. In J. Megarry (ed.), *Education of Minorities: World Yearbook of Education* (London: Kogan Page), pp. 254–78.

Price, C. (1974), *The Great White Walls Are Built* (Canberra: Australian National University Press).

Reitz, J. (1998). *Warmth of the Welcome: the Social Causes of Economic Success for Immigrants in Different Nations and Cities* (Boulder: Westview Press).

Richmond, K. (1974), 'The workforce participation of married women in Australia'. In D. Edgar (ed.), *Social Change in Australia: Readings in Sociology* (Melbourne: Cheshire), pp. 267–308.

Sturman, A. (1985), 'Immigrant Australians: education and the transition to work', *Discussion Paper No. 3* (Canberra: National Advisory and Coordinating Committee on Multicultural Education).

Wooden, M., Holton, R., Hugo, G., and Sloan, J. (1994), *Australian Immigration: A Survey of the Issues* (Canberra: Australian Government Publishing Service).

3

Continuing Ethnic Segmentation in Austria

IRENA KOGAN

Summary. Austria has fairly complex patterns of post-Second World War immigration. In addition to classic labour migrants from Turkey and the former Yugoslavia, there have been considerable inflows of refugees and displaced persons, for example Hungarians or Czechs migrating to Austria from communist countries as well as more recent refugee groups from the Middle East and Africa. Four main second-generation groups can be distinguished—the descendants of the Turkish and Yugoslavian labour migrants, those originating from Eastern Europe, and some from neighbouring developed countries (including many German speakers). The second-generation labour migrant groups have made considerable progress in education compared with the first generation, but, unlike the other two groups, still lag some way behind their native Austrian counterparts. They also continue to experience considerable ethnic penalties in the labour market, especially in access to the salariat. These penalties may be due partly to discrimination but also to the fact that people who do not hold Austrian citizenship are excluded from public sector ('Beamte') jobs many of which are in the salariat.

Introduction

FOR CENTURIES SEVERAL ETHNIC GROUPS, among them Croats, Hungarians, Slovenes, Czechs and Slovaks, have been residing on today's Austrian territory, largely near its eastern and southern borders, and have been officially recognised as ethnic minorities (Herzog-Punzenberger

2003). Other minorities, such as the Gypsies (Roma and Sinti) and Jews, although numerous in the beginning of the twentieth century, were hardly found after the Second World War. During the Nazi period, when Austria was a part of the Third Reich, about 130,000 Jews had to flee the country, while another 65,000 lost their lives[1] (Albrich 1997). In the upshot of Hitler's rule, about 20,000 Austrian intellectuals left the country, mostly overseas,[2] while tens of thousands of people were forced to work for the Nazis on Austrian soil.

After Austria gained its independence in 1945, streams of refugees and displaced persons passed through the country and thousands settled in Austria. At the same time, due to economic hardships, emigrants continued to outnumber newcomers and their main destinations were either overseas or Switzerland and Germany (Butschek 1992). Only from the late 1960s did Austria become a country of net immigration (Münz 2001). Since the Second World War some 3.8 million people have come to Austria as refugees, displaced persons, trans-migrants, recruited workers and their family dependants; of those, about 1.2 million have stayed in the country permanently.

Ex-Yugoslavs have been the largest immigrant group to Austria, with a particularly high number of immigrants arriving between the late 1960s and the early 1970s.[3] As shown in Figure 3.1, after the economic crisis of 1973 the number of immigrants from the former Yugoslavia residing in Austria fell substantially as some people returned home. However, from the late 1980s to the early 1990s, the number of ex-Yugoslavs residing in Austria increased once more.

Turks began immigrating to Austria in the late 1960s and their numbers have gradually increased throughout the second part of the twentieth century. A similar trend has been observed amongst other immigrant groups, particularly those coming from Eastern and Central European countries and, starting in the mid-1990s, newcomers from Asia, the number of whom significantly increased from the early 1990s. The inflow of

---

[1] Ethnic minorities of Slavic descent were also suppressed during the Second World War.
[2] In fact, the Americas were a destination for Austrian emigrants starting from the beginning of the nineteenth century.
[3] Austrian official statistics differentiate between Austrian citizens and foreigners, i.e. persons without Austrian citizenship. The latter might include also second-generation minorities, people who are born in Austria but retain the citizenship of their parents. Once naturalised, second-generation minorities disappear from official statistical sources, making it impossible to present exact figures of the first-generation immigrants, defined according to the country of birth, and second-generation minorities, defined as children in families with both immigrant parents.

Germans, on the other hand, has remained rather constant throughout the second half of the twentieth century.

While in 1961 foreigners constituted about 1% of the total population in Austria, their proportion grew to about 3% in 1971, and reached nearly 7% in 1991. Throughout this same period, the proportion of the foreign population in the labour force has been markedly higher. In 1971, 6% of the labour force was foreigners; by 1991 this proportion had grown to almost 9% (Statistik Austria 2001; Fassmann et al. 1999). In 2000 the total proportion of the foreign population in Austria reached 9.3%: 4.2% of the Austrian resident population was of ex-Yugoslavian origin, 1.7% arrived from Turkey, 1.3% from EU countries, and 2.3% from other countries (Statistik Austria 2001). Two major types of immigrants to Austria, refugees (or asylum seekers) and labour migrants, are discussed in more detail below.

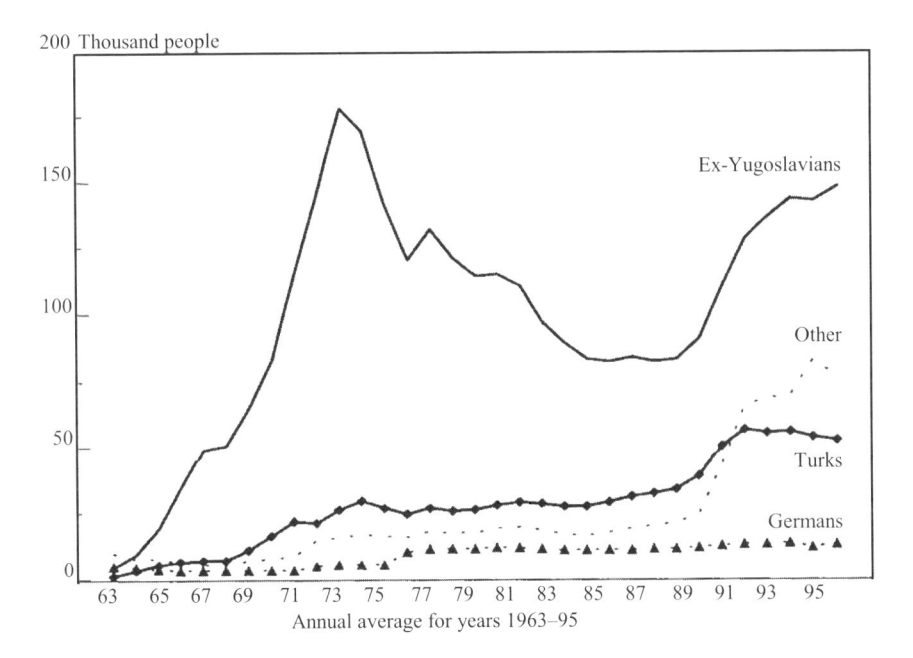

Figure 3.1. Foreign labour force in Austria, by country of origin.
Note: The most prominent countries in the category 'Other' are Poland, Czech Republic, Slovakia, Hungary and Romania.
Source: Münz et al. 1997.

Refugees and asylum seekers

Like Germany, immediately after the end of the Second World War Austria became a destination for hundreds of thousands of refugees and displaced persons, the majority of whom were either ethnic Germans or Eastern Europeans. For the Eastern Europeans, neighbouring Austria remained an attractive destination long after the end of the war. The years 1956 to 1957 were marked by a mass exodus of Hungarians, 180,000 of whom found asylum in Austria. From 1968 to 1969, 12,000 Czechs and Slovaks, of the 162,000 total who fled their homeland, settled in Austria. In 1981–2 between 120,000 and 150,000 Poles entered Austria on tourist visas, many of whom later applied for asylum (Fassmann and Münz 1994). The neighbouring countries of Eastern Europe, and largely Poland, Hungary, Romania and Czechoslovakia, remained the main countries of origin for asylum seekers to Austria through the early 1990s. In addition, since 1972 Austria has accepted refugees from other troubled regions, e.g. Chile, Argentina, Uganda, Iran, and Afghanistan, through a quota system (Münz *et al.* 1997).

Since 1992 restrictive administrative measures have decreased the absolute number of persons applying for asylum in Austria; however the numbers of foreigners entering illegally or those entering as de facto refugees have increased. This increase occurred mainly due to the inflow of refugees and asylum seekers from the war zones of Croatia, Bosnia-Herzegovina and—from 1998 to 1999—Kosovo.[4] Starting in the mid-1990s a substantial increase in the number of asylum seekers from non-European countries, mostly from Iran, Iraq, Afghanistan, India, and Nigeria, is noticeable. Figure 3.2 shows the dynamics and composition of the inflow of asylum seekers from 1970 to 2000.

While refugees recognised under the Geneva Convention have rights similar to Austrian citizens (the same right of access to the Austrian labour market, the same right of financial support from the federal government, etc.), with the exception of the right to vote, and are subjected to integration measures (e.g., language courses, social housing), asylum seekers have a much more precarious position, with an increasingly smaller number being provided with accommodation or financial support. Moreover, more recently the chances of receiving recognised refugee status have been falling for asylum seekers: until 1984 asylum seekers had

---

[4] Even in this case an entry or passage was refused to many displaced persons from the former Yugoslavia.

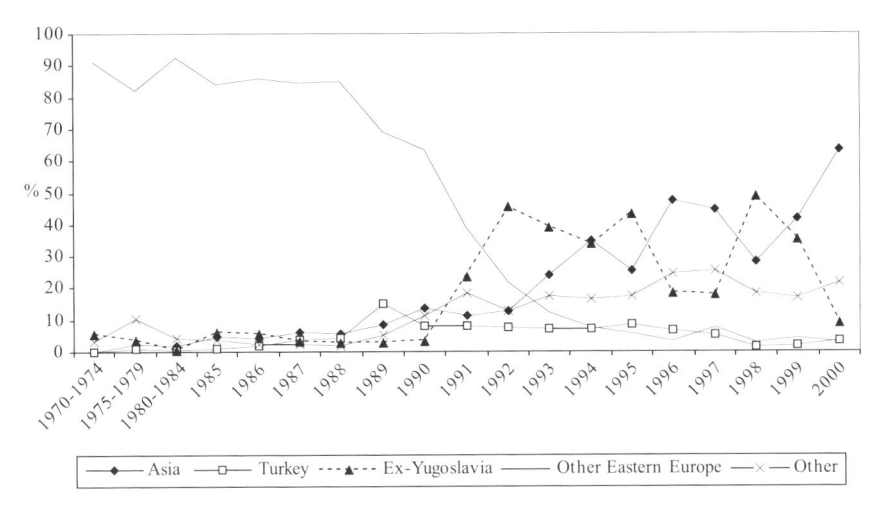

Figure 3.2. Origin of asylum seekers in Austria, 1970–2000.
Source: Münz et al. 2003.

a 50–80% chance of being recognised as refugees; by 1992 that figure had fallen to 10%, although it had increased slightly by the end of the century (Fassmann and Münz 1994; Münz et al. 2003).

Labour migrants

Immigrant labour recruitment started later in Austria than in the rest of Western Europe. In 1962 recruitment agreements were concluded with Spain,[5] in 1964 with Turkey and in 1966 with Yugoslavia, which sent the largest proportion of guest workers (see Fig. 3.1) (Münz et al. 1997; Parnreiter 1994). Guest-worker quotas were negotiated for individual branches by trade unions and employer organisations, while individual work permits made up only a small fraction (30%) of all foreign workers (Fassmann and Münz 1995). Labour migrants were recruited to low-skilled jobs in textile, leather, clothing, and heavy industry, agriculture and construction (SOPEMI 1993; Fassmann 1999; Fassmann et al. 1999).

As in other immigrant-recruiting countries such as Germany, Austria adopted the principle of short-term working residence, the so-called 'rotation principle', under which work and residence permits had to be renewed periodically. The aim of rotation was, during times of growing

---

[5] Only a small number of Spaniards was recruited (Münz 2001).

labour demand, to attract a maximal proportion of foreign workers with a low proportion of spouses and children. At times of declining demand, foreign workers have to be sent home. In reality, however, the rotation principle did not work as desired: Austrian firms themselves were interested in immigrants staying more permanently, given the costs connected to new recruitment and training. As a result, only half of foreign workers recruited between 1965 and 1985 returned to their respective countries of origin (Fassmann 1999). In 1974 employment of guest workers reached its peak[6] but by the mid-1980s the number of guest workers had significantly fallen (Kofler 2002). This halt in recruitment resulted in the rise of family reunifications, which became one of the few legal ways to enter the country. Legal reforms at the end of 1980s proclaimed a move away from the rotation principle to integration policies, albeit only for longstanding immigrants, while more restrictive measures were introduced for new entrants.

A revival of foreign worker migration, mostly from Eastern and Central Europe, started in the early 1990s (Currle 2004). The majority of these immigrants arrived on their own initiative, as official recruitment is no longer practised, and they typically have occasional or seasonal jobs and stay only temporarily in Austria. Immigrants remain over-represented in the manufacturing sector, but their proportion in the service sector, including the hotel and restaurant business, catering, tourism and cleaning, has also increased. Under current law, the number of legally employed foreigners from non-EU countries cannot exceed a certain percentage of the domestic labour force, a quota calculated for each of the Austrian federal states and based on the annual demand for foreign labour in each state (König and Stadler 2003).

Immigration, integration and citizenship policies

Like Germany, Austria, whose mass foreign immigration started with the recruitment of the guest workers, has unwillingly become an immigrant country. Though many immigrants have lived in Austria for long periods of time, and some even became Austrian citizens, the idea of temporariness of immigrant presence was until recently apparent in Austrian discourse (Fassmann and Münz 1994; Bauböck 1996, 2000; Herzog-

---

[6] About 10% of all labour force was foreign at that time.

Punzenberger 2003). Reforms in 1988 to the 1975 foreign labour law reflected a shift from the former perception of immigration as short-run work to the realisation that foreign inflow is proper immigration (SOPEMI 1988). This, however, did not result in a substantial revision of the integration policies for the majority of newcomers. To avoid permanent settlement of immigrant workers, Austria has demanded constant renewal of residence and work permits (Tazi-Preve *et al.* 1999). Immigration has been encouraged only during periods of growing labour demand in the Austrian labour market, and halted at times of slowdown; these dynamics have been achieved by means of annual quotas, set by the federal government. Thus, maximal economic gain from immigrant labour with minimal spending on the integration of immigrants became a pattern for the treatment of migration to Austria (Fassmann 1999). The temporary and labour-nature of migration determines the scarcity of integration measures for the majority of newcomers (Lischke and Rögl 1993) with the exception of recognised political refugees, who enjoy rights similar to the native-born Austrians (Fassmann 1999). Just to obtain a residence permit, immigrants must demonstrate a certain degree of integration, having a secure source of income in Austria as well as a place to reside.

On first immigrating, employed persons are granted a renewable residence permit, which can become of unlimited duration after five years of residence. If non-EU immigrants happen to lose their employment and cannot find any, they are in danger of losing their right of residence and can be forced to leave the country. As a rule, after residing in Austria for more than ten years and fulfilling other demands—such as having a regular income and place of residence, the absence of criminal record, the renouncement of former nationality and integration into the community—immigrants can apply for Austrian citizenship (SOPEMI 1995). At least partially because of the difficulties in gaining access to naturalisation in Austria and regulations in their home countries,[7] a lot of immigrants, even those residing in the country for some decades, have retained their original citizenship; nevertheless significantly more people become

---

[7] Thus, for example, until 1995 Turks taking citizenship of other countries were deprived of their rights on inheritance and estate in Turkey. Since then these regulations have been changed and retaking Turkish citizenship has become easier (Tazi-Preve *et al.* 1999). These changes resulted in the substantial increase in the number of naturalised Turkish immigrants (for more see Waldrauch and Çinar 2003).

naturalised in Austria than in Germany.[8] Generally, Turks and ex-Yugoslavs[9] tend to become naturalised in larger numbers than the rest of the immigrant population, followed by East Europeans. Only a small proportion of EU nationals or immigrants from other industrialised countries apply for Austrian citizenship (Statistik Austria 2001). The automatic naturalisation of second-generation minorities at birth is not allowed under the *jus soli* mechanism, practised in Austria, yet one third of all naturalisations are undergone by children of naturalised parents (Waldrauch and Çinar 2003). Overall, Austrian citizenship, together with the granting of an unconditional residence permit, equal political and social rights, opens a wider range of job opportunities for the immigrant population and their children, with access to public sector employment being one of the most important.

As the number of immigrants in Austria increased considerably throughout the 1990s, so grew the public and political concerns. Results of the 1997 Eurobarometer opinion poll on 'Racism and Xenophobia in Europe' demonstrated that 42% of Austrians openly described themselves as 'quite racist' or 'very racist', compared to only 33% within the European Union as a whole.[10] Seventy per cent of Austrians believe that their country has reached its limit for accepting people of other races, religions and cultures and that 'if there were to be more people belonging to these minority groups the country would have problems' (Melich 2000). With respect to this question, the European Union average for this item was 65%, and only the Greeks, Belgians and Germans had a larger percentage of individuals agreeing with the item. More optimistically, however, other public opinion studies conducted during the 1990s have documented a decreasing trend in xenophobia, and a growing openness among Austrians towards immigrants, particularly towards second and third-generation minorities (Lebhart and Münz 2003; Tazi-Preve *et al.* 1999).

Surprisingly or not, in 1999 the far-right Freedom Party, with an open anti-immigration agenda, received 27% of the public vote, the largest share of any far-right party in Europe up to this time. The Freedom Party

---

[8] Since 1980, 2–3% of all foreigners have been naturalised each year. In 2001, 4.6% of all Austrian citizens were born abroad, while the proportion of all immigrants was 11.2% (Münz *et al.* 2003).

[9] Between 1992 and 1995 the number of naturalisations among ex-Yugoslav immigrants doubled (Waldrauch and Çinar 2003), as the Austrian government eased this process for Yugoslav nationals reacting to the situation in the Balkans.

[10] Only in Belgium and France was the degree of expressed racism higher than in Austria.

received only 6% less support than the ruling Social Democratic Party. This shocking fact triggered alarm and led EU countries to impose sanctions against Austria. Three years later, in the November 2002 parliament elections, Jörg Haider's Freedom Party lost two thirds of its seats. It should be noted, however, that the right-wing governing coalition itself adopted harsher immigration policies[11] at least partially stolen from the Freedom Party's agenda.

Data and population

The data used for this study are Austrian microcensuses, pooled for the years 1995, 1997, 1999 and 2001. The microcensuses are valuable for their large sample sizes, ensuring sufficient representation of the immigrant population. Since 1995, the year Austria joined the European Union, a number of questions have annually (in March of each year) been added to the regular Austrian microcensus questionnaire covering, among other things, information on the country of birth and year of migration for the immigrant population. Hence, the data facilitates the identification of first-generation immigrants, who include people born outside Austria and who immigrated after the age of six. Defining second-generation minorities is, however, a challenge in that only those persons who arrived in Austria at age six or earlier, or were born in Austria but retain a nationality other than Austrian, are assigned to this category. Such a definition excludes persons born and naturalised in Austria but whose parents are born abroad since no information on parents' country of birth is present in the microcensus. Excluding naturalised second-generation minorities might introduce a certain bias into the analyses and might potentially underestimate the socio-economic integration of immigrant offspring. To verify if this is the case, additional analyses have been conducted with the variable pertaining to citizenship status for those second-generation minorities who were not born on the Austrian soil but arrived at or before the age of six. Within this group we can distinguish those who retained the citizenship of their parents from those who have Austrian citizenship (see Table 3.A2 in Appendix 2 to this chapter).

---

[11] This includes restrictions to the new permanent settlement, but increase in seasonal immigration. Moreover, German language courses have been made obligatory for all newcomers (König and Stadler 2003).

From these data, a number of ancestry groups and generations can be differentiated in this study: (1) Native-born Austrians, who will serve as our benchmark category; (2) first- and second-generation Eastern Europeans; (3) first- and second-generation (ex-)Yugoslavs; (4) first- and second-generation Turks; (5) first- and second-generation immigrants from other developed countries; (6) first-generation immigrants from the Middle East and Southern Asia; (7) first-generation Africans; and (8) first-generation East Asians.

Immigrants from Eastern and Central European countries include large proportions of Poles, Czechs, Slovaks, Hungarians, and Romanians. Due to the peculiarities of migration from the former Yugoslavia immigrants from ex-Yugoslavian republics, namely Slovenia, Croatia, Bosnia-Herzegovina, Macedonia, Serbia and Montenegro, are assigned to a separate group. The group of Turkish immigrants includes persons born in Turkey and does not necessarily pertain to ethnic Turks only. Some Kurds born in Turkey arrived in Austria as refugees, particularly in the early 1990s. Immigrants from the so-called 'developed countries' include those arriving from Western European countries, the USA, Canada, Australia and New Zealand and largely represent migrants from Germany or German-speaking parts of Switzerland or Italy. Proportions of immigrants from the Middle East (mostly Iran, Iraq and Lebanon) and Southern Asia (mostly India and Pakistan), Africa (largely Maghrebians and Nigerians) and Eastern Asia (largely women from Philippines) are relatively small, so their analyses have to be limited. Due to the heterogeneity and rather small numbers immigrants from countries other than those mentioned in the list above are excluded from the analyses.

Table 3.1 presents details of the sample characteristics and time of arrival of each of the analysed groups. Thirty per cent of the first-generation Eastern Europeans came between 1976 and 1988 as refugees, while almost half arrived after the fall of the Iron Curtain. Second-generation Eastern Europeans, in general, are not the children of the immigrants mentioned above. Rather, they belong to a different cohort— they are people who settled in Austria as minors (before or at the age of six) after the Second World War. (We should note that the group of second-generation Eastern Europeans contains almost no people born in Austria, as all those native-born were naturalised, and thus are no longer recognisable in the dataset. The only ones that are recognisable are those who arrived at or before the age of six.) For ex-Yugoslav immigrants, three main cohorts are found in the data: recruited labour migrants who

Table 3.1. The composition and period of migration of the first and second generations (row percentages).

	Born in Austria	Period of migration					N
		Before 1960	1961–1975	1976–1988	After 1989	Unknown	
East European, 1st generation		8.0	12.0	30.4	48.3	1.4	1,521
East European, 2nd generation	0.9	85.8	3.2	8.3	0.3	1.5	339
Yugoslav, 1st generation		1.9	34.6	18.5	44.0	1.0	3,850
Yugoslav, 2nd generation	52.3	22.6	15.7	9.4		1.0	491
Turkish, 1st generation		0.2	26.1	40.2	32.5	1.0	1,819
Turkish, 2nd generation	60.2	1.3	14.4	23.8	0.3		319
Developed, 1st generation		5.9	26.4	31.5	34.6	1.6	1,855
Developed, 2nd generation	10.9	52.0	28.9	7.6		0.6	854
Middle Eastern/S. Asian, 1st generation		1.0	13.3	41.6	42.3	1.7	293
East Asian, 1st generation		2.4	12.8	31.2	52.0	1.6	125
African, 1st generation		2.8	7.3	45.0	44.0	0.9	109

Note: 196 Yugoslavs for whom information on generation and arrival were not available, and 371 Turks for whom this information was not available, have been excluded.

arrived between 1961 and 1975, their family members who joined them between 1976 and 1988, and more recent newcomers, largely from Serbia and Bosnia-Herzegovina. Among second-generation ex-Yugoslavs, about 22% belong to a different cohort—a post-war inflow. Others are most likely children of ex-Yugoslav guest workers, with 52% being born in the country but retaining their nationality. Among Turks, the labour migrations of 1961 to 1975 and subsequent family reunifications are reflected in the data; second-generation Turks are largely children of guest workers. We should note that with Turkish and Yugoslavian nationals for whom there was no information on the country of birth, the fact of migration or the year of migration is excluded from the analyses (371 and 196 individuals, respectively).

The inflow of first-generation immigrants from developed countries has been steady since the 1960s, while the second generation mostly arrived immediately after the Second World War or in the 1960s and 1970s. The data show that migration from other regions, including the Middle East, South and East Asia and Africa, to Austria is a more recent phenomenon with almost half of all immigrants having arrived in the last decade of the twentieth century.

Educational and labour-market profile of immigrants

There is considerable variation in the educational attainment of immigrants, second-generation minorities and the native-born in Austria (see Tables 3.2A for men and 3.2B for women). First, it is apparent that the proportion of tertiary-educated persons is relatively low among the native Austrian population, while the percentage of those with some secondary vocational education is quite high. Ethnic minorities divide into two groups, one more educated than the native Austrians (East Europeans, those coming from developed countries, Middle East and Africa) and one less educated (Turks and ex-Yugoslavs). Among immigrants from the Middle East, Southern and Eastern Asia and Africa, who arrived largely as refugees, there are also a considerable proportion of people with compulsory education only, while at the same time large numbers possess full secondary and tertiary education compared to the native-born Austrians. It is not surprising that the second-generation from Eastern Europe and from Western developed countries appear to be less educated than the first generation. The majority of these people come from the older inflow of post-World War immigration; they were certainly less educated than direct immigrants who arrived later on.

Immigrants from the former Yugoslavia have lower levels of education, which is at least partially attributable to negative selection with respect to education during the times of guest worker recruitment. Educational attainment among second-generation Yugoslavs improved compared to the first generation but it has not yet converged with the educational attainment of native-born Austrians. Even though more male second-generation Yugoslav immigrants are found among secondary school graduates, they still outnumber the native-born among the lower educated and do not reach parity with the benchmark group in the proportion of tertiary educated. Second-generation female ex-Yugoslav immigrants are even more worse off than their male counterparts with a larger proportion possessing only compulsory education than among the first-generation.

The level of educational attainment among Turkish immigrants is very low as compared to the native-born Austrians and is lower relative to the other immigrant groups including ex-Yugoslavs. A majority of Turkish men and women possess compulsory education only, while the proportion of tertiary educated is rather negligible, particularly among Turkish women. Rather few of them have a maturity certificate. However, some improvement in educational attainment among second-generation Turkish immigrants is noticeable. Sons and daughters of Turkish migrants are found among lower secondary school graduates more often than in the

Table 3.2A. Highest educational qualification, by ancestry and generation: Men (row percentages).

	Compulsory	Some secondary	Full secondary	Tertiary	N
Native Austrian	15.4	61.1	16.3	7.2	57,915
First generation					
East European	11.3	45.3	26.0	17.4	620
Yugoslav	46.2	43.7	7.1	2.9	1,838
Turkish	70.8	21.3	5.1	2.9	1,002
Developed	9.1	37.9	25.2	27.8	691
Middle Eastern/S. Asian	26.8	21.3	26.2	25.6	164
African	21.1	24.8	31.2	22.9	109
Second generation					
East European	11.9	57.4	18.2	12.5	176
Yugoslav	32.8	55.6	8.9	2.7	259
Turkish	57.9	34.2	6.4	1.5	202
Developed	13.6	54.0	19.9	12.6	428

Table 3.2B. Highest educational qualification, by ancestry and generation: Women (row percentages).

	Compulsory	Some secondary	Full secondary	Tertiary	N
Native Austrian	28.8	48.7	16.3	6.1	58,784
First generation					
East European	18.0	32.5	33.0	16.5	901
Yugoslav	64.3	25.6	8.1	2.0	2,012
Turkish	87.8	7.7	3.7	0.9	817
Developed	15.6	40.6	25.3	18.5	1,164
Middle Eastern/S. Asian	33.3	18.6	34.9	13.2	129
East Asian	34.4	29.6	24.8	11.2	125
Second generation					
East European	32.5	47.9	14.7	4.9	163
Yugoslav	75.9	16.1	5.7	2.3	232
Turkish	63.2	29.1	7.7	0.0	117
Developed	26.1	45.5	20.7	7.7	426

first generation. Since the process of their educational attainment is not yet finished due to the relatively younger ages of second-generation Turks as well as of Yugoslavs (see proportion of students among the second generation in Tables 3.3A and 3.3B), the level of their educational attainment may potentially be higher than is shown in these tables.

The labour nature of migration to Austria explains the high labour market participation rates among immigrants (Fassmann 1999). Indeed, as is evident from Table 3.3A, first-generation male immigrants from nearly all immigrant groups under discussion have labour-force participation rates above 90%, which is higher than among the native-born Austrians. Among first-generation immigrants from developed countries, Middle East and Southern Asia the labour-force participation rate is similar to that among native-born Austrians. Second-generation male minorities of Turkish ancestry also have labour-force participation rates higher than among native-born Austrians. Among second-generation Yugoslavs, Eastern Europeans and other westerners the proportion of the economically active is lower than among the native-born. Due to the higher proportion of younger people, second-generation minorities are overrepresented among students. A significant proportion of second-generation minorities from Eastern Europe, the former Yugoslavia and other western developed countries are also found among other inactive in the group, and particularly among those in retirement, which can be attributed to the fact that a substantial proportion of people in these groups are of older ages.

Among women there is more substantial variation in labour-force participation (see Table 3.3B). First-generation ex-Yugoslav women and female immigrants from Eastern Asia appear much more likely to be economically active than the native-born Austrian women. Immigrant women from Eastern European countries have activity rates similar to those of the native-born, while labour-force participation rates among other immigrant women, especially among Turkish, Middle Eastern and South Asian women, are lower than among native-born women. Instead the latter are largely found among housewives, where their proportion is higher than among native-born Austrian women. Patterns of economic inactivity mean that there will be a selection bias in the characteristics of women, particularly from Turkey, the Middle East and South Asia, who are economically active, which has important implications for the analyses of women's fortunes in the labour market.

There exists significant variation in the labour-force participation of second-generation female minorities, too. Among second-generation Turks and ex-Yugoslavs it is higher than among the native-born Austrian women, while among second-generation women from developed countries and from Eastern Europe this proportion is lower, not least due to the higher proportion of retired persons (other inactive in Table 3.3B). As expected, a high proportion of students are found among second-generation women.

Having rather high labour-force participation (particularly among men), most of the immigrants to Austria (of both genders), except those coming from developed countries, are over-represented among the

Table 3.3A. Economic activity by ancestry and generation: Men (row percentages).

	Economically active	Other inactive	Looking after home	Student	N
Native Austrian	87.7	6.9	0.1	5.3	57,228
First generation					
East European	90.3	4.6	0.5	4.6	608
Yugoslav	92.4	5.6	0.7	1.3	1,800
Turkish	93.1	5.9	0.2	0.8	981
Developed	87.4	5.3	0.6	6.7	685
Middle Eastern/S. Asian	88.0	4.4	1.3	6.3	158
African	90.1	3.0	1.0	5.9	101
Second generation					
East European	76.9	19.7	0.0	3.5	173
Yugoslav	79.6	13.1	0.0	7.4	251
Turkish	90.5	2.5	0.0	7.0	200
Developed	79.6	13.1	0.0	7.4	421

Table 3.3B. Economic activity by ancestry and generation: Women (row percentages).

	Economically active	Other inactive	Looking after home	Student	N
Native Austrian	64.1	8.9	21.5	5.5	58,278
First generation					
East European	62.0	7.4	25.9	4.8	878
Yugoslav	72.9	6.3	19.9	0.9	1,988
Turkish	50.8	3.2	45.4	0.5	801
Developed	55.2	9.9	31.0	3.9	1,158
Middle Eastern/S. Asian	50.4	2.4	40.8	6.4	125
East Asian	71.0	1.6	23.4	4.0	124
Second generation					
East European	35.6	33.8	26.3	4.4	160
Yugoslav	69.9	10.6	13.7	5.8	226
Turkish	80.0	1.7	9.6	8.7	115
Developed	54.0	18.0	21.8	6.2	422

unemployed and those employed in unskilled or semi-skilled jobs (see Tables 3.4A and 3.4B). Moreover, Turkish and ex-Yugoslav immigrants are hardly found in the salariat, routine non-manual or self-employment categories, and are under-represented in skilled occupations. Eastern Europeans (both men and women) and male immigrants from the Middle Eastern and Southern Asian countries occupy salaried jobs in similar proportions to their native-born counterparts. Eastern Europeans are, however, less likely to start their own business compared to the native-born, while immigrants from the Asian continent are quite often (at least similarly to the native-born) found in the petty bourgeoisie. At the other extreme, immigrants from developed countries have much higher proportions in the salariat than any other group including native-born Austrians, and are at the same time less likely to be found in manual jobs. The same can be said about second-generation minorities from developed countries, even though they have slightly higher unemployment rates and are less likely to be found in the salariat. Overall, the occupational distribution of the second-generation minorities from developed countries is quite similar to that of the native-born Austrians. This is the case also for second-generation Eastern European men, albeit there is some over-representation in the salariat and under-representation in manual occupations.

The question is now whether second-generation Turkish and ex-Yugoslav minorities are doing better as compared to the first generation, moving closer to the employment patterns characteristic of the native-born Austrian population. Second-generation men of ex-Yugoslav ances-

Table 3.4A. Current occupation by ancestry and generation: Men (row percentages).

	Salariat	Routine non-manual	Petty bourgeoisie	Skilled manual	Semi- and unskilled	Unemployed	N
Native Austrian	23.7	10.5	10.4	30.8	20.8	3.7	48,851
First generation							
East European	22.7	5.8	4.7	27.3	32.2	7.3	550
Yugoslav	3.8	1.9	1.7	23.4	61.2	8.0	1,695
Turkish	3.9	2.1	2.6	10.9	70.2	10.3	918
Developed	46.3	8.0	7.2	17.7	17.3	3.5	577
Middle Eastern/ S. Asian	21.7	6.3	12.6	10.5	42.7	6.3	143
Second generation							
East European	40.0	10.0	9.2	23.8	13.9	3.1	130
Yugoslav	10.5	7.0	3.1	31.4	42.4	5.7	229
Turkish	3.9	2.8	1.1	28.9	54.4	8.9	180
Developed	30.2	12.9	8.1	27.0	17.4	4.5	334

Table 3.4B. Current occupation by ancestry and generation: Women (row percentages).

	Salariat	Routine non-manual	Petty bourgeoisie	Skilled manual	Semi- and unskilled	Unemployed	N
Native Austrian	19.6	30.2	11.6	3.0	31.5	4.1	39,911
First generation							
East European	19.5	16.7	6.0	3.4	44.6	9.7	616
Yugoslav	4.6	5.8	1.8	2.2	79.0	6.7	1,536
Turkish	2.4	3.7	1.3	1.1	79.8	11.7	461
Developed	32.4	23.9	10.7	1.5	25.9	5.6	675
Second generation							
Yugoslav	6.4	25.2	2.3	5.3	49.1	11.7	171
Turkish	4.0	23.2	3.0	5.1	55.6	9.1	99
Developed	26.9	27.3	6.7	2.0	30.4	6.7	253

try certainly improved their labour-market standing as compared to their fathers. They are more often found in non-manual occupations and as skilled workers and are less likely to be unemployed or unskilled. A similar trend is observed among second-generation ex-Yugoslav women, even though these face higher unemployment compared to their mothers.

Intergenerational mobility is also marked for second-generation Turkish male immigrants, but the improvement is less pronounced as compared to their Yugoslav counterparts. Sons of Turkish immigrants manage to enter skilled employment more often than their fathers and are less likely to be found among the unskilled. Other than that, their labour-market allocation is quite similar to that of their fathers. Daughters of Turkish immigrants are also less likely to be found as unskilled workers, opting instead for other jobs and particularly routine non-manual employment.

Ethnic penalties at employment entry

The question is, however, whether dissimilarity between the native-born and the majority of immigrant groups in employment and occupational attainment persists once differences in educational qualifications, age and family structure are taken into account. To calculate the ethnic penalties at employment entry, i.e. the chances of being either unemployed or employed, a binomial logistic regression is carried out, controlling for education, age and marital status. Since several years of observation are pooled to a single dataset, we also control for the year of survey. Table 3.5 reports log odds of avoiding unemployment (vs. being unemployed) among the national origin groups for men and women. Negative parameters for national origin groups thus indicate ethnic penalties at employment entry. Before turning to these ethnic penalties, the effects of control variables are discussed.

As the first column shows, amongst men, age has a curvilinear relationship with the chance of entering employment. Younger men tend to have higher risks of unemployment but the gradient flattens off after middle age. For women, shown in the second column, the effect is linear, meaning that unemployment risk decreases with the age. As expected, education has a significant impact on the employment chances for both genders: Less-educated persons are at higher risk of unemployment, while employment chances improve the higher the educational level. Marital status has the usual association with unemployment risks among men, married men tending to have lower risks of unemployment. Among women higher unemployment risks are found for divorced or separated women compared to the rest. Finally, it is evident that the year 2001 was quite a favourable year for gaining employment in Austria with unemployment risks being somewhat higher in earlier observation years.

Estimates associated with different ethnic groups are naturally of primary interest for the study. It is evident that all first-generation male immigrants, except those coming from developed countries, suffer penalties at entry to gainful employment in the Austrian labour market, other things being equal. The most disadvantaged appear to be Eastern Europeans and Turks. Second-generation men, however, are not significantly different from the native-born counterparts with respect to unemployment.

Among women the situation is less favourable for immigrants. All ethnic groups observed have higher unemployment risks compared to the native-born. Women of Eastern European origin face particularly

Table 3.5. Logistic regression of employment (parameter estimates; contrasts with unemployment).

	Model 1				Model 2			
	Men		Women		Men		Women	
Intercept	**2.39**	(0.27)	**2.77**	(0.30)	**2.47**	(0.27)	**2.79**	(0.30)
Ancestry								
Native Austrian	0		0		0		0	
East European 1	**−1.01**	(0.17)	**−1.11**	(0.14)	**−1.00**	(0.24)	**−1.22**	(0.17)
Yugoslav 1	**−0.78**	(0.10)	**−0.31**	(0.11)	**−1.43**	(0.20)	**−0.68**	(0.26)
Turkish 1	**−1.00**	(0.12)	**−0.85**	(0.15)	**−1.74**	(0.28)	−0.39	(0.76)
Developed 1	−0.14	(0.23)	**−0.47**	(0.17)	−0.19	(0.29)	−0.33	(0.24)
Middle Eastern and								
South Asian 1	**−0.78**	(0.35)			**−1.20**	(0.38)		
East European 2	−0.21	(0.51)			0.31	(0.87)		
Yugoslav 2	−0.10	(0.29)	**−0.88**	(0.24)	−0.01	(0.74)	−0.87	(0.61)
Turkish 2	−0.30	(0.27)			**−1.77**	(0.57)		
Developed 2	−0.20	(0.27)	**−0.54**	(0.25)	−0.56	(0.35)	−0.36	(0.43)
Age/10	**0.74**	(0.14)	**0.42**	(0.17)	**0.73**	(0.14)	**0.41**	(0.17)
(Age/10)^2	**−0.11**	(0.02)	−0.04	(0.02)	**−0.11**	(0.02)	−0.04	(0.02)
Education								
Compulsory	**−1.07**	(0.09)	**−0.81**	(0.08)	**−1.18**	(0.09)	**−0.83**	(0.08)
Some secondary	**−0.50**	(0.08)	**−0.37**	(0.08)	**−0.53**	(0.08)	**−0.38**	(0.08)
Full secondary	0		0		0		0	
Tertiary	**0.28**	(0.14)	**0.28**	(0.13)	**0.35**	(0.14)	**0.28**	(0.13)
Marital status								
Single	0		0		0		0	
Married/cohabiting	**0.75**	(0.06)	−0.02	(0.07)	**0.75**	(0.06)	−0.02	(0.07)
Divorced, separated	−0.15	(0.09)	**−0.46**	(0.09)	−0.14	(0.09)	**−0.45**	(0.09)
Year								
1995	−0.12	(0.06)	**−0.19**	(0.07)	**−0.13**	(0.06)	**−0.20**	(0.07)
1997	**−0.24**	(0.06)	**−0.21**	(0.07)	**−0.25**	(0.06)	**−0.21**	(0.07)
1999	**−0.24**	(0.06)	**−0.14**	(0.07)	**−0.24**	(0.06)	**−0.14**	(0.07)
2001	0		0		0		0	
Interactions between ancestry and education								
East European 1					0.02	(0.20)	−0.14	(0.15)
Yugoslav 1					**−0.46**	(0.13)	−0.23	(0.15)
Turkish 1					**−0.46**	(0.16)	0.24	(0.39)
Developed 1					−0.04	(0.24)	0.17	(0.19)
Middle Eastern and								
South Asian 1					−0.54	(0.29)		
East European 2					0.11	(0.71)		
Yugoslav 2					0.05	(0.47)	0.00	(0.38)
Turkish 2					**−0.96**	(0.36)		
Developed 2					−0.41	(0.31)	0.18	(0.32)
Chi-square (D.F.)	802.9 (19)		362.4 (16)		830.5 (28)		367.2 (22)	
N	54,485		43,485		54,485		43,485	

Note: Standard errors are given in brackets. Emboldened coefficients indicate significance at the 0.05 level or better.

high unemployment risks, higher than Turkish women. It is noteworthy that second-generation Yugoslav women, as well as second-generation women from developed countries are more at risk of unemployment than the first generation immigrants of the corresponding ethnic groups. At least for Yugoslavs, where the difference in unemployment risks is particularly large, this could be explained by varying aspirations among first- and second-generation Yugoslav women. If first-generation Yugoslav women predominantly search for jobs in the unskilled labour market, their daughters target non-manual employment more often, and there they are more likely to compete with the native-born and eventually face discrimination.[12]

The models presented in the first two columns of Table 3.5 assume that education brings the same benefits to ethnic minorities as they do to native-born Austrians. It has frequently been suggested, however, that ethnic minorities and particularly first-generation immigrants with foreign qualifications, receive lower returns on their educational investments compared to the native-born. The third and fourth columns in Table 3.5 thus demonstrate results of the analyses in which interaction effects of education with immigrant groups are included to test if immigrants' education is rewarded differently from education of the native-born Austrians. The corresponding predicted probabilities for unemployment are plotted in Figure 3.3A for men and Figure 3.3B for women.

From Figure 3.3A it is evident that the probabilities of unemployment among the native-born men, second-generation men from Eastern Europe and the former Yugoslavia and the first-generation immigrants from developed countries are quite similar. First-generation Eastern European male immigrants certainly face higher unemployment, but there is no

---

[12] Comparison of the first and second generations, as in Tables 3.3A and 3.3B, does not strictly speaking allow us to make inferences about parents and children, since the first generation will include recent arrivals who could not be the parents of the second generation. However, we can check our results by excluding these recent arrivals. We have therefore re-run the analyses excluding first-generation Turks and Yugoslavs who arrived after 1989. We include those who arrived between 1976 and 1988, since this was mainly a family reunification period and many families of recruited immigrants (those who arrived prior to 1975) arrived exactly during this period. We also dropped those younger than 40 and, for the second-generation Yugoslavs, we also dropped those who arrived prior to 1960, as those are indeed a totally different cohort. After these deletions, the standard errors for the first-generation parameter estimates become somewhat larger but there is little change in the pattern of the estimates themselves. In the case of women, the revised parameter estimates are -0.18 for first-generation Yugoslavs and -0.96 for first-generation Turkish women. In the case of men the revised estimates are -0.55 for first-generation Yugoslavs and -0.93 for first-generation Turks.

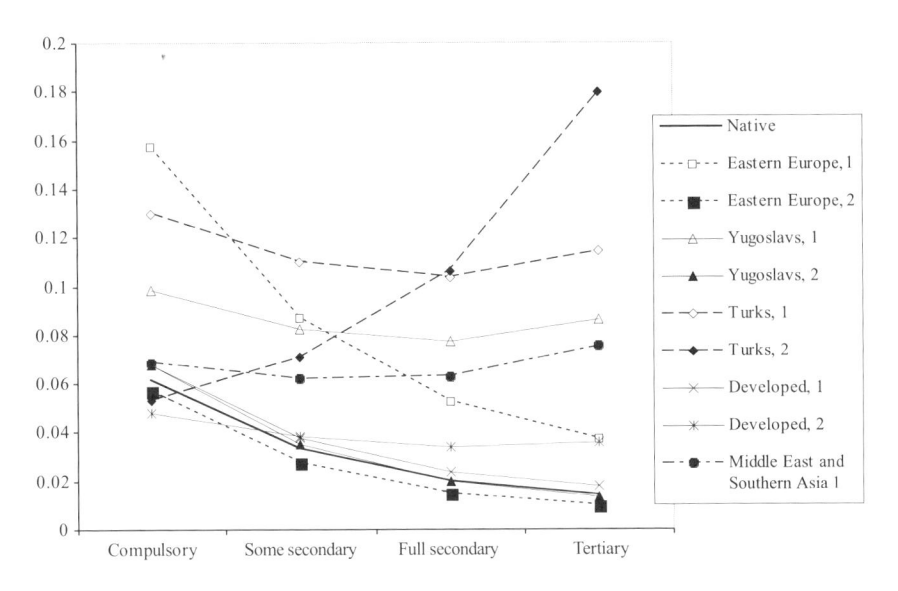

Figure 3.3A. Educational qualifications and probability of unemployment: Men.
Note: All covariates held at means.

indication that this interacts with their education. Interaction effects are, however, noticeable for the following groups: second-generation men from developed countries, first-generation immigrants from the Middle East and Southern Asia, first-generation Yugoslavs and both first- and second-generation Turks. Moreover, effects for the latter three groups prove to be statistically significant and point to the particular disadvantage of more educated ex-Yugoslav or Turkish immigrants and second-generation Turks in the access to employment.

Among women it is manifest that all minority groups appear to be disadvantaged with respect to employment entry, although there are no significant interaction effects with education to be reported. It is visible, however, that less-educated Yugoslav female immigrants have employment entry chances comparable to those of the native-born, while the relative disadvantage (compared to the native-born) among more educated women from the former Yugoslavia is more pronounced. On the other hand, the impression is that first-generation Turkish immigrant women, female immigrants from developed countries and the second-generation women from developed countries with compulsory education only face slightly higher risks of unemployment in the Austrian labour market; the effects are, however, not statistically significant.

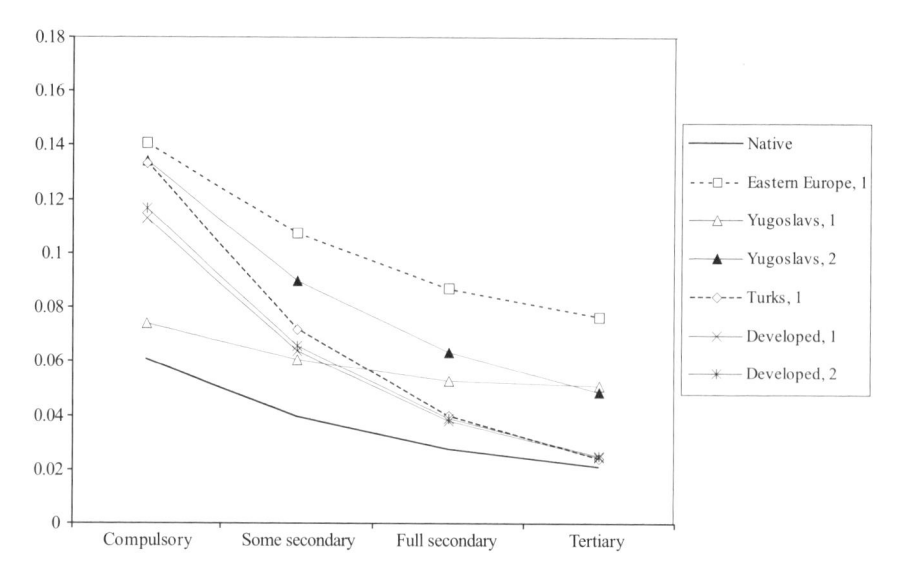

Figure 3.3B. Educational qualification and probability of unemployment: Women.
Note: All covariates held at means.

Ethnic penalties in occupational attainment

To estimate ethnic penalties with respect to immigrants' occupational attainment a multinomial logistic regression is conducted with the same set of covariates as in the model of unemployment. There are four categories for occupational outcomes—the salariat, routine non-manual, the petty bourgeoisie, and skilled work. Semi- and unskilled work serves as the reference category. Thus the chance of being found in one of the other four occupational categories relative to that of being employed as a semi- or unskilled worker are assessed, and the results can be found in Tables 3.6A and 3.6B.

Access to the salariat (vs. entry to unskilled occupations) has the expected positive association with educational qualification—i.e., the higher the level of education, the better chance a person has of landing a job in the salariat, as compared to unskilled employment. This is true for both men (Table 3.6A) and women (Table 3.6B). There is a significant curvilinear age effect of reaching salaried occupations among women, which is not the case among men. Additionally, being married increases the chances of salaried employment among men, whilst having the opposite effect among women. Moreover, divorced or separated women have

Table 3.6A. Logistic regression of occupational class: Men (parameter estimates; contrasts with semi- and unskilled manual).

	Salariat		Routine non-manual		Petty bourgeoisie		Skilled manual	
Intercept	**1.89**	(0.27)	**2.98**	(0.24)	**−1.24**	(0.27)	**4.80**	(0.18)
Ancestry								
Native Austrian	0		0		0		0	
East European 1	**−2.50**	(0.17)	**−1.59**	(0.20)	**−1.68**	(0.22)	**−0.63**	(0.12)
Yugoslav 1	**−3.51**	(0.18)	**−2.68**	(0.19)	**−2.85**	(0.19)	**−0.97**	(0.07)
Turkish 1	**−3.00**	(0.25)	**−2.16**	(0.24)	**−2.21**	(0.21)	**−1.50**	(0.12)
Developed 1	−0.30	(0.17)	−0.32	(0.19)	−0.44	(0.19)	−0.37	(0.15)
Middle Eastern and South Asian 1	**−2.97**	(0.32)	**−1.63**	(0.40)	−0.76	(0.29)	**−1.37**	(0.32)
East European 2	0.55	(0.35)	0.13	(0.39)	−0.13	(0.38)	0.12	(0.32)
Yugoslav 2	**−0.98**	(0.31)	**−0.96**	(0.28)	**−1.52**	(0.40)	**−0.78**	(0.17)
Turkish 2	**−1.62**	(0.57)	**−1.72**	(0.47)	**−2.10**	(0.72)	**−0.85**	(0.20)
Developed 2	−0.05	(0.22)	0.26	(0.22)	−0.19	(0.24)	0.08	(0.18)
Age/10	0.05	(0.14)	**−1.18**	(0.13)	**0.45**	(0.14)	**−2.14**	(0.10)
(Age/10)²	0.03	(0.02)	**0.15**	(0.02)	−0.00	(0.02)	**0.25**	(0.01)
Education								
Compulsory	**−5.91**	(0.09)	**−3.27**	(0.08)	**−1.87**	(0.08)	**−1.99**	(0.07)
Some secondary	**−3.53**	(0.06)	**−1.37**	(0.07)	**−1.05**	(0.07)	**0.18**	(0.07)
Full secondary	0		0		0		0	
Tertiary	**1.84**	(0.15)	−0.04	(0.18)	0.12	(0.19)	−0.20	(0.20)
Marital status								
Single	0		0		0		0	
Married/cohabiting	**0.43**	(0.05)	**0.21**	(0.05)	0.04	(0.05)	**0.32**	(0.04)
Divorced, separated	0.10	(0.09)	0.06	(0.09)	**−0.31**	(0.09)	0.07	(0.07)
Year								
1995	−0.03	(0.05)	−0.08	(0.05)	0.03	(0.05)	**−0.09**	(0.04)
1997	**−0.11**	(0.05)	**−0.10**	(0.05)	−0.05	(0.05)	**−0.20**	(0.04)
1999	−0.08	(0.05)	−0.03	(0.05)	**−0.10**	(0.05)	−0.07	(0.04)
2001	0		0		0		0	
Chi-square (D.F.)				33,033.94 (76)				
N				50,541				

Note: Standard errors are given in brackets. Emboldened coefficients indicate significance at the 0.05 level or better.

similarly lower chances of entering the salariat to married ones, when compared to single women.

As in the model of unemployment, the parameter estimates associated with the dummy variables for ancestry tell us about the overall ethnic penalties experienced by different immigrant groups, net of human capital characteristics. A negative parameter indicates that the group in question has a poorer chance than similarly qualified native-born peers of landing a particular occupation, compared to unskilled employment. As Table 3.6A shows, in terms of access to the salariat, these ancestry effects are negative for all male first- and second-generation minorities, with the exception of those from developed countries and second-generation

Table 3.6B. Logistic regression of occupational class: Women (parameter estimates; contrasts with semi- and unskilled manual).

	Salariat		Routine non-manual		Petty bourgeoisie		Skilled manual	
Intercept	−0.03	(0.26)	**3.04**	(0.19)	**−3.33**	(0.31)	**2.04**	(0.37)
Ancestry								
Native Austrian	0		0		0		0	
East European 1	**−2.06**	(0.16)	**−1.43**	(0.13)	**−1.28**	(0.18)	−0.43	(0.26)
Yugoslav 1	**−2.14**	(0.16)	**−2.16**	(0.12)	**−2.89**	(0.20)	**−0.75**	(0.19)
Turkish 1	**−1.93**	(0.43)	**−1.88**	(0.27)	**−2.91**	(0.41)	**−1.49**	(0.59)
Developed 1	**−0.50**	(0.15)	**−0.36**	(0.12)	−0.22	(0.15)	**−0.57**	(0.35)
Yugoslav 2	−0.58	(0.40)	−0.31	(0.22)	**−1.51**	(0.52)	−0.19	(0.41)
Developed 2	0.20	(0.22)	−0.16	(0.19)	**−0.68**	(0.28)	−0.34	(0.47)
Age/10	**0.81**	(0.15)	**−0.79**	(0.10)	**0.53**	(0.16)	**−1.96**	(0.21)
(Age/10)²	**−0.07**	(0.02)	**0.09**	(0.01)	−0.01	(0.02)	**0.23**	(0.03)
Education								
Compulsory	**−5.45**	(0.10)	**−3.33**	(0.06)	**−0.91**	(0.07)	**−1.67**	(0.14)
Some secondary	**−2.67**	(0.05)	**−0.99**	(0.05)	**−0.55**	(0.07)	0.21	(0.12)
Full secondary	0		0		0		0	
Tertiary	**2.48**	(0.13)	−0.22	(0.15)	0.15	(0.20)	0.36	(0.37)
Marital status								
Single	0		0		0		0	
Married/cohabiting	**−0.47**	(0.05)	**−0.24**	(0.04)	**1.11**	(0.06)	**−0.37**	(0.08)
Divorced, separated	**−0.44**	(0.07)	**−0.21**	(0.05)	0.04	(0.09)	**−0.46**	(0.13)
Year								
1995	0.07	(0.05)	−0.01	(0.04)	**0.27**	(0.05)	−0.06	(0.09)
1997	−0.06	(0.05)	−0.02	(0.04)	**0.19**	(0.05)	−0.09	(0.09)
1999	−0.01	(0.05)	−0.04	(0.04)	0.09	(0.05)	−0.03	(0.09)
2001	0		0		0		0	
Chi-square (D.F.)			27,214.82 (68)					
N			40,719					

Note: Standard errors are given in brackets. Emboldened coefficients indicate significance at the 0.05 level or better.

Eastern Europeans. The largest negative parameter for first-generation immigrants is observed among men of Yugoslav origin, followed by Turks, immigrants from the Middle East and Southern Asia and Eastern Europe. However, as the parameters for the second generation show, when compared to the first generation, there has been significant improvement for each of the immigrant groups under discussion; nonetheless, second-generation minorities from Turkey and ex-Yugoslavia still incur shortfalls in access to salaried jobs when compared to equally qualified native-born Austrian men. The intergenerational improvement is more pronounced for ex-Yugoslavs than for Turks.

Among women (Table 3.6B), a similar pattern of ethnic disadvantage is observed. Yugoslav, Eastern European and Turkish women having lower chances of landing salaried occupations, with immigrants from developed countries faring slightly better, but still disadvantaged when compared to the native-born. A very important finding, however, is that second-generation Yugoslav women and women from developed countries do not differ significantly from comparable native-born Austrian women in their likelihood of access to the salariat.[13]

Access to routine non-manual occupations among men and women follows slightly different patterns from those evidenced in salariat access. As the second column of the tables show, having tertiary education is less a prerequisite for entry into this type of employment. Age has a negative curvilinear effect on the odds of obtaining routine non-manual jobs among both men and women. As in the earlier analyses, it appears that married men are more prone to obtain routine non-manual jobs (as opposed to unskilled unemployment); while among the women it is rather the single women who have higher chances of obtaining routine non-manual employment.

In assessing the likelihood of entering routine non-manual employment, the negative effects of non-native birth continue to decrease, but the hierarchy remains more or less the same. Among men, ex-Yugoslavs are the most disadvantaged, followed by Turks, immigrants from the Middle East and Southern Asia and Eastern Europeans, with immigrants from developed countries being the least disadvantaged. Again, as in the earlier model, second-generation ex-Yugoslavs and Turks have a better chance, as compared to the first generation, but are still penalised relative to comparable native-born Austrian men. The likelihood of second-generation Eastern Europeans and of those originating in other developed countries attaining non-manual employment is similar to that of the native-born.

Among women, routine non-manual work is an important employment niche, more so than for men, and as such, the pattern of ethnic disadvantage observed is quite similar to the pattern observed with regard to salariat access. Again, Yugoslav women appear to be the most heavily disadvantaged, followed by Turkish women, Eastern Europeans and immigrant women from developed countries. Additionally, second-generation women of ex-Yugoslavian origin or from developed countries do not

---

[13] As in the analysis of unemployment, we have checked our results for the first generation after excluding recent arrivals. The parameter estimates all become slightly smaller, perhaps reflecting the especial difficulties that immigrants experience in the labour market at the beginning of their life in Austria, but the revised analysis confirms very substantial inter-generational improvement. In the case of men, the revised parameter estimates become -3.28 for first-generation Yugoslavs and -2.79 for first-generation Turks. In the case of women the revised estimates are -1.90 for first-generation Yugoslavs and -1.61 for first-generation Turks.

differ significantly from the native-born Austrian women in their chances of accessing routine non-manual employment.

The third columns of Tables 3.6 present the likelihood for men and women of employment within the petty bourgeoisie. As can be seen, persons with tertiary and full secondary education have the highest probability of employment in this sector (as opposed to unskilled employment), followed by individuals with some secondary and compulsory education. Age effects are linear and positive, signifying a higher propensity for self-employment with increasing age, all else being equal. Parameters for marital status, however, differ between the genders. While among men those who are divorced have the lowest probability of starting their own business, among women, *ceteris paribus*, the probability of self-employment is significantly higher for those that are married. Ancestry effects for men again indicate penalties for all immigrant groups except second-generation men from developed countries and from Eastern Europe. Ex-Yugoslav immigrants have the lowest chance of adopting self-employment, followed by immigrants from Turkey, the Central and Eastern European countries, the Middle East and southern Asia and lastly immigrants from developed countries. Second-generation Yugoslavs are more likely to be self-employed than the first, but nevertheless are less likely to adopt self-employment than native-born Austrian men. Second-generation Turks, however, do not appear to have a significantly higher likelihood of self-employment than their fathers.

As evident from Table 3.6B, Turkish women have the lowest chances for self-employment, followed by ex-Yugoslavs, and Eastern Europeans. Unlike access to the salariat and routine non-manual sectors, second-generation Yugoslav women and immigrants from developed countries have a lower probability of adopting self-employment as compared to the native-born. It is to be noted that second-generation ex-Yugoslav women have a higher chance of being self-employed compared with first-generation Yugoslavs; however for second-generation minorities from developed countries, this likelihood has decreased relative to the first generation.

The final columns in Tables 3.6 present the probabilities of being in skilled employment, as opposed to unskilled employment. Persons with compulsory education have the lowest probability of being in skilled rather than unskilled employment; among men, those with some secondary education have better prospects of landing skilled employment. The age effect is negative and curvilinear for both men and women. Married men have a higher probability of entering skilled employment, *ceteris paribus*; among women this probability is the highest for those that are single.

Overall, ethnic penalties at entry to skilled employment among male immigrants are smaller than for other occupational destinations, but the pattern is largely the same—immigrants have a higher chance of being in unskilled occupations than skilled. Unlike earlier models, however, first-generation Turkish immigrants appear to be the most highly disadvantaged, followed by newcomers from the Middle East and Southern Asia, Yugoslavs, Eastern Europeans and immigrants from developed countries. Again as earlier, the model shows improvements in the occupational positioning of second-generation Yugoslavs and Turks. Among women, for whom skilled manual employment is not so widespread, only Turkish and Yugoslav immigrants appear to be disadvantaged.

Differential returns for education?

The models presented in Tables 3.6A and 3.6B show that most first-generation and some second-generation groups appear to be penalised in accessing higher occupational groups, when compared with native Austrians. These models, however, assume that education is rewarded similarly for minority groups and the native-born Austrians. Tables 3.A1A and 3.A1B in Appendix 2 to this chapter show the results, for both men and women, of models under which this assumption is eased—that is, where interaction effects of education and ancestry are included in the model. While exact coefficients can be found in the tables mentioned above, a more straightforward way to assess whether there are differential occupational returns to specific levels of education among ethnic minorities is to plot predicted probabilities of employment in each occupational sector by level of education. Figures 3.4 and 3.5 illustrate these probabilities for both men and women in selected occupational destinations.

Figure 3.4A plots the proportion of men from various ethnic and immigrant groups (and native-born Austrians) at each level of schooling that hold salariat positions. The pattern shown in this figure is quite clear-cut; more specifically, two clusters can be identified. The first cluster, composed of the native-born, first- and second-generation minorities from developed countries, second-generation Eastern Europeans, Yugoslavs and Turks exhibit higher probabilities of entering the salariat (although some variation at the higher and lower levels of secondary education is

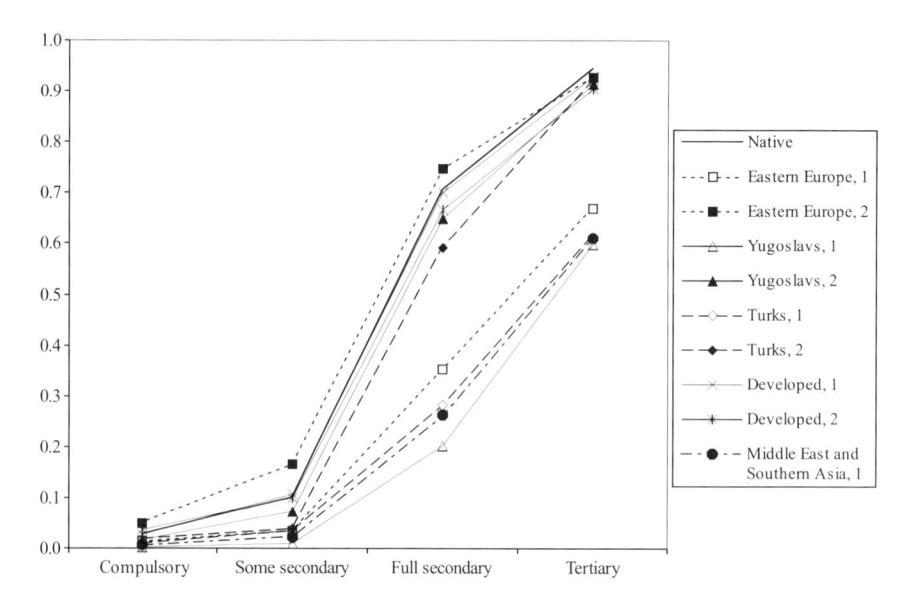

Figure 3.4A. Educational qualifications and the probability of accessing the salariat: Men.
Note: All covariates held at means.

noticeable). First-generation immigrants from Turkey, the Middle East and Southern Asia, the former Yugoslavia and Eastern Europe (the latter slightly deviating) form the second cluster, in which predicted probabilities for salariat positions are significantly lower, albeit again with some within-cluster variation. Significant negative interaction effects are found for only two of the groups under comparison, first-generation Eastern Europeans and first-generation Turks, for whom higher levels of education appear to be under-rewarded when it comes to accessing the salariat.

Among women (see Fig. 3.4B) the pattern may appear less manifest, but the underlying trends largely mimic those found amongst the men. Native-born Austrians, second-generation women from the former Yugoslavia and developed countries have similarly high probabilities of reaching the salariat. For first-generation Turkish immigrants, probabilities are proportionally lower compared to native-born Austrians. The gradient for first-generation Eastern Europeans, Yugoslavs and immigrants from developed countries appears to be flatter, meaning that at higher levels of education their entry to the salariat is disproportionately handicapped when compared to the native-born. Indeed, as the first column of

Table 3.A1A shows, a significant negative interaction with education is noticeable for these groups.

Figure 3.5A plots men's predicted probabilities of belonging to the petty bourgeoisies by level of educational attainment. The specific estimated parameters and their significance can be found in the third column of Table 3.A1A. As the figure shows, among the native-born, as well as second-generation Eastern Europeans and direct immigrants from the Middle East and Southern Asia, the probability of entering self-employment decreases as the level of education increases. Conversely, among first-generation Yugoslavs, Eastern Europeans, and first- and second-generation minorities from developed countries, those with lower levels of education have a lower probability of starting their own businesses. The effects for the first-generation Yugoslavs and immigrants from developed countries are statistically significant. These probabilities appear to suggest that more qualified immigrants from these countries perhaps turn to self-employment after experiencing difficulties gaining entry to the salariat.

In Figure 3.5B predicted probabilities for women of landing routine non-manual employment are plotted. The magnitude and the significance of the underlying interaction effects can be checked from the second column of Table 3.A1B. Manifest differences can be seen in the gradients for the native-born as opposed to first-generation Eastern Europeans,

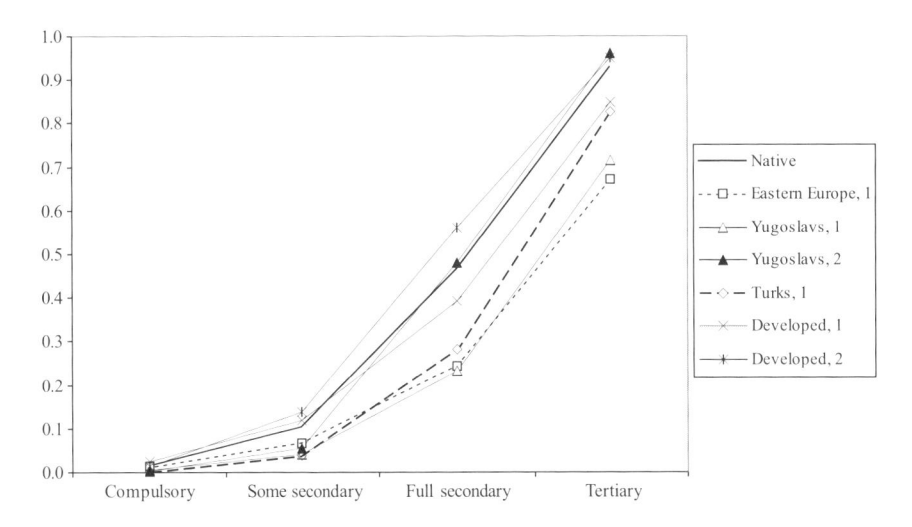

Figure 3.4B. Educational qualifications and probability of accessing the salariat: Women.
Note: All covariates held at means.

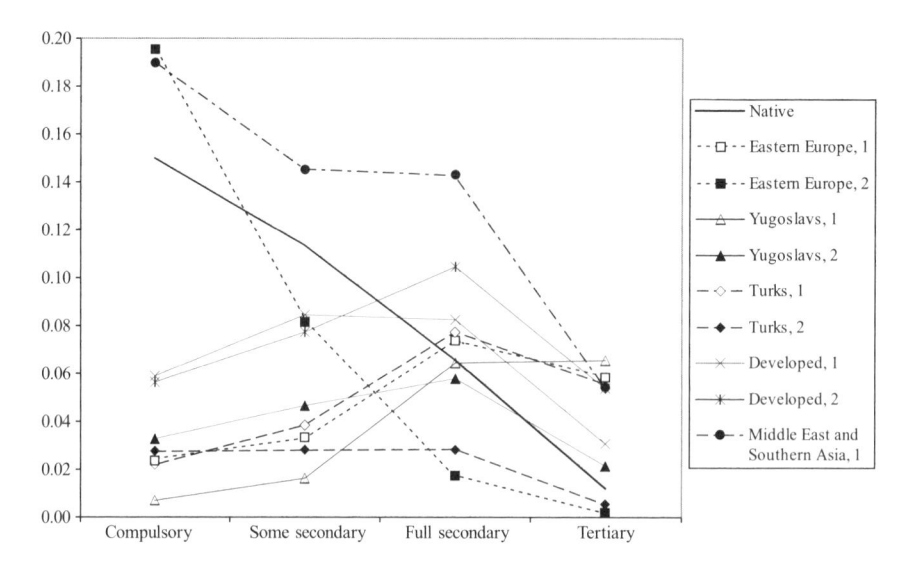

Figure 3.5A. Educational qualifications and the probability of employment in petty bourgeoisie: Men.
Note: All covariates held at means.

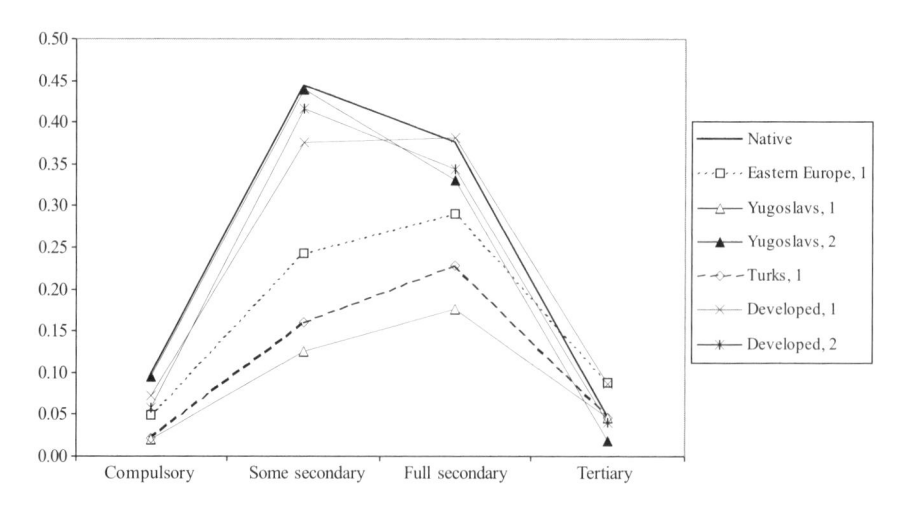

Figure 3.5B. Educational qualifications and probability of routine non-manual employment: Women.
Note: All covariates held at means.

ex-Yugoslavians and Turkish. For the former, some secondary education is quite often enough to enter routine non-manual employment, while for women from the immigrant groups, higher secondary-level education is often necessary to enter a routine non-manual job.

Discussion

The aim of this chapter was to provide a detailed description of the ethnic composition of Austrian society in the last decade of the twentieth century, and the educational and occupational profiles of Austria's various minority groups. More importantly, this chapter has evaluated the extent of convergence in employment and occupational attainment of the first and second generation and compared them to benchmark native-born Austrians. Specifically the analyses in this chapter have examined the extent of ethnic penalties, or the advantages and disadvantages associated with ethnicity or immigrant status, in the Austrian labour market after accounting for key demographic and human capital characteristics.

In Austria, mass immigration started with the official labour recruitment during which large numbers of foreigners came from the former Yugoslavia and from Turkey. Immigration from the neighbouring Eastern and Western European countries has also been substantial. Hence it was possible to conduct a meaningful comparison of the native-born Austrian population with each of these immigrant groups: Eastern Europeans, ex-Yugoslavs, Turks and immigrants from developed countries (largely German speaking). In addition to their first-generation immigrants, each of these ancestries has also fostered a growing number of second-generation members. In our data we have been able to distinguish people either born in Austria but possessing a citizenship other than Austrian, or who emigrated from their respective countries before the age of six. Male immigrants from the Middle East and Southern Asia form a final important comparator, as their presence is the result of a more recent refugee inflow.

Descriptive results show that, in general, immigrants (both men and women), particularly those not associated with guest-worker immigration, have higher levels of education than the native-born population. Nonetheless, a low level of educational attainment is a distinctive feature of Turks and immigrants from the republics of the former Yugoslavia, a pattern that is likely to reflect the fact that they were recruited for entry into low-skilled and unskilled jobs in Austria. The second generation from Turkish and Yugoslavian origins managed to improve their educational capital as compared to the first, but our analyses have shown that their educational distributions have yet to converge with those of the native Austrians. Second-generation groups from the developed countries and from Eastern Europe, on the other hand, overall have educational distributions similar to those of the native Austrians, with the men even appearing to outperform their Austrian counterparts.

Although often characterised by strong labour-market orientation, immigrants to Austria, particularly Turks and ex-Yugoslavs, are largely channelled into unskilled and semi-skilled jobs and quite often face unemployment. Immigrants are also less likely to be found in self-employment, a trend which is particularly acute amongst ex-Yugoslavs and even more so amongst Turks, whose chances of employment within the salariat are similarly negligible. A certain amount of improvement in occupational positioning of second-generation ex-Yugoslavs and Turks is visible, although for the latter this is less substantial.

In the multivariate analyses, the strategy was to test the extent to which occupational attainment of the ethnic and immigrant groups differed from that of the native-born Austrians, taking into account variance in the socio-demographic make-up of the respective groups. It appears that, after controlling for education and demographic attributes, almost all first-generation immigrants, irrespective of gender, have a lower chance of being employed and of attaining any class position other than unskilled worker than has the native population. Although immigrants from developed countries proved to have similar chances of landing employment, they remained slightly disadvantaged in regard to their occupational attainment. Second-generation Turks and ex-Yugoslavs appear to have improved their labour-market standing as compared to their parents, but are still somewhat disadvantaged when compared to the native-born Austrians. Amongst second-generation men, although unemployment appears to be less of a problem, segmentation in the unskilled and low-skilled labour market is pronounced. Amongst second-generation women, it is employment entry which is the main source of concern, as occupationally they do not differ significantly from their native Austrian counterparts.

As this study has shown, first-generation immigrants experience lower returns to education, and this can probably be explained by insufficient fluency in the host-country language and segmentation in the unskilled and low-skilled labour markets (reflecting either the 'guest worker' nature of migration or the temporary labour-oriented intentions, especially of more recent immigrants); each of these factors help to explain existing immigrant penalties. What, then, can elucidate the pattern of ethnic penalties among the second generation? It seems that if the second-generation target employment in the so-called 'secondary labour market' (Doeringer and Piore 1971), i.e. the unskilled and low-skilled jobs, they stand a good chance of obtaining employment, or at least their risk of unemployment is the same as that of the native-born Austrians. This is a common pattern amongst second-generation males, many of whom are connected (through social and ethnic networks) to the economic sectors their fathers worked in, and thus often end up in these same sectors—albeit often improving their occupational standing from the unskilled to the skilled manual sector. Indeed, Fassmann *et al.* (1999) claim that in Austria certain economic branches, mostly in the production sector, are 'reserved' for ex-Yugoslavs and Turkish nationals. Second-generation female minorities, on the other hand, often lack these long-standing networks, as women were not typically recruited during the guest-worker immigration phase. Nonetheless, being educated in Austria and (supposedly[14]) fluent in the German language they, unlike their mothers, aim at more prestigious employment and, once successful at obtaining employment, do not differ significantly from native-born women in their occupational positioning; their most serious problem remains gaining entry employment.

It might well be that discrimination is a part of the explanation for the disadvantage of both the first and second generation, and perhaps particularly for members of the Turkish minority. Results of other studies show that Turks report the highest degree of subjective discrimination, being the most marginalised group in Austria (Kolbacher and Reeger 2003). While 35.3% of Turks report experiencing discrimination in the workplace, this figure is considerably lower amongst among ex-Yugoslavs, at 13.8%. It also appears that Turkish women experience discrimination more often than men, while the situation is reversed for ex-Yugoslavs, with men reporting more unfavourable experiences.

Another explanation for the disadvantages reported above could be institutional discrimination. It should not be forgotten that non-naturalised persons in Austria might experience larger disadvantages within the labour market due to the closure of public-sector employment (*Beamte* jobs) for persons without Austrian citizenship (see also Herzog-Punzenberger 2003).[15] This is a particular concern for second-generation

---

[14] Unfortunately the data do not contain this variable seen as an important indicator of immigrants' labour-market chances.

[15] More than half of the public sector employment jobs are allocated in the salariat, while about 16% are either routine non-manual or skilled manual jobs.

groups, who are potentially more likely to look for higher status public sector employment, and hence this chapter's earlier warning that the peculiarity of the sample of second-generation minorities might result in somewhat biased estimates. To assess the nature of the bias, we conducted additional analyses, analogous to those reported in Table 3.6A, including a variable differentiating between those second-generation immigrants with Austrian citizenship and those without. These results, reported in Table 3.A2 in Appendix 2 of this chapter, show that having Austrian citizenship does improve the chances of second-generation male Turks and ex-Yugoslavs entering the salariat and routine non-manual employment (coefficients are significant at the 10% level only), but is not related to gaining entry to the petty bourgeoisie. Being naturalised also improves the chances of entering skilled manual employment, albeit insignificantly. This analysis indicates that the occupational disadvantages reported here for second-generation male Turks and ex-Yugoslavs would be somewhat lower if we could have taken into account naturalised second-generation immigrants. However, even given this finding, there remains little indication that ethnic penalties—even for naturalised second-generation ex-Yugoslav and Turkish males—ever totally disappear in Austria.

Appendix 1: Technical details

The analyses in this chapter utilise pooled Austrian microcensus data for the years 1995, 1997, 1999 and 2001. The Austrian microcensus is a continuous quarterly survey conducted by the Austrian Central Statistical Office. The data from the spring (March) quarter have been used for this chapter. The spring surveys contain a larger number of variables than surveys conducted in other quarters, particularly variables for the topic under investigation. Overall, the survey covers all residents aged 15 and older in private households (and institutions, in spring only). The sample is based on a one-stage stratified design. Stratification is conducted by the following factors: dwellings occupied or not, social position of the head of the dwelling, floor space, number of persons, quality and period of construction of the dwelling, federal state. Within strata sampling units (dwellings) are selected systematically with a random start. The sample size is approximately 30,000 dwellings, which is 0.9% of the total. After each quarterly survey, one-eighth of the addresses are substituted so that each dwelling remains in the sample for eight successive periods, and the sample is completely renewed every two years.

The survey is largely conducted via face-to-face interviews, with about 5% of interviews conducted by telephone. Mailed questionnaires are addressed only to institutions. The non-response rate of the survey ranges from 10% to 15%. Further details on the survey can be obtained at <http://www.wisdom.at/en/en_index.htm>.

In general, the variables used in this chapter are measured as laid out in the introduction of this volume. *Age* is measured in years, while the square term is included in the multivariate analyses. In presenting the parameter estimates in the logistic regressions we multiply the estimate by ten.

Marital status contains three categories, single, married or cohabiting, and other, the category that includes divorced and widowed persons.

Educational qualification pertains to the highest educational level attained by a respondent, taking into account both general educational and vocational training qualifications. Four categories are differentiated: compulsory education, some secondary education, full secondary education and tertiary education. 'Compulsory education or below' includes lower level qualifications, e.g. *Pflichtschule* or *Hauptschule*, without any vocational training. 'Some secondary education' pertains to full-time vocational schools (*berufsbildende mittlere Schulen*) or apprenticeship training in the dual system. The 'full secondary' qualification indicates a full maturity certificate obtained in higher secondary general (*allgemeinbildende höhere Schulen*) or technical (*berufsbildende höhere Schulen*) schools. With full maturity certificates individuals are entitled to enter 'tertiary education', be it traditional universities, institutions for provision of teacher, social worker or health sector professional training (i.e. non-academic tertiary education), or higher professional colleges (*Fachhochschulen*), the latter alternative introduced only in 1994.

When fitting the interaction terms between education and ethnicity shown in Tables 3.5, 3.A1A and 3.A1B, we treat educational qualifications as a continuous variable coded -2 (compulsory education), -1 (some secondary education), 0 (full secondary education), 1 (tertiary education).

The *economic activity* variable differentiates between (1) economically active respondents, i.e. those in paid work or looking for paid work even if currently unemployed, (2) other inactive, i.e. those who are retired, permanently sick or disabled, (3) student in full-time education, (4) persons looking after the home.

Unemployment is measured according to the ILO definition, thus referring to people both looking and available for work.

Occupational class is constructed on the basis of two variables in the Austrian microcensus, professional status and 3-digit occupational classification, and pertains solely to the civil labour force (i.e., excluding armed forces). Strictly following the Goldthorpe class schema, those in the salariat include professionals, administrators and managers, higher-grade technicians and supervisors of non-manual workers. The category of routine non-manual encompasses those employed in administration and commerce. The petty bourgeoisie includes small proprietors and artisans with or without employees, farmers, smallholders and other self-employed workers in primary production. Skilled workers cover the group of lower-grade technicians, supervisors of manual workers and skilled manual workers. Finally semi- and unskilled workers are lower-skilled workers in industry, construction, agriculture, including also lower grade routine non-manual employees (e.g., in sales and services).

In order to validate the occupational class schema for Austria, and above all to verify if the smaller size of the salariat reflects the Austrian reality (as opposed to being an artefact of the classification), the occupational class distribution from the microcensus data was checked against the cross-national European Union Labour Force Studies data. Results confirmed that compared to other European countries, the salariat in Austria is indeed smaller and the working class larger.

Appendix 2: Supplementary tables

Table 3.A1A. Occupational class and differential returns to education: Men.

	Salariat		Routine non-manual		Petty bourgeoisie		Skilled manual	
Main effects of ancestry								
Native Austrian	0		0		0		0	
East European 1	**−2.46**	(0.17)	**−1.71**	(0.24)	**−1.64**	(0.25)	**−0.75**	(0.19)
Yugoslav 1	**−3.51**	(0.18)	**−2.81**	(0.30)	**−2.28**	(0.27)	**−1.02**	(0.15)
Turkish 1	**−3.07**	(0.26)	**−2.05**	(0.36)	**−1.99**	(0.41)	**−1.44**	(0.27)
Developed 1	−0.24	(0.27)	−0.42	(0.34)	0.01	(0.32)	−0.28	(0.33)
Middle Eastern and South Asian 1	**−3.09**	(0.35)	**−2.01**	(0.43)	**−1.32**	(0.38)	**−1.57**	(0.40)
East European 2	0.75	(0.88)	0.83	(0.96)	−0.62	(1.02)	0.82	(0.94)
Yugoslav 2	**−1.50**	(0.46)	**−1.94**	(0.64)	−1.53	(0.80)	**−1.76**	(0.45)
Turkish 2	**−1.84**	(0.74)	**−2.60**	(1.17)	−2.49	(1.81)	**−1.22**	(0.55)
Developed 2	−0.29	(0.38)	−0.37	(0.46)	0.23	(0.44)	−0.23	(0.44)
Interaction effects between ancestry and education								
East European 1	**−0.73**	(0.21)	−0.14	(0.27)	0.25	(0.27)	−0.15	(0.19)
Yugoslav 1	−0.21	(0.22)	−0.15	(0.26)	**0.58**	(0.22)	−0.05	(0.12)
Turkish 1	**−0.55**	(0.23)	0.13	(0.28)	0.16	(0.25)	0.04	(0.19)
Developed 1	−0.04	(0.26)	−0.18	(0.31)	**0.55**	(0.28)	0.08	(0.30)
Middle Eastern and South Asian 1	−0.74	(0.42)	−0.61	(0.42)	**−0.70**	(0.27)	−0.16	(0.36)
East European 2	0.11	(0.74)	0.76	(0.83)	−0.43	(0.73)	0.68	(0.80)
Yugoslav 2	−0.43	(0.48)	−0.83	(0.50)	0.09	(0.67)	**−0.79**	(0.33)
Turkish 2	−0.05	(0.76)	−0.64	(0.75)	−0.25	(1.10)	−0.24	(0.34)
Developed 2	−0.32	(0.35)	−0.65	(0.38)	0.57	(0.38)	−0.29	(0.36)
Chi-square (D.F.)			33,102.1 (112)					
N			50,541					

Note: Standard errors are given in brackets. Emboldened coefficients indicate significance at the 0.05 level or better.

Table 3.A1B. Occupational class and differential returns to education: Women.

	Salariat		Routine non-manual		Petty bourgeoisie		Skilled manual	
Main effects of ancestry								
Native Austrian	0		0		0		0	
East European 1	**−2.00**	(0.15)	**−1.61**	(0.16)	**−1.25**	(0.21)	−0.25	(0.33)
Yugoslav 1	**−2.42**	(0.18)	**−2.49**	(0.21)	**−2.55**	(0.40)	**−1.19**	(0.43)
Turkish 1	**−2.02**	(0.48)	**−2.02**	(0.49)	−2.85	(1.59)	−0.57	(0.97)
Developed 1	**−0.53**	(0.18)	−0.35	(0.19)	0.01	(0.23)	−0.39	(0.57)
Yugoslav 2	−0.25	(0.65)	−0.41	(0.53)	−0.37	(1.17)	−0.53	(1.11)
Developed 2	0.54	(0.43)	0.26	(0.44)	−0.40	(0.65)	−1.41	(1.29)
Interaction effects between ancestry and education								
East European 1	**−0.91**	(0.19)	**−0.36**	(0.18)	0.16	(0.21)	0.34	(0.36)
Yugoslav 1	**−0.64**	(0.18)	**−0.34**	(0.17)	0.24	(0.25)	−0.37	(0.32)
Turkish 1	−0.19	(0.46)	−0.12	(0.33)	0.03	(0.84)	0.75	(0.75)
Developed 1	**−0.49**	(0.19)	0.02	(0.19)	0.28	(0.20)	0.21	(0.57)
Yugoslav 2	0.66	(0.76)	−0.12	(0.39)	0.82	(0.81)	−0.28	(0.78)
Developed 2	0.34	(0.44)	0.44	(0.41)	0.21	(0.46)	−0.99	(1.00)
Chi-square (D.F.)			27,270.5 (88)					
N			40,721					

Note: Standard errors are given in brackets. Emboldened coefficients indicate significance at the 0.05 level or better.

Table 3.A2. Effect of Austrian citizenship on the occupational class of second-generation male Turks and ex-Yugoslavs.

	Salariat		Routine non-manual		Petty bourgeoisie		Skilled manual	
Intercept	**1.94**	(0.28)	**3.04**	(0.25)	**−1.13**	(0.28)	**4.92**	(0.19)
Ancestry								
Native Austrian	0		0		0		0	
Yugoslav 2	**−0.98**	(0.31)	**−0.85**	(0.42)	**−1.07**	(0.52)	**−0.99**	(0.32)
Turkish 2	**−1.62**	(0.57)	**−1.08**	(0.57)	*−1.76*	(1.03)	**−1.02**	(0.35)
Austrian citizenship								
No citizenship	0		0		0		0	
Austrian citizenship	*0.35*	(0.21)	*0.37*	(0.21)	−0.08	(0.22)	0.27	(0.17)
Age/10	0.05	(0.14)	**−1.17**	(0.13)	**0.42**	(0.14)	**−2.16**	(0.10)
(Age/10)^2	0.03	(0.02)	**0.15**	(0.02)	−0.00	(0.02)	**0.25**	(0.01)
Education								
Compulsory	**−5.98**	(0.10)	**−3.37**	(0.09)	**−1.91**	(0.09)	**−2.07**	(0.08)
Some secondary	**−3.63**	(0.07)	**−1.47**	(0.07)	**−1.12**	(0.08)	0.07	(0.07)
Full secondary	0		0		0		0	
Tertiary	**1.98**	(0.20)	0.03	(0.24)	0.20	(0.25)	−0.01	(0.25)
Marital status								
Single	0		0		0		0	
Married/cohabiting	**0.50**	(0.05)	**0.26**	(0.05)	0.08	(0.05)	**0.38**	(0.04)
Divorced, separated	0.14	(0.09)	0.07	(0.09)	−0.31	(0.09)	0.09	(0.07)
Year								
1995	−0.02	(0.05)	−0.06	(0.05)	0.04	(0.05)	−0.08	(0.04)
1997	−0.08	(0.05)	*−0.09*	(0.05)	−0.04	(0.05)	**−0.19**	(0.04)
1999	−0.05	(0.05)	−0.02	(0.05)	*−0.09*	(0.05)	*−0.06*	(0.04)
2001	0		0		0		0	
Chi-square (D.F.)			28,228.0 (52)					
N			46,752					

Note: Standard errors are given in brackets. Emboldened coefficients indicate significance at the 0.05 level or better; italicised emboldened coefficients indicate significance at the 0.10 level.

References

Albrich, T. (1997), 'Holocaust und Schuldabwehr. Vom Judenmord zum kollektiven Opferstatus'. In R. Steininger, and M. Gehler (eds.), *Österreich im 20. Jahrhundert* Viena, Cologne, Weimar: Böhlau Verlag), pp. 39–107.

Bauböck, R. (1996), *'Nach Rasse und Sprache verschieden': Migrationspolitik in Österreich von der Monarchie bis heute*, Vienna: Institute for Advanced Studies, Political Science Series 31.

Bauböck, R. (2000), 'Immigration control without integration policy: an Austrian dilemma'. In G. Brochmann and T. Hammar (eds.), *Mechanisms of Immigration Control: A Comparative Analysis of European Regulation Policies* (Oxford: Berg), pp. 97–135.

Butschek, F. (1992), *Der österreichische Arbeitsmarkt—von der Industrialisierung bis zur Gegenwart* (Stuttgart: Gustav Fischer Verlag).

Currle, E. (2004), *Migration in Europa—Daten und Hintergründe* (Stuttgart: Lucius & Lucius).

Doeringer, P. B. and Piore, M. J. (1971), *Internal Labor Markets and Manpower Analysis* (Lexington, MA: Heath).

Fassmann, H. (1999), 'Austria'. In S. Angenendt (ed.), *Asylum and Migration Policies in the European Union* (Berlin: Research Institute of the German Society for Foreign Affairs), pp. 65–87.

Fassmann, H. and Münz, R. (1994), 'Austria: A Country of Immigration and Emigration'. In H. Fassmann and R. Münz (eds.), *European Migration in the Late Twentieth Century* (Cheltenham: Edward Elgar), pp. 149–69.

Fassmann, H. and Münz, R. (1995), 'European East–West Migration, 1945–1992'. In R. Cohen (ed.), *The Cambridge Survey of World Migration* (Cambridge: Cambridge University Press), pp. 470–81.

Fassmann, H., Münz, R., and Seifert, W. (1999), 'Was wurde aus den Gastarbeitern? Tuerken und (Ex)Jugoslawen in Deutschland und Österreich', *Demographische Informationen*, 1997/1999, 57–70.

Herzog-Punzenberger, B. (2003), 'Ethnic Segmentation in School and Labor Market: 40 Year Legacy of Austrian Guestworker Policy', *International Migration Review*, 37, 1120–44.

Kofler, A. (2002), *Migration, Emotion, Identities: The Subject Meaning of Differences* (Vienna: Braumüller).

Kohlbacher, J. and Reeger, U. (2003), 'Xenophobie aus der Perspektive der 'Anderen' —Erfahrungen und Bewältigungsstrategien betroffener AusländerInnen'. In H. Fassman and I. Stacher (eds.), *Österreichischer Migrations- und Integrationsbericht* (Vienna: Verlag Drava Klagenfurt/Celovec), pp. 356–66.

König, K. and Stadler, B. (2003), 'Entwicklungstendenzen im öffentlich-rechtlichen und demokratiepolitischen Bereich'. In H. Fassman I. Stacher (eds.) *Österreichischer Migrations- und Integrationsbericht* (Vienna: Verlag Drava Klagenfurt/Celovec), pp. 226–60.

Lebhart, G. and Münz, R. (2003), 'Migration und Fremdenfeindlichkeit in Österreich—Perzeption und Perspektiven'. In H. Fassman I. Stacher (eds.) *Österreichischer Migrations- und Integrationsbericht* (Vienna: Verlag Drava Klagenfurt/Celovec), pp. 343–56.

Lischke, U. and Rögl, H. (1993), *Multikulturalität: Diskurs und Wirklichkeit* (Vienna, IKUS Studies), 1.

Melich, A. (2000), *Eurobarometer 47.1: Images of Switzerland, Education throughout Life, Racism and Patterns of Family Planning and Work Status, March–April 1997* [computer file]. Conducted by INRA (Europe), Brussels, on request of the Europan Commission, Ann Arbor, MI: Inter-university Consortium for Political and Social Research.

Münz, R. (2001), 'Österreich: Marginalisierung von Ausländern—eine österreichische Besonderheit?' In K. Bade (ed.), *Einwanderungskontinent Europa: Migration und Integration am Beginn des 21. Jahrhunderts* (Innsbruck: Universitätsverlag Rasch).

Münz, R., Seifert, W., Ulrich, R., and Fassmann, H. (1997), 'Migrationsmuster, Integration und Exklusion von Ausländern: Deutschland und Österreich im Vergleich', *Demographie aktuell: Vorträge—Aufsätze—Forschungsberichte* 10, Berlin.

Münz, R., Zuser, P., and Kytir, J. (2003), 'Grenzüberschreitende Wanderungen und ausländische Wohnbevölkerung: Struktur und Entwicklung'. In H. Fassman and I. Stacher (eds.), *Österreichischer Migrations- und Integrationsbericht* (Vienna: Verlag Drava Klagenfurt/Celovec), pp. 20–62.

Parnreiter, C. (1994), *AusländerInnenbeschäftigung in der Weltwirtschaftskrise* (Vienna: Promedia).

SOPEMI (1988), *Trends in International Migration: Annual Report* (Paris: OECD).

SOPEMI (1993), *Trends in International Migration: Annual Report* (Paris: OECD).

SOPEMI (1995), *Trends in International Migration: Annual Report* (Paris: OECD).

Statistik Austria (2001), *Demographisches Jahrbuch 2000* (Vienna: Statistik Austria).

Tazi-Preve, I. M., Kytir, J., Lebhart, G., and Münz, R. (1999), *Bevölkerung in Österreich: Demographische Trends, politische Rahmenbedingungen, entwicklungspolitische Aspekte* (Vienna: Institut für Demographie, Österreichische Akademie der Wissenschaft).

Waldrauch, H. and Çinar, D. (2003), 'Staatsbürgerschaftspolitik und Einbürgerungspraxis in Österreich'. In H. Fassman and I. Stacher (eds.) *Österreichischer Migrations- und Integrationsbericht* (Vienna: Verlag Drava Klagenfurt/Celovec), pp. 261–83.

4

Down and Out: The Children of Migrant Workers in the Belgian Labour Market

KAREN PHALET

Summary. Belgium has three major ethnic minorities— Italians, Moroccans and Turks—originating from guest workers who came to Belgium in the post-war period. These groups continue to experience significant ethnic penalties in the Belgian labour market. For employment and occupational attainment alike, the Italian second generation experiences the smallest ethnic penalties and comes closest to achieving parity with native Belgians. In contrast, the Moroccan and Turkish second generation experience much larger ethnic penalties. Moreover, the Turkish second generation is clearly at the bottom end of the ethnic hierarchy, since it experiences at once the largest penalties on avoidance of unemployment *and* on access to the salariat. However, the generational pattern of ethnic penalties is asymmetrical. On the exclusionary side, the size of ethnic penalties suggests stagnation rather than progress across generations. Thus with regard to avoidance of unemployment, the second generation is not significantly less disadvantaged than the first generation. Moreover, relatively large portions of the second generation are not economically active. Hence, ethnic penalties are almost certainly underestimating the full extent of labour-market exclusion. In contrast, generational progress rather than stagnation is found for the inclusion of ethnic minorities in the salariat. While the second generation continues to have much less access to the salariat

Acknowledgements: We thank Patrick Deboosere and Ron Lesthaeghe of Interface Demography at the Free University of Brussels (VUB) for their support in the sampling, data handling and variable construction for this study.

than the native population, they are nevertheless significantly less disadvantaged than the first generation. Inclusionary processes at the higher end of the labour market seem to be rather less rigid, or more meritocratic, than the exclusionary processes that control labour-market entry. The persistence of ethnic disdvantage in the second generation suggests that at least part of the explanation is to be found in the receiving society. Possible explanations range from overt ethnic prejudice to citizenship status. However, civic inequality does not explain why the Turkish (rather than the Moroccan) second generation is most disadvantaged across the board. Nor does ethnic prejudice against Muslims. Possibly in the Turkish case strong ethnic ties may actually hinder the next generation, rather than helping them to avoid unemployment and to get access to stable and well-paid jobs.

Introduction

OVER THE LAST DECADES IN BELGIUM, as in other Northwest European countries, the children of migrant workers have been leaving school and entering the labour market in increasing numbers. How they make the transition from school to work is seen as a critical touchstone of the integration of ethnic minorities. Studies of migrant integration—in the narrow sense of converging socio-economic attainment levels among migrants and natives (Kalter and Granato 2002)—suggest that most changes occur at the transition between generations (Alba and Nee 2003; Crul and Vermeulen 2003). At the same time, dramatic and rising unemployment levels among low-skilled workers in general, and among migrant workers in particular, have caused concern for the prospects of the next generation (Esping-Andersen 1993; OECD 2003). In Belgium, as in some other European countries, this concern is deepened by the rise of a very significant anti-immigrant vote (Lubbers 2001; Swyngedouw 1992). While the younger generations of migrant origin are increasingly oriented towards equal rights and opportunities in Belgium (Phalet and Swyngedouw 2002), their Belgian hosts have been reluctant to accept the permanent presence of ethnic minorities in their midst (Billiet, Carton and Huys 1990).

This chapter uses data from the 1991 Census to map the varying fates of the second generation in the Belgian labour market. As a measure of ethnic disadvantage, gross and net ethnic penalties will be estimated for avoidance of unemployment and for occupational attainment. Our key research question is: does the second generation in Belgium succeed in avoiding unemployment and in gaining access to the salariat?

Migration flows and migrant groups

Up to the First World War, Belgian statistics of net migration flows were negative. At the turn of the century emigration consisted mostly of impoverished Flemish farmers. Their main destinations, aside from Brussels as an emerging urban centre and the industrial south of Belgium, were France and increasingly also the US and Canada (Caestecker 1999). Ever since the 1920s however, Belgium has known a positive migration balance (Lesthaeghe 2000). The country attracted labour migrants (or so-called guest workers) from its neighbours and from Central and Southern Europe, in particular Poland and Italy. Most labour migrants were contracted by the metal and mining industries in Wallonia and in Limburg (Flanders). The economic recession of the 1930s, however, put an end to the early recruitment of foreign labour. Workers were laid off in great numbers and Belgian trades unions supported legal restrictions on immigration, the institution of work permits, and the exclusion of migrant workers from unemployment benefits.

After the Second World War, the Belgian government made a priority of revitalising the coalmines in order to rebuild the economy (Martens 1973). In June 1946 the Belgian and Italian governments made a deal to exchange Italian guest workers for a set amount of coal to be exported to Italy. The deal resulted in the sustained active recruitment of Italian guest workers in the period 1946–9 and well into the 1950s, when the Italian government demanded better working conditions for their guest workers following the infamous 1956 mining accident at Marcinelle where 262 miners died, 136 of whom were Italians. As an indirect consequence of the Marcinelle disaster, Belgium increasingly turned to other Mediterranean countries to attract low-skilled workers.

Throughout the 1950s, immigration rates showed large annual fluctuations, reflecting the specific needs of the heavy industries for temporary labour, and the ensuing stop-and-go immigration policies of the Belgian government (see Table 4.1). From the golden sixties onward, however, Belgian migration statistics show a large and steady intake of foreign labour. The result was a stable migration surplus, in spite of significant return migration throughout the 1960s (Martens 1973). As in other Northwest European countries, the massive intake of cheap labour migrants coincided with the development of the post-war welfare state, extending social rights and fair incomes to the national working classes. The large-scale recruitment of foreign workers, and the subsequent arrival of their families, has had considerable impact on the proportion of foreigners in the total population in Belgium, which increased from roughly 5% in 1961 to over 7% in 1971 (see Table 4.1).

Up to the 1960s immigration in Belgium had been almost exclusively white, Catholic and European. But the new immigration has been much more diverse. Due to competition for foreign labour with the neighbouring countries, Belgium was forced to expand its area of recruitment (Martens 1973). Thus, in 1964 bilateral agreements were signed with Morocco and Turkey, resulting in the settlement of large numbers of Moroccan and Turkish manual workers in Belgium in the late 1960s and early 1970s. At the same time, the settlement of new migrants has spread from the Southern industrial belt to other urban and industrial areas in the North of the country (in and around the cities of Antwerp, Gent and Brussels). In parallel, the employment of migrants was no longer restricted to the heavy metal and mining industries. Increasingly, migrants were also contracted by employers in other industries, in construction, and in menial jobs.

Against the background of economic recession, the Belgian government decided to stop all immigration of new guest workers in 1974. Only the immigration of family members was still allowed. In the early 1980s, the closing of the coal mines and the rapid shrinkage of industrial labour in the South of the country marked a brutal transition to a postindustrial economy. In Belgium, the breakdown of the heavy industries was even more abrupt than in some other countries, like Germany or France (Esping-Andersen 1993). Since most migrants were employed in industrial labour, socio-economic restructuring has disproportionately

Table 4.1. Growth of the foreign population in Belgium 1947–2001 (percentages of total population and numbers (in thousands)).

	Census 1947	Census 1961	Census 1970	Census 1981	Census 1991	Population register 2001	*Census 1991[a]*
N	368	453	696	878	901	861	*1.203*
% of the total population	4.3	4.9	7.2	8.9	9.0	8.4	*12.1*

[a]National origin groups, including naturalisations and acquisitions of Belgian nationality.

affected migrant workers, leading to massive and enduring unemployment or withdrawal from the labour force (Lesthaeghe, 2000). Still, unlike in the 1930s, and except for a short dip in 1980–1, there was no significant turning point in immigration statistics. Instead, from the middle of the 1970s and well into the present, family reunification became the main source of continuing immigration. With its heavy industries Wallonia has disproportionately suffered from the restructuring of the labour market, while Flanders has more readily developed a post-industrial economy. The metropolitan region of Brussels, which has known by far the largest intake and presence of foreign workers and professionals in Belgium, has developed into an international administrative centre with a typical urban service economy.

The permanent settlement of migrant families and the birth of migrant children on Belgian soil gave rise to major South European (mainly Italian), Moroccan and Turkish communities. New immigration has continued until today through the cross-border marriages of the Moroccan and Turkish second generation (Stoop and Booms 1997). Due to the timing of successive migration waves and the differential fertility of migrant families, major migrant populations in Belgium have an atypically young age structure, as compared to the native population. Thus, a large majority of the adult second generation of Turkish and Moroccan origin were still under thirty in the 1991 Census, as compared to roughly half of the Italian second (and third) generation. Any assessment of second-generation socio-economic achievement should hence take into account differential age structures.

Typically, the settlement of migrant families and communities is marked by varying degrees of residential segregation. Studies of 'spatial assimilation' have associated residential segregation with lower quality of housing, limited social integration, and ethnic minority disadvantage in the labour market (Kalter and Granato 2002; Massey 1985). In comparison with other European cities such as Amsterdam, Paris or London, the metropolitan area of Brussels is characterised by higher levels of ethnic segregation (Breebaart and Musterd 1995). But statistical sectors in Belgium are relatively fine-grained, so that segregation indices may be inflated in comparative terms. Within Belgium, segregation indices differ between migrant communities and between regions of settlement (Eggerickx, Kesteloot and Poulain 1999). Ethnic segregation is most pronounced for Turkish migrants, and only slightly less so for Moroccan migrants, which is due to their spatial concentration in (old) industrial basins and inner cities. Segregation is much less outspoken for South Europeans, and least for

North Europeans. In the region of Brussels for example, segregation indices are 78% for the Turkish group, 69% for the Moroccan group, and 39% for the Italian group. This means that more than three in four Turkish migrants, two in three Moroccan migrants, and one in three Italian migrants in Brussels would need to move for the three minority groups to be evenly distributed across statistical sectors. Segregation indices are higher in Brussels and in Flanders than in Wallonia, where migrant settlement has been more dispersed across suburbs.

Table 4.2 shows the sizes of the most numerous groups of foreign nationals in Belgium in 1991. Under the heading of (predominantly) labour migration, the 1991 Census counts 240,000 Italians, 142,000 Moroccans, and 85,000 Turks. Taking into account naturalisations and acquisitions of Belgian nationality, the sizes of major Italian, Moroccan and Turkish minorities in 1991 were estimated at 297,000, 152,000 and 88,000 respectively (Eggerickx *et al.* 1999). Close to half of the Italian, Moroccan and Turkish minorities were born in Belgium as children of migrant parents. Finally, there is a marked decline in the numbers of foreign nationals in the 2001 population register as compared with 1991 (see Table 4.1). This is largely due to the enhanced legal access to Belgian citizenship (cf. *infra*).

As distinct from other European countries with (former) colonies, Belgium has not known a significant post-colonial immigration. The number of migrants from the former colonies (Congo, Ruanda and Burundi) was estimated at 21,000 in the 1991 Census (see Table 4.2). Most of them came in the 1980s and 1990s as part of an increasingly diversified inflow of refugees and asylum seekers (Eggerickx *et al.* 1999). The other most numerous categories of foreign nationals originate from neighbouring countries like France and the Netherlands. Finally, estimates of the numbers of undocumented migrants vary widely. Most likely, the regularisation campaign of the last government will add further to the ethnic diversity of minority populations in the new 2001 Census (which was not yet available for public use at the moment of this study).

Equal opportunities and rights: policies and practice

Hard evidence of ethnic disadvantage suggests that Belgium is not living up to its public commitment to equal opportunities for citizens of migrant origin. Maybe not surprisingly given the relatively young age of

Table 4.2. Belgium's foreign population from different national origins (numbers (in thousands) and percentages of the most important groups, within-group percentages of Belgian citizens and born in Belgium).

National origin/refugee status	Census 1991	*Census 1991*[a]	% of total population	% with citizenship	% born in Belgium
Italian	240	*297*	3.0	19.2	49.1
Moroccan	142	*152*	1.5	6.7	47.7
Turkish	85	*88*	0.9	3.5	45.9
French	93	*151*	1.5	38.3	25.1
Dutch	65	*96*	1.0	31.9	30.1
Congo/Ruanda/Burundi[b]	13	*21*	0.2	37.5	13.5
Refugees (all countries)	20	*25*	0.3	14.9	30.4
Foreign (origin) population	901	*1,203*	12.1	25.1	35.5
Total population	9,979	*9,979*	100	91.0	90.9

[a] National origin groups and refugees, including naturalisations and acquisitions of Belgian nationality
[b] Postcolonial immigration

the second generation, research on ethnic inequalities in Belgium has focused mainly on educational disadvantage (Neels 2000; Ouali and Réa 1994). Unfortunately, the only nationally representative survey of minority school careers lacks a native comparison group. But the findings clearly show the very limited access of Moroccan and Turkish minority men to higher educational qualifications, even after statistically correcting for delayed attainment (Neels, 2000). In particular, the Turkish second generation shows even lower educational attainment and less progress than their Moroccan age mates. Looking beyond school careers, national statistics give a rather bleak picture of the fortunes of the second generation in the labour market. For example, Neels and Stoop (2000) used the 1991 Census to compare unemployment risks for young Turkish, Moroccan and native men. They conclude that ethnic differences in qualifications, age structures and settlement patterns explain only part of the dramatic ethnic gap between migrant and native unemployment levels. Similarly, their findings demonstrate the overrepresentation of young Turkish and Moroccan men in unskilled work, after controlling for qualifications, age and place of residence. Furthermore, a comparative study of migrant and native self-employment levels in national survey and census data reveals that ethnic self-employment has remained a marginal phenomenon in the Belgian context (Moors 2000). On a more positive note, there is evidence that Turkish and Moroccan women of the second generation have gone a long way to closing the huge gender gap in economic activity (Stoop and Booms 1997). At the same time, the continuing immigration of partners from Turkey and Morocco keeps the overall level of female labour-market participation low.

Still, we had to wait until the early 1990s for issues of ethnic disadvantage and discrimination to become serious political concerns (Phalet and Swyngedouw 2003). Only after the electoral breakthrough of the Extreme Right in Flanders in 1991 (10% of Flemish voters supporting the Extreme Right) with a campaign which successfully exploited anti-immigrant feelings, and in direct response to the first urban riots involving minority youth in Brussels in the same year, did the Belgian government and parliament finally agree on the need for national integration policies. The framework for integration policies was prepared by the Royal Commission for Migrant policies (KCM). This Commission had published two influential reports in 1989 and 1990, documenting various forms of ethnic disadvantage and recommending positive action. In 1991, an immediate political consequence of the electoral success of the Extreme Right had been the explicit rejection of racism across all other parties in Belgium. As a consequence of this new political alignment, the symbolic authority and policy impact of the Commission was much enhanced and a national framework for integration policies could be negotiated.

The formal definition of integration, as it was approved by the Belgian government and parliament in 1991, emphasises protection from discrimination, socio-economic inclusion and the full participation of migrants and ethnic minorities as active citizens. In the cultural realm, integration would entail assimilation in the public domain, with reference to maintaining public order and to promoting core values of liberal democracies. At the same time, diverse ethnic cultures and identities are to be respected in the private domain of family and community life. This definition was a compromise between different approaches in the Flemish North and in the Francophone South of the country (Bousetta, Gsir and Jacobs 2005). While Flemish integration policies are more often explicitly targeted at ethnic groups and self-organisations, Francophone policies tend to avoid ethnic categories and target general social disadvantage instead. The ideological impact of well-established and distinct philosophies of integration in France and in the Netherlands is only part of the explanation (Favell 1998). In addition, Flemish policy making has to reckon with a strong anti-immigrant vote (no less than 25% in the last 2004 national and regional elections). The result of this is more intense political mobilisation on both sides of the ethnic divide between migrants and natives. Conversely, the Francophone South of the country has historically been characterised by a very stable and dominant social-democrat party and by relatively strong trades unions, making it more attractive for migrants or minorities to close ranks with the native working classes. By and large, distinct integration policies seem to respond to more commonly class-based identifications and political mobilisation in the South of the country, as opposed to more ethnically based identifications and forms of organisation in the Flemish North.

Within the institutional framework of Belgium as a binational state, the Flemish and Francophone Communities both have jurisdiction with regard to migrants or minorities. But depending on the policy domain (education, labour market, culture, urban renewal etc.) political authorities at all levels can be directly or indirectly involved. Thus the effective coordination and implementation of integration policies has been complicated by fragmentation and competition between local, communal, regional, national and European levels of governance (Jacobs 2000). In fact, the only area where the Royal Commission's recommendations for positive action have been consistently implemented since 1991 is in education (Martens and Caestecker 2001). Specifically, in the Flemish part of Belgium primary and secondary schools attracting many pupils with an ethnic minority background (i.e. foreign country of birth of mother) or from socially disadvantaged families (i.e. mother has less than full secondary education) receive additional funding for educational support. In the Francophone South the same applies to schools located in areas that are designated as socially disadvantaged. Although no formal ethnic criteria are used in the South, the designated areas overlap in fact with the urban and industrial areas where most migrant families live.

At the national level, policies with a view to protecting and extending the rights of migrants or minorities have been institutionalised in four ways: through anti-discrimination legislation, enhanced access to citizenship, enfranchisement of foreign residents, and state recognition of Islam. The first anti-discrimination law in 1981 condemned racism, but it was narrowly concerned with racist or xenophobic acts and did not lead to significant judicial action: of the 1,266 complaints in the period 1981–91, 987 did not qualify for treatment, and only 43 cases led to convictions (Martens and Caestecker 2001). In 1991 and more importantly in 1994, the scope of the anti-discrimination law was much broadened and more serious sanctions were specified. In 1993 the federal Centre for Equal Opportunities and against Racism (CGKR) was founded to support anti-discrimination policies. Still, of the forty-nine complaints filed by the Centre in the period 1993–9, only eight had resulted in convictions. From a European perspective, one may conclude that Belgium was late to develop effective anti-discrimination legislation; and the courts have been slow to make use of the new law.

Turning to citizenship law, we have seen a series of legislative changes since 1984 which have greatly facilitated and effectively increased the acquisition of the Belgian nationality (Jacobs 1999). Moreover, the acquisition of Belgian nationality has never implied the loss of one's old nationality. As in most European countries, *ius sanguinis*, or intergenerational transmission, constitutes the basic principle of access to Belgian citizenship (Weil 2001). Progressively, however, *ius soli*, or place of birth, has been introduced in citizenship laws. Specifically, since 1984, the third generation, i.e. children born in Belgium from parents born in Belgium, could acquire citizenship through a declaration of the parents before the age of twelve. All other legal residents had to go through a long, costly and demanding naturalisation procedure. Since 1992, the third generation automatically acquires Belgian nationality at birth; and a new optional procedure is introduced for the second generation. Finally, since 2000 all permanent residents born in Belgium, or who have been living in Belgium for at least seven years, can opt for Belgian nationality. In parallel, in 1995, 1998 and 2000, the existing discretionary naturalisation procedure for legal residents has been greatly facilitated. The recency of these legislative changes implies that nearly all adults of migrant origin in the 1991 Census still had foreign nationality at birth. The only exception is the case of Belgian citizens of mixed parentage, whose mothers have acquired Belgian nationality through marriage. Still, significant portions of the main minority groups report acquisition of Belgian nationality in 1991, ranging from 19% of the Italian minority to respectively 7% and 4% of the Moroccan and Turkish minorities (see Table 4.2).

A crucial aspect of citizenship regimes for the incorporation of migrants in the labour market is the degree to which non-nationals are formally excluded from social and economic rights (Brubaker 1989). In Belgium, most social and economic rights have been progressively decoupled from Belgian citizenship from the late 1960s onwards (Phalet and Swyngedouw 2002). Thus, foreign residents have equal legal access to social benefits, including social housing, public education and health care, and other relatively generous welfare provisions. In parallel, Belgium has pragmatically reorganised its labour market since the early 1960s in order to open up the economy to cross-border investment, thus preparing the way for the unprecedented economic prosperity of the next generations. Thus, foreigners are allowed to start their own businesses and to acquire or inherit property in Belgium. Remaining limitations for non-citizens refer to the allocation of jobs in the public sector and the right to vote and to run for office. Specifically, civil servants have to be Belgian by nationality, but this restriction only applies to the most protected tenured positions. It is commonly circumvented by offering work contracts of indeterminate duration instead. Furthermore, Belgian nationality is required to vote in national—not local—elections and to be eligible for public office. More generally, nationality, and in particular EU citizenship, makes a real difference in economic opportunities, in as far as qualifications from outside the EU are not formally recognised and cross-border mobility of third-country nationals is not guaranteed under the Schengen agreement (Hansen and Weil 2001). These restrictions imply a considerable competitive disadvantage for migrants or minorities from outside the EU, in terms of access to highly qualified jobs in international firms or organisations.

The recent facilitation of migrant access to Belgian citizenship has been politically negotiated as an alternative to enfranchising foreign residents (Jacobs 1999). In spite of European directives, the volatile political balance of power between national communities in Belgium blocked the access of EU citizens to local voting rights until 1999, and that of third-country nationals until 2004. The issue of enfranchisement is especially sensitive in the region of Brussels, where foreign nationals outnumber a national minority of Dutch-speaking Belgians.

In the religious domain, the formal recognition of Islam in Belgium dates back to 1974, when Islam was included—next to the Roman Catholic, Protestant, Anglican, Orthodox and Judaic religions—within the existing framework of state-church relationships. This framework guarantees freedom of worship to Belgian citizens and stipulates that the State provides the salaries and pensions of clergymen and secular delegates for recognised religions and secular philosophies of life. Furthermore, the Constitution provides that the State must not interfere with the internal organisation of religious communities. In practice, however, the public recognition of Islam was motivated more by international concerns as a consequence of the oil crisis than by the religious rights of Muslim migrants in Belgium. Accordingly, it would take until 1998 until Muslims got the opportunity to elect religious representatives for the Executive Office in charge of the management of issues linked to the Islamic faith (Bousetta 2000). (Due to internal conflicts between Muslim representatives, new elections had to be held in 2005.) In spite of early recognition therefore, the official status of Islam has only quite recently been fully established.

In conclusion, Belgium was late to develop coordinated integration policies, to apply anti-discrimination legislation, and to extend political and religious rights to migrants and minorities. While social and economic rights of migrants have long been decoupled from national membership, the formal distinction between EU citizens and third-country nationals introduces new forms of 'civic inequality'. In particular in Flanders, political decision-making and public debates over issues of ethnic disadvantage and discrimination have been dominated by the rise of the Extreme Right. Public xenophobia, in combination with the historical national divide between Flemings and Francophones, has made the use of ethnic categories in national statistics a sensitive issue. Although some administrations have started earlier to develop their own data on ethnicity for internal use, political decision-making with regard to migrants and minorities in Belgium has not relied on quasi-representative national data sources until the early 1990s.

The first efforts to generate special survey data on migrant populations in Belgium were a direct consequence of the rise of the Extreme Right in Flanders and the concomitant urban unrest in Brussels in 1991. In the period 1993–6, nation-wide special surveys of Turkish and Moroccan men and women documented their migration histories, family formation, education and socio-economic attainment for the first time (Lesthaeghe, 2001). In addition, the prospect of local voting rights for non-nationals raised a new interest in the political opinions, identities and languages of migrants and minorities, especially in the bilingual region of Brussels (Janssens 2001; Swyngedouw, Phalet and Deschouwer 1999). Special surveys have typically relied on samples of foreign nationals from the national register. This practice is becoming increasingly problematic however, as growing numbers of third-, second- and even first-generation citizens are granted Belgian nationality by birth, declaration or option (see Table 4.2). In parallel, anonymised records from the census have been made available for public use through Interface Demography at the Free University of Brussels (Lesthaeghe 2001). In a landmark monograph the National Institute of Statistics combined multiple criteria to identify ethnic minorities and to distinguish the second and third generation from the first generation of migrants proper, taking into account naturalisations and acquisitions (Eggerickx *et al.* 1999).

Data and measures

Our data are anonymised records from the 1991 Census, which provides general information on household composition and age, labour-market participation and employment status, educational and occupational attainment, housing and wealth. One major advantage of the census is that it includes key information about the (previous and new) nationality, nativity and length of residence of migrant populations. In 1991 this information was still sufficient to cover almost the entire second generation (Eggerickx *et al.* 1999). More generally, the obvious advantages of the census are its nationwide scope and large numbers, and hence the possibility to compare socio-economic attainment across optimally representative samples of specific migrant groups and a native reference group.

But there are some serious limitations (Stoop and Surkyn 1997). Both record and item non-response are slightly higher in migrant populations than in the national population (i.e. 3.4% overall record non-response). More frequent language and literacy problems, in particular among the first generation, are one explanation. Another explanation is the atypical composition of migrant populations, so that more respondents have little education or live in urban areas where response rates are generally lower. Importantly, the reliability of migrants' self-reported educational qualifications has been questioned, since school levels and types in the census refer to the Belgian system and hence, do not adequately reflect educational systems in the countries of origin. This mismatch has clearly resulted in higher rates of item non-response among first-generation migrants. In our analyses, we have used supplementary information on the country/countries of schooling and the age of leaving school to double-check the assignment of respondents to qualification levels. Last but not least, the census omits important information that is needed for a full analysis of an emerging ethnic stratification of Belgian society. Thus, for reasons of privacy or political sensitivity, it does not include questions on language, religion, ethnic ancestry and class origins of the parents. Consequently, we are unable to disentangle the impact of ethnicity and class origins on second-generation attainment.

Alternatively, the 1993–6 nationwide special surveys among Moroccan and Turkish minorities contain precious information on ethnic and class origins; and they provide reliable measures of the educational attainment and the language mastery of the first generation (Lesthaeghe 2001). But they have the disadvantages of much smaller numbers of respondents, narrow samples of foreign nationals, and no native comparison sample. Hence, the 1991 Census was chosen as the best currently available data source in Belgium. In light of known data constraints however, the analysis of net ethnic penalties may be rather more accurate for the second generation than for the first generation.

Specifically, 50% random samples of Italian-, Moroccan-, and Turkish-origin groups were combined with a 10% random sample of the reference population in the three regions of Belgium (Flanders, Brussels and Wallonia). Italian, Moroccan and Turkish minorities were selected because they are by far the largest groups of labour migrants in Belgium and for comparative reasons, because they are also present in the neighbouring countries. As sampling frames inclusive national-origin groups and generations were defined by combining multiple criteria: nationality at birth (Italian, Moroccan or Turkish), country of birth (Italy, Morocco, Turkey, Belgium, or other), country of schooling, and length of residence. Italian, Moroccan and Turkish samples include all respondents with Italian, Moroccan or Turkish nationality, either currently or at birth, or who were born in Italy, Turkey or Morocco. Ethnic minorities are compared with the native reference population. The latter category consists of all respondents who are born with Belgian nationality. This includes small percentages of respondents who are either born in Belgium of mixed parentage, or else born abroad (most often in the neighbouring countries or in the former colonies) of Belgian parentage.

The second generation in this study includes all respondents who are either born in Belgium with foreign nationality, or who arrived at age seven or younger and whose complete school careers took place in Belgium. It should be noted that the Italian second generation is really 'second generation plus': as the first Italian guest workers arrived before 1950, it is possible that some have adult grandchildren who are now entering the labour market. In view of considerable early return migration and most often delayed family reunion, this is probably only a small portion of the local-born Italian population. Unfortunately, there is no census question on one's parents' country/countries of birth, so it is not possible to separate the second from the third generation. Since the focus of this study is on second-generation attainment, the first generation is a very heterogeneous residual category, which should not be mistaken for the parents of the second generation. In addition to the older first generation, who were initially recruited as guest workers, this category also includes the so-called in-between generation, who joined their parents at a later age through family reunion, and the younger first generation, most of whom migrated more recently as marriage partners of the second generation.

All respondents were sampled within the age range from eighteen to fifty, which corresponds to the vast majority of the economically active population in Belgium. Government efforts to encourage sustained economic activity are in fact quite recent, so that the Belgian population of working age has remained more restricted than in most other European countries today. The main reason for this is the extension of very generous early-retirement schemes to middle-aged workers. This extension was originally considered in order to soften the social consequences of economic restructuring—and to reduce the social costs of restructuring for employers. In parallel, obligatory schooling in Belgium was extended to age eighteen.

Socio-economic profiles: gross educational and occupational disadvantage

As a first step the education, economic activity, employment and occupations of migrants and natives are briefly described. Marginal distributions give a first impression of gross ethnic disadvantage in education and in the labour market. But they should be interpreted with care, given known group differences in age structure and qualifications. In order to give more precise estimates of ethnic disadvantage, the next section will discuss an analysis of net ethnic penalties.

Tables 4.3A and 4.3B show the highest educational qualifications for migrant and native men and women of working age. Most notably, all minority groups are much less qualified than the native reference group. Of the native population, the majority has completed full secondary education or more, as against a clear majority of all three minority groups without full secondary education. As a consequence of the selective recruitment of guest workers by the Belgian government and industries, there are hardly any ethnic differences in the education of the first generation. Looking across generations, there is evidence of overall progress up to full secondary education: the second generation is more often obtaining secondary qualifications than the first generation, with the Italian second generation coming closest to parity with the native population. At the tertiary level however, the children of migrant workers are still hugely underrepresented. Across gender, over 22% of the native Belgians have tertiary qualifications, as compared to roughly 10% of the Italian, 6% of the Moroccan, and 2.5% of the Turkish second generation. But one should keep in mind that the second generation is still relatively young, so that their final educational attainment is almost certainly underestimated. Lastly, generational differences in educational attainment are most outspoken for minority women. Specifically, large gender differences between first-generation men and women, which reflect known gender inequalities in the sending societies, especially in Morocco and Turkey, have all but disappeared in the second generation. In sum and in spite of generation and gender differences, we conclude that the most important minorities in Belgium are marked by persistent educational disadvantage.

Tables 4.4A and 4.4B show the economic activity of migrant and native men and women of working age. We distinguish between men and women who are economically active, full-time students, looking after the home, or otherwise economically inactive. Overall, minorities are less often economically active than native Belgians. In addition, the partici-

Table 4.3A. Highest educational qualification, by national origin and generation: Men (row percentages).

	Primary or none	Lower secondary	Higher secondary	Tertiary	N
Belgian origin	25.8	22.0	31.2	21.0	183,844
First generation					
Moroccan	59.1	12.6	16.1	12.2	9,455
Turkish	61.4	16.8	16.0	5.8	6,257
Italian	60.3	19.4	15.2	5.1	11,791
Second generation					
Moroccan	58.8	14.3	22.1	4.8	5,352
Turkish	49.4	21.3	26.8	2.5	2,963
Italian	34.1	25.1	31.7	9.1	28,159

Table 4.3B. Highest educational qualification, by national origin and generation: Women (row percentages).

	Primary or none	Lower secondary	Higher secondary	Tertiary	N
Belgian origin	28.0	18.5	30.4	23.1	177,971
First generation					
Moroccan	79.2	9.0	8.4	3.4	7,940
Turkish	78.6	10.9	9.0	1.5	6,020
Italian	65.5	16.7	13.7	4.1	9,536
Second generation					
Moroccan	57.0	14.4	21.8	6.8	4,710
Turkish	50.8	20.2	26.5	2.5	2,477
Italian	33.1	24.5	32.3	10.1	25,118

pation of Moroccan and Turkish migrants lags behind that of Italian migrants. One plausible explanation is that the transition to a post-industrial economy has affected the former groups at a much earlier stage of their settlement in Belgium. Possible additional explanations refer to different degrees of ethnic segregation and public prejudice towards 'old' and 'new' migrants (cf. *infra*). As might be expected, female labour-market participation is lower than male participation, with the largest gender gap in Moroccan and Turkish minorities. Again, low activity levels reflect gender inequalities in Morocco and Turkey, but they are perpetuated in Belgium through cross-border marriages. Although the second generation of Moroccan and Turkish women is more active than the first generation, high inactivity levels persist in the next generation. Given the relatively small numbers of self-reported homemakers among second-generation women, the intergenerational transmission of traditional gender roles can only be part of the explanation. On the male side, we see that the second generation is rather less active than the first generation. One obvious explanation of the limited economic activity of second-generation men is the decline of the industrial sector, where the older first generation was, and still is, most frequently employed. Looking across gender, second-generation inactivity is also due in part to higher numbers of Turks and especially Moroccans staying on in school, thus postponing the transition to work. High staying-on rates among Moroccan and Turkish students are of course age-related. Additional explanations might be more frequent school failure and expected discrimination in the labour market (Vallet and Caille 1996). To sum up, the economically active migrant population is highly and differentially selective. In particular, very high inactivity levels among Moroccan and Turkish women suggest that active women of Moroccan or Turkish origin are a very select minority indeed. By implication, an analysis of the active population is bound to underestimate the full extent of ethnic and gender disadvantages.

Tables 4.5A and 4.5B show the employment status and the occupational destinations of the active population. When it comes to avoiding unemployment, the dramatic ethnic disadvantage of migrants and minorities is well known. Ethnic differences in unemployment rates are indeed considerable. Thus, over 30% of the active Moroccan and Turkish men are registered as unemployed, as against 16% of the Italian men and 6% of the native men. Hence, Turkish or Moroccan men are about five times more likely to be unemployed than native men. A similar ethnic hierarchy of unemployment rates is also found for women, although women are more often unemployed overall than men. While 17% of the

Table 4.4A. Economic activity by national origin and generation: Men (row percentages).

	Economically active	Other Inactive	Looking after home	Full-time student	N
Belgian origin	81.3	10.3	0.4	8.0	203,276
First generation					
Moroccan	79.4	13.5	1.0	6.2	10,973
Turkish	76.0	21.2	1.3	1.5	6,861
Italian	85.1	13.5	0.6	0.9	12,345
Second generation					
Moroccan	44.6	32.1	1.0	22.3	7,074
Turkish	58.4	26.7	0.6	14.3	3,547
Italian	75.4	16.0	0.5	8.1	31,012

Table 4.4B. Economic activity by national origin and generation: Women (row percentages).

	Economically active	Other Inactive	Looking after home	Full-time student	N
Belgian origin	68.5	15.4	8.1	7.9	196,702
First generation					
Moroccan	28.4	10.3	57.7	3.6	9,500
Turkish	31.7	10.7	56.6	1.0	6,717
Italian	52.5	18.2	28.3	1.0	10,040
Second generation					
Moroccan	37.9	24.7	14.2	23.2	6,296
Turkish	52.4	23.5	10.8	13.4	2,935
Italian	67.2	16.4	7.6	8.9	27,941

active native women are unemployed, unemployment levels for active Turkish women are over 60%. This picture does not change much when we focus on the second generation. Except for Italian and Moroccan women, the second generation is not more able, or even less able to avoid unemployment than the first generation. Again, the overall loss of employment across generations coincides with economic restructuring. As distinct from the older first generation, the second generation has entered the labour market at the time when industrial work was already in short supply.

Another notable feature of Tables 4.5A and 4.5B is the dramatic under-representation of ethnic minorities in the salariat. Of the active native population over 30% is in the salariat, whereas percentages of ethnic minorities in the salariat range from 3% (among first-generation Turkish women) up to 16% (among second-generation Italian men). Here too, Italians seem to have a competitive advantage over Moroccans and Turks; and Turks are at the bottom end of the ethnic hierarchy. Across the board, the second generation is only slightly more successful in gaining access to the salariat than the first generation. But the Italian second generation is making most progress, and the Turkish second generation least. In view of the younger age of the second generation however, the figures may underestimate an upward generational trend. Interestingly, minority women of the second generation appear to have caught up with—and in the case of Moroccan women even surpassed—minority men in the salariat.

A similar, though somewhat less dramatic, under-representation of ethnic minorities is also apparent in routine non-manual work. Again, the Turkish minority forms the bottom of the ethnic hierarchy, while the Italians are almost on a par with the native population. It is well known that women are more often employed in routine non-manual work than men. Accordingly, most second-generation progress in access to routine non-manual work is observed for minority women. At the lower end of the labour market, ethnic minorities are dramatically over-represented in unskilled and semi-skilled manual work, as might be expected of labour migrants. The over-representation is much reduced however in the second generation, which is due in part to the declining demand for low-skilled work. In part too, the second generation may be discouraged by ethnic discrimination in a segmented labour market (Piore 1979). Being more qualified and more like native workers than new migrants, they should be less ready to settle for unskilled or underpaid work. Or they may simply be less inclined to endure the harsh working conditions of migrant workers in order to avoid unemployment (Kasinitz, Mollenkopf and Waters 2004). If the ethnic discrimination hypothesis were true, one would expect that qualifications do not protect the second generation against unemployment to the same extent as they do for native workers. We will return to the role of qualifications in the next section.

Turning to skilled manual work, we find much smaller ethnic and generational differences. Interestingly, the three minority groups differ in their propensities to take up skilled manual work: Turkish and Italian men are rather more likely than native men to be in skilled manual work, but Moroccan men rather less. Table 4.5b shows a similar pattern for minority women, although fewer women than men are in skilled manual work. Finally, formal self-employment, as it is reported in the census, is rather weakly developed in the Belgian context. According to Tables 4.5a and 4.5b, only 5% of the active native men and 4% of the women are categorised as petty bourgeoisie. Running counter to the notion of ethnic enterprise as a way to circumvent ethnic discrimination in regular careers

(Clark and Drinkwater 1998; Light 1984), the tables show that ethnic minorities in Belgium are even less often self-employed overall than the native population. At the same time, there are notable ethnic differences, with most self-employment in the Italian group and least in the Moroccan group. Given the young age of the second generation, it is too early to draw any conclusions about future trends in ethnic self-employment.

To conclude, the marginal distributions of labour-market outcomes document gross disadvantage of ethnic minorities. Moreover, ethnic minority disadvantage persists in the second generation. Not only is the

Table 4.5A. Current occupation by national origin and generation: Men (row percentages).

	Salariat	Routine non-manual	Petty bourgeoisie	Manual supervisor/ skilled manual	Semi- and unskilled	Unemployed	N
Belgian origin	31.6	12.8	5.0	29.0	15.2	6.4	165,171
First generation							
Moroccan	6.6	8.1	2.8	25.0	25.5	31.9	8,708
Turkish	5.4	3.8	2.5	31.8	22.6	34.0	5,213
Italian	9.6	8.0	3.9	44.8	17.8	15.8	10,502
Second generation							
Moroccan	7.2	8.7	1.7	24.5	19.7	38.2	3,157
Turkish	3.7	5.1	1.5	32.7	18.9	38.0	2,089
Italian	15.8	10.3	2.5	40.4	15.8	15.2	23,381

Table 4.5B. Current occupation by national origin and migration generation: Women (row percentages).

	Salariat	Routine non-manual	Petty bourgeoisie	Manual supervisor/ skilled manual	Semi- and unskilled	Unemployed	N
Belgian origin	30.6	28.7	3.5	7.1	12.9	17.2	134,825
First generation							
Moroccan	5.8	9.4	0.9	4.0	25.9	54.0	2,694
Turkish	3.0	4.6	2.3	4.8	22.0	63.4	2,131
Italian	9.0	17.1	3.0	9.9	19.1	42.0	5,266
Second generation							
Moroccan	9.9	19.3	1.0	4.1	17.7	48.0	2,389
Turkish	3.8	6.6	1.4	8.0	14.3	65.0	1,537
Italian	15.3	26.0	2.2	7.6	11.2	37.7	18,773

second generation more often excluded from the labour market, as evident from the elevated levels of economic inactivity and unemployment. But they are also much less included in terms of access to better jobs in general and to the salariat in particular. Looking beyond common disadvantage, the patterning of labour-market destinations suggests some interesting ethnic differences. Across the board, Italians are closest to achieving parity with native Belgians, in line with expectations of more limited discrimination or disadvantage for less recent and less visible migrants (Alba 2005; Alba and Nee 2003). Nevertheless, the Italian second generation continues to be underrepresented in tertiary education; they are less protected against unemployment than native Belgians; and access to the salariat is still a major bottleneck. In the Italian case, it seems plausible that persistent disadvantage is at least in part class-based, given the working-class background of Italian migrant workers.

In contrast, Moroccan and Turkish minorities are undoubtedly the most disadvantaged groups in the Belgian labour market. Given the common working-class background of the Italian, Moroccan and Turkish second generation, possible explanations of the additional disadvantage of Moroccans and Turks are their more recent entry in the Belgian labour market, in combination with typically higher levels of ethnic segregation and ethnic prejudice against racial or religious minorities (Alba 2005; Model and Lin 2002). In addition, institutionalists have emphasised the role of citizenship regimes as exclusionary devices (Brubaker 1989; Hansen and Weil 2001). In the case of Turkish and Moroccan minorities, ethnic disadvantage is to some extent institutionalised by the more restricted access to citizenship rights of non-EU residents, the so-called third-country nationals. But common civic, ethnic and class barriers cannot fully explain Turkish disadvantage, since there are also consistent ethnic differences between Moroccans and Turks. Overall, the Turkish second generation is at the bottom end of the ethnic hierarchy with the lowest qualifications, the most dramatic rates of unemployment, and with least access to higher occupations. The fact that Turks, much like Italians, are outnumbering Moroccans in skilled manual work and in ethnic business suggests a Turkish route to socio-economic improvement with limited educational investment. In contrast, the Moroccan second generation is slightly less underrepresented in the salariat and in routine non-manual work than their Turkish counterpart, in line with an initial (French) language advantage and more sustained educational investment. In light of the extremely poor representation of both minorities in the salariat however, another way to look at the same pattern is from the perspective of differential discrimination. Possibly, Turkish disadvantage is, to a greater extent than Moroccan disadvantage, accounted for by the lack of individual and contextual human capital in ethnically most cohesive and segregated Turkish migrant communities (Lesthaeghe 2000). If this is indeed the case, the Moroccan minority may turn out to be most 'truly disadvantaged' or discriminated after all, if we were to control for group differences in human capital.

Ethnic penalities in the labour market: the avoidance of unemployment

We now turn to an analysis of net ethnic penalties in the labour market. Using the cross-national model specifications in the introductory chapter to this volume, logistic regressions are carried out. To estimate the extent of net ethnic disadvantage after taking into account human capital, ethnic penalties are calculated while controlling for education (with full secondary as a reference category), age (with age centred and age squared as covariates), and marital status (married, widowed or divorced with single as a reference category). As a measure of education, cross-national CASMIN codes were used to assign respondents' highest qualifications to four categories (i.e. primary or none, lower secondary, full secondary, and tertiary). Due to problems of small numbers in the minority populations, lower and higher tertiary levels had to be collapsed. Although human capital controls in the cross-national model do not adequately assess the selection of the first generation, they should be fairly complete for the second generation, whose labour-market destinations constitute the main focus of this study. Finally, differential disadvantage across receiving contexts has been well documented (Reitz 1998; Van Tubergen, Maas and Flap 2004). Hence, we take into account regional discrepancies in socio-economic opportunities between the Francophone South of the country and the more prosperous and more post-industrial Flemish North. To this end, regions were added to the models as a contextual control variable (i.e. Flanders and Wallonia with the metropolitan area of Brussels as a reference category).

To keep the number of interaction terms down to a minimum, separate regressions were carried out for men and women. Ethnic penalties were estimated for two types of labour-market outcomes, in line with a conceptual distinction between exclusionary and inclusionary mechanisms (Heath, McMahon and Roberts 1997). To capture processes of socio-economic exclusion, we look at ethnic penalties in avoiding unemployment. To this end, we exclude all those who are economically inactive from the analysis, and we consider the odds of paid employment or self-employment versus unemployment. Turning to processes of socio-economic inclusion, we consider the likelihood of gaining access to the different occupational classes. The latter analysis includes all those who are either self-employed or employed in paid work. In line with cross-national model specifications, collapsed EGP class categories are used to estimate the odds of being either in the salariat, or in routine non-manual work, or in the petty bourgeoisie, or in supervisory or skilled manual work, rather than in semi- or unskilled manual work.

The results of the analysis of unemployment risks can be seen in Table 4.6. What has been modelled is actually the likelihood of avoiding unemployment. Hence, negative parameters are to be interpreted as ethnic penalties: they indicate that minority groups are more often unemployed than the native reference group. As predicted by human capital theory, the analysis confirms a curvilinear age effect with younger, hence less experienced people being more often unemployed. Also in line with expectations from human capital, more education means more protection against unemployment. Thus, people without full secondary education, and in particular those with only primary education or none, are more often unemployed. Conversely, men and especially women with higher qualifications are more likely to avoid unemployment. In line with most other studies, we find that unemployment is less likely among married men and among single women. In addition, regional effects show the well-known discrepancies between North and South, with people in Flanders being most likely to avoid unemployment, and people in Wallonia least. Interestingly, significant interactions of regions with national origins—which are not reported in Table 4.6—indicate that all three minority groups are most exposed to unemployment as compared with natives in the North, which makes Flanders at once the most prosperous and the most exclusionist region. More fine-grained multi-level analysis at the level of municipalities is needed, however, to identify which contextual factors make a difference in ethnic penalties.

What happens to ethnic disadvantage after controlling for human capital? Overall, ethnic penalties in avoiding unemployment remain significant and large. They reveal that ethnic minorities are much more exposed to unemployment than native Belgians with a similar education, age and marital status and who are living in the same region. Looking across generations, net ethnic penalties are only slightly less severe in the

Table 4.6. Logistic regression of employment and unemployment (parameter estimates; contrasts with unemployment).

	Men	Women	Men	Women
Constant/Intercept	**4.82 (0.13)**	**4.13 (0.12)**	**4.84 (0.12)**	**4.15 (0.12)**
National origin				
Belgian origin	0	0	0	0
Moroccan 1	**−1.86 (0.03)**	**−1.48 (0.05)**	**−2.09 (0.04)**	**−1.72 (0.07)**
Turkish 1	**−2.06 (0.04)**	**−1.67 (0.05)**	**−2.24 (0.06)**	**−2.05 (0.07)**
Italian 1	**−0.61 (0.03)**	**−0.79 (0.03)**	**−0.59 (0.03)**	**−0.79 (0.03)**
Moroccan 2	**−1.49 (0.04)**	**−1.10 (0.05)**	**−1.49 (0.04)**	**−1.10 (0.05)**
Turkish 2	**−1.75 (0.05)**	**−1.63 (0.06)**	**−1.93 (0.07)**	**−1.84 (0.08)**
Italian 2	**−0.45 (0.02)**	**−0.63 (0.02)**	**−0.45 (0.02)**	**−0.63 (0.02)**
Age centred	**0.18 (0.01)**	**0.17 (0.01)**	**0.18 (0.01)**	**0.07 (0.01)**
Age squared	−0.00 (0.00)	−0.00 (0.00)	−0.00 (0.00)	−0.00 (0.00)
Marital status				
Married	**1.07 (0.02)**	**−0.12 (0.02)**	**1.07 (0.02)**	**−0.12 (0.02)**
Widowed/divorced	**0.15 (0.04)**	**−0.37 (0.03)**	**0.16 (0.04)**	**−0.37 (0.03)**
Single	0	0	0	0
Qualification				
Tertiary	**0.37 (0.03)**	**1.07 (0.03)**	**0.30 (0.08)**	**1.27 (0.06)**
Higher secondary	0	0	0	0
Lower secondary	**−0.35 (0.02)**	**−0.45 (0.02)**	**−0.30 (0.06)**	**−0.62 (0.05)**
Primary/None	**−1.09 (0.02)**	**−0.92 (0.02)**	**−1.00 (0.11)**	**−1.28 (0.10)**
Region				
North (Flanders)	**0.63 (0.03**	**0.10 (0.03)**	**0.63 (0.03)**	**0.11 (0.03)**
South (Wallonia)	**−0.14 (0.03)**	**−0.45 (0.03)**	**−0.14 (0.03)**	**−0.45 (0.03)**
(Metropolitan area of) Brussels	0	0	0	0
Significant interactions between origin and qualifications				
Moroccan 1			**−0.19 (0.02)**	**−0.20 (0.04)**
Turkish 1			*−0.14 (0.04)*	**−0.28 (0.06)**
Turkish 2			**−0.19 (0.05)**	**−0.28 (0.06)**
Chi-square (D.F.)	23192 (15)	22659 (15)	23278 (18)	22736 (18)
Chi-square # (D.F.)			86 (3)[a]	77 (3)[a]
N	213861	164604	213861	164604

Note: standard errors are given in brackets. Emboldened parameter estimates are significant at $P < 0.0001$, italicised parameters at $P < 0.001$.
[a] compared to model with main effects only.

second generation. This may be due to somewhat less reliable human capital controls in the first generation, since the model fit is not significantly worse when generations are collapsed. Also in light of stable or rising levels of gross unemployment across generations, it seems safe to conclude that socio-economic exclusion persists in the second generation. While all children of migrant workers are more exposed to unemployment than native Belgians with a similar background, ethnic community contexts also make a difference. In line with ethnic differences in gross disadvantage, ethnic penalties are largest for second-generation Turks, somewhat smaller for Moroccans, and much smaller for Italians. Even after taking into account human capital, the Turkish second generation is still least likely; and the Italian second generation is most likely to avoid unemployment. Finally, large gender differences in gross unemployment do not affect the pattern of net ethnic penalties, which is very similar for minority women.

The models discussed so far assume similar returns to educational investment across groups and generations. But ethnic minorities, and in particular the first generation, may actually receive lower returns on their educational investments than does the native population. To find out whether educational investment offers as much protection against unemployment to minorities as it does to native Belgians, we have tested the interaction effects of qualifications and national origins on employment. (For reasons of parsimony education is centred and treated as a continuous variable in interaction effects, but not in the main effects.) Results of the analysis with interactions added are shown on the right-hand side of Table 4.6.

Across gender, three of the interaction terms turn out to be significant. Accordingly, the models with these interaction terms added, fit the data significantly better. As expected, interaction effects are negative in all three cases. Specifically, first-generation Turks and Moroccans receive lower returns on their educational qualifications when it comes to avoiding unemployment in the Belgian labour market. And so do second-generation Turks. For the first generation, less reliable measures of foreign qualifications in the Belgian census are one possible explanation which cannot be entirely excluded. If we assume that Moroccan and Turkish qualifications are reliably measured, lower returns in the first generation may be best explained by a tendency of Belgian employers to discount foreign qualifications, in particular qualifications from outside the EU. Such a tendency would not necessarily be ethnocentric, since employers may be risk averse in the absence of sufficient information about Turkish or Moroccan qualifications.

But such reasonable doubt cannot explain why higher qualifications fail to protect the Turkish second generation to the same extent as they protect native Belgians. We know that the Turkish group has a lower percentage of people with tertiary education than all other groups. One explanation of persistent lower returns across generations may therefore be that individual human capital makes less of a difference in a community context where a majority is poor in human capital (Portes 1998; Van

Tubergen *et al.* 2004). The impact of community contexts on the access to employment may work either way: through the presence or absence of ethnic social capital that is readily convertible into paid work, or through the influence of positive or negative ethnic stereotyping on the perceived productivity and work attitudes of job applicants (Waldinger 1996). Yet, no significant interactions are found for the Moroccan second generation, who also originate from ethnic communities with very limited human capital. Ultimately, it is possible that the ethnic community context of Turkish migrants has a more pervasive negative impact on the odds of employment, as a consequence of its particularly high degrees of ethnic cohesion and ethnic segregation across generations. Telling examples of intergenerational continuity are the high likelihood for children of Turkish migrants to marry partners from Turkey and to settle down in the same urban or former industrial areas where the first generation also lives (Eggerickx *et al.* 1999; Lesthaeghe 2000).

Ethnic penalties in the labour market: occupational destinations

Next, we examine what kinds of jobs are achieved by those who have obtained employment: who is gaining access to the most stable and well-paid professional, managerial or administrative jobs in the salariat? Who is filling the least secure and least well-paid semi- or unskilled jobs? And who is becoming self-employed? The primary focus of our analysis is the impact of national origins on the class destinations of the second generation, while controlling for human capital and regional context of reception. As semi- or unskilled work is the reference category, negative effects for access to the salariat and self-employment are interpreted as ethnic penalties. Tables 4.7A and 4.7B show the results of the analysis of occupational destinations.

Before turning to our main interest, we note that all significant effects of the control variables are in the expected direction (except for the lower likelihood of married men to be self-employed). Most notably, the transition to tertiary education has a very strong impact on the likelihood of gaining access to the salariat. The expected effects of age and education are also found for the other occupational destinations. Accordingly, older people and people with higher qualifications are more likely to be self-employed than younger or less qualified people. In addition, regional differences document a distinct class structure in the metropolitan area of

Table 4.7A. Logistic regression of occupational class: Men (parameter estimates: contrasts with semi- and unskilled class).

	Salariat	Routine non-manual	Petty bourgeoisie	Manual supervisor or skilled manual
Constant/Intercept	**3.11 (0.15)**	**1.06 (0.16)**	−0.33 (0.21)	**−1.08 (0.12)**
National origin				
Belgian origin	0	0	0	0
Moroccan 1	**−2.36 (0.06)**	**−1.15 (0.05)**	**−0.87 (0.08)**	**−0.35 (0.04)**
Turkish 1	**−1.95 (0.08)**	**−1.46 (0.08)**	**−0.79 (0.10)**	**−0.10 (0.04)**
Italian 1	**−1.05 (0.05)**	**−0.37 (0.05)**	**−0.35 (0.06)**	**0.46 (0.03)**
Moroccan 2	**−1.32 (0.09)**	**−0.73 (0.08)**	**−0.96 (0.15)**	**−0.20 (0.06)**
Turkish 2	**−1.44 (0.14)**	**−0.94 (0.12)**	**−0.85 (0.19)**	−0.01 (0.09)
Italian 2	**−0.56 (0.03)**	**−0.17 (0.03)**	**−0.66 (0.05)**	**0.35 (0.02)**
Age centred	**0.19 (0.01)**	**0.04 (0.01)**	**0.08 (0.01)**	**−0.09 (0.01)**
Age squared	**−0.00 (0.00)**	0.00 (0.00)	−0.00 (0.00)	**0.00 (0.00)**
Marital status				
Married	**0.10 (0.02)**	*−0.08 (0.02)*	**−0.19 (0.03)**	**0.25 (0.02)**
Widowed/divorced	−0.05 (0.04)	*−0.16 (0.05)*	**−0.40 (0.06)**	0.04 (0.04)
Single	0	0	0	0
Qualification				
Tertiary	**2.71 (0.04)**	**1.72 (0.04)**	**0.81 (0.05)**	0.13 (0.04)
Higher secondary	0	0	0	0
Lower secondary	**−1.11 (0.02)**	**−0.77 (0.02)**	**−0.38 (0.03)**	**−0.16 (0.02)**
Primary/None	**−2.27 (0.02)**	**−1.43 (0.02)**	**−0.82 (0.03)**	**−0.58 (0.02)**
Region				
North (Flanders)	**−0.54 (0.03)**	**−0.61 (0.03)**	**0.24 (0.06)**	**0.34 (0.03)**
South (Wallonia)	**−0.32 (0.03)**	**−0.60 (0.04)**	**0.29 (0.06)**	**0.28 (0.03)**
(Metropolitan area of) Brussels	0	0	0	0
Chi-square (D.F.)			78733 (60)	
N			192462	

Note: standard errors are given in brackets. Emboldened parameter estimates are significant at $P < 0.0001$, italicised parameters at $P < 0.001$.

Brussels, where more people are employed in the salariat and in routine non-manual work rather than in semi- or unskilled work than in the Northern or Southern periphery. Conversely, Brussels counts relatively fewer manual workers and self-employed workers than the periphery. As a capital city of the European Union, Brussels has attracted a high concentration of international administrative and managerial functions, which gave rise to a typical urban service economy (Waldinger 1996). As might be expected, a closer look at the jobs that are typically taken up by ethnic minorities in Brussels reveals relatively high numbers of minority men and also women in low-end service jobs, such as the cleaning and catering business. Interestingly, significant interactions of region with

Table 4.7B. Logistic regression of occupational class: Women (parameter estimates: contrasts with semi- and unskilled class).

	Salariat	Routine non-manual	Petty bourgeoisie	Manual supervisor or skilled manual
Constant/Intercept	**3.11 (0.15)**	**1.06 (0.16)**	−0.33 (0.21)	**−1.08 (0.12)**
Constant/Intercept	**4.06 (0.19)**	**2.09 (0.16)**	**−1.71 (0.29)**	**−2.08 (0.21)**
National origin				
Belgian origin	0	0	0	0
Moroccan 1	**−1.96 (0.12)**	**−1.65 (0.09)**	**−1.44 (0.22)**	**−0.81 (0.12)**
Turkish 1	**−1.78 (0.17)**	**−1.87 (0.12)**	−0.14 (0.16)	−0.33 (0.12)
Italian 1	**−1.06 (0.07)**	**−0.61 (0.05)**	**−0.54 (0.09)**	**0.48 (0.06)**
Moroccan 2	**−1.18 (0.11)**	**−0.92 (0.08)**	**−0.79 (0.22)**	**−0.78 (0.12)**
Turkish 2	**−1.33 (0.18)**	**−1.63 (0.13)**	−0.15 (0.23)	−0.01 (0.12)
Italian 2	**−0.53 (0.04)**	−0.07 (0.03)	**−0.23 (0.06)**	**0.49 (0.04)**
Age centred	**0.22 (0.01)**	0.02 (0.01)	**0.06 (0.02)**	**−0.09 (0.01)**
Age squared	−0.00 (0.00)	0.00 (0.00)	0.00 (0.00)	**0.00 (0.00)**
Marital status				
Married	**−0.39 (0.03)**	**−0.36 (0.03)**	0.04 (0.06)	*−0.12 (0.04)*
Widowed/divorced	**−0.37 (0.05)**	**−0.29 (0.04)**	−0.11 (0.08)	**−0.24 (0.06)**
Single	0	0	0	0
Qualification				
Tertiary	**3.45 (0.05)**	**1.76 (0.05)**	**1.42 (0.09)**	**0.43 (0.07)**
Higher secondary	0	0	0	0
Lower secondary	**−1.38 (0.03)**	**−0.79 (0.02)**	**−0.33 (0.04)**	**−0.19 (0.03)**
Primary/None	**−2.78 (0.03)**	**−1.75 (0.02)**	**−0.79 (0.08)**	**−0.55 (0.03)**
Region				
North (Flanders)	**−0.44 (0.04)**	**−0.58 (0.04)**	**0.68 (0.08)**	**0.50 (0.05)**
South (Wallonia)	*0.14 (0.04)*	**−0.29 (0.04)**	**0.78 (0.08)**	0.05 (0.06)
(Metropolitan area of) Brussels	0	0	0	0
Chi-square (D.F.)		60705 (60)		
N		128127		

Note: standard errors are given in brackets. Emboldened parameter estimates are significant at $P < 0.0001$, italicised parameters at $P < 0.001$.

national origin—which are not reported in the tables—indicate that Moroccans and Turks, but not Italians, have much less access to the salariat in Brussels than in the periphery, with the Turkish second generation being most differentially disadvantaged in Brussels. This regional pattern of higher overall employment levels in the salariat, along with increased ethnic penalties for Turkish and Moroccan minorities in Brussels, is suggestive of fierce ethnic competition at the higher end of the urban labour market, apparently to the disadvantage of migrants from outside the EU.

What happens to ethnic occupational disadvantage after controlling for human capital and regional opportunity structures? Looking across gender and generations, ethnic penalties on occupational attainment are mostly significant and large for all three minorities. As might be expected, the largest penalties are incurred in gaining access to the salariat, but ethnic minorities are also less likely to be included in routine non-manual work and in self-employment (except for the small and highly selective group of Turkish women in paid employment). Only Moroccans are also penalised at the transition from semi- or unskilled to supervisory or skilled manual work. Overall, the sizes of ethnic penalties are smaller for the Italian minority than for the Moroccan and Turkish minorities. As distinct from our finding of stagnation for avoidance of unemployment, generational progress rather than stagnation seems the predominant pattern for inclusion into the salariat. The same pattern of ethnic penalties is largely replicated among women, in spite of notable gender differences in the gross occupational attainment of the second generation. Across gender, those of the second generation who succeed in finding a job are more likely to gain access to better jobs than the first generation. Accordingly, the model fit for occupational destinations was significantly worse when generations were collapsed.

Nevertheless, significant and often considerable penalties persist in the second generation. Focusing on the second generation, we find the same ethnic hierarchy that was already described for gross occupational attainment levels in the previous section. In particular, the Turkish second generation makes least progress and is most underrepresented in the salariat and also in routine non-manual work, even after taking into account human capital. Moreover, and running counter to an expected competitive advantage of cohesive ethnic communities in setting up ethnic business (Flap, Kumcu and Bulder 2000; Sanders and Nee 1996), we find that the Turkish second generation is not more often self-employed than other groups. In complete contrast, the Italian second generation makes most progress and comes closest to parity with native Belgians across the board. But significant penalties remain, in particular in gaining access to the salariat. Finally, the Moroccan second generation is only slightly less severely penalised than their Turkish counterpart. While they make more significant progress than Turks in gaining access to the salariat and to routine non-manual work, they continue to be underrepresented in all four occupational classes.

To conclude, we consider the possibility that ethnic minorities get lower returns on their educational investments than do the native populations. To this end, interaction effects of qualifications with national origin are tested for occupational destinations in the same way in which they were tested for employment. Table 4.8 shows the results of an analysis with added interaction terms for the male (self-)employed population. Due to scarcity problems, interactions could not be reliably tested for the female (self-)employed population.

Again, all significant interactions are negative, indicating lower returns on the educational investment of ethnic minorities. Specifically, Moroccan and Turkish migrants get significantly lower returns on their qualifications in terms of inclusion in all four occupational classes (except for the access of Turkish migrants to the salariat). For the first generation, unreliable measures or more common discounting of foreign qualifications by employers are the most likely explanation. Interestingly, lower returns are also found for second-generation Moroccan men, who get less out of higher qualifications in terms of access to the salariat and to routine non-manual work than native Belgians. The same is not true of the Turkish second generation. Apparently, those few Turkish men who have obtained higher qualifications *and* who are fortunate enough to be

Table 4.8. Occupational class and differential returns to education: Men (parameter estimates: contrasts with semi- and unskilled class).

	Salariat	Routine non-manual	Petty bourgeoisie	Manual supervisor or skilled manual
Main effects of national origin				
Belgian origin	0	0	0	0
Moroccan 1	**−2.71 (0.06)**	**−1.77 (0.06)**	**−1.42 (0.11)**	**−0.75 (0.05)**
Turkish 1	**−2.09 (0.09)**	**−1.82 (0.11)**	**−1.07 (0.15)**	**−0.37 (0.07)**
Italian 1	**−1.09 (0.07)**	**−0.64 (0.08)**	−0.29 (0.10)	**0.37 (0.06)**
Moroccan 2	**−1.56 (0.10)**	**−1.17 (0.10)**	**−1.27 (0.19)**	**−0.36 (0.08)**
Turkish 2	**−1.36 (0.16)**	**−0.91 (0.15)**	−0.72 (0.24)	0.21 (0.10)
Italian 2	**−0.65 (0.04)**	**−0.32 (0.04)**	**−0.86 (0.07)**	**0.29 (0.03)**
Significant interactions between origin and qualifications				
Moroccan 1	**−0.38 (0.05)**	**−0.67 (0.04)**	**−0.44 (0.09)**	**−0.30 (0.03)**
Turkish 1	−0.13 (0.07)	**−0.39 (0.07)**	**−0.22 (0.05)**	**−0.21 (0.05)**
Italian 1	−0.02 (0.05)	**−0.27 (0.05)**	0.05 (0.06)	−0.07 (0.04)
Moroccan 2	**−0.37 (0.09)**	**−0.66 (0.07)**	−0.35 (0.15)	−0.15 (0.06)
Italian 2	**−0.16 (0.03)**	**−0.22 (0.03)**	**−0.22 (0.05)**	−0.05 (0.02)
Chi-square (D.F.)	80628 (80)			
Chi-square # (D.F.)	1895 (20)			
N	192462			

Note: standard errors are given in brackets. Emboldened parameter estimates are significant at $P < 0.0001$, italicised parameters at $P < 0.001$.

employed, get similar returns to those of native Belgians. Finally, the Italian pattern is rather puzzling, with similar returns on their qualifications for the first generation (except for routine non-manual work) but with significantly lower returns for the second generation. They are less rewarded for their investments in higher education, not only in terms of gaining access to the salariat, but also in terms of being included in routine non-manual work and in self-employment. A common explanation of lower returns on the qualifications of the Moroccan and Italian second generation refers to ethnic community effects: for both groups, lack of human capital at the community level may decrease the pay-off of individual investment in human capital. But this should also be the case for the Turkish second generation. One possible reason why the interaction does not reach significance in the Turkish case could be derived from a systemic need to maintain the ethnic status hierarchy in segmented labour markets (Piore 1979). If we accept this postulate of segmented labour market theory, ethnic discrimination should only occur when the numbers of a minority group entering more privileged segments of the labour market, are sufficient to threaten the superior status of their native colleagues. In comparison with Moroccans and Italians, the 'happy few' Turks who are at once highly qualified and employed, may have the somewhat dubious comparative advantage of their small numbers (in relative as well as absolute terms, given their smaller group size).

Conclusion

The main conclusion of this study is that ethnic minorities experience significant and dramatic ethnic penalties in the Belgian labour market. Much of the disadvantage of the older first generation is explained by their lack of human capital, since low-skilled 'guest workers' were selectively recruited from less-developed regions or countries. Also for the younger first generation, most of whom migrated through family reunion or family formation, disadvantage is associated with limited human capital. Most often, they lack local language skills, local qualifications and experience in the local labour market, which are needed to compete on an equal footing with the native population. But this is not the case for the second generation, who have completed their school careers in Belgium. Still, significant and often large ethnic penalties persist in the second generation.

Additional evidence of disadvantage comes in the form of significantly lower returns on the educational investment of ethnic minorities in the Belgian labour market. Among the first generation, lower returns are limited mostly to Turkish and Moroccan qualifications, which may be more unreliably measured and/or more frequently discounted by employers than national and (formally equivalent) European qualifications. Turning to the second generation, we find that Turks get less protection against unemployment out of additional educational investment than native Belgians of similar age and qualifications. In parallel, Italians and Moroccans get less out of their educational investments than natives in terms of access to better jobs. Regardless of their individual qualifications, the children of labour migrants have in common their working-class background and their membership of ethnic communities that are relatively poor in human capital. From the perspective of social capital theory, individual investments in human capital are less rewarding when human capital within one's family or community is limited (Portes 1998; Van Tubergen *et al*. 2004). The other side of the same coin is ethnocentric bias or class bias in recruitment and employment procedures. Indeed, the same effect of community context has been attributed to a lack of ethnic social capital that is readily convertible into well-paid jobs, or alternatively, to negative effects of ethnic or class stereotypes on perceived productivity in the eyes of employers (Waldinger 1996).

Furthermore, the analyses support the relevance of a conceptual distinction between exclusionary and inclusionary processes in the labour market (Heath *et al*. 1997). In line with expectations from selective constraints on class fluidity, the pattern of ethnic penalties is asymmetrical. On the exclusionary side, the sizes of ethnic penalties suggest stagnation rather than progress across generations. With regard to avoidance of unemployment, the second generation is not significantly less disadvantaged than the first generation. Moreover, relatively large portions of the second generation are not economically active. Hence, ethnic penalties are almost certainly underestimating the full extent of labour-market exclusion. In contrast, generational progress rather than stagnation is found for the inclusion of ethnic minorities in the salariat. While the second generation continues to have much less access to the salariat than the native population, they are nevertheless significantly less disadvantaged than the first generation. Accordingly, we find that higher qualifications greatly increase access to the salariat. But they only offer limited protection against unemployment. To conclude, inclusionary processes at the higher end of the labour market seem to be rather less rigid, or more meritocratic, than the exclusionary processes that control labour-market entry.

The persistence of ethnic disdvantage in the second generation suggests that at least part of the explanation is to be found in the receiving society. Possible explanations range from social-class origins and ethnic prejudice to citizenship status. This study was not aimed at testing competing explanations of ethnic disadvantage. Still, the pattern of ethnic penalties is in line with expectations from all three perspectives. Importantly, ethnic penalties document the differential impact of ethnic community contexts on the labour-market destinations of the second generation. For employment and occupational attainment alike, the Italian second generation experiences the smallest ethnic penalties and comes closest to achieving parity with native Belgians. In contrast, the Moroccan and Turkish second generation experiences much larger ethnic penalties. Moreover, the Turkish second generation is clearly at the bottom end of the ethnic hierarchy, since they experience at once the largest penalties on avoidance of unemployment *and* on access to the salariat. Although the educational investment of Turkish migrant families in the next generation lags behind the investments made by Moroccans and Italians, the ethnic hierarchy holds after controlling for human capital. Consequently, lack of human capital cannot fully explain why the children of Turkish migrants are most disadvantaged.

Looking beyond human capital, the literature on the integration of the second generation suggests three possible explanations of differential disadvantage. The first explanation refers to the restructuring of post-industrial labour markets and the timing of 'old' and 'new' migration (Alba and Nee 2003). In the case of Belgium, more recent labour migrants from Morocco and Turkey have been disproportionately affected by the transition to a post-industrial economy at an early stage of their settlement. As a consequence, more widespread economic inactivity and unemployment in Moroccan and Turkish communities may complicate the transition from school to work for the next generation. An alternative explanation of differential disadvantage is derived from ethnic prejudice. As visible Muslim minorities, Moroccan and Turkish minorities may encounter more pervasive ethnic prejudice than Italians, due to the existence of bright racial or religious boundaries in the receiving society (Alba 2005). Lastly, differential disadvantage has been attributed to 'civic inequalities' between EU citizens and third-country nationals

(Hansen and Weil 2001). In comparison with Moroccans and Turks, Italians have the competitive advantage of free movement and formally equivalent qualifications within the EU.

Citizenship regimes may directly influence ethnic minority disadvantage by restricting the social and economic rights of non-citizens, or they may exert more indirect influence by identifying migrants or minorities as outsiders who do not belong (Brubaker 1989). Table 4A1 (see Appendix below) shows the percentages of migrants of working age in the Belgian census who have naturalised or otherwise acquired citizenship, ranging from 4% of the Turkish women up to 31% of the Italian women. As a preliminary test of the relevance of civic inequality, citizenship status (i.e. foreign vs. national, with native Belgians as a reference category) was added to logistic regressions with national origin and generation. Including citizenship status significantly improved the model fit. After taking into account human capital, migrants who have naturalised or acquired citizenship were found to experience somewhat smaller ethnic penalties on avoidance of unemployment, and much smaller penalties on access to the salariat. It should be noted however, that the causal direction of these associations is uncertain—as Belgian nationality is acquired by declaration or option during childhood or young adulthood but naturalisation is not limited by age.

But civic inequality does not explain why the Turkish (rather than the Moroccan) second generation is most disadvantaged across the board. Nor does ethnic prejudice against Muslims. Possibly then, the Turkish second generation has been most affected by the combined impact of limited human resources and economic restructuring, because the Turkish community exhibits the highest levels of ethnic cohesion and ethnic segregation across generations. Converging evidence on the strength of Turkish communities in Belgium comes from studies of residential segregation, cross-border marriage, ethnic language retention, and ethnic associational life (Eggerickx *et al.* 1999; Lesthaeghe 2000; Phalet and Swyngedouw 2003). In the Turkish case, strong ethnic ties may actually hinder the next generation, rather than helping them to avoid unemployment and to get access to stable and well-paid jobs. To throw more light on the role of ethnic community contexts, future studies of the second generation should include measures of ethnic segregation and social capital.

Finally, the estimates of ethnic penalties in this study should be interpreted with caution in view of data constraints and methodological limitations. For a number of reasons, the ethnic penalties of the first generation are probably less reliably estimated and also more difficult to interpret. One reason is the omission of important control variables, such as language mastery or duration of stay, from the analysis. Moreover, educational qualifications abroad were less reliably measured by the census. And one should keep in mind that the first generation is a rather heterogeneous reference category, which not only includes the parents of the second generation, but also the younger first generation who are joining their families or partners in Belgium. Clearly, the main contribution of this study lies in estimating the ethnic penalties of the second generation. Although ethnic penalties cannot be unambiguously interpreted as measures of ethnic discrimination, the analysis convincingly shows that human-capital theory leaves much ethnic disadvantage unexplained, in particular among the second generation. As more and more children of migrants are leaving school, persistent ethnic disadvantage in the labour market poses a serious threat to the future of the next generation.

Appendix: Supplementary table

Table 4.A1. Citizenship status by national origin and generation: men and women of working age (percentages with Belgian citizenship).

	Moroccan origin	Turkish origin	Italian origin
Men			
First generation	11.7	5.6	6.2
Second generation	11.4	4.5	20.2
Total	11.4	5.2	16.1
Women			
First generation	7.0	2.8	18.2
Second generation	14.9	7.7	35.5
Total	10.1	4.3	30.9

References

Alba, R. (2005), 'Bright versus blurred boundaries: Second-generation assimilation and exclusion in France, Germany and the United States'. *Ethnic and Racial Studies*, 28(1), 20–49.

Alba, R. and Nee, N. (2003), *Remaking the American mainstream: Assimilation and contemporary immigration* (Cambridge, MA: Harvard University Press).

Billiet, J., Carton, A., and Huys, R. (1990), *Onbekend of onbemind?* (KU Leuven: Sociologisch Onderzoeksinstituut).

Bousetta, H. (2000), 'Institutional theories and immigrant ethnic mobilisation: Relevance and limitation'. *Journal of Ethnic and Migration Studies*, 25, 229–45.

Bousetta, H., Gsir, S., and Jacobs, D. (2005), 'Active civic participation of immigrants in Belgium'. Country report prepared for the POLITIS project. www.uni-oldenburg.de/politis-europe.

Breebaert, M. and Musterd, S. (1995), *Etnische segregatie in metropolitane gebieden: Een internationaal perspectief* (Amsterdam: Working Papers Amsterdam Study Center for the Metropolitan Environment).

Brubaker, R. W. (1989), 'Membership without citizenship: The economic and social rights of non-citizens'. In R. W. Brubaker (ed.), *Immigration and the politics of citizenship in Europe and North America* (Lanham, Md.: The German Marshall Fund and University Press of America), pp. 143–62.

Caestecker, F. (1999), 'Migratiecontrole in Europa in de 19de eeuw'. In J. Art and L. François (eds.), *Docendo discimus* (Gent: Academia Pers), pp. 241–56.

Clark, K. and Drinkwater, S. (1998), 'Ethnicity and self-employment in Britain'. *Oxford Bulletin of Economics and Statistics*, 60(3), 383–407.

Crul, M. and Vermeulen, H. (2003), 'The future of the second generation: the integration of migrant youth in six European countries'. *International Migration Review*, 37 (special issue).

Eggerickx, T., Kesteloot, C., and Poulain, M. (1999), *De allochtone bevolking in België*. Censusmonografie nr. 3 (Brussels: National Institute of Statistics).

Esping-Andersen, G. (1993) (ed.), *Changing classes: Stratification and mobility in post-industrial societies* (London: Sage).

Favell, A. (1998), *Philosophies of integration: Immigration and the idea of citizenship in France and Britain* (London: Macmillan).

Flap, H., Kumcu, A., and Bulder, B. (2000), 'The social capital of ethnic entrepreneurs and their business success'. In J. Rath (ed.), *Immigrant business* (Houndmills, UK: Macmillan) pp. 142–61.

Hansen, R. and Weil, P. (2001) (eds.), *Towards a European nationality: Citizenship, immigration and nationality law in the EU* (New York: Palgrave).

Heath, A., McMahon, D., and Roberts, J. (1997), 'Education and occupational attainments: the impact of ethnic origins'. In V. Karn (ed.), *Ethnicity in the 1991 Census, Vol. 4, Education, employment and housing* (London: HMSO), pp. 91–113.

Jacobs, D. (1999), 'The debate over enfranchisement of foreign residents in Belgium. *Journal of Ethnic and Migration Studies*, 25(4), 649–883.

Jacobs, D. (2000), 'Multinational and polyethnic politics entwined: Minority representation in the Region of Brussels-Capital'. *Journal of Ethnic and Migration Studies*, 26(2), 289–304.

Janssens, R. (2001), *Taalgebruik in Brussel* (Brussels: VUB Press).
Kalter, F. and Granato, N. (2002), 'Demographic change, educational expansion and structural assimilation of immigrants: The case of Germany'. *European Sociological Review*, 18(2), 199–216.
Kasinitz, P., Mollenkopf, J. H., and Waters, M. C. (2004), *Becoming New Yorkers: Ethnographies of the new second generation* (New York: Russell Sage Foundation).
Lesthaeghe, R. (2001), 'Die FWGM und MHSM Erhebungen unter türkischen und marokkanischen Bevölkerungen in Belgien'. *Zeitschrift für Bevölkerungswissenschaft*, 26(3), 453–62.
Lesthaeghe, R. (2000) (ed.), *Communities and generations: Turkish and Moroccan populations in Belgium* (Brussels: VUB Press).
Light, I. (1984), 'Immigrant and ethnic enterprise in North America'. *Ethnic and Racial Studies*, 7, 195–216.
Lubbers, M. (2001), *Exclusionistic electorates: Extreme right-wing voting in Western Europe* (Nijmegen: ICS Dissertation Series).
Martens, A. (1973), *25 jaar wegwerparbeiders: Het Belgische immigratiebeleid na 1945* (Leuven: KU Leuven).
Martens, A. and Caestecker, F. (2001), 'De algemene beleidsontwikkelingen sinds 1984'. In J. Vranken, C. Timmerman and K. Van der Heyden (eds.), *Komende generaties* (Leuven: Acco), pp. 99–128.
Massey, D. S. (1985), 'Ethnic residential segregation: A theoretical synthesis and empirical review'. *Sociology and Social Research*, 69, 315–50.
Model, S. and Lin, L. (2002), 'The cost of not being Christian: Hindus, Sikhs and Muslims in Britain and Canada'. *International Migration Review*, 36, 1061–92.
Moors, G. (2000), 'Turkish and Moroccan ethnic enterprises in Belgium'. In R. Lesthaeghe (ed.), *Communities and generations* (Brussels: VUB Press), pp. 321–39.
Neels, K. (2000), 'Education and the transition to employment: young Turkish and Moroccan adults in Belgium'. In R. Lesthaeghe (ed.), *Communities and generations* (Brussels: VUB Press), pp. 243–77.
Neels, K. and Stoop, K. (2000), 'Reassessing the ethnic gap: employment of younger Turks and Moroccans in Belgium'. In R. Lesthaeghe (ed.), *Communities and generations* (Brussels: VUB Press), pp. 279–313.
OECD (2003), *Employment outlook: Toward more and better jobs* (Paris: OECD).
Ouali, N. and Réa, A. (1994), 'La scolarité des élèves d'origine étrangère: différenciation et discrimination ethnique'. *Cahiers de Sociologie et d'Economie Régionales*, 21–22, 7–55.
Phalet, K. and Swyngedouw, M. (2002), 'National identities and representations of citizenship: A comparison of Turks, Moroccans and working-class Belgians in Brussels'. *Ethnicities*, 2(1), 5–30.
Phalet, K. and Swyngedouw, M. (2003), 'Measuring immigrant integration: The case of Belgium'. *Migration Studies—Studi Emigrazione,* Vol. XL (152), 773–803.
Piore, M. J. (1979), *Birds of passage: Migrant labour in industrial societies* (New York: Cambridge University Press).
Portes, A. (1998), 'Social capital: Its origins and applications in modern sociology'. *Annual Review of Sociology*, 24, 1–24.
Reitz, J. G. (1998), *Warmth of The Welcome* (Boulder: Westview Press).

Sanders, J. M. and Nee, V. (1996), 'Immigrant self-employment: The family as social capital and the value of human capital'. *American Sociological Review*, 61, 231–49.
Stoop, R. and Booms, B. (1997), 'Arbeidsparticipatie en arbeidsmobiliteit bij Turkse en Marokkaanse vrouwen'. In R. Lesthaeghe (ed.), *Diversiteit in sociale verandering* (Brussels: VUB Press).
Stoop, K. and Surkyn, J. (1997), *In de wetenschap het niet te weten: Achtergronden van de non-respons in de Volkstelling van 1991* (Leuven: Steunpunt Werkgelegenheid, Arbeid, Vorming).
Swyngedouw, M. (1992), 'National elections in Belgium: The breakthrough of the Extreme Right in Flanders'. *Regional Politics and Policy*, 2/3, 62–75.
Swyngedouw, M., Phalet, K., and Deschouwer, K. (1999), *Minderheden in Brussel* (Brussels: VUB Press).
Vallet, L.-A. and Caille, J.-P. (1996), *Les élèves étrangers ou issues de l'immigration dans l'école et le collège francais I/II/III*. Documents de Travail INSEE/CREST, 9614/9615/9616.
Van Tubergen, F., Maas, I., and Flap, H. (2004), 'The economic incorporation of immigrants in 18 Western societies: Origin, destination and community effects'. *American Sociological Review*, 69, 704–47.
Waldinger, R. (1996), *Still the promised city?* (Cambridge, MA: Harvard University Press).
Weil, P. (2001), 'Access to citizenship: A comparison of twenty-five nationality laws'. In T. A. Aleinikoff and D. Klusmeyer (eds.), *Citizenship today: Global perspectives and practices* (Washington, DC: Carnegie Endowment for International Peace), pp. 17–35.

5

Inclusion for all but Aboriginals in Canada

SOOJIN YU & ANTHONY HEATH

Summary. Canada is a classic country of immigration with 21% of its working-age population being first generation and a further 9% second generation. Canada has also been notable in the last quarter of the twentieth century for its 'point system' for selection of economic immigrants, and indeed the first generation proves to be highly educated (more so indeed than the charter population). While a number of visible minority groups in the first generation experience substantial disadvantages, in the second generation the one clearly disadvantaged group (in net terms) are the Caribbeans where both men and women experience substantial and statistically significant disadvantages with respect to employment. Almost every other group in the second generation has achieved or surpassed parity with the charter group of the British. Whether this success of the second generation is due to Canadian policies of multiculturalism or to the lagged effects of the 'point system' for entry is impossible to determine from these data. However, major disadvantages continue to be experienced by the Aboriginals both in employment and in occupational attainment.

Canada, a country of immigration

CANADA IS A CLASSICAL COUNTRY OF IMMIGRATION, along with the United States and Australia. Apart from the Aboriginal population, who crossed the Bering Strait from Asia around 40,000 BCE (Isajiw 1999: 77; Knowles 1997: 1), most of its population arrived relatively recently. The two charter groups—French and British—may be considered as exceptions, as substantial numbers started to arrive as early as the mid-1600s. The French colonisers came first[1] and their settlement increased from 6,000 people in 1672 to 60,000–70,000 by 1760 (Isajiw 1999: 78; Knowles 1997: 6–12). Their main occupations were fishing, farming, fur trading, and other supporting occupations, such as the military and blacksmithing (Herberg 1989: 63). Colonisers from the British Isles started to arrive later, but since the British conquest of New France in 1759, they have had by far the strongest influence in Canada (Satzewich 1990: 327).

The very first wave of 'newcomers' was composed of American 'refugees': the United Empire Loyalists fleeing the American Revolution. A total of some 40,000–50,000 English-speaking Loyalists arrived between 1775, when hostilities broke out, and 1784, the year after the peace treaty (Knowles 1997: 20).[2] The first wave of immigrants to Canada from a neither-English-nor-French-speaking background came from Germany: Mennonites, Moravians and Tunkers started to come from about 1780 until well into the 1800s (Herberg 1989: 63; Angelini and Broderick 1997: 107). They were followed by Irish farmers, who started to arrive in the 1830s. The Irish wave peaked between 1846 and 1854, bolstered by the infamous Potato Famine (1845–6). Finally, with the 1850s' Gold Rush in British Columbia, Chinese, followed by Sioux Indians, arrived in numbers, both initially from the US (Isajiw 1999: 79). Therefore, on the eve of the Confederation in 1867, Canada's four main segments were all present: the Aboriginal people, the French and British charter groups, and the 'newcomers'. The charter groups were numerically dominant however, as only 8% of the population was neither French nor British at that time (Kalbach and Kalbach 1999: 5).

With the enactment of the 1867 British North America Act, the present-day Canada was born. As an emerging nation-state with a population of just over three million spread across a large territory, Canada's priority was to expand the labour force through immigration from Europe (Fleras and Elliot 1996: 290–1; Simmons 1999: 42; Kelley and Trebilcock 2000: 13). Therefore, immigration was perceived as an integral part of its long-term national development. Government sought to recruit immigrants actively, offering free land and even transportation assistance at times, and once arrived, immigrants were welcomed as permanent, future

---

[1] Samuel de Champlain, the first French coloniser, arrived in 1609.
[2] Less well known is the fact that about 10% of them were black (Angelini and Broderick 1997: 107).

citizens. (Reitz 1988; Richmond 1990; Kelley and Trebilcock 2000: 68). These traits characterise a classical country of immigration.

Figure 5.1 shows the annual immigration flows to Canada since Confederation. The inflow's absolute (solid line) and relative (dotted line) size has varied greatly over the past one and a half centuries. A brief description of some important influxes will help to understand Canada's current ethno-cultural fabric. The first period in which annual immigrant intake exceeded 1% of the total population was 1881–91. The influx was a mixed flow, consisting of, among others, Chinese who worked in the Canadian Pacific; Jewish refugees from Russia in the 1880s, Hungarian settlement in Saskatchewan in 1886, and the arrival of Mormons in Alberta from 1887.

The second, and by far the highest, influx occurred during the period 1901 to 1914, with Canada's historic record of over 400,000 immigrants (or 5.3% of total population) in 1913, a result of aggressive recruitment efforts from North, Central, East and South Europe. For example, Ukrainians had begun to arrive in Manitoba in 1891, but much larger groups came from 1896 onwards. Italians numbered about 11,000 in 1901; by 1911, they were about 46,000 (Isajiw 1999: 81). Various non-European groups also started to arrive. For example, approximately 5,000 Sikhs from the Punjab arrived in British Columbia between 1905 and 1908 (Kurian 1991) and over 8,000 Japanese arrived in 1907. Consequently,

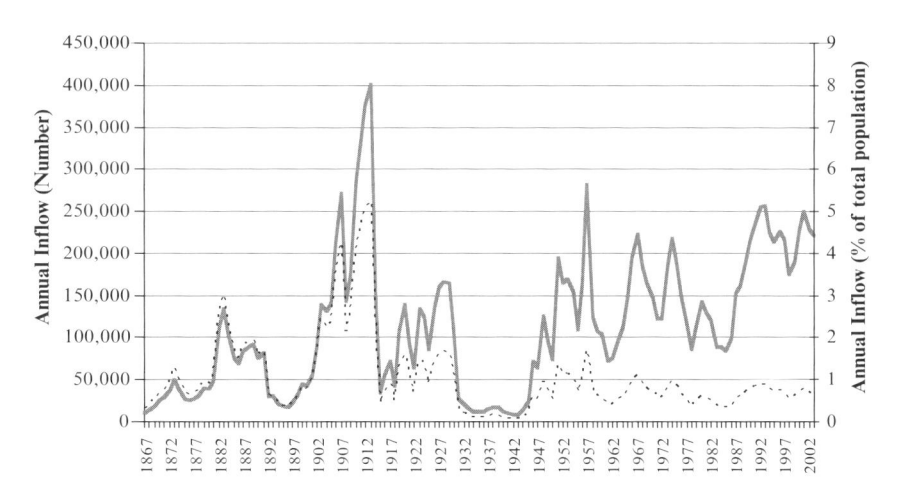

Figure 5.1. Annual immigrant inflow to Canada, 1867–2003 (number and percentage of total population).
Source: *Citizenship and Immigration Canada, Facts and Figures 2003.*

immigration's ethnic composition changed: compared to 1867–90, when 60% were from the British Isles, in 1914 only 38% were from the British Isles, 34% were from America, and 28% from other parts of Europe (but mostly Central, East and South Europe) and elsewhere in the world (Kelley and Trebilcock 2000: 113; Angelini and Broderick 1997: 108–9).

In the period ranging from the beginning of the First World War to end of the Second World War inclusive (1914–45), immigration was low. During the two wars (1914–18, 1939–45), immigration was discouraged for national security reasons. The Great Depression years of the 1930s discouraged further immigration. In addition, this inter-war period saw a series of restrictive actions: Germans and Japanese (and Italians to a lesser extent) were either deported or interned while German subgroups and other ethnic groups which had the remotest resemblance to Germans (e.g. Mennonites, Doukhobors, Hutterites, Ukrainians, Russians and Finns) were discouraged from coming to Canada; the 1923 Chinese Exclusion Act effectively terminated immigration from China; an Order-in-Council restricted immigration to only British subjects and American citizens in 1931 (Kelley and Trebilcock 2000: 175; Isajiw 1999: 82; Taylor 1991: 2).

The Second World War, however, was followed by a huge economic and immigration boom. Among others, Polish immigrants came between 1945 and 1950 as skilled trade-persons, factory workers or miners. They were followed by Hungarian refugees in 1956–7. Italians, Portuguese, and Greek immigrants came in the period from the 1950s to the 1970s as construction and factory workers and other service workers (Driedger 1996: 59; Tastsoglou and Stubos 1992: 160). This period was also marked by substantial immigration from less traditional source countries. For example, in the 1950s a large number of West Indians started to come to fill vacancies in domestic, nursing, and factory work (Kalbach and Kalbach 1999: 4). Figure 5.1 shows that the years 1951 through 1957 (except 1955) saw immigration levels at above 1% of the total population.

Anti-discriminatory changes in policy and legislation followed. For example, the new immigration regulations in 1967 abolished all types of discrimination in immigrant selection by introducing the innovative 'point system' (D'Costa 2000: 50). The Royal Commission on Bilingualism and Biculturalism was followed by the 1971 Multiculturalism Act, setting Canada to be a 'multicultural society within a bilingual framework' (Roberts and Clifton 1990: 137; Knowles 1997: 177; Driedger 2001: 429; Garcea 2003: 61).

Thereafter, the source of immigration waves continued to diversify, increasingly coming from the developing world. For example, by 1968 Hong Kong made it to the top ten source countries, becoming the first non-European country to do so (Kalbach and Kalbach 1999: 4). From the 1970s Central and South Americans started to come in numbers, and in the late 1970s to 1980s, a Vietnamese influx came after the Vietnam War (Herberg 1989: 64). Among immigrants who arrived between 1981 and 1991, 88% were of neither British nor French origins. Currently, the largest immigration inflows to Canada originate from Asia.

Therefore, given its relatively short history of nationhood and comparatively long history of immigrant arrivals from different corners of the world, Canada is rightly referred to as a country of immigration.

Research questions and expectations

Ultimately, this book seeks to examine whether the economic fate of immigrants and their descendants differs from one 'host' country to another. For example, are immigrants and their native-born descendants in Canada, a classical country of immigration, faring better than (or worse than or no different from) their counterparts in other countries of destination with shorter immigration histories? However, before such cross-national comparison is undertaken, various ethnic groups in Canada, some of whose respective histories were briefly mentioned above, must be compared.

The first and foremost question to address in this intra-national investigation is a generational one. Do the native-born second-generation fare better than the immigrant, foreign-born first generation? There are a number of reasons to hypothesise that the second generation would outperform the first-generation. The foreign-educated first generation has distinctive disadvantages in the labour market compared to their domestically educated second-generation peers due to linguistic barriers, unequal recognition of foreign credentials, psychological shock of migration and cultural differences.

The second question is an ethno-generational one. Do ethnic groups show similar or different generational patterns? Ethnic groups may differ in their economic performance due to a number of factors: groups may differ in terms of their various human, cultural and social capital levels; their cultural perceptions of what constitutes economic success may differ; also, various ethnic groups may be subject to differing levels of discrimination and barriers. Do data show that some ethnic groups fare markedly better or worse than others? For which ethnic groups do the second generation fare better than the first generation? Are there some ethnic groups for whom that generational trend is reversed? Are visible minorities faring worse than non-visible minorities?

Thirdly, are differential returns to education likely to be a part of the reason behind the interethnic patterns, if any? In other words, if an ethnic group lags behind others economically even after controlling for age, education and marital status, is it because their education is harder to translate into employment or occupational attainment than others?

Finally, the fourth question concerns gender. Are the generational and ethno-generational patterns different between women and men? Because factors influencing labour market performance may play differently for women and men, gender differences are expected. However, while gender differences may be large among some ethnic groups, they may be insignificant in others. Hence, some interethnic differences in gender patterns are also expected.

Data and methods

Analyses are based on the public use sample of the 2001 Canadian Census.[3] This is a 2.7% sample of individuals and covers non-institutional residents in Canada.[4] In line with other chapters of this book, the sample was cut to female and male adults aged 18 to 59, resulting in the final sample of 452,578.

---

[3] The analyses were also replicated using the entire 1996 Census of Population and Housing Sample Retrieval Data Base, also known as 'Census 2B' (Statistics Canada 1999) which contains information about *all* 'non-institutional individuals' who were living in the randomly selected 20% of households at the time of census-taking (N=6,025,567). We are grateful to Statistics Canada's Graduate Research Stipend Programme for allowing us to access this dataset.

[4] The target population consisted of Canadian citizens and landed immigrants who had a usual place of residence in Canada or who were abroad, either on a military base or on a diplomatic mission. The file also includes data on non-permanent residents of Canada, for example persons who hold a student or employment authorisation or a Minister's permit or who are refugee claimants, and members of their family living with them. The file excludes institutional residents, employees who reside in the institution in which they work, residents of incompletely enumerated Indian reserves or Indian settlements, and foreign residents (e.g. foreign diplomats). We are grateful to Statistics Canada for permission to use these data.

As in the rest of the book, the first generation includes all foreign-born individuals except those who arrived in Canada during the pre-school years. Since age of arrival is provided only in grouped categories, however, our measure of pre-school years covers only those aged 0–4 inclusive. The second generation includes all the Canadian-born population (as well as the foreign-born who arrived during the pre-school years) who had two foreign-born parents, while the third and higher generations include those with one or both parents Canadian-born. For economy, we shall simply term these the third generation.

The generational question raised in the previous section seeks to answer whether the native-born offspring fare better than their foreign-born parents. There are a number of reasons why using the current definition and cross-sectional data to answer this question would not be appropriate. For example, an immigrant wave from the 'same' ethnic background may drastically change in its labour market-relevant characteristics (e.g. socio-economic profile) over time. In this case, the experience of the current first generation would not be a good guide to that of the parents of the second generation. We can, however, check our results by excluding recent arrivals from the first generation and thus limiting our analysis to older immigrants who are, potentially at least, parents of the current second generation.

Table 5.1 shows that almost 21% of the sample was first generation while a further 9% was second generation. Ethnic groups whose proportion of second or later generation members exceeds that of their first generation are groups that arrived earlier in Canadian history and whose flows subsequently stopped or dropped substantially. Most European groups except the Polish and 'Other Europeans' are in this category as is the 'Other multiple' category (likely to come from interethnic families). The remaining groups, mostly visible minorities, show the opposite trend with the proportion of first-generation being higher than the second or later generations.

Table 5.1 also shows the sample's ethnic composition by generation, but before discussing the figures, this central variable deserves an elaboration. 'Ethnicity' was derived from a question which asks: 'To which ethnic or cultural group(s) did this person's *ancestors* belong? Specify as many as applicable' (original emphasis). Respondents were provided with twenty-four concrete examples of ethnic or cultural groups, such as German, Inuit or East Indian alongside the question. Three aspects are noteworthy: the question was open-ended; multiple ethnic identification was encouraged; and the question relied on self-identification, but with a

Table 5.1. Canada's population from different origins by generation, 2001 (percentages).

	First generation	Second generation	Third generation	Total
British	1.5	1.1	9.1	53,322
French	0.2	0.1	3.5	17,127
Canadian	0.2	0.3	20.7	95,759
Multiple charter	0.2	0.1	13.5	62,590
Irish	0.2	0.1	1.2	6,856
German	0.4	0.5	1.4	10,306
Ukrainian	0.1	0.1	0.8	4,895
Polish	0.6	0.2	0.2	4,158
Italian	0.8	1.5	0.4	11,942
Other European	2.6	1.9	1.1	25,342
Jewish	0.2	0.1	0.3	2,617
Lebanese	0.3	0.0	0.0	1,464
Chinese	3.1	0.4	0.1	16,400
Indian	1.8	0.3	0.0	9,863
Other Asian	2.8	0.3	0.1	14,430
Caribbean	1.0	0.2	0.1	5,663
African	0.6	0.0	0.0	2,907
Filipino	0.9	0.1	0.0	4,818
South & Central American	0.5	0.1	0.0	2,690
Aboriginal	0.0	0.0	1.6	7,264
Multiple Aboriginal	0.0	0.0	2.3	10,868
Other single	0.1	0.0	0.3	1,906
Other multiple	2.6	1.7	13.2	79,391
Total %	20.7	9.4	69.9	100
Total N	93,743	42,499	316,336	452,578

First generation includes all foreign-born who arrived in Canada at over 4 years of age. Second generation includes all Canadian-born *and* foreign-born who arrived in Canada at 4 years of age or younger. Respondents aged 18–59.
Source: *Statistics Canada*, Individual File (Flat ASCII File), 2001 Census (Public Use Microdata Files), 95M0016XCB.

clear emphasis on identifying 'ancestors'. Consequently, more than 180 different ethnic or cultural groups were reported and up to six groups were identified per individual. In order to maintain a manageable number and to sustain fairly homogenous groups for meaningful analyses, those with single responses were classified into the sixteen most numerous single-ethnicity groups (and four composite single-ethnicity groups such as Other European and Other Asian). The rest were aggregated into multiple ethnic background categories as shown in Table 5.1. (In order to reduce the amount of material we shall not in subsequent tables show the results for the 'other single' and 'other multiple' groups as they are highly heterogeneous and therefore hard to interpret.)

Third-generation British was chosen as the reference group in order to keep in line with the tradition observed in the relevant Canadian literature (Porter 1965; Darroch 1979; Richmond 1986; Nakhaie 1995: 173; Geschwender and Guppy 1995). We also distinguish three other categories of charter groups: French Canadian and multiple (that is, respondents who gave multiple responses including more than one of British, French and Canadian).

Two seemingly incongruent figures warrant caveats. First, while 'Aboriginals' are expected to have been born in Canada for generations, approximately 500 respondents identified themselves as first-generation Aboriginals. Further disaggregation showed that over 97% of them were Amerindians born in the United States (not shown).[5] Given this peculiarity and the small size of this group, no comparison with the 'third-generation' Aboriginals will take place. The second irregularity concerns the few first-generation respondents who, despite being asked about their 'ancestors', identified themselves as 'Canadians' only. Before explaining this group further, it must be noted that 'Canadians' are a recently formed group and that it seems to be subject to self-selection. Boyd and Norris (2001) show that only 0.5% of the total population identified themselves as 'Canadians' in 1981, but it grew to 4% in 1991 and 31% in 1996 (figure includes multiple responses and all ages). Quebec residents (Yu 2004) and 'French' and 'British' with lower socio-economic characteristics (Boyd 1999) seem to be over-represented in this category. Figures in the following section confirm these observations. In addition, Boyd (1999) further notes that Canadian in English and Canadien in French may contain different connotations. Based on the rather indistinct character of this group and their small size, the few first-generation individuals who identified themselves as 'Canadians' only will not be discussed further.

In line with the rest of the book, economic success, the main outcome variable, will be measured by two indicators: avoidance of unemployment and occupational attainment, assessed by a reduced Goldthorpe class schema. After controlling for educational attainment (CASMIN schema), age and marital status, a regression coefficient will express how that ethno-generational group's net economic performance compares to that of the charter group. All ethno-generational groups' coefficients, or

---

[5] Any Aboriginal individual who is registered as an Indian under Canada's Indian Act is granted entry to Canada under Immigration and Refugee Protection Act Section 19(1). Most of these individuals are American-born Aboriginals within a number of tribes that are present in Canada too.

their relative measures of economic performance, will be compared to answer the research questions: Which generation fares better? Are the generational patterns different among different groups? Are the inter-ethnic differences due to differential returns to education? Are patterns for women different from men?

Profile of the first and later generations

Before the 'net' differences between ethnic groups are discussed, this section first reports on the 'gross differences' or the profile of Canada's ethnic groups by generation with regards to their educational attainment, economic activity and current occupation.

Educational attainment

Educational attainment, the most important control variable in the subsequent regression analysis, shows interesting trends and exceptions in Tables 5.2A and 5.2B. We distinguish five levels of education: no education or primary only, incomplete secondary, full secondary, some tertiary and full tertiary. One striking feature is that the first generation is generally highly educated. In several cases the first generation shows a higher proportion with tertiary (part or full) education and a smaller proportion with lower educational level than do the second or third generations. This overall pattern is different from other countries where the first generation consists of migrant workers with relatively low educational levels while the second generation have 'caught up' with the charter population. This distinctive feature may in part be a reflection of Canada's economic immigrant selection criteria which emphasise education and skills through the point system.

Furthermore, compared with the third generation British (the reference group), most of the first-generation ethnic groups show higher proportions with full tertiary education. Among them, the first generation with Jewish, Ukrainian, French and Chinese ancestry show the highest figures. Only two first-generation ethnic groups show substantially lower figures than the reference group: Italian and Caribbean.

Second-generation ethnic groups show somewhat smaller intergroup variations than the first generation, although they still tend to exceed the reference group of third generation British in their proportions with full

Table 5.2A. Highest educational level, by ancestry and generation: Men (row percentages).

	Primary	Incomplete secondary	Secondary	Some tertiary	Full tertiary	N
First generation						
British	1.0	12.2	18.3	43.0	25.5	3,365
French	0.7	7.0	14.0	39.9	38.4	542
Irish	0.8	12.7	20.5	40.5	25.5	385
German	10.0	14.0	13.1	38.4	24.5	838
Ukrainian	1.3	9.4	16.7	32.6	39.9	233
Polish	1.5	13.0	25.9	37.5	22.1	1,226
Italian	23.1	18.5	17.6	30.5	10.3	1,833
Jewish	0.7	8.7	16.9	23.3	50.4	450
Lebanese	7.7	14.6	24.2	26.8	26.7	652
Chinese	6.1	14.6	22.4	19.6	37.2	6,682
Indian	5.9	17.5	21.9	22.3	32.4	4,121
Caribbean	6.0	23.8	23.5	35.3	11.3	1,809
African	3.2	14.5	25.7	29.3	27.3	1,324
Filipino	1.2	9.6	28.3	29.8	31.1	1,629
Second generation						
British	1.5	16.5	26.4	34.8	20.9	2,690
French	2.6	8.6	23.3	37.1	28.4	116
Irish	0.3	16.4	26.7	30.5	26.0	311
German	4.2	16.4	18.5	40.9	19.9	1,275
Ukrainian	3.1	14.1	18.1	37.7	27.0	326
Polish	1.3	11.7	27.6	32.8	26.6	384
Italian	1.5	12.8	30.0	35.6	20.2	3,442
Jewish	2.0	7.5	19.4	17.8	53.4	253
Lebanese	0.0	21.3	30.6	26.9	21.3	108
Chinese	0.2	7.9	31.6	20.6	39.8	1,036
Indian	0.3	13.6	37.4	21.0	27.7	737
Caribbean	2.1	17.4	39.5	28.1	12.8	516
African	0.9	13.8	47.7	19.3	18.3	109
Filipino	0.0	9.4	43.8	30.3	16.5	267
Third or later generation						
British	2.4	20.6	25.0	33.4	18.6	20,817
French	6.1	17.0	23.0	35.9	18.0	8,081
Canadian	6.6	23.0	27.4	32.0	11.0	46,998
Multiple charter	4.8	18.0	25.2	34.9	17.1	29,656
Irish	3.3	22.7	25.1	33.2	15.7	2,989
German	8.6	26.8	21.6	31.9	11.2	3,238
Ukrainian	2.6	24.7	23.7	32.3	16.7	2,055
Polish	2.6	22.1	25.4	31.7	18.3	426
Italian	2.5	17.5	31.8	32.3	15.8	867
Jewish	1.1	6.3	20.9	15.8	55.8	631
Chinese	1.3	12.8	28.8	30.1	26.9	156
Caribbean	5.2	32.8	29.9	26.9	5.2	134
Aboriginal	15.4	39.4	17.5	25.4	2.3	3,435
Multiple Aboriginal	4.0	29.3	24.2	34.1	8.4	4,953

Source: *Statistics Canada*, 2001 Census (PUMF), 95M0016XCB.

Table 5.2B. Highest educational level, by ancestry and generation: Women (row percentages).

	Primary	Incomplete secondary	Secondary	Some tertiary	Tertiary	N
First generation						
British	0.9	15.4	25.8	39.3	18.6	3,513
French	2.2	5.7	17.6	36.8	37.8	495
Irish	0.7	17.0	22.1	40.0	20.1	412
German	11.2	17.4	18.1	38.0	15.3	940
Ukrainian	1.9	8.9	15.9	36.4	36.8	258
Polish	1.4	10.6	27.1	41.2	19.7	1,348
Italian	36.7	17.3	22.5	17.0	6.4	1,660
Jewish	1.8	6.5	22.2	26.8	42.7	433
Lebanese	12.3	19.3	27.1	22.3	18.9	528
Chinese	8.4	16.3	23.1	23.6	28.6	7,457
Indian	8.7	18.4	24.3	21.4	27.3	4,129
Caribbean	6.4	19.8	22.1	42.9	8.9	2,553
African	6.4	17.4	31.4	30.8	13.9	1,216
Filipino	1.6	7.4	19.7	34.3	37.1	2,648
Second generation						
British	1.1	14.7	28.1	34.0	22.1	2,474
French	3.1	9.9	16.8	36.6	33.6	131
Irish	0.7	13.5	25.3	38.0	22.6	297
German	3.8	13.5	28.0	33.2	21.5	1,119
Ukrainian	1.0	11.3	23.0	35.3	29.3	300
Polish	1.0	10.2	30.2	31.0	27.6	420
Italian	0.7	8.0	28.7	36.1	26.5	3,310
Jewish	0.5	7.7	28.2	20.5	43.2	220
Lebanese	3.1	12.2	36.7	31.6	16.3	98
Chinese	0.6	6.9	31.8	18.8	41.9	943
Indian	0.7	7.6	36.8	21.3	33.6	752
Caribbean	1.0	13.9	35.5	34.1	15.5	510
African	0.9	12.8	38.5	28.4	19.3	109
Filipino	0.9	8.1	37.7	29.1	24.2	223
Third or later generation						
British	1.6	17.7	27.3	33.6	19.8	20,463
French	5.5	15.1	26.3	34.3	18.9	7,762
Canadian	5.8	19.7	29.9	32.9	11.6	46,753
Multiple charter	3.5	14.7	27.3	35.4	19.1	31,415
Irish	2.3	18.9	27.4	33.8	17.7	2,462
German	8.0	24.4	24.4	30.5	12.6	2,896
Ukrainian	2.2	22.1	24.5	34.6	16.6	1,723
Polish	3.1	19.8	28.5	31.4	17.2	354
Italian	1.9	14.1	34.0	29.8	20.2	830
Jewish	0.5	6.5	22.2	17.6	53.2	630
Chinese	0.0	11.1	23.8	28.6	36.5	126
Caribbean	4.3	24.1	30.5	31.9	9.2	141
Aboriginal	13.2	37.9	20.6	23.9	4.4	3,719
Multiple Aboriginal	2.7	22.9	27.7	35.7	11.0	5,598

Source: *Statistics Canada*, 2001 Census (PUMF), 95M0016XCB.

tertiary education. Among these groups, the second generation of Jewish and Chinese origins show the highest proportions with full tertiary education. Among the two first-generation groups that showed substantially lower figures than the reference group (Italian and Caribbean), second-generation Italians now show comparable figures to the third-generation British. While second-generation Caribbeans still show lower figures than the British, they do so to a lesser extent.

Somewhat similar patterns are present among the third generation. The third-generation Jewish and Chinese groups outstrip the British by a considerable margin. Most of the other groups, especially the Canadian, lag some way behind the British while the Aboriginals have notably low levels of education.

The above-reported patterns along generational and ethnic lines are present among both women and men. Interestingly, consistent with the interethnic variation that was greater among the first generation than the second, men are slightly more educated than women among the first generation while no such gender difference is observed among the second generation.

Economic activity

Before the different groups' avoidance of unemployment is examined, it is important to know the 'denominator': the economically active population. The economically active are defined as either employed or unemployed (not employed, looking for a job and available to work) during the reference week of the census.

Table 5.3A shows that, compared to the third-generation British male reference group, 84.7% of whom are economically active, most second-generation groups show lower rates of economic activity and correspondingly higher rates of full-time education, with the Indian, Jewish and Chinese groups showing the highest rates, partly reflecting their relatively young age profiles but also, we suspect, reflecting their strategy of upward mobility through education. Interestingly they are also joined by the Caribbean and Filipino groups, who are not normally regarded as being especially ambitious educationally.

Turning to the 'other inactive category', which we can perhaps think of as representing discouraged workers, one figure stands out above all the others—the 23.4% of the third-generation Aboriginals. This is an alarming figure, although not entirely unexpected given Aboriginals' long history of exploitation and life in reserves.

As expected, women show much lower proportions being economically active than do men, but their generational patterns are more or less similar to men's. In particular, we see the same tendency towards high rates of full-time education among the second generation and we also see that the African, Caribbean and Filipino women have especially high rates, approaching or exceeding those of the Chinese and Indian women.

Again, as among the men, the aboriginal women are notable for their very high rate of 'other inactivity' but their figure of 35% is exceeded by that for the first-generation Lebanese women, a predominantly Muslim group. Lebanese women also show the highest rate of 'other inactivity' in the second generation, although their distinctiveness in this respect is not as noticeable as it is in the first generation.

These variations in rates of economic activity will introduce some important selection biases that will be important to keep in mind when we later turn to the analysis of net disadvantages in unemployment and occupational attainment. In the case of men, compared with the figure of 85% for the reference group of third-generation British, several second-generation groups—the Chinese, Indian and Caribbeans—have activity rates below 60%. In the case of women too there are several groups with rates well below the 74% of the reference group. However, the nature of the selection processes may vary from group to group. In some cases, where low economic activity is a result of high rates of full-time education, it may be the less ambitious individuals who are economically active. In contrast, where the low economic activity rates are due to high proportions in the 'other inactive' category, it may be the more ambitious individuals who are in the labour market.

Current occupational status

Finally, Tables 5.4A and 5.4B show the occupational distributions by ethnicity and gender. Perhaps the most interesting figures are the proportions in the salariat and proportions unemployed.

As expected, the proportions in the salariat show somewhat similar patterns to those for tertiary education. First, some first-generation ethnic groups show higher proportions in the salariat than the respective second generation, but this generational pattern is neither as pronounced nor as prevalent as with education. Secondly, similarly to education, the

Table 5.3A. Economic activity, by ancestry and generation: Men (row percentages).

	Employed	Unemployed	FT education	Other inactive	N
First generation					
British	85.3	3.5	3.1	8.1	3,365
French	76.6	5.9	7.0	10.5	542
Irish	86.8	2.3	2.1	8.8	385
German	83.3	3.1	3.1	10.5	838
Ukrainian	73.4	6.0	9.4	11.2	233
Polish	81.2	3.6	8.8	6.4	1,226
Italian	83.0	2.6	0.9	13.5	1,833
Jewish	80.4	2.7	10.0	6.9	450
Lebanese	66.6	7.5	14.1	11.8	652
Chinese	65.8	4.4	15.9	13.9	6,682
Indian	78.8	4.5	7.8	8.8	4,121
Caribbean	78.1	5.3	6.9	9.7	1,809
African	61.0	7.5	21.1	10.3	1,324
Filipino	79.3	4.3	7.7	8.7	1,629
Second generation					
British	80.9	3.3	7.6	8.3	2,690
French	80.2	1.7	8.6	9.5	116
Irish	76.5	3.9	11.6	8.0	311
German	87.1	2.5	3.8	6.7	1,275
Ukrainian	78.5	5.2	3.4	12.9	326
Polish	74.0	5.5	13.0	7.6	384
Italian	83.5	3.0	7.8	5.7	3,442
Jewish	69.6	2.4	20.9	7.1	253
Lebanese	67.6	4.6	23.1	4.6	108
Chinese	55.8	2.9	36.1	5.2	1,036
Indian	50.6	3.7	40.3	5.4	737
Caribbean	51.9	7.0	31.0	10.1	516
African	60.6	5.5	27.5	6.4	109
Filipino	58.4	2.2	33.7	5.6	267
Third or later generation					
British	80.3	4.4	6.7	8.5	20,817
French	76.5	5.2	7.8	10.5	8,081
Canadian	76.5	5.5	8.5	9.5	46,998
Multiple charter	76.9	5.6	8.4	9.1	29,656
Irish	81.3	4.4	5.1	9.2	2,989
German	83.8	3.4	5.1	7.7	3,238
Ukrainian	83.9	2.9	5.3	7.9	2,055
Polish	81.7	4.9	5.4	8.0	426
Italian	73.4	4.6	13.8	8.2	867
Jewish	76.9	2.7	13.8	6.7	631
Chinese	72.4	3.2	12.2	12.2	156
Caribbean	79.1	4.5	10.4	6.0	134
Aboriginal	50.6	16.5	9.4	23.4	3,435
Multiple Aboriginal	71.7	8.8	9.5	9.9	4,953

Source: *Statistics Canada*, 2001 Census (PUMF), 95M0016XCB.

Table 5.3B. Economic activity, by ancestry and generation: Women (row percentages).

	Employed	Unemployed	FT education	Other inactive	N
First generation					
British	71.9	2.7	3.1	22.3	3,513
French	65.1	4.0	11.5	19.4	495
Irish	73.8	3.2	2.2	20.9	412
German	63.8	3.1	3.8	29.3	940
Ukrainian	60.5	5.8	14.3	19.4	258
Polish	68.4	3.9	10.6	17.1	1,348
Italian	59.1	2.8	1.1	37.0	1,660
Jewish	68.4	2.8	8.5	20.3	433
Lebanese	43.2	3.4	10.4	43.0	528
Chinese	55.2	4.5	13.1	27.2	7,457
Indian	62.7	6.8	6.5	24.0	4,129
Caribbean	68.7	6.7	8.9	15.7	2,553
African	47.9	8.4	22.1	21.5	1,216
Filipino	78.0	3.4	5.4	13.3	2,648
Second generation					
British	73.1	3.0	7.7	16.1	2,474
French	74.8	3.1	7.6	14.5	131
Irish	74.1	2.7	8.8	14.5	297
German	76.2	2.1	3.8	17.9	1,119
Ukrainian	74.7	1.3	1.3	22.7	300
Polish	69.0	2.6	13.8	14.5	420
Italian	74.2	2.9	8.8	14.1	3,310
Jewish	61.8	1.8	15.5	20.9	220
Lebanese	43.9	7.1	24.5	24.5	98
Chinese	53.2	2.9	37.3	6.6	943
Indian	43.5	2.7	45.6	8.2	752
Caribbean	48.4	5.3	36.9	9.4	510
African	48.6	3.7	39.4	8.3	109
Filipino	48.4	2.2	41.3	8.1	223
Third or later generation					
British	71.1	3.3	7.2	18.5	20,463
French	66.5	3.8	9.0	20.7	7,762
Canadian	65.8	3.8	9.8	20.6	46,753
Multiple charter	67.6	4.0	9.7	18.6	31,415
Irish	72.3	3.5	5.9	18.4	2,462
German	70.4	2.6	5.8	21.2	2,896
Ukrainian	74.8	3.8	4.8	16.6	1,723
Polish	70.6	2.5	7.6	19.2	354
Italian	67.0	3.9	15.3	13.9	830
Jewish	68.7	3.5	14.4	13.3	630
Chinese	65.1	3.2	18.3	13.5	126
Caribbean	63.8	5.0	14.9	16.3	141
Aboriginal	42.4	9.7	13.0	34.9	3,719
Multiple Aboriginal	61.7	6.3	12.2	19.8	5,598

Source: *Statistics Canada*, 2001 Census (PUMF), 95M0016XCB.

second generation shows less intergroup variation than the first-generation. Thirdly, the second-generation groups all (with the one exception of the Jewish group) show higher levels of access to the salariat than do the third generation

However, a similar ethnic hierarchy is noticeable across the three generations: Jews consistently show the highest figures in the salariat while Chinese are also ahead of the third-generation British in all three generations. Groups of European ancestry are fairly similar to the charter populations, while the visible minorities of Africans, Caribbeans, Lebanese and Filipinos tend to lag behind. However all four of these groups are more successful than the third-generation Aboriginals, who come at the bottom of the ethnic hierarchy. It is also important to note that, among the four third-generation charter groups, the French are more or less on a par with the British while the Canadians lag some way behind. People reporting multiple charter ancestry fall in between.

Finally, most of these patterns operate in the same way among women as among men (although the overall occupational distributions are rather different). In particular we see the same ethnic hierarchy with the Jews and Chinese being well ahead of the third-generation British in access to the salariat, the European groups being rather similar to the British and French charter groups, and the visible minorities of Africans, Caribbeans, Lebanese and Filipinos being the least successful. The Aboriginal women are also relatively near the bottom of the ethnic hierarchy but do not actually lag far behind in the way that Aboriginal men do. However, this may reflect the different selection processes that operate for men and women of Aboriginal ancestry.

Somewhat similar patterns are present in the unemployment figures. Jews stand out in all three generations with very low rates of unemployment while the various groups of European ancestry are not dissimilar from the British and French charter groups. Africans and Caribbeans show high unemployment figures but once again it is the Aboriginals who stand out with remarkably high unemployment rates of 21% for men and 15% for women. In the case of men this is over twice the unemployment rate of the next most disadvantaged group, the first-generation Africans.

There are also some distinctive patterns of self-employment with considerable intergroup differences. Many first-generation groups have higher proportions in the petty bourgeoisie than the 11% of the reference group, perhaps reflecting difficulties in gaining salaried employment. The Lebanese are notable for their high rate of self-employment in both generations (a pattern that is also apparent for Lebanese in Australia) while,

Table 5.4A. Current occupation by ancestry and generation: Men (row percentages).

	Salariat	RNM	PB	Skilled manual	Less skilled manual	Unemployed	N
First generation							
British	46.6	11.1	11.2	15.0	12.3	3.7	3,202
French	47.8	17.1	10.0	8.1	10.6	6.5	492
Irish	43.3	10.1	15.3	16.2	12.6	2.5	365
German	32.8	9.1	19.7	16.8	18.3	3.3	778
Ukrainian	37.9	6.5	12.1	14.5	22.4	6.5	214
Polish	26.0	8.8	16.1	20.2	25.1	3.8	1,159
Italian	24.5	11.1	18.7	20.8	22.0	2.9	1,637
Jewish	53.1	10.6	20.0	4.0	9.4	2.8	424
Lebanese	34.7	14.0	18.5	7.1	17.3	8.5	579
Chinese	41.8	18.6	12.1	6.3	15.8	5.4	5,484
Indian	29.8	13.1	11.3	10.2	30.7	4.9	3,839
Caribbean	21.8	17.1	6.4	17.0	32.0	5.8	1,668
African	29.1	14.8	7.0	8.3	31.8	8.9	1,115
Filipino	22.2	17.9	3.1	14.2	38.1	4.6	1,531
Second generation							
British	39.8	15.7	8.8	15.0	17.2	3.5	2,526
French	46.4	9.1	12.7	12.7	17.3	1.8	110
Irish	38.6	16.4	6.8	16.4	17.7	4.1	293
German	35.6	11.7	15.0	18.0	17.2	2.6	1,217
Ukrainian	37.7	11.8	17.2	14.5	13.1	5.7	297
Polish	39.4	13.9	8.1	12.5	20.3	5.8	360
Italian	36.4	17.8	11.7	13.7	17.3	3.1	3,298
Jewish	58.6	16.7	11.0	1.8	9.3	2.6	227
Lebanese	31.3	19.2	19.2	8.1	17.2	5.1	99
Chinese	50.5	23.9	4.5	5.6	12.2	3.3	911
Indian	38.4	24.5	3.8	4.3	24.8	4.1	653
Caribbean	26.5	30.5	2.7	6.5	25.8	8.1	446
African	30.2	24.0	4.2	8.3	27.1	6.3	96
Filipino	31.8	33.1	1.7	8.7	22.3	2.5	242
Third generation							
British	33.0	14.2	11.2	15.5	21.4	4.7	19,513
French	32.5	14.2	9.8	15.3	22.5	5.7	7,335
Canadian	24.3	13.9	9.6	18.0	28.2	6.0	43,145
Multiple charter	31.1	14.5	9.2	15.6	23.6	6.1	27,435
Irish	29.0	15.6	10.8	17.3	22.5	4.7	2,779
German	22.9	10.5	20.9	18.6	23.6	3.6	3,094
Ukrainian	30.8	13.2	14.6	18.1	20.3	3.0	1,941
Polish	32.9	10.2	15.5	16.5	19.7	5.2	401
Italian	30.0	19.2	9.3	13.5	23.0	4.9	813
Jewish	62.3	14.9	10.5	3.5	5.9	2.9	592
Chinese	42.4	21.5	6.9	6.9	18.8	3.5	144
Caribbean	24.8	19.2	3.2	8.8	39.2	4.8	125
Aboriginal	15.3	10.4	4.9	15.1	33.7	20.7	2,750
Multiple Aboriginal	20.9	15.1	8.1	16.9	29.5	9.6	4,571

Source: *Statistics Canada*, 2001 Census (PUMF), 95M0016XCB.

Table 5.4B. Current occupation by ancestry and generation: Women (row percentages).

	Salariat	RNM	PB	Skilled manual	Less skilled manual	Unemployed	N
First generation							
British	47.8	29.0	8.8	2.9	8.3	3.2	2,925
French	58.7	22.4	5.0	2.0	6.8	5.0	397
Irish	49.1	31.0	6.8	2.0	7.4	3.7	352
German	39.0	26.8	13.2	2.8	14.2	4.0	720
Ukrainian	38.7	27.9	4.4	1.0	20.6	7.4	204
Polish	33.0	27.9	7.7	4.1	22.6	4.6	1,144
Italian	30.5	29.6	9.3	3.9	22.6	4.1	1,124
Jewish	54.5	23.8	12.3	1.8	4.1	3.5	341
Lebanese	35.0	34.0	11.7	3.2	10.4	5.8	309
Chinese	36.0	26.6	7.8	2.8	20.6	6.3	5,367
Indian	28.1	26.6	5.6	3.1	28.1	8.6	3,286
Caribbean	28.8	34.2	2.8	4.1	22.3	7.7	2,211
African	24.9	32.2	3.4	2.2	25.8	11.4	891
Filipino	26.3	42.7	3.2	3.0	21.1	3.7	2,412
Second generation							
British	45.9	31.9	7.4	2.1	9.2	3.5	2,151
French	61.5	16.2	5.1	5.1	8.5	3.4	117
Irish	51.0	31.4	5.7	1.9	6.9	3.1	261
German	45.7	28.1	10.7	4.5	8.5	2.5	974
Ukrainian	52.9	27.5	7.4	3.7	7.0	1.6	244
Polish	44.2	35.7	5.2	2.2	9.6	3.0	364
Italian	49.2	34.1	4.1	3.2	6.2	3.3	2,948
Jewish	54.9	26.3	10.9	0.0	5.7	2.3	175
Lebanese	27.4	42.5	2.7	4.1	13.7	9.6	73
Chinese	49.2	34.3	2.5	2.0	8.8	3.2	842
Indian	41.4	41.9	1.1	1.1	11.5	3.1	654
Caribbean	35.8	38.7	1.8	2.9	14.6	6.1	444
African	31.9	41.5	2.1	0.0	20.2	4.3	94
Filipino	28.7	48.5	1.0	1.5	17.8	2.5	202
Third or later generations							
British	42.8	30.9	7.2	2.9	12.4	3.9	17,547
French	44.0	29.7	5.9	2.6	13.1	4.7	6,344
Canadian	36.7	32.5	6.0	3.3	16.8	4.7	38,311
Multiple charter	42.9	30.3	6.0	2.9	13.2	4.8	26,510
Irish	42.8	31.4	6.3	3.5	11.9	4.0	2,113
German	36.5	31.1	12.8	3.4	13.2	3.0	2,508
Ukrainian	41.8	33.3	7.4	3.3	9.8	4.4	1,504
Polish	40.5	33.2	5.3	3.0	15.0	3.0	301
Italian	39.9	34.4	6.2	2.3	12.9	4.4	730
Jewish	58.7	25.1	7.7	0.9	3.6	3.9	557
Chinese	50.0	33.6	5.2	1.7	6.0	3.4	116
Caribbean	31.1	41.0	1.6	1.6	18.9	5.7	122
Aboriginal	29.4	30.0	3.7	2.1	20.3	14.5	2,490
Multiple Aboriginal	33.9	33.9	6.0	2.5	16.2	7.6	4,671

Source: *Statistics Canada*, 2001 Census (PUMF), 95M0016XCB.

as in other countries, Caribbeans and Filipinos have very low rates of self-employment. Interestingly Chinese and Indians, who in Britain have relatively high rates of self-employment, are not notable in Canada for their self-employment. This may reflect the different selection processes for immigrants to the two countries.

Economic performance: findings from logistic and multinomial regression

Avoidance of Unemployment

Now that the 'gross' differences have been outlined, regressions examine the 'net' differences or 'ethnic penalties'. First, logistic regression is used to calculate the log-odds of being in employment versus unemployment. Employment is coded 1 and unemployment 0. Therefore, groups with positive estimates are more likely to be employed than the reference group of third-generation British (that is, experience an ethnic 'premium' while negative estimates indicate an ethnic penalty and a lower likelihood of gaining employment. Table 5.5 shows the parameter estimates from a model with main effects only.[6] Interactions between ethnicity and education are added in Table 5.A1, shown in the Appendix to this chapter.

Table 5.5. Logistic regression of employment and unemployment (parameter estimates: contrasts with unemployment).

	Men		Women	
Intercept	**1.37**	(0.12)	**1.28**	(0.14)
Ancestry				
British 3	0		0	
British 1	0.06	(0.10)	0.08	(0.11)
French 1	**−0.57**	(0.19)	**−0.46**	(0.23)
Irish 1	0.49	(0.34)	−0.07	(0.29)
German 1	0.32	(0.20)	−0.08	(0.20)
Ukrainian 1	**−0.62**	(0.28)	**−0.86**	(0.28)
Polish 1	0.07	(0.16)	**−0.30**	(0.15)
Italian 1	**0.57**	(0.15)	0.07	(0.16)
Jewish 1	0.19	(0.30)	−0.12	(0.30)
Lebanese 1	**−0.79**	(0.16)	**−0.44**	(0.25)

[6] We have not shown the coefficients for some smaller groups or for various composite groups such as the 'other single' or 'other multiple' groups.

CANADA: INCLUSION FOR ALL BUT ABORIGINALS

Chinese 1	**−0.37**	(0.07)	**−0.54**	(0.07)
Indian 1	**−0.22**	(0.08)	**−0.80**	(0.08)
Caribbean 1	−0.16	(0.11)	**−0.63**	(0.09)
African 1	**−0.83**	(0.11)	**−1.18**	(0.12)
Filipino 1	−0.17	(0.13)	−0.03	(0.12)
British 2	**0.31**	(0.11)	0.11	(0.12)
French 2	0.97	(0.72)	0.16	(0.51)
Irish 2	0.08	(0.30)	0.23	(0.36)
German 2	**0.57**	(0.18)	**0.47**	(0.21)
Ukrainian 2	−0.30	(0.26)	0.76	(0.51)
Polish 2	−0.34	(0.23)	0.10	(0.31)
Italian 2	**0.46**	(0.11)	0.20	(0.11)
Jewish 2	0.22	(0.42)	0.31	(0.51)
Lebanese 2	0.11	(0.47)	**−1.02**	(0.41)
Chinese 2	0.14	(0.19)	−0.08	(0.20)
Indian 2	−0.03	(0.20)	−0.03	(0.24)
Caribbean 2	**−0.49**	(0.18)	**−0.48**	(0.21)
African 2	−0.05	(0.43)	−0.21	(0.52)
Filipino 2	0.77	(0.42)	0.37	(0.46)
French 3	**−0.19**	(0.06)	**−0.23**	(0.07)
Canadian 3	**−0.16**	(0.04)	**−0.11**	(0.05)
Multiple charter 3	**−0.27**	(0.04)	**−0.22**	(0.05)
Irish 3	0.04	(0.10)	0.00	(0.12)
German 3	**0.42**	(0.10)	**0.35**	(0.12)
Ukrainian 3	**0.51**	(0.14)	−0.07	(0.13)
Polish 3	−0.09	(0.23)	0.31	(0.34)
Italian 3	−0.05	(0.17)	−0.14	(0.19)
Jewish 3	0.24	(0.25)	−0.30	(0.22)
Chinese 3	0.32	(0.46)	−0.11	(0.52)
Caribbean 3	0.34	(0.42)	−0.24	(0.40)
Aboriginal 3	**−1.50**	(0.06)	**−1.28**	(0.07)
Multiple Aboriginal 3	**−0.65**	(0.06)	**−0.60**	(0.07)
Age/10	**0.53**	(0.07)	**0.63**	(0.08)
(Age/10)^2	**−0.06**	(0.01)	**−0.05**	(0.01)
Marital status				
Single	0		0	
Married	**0.80**	(0.03)	**0.16**	(0.03)
Divorced/separated/widowed	**0.17**	(0.04)	**−0.15**	(0.04)
Educational qualifications				
Primary or none	**−0.82**	(0.04)	**−0.71**	(0.05)
Incomplete secondary	**−0.41**	(0.03)	**−0.47**	(0.03)
Secondary	0		0	
Incomplete tertiary	**0.09**	(0.03)	**0.18**	(0.03)
Full tertiary	**0.49**	(0.04)	**0.42**	(0.04)
Chi-square (d.f.)	4751.2 (55)		2,746.9 (55)	
N	181,848		160,373	

For both women and men the control variables have the expected effects. Age has a curvilinear effect, and higher education and being married/cohabiting are correlated with a higher chance of being employed. As far as the ethnic differences are concerned, however, parameter estimates vary widely. Figures for men are reported in detail below, but women's intergroup and intergenerational patterns are remarkably similar to those of men.

Compared with the third-generation men of British origins, only one first-generation group shows a significant positive parameter estimate (Italian men) while a number show estimates that are not significantly different from the reference group: Irish, German, Polish, British, Jewish, Caribbean and Filipino. All other first-generation ethnic groups show significant negative estimates, that is are more likely than the reference group to be unemployed after taking into account their age, education and marital status. Among them, first-generation Africans show the largest ethnic penalties, closely followed by the Lebanese.

The picture changes a good deal when the second-generation men are examined. Compared with the third-generation British, only one group—the second-generation Caribbeans—shows a significant ethnic penalty. Many ethnic groups that showed negative estimates among the first generation now show positive estimates or estimates not significantly different from zero: these include French, Ukrainian, Lebanese, Chinese, Indian and African men. This general pattern shows a generational 'improvement' and this is confirmed by a formal test.[7]

Turning next to the interactions between ethnicity and education, we find that a number of first-generation groups show ethnic and interaction parameter estimates which are both statistically significant and same-signed (negative in all cases). The case of these groups is disconcerting as this pattern means that their high-school educated members possess significantly lower chances of being employed than the reference group and that gap widens as educational level increases. The first-generation Chinese, Indians, Caribbeans and Africans are in this category. No second-generation groups are in this situation, which is encouraging.

---

[7] If we fit ethnic group and generation as separate variables in place of the combined ethno-generational variable used in the analysis for Table 5.5 we find for first-generation men a significant negative parameter estimate of -0.21 (s.e. 0.04), and for the second-generation men a non-significant positive estimate of 0.09 (s.e. 0.05) (both contrasted with the third generation). In the case of women the first-generation estimate is -0.43 (s.e. 0.04) and for the second generation $+0.06$ (s.e. 0.05).

Other groups show a combination of significant negative interactions with either positive or non-significant main effects for ethnicity. For them, those with full secondary education are either more likely (positive estimates) or as likely (non-significant estimates) to be employed than the reference group. However, among those with higher education, this relative advantage dwindles, and in some cases, disappears altogether.

Occupational attainment

Leaving the unemployed apart, this section examines the occupational attainment of those who are actually in work. Using a simplified Erikson/Goldthorpe class schema, multinomial logistic regression is used to estimate each ethnic group's likelihood of attaining the salariat, routine non-manual, petty bourgeoisie or skilled manual classes rather than the semi- and unskilled class. Tables 5.6A and 5.6B show the main effects for men and women respectively.

The control variables—age, education and marital status—behave as expected. Age, education and being married all have a positive effect on attaining classes other than the semi- and unskilled class. As shown in other chapters in this book, education has the strongest effect on attaining access to the salariat for both women and men. Interestingly, full tertiary education has a much larger positive effect on women's access to skilled manual (rather than low/semi-skilled) than it does for men's, suggesting that the kinds of skilled manual occupations that women access may differ from those held by men.

The overall occupational patterns are similar to the employment patterns. Several of the first-generation groups show negative (and often statistically significant) estimates, suggesting a lower likelihood of attaining the salariat, routine non-manual, petty bourgeoisie or skilled manual occupations relative to unskilled manual occupations when compared to the third-generation British reference group. As with employment the overall picture changes when the second-generation groups are examined: most of them now show positive (and often statistically significant) estimates. Perhaps most remarkably every single visible minority group—Lebanese, Chinese, Indian, Caribbean, African and Filipino—show positive estimates for access to the salariat. Only in the case of skilled manual work do we find substantial negative estimates.

Once again, then, we see generational improvement and, in the case of access to the salariat, the difference between the first and second generation

Table 5.6A. Logistic regression of occupational class: Men (parameter estimates; contrasts with semi and unskilled work).

	Salariat		RNM		PB		Skilled manual	
Intercept	−2.91	(0.09)	−0.54	(0.09)	−6.75	(0.13)	−2.97	(0.09)
Ancestry								
British 3	0		0		0		0	
British 1	**0.54**	(0.07)	**0.19**	(0.08)	**0.19**	(0.08)	**0.26**	(0.07)
French 1	**0.34**	(0.17)	**0.58**	(0.18)	0.26	(0.20)	−0.27	(0.21)
Irish 1	**0.46**	(0.18)	0.09	(0.22)	**0.50**	(0.20)	0.35	(0.20)
German 1	−0.12	(0.12)	−0.25	(0.15)	**0.51**	(0.12)	0.13	(0.13)
Ukrainian 1	**−0.76**	(0.22)	**−1.10**	(0.31)	−0.20	(0.26)	−0.28	(0.24)
Polish 1	**−0.80**	(0.10)	**−0.79**	(0.12)	0.05	(0.10)	−0.04	(0.09)
Italian 1	−0.06	(0.09)	−0.01	(0.10)	**0.18**	(0.08)	**0.24**	(0.08)
Jewish 1	**0.60**	(0.19)	0.31	(0.22)	**1.26**	(0.20)	−0.55	(0.29)
Lebanese 1	0.18	(0.14)	0.17	(0.15)	**0.86**	(0.15)	**−0.51**	(0.19)
Chinese 1	**0.15**	(0.05)	**0.55**	(0.05)	**0.26**	(0.06)	**−0.57**	(0.07)
Indian 1	**−1.03**	(0.06)	**−0.55**	(0.06)	**−0.50**	(0.06)	**−0.81**	(0.06)
Caribbean 1	**−0.72**	(0.08)	**−0.16**	(0.08)	**−1.01**	(0.11)	**−0.38**	(0.08)
African 1	**−1.01**	(0.09)	**−0.51**	(0.10)	**−0.92**	(0.13)	**−1.11**	(0.12)
Filipino 1	**−1.86**	(0.08)	**−0.65**	(0.08)	**−2.18**	(0.16)	**−0.85**	(0.09)
British 2	**0.42**	(0.07)	**0.29**	(0.07)	0.07	(0.09)	**0.20**	(0.08)
French 2	0.32	(0.30)	−0.40	(0.39)	0.47	(0.36)	−0.02	(0.36)
Irish 2	0.26	(0.19)	0.26	(0.20)	−0.10	(0.27)	0.32	(0.21)
German 2	0.16	(0.10)	0.00	(0.11)	**0.40**	(0.11)	**0.22**	(0.10)
Ukrainian 2	0.19	(0.21)	0.18	(0.24)	**0.56**	(0.22)	0.23	(0.23)
Polish 2	0.04	(0.17)	−0.09	(0.19)	−0.25	(0.23)	−0.15	(0.20)
Italian 2	**0.33**	(0.06)	**0.36**	(0.06)	**0.52**	(0.07)	0.11	(0.07)
Jewish 2	**0.96**	(0.27)	**0.85**	(0.28)	**1.06**	(0.31)	−1.05	(0.55)
Lebanese 2	0.64	(0.34)	0.53	(0.34)	**1.84**	(0.36)	0.07	(0.44)
Chinese 2	**0.96**	(0.12)	**0.93**	(0.12)	**0.51**	(0.19)	−0.01	(0.17)
Indian 2	**0.32**	(0.12)	**0.33**	(0.12)	0.02	(0.22)	**−0.91**	(0.21)
Caribbean 2	0.12	(0.15)	**0.55**	(0.13)	−0.45	(0.31)	**−0.63**	(0.21)

CANADA: INCLUSION FOR ALL BUT ABORIGINALS

	(1)	SE	(2)	SE	(3)	SE	(4)	SE
African 2	0.15	(0.31)	0.26	(0.29)	−0.07	(0.55)	−0.28	(0.41)
Filipino 2	**0.45**	(0.20)	**0.72**	(0.18)	−0.58	(0.52)	−0.13	(0.26)
French 3	**−0.10**	(0.04)	−0.06	(0.05)	**−0.21**	(0.05)	**−0.10**	(0.05)
Canadian 3	**−0.33**	(0.03)	**−0.23**	(0.03)	**−0.29**	(0.03)	**−0.07**	(0.03)
Multiple charter 3	**−0.15**	(0.03)	**−0.09**	(0.03)	**−0.24**	(0.04)	**−0.11**	(0.03)
Irish 3	**−0.13**	(0.06)	0.07	(0.07)	−0.09	(0.08)	0.05	(0.07)
German 3	−0.12	(0.06)	**−0.25**	(0.07)	**0.68**	(0.06)	**0.18**	(0.06)
Ukrainian 3	0.08	(0.08)	0.02	(0.08)	**0.34**	(0.08)	**0.23**	(0.08)
Polish 3	0.08	(0.16)	−0.25	(0.20)	**0.42**	(0.18)	0.16	(0.17)
Italian 3	0.04	(0.11)	**0.23**	(0.11)	0.04	(0.14)	−0.08	(0.13)
Jewish 3	**1.42**	(0.19)	**1.16**	(0.20)	**1.39**	(0.22)	0.08	(0.28)
Chinese 3	0.33	(0.27)	0.48	(0.27)	−0.03	(0.38)	−0.49	(0.38)
Caribbean 3	−0.18	(0.26)	−0.13	(0.25)	**−1.44**	(0.53)	**−0.94**	(0.34)
Aboriginal 3	**−0.45**	(0.07)	**−0.51**	(0.07)	**−0.94**	(0.10)	**−0.32**	(0.07)
Multiple Aboriginal 3	**−0.41**	(0.05)	**−0.18**	(0.05)	**−0.36**	(0.07)	**−0.15**	(0.05)
Age/10	**1.12**	(0.05)	0.06	(0.05)	**2.40**	(0.07)	**1.00**	(0.05)
(Age/10)^2	**−0.12**	(0.01)	−0.01	(0.01)	**−0.24**	(0.01)	**−0.12**	(0.01)
Marital status								
Married/common law	**0.34**	(0.02)	0.01	(0.02)	**0.52**	(0.03)	**0.49**	(0.02)
Divorced etc	0.00	(0.03)	−0.06	(0.04)	**0.21**	(0.04)	**0.30**	(0.03)
Single	0		0		0		0	
Qualifications								
Primary or none	**−1.95**	(0.06)	**−1.24**	(0.05)	**−0.28**	(0.04)	**−0.24**	(0.04)
Incomplete secondary	**−0.98**	(0.02)	**−0.59**	(0.02)	**−0.22**	(0.02)	**−0.17**	(0.02)
Full secondary	0		0		0		0	
Some tertiary	**1.02**	(0.02)	**0.37**	(0.02)	**0.54**	(0.02)	**1.06**	(0.02)
Full tertiary	**3.09**	(0.03)	**1.14**	(0.03)	**1.14**	(0.03)	**0.21**	(0.04)
Chi-square (d.f.)					73,779.054 (220)			
N					194,629			

Table 5.6B. Logistic regression of occupational class: Women (parameter estimates; contrasts with semi and unskilled work).

	Salariat		RNM		PB		Skilled manual	
Intercept	−3.42	(0.09)	−0.36	(0.08)	−6.98	(0.16)	−4.45	(0.18)
Ancestry								
British 3	0		0		0		0	
British 1	**0.31**	(0.08)	**0.23**	(0.08)	**0.28**	(0.10)	**0.29**	(0.14)
French 1	0.29	(0.22)	0.01	(0.23)	−0.09	(0.30)	0.02	(0.41)
Irish 1	**0.44**	(0.22)	**0.43**	(0.22)	0.12	(0.29)	0.03	(0.43)
German 1	−0.23	(0.13)	−0.18	(0.13)	**0.31**	(0.15)	−0.17	(0.25)
Ukrainian 1	**−1.36**	(0.22)	**−0.86**	(0.21)	**−1.41**	(0.38)	**−1.80**	(0.73)
Polish 1	**−1.22**	(0.09)	**−0.89**	(0.09)	**−0.81**	(0.13)	**−0.40**	(0.17)
Italian 1	**−0.19**	(0.10)	−0.15	(0.09)	**−0.35**	(0.12)	−0.13	(0.17)
Jewish 1	**0.65**	(0.29)	**0.64**	(0.29)	**1.25**	(0.32)	0.44	(0.49)
Lebanese 1	0.14	(0.22)	**0.41**	(0.21)	**0.79**	(0.25)	0.33	(0.37)
Chinese 1	**−0.87**	(0.05)	**−0.59**	(0.05)	**−0.50**	(0.07)	**−0.57**	(0.10)
Indian 1	**−1.54**	(0.06)	**−0.96**	(0.06)	**−1.18**	(0.09)	**−0.80**	(0.12)
Caribbean 1	**−0.93**	(0.07)	**−0.52**	(0.07)	**−1.52**	(0.14)	**−0.27**	(0.13)
African 1	**−1.26**	(0.11)	**−0.71**	(0.10)	**−1.32**	(0.20)	**−0.98**	(0.24)
Filipino 1	**−1.99**	(0.07)	**−0.56**	(0.06)	**−1.83**	(0.13)	**−0.83**	(0.14)
British 2	**0.32**	(0.09)	**0.29**	(0.09)	**0.34**	(0.11)	−0.05	(0.17)
French 2	0.52	(0.37)	−0.37	(0.40)	0.12	(0.53)	0.91	(0.52)
Irish 2	**0.81**	(0.27)	**0.59**	(0.26)	0.47	(0.36)	0.20	(0.51)
German 2	**0.40**	(0.13)	**0.29**	(0.13)	**0.68**	(0.16)	**0.77**	(0.19)
Ukrainian 2	0.32	(0.28)	0.30	(0.28)	0.18	(0.35)	0.65	(0.42)
Polish 2	0.08	(0.20)	0.31	(0.20)	−0.08	(0.29)	−0.04	(0.40)
Italian 2	**0.70**	(0.09)	**0.68**	(0.09)	0.24	(0.12)	**0.72**	(0.14)
Jewish 2	**0.75**	(0.36)	0.58	(0.35)	**1.34**	(0.41)	−19.23	(0.00)
Lebanese 2	−0.18	(0.42)	0.25	(0.37)	−0.09	(0.79)	0.56	(0.66)
Chinese 2	**0.57**	(0.14)	**0.51**	(0.14)	0.17	(0.26)	0.29	(0.28)
Indian 2	**0.38**	(0.15)	**0.48**	(0.14)	−0.61	(0.40)	−0.54	(0.40)
Caribbean 2	**0.32**	(0.17)	0.21	(0.15)	−0.28	(0.38)	0.25	(0.31)

CANADA: INCLUSION FOR ALL BUT ABORIGINALS

	Model 1		Model 2		Model 3		Model 4	
African 2	−0.30	(0.33)	−0.09	(0.29)	−0.59	(0.76)	−20.27	(0.00)
Filipino 2	−0.31	(0.24)	0.18	(0.20)	−1.03	(0.73)	−0.63	(0.60)
French 3	−0.04	(0.05)	**−0.10**	(0.05)	**−0.28**	(0.07)	−0.16	(0.10)
Canadian 3	**−0.18**	(0.03)	**−0.18**	(0.03)	**−0.31**	(0.04)	−0.09	(0.06)
Multiple charter 3	−0.05	(0.03)	**−0.10**	(0.03)	**−0.19**	(0.05)	−0.05	(0.06)
Irish 3	0.11	(0.08)	0.08	(0.08)	−0.08	(0.12)	0.24	(0.14)
German 3	**0.25**	(0.08)	**0.20**	(0.07)	**0.76**	(0.09)	0.25	(0.13)
Ukrainian 3	**0.32**	(0.10)	**0.36**	(0.10)	**0.26**	(0.13)	**0.38**	(0.17)
Polish 3	−0.08	(0.20)	−0.04	(0.19)	−0.40	(0.30)	−0.09	(0.37)
Italian 3	0.07	(0.13)	0.12	(0.13)	0.13	(0.19)	−0.13	(0.27)
Jewish 3	**1.07**	(0.24)	**0.94**	(0.24)	**1.33**	(0.28)	0.08	(0.50)
Chinese 3	0.75	(0.43)	0.78	(0.42)	0.69	(0.57)	0.26	(0.81)
Caribbean 3	−0.29	(0.29)	0.00	(0.26)	**−1.44**	(0.74)	−0.83	(0.74)
Aboriginal 3	−0.08	(0.07)	**−0.19**	(0.07)	**−0.63**	(0.12)	**−0.56**	(0.15)
Multiple Aboriginal 3	**−0.15**	(0.06)	−0.07	(0.05)	−0.11	(0.08)	**−0.29**	(0.11)
Age/10	**1.75**	(0.05)	**0.58**	(0.05)	**2.47**	(0.09)	**1.44**	(0.10)
(Age/10)^2	**−0.18**	(0.01)	**−0.06**	(0.01)	**−0.25**	(0.01)	**−0.16**	(0.01)
Marital status								
Married/common law	**0.11**	(0.02)	**−0.04**	(0.02)	**0.72**	(0.04)	0.08	(0.04)
Divorced etc	−0.01	(0.03)	0.00	(0.03)	**0.25**	(0.05)	−0.04	(0.06)
Single	0		0		0		0	
Qualifications								
Primary or none	**−2.26**	(0.06)	**−1.44**	(0.04)	**−0.66**	(0.05)	**−0.52**	(0.07)
Incomplete secondary	**−1.01**	(0.02)	**−0.61**	(0.02)	**−0.49**	(0.03)	**−0.34**	(0.04)
Full secondary	0		0		0		0	
Some tertiary	**1.28**	(0.02)	**0.64**	(0.02)	**0.85**	(0.03)	**0.45**	(0.04)
Full tertiary	**2.95**	(0.03)	**0.92**	(0.03)	**1.46**	(0.03)	**0.91**	(0.06)
Chi-square (d.f.)					52,936.645 (220)			
N					181,127			

is considerably larger than that which we found previously with respect to unemployment. If we carry out a formal test of generational differences as we did for employment we find that for first-generation men the parameter estimate is −0.10 (s.e. 0.03) while for the second generation it is +0.38 (s.e. 0.03), both being contrasted with the third generation. In the case of women the difference is even larger with estimates of −0.53 (s.e. 0.03) and +0.43 (s.e. 0.03) for the first and second generations respectively. (Similar patterns hold for the routine nonmanual class.) This suggests that the second generation is more successful than either the first or later generations, a pattern that has been found in the USA as well. One possible interpretation of this is that the first, immigrant generation is positively selected with unusual levels of drive and ambition but is unable to translate this into economic success perhaps because of the handicaps imposed through foreign qualifications or lack of fluency in English. The second generation does not have the same handicaps but is influenced by the ambition and drive of their parents to excel in the labour market. By the time of the third generation, however, there is some 'regression to the mean' as the grandchildren of the original immigrants become more fully assimilated and culturally indistinct from the charter population. To be sure, our evidence on the third and later generations is restricted to the longer-established groups of European ancestry and we have no way of knowing whether this pattern of 'regression to the mean' will also apply to the groups from non-European origins.

Finally, we should note that Aboriginals show significant ethnic penalties for all outcomes, reinforcing the pessimistic account of Aboriginal fortunes that we have already obtained from our analyses of economic activity and employment.

Are these interethnic differences in occupational attainment complicated by differential returns to education? Tables 5.7A and 5.7B show the significant interactions between ethnicity and education. Again, exactly as with unemployment, we find a considerable number of negative interactions indicative of lower returns to education in the first generation. These are particularly prevalent among men in access to skilled manual work, where all the visible minorities—Lebanese, Chinese, Indians, Caribbeans, Africans and Filipinos—experience significantly lower returns on their educational investments than does the reference group. However, this pattern is not apparent in the second or in later

CANADA: INCLUSION FOR ALL BUT ABORIGINALS 209

Table 5.7A. Differential returns to education: Men (parameter estimates).

	Salariat		RNM		PB		Skilled manual	
Main effects of ancestry								
German 1	−0.24	(0.16)	−0.27	(0.17)	**0.55**	(0.13)	0.24	(0.13)
Polish 1	**−0.63**	(0.13)	**−0.67**	(0.13)	0.03	(0.12)	0.08	(0.10)
Jewish 1	**0.84**	(0.24)	**0.57**	(0.25)	**1.38**	(0.24)	−0.31	(0.33)
Lebanese 1	0.15	(0.16)	0.18	(0.16)	**0.83**	(0.15)	**−0.51**	(0.19)
Chinese 1	0.08	(0.06)	**0.59**	(0.05)	**0.21**	(0.06)	**−0.58**	(0.07)
Indian 1	**−0.89**	(0.07)	**−0.58**	(0.06)	**−0.50**	(0.07)	**−0.78**	(0.07)
Caribbean 1	**−0.81**	(0.10)	**−0.21**	(0.08)	**−0.99**	(0.11)	**−0.33**	(0.08)
African 1	**−0.83**	(0.13)	**−0.48**	(0.11)	**−0.77**	(0.14)	**−0.98**	(0.13)
Filipino 1	**−1.04**	(0.11)	**−0.47**	(0.10)	**−1.89**	(0.19)	**−0.73**	(0.11)
Irish 2	**0.46**	(0.21)	0.34	(0.21)	−0.13	(0.30)	0.28	(0.23)
German 2	0.13	(0.11)	−0.09	(0.12)	**0.46**	(0.11)	0.18	(0.11)
Ukrainian 2	0.03	(0.26)	0.20	(0.26)	**0.64**	(0.23)	−0.01	(0.28)
Italian 2	**0.32**	(0.07)	**0.34**	(0.07)	**0.57**	(0.08)	**0.14**	(0.07)
French 3	**−0.23**	(0.05)	−0.09	(0.05)	**−0.17**	(0.05)	−0.06	(0.05)
Canadian 3	**−0.40**	(0.03)	**−0.25**	(0.03)	**−0.26**	(0.03)	−0.04	(0.03)
Multiple charter 3	**−0.22**	(0.03)	**−0.10**	(0.03)	**−0.23**	(0.04)	**−0.08**	(0.03)
Irish 3	−0.09	(0.07)	0.02	(0.07)	−0.09	(0.08)	0.08	(0.07)
German 3	**−0.15**	(0.07)	**−0.30**	(0.07)	**0.64**	(0.07)	**0.16**	(0.06)
Aboriginal 3	**−0.46**	(0.07)	**−0.57**	(0.07)	**−1.03**	(0.10)	**−0.36**	(0.07)
Multiple Aboriginal 3	**−0.44**	(0.06)	**−0.19**	(0.05)	**−0.34**	(0.07)	**−0.13**	(0.05)
Ancestry/education interactions								
German 1	**0.35**	(0.13)	**0.34**	(0.14)	**0.24**	(0.11)	−0.01	(0.11)
Polish 1	**−0.29**	(0.10)	**−0.31**	(0.13)	−0.12	(0.11)	**−0.33**	(0.10)
Jewish 1	**−0.46**	(0.19)	**−0.56**	(0.22)	**−0.39**	(0.19)	−0.58	(0.31)
Lebanese 1	−0.08	(0.14)	−0.15	(0.15)	−0.03	(0.13)	**−0.61**	(0.17)
Chinese 1	**−0.13**	(0.05)	**−0.36**	(0.05)	−0.08	(0.05)	**−0.20**	(0.06)
Indian 1	**−0.18**	(0.05)	−0.04	(0.05)	−0.10	(0.05)	**−0.15**	(0.06)
Caribbean 1	0.11	(0.09)	0.14	(0.08)	−0.04	(0.11)	**−0.26**	(0.08)

Table 5.7A. Differential returns to education: Men (parameter estimates) (cont.)

	Salariat		RNM		PB		Skilled manual	
African 1	−0.28	(0.10)	−0.17	(0.10)	−0.42	(0.11)	−0.38	(0.12)
Filipino 1	−0.76	(0.08)	−0.33	(0.08)	−0.49	(0.15)	−0.26	(0.10)
Irish 2	−0.46	(0.19)	−0.44	(0.22)	−0.21	(0.28)	−0.12	(0.23)
German 2	0.03	(0.10)	0.17	(0.12)	−0.25	(0.10)	0.07	(0.11)
Ukrainian 2	0.40	(0.24)	0.25	(0.25)	0.10	(0.22)	0.59	(0.27)
Italian 2	−0.04	(0.07)	0.01	(0.07)	−0.18	(0.08)	−0.14	(0.08)
French 3	0.25	(0.05)	0.18	(0.05)	0.02	(0.05)	−0.01	(0.05)
Canadian 3	0.13	(0.03)	0.10	(0.03)	−0.08	(0.03)	−0.05	(0.03)
Multiple charter 3	0.12	(0.03)	0.07	(0.03)	0.01	(0.04)	−0.03	(0.03)
Irish 3	−0.02	(0.07)	0.14	(0.07)	0.04	(0.08)	−0.06	(0.07)
German 3	−0.04	(0.06)	0.10	(0.07)	−0.32	(0.06)	0.05	(0.06)
Aboriginal 3	−0.34	(0.07)	−0.04	(0.07)	−0.25	(0.09)	−0.21	(0.06)
Chi-square (d.f.)			74,600.396 (408)					
N			194,629					

Source: Statistics Canada, 2001 Census (PUMF), 95M0016XCB.

CANADA: INCLUSION FOR ALL BUT ABORIGINALS   211

Table 5.7B. Differential returns to education: Women (parameter estimates)

	Salariat		RNM		PB		Skilled manual	
Main effects of ancestry								
Ukrainian 1	−0.46	(0.26)	−0.76	(0.26)	−1.01	(0.45)	−1.80	(1.00)
Polish 1	−1.09	(0.12)	−0.86	(0.10)	−0.85	(0.17)	−0.27	(0.17)
Italian 1	−0.05	(0.13)	0.01	(0.12)	−0.11	(0.16)	−0.02	(0.22)
Lebanese 1	0.10	(0.23)	0.35	(0.20)	0.75	(0.25)	0.24	(0.37)
Chinese 1	−0.85	(0.06)	−0.61	(0.05)	−0.45	(0.07)	−0.55	(0.10)
Indian 1	−1.28	(0.07)	−1.02	(0.06)	−1.20	(0.10)	−0.80	(0.12)
Caribbean 1	−0.87	(0.08)	−0.53	(0.07)	−1.49	(0.15)	−0.27	(0.13)
African 1	−1.22	(0.13)	−0.75	(0.10)	−1.15	(0.20)	−1.02	(0.26)
Filipino 1	−1.27	(0.10)	−0.61	(0.08)	−1.49	(0.16)	−0.74	(0.17)
Italian 2	0.82	(0.09)	0.61	(0.09)	0.18	(0.15)	0.49	(0.16)
French 3	−0.14	(0.06)	−0.07	(0.05)	−0.20	(0.08)	−0.18	(0.10)
Canadian 3	−0.23	(0.03)	−0.17	(0.03)	−0.28	(0.05)	−0.09	(0.06)
German 3	0.17	(0.08)	0.14	(0.08)	0.65	(0.10)	0.22	(0.14)
Aboriginal 3	−0.13	(0.07)	−0.27	(0.07)	−0.73	(0.13)	−0.60	(0.16)
Ancestry/education interactions								
Ukrainian 1	−0.96	(0.19)	−0.28	(0.20)	−0.67	(0.33)	−0.18	(0.70)
Polish 1	−0.20	(0.11)	−0.09	(0.10)	−0.04	(0.15)	−0.34	(0.17)
Italian 1	0.15	(0.10)	0.20	(0.09)	0.17	(0.11)	0.11	(0.16)
Lebanese 1	−0.33	(0.19)	−0.33	(0.18)	−0.41	(0.21)	−0.08	(0.31)
Chinese 1	0.06	(0.05)	0.15	(0.05)	0.00	(0.06)	−0.07	(0.09)
Indian 1	−0.28	(0.06)	0.05	(0.05)	−0.05	(0.08)	−0.07	(0.10)
Caribbean 1	0.10	(0.08)	0.22	(0.07)	0.14	(0.14)	0.26	(0.13)
African 1	0.01	(0.12)	0.13	(0.10)	−0.45	(0.18)	0.17	(0.24)
Filipino 1	−0.58	(0.07)	0.01	(0.06)	−0.43	(0.12)	−0.14	(0.13)
Italian 2	−0.02	(0.10)	0.22	(0.10)	0.16	(0.14)	0.47	(0.16)

Table 5.7B. Differential returns to education: Women (parameter estimates) (cont.)

	Salariat		RNM		PB		Skilled manual	
French 3	**0.23**	(0.06)	0.06	(0.05)	−0.04	(0.07)	**0.24**	(0.10)
Canadian 3	**0.11**	(0.04)	0.00	(0.03)	0.00	(0.05)	0.06	(0.06)
German 3	0.03	(0.08)	0.10	(0.07)	**−0.57**	(0.09)	−0.02	(0.13)
Aboriginal 3	**−0.18**	(0.07)	−0.13	(0.07)	**−0.38**	(0.11)	**0.40**	(0.15)
Chi-square (d.f.)				53,645.002 (408)				
N				181,127				

Source: Statistics Canada, 2001 Census (PUMF), 95M0016XCB.

generations,[8] nor is it so apparent for women. The most likely interpretation is that foreign qualifications from non-European countries do not have the same value in the Canadian labour market as do domestic or European qualifications.

Once again, however, we find a different and much more pessimistic picture for Aboriginals. Aboriginal men in particular display a pattern of significant negative interactions as well as negative main effects. This clearly cannot be attributed to foreign qualifications and suggests a more fundamental process of disadvantage and social exclusion, perhaps resulting from their geographical concentration in regions where there are few opportunities for economic advance for the highly educated.

Conclusion

With the caveat in mind that the second-generation referred to in this chapter is not composed of the offspring of the current first-generation but is the offspring of older waves of immigrants, this chapter sought to answer four questions. First, do the second generation fare better than the first generation in terms of their access to employment and occupational attainment? Secondly, for which ethnic groups is that generational trend present, absent or reversed? Thirdly, are differential returns to education likely to be a part of the reason behind the interethnic patterns? Finally, are these generational and ethno-generational patterns different between women and men?

Regarding the first question, overall the second-generation ethnic groups fared better than the first-generation groups on both access to employment and occupational attainment. This was particularly noticeable in the case of occupational attainment, where the second generation were noticeably more successful than either the first or the third (and later) generations. As we suggested, this second-generation success may be because they have inherited the drive and determination of their parents and have not yet fully assimilated into the charter populations.

---

[8] However, we should note that the sample sizes for the second-generation groups tend to be somewhat smaller in the case of the visible minorities than those for the first generation (see Table 5.1). One will thus be less likely to find significant interaction effects in the second generation than in the first. Inspection of the standard errors in Tables 5.7A and 5.7B, however, suggests that there is a real difference between the generations and that this is not simply a methodological artefact.

One problem with our analysis, as we have repeatedly emphasised, is that our first generation are not the parents of the second generation and include recent arrivals. Recent arrivals may have particular difficulties in the labour market as they have had little time to learn about the workings of the Canadian labour market and little opportunity to acquire Canadian work experience. However, over the course of their careers they may gradually improve their position, so it may be somewhat misleading to see the improvement between the first and second generations as wholly generational in character since it may in part reflect life-cycle phenomena as the migrants gradually 'acculturate' the longer they stay in Canada.[9] We can check on this argument by excluding recent arrivals from our analysis of the first generation. When we do so, we find that the apparent generational improvement with respect to employment disappears while that with respect to access to the salariat remains quite substantial and highly significant (albeit somewhat reduced in magnitude).[10] This confirms the hypothesis that recent arrivals have particular difficulties in the labour market but suggests that there may nonetheless be real generational improvement in occupational attainment.

Is this pattern of intergenerational 'improvement' in access to the salariat consistently present for all ethnic groups? Tables 5.8A and 5.8B summarise the intergenerational patterns in the ethnic penalties for access to the salariat for men and women respectively. Among the nine cells of these three-by-three tables, those in the top-left to bottom-right diagonal cells show no intergenerational difference: if their first generation showed a significant ethnic 'premium', the second generation did so too; if the first generation showed a significant ethnic penalty, the second generation did too, and so on. The groups in the three cells below that diagonal line are those for whom the aforementioned generational 'improvement' holds true: the second generation fared better than the first generation. Finally, the groups in the three cells above the diagonal line are those for whom generational 'deterioration' occurred, where the second generation fared

---

[9] In the American literature it has been suggested that there has been a deterioration over time in the 'quality' of immigrants to the USA. This would of course further invalidate any comparison of the first and second generations as indicative of change between parents and children. However, there has been no suggestion that this deterioration in quality applies to Canada. See Borjas 1993; Reitz 1998.

[10] If we exclude from the first generation those who arrived after 1980, we find that for men with respect to employment the first generation parameter estimate is 0.03 (s.e. 0.06) and for the second generation 0.05 (s.e. 0.05) while for women the coefficients are -0.11 (s.e. 0.06) and 0.00 (s.e. 0.05) respectively. With respect to access to the salariat the coefficients for men are $+0.03$ (s.e. 0.04) and 0.33 (s.e. 0.04) while for women they are -0.37 (s.e. 0.04) and 0.33 (s.e. 0.03).

worse than the respective first generation. The results shown in these tables are those obtained when arrivals post-1980 are excluded from the first generation so that we do not confuse intergenerational change with gradual acculturation by new immigrants the longer they stay in Canada.[11]

The striking feature shown in these tables is that every single group that had experienced an ethnic penalty in the first generation has improved its position in the second generation, moving either to being not significantly different from the reference group of third-generation British (Poles, Caribbeans and the composite group of other single ancestries in the case of men) or significantly surpassing them (Indian and Filipino men).[12] In contrast, most groups that were competing on equal terms with the charter populations in the first generation (French, Irish, German, Ukrainian, Lebanese and African men) have remained in that situation. In other words, the intergenerational improvement has been most marked among those groups that were most disadvantaged in the first generation. A similar pattern holds for women although in the case of women even more groups have moved from significant negative estimates in the first generation to significant positive ones in the second.

Is this encouraging story undermined by differing returns to education? As we saw earlier, a number of groups obtained lower returns on their educational investments in the first generation but only one—the Irish men—received significantly lower returns in the second generation. In other words, highly qualified members of the first generation tended to have even larger disadvantages than those on which Table 5.8A is based. Since it is the highly qualified who are best placed to enter the salariat, this in effect means that the generational progress is even greater than apparent from Table 5.8A.

On the final question of gender, the answer is that the process of ethnic stratification appears to operate very similarly for women and men.

---

[11] The groups which changed the cell of the table in which they are located once recent arrivals are excluded are in the case of men: French (first-generation estimate not significant after exclusions), Irish (first-generation estimate no longer significant), Ukrainian (first-generation estimate substantially reduced and no longer significant), African (first-generation estimate substantially reduced and no longer significant). There were only two changes in cell location for women after the exclusion of recent arrivals: Irish (first-generation estimate no longer significant after exclusions) and Ukrainian (first-generation estimate substantially reduced and no longer significant).

[12] It is important to recognise that one parameter estimate may not be significantly different from zero and a second one be significantly different from zero, but the two estimates need not necessarily be significantly different from each other. We have therefore checked for this and in all five cases mentioned the inter-generational change in the estimate is statistically significant.

Table 5.8A. Ethnic penalties in access to the salariat: Men.

		Second generation		
		Positive	Not significantly different from zero	Negative
First generation	Positive	British Jewish Chinese		
	Not different from zero	Italian	French Irish German Ukrainian Lebanese African	
	Negative	Indian Filipino	Polish Caribbean Other single	

Table 5.8B. Ethnic penalties in access to the salariat: Women.

		Second generation		
		Positive	Not significantly different from zero	Negative
First generation	Positive	British Jewish		
	Not different from zero	German Irish	French Ukrainian Lebanese	
	Negative	Italian Chinese Indian Caribbean Other single	Polish African Filipino	

While, as might be expected given the very large number of coefficients being estimated, a number of ethnic group coefficients vary by gender, there is no general pattern either for men's coefficients to be larger than the women's or for particular groups of men (e.g. visible minorities) to show distinctive patterns of gender inequality.

Overall, then, ethnic groups in Canada have shown remarkable success in the second generation, most groups in net terms equalling or surpassing the third-generation British. While a number of visible minority groups in the first generation experience substantial disadvantages, in the second generation the one clearly disadvantaged group are the

Caribbeans where both men and women experience substantial and statistically significant disadvantages with respect to employment.

Whether this success of the second generation is due to Canadian policies of multiculturalism or to the lagged effects of the 'point system' for entry is impossible to determine from these data. We have also checked to see whether these patterns vary between Quebec and the other provinces of Canada and we find that the results are broadly consistent across provinces, with much the same patterns of generational improvement and ethnic disadvantage in Quebec as in the rest of Canada.

Finally, we must conclude by emphasising the major disadvantages that continue to be experienced by the Aboriginals. The possible benefits of multiculturalism do not appear to apply to the indigenous peoples.

Appendix

Table 5.A1. Differential returns to education with respect to employment (parameter estimates: contrasts with unemployment).

	Men		Women	
Intercept	**1.39**	(0.14)		
Ancestry				
British 3	0		0	
British 1	0.11	(0.11)	0.19	(0.13)
Irish 1	**1.11**	(0.29)	−0.06	(0.31)
German 1	**0.42**	(0.20)	−0.04	(0.20)
Polish 1	0.10	(0.15)	−0.08	(0.19)
Italian 1	**0.50**	(0.16)	0.06	(0.17)
Jewish 1	0.92	(0.30)	0.13	(0.46)
Chinese 1	**−0.25**	(0.07)	**−0.45**	(0.07)
Indian 1	**−0.19**	(0.08)	**−0.74**	(0.08)
Caribbean 1	−0.14	(0.09)	**−0.60**	(0.09)
African 1	**−0.68**	(0.12)	**−1.02**	(0.13)
Filipino 1	−0.07	(0.12)	0.16	(0.16)
Irish 2	0.39	(0.36)	0.50	(0.50)
German 2	**0.60**	(0.21)	**0.99**	(0.31)
Caribbean 2	**−0.48**	(0.21)	**−0.51**	(0.22)
Multiple charter 3	**−0.27**	(0.05)	**−0.25**	(0.05)
German 3	**0.41**	(0.12)	**0.38**	(0.13)
Significant interactions with education				
British 3	0		0	
British 1	−0.15	(0.10)	**−0.25**	(0.11)
Irish 1	**−0.84**	(0.41)	−0.05	(0.28)
German 1	**−0.40**	(0.16)	−0.18	(0.16)
Polish 1	−0.14	(0.15)	**−0.36**	(0.16)
Italian 1	**−0.33**	(0.11)	−0.16	(0.13)

Table 5.A1. Differential returns to education with respect to employment (parameter estimates: Contrasts with unemployment). (*cont.*)

	Men		Women	
Jewish 1	**−0.73**	(0.35)	−0.29	(0.30)
Chinese 1	**−0.34**	(0.13)	−0.20	(0.20)
Indian 1	**−0.36**	(0.06)	**−0.28**	(0.06)
Caribbean 1	**−0.18**	(0.07)	**−0.21**	(0.06)
African 1	**−0.23**	(0.10)	−0.03	(0.08)
Filipino 1	**−0.40**	(0.10)	**−0.42**	(0.11)
British 2	**−0.59**	(0.30)	**−0.42**	(0.39)
Irish 2	−0.15	(0.16)	**−0.76**	(0.23)
German 2	**0.52**	(0.21)	0.07	(0.21)
Caribbean 2	0.07	(0.04)	**0.11**	(0.05)
Multiple charter 3	**−0.19**	(0.09)	−0.16	(0.11)
German 3	**−0.44**	(0.04)	**−0.35**	(0.05)
Chi-square (d.f.)	5,115.1 (102)		3,032.1 (102)	
N	181,848		160,373	

Note: Emboldened coefficients indicate significance at the 0.05 level or better; standard errors are given in parentheses.
Source: *Statistics Canada*, 2001 Census (PUMF), 95M0016XCB.

References

Angelini, P. U. and Broderick, M. (1997), 'Race and Ethnicity: the obvious diversity'. In P. U. Angelini (ed.), *Our Society: Human Diversity in Canada* (Toronto: Nelson), pp. 105–29.

Borjas, G. J. (1993), 'Immigration policy, national origin, and immigrant skills: a comparison of Canada and the United States'. In D. Card and R. B. Freeman (eds.), *Small Differences that Matter: Labor Markets and Income Maintenance in Canada and the United States* (Chicago: University of Chicago Press), pp. 21–43.

Boyd, M. (1999), 'Canadian eh? Ethnic origin shifts in the Canadian census'. *Canadian Ethnic Studies*, 31, 1–19.

Boyd, M. and Norris, D. (2001), 'Who are the "Canadian"? Changing census responses, 1981–1996'. *Canadian Ethnic Studies*, 33, 1–24.

Citizenship and Immigration Canada (2004), *Facts and figures 2003: Immigration overview* (Ottowa: Minister of Public Works and Government Services Canada).

Darroch, G. A. (1979), 'Another look at ethnicity: stratification and social mobility in Canada'. *Canadian Journal of Sociology*, 4, 1–25.

D'Costa, R. (2000), 'Canadian immigration policy: a chronological review with particular reference to discrimination'. In O. P. Dwivedi, R. D'Costa, C. Lloyd Standford and E. Tepper (eds.), *Canada 2000: Race Relations and Public Policy*. Conference Proceedings. Guelph: Department of Political Studies, University of Guelph, pp. 44–52.

Driedger, L. (1996), *Multi-Ethnic Canada: Identities and Inequalities* (Toronto: Oxford University Press).

Driedger, L. (2001), 'Changing visions in ethnic relations'. *Canadian Journal of Sociology*, 26, 421–51.

Fleras, A. and Elliott, J. L. (1996), *Unequal Relations: An Introduction to Race, Ethnic and Aboriginal Dynamics in Canada*. 2nd edn. (Scarborough, ON: Prentice Hall Canada).

Garcea, J. (2003), 'The construction and constitutionalization of Canada's citizenship regime: reconciliation of diversity and equality', *Canadian Diversity/Diversité canadienne*, 2, 59–64.

Geschwender, J. A. and Guppy, N. (1995), 'Ethnicity, Educational Attainment, and Earned Income among Canadian-born Men and Women'. *Canadian Ethnic Studies*, 27, 67–83.

Herberg, E. N. (1989), *Ethnic Groups in Canada: Adaptations and Transitions* (Scarborough, ON: Nelson Canada).

Isajiw, W. W. (1999). *Understanding Diversity: Ethnicity and Race in the Canadian Context* (Toronto: Thompson Educational Publishing).

Kalbach, M. A. and Kalbach, W. E. (1999). 'Becoming Canada: Problems of an Emerging Identity', *Canadian Ethnic Studies*, 31, 1–16.

Kelley, N. and Trebilcock, M. (2000), *The Making of the Mosaic: A History of Canadian Immigration Policy* (Toronto: University of Toronto Press).

Knowles, V. (1997), *Strangers at Our Gates: Canadian Immigration and Immigration Policy, 1540–1997*. Rev. edn. (Toronto: Dundurn Press).

Kurian, G. (1991), 'South Asians in Canada', *International Migration*, 29, 421–33.

Nakhaie, M. R. (1995), 'Ownership and Management Position of Canadian Ethnic Groups in 1973 and 1989', *Canadian Journal of Sociology*, 20, 167–92.

Porter, J. (1965), *Vertical Mosaic: An Analysis of Social Class and Power in Canada* (Toronto: University of Toronto Press).

Reitz, J. (1988), 'The Institutional Structure of Immigration as a Determinant of Inter-Racial Competition: A Comparison of Britain and Canada', *International Migration Review*, 22, 117–46.

Reitz, J. G. (1998), *Warmth of the Welcome: The Social Causes of Economic Success for Immigrants in Different Nations and Cities* (Boulder, Colorado: Westview Press).

Richmond, A. H. (1986), 'Ethnogenerational Variation in Educational Achievement', *Canadian Ethnic Studies*, 18, 75–89.

Richmond, A. H. (1990), 'Race Relations and Immigration: A Comparative Perspective', *International Journal of Comparative Sociology*, 31, 156–76.

Roberts, L. W. and Clifton, R. A. (1990), 'Multiculturalism in Canada: A Sociological Perspective'. In P. S. Li (ed.), *Race and Ethnic Relations in Canada* (Toronto: Oxford University Press), pp. 120–47.

Satzewich, V. (1990), 'Rethinking Post-1945 Migration to Canada: Towards a Political Economy of Labour Migration', *International Migration*, 28, 327–45.

Simmons, A. B. (1999), 'Immigration Policy: Imagined Futures'. In S. S. Halli and L. Driedger (eds.), *Immigrant Canada: Demographic, Economic, and Social Challenges* (Toronto: Toronto University Press), pp. 21–50.

Statistics Canada (1999), *1996 Census Dictionary*, final edn. (Ottawa): Minister of Industry).

Tastsoglou, E. and Stubos, G. (1992), 'The Greek Immigrant Family in the United States and Canada: The Transformation from an "Institutional" to "Relational" Form, 1945–1970', *International Migration*, 30, 155–73.

Taylor, K. W. (1991), 'Racism in Canadian Immigration Policy'. *Canadian Ethnic Studies*, 23, 1–20.

Yu, S. (2004), *Economic success and socio-cultural retention among native-born ethnic groups in Canada and Britain*. D.Phil. thesis. Oxford: Department of Sociology, University of Oxford.

6

Is French Society Truly Assimilative? Immigrant Parents and Offspring on the French Labour Market

ROXANE SILBERMAN & IRENE FOURNIER[1]

Summary. France is unusual among Western European countries in having experienced net immigration for much of the twentieth century. Migrants have come from three main sources, firstly from other European countries (especially Portugal), second from former French territories and colonies in Maghreb, Sub-Saharan Africa and South East Asia, and thirdly from some less-developed non-European countries in the Near East. It is also important to distinguish Repatriates (of European origin) from other migrants from the Maghreb. France's 'Republican Model' of assimilation runs counter to the active recognition of distinct ethnic groups but a number of datasets enable us to identify with reasonable accuracy the major second-generation groups. The French data also enable us to distinguish the natural parents of the second generation, thus enabling a precise generational comparison to be made. The results of this comparison indicate that, while the second generation have made considerable absolute gains in educational and occupational level, in relative terms the second-generation Maghrebins remain just as disadvantaged as their parents. Groups of European ancestry on the other hand experience much reduced ethnic penalties, and in several cases no penalty at all.

---

[1] The authors thank Anthony Heath for his help in dealing with some methodological problems: his contribution to this chapter has been considerable.

Introduction

UNLIKE MANY OTHER EUROPEAN COUNTRIES WHICH only first hosting immigrants after 1945, immigration has been a permanent feature of France since the late nineteenth century. In the 1920s foreigners accounted for over 7% of the population, thus putting France on the highest rate after the USA (Tapinos 1975; Noiriel 1988). After a decline, the proportion recovered to the 7% level in the 1960s. By the close of the twentieth century an estimated 25% of the population was either an immigrant or had at least one parent or grandparent born abroad (Tribalat 1991*a*).

However, only recently has anyone wondered about the outcomes experienced by the second generation or about the ethnic penalties facing particular groups of immigrants and their offspring. Despite a long history of xenophobia (Noiriel 1988; Schor 1985), France sees itself as an assimilative society and presents itself as such. It was long held that the French school system and relatively accessible citizenship would ensure adequate mechanisms for full assimilation, defined as the disappearance of any distinctive ethnic trait or even the loss of memory of any ethnic origin (Renan 1882). This largely explains the long delay in raising the issue of whether ethnic penalties affected any more or less visible ethnic minorities.

Nonetheless, the issue did emerge in the late 1980s when second-generation Maghrebins and their peers from elsewhere began experiencing difficulties in the suburbs, triggering defensive responses. Heated debate developed between supporters of the so-called Republican Model who held that ethnic origins were a personal matter (Schnapper 1991) and advocates of a more open model based on multiculturalism (Lapeyronnie 1993; Wieviorka 1996). This debate clouded research and discussion of the condition of the second generation and the touchy question of any discrimination that they might be experiencing. There was even dispute over distinguishing the second generation by country of birth or citizenship at birth since that might negate the value of French citizenship subsequently acquired by naturalisation or might be thought to give official recognition to second-class citizenship based on ethnic origin.

Nonetheless, the obvious handicaps facing neighbourhoods with high proportions of first and second-generation minority groups triggered research in the mid-1980s just as new variables were coming online to better identify minorities in major national surveys. This research was of two broad types: the first focused on access to education and stressed that, encouraged by their parents' hopes for upward social mobility, the second-generation groups scored at least as well as native French children of comparable social origin (Mingat 1984; Boulot & Fradet 1988; Vallet & Caille 1996; Brinbaum 2002; Brinbaum & Kieffer 2005). Along the same lines, research also focused on the success stories of some second-generation groups despite the stigma of immigration (Zeroulou 1988; Santelli 2001). A different stream of research examined how strong conflict situations develop within the school and on the streets where high aspirations meet the reality of the educational selection process (Van Zanten 2001) and where such conflict could reinforce stigmatisation in a context of long-term hostility towards Maghrebins and certain others, as consistently shown in surveys since 1945 (Girard & Stoetzel 1953; Mayer 1994).

Turning now to the outcomes on the job market, research converges on the finding that differences in diploma levels or social capital fail to explain entirely the obstacles facing these groups on a job market that has been ever slacker since the late 1970s. Research also consistently reports a contrast between second-generation Maghrebins facing a strong ethnic penalty and second-generation Southern Europeans who secure jobs more easily despite low scholastic achievements (Richard 1997; Silberman & Fournier 1999 and 2006; Meurs, Pailhé & Simon 2006; Silberman, Alba and Fournier 2007). This parallels findings for the first generation (Dayan, Échardour & Glaude 1996).

The analyses presented in this chapter hope to expand the scope of research in three ways: firstly, our analyses include second-generation groups from the latest migration waves who are only now entering the job market, thus enabling us to get new insights on the varying paths of assimilation trodden by a wide variety of groups rather than restricting ourselves to the contrast between South Europeans and Maghrebins as in previous research; second, our analyses compare the current first and second generations as in the other chapters of this book, but we are also able to extend this by comparing the current second generation with their natural parents; and, third, our analyses incorporate methodological adjustments to enable comparison with data from other host countries in order to set our understanding of the assimilation process and of the Republican Model within a comparative framework.

Overview of immigration to France

Most West European countries only saw immigrants in any large number from the 1960s onwards while France has seen several major waves since 1880. The reasons for the early start and persistence over time of migration to France are subjects of discussion: the most frequently cited factors are the precocious decline in domestic birth rates and labour shortages. Both these factors were grounded in the long term effects of the French Revolution of 1789, which rooted rural populations into small farm ownership, restricting their birth rates to contain the effect of inheritance laws that induced subdivision of land among heirs, finally making them unavailable for industrialisation of the economy.

While immigration from neighbouring Belgium, Italy and Spain has been a permanent feature of French history, a new wave that arrived before the First World War included migrants from Central Europe who either continued to the USA or settled in France. The First World War stimulated immigration and saw arrivals from a wider variety of origins who found work in farms and arms factories, where they replaced manpower drafted into the army to serve in the trenches. This period also witnessed the first arrivals from French-ruled North Africa. The end of the war saw a surge of immigration from Belgium, Italy and Poland but also included populations from the French colonies. The 1929 depression reduced, but did not entirely end, these flows despite the growing hostility against foreigners that accompanied the rise of xenophobic political parties and the restricted access to liberal professions, self-employment and freelancing in trades such as film-making. (Essentially the restrictions targeted professions exercised by Jews fleeing the pogroms and Nazism in Eastern Europe.) The Spanish Civil War also drove many of General Franco's opponents into exile just over the border in southern France, where they remain an important component of the local population.

The Second World War brought a halt to immigration until 1945 when national reconstruction and proactive government policy led to the establishment of a National Immigration Office with branch offices abroad. Throughout the 1950s 'populationist' immigration policy sought to boost inflows from European countries and to reduce the massive arrivals from North Africa (Tapinos 1975), which nonetheless continued to climb. Immigration rose to new highs in the early 1970s until the 1974 oil crisis induced a cutback throughout Western Europe. Although labour immigration was officially halted, family dependants could still rejoin established immigrants, despite a failed attempt to cap these entries in

1975. Note that family immigration was in no way a new phenomenon in France as is often suggested nowadays. Families simply became an increasingly visible component when the other flows slowed down. Immigration persisted however: asylum seekers rose to predominate among the legal migration flow while the chronic inflow of illegals continued (Tapinos 1975; Moulier-Boutang, Garson & Silberman 1986), leading to a general amnesty in 1981-2, followed by a succession of small-scale amnesties. At this time an increasing proportion of immigrants came from urban backgrounds, reflecting tougher French immigration policy plus urbanisation and better schooling in the countries of origin. The inflows also included students coming for secondary or tertiary education, especially from the Maghreb and Sub-Saharan Africa.

In the 1990s, inflows increased in size despite the absence of any change in immigration laws and despite growing hostility to aliens and the rise of xenophobic political parties. Moreover, as the authorities became tougher on illegal aliens, some left- and right-wing political leaders began calling for more liberal immigration policy in certain sectors of the job market and even for a radical overhaul of policy, with proposals to base immigration on quotas and selection criteria (Weil 2002).

Today's second generation thus originates in three different types of populations. The largest population comes from the Maghreb, that is ex-French North Africa, led by immigration from Algeria and Morocco dating back to World War I. However, the first major wave of Algerian immigration began after the Second World War when, legally speaking, Algeria was still an integral part of France as a French department. Algerian inflows dropped from 1958, at the start of the Algerian insurgency, until independence in 1962 but Algerians remained a substantial population of the mainland throughout that war. Algerian independence then triggered inflows of French Repatriates (individuals of French or European ancestry) and of Harkis, native Algerians who had served in the French armed forces and who were resettled in remote villages in mainland France where many still live today. For a limited period, non-European Algerians living in France could opt for French nationality while citizenship was automatic for Repatriates, thus cloning the first- and second-class citizenships that had existed in Algeria (in patent violation of the principle of equality enshrined in the Republican Model). After Algerian independence, the vast majority of beneficiaries of the French nationality option were Harkis. Immigration levels then boomed with the liberalisation of French immigration policy until 1973 when Algeria restricted departures on the pretext of rising French racism. At this point, high numbers of dependants arrived to rejoin established immigrant relatives alongside higher inflows from Morocco, stimulated partly by Repatriates from that country. Tunisian immigrants came later; they tended to be relatively well-educated urbanites. The general view however is that Maghrebins do not readily adjust to French society. Many have little schooling and held or hold unskilled jobs in mining and industry. Relatively high percentages of the fathers of the second generation were unemployed or were laid off on early retirement plans: indeed, they were highly vulnerable to the economic restructuring of the 1970s and 1980s. Nonetheless, Maghrebins were entitled to relatively easy access to self-employment and many opted into small business—Algerians tended to open cafés and restaurants while Tunisians preferred grocery shops (rooted in the commercial tradition in the south of Tunisia). These populations also tended to be concentrated in substandard low-income housing projects on the outskirts of cities. It is also important to note that Maghrebins are not homogeneous: strong social, ethnic (for example the distinction between Berbers and Arabs) and historical differences subsist between Algerians, Moroccans and Tunisians, while the Algerian independence war proved particularly gruesome.

Ex-French possessions went on to supply two more major groups. The collapse of the US presence in South East Asia in 1975 largely explains the major inflow of South East Asians. This population comprises Cambodians, Laotians and Vietnamese, some of whom are ethnic Chinese (Ma Mung 2000). Their second-generation members come from parents of widely varying educational or social backgrounds and with far more diverse social status than Maghrebins. In the case of pre-1975 South East Asian immigrants, over one third of their parents held middle or upper-level professional occupations, a proportion that began dipping as the share of economic refugees rose (Tribalat 1995). These populations quickly organised businesses and residential neighbourhoods such as the Chinatown of Paris (rooted in the old as well in the new Chinese immigration), while Maghrebins developed some ethnic neighbourhoods of their own in the capital and in Marseille, although they covered a narrower range of economic activity.

Sub-Saharans are the third population from ex-French possessions, coming especially from Cameroon, Ivory Coast, Mali and Senegal. Many came from rural backgrounds but artisans and craftsmen are not rare. Schooling varies. These second-generation groups are now starting to enter the job market in large numbers. Most of their parents held unskilled jobs in construction and services. The youth constitute a substantial proportion of the non-white component of the national population. It should also be noted that migration from the French Antilles (Guadeloupe and Martinique, two overseas departments of France) and other possessions has also been rising since the 1970s, thus boosting the share of the non-white mainland population working in public hospitals and other government agencies. Yet these non-whites often face discrimination, especially in access to housing. Little comparative analysis is available on the condition of these domestic immigrants from the Antilles and that of foreign immigrants because of French reluctance to identify non-white French citizens as a separate category and create a stigma of second-class citizenship. However, such analysis would be very useful to assess the condition of non-whites in French society today. Recently, a new Black movement, CRAN (Conseil Representatif des Associations Noires) has advocated the identification of Blacks and funded a first poll in order to count this population.

Another very different set of second-generation groups are the offspring of parents who arrived in the 1960s and 1970s from Italy, Spain and Portugal in that order. All three are EU member states today, giving their citizens the right to settle freely and to work in France without holding French citizenship; further immigration from these countries therefore continues although at a lower level. The largest component is Portuguese. Most are skilled workers with an established presence in the construction industry where some have started their own contracting firms. Because of their longstanding presence in France, Portuguese also have the highest share of offspring from intermarriage with French nationals (Silberman & Fournier 2006).

Further second-generation groups are the product of inflows from the Near and Middle East plus more recent arrivals from Poland, Romania and elsewhere in Eastern Europe as well as Yugoslavians who began coming in the 1970s. Turks are currently the most numerous and first arrived in the late 1960s. On the upswing until the 1974 immigration shutdown, Turkish inflows persisted for several years through illegal migration and legal arrivals of dependants. However, Turks are far fewer than in Germany and most have concentrated in Greater Paris or eastern France. The first-generation parents were unskilled workers in factories, small business and the garment industry.

Finally, France has had very small-scale immigration from Mauritius, Pakistan, Sri Lanka and further afield since the 1970s. These second-generation groups too are now on the job market.

Immigrants differentiate strongly according to whether they come from an EU member state, a non-EU member state or an ex-French colony. Second-generation groups also stand apart if they come from a Muslim country, as is often the case. The final consideration that overlaps with the preceding is 'visibility', a term avoided in the French literature which is uncomfortable with such distinctions, although skin color is an obvious target for discrimination (Silberman and Fournier 2006).

Immigration policy

French immigration policy has always been governed and regulated by the needs of the labour market even though it has been a permanent feature of French society, even though many of these immigrants have settled permanently and raised families here, and even though they were encouraged to do so by other national policies aimed at boosting birth rates. Except in the case of political refugees, access to work and residence rights depended on the needs of the labour market throughout the twentieth century. There was no overall policy such as that of Australia, Canada or the USA with any upfront offers of speedy naturalisation and other enticements to settle permanently. Nor were there any free migration rights within a given area of the sort that prevailed between the UK and the Commonwealth. The one major exception was Algeria which was legally part of mainland France until 1962, after which its inhabitants enjoyed special entry privileges until 1973. Somewhat similar provisions also applied to ex-French Sub-Saharan countries albeit more restrictively. Because domestic job market needs determined immigration policy, work and residence permits did not initially entitle their holders to change type of job or area of residence at will. Nor was renewal automatic. Only in 1981 did immigrants become directly eligible for a ten–year permit after an initial permit valid for one year. Immigrants moved through a system of one-, three- and ten-year permits, without automatic entitlement to upgrading at any stage. Upgrades depended principally on the applicant's employment status. Access to self-employment has always been regulated and subject to special authorisation, with exceptions for certain nationalities who also had easier access to dependant visas and other benefits. Restrictions were also the case for family dependants even if entrance was easier than in Germany. Only direct dependants (children under 16 or in some case 18 years old, wife or husband, and dependent parents) were allowed to apply for entry. Entrance was subject to resources and housing.

Access to the labour market was also subject to restrictions for a long time. A great number of family dependants entered illegally and still now we regularly find immigrants' children who have been raised in France but have no legal status as shown by the recent parents' movement to oppose expulsions of children with illegal status in the schools during summer 2006. All of the above fluctuated in line with the mood of diplomatic relations between France and the origin countries, the vital interests of the moment and historical considerations.

France presents as a country where naturalisation comes more easily than was the case in Germany (Brubaker 1992; Schnapper 1991). This is because French law provides for citizenship by right to anyone born on its soil. However, assuming the individual files no objection, citizenship is only conferred at the age of majority, not at birth as in the USA. In the 1980s and 1990s, the French citizenship commission moved to require that individuals had to proactively apply for citizenship in order to receive it; a conservative government later enacted this provision— before it was quickly abrogated by a left government. One contribution to the long-term integration of immigrant offspring was the so-called 'double jus soli' extending automatic citizenship at birth to anyone born in France from at least one French-born parent. This provision was particularly relevant to Algerian immigrants: any such person born in Algeria before independence in 1962 was legally born on French soil and 'double jus soli' entitled his French-born children to automatic citizenship at birth. Despite multiple revisions, other provisions facilitated naturalisation through marriage. Finally, immigrants have the option of including their offspring in their naturalisation applications and registering them at birth as French citizens. All in all, a large proportion of second-generation individuals born in France hold French citizenship once they reach the age of majority, although often no sooner. Other second-generation individuals can also apply for citizenship but, as with the first generation, the procedure is more restrictive and the processing is more arbitrary than widely claimed (Noiriel 1988; Weil 2002).

Conversely, the French authorities are most reluctant to intervene against racial and ethnic discrimination or to set up indicators that would measure its extent although there has been no shortage of commissions, think tanks and official reports.[2] While some legal improvements have

---

[2] Founded in 1989, the Haut conseil à l'integration noted these issues in its annual report. See 'Lutter contre les discriminations: faire respecter le principe d'égalité' (1998). See also the report by J. P. Belorgey 'Lutter contre la discrimination' (1999) commissioned by Social Affairs &

been made regarding the burden of proof (Henry 2001), the number of complaints on file remains ridiculously low (Garner-Moyer 2003). Any policy that smacks of affirmative action (usually translated into French as 'positive discrimination') is considered an unconstitutional violation of the right to equality. Only recently has the Government started to track hiring discrimination with testing methods or operating discrimination awareness campaigns for employers.[3] Alongside this, the major media only started in 2004 to debate public policies to fight discrimination through quotas and other means.[4]

The delayed interest in discrimination is intertwined with public debate about the Republican Model, which became an issue in the 1980s through the activism of SOS Racisme after the immigration shutdown and just when second-generation Maghrebins were entering the job market. Against a backdrop of increasing violence, arson and carjackings in the high-unemployment suburbs of major cities, Dominique Schnapper's book was released, presenting the 'French model of assimilation' as uniquely and diametrically opposed to the German model or the US model with its essential 'multiculturalism'.

That ethnic minorities should become a 'problem' now suggested that the Republican Model was falling apart because it held that ethnic background was supposed to fade away, or at least confine itself to the privacy of the immigrant's home. Debate then shifted imperceptibly from whether it was a matter of public life vs. personal privacy to one of visibility vs. invisibility, triggered by extensive coverage of whether Muslim schoolgirls should wear Islamic headscarves to school. We also find increasing debate

---

Employment Minister Martine Aubry, which led to the creation of the discrimination investigation commission, renamed GELD (Groupe d'etudes et de lutte contre les discriminations) in 2000. It has been operating a toll-free hotline since 2001 for anyone who feels s/he has been a victim of discrimination. For its part, the National Consultative Commission on Human Rights incorporates data in its annual reports on discrimination due to national origin. It commissions annual racism surveys from the CSA polling agency. Finally, a new anti-racism agency, la HALDE (Haute autorité de lutte contre les discriminations et pour l'égalité), was set up in 2004 with very limited means when compared with corresponding organisations in the UK for example.

[3] Testing involved submitting job applications with name changes to employers (Bovenkerk 1992; De Schutter 2001). See also statements by an actual job applicant and graduate of the Institut d'Etudes Politiques (Libération 2004). A recent study by the Observatoire de la Discrimination also found strong discrimination against Maghrebins and a national survey using testing was set up (Cediey and Foroni 2007).

[4] It first became an issue when the topnotch Institut d'Etudes Politiques elected to diversify student intake by proactively seeking out applicants from schools in low-income neighbourhoods.

about the organisational structure of Islam in France and the financing of new mosques or land for Muslim cemeteries. In this context, bids to tighten up naturalisation laws arose alongside particularly heated debate over the legality of wearing Islamic headscarves in secular public school classrooms, an issue unseen anywhere else in Europe with this importance. In 2004, new legislation banned any distinctive religious symbols in the classroom and it was represented as a move to clarify the separation of church and state as well as to support women's rights. In practice, it mostly affected Muslim women, but it required the odd Sikh male to remove his turban too. Other government agencies then chimed in to ban headscarves on the job or when executing official duties or participating in public events such as civil marriages.

This public issue also had some implications for research: second-generation surveys needed grounding in data about parents' country of birth (Tribalat 1989 and 1995) but this upset French 'fade away' assimilationists (Silberman 1989, 1992; Simon 1997*a* and 1998; Héran 2002) and angered colleagues who saw this as a form of racism fraught with risks of stigmatisation (Le Bras 1998) even if the bottom line was merely to map out who discriminates against which generation(s). Recently, the debate seemed to move as shown with the hearings about ethnic variable undertaken in 2006 by the CNIL (Commission Nationale de l'Informatique et des Libertés). But any discussion of preferential quotas in this arena still quickly reaches thermonuclear temperatures.

As battle lines hardened in this debate, xenophobic political parties were gaining ground, which is hardly new to France (Schor 1985) despite the nation's allegedly assimilationist tradition. We need only look back to the de-naturalisation policy of the Vichy Government in the early 1940s. The far-right National Front Party has been an established presence on the political scene since the 1980s and puts anti-immigration legislation at the top of its agenda. That said, the left-wing parties also want shutdowns on immigration and illegal aliens in the name of fighting unemployment and allocating existing resources so as to better integrate established immigrants. Nor did these parties ever deliver once in office on their election promise to grant 'local citizenship' to non-EU alien residents.[5]

---

[5] EU law provides that aliens shall be entitled to vote in local elections if only because they are taxpayers with a right of vote on how their tax euros are spent and by whom, and a prominent right-wing political leader has already openly advocated such voting rights for long-term resident aliens.

Data

The general misconception is that little or no data exist on immigrant populations or their offspring. This is largely due to violent debate about the Republican Model and the ethnic 'fade-away' effect it should engender. However, several researchers argue that long-existing data allowed identification of immigrants, their offspring and nationalities, e.g. census data identifies people born in France and having acquired citizenship at a later date, thereby pinpointing a healthy number of second-generation individuals. Moreover, there is a permanent demographic sample (EDP) that has been matching data for 1% of the population since 1968 and enables follow-up of the second generation, defined as those having at least one foreign-born parent (Tribalat 1991b; Silberman 1992; Héran 2002).

Above all, growing numbers of major government surveys now incorporate indicators that identify immigrants and aliens by place of birth, nationality and date of entry into France as well as second-generation individuals by place of birth and parents' citizenship at birth. Second-generation data has been available since the INSEE (Institute National de la Statistique et des Etudes Economiques) 'Situations Défavorisées' surveys of the 1980s. They further stand out easily in the 1980 panels of the Education Ministry, in the INSEE 'Jeunes et Carrières' surveys or the CEREQ 'Générations' and 'Eva' surveys that track youth job histories from school exit, as well as from the INSEE 'Formation Qualification Professionnelle' surveys since 1993. More recently, the 'Enquête Familiale', run along with the national census, identifies second-generation individuals from demographic indicators and since 2005/6 the Labour Force surveys have questions about parents' country of birth and citizenship. However, France does not classify by ethnic or racial traits and there is widespread opposition to doing so. The recent INSEE 'Histoire de Vie' survey contained questions about perceived identity with very limited investigation of the racial or ethnic dimension and CEREQ (Centre d'Études et de Recherche sur les Qualifications) surveys did ask about perceived discrimination based on skin colour or name. A recent INED survey has investigated how questions about race and ethnicity are perceived (Simon and Clément 2006). However, there is still strong hostility towards introducing any element that will allow identification of the second generation, as witnessed during recent revision of the French census-taking system (Héran 2002). This raises the issue of sample sizes available to researchers using major surveys that cover minorities. Moreover, the

CNIL (Commission Nationale de l'Informatique et des Libertés) data privacy watchdog compounds the difficulty by considering national origin as sensitive information, requiring ever more drastic aggregation of survey data before release to researchers even if discussion seems now to be more opened.

For this chapter we use data from the latest INSEE 'Formation Qualification Professionnelle' survey (2003). This survey of social and professional mobility has been conducted every seven to ten years since 1960 and its results have enabled clear identification of the second generation since 1993. It gives details about respondents' parents and grandparents. It not only lets us compare first and second generations according to place of birth and age at entry into France, it further enables real comparison between parents and offspring. In practice, the current first generation now on the job market are not the parents of the second generation who are also currently on the job market, although they share the same countries of origin. Today's first generation includes immigrants who, at best, only partially resemble the parents of the second generation. First-generation immigrants from some longstanding countries of origin are now rare in France because inflows have ceased and many of the original migrants now exceed the cut-off age used in this study of 59 years.

Population composition

The 2003 survey went back to larger sample sizes after a cutback for the 1993 edition. The number of first- and second-generation respondents is adequate if nationalities are aggregated, as the CNIL watchdog requires anyhow. Unfortunately, due to an error in the questionnaire, date of entry to mainland France was only asked of French citizens living in French overseas departments and was not asked of all respondents born abroad. We resolved this problem by using schooling data that broadly establishes respondent's age at entry to France and distinguishes which foreign-born children were entirely schooled on the mainland. School records note every year of schooling from primary level onwards, including the country in which the schooling occurred. This provides a good idea in certain cases and a rough idea in others of which immigrants entered France at school age. We therefore approximated age at entry through comparison of several different responses. Foreign-born respondents reporting no mainland schooling were classed as having landed after minimum school-leaving age and therefore considered as first generation. Those reporting full schooling abroad were also considered as first generation. Foreign-born respondents reporting full schooling on the mainland were classed as having entered before the age of 6 years, whereas those reporting some mainland schooling were classed according to age at entry as provided through school records; in cases of multiple dates of mainland schooling, we used the earliest date. Immigrants' offspring who were born in France are naturally classified as second generation. Finally, we cross-checked the data against the country of the respondent's first job, causing a few reclassifications. But we cannot establish a precise date of entry for those who entered after completing school or who never went to school, i.e. the first generation.

For international comparisons, we have used the standard definition used in the present volume of a first-generation immigrant as anyone born abroad and entering the host country after the primary school entry age of 5 years; second-generation is anyone entering the country before the age of 6 years or any French-born offspring of foreign-born aliens. We considered someone as second-generation if at least one parent was an immigrant—this is less restrictive than requiring two immigrant parents but offers two interrelated advantages. First, it obtains bigger sample sizes for quantitative analysis. Second, it enables inclusion of older migration waves with high rates of intermarriage. Usually, the North American literature refers to this population as Generation 2.5, just short of Generation 3 where both parents are born in the destination country.

Turning next to our classification of ethnic groups, we take into account both sample sizes and the problems of mandatory CNIL/INSEE pre-release aggregations.[6] We have also retained some smaller groups for their intrinsic comparison value but discarded any results deemed statistically unreliable.

The Maghrebin group covers ex-French Algeria, Morocco and Tunisia with no way of distinguishing individual countries. Delimitation of this group was complicated by the presence of Repatriates, including about 1 million who entered from Algeria alone immediately after independence. Repatriates are mostly Europeans and are quite reliably distinguishable by parental citizenship at birth. They differ widely from the Maghrebins. Fortunately the FQP survey provides the citizenship at birth

---

[6] The authors thank INSEE, the national statistical institute, for adopting our suggestions about aggregation and adjusting its categories.

of the respondent's parent (which is not the case in some other surveys).[7] As a complementary indicator we were also able to use the report about the language that was spoken at home when a child (Arab, Berberian or French).

Southern Europeans form the third group. It covers Italy and Spain, whose nationals first arrived in large numbers during the 1950s and 1960s, with the oldest dating back to before the Second World War. Greece has supplied only a small number of political refugees. However the largest component here is the Portuguese. Unrestricted entry rights now facilitate movement both ways as well as further arrivals.

The East European group covers all ex-Comecon countries, regardless of EU membership status. Poland, Romania and ex-Yugoslavia predominate. This population comes from a wide range of countries and some have a longer history of migration to France than others. The Yugoslavian wave began in the late 1960s/early 1970s. Polish migration dates way back to pre- and post-Second World War waves triggered by Nazism and its aftermath, plus more recent waves now rising sharply. Romanian migration is largely recent, but also incorporates a wartime wave, as holds for the rest of Eastern Europe.

Then we have a population of Sub-Saharan Africans that covers Cameroon, Ivory Coast, Mali, Niger, Senegal and other ex-possessions in Africa. Here we do not distinguish immigrants born abroad according to citizenship at birth. Under colonial rule, entitlement to French citizenship was complex and it would not be feasible to try to distinguish them from Europeans. Moreover the samples would be too small to be useful.

The Near and Middle Eastern group covers an unfortunately more motley mix. For statistical reasons and because of CNIL restrictions, we could not isolate Turks, the largest component of this population, from Lebanese and other nationalities.

South East Asians form the final group. It covers Cambodia, Laos and Vietnam. Sample sizes prohibit a detailed breakdown but this group includes a handful of Europeans who returned to France after decolonisation: as with Sub-Saharan Africa, it is difficult to distinguish individual populations on the basis of place of birth and citizenship at birth.

---

[7] Order of construction begins with immigrants having one or both parents born in North Africa and holding a Maghrebin citizenship at birth, bearing in mind that intermarriages with mainlanders were rare in these populations but common among Repatriates (Alba & Silberman 2002). Next, the Repatriate population covers people of European ancestry, including Jews, some Harkis and a handful of other non-Europeans whose parents held French citizenship at birth. Note that parents' citizenship at birth is based on respondents' answers only.

We have discarded West European immigrants who are very diverse and of less interest Another fringe wave came in from the Indian Ocean during the 1970s and 1980s followed by more recent waves but again numbers are too small and any aggregation with other groups would overdiversify origins and composition.

Table 6.1 gives breakdowns by country of origin and generation for the 17–59 age range in our survey (yielding a sample of 35,065 persons). First- and second-generation respondents total 22.2% of the national population. Maghrebins and South Europeans contain high numbers of long-established first generation individuals, as already noted. The largest group of recent first generation arrivals are the Sub-Saharan Africans. The length of presence in France also explains first/second-generation imbalances between the different populations. Among groups such as Italians, Portuguese and Spaniards over 70% are second-generation. In the case of Maghrebins and other populations with a long-standing presence but still on the job market, or making a comeback to it, the generation balance is about 50%/50%. For recent waves such as the Sub-Saharans, second-generation adults are still scarce. On the other hand, Repatriates exemplify the outcome of a one-off migration wave now largely off the job market where the second generation exceeds 85%. This underscores the imperative to isolate this sizable population from other Maghrebins. We must also pay some attention to the age distribution. We do not provide tables here, but note for instance, that second-generation individuals of the oldest waves (the South Europeans for instance) do have a greater proportion of individuals more that 35 years old than in the recent waves such as the Turks.

Table 6.1. French population (aged 17–59), by origin and generation (percentage of total population (weighted)).

	First generation	Second or later generation	N
Native-born French		76.5	27,290
Maghrebin	2.2	2.2	1,287
Repatriate	0.7	3.9	1,568
South European	1.6	4.9	2,299
East European	0.5	0.9	457
Sub-Saharan African	1.3	0.6	569
Near Eastern	0.6	0.3	274
South East Asian	0.3	0.4	216
Other	1.4	1.8	1,105
Sample N	2,770	32,295	35,065

Source: FQP Survey 2003.

Group characteristics

Education

The populations we compare in this chapter have encountered very different school systems.. There are to be sure considerable methodological difficulties facing an immigration survey trying to pin down scholastic achievement in populations educated abroad in seriously deficient school systems. Like their native French peers, however, the second generation went through the French school system, which has been steadily expanding post-secondary education since the 1950s. Insofar as immigrants belong to populations of longer or shorter presence in France, the profiles of their second-generation members will vary widely in terms of age and their eldest members (whose proportion varies from group to group) will have benefited less from the recent liberalisation of the school system.

To review the French school system briefly, liberalisation (or démocratisation) refers to the major standardisation of education at lower levels, postponement of streaming into academic and vocational tracks until a later stage in the educational process and a multiplication of diplomas at the secondary and tertiary levels. This all started in the 1950s and has educated greater numbers of youth to higher levels of attainment despite continuing inequalities. After standardisation of lower secondary schooling came easier access to upper secondary school diplomas (the baccalauréat), which secured admission to lower tertiary education. Standardisation delayed until later ages the sharp distinction between an academic track leading to academic secondary and tertiary education on the one hand and a shorter vocational track that speedily puts youth on the job market on the other hand. Standardisation of the first two years of lower secondary schooling in the 1960s was extended to the whole lower secondary school in the 1970s, followed by standardisation of the first year of upper secondary schooling. Only later did separation reappear between the academic and vocational tracks leading to lower secondary vocational diplomas such as the CAP (Certificat d'aptitude professionelle) and BEP (Brevet d'etudes professionelles); the separation was accompanied by crossover options. Moreover, as the school system facilitated a wider range of post-secondary options, it became more diverse through a system of elective courses and language options (Duru-Bellat & Kieffer 1999). Numbers of secondary school graduates continued to grow thanks to diversification of diploma types through the creation of vocational and technological baccalaureats, although French graduations still lag behind those of some other countries and France remains well short of graduating 80% of students, a target set by the Education Ministry in 1986. Liberalisation facilitated access to tertiary education, especially through the creation of two-year scientific and technological vocational degrees (the Brevet de technicien superieur (BTS) and the Diplome universitaire de technologie (DUT)). This is in line with a national school system traditionally divided into an academic track leading to tertiary studies and a short, low-prestige vocational track primarily intended for less able students. The new feature is that the lower secondary vocational CAP and BEP or higher secondary vocational and technological diplomas now secure jobs faster and offer better guarantees against unemployment than do comparable academic diplomas; this is even more true for the lower tertiary vocational BTS and DUT. Nevertheless, French upper secondary school diplomas automatically entitle holders to admission to a tertiary institution, but the downside of this policy is very high dropout rates for first and second year students, especially those from working-class families including the second-generation Maghrebins (Beaud 2002). Finally, the surge in women's tertiary enrolments continues (Baudelot and Establet 1992; Duru-Bellat, Kieffer & Marry 2001).

Differences between second-generation groups and other immigrant waves show up imperfectly in the education categories used in this volume for international comparison. They fudge some distinctions in the French school system that would help to differentiate the first and second generations. For example, the primary schooling category lumps together persons having at least some primary schooling with those having none and, as will be seen, this distinction is important in the case of some first-generation groups. The lower secondary category lumps together general school leaving certificates of minimal job-finding value (the Brevet d'Etudes du Premier Cycle (BEPC) with the job-clinching lower vocational CAP and BEP, popular with Portuguese and other ethnic groups. The higher secondary category covers all manner of secondary diplomas (baccalauréats), masking the new vocational and technological diplomas held by younger second-generation individuals—here too certain ethnic groups gravitate towards certain diplomas. The problem recurs at the lower tertiary level. Finally, the upper tertiary category covers all higher degrees including those issued by a core of elite universities (so-called Grandes Ecoles) whose graduates form a distinctly privileged socio-professional class on the job market.

For comparison purposes, our cross-tabulations use the standard classification used in this volume. However, we also provide as an Appendix to this chapter more detailed classifications which yield further insights into differences between groups. We also compare the characteristics of the current first-generation groups with those of the natural parents of the second-generation survey respondents.

Table 6.2A shows the distribution of schooling of the current first-generation men, of the second-generation men, and also of the fathers of the current second generation (who can be thought of as the original first generation). Overall, the current first generation has less education than their native French peers. Among first-generation men, Portuguese and other South Europeans show the highest proportion with little or very little education. Next come Maghrebins and Near Easterners, including

Table 6.2A. Highest educational qualification, by ancestry and generation: Men (row percentages (weighted)).

	Primary or none		Lower secondary	Higher secondary	Lower tertiary	Higher tertiary	N
Native-born French	24.0	(0.2)	39.0	16.0	9.8	11.2	12,899
First-generation							
Maghrebin	63.3	(12.2)	15.9	8.5	2.6	9.7	334
Repatriate	38.9	(3.1)	25.1	13.5	3.3	17.2	106
South European	76.3	(3.3)	16.3	3.8	1.1	2.5	277
East European	34.0	(1.6)	26.2	23.3	14.5	12.0	51
Sub-Saharan African	32.5	(8.1)	14.0	20.6	8.1	24.9	183
Near Eastern	48.8	(2.7)	20.2	12.1	3.2	15.7	102
South East Asian	36.7	(2.4)	10.4	33.7	3.2	16.0	48
Fathers of the second generation							
Maghrebin	*86.9*	*(35.5)*	*8.9*	*1.6*	*0.0*	*2.7*	*279*
Repatriate	*46.2*	*(4.4)*	*23.4*	*12.0*	*3.5*	*15.0*	*609*
South European	*79.4*	*(8.5)*	*15.7*	*2.6*	*0.6*	*1.8*	*838*
East European	*71.8*	*(4.1)*	*13.6*	*5.7*	*1.5*	*7.4*	*142*
Sub-Saharan African	*44.9*	*(8.1)*	*16.7*	*18.0*	*2.9*	*17.5*	*64*
Near Eastern	*72.3*	*(11.0)*	*7.7*	*6.5*	*7.4*	*6.1*	*42*
South East Asian	*39.1*	*(2.9)*	*18.2*	*15.2*	*8.9*	*18.5*	*62*
Second-generation							
Maghrebin	33.3	(0.0)	40.9	14.0	4.1	7.7	279
Repatriate	20.6	(0.3)	33.7	21.2	8.4	16.0	609
South European	30.7	(0.2)	41.1	14.0	7.1	7.1	838
East European	23.7	(0.0)	38.3	15.4	11.1	11.6	142
Sub-Saharan African	23.3	(0.0)	28.9	22.2	6.6	19.1	64
Near Eastern	29.8	(0.0)	29.4	16.7	7.4	16.7	42
South East Asian	12.3	(0.0)	16.8	27.8	6.9	36.2	62

Note: figures in brackets give the percentage with no formal schooling.

Turks. However, the breakdown between some and no primary schooling presents a rather different picture since 12.2% of Maghrebin respondents and 8.1% of Sub-Saharan Africans had no formal schooling, these two groups thus taking the lead, far ahead of South Europeans and other groups, which only score from 2% to 3% with no formal schooling. At the highest educational levels we find that South Europeans and Maghrebins are less numerous than other groups. These other groups appear in the same proportions at these levels and in some cases at higher levels than their native French peers. The explanation may lie in the presence of Jews among the Repatriate and East European populations as well as in the immigration of highly educated persons after the Comecon collapse and more open borders. For other groups, the explanation clearly lies in the effect of tighter, more selective immigration policy and procedures, plus the presence of well-educated persons, in recent or ongoing migration waves. Comparison with the natural parents of the second generation is instructive here. Table 6.2A shows the gap between the characteristics of current first-generation groups with those of the natural parents of the second generation. With exceptions for the one-off wave of Repatriates and for the first wave of South East Asian refugees, the educational levels of the parents of the second generation are generally substantially lower than those of the current first generation. This is to be expected since the parents will generally be rather older than the current first generation and will not have had the benefit of the recent world-wide increase in educational levels. Most notably, the parents show markedly larger proportions with no formal schooling whatsoever. Thus, this proportion rises from 12% to 36% for Maghrebins and from 3% to 9% for South Europeans

The tables for women are broadly similar with only a few notable differences. For example, the proportion of well-educated women is very low among South East Asians of the current first generation and for mothers of the second generation. The proportion of well-educated women from Eastern Europe is very high but only for the current first generation, reflecting a change over time in the character of the migration flows from Eastern Europe. Several groups average lower levels of education for women than was the case for men but this is less pronounced among current first-generation groups than it was for mothers of the second generation. For the parental generation we find especially large proportions of women with no formal schooling: Maghrebins 48%, Near Easterners 20%, Sub-Saharan Africans 15% and South Europeans 11%.

Differences in education between the current first generation and the parents of the current second generation clearly show the limits of comparison between the current first and second generation: such a comparison does not provide a good measure of the intergenerational changes.

The second generation are more educated than the current first generation and far more so than their parents. The proportion with little education is lower and recourse to the more detailed classification shows that scarcely any have no formal schooling. We see the same improvement for women as for men. One remarkable feature is the generational decline in the proportion with low education. The proportion falling into our lowest educational level (primary or none) is 40 percentage points lower among the second-generation Maghrebins, South Europeans, East Europeans and Near-Eastern women than it was among their mothers, and there are large declines too among the remaining groups. This leap between generations is remarkable.

Table 6.2B. Highest educational qualification, by ancestry and generation: Women (row percentages (weighted)).

	Primary or none		Lower secondary	Higher secondary	Lower tertiary	Higher tertiary	N
Native-born French	22.6	(0.2)	35.3	19.6	10.8	11.8	14,391
First-generation							
Maghrebin	69.7	(26.6)	16.8	5.7	3.0	4.8	313
Repatriate	30.4	(3.5)	31.9	10.8	5.7	21.3	130
South European	77.9	(1.7)	13.4	4.2	1.1	6.5	290
East European	24.8	(1.0)	12.6	20.4	13.8	28.5	93
Sub-Saharan African	39.9	14.7)	20.8	18.5	8.4	12.4	221
Near Eastern	62.6	(11.1)	10.5	10.8	2.5	13.6	80
South East Asian	52.2	(3.4)	23.5	16.9	4.0	3.4	46
Mothers of the							
second generation							
Maghrebin	*87.9*	*(47.8)*	*7.3*	*2.5*	*0.0*	*2.3*	*361*
Repatriate	*52.6*	*(6.7)*	*24.4*	*13.4*	*3.2*	*6.4*	*723*
South European	*84.4*	*(11.1)*	*10.8*	*3.3*	*0.7*	*0.8*	*894*
East European	*77.6*	*(6.1)*	*14.1*	*4.8*	*0.6*	*3.0*	*171*
Sub-Saharan African	*43.2*	*(14.8)*	*28.9*	*15.9*	*5.4*	*6.7*	*101*
Near Eastern	*68.0*	*(20.1)*	*15.3*	*6.2*	*6.3*	*4.2*	*50*
South East Asian	*54.7*	*(13.3)*	*18.0*	*19.1*	*1.4*	*6.9*	*60*
Second-generation							
Maghrebin	30.8	(0.5)	33.6	17.6	9.4	8.6	361
Repatriate	15.8	(0.0)	31.0	22.7	13.0	17.4	723
South European	23.5	(0.2)	41.3	16.3	9.9	9.0	894
East European	35.1	(1.0)	32.1	16.3	7.5	9.1	171
Sub-Saharan African	22.2	(0.0)	26.1	27.6	9.6	14.6	101
Near Eastern	28.7	(0.0)	41.5	18.3	0.0	11.6	50
South East Asian	16.7	(0.0)	14.2	15.0	19.6	34.5	60

Note: figures in brackets give the percentage with no formal schooling.

Turning to the more detailed distinctions (shown in the Appendix) we find that results depend to some extent on whether the detailed or aggregate classifications are used. If we compare second-generation Maghrebins and their South Europeans peers, we see that the percentages are similar at the higher tertiary level although South Europeans have a slight edge over Maghrebins at the lower tertiary level. However, when we disaggregate we find the classical opposition between the South Europeans, who have a greater preference for vocational over academic qualifications, and the Maghrebins. The same pattern is apparent at the lower secondary level. This difference is of interest on the job market where vocational diplomas, for this level of education, are a better guarantee against unemployment, a factor in favour of the South European second generation. However, these data give only an incomplete view of current trends. The second-generation men now leaving school (Silberman & Fournier 2006) have been entering vocational and technological programmes more extensively. The Portuguese in particular have exploited tertiary vocational options thanks to the creation of new programmes where their presence is stronger than that of Maghrebins who continue to focus more on academic diplomas, although, unlike South East Asians, without making real headway at the highest levels. The trend we see in our tables is now accentuated and the South European second generation is now surpassing the Maghrebins at the tertiary level. Vocational programmes no longer leave the Portuguese with a short length of education. The situation for second-generation women is much the same. Note that these data also confirm a growing proportion of the Sub-Saharan Africans and Turks achieving higher secondary vocational diplomas among cohorts now leaving school.

South-East Asians are clearly the most successful in education. Finally, we must note the difference in educational attainment between the Maghrebin second generation and Repatriates' children. Once again this stresses the importance of clearly identifying the two populations in the data.

Employment

These changes have occurred in the context of the high unemployment prevailing in France since the 1970s which has affected youth more markedly here than in other European countries (Goux & Maurin 1998). First-time jobseekers have been particularly vulnerable to the general decline in job security even though France offers a greater number of youth programmes. A significant share of these programmes involves public sector employment.

Tables 6.3A and 6.3B show the patterns of economic activity in our sample. We do not however include information on parents' economic activity since in many cases the parents are retired and comparisons with the current first or second generations therefore become problematic. Except in the case of East Europeans, the first-generation men show slightly higher activity levels than their native French peers; as is widely known, a major motivation of immigration is to find work. However, students increasingly form part of recent and ongoing immigrant waves, especially those coming from Eastern Europe, the Near East, South East Asia and Sub-Saharan Africa. Economic activity levels drop noticeably, however, for the second-generation groups. Many contain a substantial proportion of young people still in school, e.g. South East Asians and Sub-Saharan Africans as well as Near Easterners and Maghrebins. Only South Europeans and, unlike the first generation, East Europeans show high economic activity levels in the second generation.

High inactivity levels are the key issue for women, most notably for Near Easterners, Maghrebins and Sub-Saharan Africans. Most are Muslims. For all groups, the second generation show lower inactivity levels than the first generation, although in most cases still not reaching native French levels of economic activity. Inactivity remains noticeably high for young Near Eastern women but plummets for their Sub-Saharan sisters.

For the mothers of the FQP (Formation Qualification Professionnelle survey) respondents there is a survey question to establish whether they were working at the moment the respondent left school, at the moment of the survey (if the respondent was still at school) or whether they had never worked. The proportions who had never worked are shown in Table 6.3A in the Appendix and demonstrate that the mothers of the second generation almost invariably show higher inactivity levels than do the current first-generation from the same country of origin. This implies that, comparing mothers with daughters, there has been a greater intergenerational change for the second generation than there has been for the recent arrivals. Another interesting point is that, although the mothers (most of them in France) of the second generation have a high level of inactivity, their activity rates are higher than that of the mothers (most of them not in France) of the current first generation. This is true whether we consider those who have never worked or those who did not work at the moment the respondent was finishing school. This warns us against writing off

Table 6.3A. Economic activity, by ancestry and generation: Men (row percentages (weighted)).

	Economically active	Full-time student	Retired etc.	Other inactive	N
Native-born French	85.5	9.3	2.2	3.0	12,899
First-generation					
Maghrebin	88.5	2.7	2.0	6.8	334
Repatriate	87.8	1.4	6.5	4.3	106
South European	87.7	1.1	2.0	8.1	277
East European	77.7	11.6	2.8	8.0	51
Sub-Saharan African	88.1	7.7	0.8	3.5	183
Near Eastern	88.7	7.0	0.0	4.3	102
South East Asian	84.2	14.3	0.0	1.6	48
Second-generation					
Maghrebin	78.4	19.2	0.2	2.2	279
Repatriate	80.3	16.4	1.6	1.8	609
South European	89.6	5.7	1.8	2.9	838
East European	88.0	5.3	3.6	3.1	142
Sub-Saharan African	60.6	36.9	0.9	1.6	64
Near Eastern	80.0	20.0	0.0	0.0	42
South East Asian	67.5	30.3	0.0	2.1	62

Table 6.3B. Economic activity, by ancestry and generation: Women (row percentages (weighted)).

	Economically active	Full-time student	Retired etc.	Other inactive*	Never worked*	N
Native-born French	72.8	10.5	1.9	14.9	2.5	14,391
First-generation						
Maghrebin	46.5	2.3	0.2	51.0	37.5	313
Repatriate	62.9	1.5	8.4	27.3	8.4	130
South European	72.8	2.2	0.5	24.5	6.3	290
East European	66.8	6.2	0.0	27.1	8.1	93
Sub-Saharan African	59.4	7.6	0.7	32.4	19.2	221
Near Eastern	45.7	7.2	0.0	47.1	29.6	80
South East Asian	73.5	10.0	1.6	14.9	1.8	46
Second-generation						
Maghrebin	57.7	20.2	0.3	21.8	7.9	361
Repatriate	70.6	16.1	0.2	13.1	0.9	723
South European	75.4	7.9	1.5	15.2	2.5	894
East European	71.2	2.4	5.4	21.1	2.2	171
Sub-Saharan African	49.5	42.1	0.0	8.4	4.6	101
Near Eastern	48.0	18.1	2.2	31.8	11.8	50
South East Asian	70.0	16.0	0.0	14.0	5.5	60

*Other inactive include all women that are currently inactives. Figures in the next column give the percentages of the total population who have never worked.

Muslim women's economic activity as simply 'part of the culture': the selective nature of migration and the opportunities available on the host country's job market both contribute to shape the activity levels of immigrant women.

Turning now to unemployment, Table 6.4 shows the unemployment levels of those sample members who are economically active (that is excluding the fulltime students, retired or other inactive). We see that current first-generation men experience very high levels of unemployment, in most cases over twice those of the native French. We must remember that we are comparing populations of very differing education levels but nonetheless South Europeans predictably show the lowest unemployment rates. Maghrebins and more recent waves from the Near East and Sub-Saharan Africa are in the least enviable situation but South East Asians also face barriers. Moreover, barriers carry over to the second generation. Unemployment among second-generation Maghrebins and Sub-Saharan Africans is barely lower than among the first generation while among South East Asians it is higher than in the first generation. We cannot compare the second generation with their fathers here because of the diversity of their situations.[8]

As a rule, in France women fare less well than men in an environment of high unemployment. Table 6.4 shows that native Frenchwomen's unemployment rate is 3 percentage points higher than men's. Current first-generation women are far more vulnerable than native-born women of French ancestry to unemployment, displaying a pattern quite comparable to that for men, with very high rates for Maghrebin, East European and Sub-Saharan African women against a relatively low rate for their South European sisters. (In Table 6.4 we do not show the figures for the Near Eastern and South East Asian women as the numbers involved are so low.) The patterns remain rather similar in the second generation, with the Maghrebin women continuing to have rates of unemployment three times those of the native French.

---

[8] The respondent was asked to report the situation of the parents at the moment he or she was finishing school but some of the fathers had already retired at that time. Moreover, at the time the parents had been on the labour market, the state of the economy had been radically different.

Table 6.4. Unemployment, by ancestry, generation and gender (row percentages (weighted)).

	Men		Women	
	% Unemployed	N	% Unemployed	N
Native-born French	7.6	11,209	10.7	10,657
First generation				
Maghrebin	26.0	298	31.6	157
Repatriate	11.8	91	14.7	90
South European	5.8	245	8.7	215
East European	22.4	42	25.3	62
Sub-Saharan African	19.8	163	25.3	136
Near Eastern	27.1	91	–	–
South East Asian	10.0	42	–	–
Second generation				
Maghrebin	23.2	230	33.2	212
Repatriate	13.3	504	15.0	525
South European	8.5	758	12.7	682
East European	7.0	126	10.0	123
Sub-Saharan African	14.9	43	20.3	57
Near Eastern	4.4	36	–	–
South East Asian	25.5	45	–	–

Note: economically inactive are excluded from the base.

Occupational class

We turn next, in Tables 6.5A and 6.5B, to consider the occupational distributions of those sample members who actually have (or had) jobs.[9] The first key observation concerns the distribution between skilled and unskilled manual jobs. In general, first-generation men are over-represented (in comparison with the native-born French) in semi and unskilled manual work. This pattern holds for Maghrebin, East European, Sub-Saharan African and Near Eastern men, and tends to be even more marked among the fathers of the second generation than it is among the current first generation. We also see the familiar difference between Maghrebins and Portuguese with the South Europeans being markedly over-represented in skilled manual work.

A number of groups, however, are well-represented in non-manual work. Access to routine non-manual work is strongest for Sub-Saharan

---

[9] Note that using the EGP (Erickson-Goldthorpe-Portocarero) classification for international comparison, we have had to recode the French categories. Our recoding differs slightly from previous recodings that have been used because we systematically use the parallel information about employment status (waged or independent) thus including more respondents in the petty bourgeoisie category.

Table 6.5A. Current occupational class, by ancestry and generation: Men (row percentages (weighted)).

	Salariat	Routine non-manual	Petty bourgeoisie	Skilled manual	Semi- and unskilled manual	N
Native-born French	30.2	10.1	10.3	37.9	11.4	10,401
First generation						
Maghrebin	16.0	6.9	9.5	42.3	25.4	220
Repatriate	43.9	6.0	15.0	28.6	6.5	81
South European	12.4	2.7	14.5	54.8	15.6	230
East European	14.8	9.3	5.8	47.0	23.1	37
Sub-Saharan African	28.2	15.5	4.3	31.8	20.3	130
Near Eastern	19.5	1.6	18.9	32.3	27.7	69
South East Asian	40.0	2.6	8.6	35.9	12.9	37
Fathers of the second generation						
Maghrebin	*13.7*	*3.2*	*3.4*	*43.9*	*35.8*	*193*
Repatriate	*41.5*	*12.7*	*6.1*	*30.0*	*9.8*	*500*
South European	*10.8*	*4.6*	*14.9*	*49.5*	*20.0*	*701*
East European	*16.5*	*6.0*	*12.1*	*44.6*	*20.8*	*112*
Sub-Saharan African	*48.5*	*10.8*	*3.0*	*22.2*	*15.6*	*48*
Near Eastern	*13.8*	*3.7*	*9.9*	*38.4*	*34.2*	*35*
South East Asian	*50.6*	*7.0*	*9.8*	*26.1*	*6.6*	*48*
Second generation						
Maghrebin	15.4	9.1	10.4	44.8	20.4	183
Repatriate	42.3	10.5	5.5	31.6	10.2	444
South European	26.8	8.7	10.2	41.4	13.0	698
East European	29.5	8.7	7.2	48.4	6.2	118
Sub-Saharan African	47.1	16.0	5.3	22.8	8.8	37
Near Eastern	24.8	6.2	8.1	29.5	31.5	34
South East Asian	52.8	11.5	9.8	21.2	4.7	37

Africans although this may result from inclusion of Europeans born in the Sub-Saharan region.[10] The bimodal nature of current Sub-Saharan migration is another probable factor. In the salariat, the best-represented groups are the South East Asians and the Repatriates from North Africa, both of which show higher proportions than do the native-born French. Once again, this pattern is evident both among the current first generation and among the fathers of the second generation.

---

[10] As noted earlier, because of the sample size and differing regulations governing attribution of citizenship, it is harder to distinguish ancestry among Sub-Saharan populations than among Maghrebins.

Table 6.5B. Current occupational class, by ancestry and generation: Women (row percentages (weighted)).

	Salariat	Routine non-manual	Petty bourgeoisie	Skilled manual	Semi- and unskilled manual	N
Native-born French	35.9	30.1	5.2	5.9	22.8	9,554
First-generation						
Maghrebin	17.7	22.8	3.1	4.7	51.7	106
Repatriate	48.4	20.5	4.9	7.2	19.0	76
South European	8.6	15.2	2.8	6.8	66.7	197
East European	27.1	24.2	1.8	8.5	38.4	48
Sub-Saharan African	14.0	31.1	0.0	4.1	50.8	101
Mothers of the second generation						
Maghrebin	*16.4*	*23.4*	*1.6*	*4.2*	*54.5*	*73*
Repatriate	*36.6*	*34.5*	*3.4*	*3.4*	*22.1*	*353*
South European	*12.2*	*20.6*	*6.0*	*7.4*	*53.9*	*382*
East European	*18.2*	*17.8*	*11.4*	*6.4*	*46.3*	*72*
Sub-Saharan African	*37.0*	*25.8*	*2.3*	*6.0*	*28.8*	*60*
Second-generation						
Maghrebin	23.4	36.2	3.1	4.1	33.2	150
Repatriate	40.8	32.5	5.8	2.0	19.0	452
South European	29.8	31.7	3.9	4.8	29.8	597
East European	37.7	26.2	7.5	3.7	24.9	110
Sub-Saharan African	44.7	31.8	0.0	3.9	19.6	47

The second key point is access to small business, which falls into the general category of the petty bourgeoisie. In the lead, we find first-generation Turks, Lebanese and other Near Easterners, South Europeans (operating small businesses in the construction and mechanical industries), as well as South East Asians and Maghrebins in the restaurant industry, with the lattermost also operating cafés. In the second generation the proportions in the petty bourgeoisie are generally lower but we still find some continuity for South European and Near Eastern men. However, we must remember that many of the second generation are relatively young and that self-employment tends to increase with age.

Another basis for comparison is between the current first generation and the fathers of the second generation (more or less representing the original first generation). The FQP survey included a question asking what job parents held when the respondent left school, currently holds if the respondent is still in school, or the last job if unemployed or retired. This comparison yields a rather different picture of the generation gaps. To grasp this, consider the example of the Maghrebins where 36% of the fathers of second-generation respondents were semi- or unskilled manual workers compared with barely 26% among the current first generation. This reflects both structural change in the job market and in the social composition of the immigration waves themselves. The distance between fathers and sons or mothers and daughters is thus greater than that between the second generation and the current first generation.

Nevertheless the comparison between the second generation and their fathers suggests that there is very substantial intergenerational continuity. The similarity is most marked in the case of the more successful groups such as the Repatriates, the South East Asians and the Sub-Saharan Africans. The other groups all show some intergenerational progress, albeit from relatively low starting points. The Maghrebins are of particular interest. Their share in semi and unskilled manual work has declined from 36% in the fathers' generation to 20% in the second generation but they still remain markedly under-represented in the professional and managerial jobs of the salariat.

As usual, women generally are more concentrated than men in services and unskilled jobs. In addition we find that all first-generation groups other than the Repatriates are over-represented in this lowest class category when compared to native-born women of French ancestry. This pattern holds true whether we consider the current first generation or the mothers of the second generation. (As with unemployment we exclude the Near Eastern and South East Asian women because of the small sample numbers.) Conversely the Repatriates are the one group that is over-represented in the salariat. Interestingly rates of self-employment are very low for all these groups of women, including the native-born French.

Is the second generation more present at the top than the first generation was? The answer is a strong yes for South and East Europeans who are increasing their share of professional and managerial jobs (both in comparison with the current first generation and with their mothers). The answer is less clear for Maghrebins. As with the men, the percentage of Maghrebin women to be found in the semi and unskilled manual class has declined from over 50% in the first generation to 33% in the second generation. However, the resulting upwards shift only goes as far as the routine non-manual class, where they have greatly increased their representation, and they remain markedly under-represented in the salariat.

Ethnic penalties

Having outlined the gross differences between the various groups and generations that can be identified in the French data, we now turn to the ethnic penalties, that is to the net differences after controlling for age, education and marital status. As with the other chapters in this volume, we begin with an analysis of unemployment before moving on to a discussion of occupational class.

The avoidance of unemployment

Following the standard approach adopted in this volume, we focus on the avoidance of unemployment. We restrict our analysis to respondents who were economically active (that is who were either in work or were available and looking for work) and use logistic regression to explore the factors associated with being in work rather than being unemployed. The results are shown in Table 6.6. Positive coefficients indicate that the group in question was more likely than the reference group to be in work while negative coefficients indicate that the group was more likely than the reference group to be unemployed. In essence, then, negative coefficients indicate disadvantage. As explained earlier, we are not able to include the parents of the second generation in these analyses.

Looking first at our control variables we see that age has the usual curvilinear association with unemployment, both young people and those closer to retirement age being relatively prone to unemployment while those in middle age had greater likelihood of being in work. We also see that qualifications provide some protection against unemployment, people without any qualification being particularly at risk of unemployment.[11] As is common elsewhere, married people are more likely to be in work than the single. These patterns apply in broadly similar fashion to both men and women.

Turning next to our various categories of ancestry, a clear picture of ethnic stratification emerges. Groups of European ancestry tend to be relatively successful in avoiding unemployment whereas groups of

---

[11] As noted earlier the standard classification of educational qualifications that we follow in this volume does not altogether do justice to the structure of French education, with its crucial divisions into vocational and educational tracks. If we use a more refined classification that corresponds better to the French situation, we do find stronger relationships between qualification and employment, but the pattern and magnitude of the ethnic parameter estimates remains fundamentally unchanged.

Table 6.6. Logistic regression of unemployment (parameter estimates; contrasts with unemployment).

	Men Model 1		Women Model 1		Model 2	
Intercept	**5.15**	(0.40)	**4.49**	(0.36)	**4.54**	(0.36)
Ancestry						
Native-born French	0		0		0	
Maghrebin 1	**−0.84**	(0.18)	**−0.73**	(0.20)	**−1.02**	(0.22)
Repatriate 1	−0.02	(0.36)	−0.19	(0.31)	−0.18	(0.31)
South European 1	**1.53**	(0.33)	**1.50**	(0.29)	**0.87**	(0.33)
East European 1	−0.63	(0.49)	**−1.08**	(0.32)	**−1.08**	(0.32)
African 1	**−1.26**	(0.21)	**−1.45**	(0.22)	**−1.45**	(0.22)
Near Eastern 1	**−2.09**	(0.26)	**−1.68**	(0.38)	**−1.69**	(0.38)
Southeast Asian 1	−0.36	(0.49)	−0.12	(0.49)	−0.11	(0.49)
Maghrebin 2	**−1.67**	(0.20)	**−1.69**	(0.18)	**−1.70**	(0.18)
Repatriate 2	**−0.87**	(0.15)	**−0.65**	(0.14)	**−0.66**	(0.14)
South European 2	−0.13	(0.14)	**−0.28**	(0.12)	**−0.28**	(0.12)
East European 2	0.60	(0.39)	0.35	(0.31)	0.36	(0.31)
Sub-Saharan African 2	**−1.21**	(0.46)	**−0.93**	(0.38)	0.38	(0.85)
Near Eastern 2	−0.33	(0.74)	**−1.45**	(0.61)	**−1.46**	(0.61)
South East Asian 2	**−1.46**	(0.42)	0.02	(0.61)	0.02	(0.61)
Age /10	**1.53**	(0.21)	**1.51**	(0.19)	**1.54**	(0.19)
(Age/10)^2	**−0.16**	(0.02)	**−0.13**	(0.02)	**−0.13**	(0.02)
Qualifications						
Higher tertiary	**0.35**	(0.14)	**0.42**	(0.12)	**0.47**	(0.12)
Lower tertiary	**0.48**	(0.16)	**0.71**	(0.13)	**0.73**	(0.13)
Higher secondary	0		0		0	
Lower secondary	−0.12	(0.10)	**−0.25**	(0.09)	**−0.24**	(0.09)
No qualification	**−0.67**	(0.10)	**−0.81**	(0.09)	**−0.82**	(0.09)
Marital Status						
Married/cohabiting	**1.13**	(0.08)	**0.53**	(0.07)	**0.53**	(0.07)
Divorced/widowed	**0.30**	(0.12)	0.02	(0.10)	0.02	(0.10)
Single	0		0		0	
Significant interactions with education						
Maghrebin 1					**−0.29**	(0.11)
South European 1					**−0.47**	(0.15)
Sub-Saharan African 2					**1.39**	(0.59)
Chi-square (D.F.)	680.1 (22)		586.3 (22)		610.1 (25)	
N	13,923		13,053		13,053	

Note: Standard errors are given in brackets; emboldened coefficients indicate significance at the 0.05 level or higher.

Maghrebin, Sub-Saharan African and Near Eastern ancestry tend to experience quite major disadvantages. The repatriates from North Africa, most of whom will have European ancestry, fall somewhere in between. Broadly speaking, this pattern holds both for the current first and second generations and for both men and women. Moreover there is no sign that, compared with the first generation, the second generation in general has improved its position relative to the native-born French.[12]

Looking at the results in more detail we see that the South Europeans actually show an ethnic 'premium' in the first generation, possibly related to the niche they occupy in the building industry and small firms. But, interestingly, the second-generation men have lost this 'premium' and the second-generation women even show a modest penalty. East Europeans show some disadvantage in the first generation, although their disadvantage may be exacerbated by the fact that many of them will be rather recent arrivals; their disadvantage may tend to decline as their length of experience in the French labour market increases. Second-generation East Europeans appear to compete on equal terms with the native-born French. The repatriates from North Africa experience some marked disadvantages in the second generation in gaining employment. Given the mixed nature of this group, it is hard to be sure of the interpretation for this disadvantage although Silberman and Fournier have found that the Repatriate second generation expresses some feelings of discrimination (Silberman and Fournier 2006).

Among the other groups we see very substantial disadvantages for both generations of Maghrebins, Sub-Saharan Africans and groups from the Near East (including people from Turkey and the Lebanon) with coefficients around -1.00. Given the small numbers in our sample, and the consequent large standard errors, we must be cautious in drawing conclusions about the relative scale of the disadvantages but the ethnic penalty experienced by the second-generation Maghrebins appears to be particularly large.

Finally we should note that the results for the East Asians, many of whom will be ethnic Chinese from Vietnam, are rather mixed and do not tell a clear story. Whereas the first generation does not seem to suffer any ethnic penalty, this is not the case for the second-generation men, a result that we have also found for recent cohorts of school-leavers where a significant proportion of the East Asian second generation report discrimination in finding a job (Silberman and Fournier 2006). This does not

---

[12] If we amalgamate our fourteen ethnic-cum-generation groups into seven ethnic groups and add a variable for generation (distinguishing first generation from the second generation) we find that there is no significant difference between the generations, either in the case of men or of women. However this model does not give as good a fit to the data as the one which distinguishes the individual ethnic-cum-generation groups. In other words, the effect of generation varies across ethnic groups. Note that in this analysis we exclude the native-born French so that the analysis covers only the seven ethnic minority groups.

completely fit the success story that is often told about this ethnic group. Again, the number of East Asians in our sample is very small and we need to await larger samples before drawing any firm conclusions.

We have also checked whether any of these groups receive differential returns on their educational investments. In the case of men we find that in none of our groups is there a significant interaction with education, but in the case of women three groups have significant interactions. These are shown in the second model in Table 6.6. First-generation Maghrebin and South European women obtain lower returns on their educational investments than do the native-born French but second-generation Africans receive greater returns. While lower returns in the first generation fit with our general theoretical expectations, higher returns in the second generation are somewhat puzzling. However, given the very small number of second-generation African women in our sample, and the risk of selection biases, we feel it would be wise to defer interpreting this finding until it has been confirmed by other research.

Occupational attainment

Finally we turn to models of occupational class. In line with other chapters in this volume we distinguish five classes—the salariat, the routine non-manual class, the petty bourgeoisie, the skilled manual class and the semi- and unskilled class. We restrict our analysis to respondents who were actually in work, excluding the unemployed. It is thus an analysis of the occupational positions of those who were fortunate enough to have jobs. Table 6.7A shows the results for men.

In many ways the picture is the same as for unemployment, with groups of European ancestry having greater occupational success than the groups from less-developed countries, and, as with unemployment, there is not a great deal of evidence of generational progress. Moreover, disadvantages appear to be present at most levels of the class structure.

Among the groups of European ancestry, the current first-generation East Europeans stand out as having major disadvantages in access to the salariat although in the second generation they appear to compete on equal terms with the native-born French. Again we must remember that these first-generation East Europeans are very recent arrivals (and are very unlikely to be the parents of the second generation). Their disadvantages in gaining access to salaried positions may well reflect their lack of fluency in the French language and their limited experience of the French labour market. When we examine the ethnic penalties experienced

Table 6.7A. Logistic regression of occupational class: Men (parameter estimates; contrasts with unskilled manual).

	Salariat		Routine non-manual		Petty bourgeoisie		Manual supervisor or skilled manual	
Intercept	**2.49**	(0.50)	**1.88**	(0.55)	**1.99**	(.56)	**2.57**	(0.43)
Ancestry								
Native-born French	0		0		0		0	
Maghrebin 1	**−0.96**	(0.32)	**−0.67**	(0.34)	−0.23	(0.31)	−0.33	(0.22)
Repatriate 1	0.67	(0.52)	0.11	(0.63)	0.56	(0.55)	0.31	(0.48)
South European 1	**0.80**	(0.36)	−0.66	(0.51)	**1.23**	(0.36)	**0.90**	(0.28)
East European 1	**−2.87**	(0.67)	−0.89	(0.63)	**−1.89**	(0.82)	−0.73	(0.44)
African 1	**−1.48**	(0.35)	−0.10	(0.33)	**−1.76**	(0.52)	**−0.63**	(0.28)
Near Eastern 1	**−1.65**	(0.48)	**−2.89**	(1.03)	−0.55	(0.41)	**−1.21**	(0.33)
East Asian 1	−0.22	(0.66)	−1.25	(1.11)	−0.18	(0.77)	0.02	(0.54)
Maghrebin 2	**−1.19**	(0.34)	**−0.70**	(0.33)	**−0.87**	(0.35)	−0.46	(0.24)
Repatriate 2	0.32	(0.21)	0.02	(0.23)	**−0.72**	(0.28)	−0.19	(0.19)
South European 2	0.07	(0.16)	−0.29	(0.18)	−0.09	(0.17)	0.03	(0.13)
East European 2	0.60	(0.47)	0.67	(0.50)	0.29	(0.53)	**0.94**	(0.42)
Sub-Saharan African 2	0.38	(0.67)	0.40	(0.67)	−0.78	(0.92)	−0.51	(0.62)
Near Eastern 2	**−1.42**	(0.67)	−1.18	(0.70)	−1.20	(0.72)	**−1.17**	(0.48)
East Asian 2	0.09	(0.85)	0.44	(0.90)	0.13	(0.93)	0.05	(0.81)
Age /10	**1.58**	(0.27)	**1.13**	(0.29)	**1.93**	(0.30)	**1.08**	(0.22)
(Age/10)²	−0.03	(0.03)	**−0.07**	(0.03)	−0.08	(0.03)	**−0.06**	(0.02)
Qualification								
Higher tertiary	**2.72**	(0.24)	0.23	(0.29)	**0.99**	(0.28)	0.08	(0.27)
Lower tertiary	**1.55**	(0.20)	**0.48**	(0.23)	**0.72**	(0.23)	**1.09**	(0.20)
Higher secondary	0		0		0		0	
Lower secondary	**−1.79**	(0.11)	**−0.77**	(0.13)	**−0.63**	(0.13)	−0.11	(0.11)
No qualification	**−3.57**	(0.13)	**−1.46**	(0.13)	**−1.79**	(0.14)	**−0.77**	(0.11)
Marital Status								
Married/cohabiting	**0.59**	(0.09)	**0.39**	(0.10)	**0.58**	(0.10)	**0.49**	(0.07)
Divorced/separated	**0.41**	(0.17)	**0.63**	(0.18)	**0.43**	(0.18)	**0.42**	(0.14)
Single	0		0		0		0	
Chi-square (D.F.)				5,879.6 (88)				
N				12,756				

Note: Standard errors are given in brackets; emboldened coefficients indicate significance at the 0.05 level or higher.

by the fathers of the second generation (shown in Table 6.A4 in the Appendix), we find that East Europeans were not especially disadvantaged in the father's generation.

The other major discrepancy between results for the current first generation and the fathers of the second generation occurs among the South

Europeans, who experienced substantial ethnic penalties in the fathers' generation but an ethnic premium in the current first generation. This may well reflect a change in the patterns of migration from South Europe with recent arrivals being highly skilled migrants taking advantage of the EU's free labour market. In contrast, for the other long-established groups such as the Maghrebins and the Repatriates, the penalties experienced by the current first generation and the fathers' generation are remarkably similar.

In the second generation we find that none of the groups of predominantly European ancestry—the East Europeans, South Europeans and the Repatriates—experience ethnic penalties in access to the salariat, routine non-manual class or the skilled manual class. The East Asian group is also very similar to the groups of European ancestry: none of the parameter estimates in either generation (or for the fathers' generation) is statistically significant. While we have to be cautious because of the small numbers involved (and large standard errors) this does seem to be similar to patterns found in other countries where East Asians prove to be relatively successful (although as we noted earlier the second generation may experience some difficulties entering the labour market).

Among some of our other groups, however, substantial penalties remain. For example, among Maghrebins the first generation have a penalty of -0.96 compared with -1.19 in the second generation (and -1.01 in the fathers' generation) with respect to salariat occupations (and the story is more or less repeated for the other class positions). Similarly among groups from the Near East the ethnic penalty for access to the salariat is -1.65 in the first generation and -1.42 in the second generation (and -2.55 for the fathers' generation). Only the sub-Saharan Africans show marked differences between generations although, as in the case of the East Europeans, we need to remember that the first generation are relatively recent arrivals and that we are not comparing parental and filial generations. The parental analysis in fact indicates that the fathers of the second generation were also relatively successful in the labour market just like the second generation.[13] Overall, then, these results show very high levels of intergenerational continuity in the nature and size of the ethnic penalties.

The picture for women is shown in Table 6.7B, and the results are fairly similar to those for men with one or two detailed exceptions. The

---

[13] Here we must note that some parents may well not be immigrants but well-off individuals who have sent their children to France.

Table 6.7B. Logistic regression of occupational class: Women (parameter estimates; contrasts with unskilled manual).

	Salariat		Routine non-manual		Petty bourgeoisie		Manual supervisor or skilled manual	
Intercept	**2.11**	(0.42)	**2.21**	(0.37)	−1.19	(.67)	**−0.53**	(0.63)
Ancestry								
Native-born French	0		0		0		0	
Maghrebin 1	−0.43	(0.36)	−0.35	(0.27)	−0.58	(0.54)	−0.66	(0.49)
Repatriate 1	0.27	(0.23)	−0.12	(0.38)	−0.45	(0.65)	0.32	(0.54)
South European 1	**−0.90**	(0.38)	**−0.60**	(0.24)	**−1.16**	(0.52)	−0.39	(0.37)
East European 1	**−1.83**	(0.46)	**−0.81**	(0.40)	−1.69	(1.04)	−0.44	(0.57)
Sub-Saharan African 1	**−2.64**	(0.39)	**−0.95**	(0.25)	–		**−1.17**	(0.49)
Maghrebin 2	**−1.13**	(0.29)	**−0.63**	(0.22)	−0.60	(0.47)	**−0.99**	(0.46)
Repatriate 2	−0.24	(0.17)	−0.04	(0.15)	0.22	(0.26)	**−0.99**	(0.35)
South European 2	**−0.43**	(0.14)	**−0.24**	(0.11)	**−0.57**	(0.23)	**−0.40**	(0.20)
East European 2	0.14	(0.31)	−0.12	(0.28)	0.31	(0.40)	−0.27	(0.50)
African 2	−0.22	(0.52)	−0.07	(0.47)	–		−0.20	(0.81)
Age /10	**1.46**	(0.23)	**1.05**	(0.20)	**1.07**	(0.38)	0.60	(0.34)
(Age/10)^2	**−0.04**	(0.02)	**−0.06**	(0.02)	−0.01	(0.04)	−0.03	(0.03)
Qualification								
Higher tertiary	**2.69**	(0.16)	0.29	(0.18)	**1.25**	(0.26)	1.19	(0.25)
Lower tertiary	**1.97**	(0.14)	**0.82**	(0.15)	**0.90**	(0.24)	**1.45**	(0.21)
Higher secondary	0		0		0		0	
Lower secondary	**−1.75**	(0.09)	**−0.72**	(0.08)	**−0.53**	(0.14)	−0.33	(0.14)
No qualification	**−3.66**	(0.12)	**−1.62**	(0.09)	**−1.35**	(0.16)	**−0.45**	(0.15)
Marital Status								
Married/cohabiting	−0.13	(0.08)	**−0.22**	(0.07)	**0.52**	(0.13)	**−0.10**	(0.11)
Divorced/separated	−0.03	(0.11)	0.07	(0.10)	−0.05	(0.19)	−0.07	(0.16)
Single	0		0		0		0	
Chi-square (D.F.)				5,424.9 (88)				
N				11,551				

Note: Standard errors are given in brackets; emboldened coefficients indicate significance at the 0.05 level or higher.

main differences from the male results are that South European women are quite disadvantaged in both generations while Maghrebin women in the first generation do not experience any major ethnic penalties. The Maghrebin pattern may be a consequence of the selection bias that we noted in Table 6.3B: only a small proportion of first-generation Maghrebin women are economically active, and those who are active may be unusually talented or motivated. However, similar selective processes are probably at work among women from the Near East, who also have a low rate of economic activity but experience very large ethnic penalties.

The explanation for these results, therefore, remains somewhat unclear, and once again it would be desirable to check them from other sources before reaching any definitive conclusion.

We have also checked whether ethnic minority men and women obtain lower occupational returns on their educational investments than do the native-born French. In the case of men, none of the interaction terms proved to be statistically significant, and in the case of women only one (for second-generation East European women with respect to positions in the salariat) was significant. Failure to find significant interactions may reflect our lack of statistical power, since we have a relatively small dataset and a number of our ethnic groups are therefore rather small. Nonetheless, we do have fairly large numbers of second-generation Maghrebins, Repatriates and South Europeans and it is striking that for none of these groups do we find significant interactions. On balance, then, we are reasonably confident that second-generation ethnic minorities receive similar returns on their education to those of the native-born French.

Public employment

Public employment is highly developed in France, covering large sectors of activity. Hence it is useful to have complementary insights about the disadvantage ethnic groups may have in gaining access to public employment and any intergenerational changes that have occurred. Remember that French (and more recently European) nationality is necessary in order to apply for a civil service post, although some unskilled jobs are accessible through short-term contracts for foreigners. Another important feature is that anonymous selection procedures are often used for entering the public sector. Table 6.A6 in the Appendix shows that there are negative coefficients for all first-generation groups except the Repatriates. South European and Sub-Saharan African men and women together with South East Asian men show particularly large and statistically significant negative coefficients, although this is not the case for the Maghrebins.

The pattern is fairly similar for the parents of the second generation. Here also we find that all groups apart from Repatriates show negative coefficients and these coefficients are quite substantial for Maghrebins, South Europeans and South East Asian men. However, the mothers and fathers of the Repatriates show substantial 'premiums'. This reflects the pattern for the people who subsequently became Repatriates to be employed in the public sector in the Maghreb before Independence.[14]

Turning to the second generation we see an interesting pattern of intergenerational change. While all the coefficients are once again negative except for Repatriate men, we find no major disadvantages for second-generation men (about 80% of whom have French citizenship although often gaining citizenship only when they are 18 years old). There are significant coefficient for Maghrebin and South European men but both of these are substantially lower than in their parents' generation. We must be cautious in our interpretation but it does appear that the second generation have improved chances of access to public sector employment.

Conclusion

France is unusual among Western European countries in having experienced net immigration for much of the twentieth century. Migrants have come from three main sources: firstly from other European countries (especially Portugal), second from former French territories and colonies in the Maghreb, Sub-Saharan Africa and South East Asia, and thirdly and more recently from some less-developed non-European countries in the Near East such as Turkey. It is also important to distinguish Repatriates (largely of European origin) from other migrants from the Maghreb.

France's 'Republican Model' of assimilation runs counter to the active recognition of distinct ethnic groups but a number of datasets enable us to identify with reasonable accuracy the major second-generation groups. The French data also enable us to distinguish the natural parents of the second generation, thus enabling a precise generational comparison to be made. It also shows how cautious one should be when it is only possible to compare current first and second generations. Comparisons between the second generation, their parents and the current first generation shows that the distance between the second generation and their parents is generally rather greater than the distance between the second generation and the current first generation. But we

---

[14] Civil Service employees coming from the mainland often married in Algeria. There is also the well-known tendency for public sector employment to run in families, which could well account for the intergenerational continuity in the case of Repatriates.

also see that there is a strong continuity in the penalty that the different ethnic groups experienced on the labour market. In line with previous analysis we find that among Maghrebins the parents' generation, the current first generation and the second generation all endure an ethnic penalty. But the results of this comparison also indicate that, while the second generation have made considerable absolute gains in educational and occupational level, in relative terms the second-generation Maghrebins remain just as disadvantaged as their parents. The disadvantage they suffer is not just at the entrance of the labour market but also in the competition for higher-level occupational positions. The second-generation men also suffer an ethnic penalty in securing public employment in spite of their involvement in youth scheme programmes

The results are still uncertain for the Sub-Saharan Africans where different waves of immigrants are also mixed and where we are not able in this survey to isolate those of European ancestry. Groups such as the South and Eastern Europeans on the other hand experience much reduced ethnic penalties in the second generation, and in several cases no penalty at all except for minorities from the Near East (although the numbers in our sample are too small for us to be sure). This certainly calls into question the assimilationist credentials of the French Republican Model. While the various groups of European ancestry certainly appear by the second generation to compete on equal terms with the native-born population of French ancestry, this is certainly not true of the second generation from the Maghreb where unfortunately, because of data restrictions, we cannot distinguish between the Algerians, who experienced a bloody war of Independence, from the Moroccans and the Tunisians. What is worse, there is very little sign of intergenerational progress for the Maghrebins towards this objective of equal opportunity. A decade ago the French Presidential candidate Jaques Chirac campaigned on the theme of 'la fracture sociale'. In 2003 there is little evidence of progress but one aspect of this fracture seems more clearly to be a coloured one, as the 2005 urban riots have demonstrated, involving mostly Maghrebin and also Sub-Saharan youth who are just now arriving in greater numbers on the labour market. Segmented assimilation could well be the case in France in a context of long-lasting high levels of unemployment.

Appendix 1: Supplementary tables

Table 6.A1. Highest educational qualification: second-generation men (row percentages (weighted)).

	None	Primary	Lower secondary academic	Lower secondary vocational	Higher secondary vocational	Higher secondary academic	Lower tertiary voc.	Lower tertiary acad.	Higher tertiary	N
Native-born French	0.2	23.8	9.9	29.1	8.5	7.5	8.3	1.5	11.2	12,899
Second generation										
Maghrebin	0.0	33.3	13.5	27.5	7.3	6.6	3.3	0.9	7.7	279
Repatriate	0.3	20.4	13.9	19.8	9.0	12.3	6.6	1.8	16.0	609
South European	0.2	30.5	8.8	30.2	7.1	6.9	6.6	0.5	7.1	838
East European	0.0	23.7	11.3	27.0	9.2	6.2	10.4	0.6	11.6	142
African	0.0	23.3	15.1	13.7	11.0	11.2	5.1	1.5	19.1	64
Near Eastern	0.0	29.8	16.2	13.2	5.9	10.8	7.4	0.0	16.7	42
South East Asian	0.0	14.5	11.3	8.1	8.1	17.7	9.7	0.0	30.7	62

Table 6.A2. Highest educational qualification: second-generation women (row percentages (weighted)).

	None	Primary	Lower secondary academic	Lower secondary vocational	Higher secondary vocational	Higher secondary academic	Lower tertiary voc.	Lower tertiary acad.	Higher tertiary	N
Native-born French	0.2	22.4	11.8	23.5	8.8	10.8	9.1	1.7	11.8	14,391
Second generation										
Maghrebin	0.5	30.3	8.9	24.7	7.0	10.6	6.3	3.2	8.6	361
Repatriate	0.0	15.8	12.8	18.2	8.2	14.5	9.9	3.1	17.4	723
South European	0.2	23.3	10.9	30.4	8.2	8.1	8.0	1.8	9.0	894
East European	0.8	34.3	9.9	22.2	8.7	7.6	7.1	2.4	9.1	171
African	0.0	22.2	14.1	11.9	10.8	16.8	6.7	2.9	14.6	101
Near Eastern	0.0	28.7	15.2	26.3	4.6	13.7	0.0	0.0	11.6	50
South East Asian	0.0	16.7	7.5	6.7	7.8	7.3	10.2	9.4	34.5	60

Table 6.A3. Mothers' economic activity: Mothers of the first and second generations (percentages (weighted)).

	Does not work at the moment[a]	Never worked[b]	N
Mothers of native born French	42.1	22.6	14,383
Mothers of the first generation			
Maghrebin	90.7	87.7	312
Repatriate	73.0	52.5	130
South European	52.6	44.6	290
East European	31.4	27.5	93
Sub-Saharan African	62.5	53.8	221
Near Eastern	83.6	79.2	80
South East Asian	54.2	46.9	46
Mothers of the second generation			
Maghrebin	75.4	64.4	361
Repatriate	48.0	30.4	723
South European	49.8	33.1	894
East European	53.7	31.1	171
Sub-Saharan African	38.8	21.0	101
Near Eastern	67.7	51.8	50
South East Asian	44.2	34.5	60

Notes:
[a] But has worked before.
[b] Including mothers who were dead when the respondent was finishing school.

Table 6.A4. Logistic regression of fathers' occupational class (parameter estimates; contrasts with unskilled manual).

	Salariat		Routine non-manual		Petty bourgeoisie		Manual supervisor or skilled manual	
Intercept	**3.23**	(0.23)	**1.54**	(0.25)	**1.61**	(0.24)	**2.14**	(0.23)
Father's ancestry								
Native-born French	0		0		0		0	
Maghrebin	**−1.01**	(0.26)	**−2.03**	(0.42)	**−2.55**	(0.37)	**−0.65**	(0.17)
Repatriate	**0.58**	(0.18)	**0.51**	(0.20)	**−0.88**	(0.23)	0.18	(0.17)
South European	**−0.78**	(0.16)	**−1.01**	(0.20)	**−0.72**	(0.13)	0.04	(0.10)
East European	**−0.79**	(0.38)	−0.84	(0.43)	**−0.85**	(0.33)	−0.07	(0.25)
Sub-Saharan African	0.23	(0.54)	0.13	(0.59)	−1.62	(0.82)	−0.48	(0.52)
Near Eastern	**−2.55**	(0.81)	**−1.69**	(0.77)	**−1.72**	(0.57)	**−1.02**	(0.40)
South East Asian	0.62	(0.61)	0.09	(0.72)	−0.32	(0.67)	−0.01	(0.59)
Qualification								
Higher tertiary	**2.32**	(0.62)	0.68	(0.66)	1.15	(0.64)	−0.04	(0.65)
Lower tertiary	1.11	(0.75)	0.98	(0.78)	1.22	(0.77)	1.00	(0.76)
Higher secondary	0		0		0		0	
Lower secondary	**−2.35**	(0.24)	**−1.25**	(0.26)	**−0.85**	(0.25)	**−0.54**	(0.24)
No qualification	**−3.82**	(0.23)	**−2.13**	(0.25)	**−1.33**	(0.25)	**−1.50**	(0.24)
Chi-square (D.F.)				3856.98(44)				
N				12,274				

Note: Standard errors are given in brackets; emboldened coefficients indicate significance at the 0.05 level or higher.

Table 6.A5. Logistic regression of mothers' occupational class (parameter estimates; contrasts with unskilled manual).

	Salariat		Routine non-manual		Petty bourgeoisie		Manual supervisor or skilled manual	
Intercept	**2.80**	(0.17)	**1.90**	(0.18)	**−0.49**	(0.24)	−0.32	(0.26)
Mothers' ancestry								
Native-born French	0		0		0		0	
Maghrebin	**−1.33**	(0.43)	−0.50	(0.29)	**−3.21**	(1.01)	−0.90	(0.60)
Repatriate	0.13	(0.17)	0.28	(0.15)	**−1.45**	(0.31)	−0.32	(0.30)
South European	**−0.99**	(0.19)	**−0.70**	(0.14)	**−1.75**	(0.22)	−0.28	(0.20)
East European	−0.50	(0.37)	**−0.79**	(0.35)	**−0.75**	(0.36)	−0.45	(0.53)
Sub-Saharan African	0.12	(0.38)	−0.20	(0.37)	**−2.25**	(1.03)	−0.09	(0.56)
Qualification								
Higher tertiary	**1.60**	(0.53)	−0.39	(0.58)	0.22	(0.75)	−1.01	(1.15)
Lower tertiary	0.85	(0.61)	0.60	(0.63)	0.48	(0.80)	0.88	(0.77)
Higher secondary	0		0		0		0	
Lower secondary	**−2.66**	(0.18)	**−1.23**	(0.19)	**−0.78**	(0.26)	**−0.89**	(0.27)
No qualification	**−3.99**	(0.18)	**−2.50**	(0.18)	−0.35	(0.25)	**−1.47**	(0.27)
Chi-square (D.F.)				3123.26 (44)				
N				8,700				

Note: Standard errors are given in brackets; emboldened coefficients indicate significance at the 0.05 level or higher.

Table 6.A6. Logistic regression of public sector employment (parameter estimates; contrasts with private sector employment).

	Men		Women		Fathers of second generation men		Mothers of second generation women	
Intercept	**−0.78**	(0.30)	**−0.59**	(0.28)	**−0.77**	(0.07)	**−0.93**	(0.07)
Ancestry								
Native-born French	0		0		0		0	
Maghrebin 1	−0.29	(0.23)	−0.06	(0.24)				
Repatriate 1	0.29	(0.27)	0.14	(0.25)				
South European 1	**−1.69**	(0.43)	**−0.83**	(0.26)				
East European 1	−0.81	(0.54)	−0.55	(0.35)				
Sub-Saharan African 1	**−1.73**	(0.59)	**−1.38**	(0.62)				
Near Eastern 1	**−0.73**	(0.27)	−0.32	(0.24)				
South East Asian 1	**−1.54**	(0.73)	−0.60	(0.49)				
Maghrebin 2	**−0.52**	(0.24)	−0.24	(0.20)	**−0.86**	(0.27)	−0.60	(0.38)
Repatriate 2	**0.28**	(0.12)	−0.09	(0.11)	**0.56**	(0.10)	**0.68**	(0.11)
South European 2	**−0.31**	(0.11)	**−0.20**	(0.09)	**−0.98**	(0.15)	**−0.90**	(0.20)
East European 2	−0.17	(0.25)	−0.19	(0.22)	−0.34	(0.28)	**−1.03**	(0.47)
Sub-Saharan African 2	−0.70	(0.55)	−0.74	(0.66)	−0.20	(0.36)	0.08	(0.31)
Near Eastern 2	−0.05	(0.42)	**−0.80**	(0.39)	–	–	−1.19	(1.06)
South East Asian 2	−0.26	(0.42)	−0.44	(0.36)	**−0.82**	(0.44)	−0.40	(0.50)

	(1)	(2)	(3)	(4)
Age/10	**0.46** (0.17)	**0.44** (0.15)		
(Age/10)²	−0.00 (0.01)	−0.00 (0.01)		
Qualifications				
Higher tertiary	**0.31** (0.08)	**0.79** (0.07)	**1.11** (0.10)	**0.58** (0.13)
Lower tertiary	**−0.29** (0.09)	**0.23** (0.07)	−0.14 (0.16)	0.12 (0.19)
Higher secondary	0 (0.07)	0 (0.06)	0	0
Lower secondary	**−0.54** (0.07)	**−0.28** (0.06)	**−0.70** (0.09)	**−0.36** (0.09)
Primary	**−0.91** (0.08)	**−0.59** (0.07)	**−0.95** (0.08)	**−0.93** (0.09)
Marital Status				
Married/cohabiting	**0.15** (0.06)	−0.01 (0.52)		
Divorced/widowed	**0.27** (0.10)	0.04 (0.08)		
Single	0	0		
Chi−square (D.F.)	496.5 (22)	528.2 (22)	429.02 (11)	368.5 (11)
N	12,762	11,563	12,300	8,754

Note: Standard errors are given in brackets; emboldened coefficients indicate significance at the 0.05 level or higher.

References

Alba, R. and Silberman, R. (2002), 'Decolonization, immigration and the social origins of the second generation: the case of North Africans in France', *International Migration Review*, 36, 1169–93.

Baudelot, C. and Establet, R. (1992), *Allez les filles* (Paris: Le Seuil).

Beaud, S. (2002), *80 % au bac ? Et après ? Les enfants de la démocratisation scolaire* (Paris: La Découverte).

Belorgey, J. P. (1999), *Lutter contre la discrimination* (Paris: Social Affairs and Employment Ministry).

Boulot, S. and Fradet, D. (1988), *Les immigrés et l'école: une course d'obstacles* (Paris: L'Harmattan).

Bovenkerk, F. (1992), *Testing Discrimination in Natural Experiments: A Manual for International Research on Discrimination on the Grounds of 'Race' and 'Ethnic origin'* (Genève: Bureau International du Travail (BIT)).

Brinbaum, Y. (2002), *Au cœur des parcours migratoires, les investissements éducatifs des familles immigrées: attentes et désillusions*. Thèse pour le doctorat de sociologie (Paris: Université René Descartes)**.**

Brinbaum, Y. and Kieffer, A. (2005), 'D'une génération à l'autre, les aspirations éducatives des familles immigrées: ambitions et persévérances', *Éducation et Formation* (Paris: Ministère de l'Éducation Nationale).

Brubaker, W. R. (1992), *Citizenship and Nationhood in France and Germany* (Cambridge, MA: Harvard University Press).

Cediey, E. and Foroni, F. (2007), 'Les discriminations à raison de l'origine dans les embauches en France. Une enquête nationale par tests de discrimination selon la méthode du Bureau International du Travail', BIT/ILO.

Coleman, J. (1988), 'Social capital in the creation of human capital'. *American Journal of Sociology*, 94, 95–121.

Commission Nationale Consultative des droits de l'homme (1996), *La lutte contre le racisme et la xénophobie*. Rapport annuel (Paris: La Documentation Française).

Dayan, J. L., Échardour, A., and Glaude, M. (1996), 'Le parcours professionnel des immigrés en France: une analyse longitudinale', *Économie et Statistique, n°259* (Paris: INSEE).

De Schutter, O. (2001), *Discriminations et marché du travail: Liberté et égalité dans les rapports d'emploi* (Bruxelles: Lang).

Dupray, A. and Moullet, S. (2004), 'Quelles discriminations à l'encontre des jeunes d'origine maghrébine à l'entrée du marché du travail en France'. *Marché du travail et genre, Maghreb-Europe*. Actes du Colloque international de Rabat (Bruxelles: DULBEA éditions).

Duru-Bellat, M. and Kieffer, A. (1999), 'La démocratisation de l'enseignement 'revisitée': une mise en perspective hstorique et internationale des inégalités scolaires en France' (Paris et Dijon: Cahier IREDU-LASMAS), n° 60.

Duru-Bellat, M., Kieffer, A., and Marry, C. (2001), 'La dynamique des scolarités des filles: le double handicap questionné', *Revue Française de Sociologie*, 42, 251–80.

Garner-Moyer, H. (2003), 'Discrimination et emploi: revue de la literature', *Documents d'études, n°69* (Paris: DARES, Ministère des affaires sociales, du travail et de la solidarité).

Girard, A. and Stoetzel, J. (eds.) (1953), 'Français et immigrés : l'attitude française, l'adaptation des italiens et des polonais', *Travaux et Documents n°19* (Paris: INED et PUF).

Goux, D. and Maurin, E. (1998), 'From Education to First Job: The French Case'. In Y. Shavit and W. Müller (eds.), *From School to Work* (Oxford: Clarendon Press), pp. 103–41.

Haut Conseil à l'integration (1998), 'Lutter contre les discriminations: faire respecter le principe d'égalité' (Paris: La Documentation Française).

Henry, M. (2001), 'Le nouveau régime probatoire applicable aux discriminations', *Le droit ouvrier (633)*, pp. 194–200.

Héran, François (2002), 'Les immigrés et leurs descendants dans le système statistique français: réflexions sur les pratiques et les principes'. In François Héran (ed.), *Immigration, Marché du Travail, Intégration* (Paris: La Documentation Française), pp. 121–33.

Lapeyronnie, D. (1993), *La France et la Grande-Bretagne face à leurs immigrés* (Paris: Presses Universaires de France).

Le Bras, H. (1998), *Le démon des origines: Démographie et Extrême Droite* (Paris: Éditions de l'Aube).

Ma Mung, E. (2000), *La diaspora chinoise, géographie d'une migration* (Paris: Éditions Oprhys).

Mayer, N. (1994), 'Racisme et xénophobie dans l'Europe des Douze: Étude sociologique'. In *La lutte contre le racisme et la xénophobie 1993: Exclusion et Droits de l'Homme* (Paris: Rapport de la Commission Consultative des Droits de l'Homme), pp. 65–70.

Marie, C. V. (2002), 'Les Antillais en France: Une nouvelle donne, Adri. Nouvelle version de "Les Antillais de l'Hexagone"'. In P. Dewitte (ed.) (1999), *Immigration et intégration, l'état des savoirs* (Paris: La Découverte).

Meurs, D., Pailhé, A., and Simon, P. (2006), 'Persistance des inégalités entre générations liées à l'immigration: l'accès à l'emploi des immigrés et de leurs descendants en France', *Population n° 5–6–2006* (Paris: INED).

Mingat, A. (1984), 'Les acquisitions scolaires de l'élève au CP: les origines des différences', *Revue française de pédagogie*, 69, 49–62.

Moulier-Boutang, Y., Garson, J. P., and Silberman, R. (1986), *Economie politique des migrations clandestines de main d'œuvre: Comparaisons internationales et exemple français*, Préface de G. Tapinos (Paris: Publisud).

Noiriel, G. (1988), *Le Creuset Français: Histoire de l'Immigration xix–xx Siècles* (Paris: Éditions du Seuil).

Renan, E. ([1882] 1992), *Qu'est ce qu'une nation?*, réédition 1992 (Paris: Presses Pocket).

Richard, J.-L. (1997), *Dynamiques démographiques et socioéconomiques de l'intégration des jeunes générations d'origine immigrée en France*. Thèse pour le Doctorat de sciences économiques (Paris: Institut d'Études Politiques).

Richard, J.-L. (2004), *Partir ou rester? Destinées des jeunes issus de l'immigration* (Paris: Presses Universitaires de France (PUF)).

Santelli, E. (2001), *La mobilité sociale dans l'immigration: Itinéraires de réussite des enfants d'origine algérienne* (Toulouse: Presses Universitaires du Mirail).

Schnapper, D. (1991), *La France de l'intégration* (Paris: Gallimard).

Schor, R. (1985), *L'Opinion française et les étrangers 1919-1939*, Thèse d'Etat (Paris: Publications de la Sorbonne).
Silberman, R. (1989), 'Statistiques, immigration et minorités'. In P. Vieille (ed.), *L'immigration à l'université et dans le recherche, Babylone n° 6-7* (Paris: Christian Bourgois), pp. 10-18.
Silberman, R. (1992), 'French Immigration Statistics'. In D. L. Horowitz and G. Noiriel (eds.), *Immigrants in Two Democracies: French and American Experience* (New York: New York University Press), pp. 112-17.
Silberman, R. (2002), 'Les enfants d'immigrés sur le marché du travail'. In F. Héran (ed.), *Immigration, marché du travail, intégration*. Commissariat Général du Plan (Paris : La Documentation Française.
Silberman, R. and Fournier, I. (1999), 'Les enfants d'immigrés sur le marché du travail: les mécanismes d'une discrimination sélective', *Formation Emploi*, 65, 31-55.
Silberman, R. and Fournier, I. (2006), 'Les secondes génération sur le marché du travail en France: une pénalité ethnique qui persiste', *Revue Française de Sociologie*, 47, 243-92.
Silberman, R., Alba, R., and Fournier, I. (2007), 'Segmented assimilation in France? Discrimination in the labour market against the second generation', *Ethnic and Racial studies*, 30, 1-27.
Simon, P. (1997a), 'La répresentation statistique de l'immigration: Peut-on comptabiliser l'ethnicité?' In J. L. Rallu, Y. Courbage and Y. Piche (eds.), *Old and New Minorities* (Paris: INED), pp. 11-30.
Simon, P. (1997b), 'La statistique des origines: l'ethnicité et la "race" dans les recensements aux États-Unis, Canada et Grande-Bretagne'. In *Sociétés Contemporaines*, 26, 11-44.
Simon, P. (1998), 'Nationalité et origine dans la statistique française: les catégories ambiguës', *Population*, 53, 541-68.
Simon, P. and Clément, M. (2006), 'Comment décrire la diversité des origines en France? Une enquête exploratoire sur les perceptions des salariés et des étudiants', *Population et Sociétes*, n° 425 (Paris: INED).
Tapinos, G. (1975), 'L'immigration étrangère en France', *Travaux et Documents* (Paris: INED).
Tribalat, M. (1989), 'Immigrés, étrangers, français: l'imbroglio statistique'. *Population et Sociétés, n°241*.
Tribalat, M. (1991a), 'Combien sont les Français d'origine étrangère?' In *Économie et Statistique n° 242*, Paris INSEE.
Tribalat, M. (ed.) (1991b), *Cent ans d'immigration, Étrangers d'hier, Français d'aujourd'hui : apport démographique, dynamique familiale et économique de l'Immigration Étrangère*, Travaux et Documents, Cahier n°131 (Paris: INED-PUF).
Tribalat, M. (1995), *Faire France: Enquête sur les Populations d'Origine Étrangère en France* (Paris: La Découverte).
Tribalat, M. avec la participation de P. Simon et B. Riandey (1996), *De l'immigration à l'assimilation* (La Paris: La Découverte/INED).
Vallet, L.-A. and Caille, J.-P. (1996), 'Les élèves étrangers ou issus de l'immigration dans l'école et le collège français'. *Les Dossiers d'Éducation et Formation, n° 67*, Paris.

Van Zanten, A. (2001), *L'école de la périphérie: Scolarité et ségrégation en banlieue* (Paris: Presses Universitaires de France (PUF)).
Weil, P. (2002), *Qu'est ce qu'un Français ? Histoire de la Nationalité française depuis la Révolution.* Réédition augmentée 2004. (Paris: Grasset).
Wieviorka, M. (1996), 'Culture, société et démocratie'. In M. Wieviorka (ed.), *Une société fragmentée: Le multiculturalisme en débat* (Paris: La Découverte), pp. 11–60.
Zeroulou, Z. (1988), 'La réussite scolaire des enfants d'immigrés: L'apport d'une approche en termes de mobilisation', *Revue Française de Sociologie*, 29, 447–70.

7

Educational Hurdles on the Way to Structural Assimilation in Germany

FRANK KALTER & NADIA GRANATO

Summary. Five major groups of classic 'labour migrants' are established in Germany—Greeks, Italians, (ex-)Yugoslavs, Turks and Iberians, of which the largest single group are the Turks. There now are significant numbers of second-generation men and women from these origins in the German labour market. More recently they have been joined by a more diverse group of migrants from Western Europe, Eastern Europe, the (middle) East and Africa. In the first generation the labour-migrant groups had relatively low levels of education leading to marked ethnic stratification within the labour market. This ethnic stratification continues in the second generation although on a reduced scale. While the second generation has acquired higher levels of education than the first, they still lag some way (the Turks especially so) behind native Germans in their education. Ethnic penalties in the labour market itself are also much reduced in the second generation, although significant penalties remain for Turks. However most of the continuing ethnic stratification is due to processes that operate prior to entry into the labour market.

Introduction

LOOKING AT THE GERMAN LABOUR MARKET, the existence of ethnic inequality is highly visible. No matter which specific indicator one chooses, almost all empirical studies arrive at the general conclusion that nearly all of the distinguishable immigrant groups are less successful than the indigenous population (e.g., Diekmann *et al.* 1993; Velling 1994;

Bender and Seifert 1996; Constant and Massey 2003). This does not only hold true for the 'typical' labour migrants of the 1960s and early 1970s—on which most research to-date has focused—but also for the 'new' immigrant groups, e.g., those from Eastern Europe. Moreover (and most importantly), recent research clearly indicates that not only are direct migrants themselves disadvantaged, but also that their descendants—although improving upon their parents' generation—are still much worse off than indigenous youth (cf. Seifert 1992; Szydlik 1996). As a consequence, many authors tend to come to the conclusion that ethnic stratification may very well become a permanent feature of the German labour market.

In contrast to the empirical facts, however, the theoretical reasons behind the existence and persistence of ethnic inequality in Germany have been far less clear—until now. 'Obvious' explanations for ethnic stratification in former decades, and above all explanations of strong negative selectivity with respect to qualifications, have neither sufficiently accounted for why former immigrants have failed to improve their chances over time nor accounted for the situation of more recent immigrants or the continuing disadvantages of the second and third generations. So far, surprisingly little research has tried to disentangle the main mechanisms through which observable inequalities come into being or are reproduced—the most important question being whether this disadvantage may result from labour-market discrimination or from processes associated with human capital assets.

One of the main reasons for this is the fact that large-scale data sets have not been available until recently. As a consequence, many studies were unable to include differentiated measures of educational qualifications or to differentiate between different ethnic groups and different generations; almost all studies were unable to combine both aspects. Recently this situation has changed and new attempts have been made in order to consider more systematically the mechanisms accounting for ethnic disadvantages (Granato 2003; Granato and Kalter 2001; Kalter and Granato 2002; Konietzka and Seibert 2003). Therefore, the general aim of this chapter is to continue this work and contribute to still-open questions regarding ethnic inequality in the German labour market.

Given this general aim, this chapter is structured as follows: the first section will briefly describe the history of post-war immigration to Germany, specifying the background conditions against which the patterns of ethnic inequality have developed. The second section will sketch out the general mechanisms which may account for ethnic disadvantage and their plausibility—given the immigration patterns and institutional labour market setting—in the German case. Following the general scheme of analysis outlined in the introduction to this volume, we then analyse the patterns of ethnic inequality empirically, relying on data from the German microcensus. A description of the foreign population (i.e., its ethnic and socio-economic structure) is provided first, followed by analyses addressing the degree of ethnic disadvantage with respect to unemployment and occupational attainment, and discussing specifically those mechanisms related to formal education and labour market discrimination. Our final section will discuss the main findings of this chapter and possible tasks for future research.

Immigration history and immigration context in post-war Germany

For much of its history with regard to migration, Germany has largely been a 'sending' rather than a 'receiving' country (Bade 1992). Like many other European countries, the switch to a country of immigration happened soon after the end of the Second World War. While it is true that emigration was predominant in Germany for many years prior, it is worth noting that even before the Second World War immigration to Germany was far from absent and played an important part in the country's socio-economic and demographic development. For example, the census of 1910 reported a total of 1.3 million foreigners living in Germany, nearly half of them stemming from Austria. In 1925, between the wars, about one million foreigners were living in Germany, with the Poles (more than one-quarter of all foreigners) being the predominant group (Münz 2002: 21).

Substantial inflow to Germany started soon after 1945, and one can distinguish (roughly) five different phases of post-war immigration to Germany. In the aftermath of the war the first important phase was the 'immigration' of Germans, or the refugees and expellees from former German territories in Eastern Europe. The beginning of the Cold War led to many additional Germans from the Soviet sector entering the Western sector, and after 1949 GDR citizens became the most important immigrant group in the Federal Republic (Velling 1994: 33). However, in 1961 these movements ended dramatically with the construction of the Berlin wall.

The erection of the Berlin wall thus marks the starting point of the second phase of immigration, largely one of massive labour migration from Southern Europe. As early as the 1950s West Germany experienced a growing shortage of labour in its lower and less qualified sectors of the economy due to extremely quick economic growth—its so-called 'economic miracle'. As a consequence Germany, like other Western European countries, began to recruit workers from Southern Europe to fill these specific labour-market gaps. The first recruitment agreement between the FRG and Italy was made in 1955, to be followed by agreements with Spain and Greece, both in 1960. However, because of the aforementioned parallel integration of refugees, expellees, and GDR-citizens into the labour market, as Figure 7.1 shows, the number of foreigners in Germany rose only slightly in the period up until 1961, remaining well below one million.

This trend, however, changed dramatically over the next few years. Additional recruitment agreements with Turkey (1961), Morocco (1963), Portugal (1964), Tunisia (1965) and Yugoslavia (1968) were made and subsequently the number of foreigners in Germany increased sharply. In 1973 there were already four million foreign-born living in Germany. Whilst inflow from Morocco and Tunisia never played a (numerically) important part, around three million came from the six other recruitment countries, constituting the amalgam group of 'labour migrants' (Borjas 1987) (again see Figure 7.1). While the early years of recruitment were dominated by migrants from Italy, Spain and Greece, Turkish and Yugoslav migrants became the dominant groups after the economic recession in 1967. The labour migration was intended to fill specific shortages in the domestic labour market in a flexible way; therefore the so-called 'rotation model' was designed, based on a temporary 'stay-and-return' migration. This model explains the high rates of annual in- and outflows throughout the 1960s and early 1970s, as well as why those migrants were referred to as 'guest workers' (Bade 1992: 394). As 'guest-workers' were explicitly recruited into unskilled positions, concentrated in a few industrial sectors, with unfavourable working conditions, it is not surprising that over the course of this immigration phase, a severe ethnic stratification (*Unterschichtung*) emerged in the German labour market.

This second phase of immigration ended in 1973 when, as a consequence of the OPEC oil embargo and its negative effect on labour demand, the government of the FRG stopped the guest-worker recruitment. But, contrary to the government's intentions, the influx of

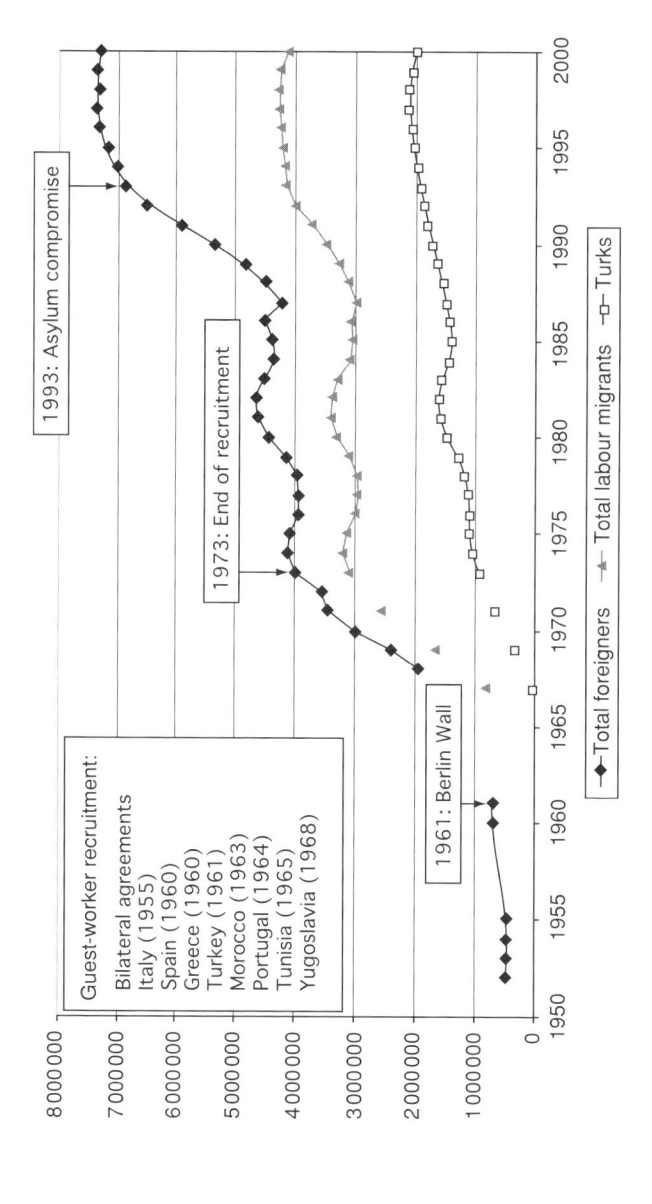

Figure 7.1. The growth of the foreign population in Germany.

migrants decreased only slightly and only in the short run. By 1976 the number of migrants coming to Germany was rising again, and return migration was decreasing; the reason for this reversal was that, although direct recruitment had been stopped, spouses and children of immigrant workers living in Germany were allowed to immigrate. Thus, the most prevalent type of immigration in this third phase was family reunification, constituting 50 to 70% of the influx between 1975 and 1981 (Velling 1993). As a consequence the stock of foreigners living in Germany decreased only slightly between 1974 and 1977 and started to rise slightly again by 1978.

Due to the process of family reunification, the demographic composition of migrants changed considerably, and their overall rate of labour force participation declined. Additionally, with the recession of 1974–5, the unemployment rate of migrants became higher than that of native Germans for the first time; this strong rise in migrant unemployment also reflected the government's policy to favour German job applicants—in other words, migrants were typically only able to get a work permit if no Germans were applying for the same job. At the beginning of the 1980s, with family reunification migration ceasing but migrant unemployment continuing to rise, the German government used financial incentives to promote 'return migration'. The impact of these incentives, however, was rather small as they tended to influence only the time of return for those migrants who had already decided to go back, and not the actual decision to return. The fact that coming back to Germany after returning to one's home country was almost impossible also probably decreased the impact of the incentives. Overall, the length of immigrants' stays was extending, and more and more guest workers were making plans to stay in Germany permanently.

Beginning in the mid 1980s a fourth phase of immigration began, with a shift from classical labour migration to a new influx of asylum seekers and 'ethnic' Germans (i.e., people with German ancestry living in Eastern European states, the so-called *Aussiedler*). With the fall of the Iron Curtain and the liberalisation of travel regulations, migration of ethnic Germans from the former Soviet Union (and its successor states), Poland and Romania increased considerably, especially as according to German law they were granted German citizenship almost immediately (Münz 2002). When more than 377,000 *Aussiedler* came in 1989 the government reacted by imposing a number of restrictions. These restrictions led to the implementation of a new law in 1993 which outlined how to deal with the consequences of war. The law set forth both a quota for the annual admission of ethnic Germans and a new definition as to who belongs to that group. The rise in the number of asylum seekers was largely due to the civil war in Yugoslavia, the conflicts in Kurdish territories of Turkey and northern Iraq as well as the fall of the Iron Curtain. Again in 1993 however, this massive inflow was reduced by the so-called German 'Asylum Compromise', which replaced the relatively liberal regulations (at least when compared to those of other European countries) with strict admission criteria.

Given the two major legislative changes taking place in 1993, immigration thereafter declined considerably. These changes marked the beginning of the fifth phase of migration, composed predominantly of new labour migrants from Poland, the Czech Republic and other Eastern European states. Although many still come to Germany with intentions of permanent residency, temporary forms of migration, such as seasonal workers or new guest-workers with time-limited working contracts, have recently become increasingly important.

Explaining ethnic disadvantages in the German labour market

Essentially there are two starting points explaining ethnic disadvantages in the labour market—first, immigrants may lack the resources which are necessary to succeed, above all human capital; or second, they may receive different returns for their human capital. Against the background of this general distinction, this chapter attempts two things. On the one hand, we try to sketch more precise theoretical mechanisms distinguishing why investments in human capital or the returns to human capital may differ. On the other, we briefly discuss whether, in the German case, the necessary conditions under which these particular mechanisms come to bear are met.

We begin this section by examining the first point, i.e., why immigrants might differ from natives with respect to investment in human capital. In the literature on economic assimilation there are at least three prominent explanations for this differential; we refer to them as the 'standard explanations' in the following. First, following Borjas (1987) in-migration might be 'negatively selected' with respect to human capital; i.e., the differential might be due to differences in average human capital investment between the home country and the host country or to an increased likelihood of individuals with lower levels of human capital immigrating. A second explanation argues that some aspects of human capital (e.g. language skills) are culturally specific, and thus these skills are more useful in some societal contexts than in others. The act of migration leads to a devaluation of these human capital aspects specific to the country of origin and, as a consequence, to a devaluation of human capital overall (Chiswick 1978, 1991; Friedberg 2000). Finally, a third mechanism asserts that immigrants might consider their stay in the host country as temporary, and thus might be more reluctant to invest in aspects of human capital that are specific to the host country (Bonachich 1972; Dustmann 1993; 2000).

Surely in the case of labour migration to Germany in the 1960s and 1970s all three mechanisms are relevant. First, there is no doubt—due to the specific historical demand—that in-migration in the 1960s and 1970s was dominated by low-qualified workers, resulting in an instant ethnic stratification (*Unterschichtung*) in the labour market (Hoffmann-Nowotny 1973; Heckmann 1992: 81). Second, German is not spoken in any of the six recruitment countries and three or four decades ago cultural contexts were also rather dissimilar to the German society. Third, as outlined in the previous section of this chapter, the workers initially entered Germany under the conditions of the rotation principle which explicitly required return migration after a short number of years.

For more recent immigrant groups, e.g., Eastern Europeans, however, the situation is different. As compared to former labour migrants these groups not only arrived with more permanent orientations, but also with considerably higher levels of formal qualifications as shown in Tables 7.2A and 7.2B below. Here, then, the question at-hand is whether these qualifications are rightfully acknowledged and compensated in the labour market. In this respect the German labour market provides especially high hurdles, as it is strongly segmented along professional lines, and access to particular occupations is strongly correlated with the German vocational training system. This arrangement has proved to be a major obstacle for labour market integration of the *Aussiedler* (Konietzka and Kreyenfeld 2001).

It should also be noted that all three 'standard explanations' only hold true for newcomers with direct migration experience, i.e. the first generation of immigrants. In contrast, the second generation never experiences migration, nor do they, generally, harbour ideas of return migration. Nonetheless, there are multiple ways in which disadvantages may be transmitted from generation to generation. Although much research remains to be done to explicate the exact mechanisms through which these transmission processes operate,[1] general research on social mobility has shown clearly that Germany provides a societal context where barriers to intergenerational social mobility and impacts of social origin on educational attainment are relatively strong (cf. Erikson and Goldthorpe 1992; Müller *et al.* 1989; Müller and Pollak 2004) and thus affect immigrant groups in particular. Although there are few quantitative studies examining the educational attainment of immigrants' children, these studies show that disadvantages are mainly (Alba *et al.* 1994) or even completely (Kristen and Granato 2004) due to socio-economic background differences rather than ethnicity.

We now turn to our second point—whether ethnic minorities receive different returns on their human capital investments within the German labour market. Here, economic theory has made great strides in understanding the main mechanism of discrimination and the conditions under which discrimination is most likely to occur. The neo-classical approach clearly predicts that discrimination will not exist in perfect markets. Turning it the other way round, this implies that market failure is a necessary condition for discriminative behaviour to exist and most of the prominent discrimination theories can easily be fitted into this general idea. To begin, theories of monopsonistic discrimination start from the assumption that there is a lack of competition on the demand side for labour (Madden 1973).[2] With respect to the situation in Germany, however, one may expect that this source of discrimination is relatively weak in comparison to other countries. As discussed above, the German labour market is strongly segmented along occupational lines rather than segmented between firms (Marsden 1990); thus the monopsonistic power of the firms can be expected to be relatively low.

In his seminal work on the 'economics of discrimination', Becker (1971) relies on personal preferences, or 'tastes for discrimination', as the mechanism fostering discrimination. Becker shows that such tastes—appearing on the side of employers, employees or customers—will result in effective market discrimination. There is some doubt, however, as to whether tastes for discrimination will persist over time in markets that are otherwise competitive (Arrow 1972: 192; Arrow 1998). This same doubt

---

[1] Here, decision models of investment under uncertainty (e.g., Breen and Goldthorpe 1997; Erikson and Jonsson 1996; Esser 1999: 265 ff.; Kalter 2003: 59 ff.) seem to provide a fruitful framework.
[2] The arguments do not only hold true for monopsonies in a narrower sense, but also if cartels or mobility barriers for labour exist.

holds true for a third form of discrimination, namely the so-called 'error discrimination' where employers have false beliefs about workers' qualities (England 1992: 60). As this critique argues, if there are no other market failures (e.g., monopsonies), actors with either tastes for discrimination or 'false beliefs' will not be able to compete successfully against other actors having no tastes and 'true beliefs'.[3] Therefore, the explanatory power of taste discrimination and error discrimination seems to be questionable in the middle- to long-run. Thus with respect to Germany, these explanations are especially unconvincing in explaining the disadvantage faced by longer-established groups of migrants, such as the labour migrants.

Closely related to the idea of error discrimination, but different in consequence, are theories of statistical discrimination. As in error discrimination, these approaches assume that employers do not have full information on the productivity of workers and subsequently impute other information instead. However, in contrast to error discrimination the imputed values are not really seen as 'false' but rather as being a 'statistical approximation'. In principle, at least three different models of statistical discrimination can be distinguished (Phelps 1972; Arrow 1972; Aigner and Cain 1977; England 1992: 56 ff.). Groups are assumed to differ with respect to (1) their mean productivity, (2) variances in productivity or (3) the reliability of tests trying to measure productivity. If one uses formal education as the test variable in the third type, this leads to an application of the so-called 'signalling theory' (Arrow 1973). In contrast to the concepts of taste discrimination and error discrimination, the idea of statistical discrimination seems to be more important for empirical applications. However, especially as compared with other countries, in Germany the link between educational/vocational qualifications and the labour market is especially close (Müller *et al.* 1998). Thus, the signalling power of educational qualifications (or the reliability of the test variable) is subsequently strong, at least with respect to those qualifications that have been acquired in Germany (and thus applicable for the second generation).

To summarise, the specific context of immigration and the institutional labour-market setting in Germany suggest that in order to explain ethnic disadvantage, processes related to human capital seem more important than processes related to discrimination. Therefore, in our

---

[3] Recently, some models have been suggested that show that tastes could be stable over time if search costs exist (Black 1995; Borjas and Bronars 1989).

analysis, ethnic disadvantages are expected to be severely reduced upon controlling for educational qualifications.

Note, however, that residual effects of ethnicity—the so-called 'ethnic penalties'—might exist even if discrimination (in a narrower sense) were absent. First, it should be noted that formal educational qualifications are only a proxy variable for human capital, defined as the whole of abilities and skills which account for a worker's productivity. Therefore unmeasured aspects of human capital may account for ethnic differences—perhaps above all those aspects which are culturally specific, such as language proficiency or other cultural knowledge.[4] Second, (one's own) human capital is not the only relevant resource for achieving good labour market positions. Most obviously, there might be a direct impact of parental resources on a child's success which is not mediated by the child's actual level of human capital. Further, job searchers might also mobilise the resources of others, or their social capital, to aid in their search. It is well known in the economic literature that social networks play a decisive role in the labour market, as empirically many jobs are found with the help of friends and relatives. Networks of immigrants and their children might differ from those of the indigenous youth with respect to ethnic composition. As ethnically homogenous ties may only give access to information and resources available in the ethnic community they might not be as helpful as ties to the indigenous population and thus subsequently lead to disadvantage (Portes and Rumbaut 2001: 48; Petersen and Saporta 2000).

Characteristics of the foreign population in Germany

Following on from the migration processes discussed earlier, this section will describe the structure of the foreign population in Germany resulting from these processes. We will start with a more detailed look at the ethnic composition of Germany, followed by a description of the central

---

[4] This argument has already been mentioned above and basically, it is the most obvious explanation why residual effects of ethnicity (controlling for education) may be observed for the first generation. Although immigrants' children do much better than their parents with respect to such culturally specific skills, there might still be a considerable gap between them and the indigenous youth and this might be important also for the second generation to succeed in the labour market.

socio-economic characteristics of ethnic groups, such as educational qualification, economic activity and occupational attainment.

The composition of the foreign population

To examine ethnic differences in labour market success we rely on data from the 1993 and 1996 German Microcensuses (MZ). The German MZ is an annual survey of 1% of households in Germany (Lüttinger and Riede 1997). Scientific-use files exist for several recent years, each consisting of a 70% subsample. The German Microcensus is an appropriate data source for the specific aims of comparative analysis as it contains detailed information on educational attainment as well as on a range of labour market variables. In addition, the sample size is large enough to obtain a sufficient number of immigrants and their children and to allow distinction between several relevant subgroups. Additionally, being an obligatory survey, the Microcensus delivers a largely unbiased picture of the population—another advantage compared to other available survey data.

Our analysis is constrained to respondents aged 18–59, leaving a total of 476,127 respondents in the pooled 1993 and 1996 datasets. Of those, 31,852 (7.4%) can be defined as immigrants and their descendants. Note, however, that for the purposes of this analysis the definition of immigrants and their descendants must rely on nationality, as the MZ—like most other German data sets—does not contain information on parents' country of birth for most respondents. This deviates from the concept of 'ethnicity' used in many of the other contributions to this volume and in general seems to lead to a rather restricted understanding of 'minority groups'. However, in our case this deviation from the concept of parents' country of birth may not be severe as naturalisation of immigrants in Germany was not common until the end of the 1990s.[5]

---

[5] Traditionally, in Germany citizenship has been based on the rules of 'ius sanguinis' and until 1993 naturalisation of those without at least one German parent or German ancestry was exceptional and a matter of discretion (Diehl and Blohm 2003). In the period from 1974 (one year after the stopping of recruitment) to 1992 only 311,000 immigrants were naturalised and the yearly rates ranged between 0.3% and 0.6% with respect to the total foreign population (Münz et al. 1999: 125). Since the first revision of the citizenship law in 1993 immigrants with a duration of stay of fifteen years or more were legally entitled to become naturalised resulting in slightly increasing figures. However, from 1993 until 1997 the yearly rates were still very low-ranging between 1.0% and 1.2%. Only recently, the situation has changed more dramatically as the figures e.g. for Turks noticeably increased since 1999 and a second—more liberal—revision of the citizenship law took place in 2000. However, these recent developments do not concern our data.

The large sample size allows us to classify the non-Germans into eleven different groups. Five of these groups (Italian, Greek, (ex-) Yugoslav, Turkish and Iberian (combination of either Spanish or Portuguese)) represent the classical labour-migrant population; in the following we refer to this group of nationalities as 'labour migrants'. Together they constitute more than two thirds of the foreign population, with nearly half of them (one-third of the total foreign population) being Turkish (see also Figure 7.1). The category of 'Western Europe' covers respondents from France, Britain, the Netherlands, Austria, Belgium, Denmark, Finland, Sweden, Ireland, Luxembourg and the US. This group represents 10% of the foreign population in Germany, followed by those coming from the (mid) East (Table 7.1). With more than 6% of respondents coming from Eastern European countries, immigrants from the former USSR, Poland, Romania and Slovakia represent a notable share. Migrants from African countries form a rather small group, making up nearly 3% of the non-German population. All other respondents are classified into the residual categories 'Other European countries' (including the Western countries not mentioned above (e.g., Switzerland) and other Eastern and Middle European countries) or 'Other non-European countries'.[6]

Table 7.1. The composition of the foreign population in Germany, aged 18–59 (percentages of sample).

	First generation	Second generation	Total
Italian	7.4	2.0	9.4
Greek	4.7	1.4	6.1
Yugoslav	14.3	2.1	16.4
Iberian	3.0	0.9	3.9
Turkish	26.6	6.7	33.3
W. European & US	8.3	1.7	10.0
E. European	6.0	0.1	6.1
Other European	2.6	0.3	2.8
African	2.6	0.2	2.8
(Mid) Eastern	7.2	0.2	7.4
Other non-European	1.6	0.1	1.7
Total	84.2	15.8	100.0
Total N	26813	5039	31852

Note: Cases are weighted; foreign population (defined as respondents of non-German nationality) aged 18–59 accounts for 7.4% of the total population aged 18–59.

[6] The residual category of 'other European countries' results from the fact that in the scientific use files of the MZ several European nationalities are not listed separately but classified in such a way that a distinction between Western and Eastern Europe is not possible.

Among all ethnic groups living in Germany, the share of the second generation is still small. Only one in six can be designated as belonging to the second generation if one defines it by either being born in Germany or immigrating before the age of six. Not surprisingly, the share is a bit higher for the five classical labour-migrant groups, save immigrants from the former Yugoslavia. This might be due to the fact that a large number of refugees came to Germany during the civil war in former Yugoslavia. As the numbers of second-generation respondents from Eastern Europe, other European countries, Africa, the (middle) East and other non-European regions are very low, we pool these five categories in all subsequent analyses of the second generation.

Educational attainment

Looking at the educational attainment of the different minority groups, distinctive patterns of selectivity, especially as compared to the indigenous population, can be seen. Beginning with first-generation male immigrants (Table 7.2A), groups are observed which are clearly less educated, clearly more educated, and which differ in distribution from the Germans, mostly in a U-shaped way indicating over-representation at both the lower and upper ends of the educational qualification ladder. First-generation male labour migrants clearly belong to the disadvantaged groups. This is not very surprising considering the fact that—as discussed in the first section—labour recruitment in the sixties and early seventies was explicitly negatively selective with respect to qualifications. In Table 7.2A these historical traces become apparent when comparing the proportions of lowest and highest degrees within these groups with those of the indigenous population. While only a minor proportion of German men aged 18–59 have no or only primary school education, nearly half of first-generation Italians, Greeks, Iberians and Turks, and nearly one-third of first-generation ex-Yugoslavs are at the lowest level of education. At the other extreme, while more than 9% of the Germans have higher tertiary education, the respective shares are much lower amongst first-generation labour-migrant groups, ranging from 2 to 4%. Among the remaining first-generation groups only Africans are likewise disadvantaged, but even they do slightly better on average than first-generation labour migrants as their share of highly educated respondents (7.5%) is only slightly lower than that of native Germans.

In sharp contrast, first-generation Western European immigrants are clearly positively selected in comparison to benchmark Germans.

Table 7.2A. Highest educational qualification, by ancestry and generation: Men (row percentages).

	Primary/None	Lower secondary	Higher secondary	Lower tertiary	Higher tertiary	N
Native German	8.7	64.2	11.4	6.4	9.3	174653
First generation						
Italian	53.6	41.1	2.6	0.7	2.1	1395
Greek	49.0	38.0	7.8	1.7	3.5	760
Yugoslav	31.6	58.7	5.3	1.7	2.8	2167
Iberian	53.6	38.4	5.4	0.8	1.8	436
Turkish	59.7	32.8	4.7	1.0	1.9	4144
W. European & US	8.4	43.8	16.3	10.6	20.9	1307
E. European	13.4	49.4	16.5	7.4	13.4	733
Other European	29.5	43.9	10.0	4.3	12.4	368
African	41.8	28.6	19.4	2.7	7.5	511
(Mid) Eastern	28.9	22.4	23.8	5.7	19.2	1079
Other non-European	22.6	22.2	23.1	6.1	25.9	186
Second generation						
Italian	31.2	57.7	7.7	2.5	0.8	317
Greek	29.3	47.0	17.3	2.0	4.4	218
Yugoslav	30.0	62.0	6.9	1.1	0.0	318
Iberian	21.7	60.9	11.2	4.4	1.9	141
Turkish	42.4	48.3	8.6	0.2	0.5	997
W. European & US	12.8	50.6	22.0	3.1	11.6	287
All Other	33.8	37.4	21.6	2.9	4.3	122

Although both groups show similar proportions with no or low-level qualifications, the proportion of migrants from Western Europe with higher tertiary education is more than twice that of German natives. For the remaining first-generation groups, the Eastern Europeans, other Europeans, Eastern migrants, and the remaining category of 'other', the question of whether there is a relative advantage or disadvantage is less clear, especially as we find the above-mentioned pattern of U-shaped selectivity, with proportions of the lowest and highest educational groups notably higher than in the German reference group.

Surely one of the most telling indicators of a minority group's integration is the difference between generations. If we look now at the educational attainment of the second generation, amongst all of the five labour-migrant groups we find a rather similar pattern: overall, the second generation does better than the first; however, when compared to the German reference group there remains a remarkable gap in human capital assets. Second-generation male Turks are especially disadvantaged with more than 40% holding no or only primary education and more than 90% holding qualifications no higher than lower secondary. The four other labour-migrant groups do slightly better, with proportions holding no or only primary qualifications varying between 22% (Iberians) and 31% (Italians). These findings are even more important considering that these figures do not take into account different age structures. If one were to compare second-generation groups to similarly aged Germans the educational gap would probably be even more pronounced due to educational expansion. Thus, already at this early point of our analyses we get a hint that proper access to educational qualifications seems to be a very severe problem with respect to the labour market integration of second-generation labour migrants. Second-generation migrants from other (non-European) countries, who are highly heterogeneous with respect to ethnicity, also tend to be less educated than German respondents with more than two-thirds having qualifications at or below lower secondary.

As Table 7.2B shows, although the educational qualifications of women, on average, are notably lower than those of men, in most cases similar patterns with respect to immigrant selectivity can be found. For the first generation we find that female labour migrants and Africans are clearly disadvantaged in terms of educational qualifications as compared to German women. This is most obvious at the lowest educational level, which is held by between 57% (ex-Yugoslavs) and 80% (Turks) of labour-migrant women, compared to only 18% of the German women. Conversely, Western European women are clearly advantaged in terms of qualifications, as are Eastern European women, albeit in a less-pronounced manner. While this latter finding deviates from the results for men, again we find a U-shaped pattern for the remaining three first-generation groups.

Save the Turks, second-generation labour-migrant men and women have rather similar educational qualifications. The fact that, roughly, first-generation women have lower educational qualifications than men indicates that improvement across generations is stronger for women. Moreover, the gap with the indigenous population seems to be smaller as German women are less educated than German men. However, in order to give an accurate assessment controlling for birth cohorts would be necessary.

Economic activity and occupational attainment

Turning to economic activity, Table 7.3A clearly shows that male immigrants are highly involved in the German labour market. Among the first

Table 7.2B. Highest educational qualifications, by ancestry and generation: Women (row percentages).

	Primary/None	Lower secondary	Higher secondary	Lower tertiary	Higher tertiary	N
Native German	17.8	62.2	10.9	2.9	6.3	172716
First generation						
Italian	70.1	20.2	4.6	0.8	4.3	851
Greek	69.3	21.4	5.2	0.8	3.3	638
Yugoslav	57.2	34.8	4.7	0.9	2.4	2040
Iberian	60.4	25.7	7.8	0.6	5.6	440
Turkish	80.5	15.9	2.7	0.2	0.7	3658
W. European & US	12.6	39.7	20.9	5.4	21.5	1190
E. European	16.6	38.7	23.5	6.7	14.5	989
Other European	37.0	28.5	15.6	6.2	12.6	381
African	65.6	20.4	9.6	0.7	3.7	236
(Mid) Eastern	36.8	20.7	22.0	3.4	17.2	962
Other non-European	24.1	26.3	21.9	3.4	24.4	280
Second generation						
Italian	32.3	57.1	8.2	1.4	1.0	257
Greek	27.4	44.1	24.7	1.1	2.7	163
Yugoslav	18.0	65.3	15.3	1.0	0.3	257
Iberian	24.3	59.0	14.6	2.1	0	126
Turkish	51.6	41.0	6.8	0.1	0.5	866
W. European & US	16.7	52.4	19.9	4.1	6.9	215
All Other	33.6	38.3	22.7	0.8	4.7	112

generation, activity rates of Western Europeans and the labour-migrant groups—except for the ex-Yugoslavs—are clearly higher than the rate of the reference population. In contrast, however, the remaining groups show lower rates of economic activity than the Germans. It is reasonable to assume that this lower rate mainly reflects differences between minority groups with respect to their legal status in Germany; this also explains the deviation of former Yugoslavs from the overall labour-migrant pattern. High rates of studentship also contribute to lower levels of economic activity for African and Eastern immigrants. It is not surprising that second-generation groups show much lower activity rates than both first-generation groups and native Germans; as Table 7.3A clearly indicates, this divergence is due to higher rates of studentship rather than other reasons for economic inactivity. Again this finding points to the fact that the age structure of the second-generation groups strongly deviates from that of the German reference population.

In contrast to men, female immigrants (shown in Table 7.3B) of the first generation do not show higher rates of economic activity than German women, with Greeks the only exception. While the differences

Table 7.3A. Economic activity by ancestry and generation: Men (row percentages).

	Economically active	Student	Other inactive	N
Native German	88.8	6.0	5.1	194968
First generation				
Italian	95.5	0.4	4.1	1477
Greek	94.5	0.8	4.8	809
Yugoslav	88.2	0.8	10.9	2336
Iberian	93.4	1.1	5.6	473
Turkish	90.1	1.3	8.7	4442
W. European & US	92.1	3.6	4.3	1374
E. European	86.6	5.5	7.9	808
Other European	81.3	5.0	13.7	403
African	76.8	12.4	10.8	557
(Mid) Eastern	77.9	11.2	10.9	1209
Other non-European	78.2	8.8	13.0	209
Second generation				
Italian	86.3	9.8	4.0	350
Greek	76.7	21.2	2.1	248
Yugoslav	81.1	15.7	3.2	361
Iberian	88.3	10.6	1.1	157
Turkish	84.0	12.8	3.2	1138
W. European & US	82.6	15.2	2.2	318
All Other	66.7	25.0	8.3	147

Table 7.3B. Economic activity, by ancestry and generation: Women (row percentages).

	Economically active	Student	Other inactive	N
Native German	67.9	4.9	27.2	193772
First generation				
Italian	62.4	1.1	36.5	891
Greek	73.2	1.4	25.4	692
Yugoslav	64.9	0.9	34.2	2219
Iberian	63.8	2.6	33.6	474
Turkish	42.2	1.1	56.7	4016
W. European & US	65.6	4.4	30.1	1264
E. European	58.5	4.2	37.3	1087
Other European	52.1	5.1	42.8	413
African	41.9	5.6	52.5	265
(Mid) Eastern	39.1	7.8	53.1	1082
Other non-European	43.4	7.3	49.3	312
Second generation				
Italian	68.9	9.5	21.7	287
Greek	57.1	27.0	15.9	198
Yugoslav	68.1	21.9	10.0	307
Iberian	67.5	13.5	19.0	143
Turkish	59.8	14.6	25.7	1010
W. European & US	70.2	10.7	19.1	238
All Other	56.3	23.4	20.3	138

from the indigenous population are only minor for Western Europeans and most labour-migrant groups, they are of considerable size for Turks and the other remaining groups. Looking at the second generation we find another important deviation from the male pattern. Except for Greeks, all second-generation female groups show higher rates of economic activity than their respective first-generation groups—even though the rates of studentship are also higher. In other words, for second-generation women the likelihood of belonging to the 'other inactive' group is clearly reduced compared to that of the first generation. It would be useful to know, however, whether this is a pure age effect or also a cohort effect. Unfortunately the cross-sectional nature of our data means that this question cannot be answered.

Tables 7.4A and B report the current occupational attainment of those characterised as economically active. The general picture here is that, compared to the indigenous population, all minority groups except for the Western Europeans are by some means or other disadvantaged; this holds true for men as well as women. Examining likelihoods of unemployment, for example, nearly all groups show higher proportions of unemployed respondents than the Germans. This pattern especially applies to four groups—Eastern Europeans, Africans, (middle) Easterners, and immigrants from other (non-European) countries—whose rates of unemployment are up to four times higher. Amongst labour migrants, unemployment rates are moderate with Turks being the most affected group. With respect to generational differences we find a slight improvement for second-generation women, but there is no such trend for the men. Otherwise the unemployment patterns for men and women are roughly the same.

As might be expected given the history of guest-worker recruitment and the strong segmentation of the German labour market, first-generation labour migrants are mainly found in the semi- and unskilled sector. Among men this proportion is above 50%, and among women nearly two-thirds. We find, however, that the respective shares for the second-generation groups are clearly lower, albeit still higher than for the indigenous population.

In the salariat, only first-generation male migrants from Western European countries (and the US) have a higher share (43%) than the Germans (28%), whereas first-generation labour migrants are strongly under-represented, with proportions ranging only between almost 3 and 6%. Among second-generation labour migrants, Iberian and Italian men have the highest share in the salariat, whereas Turks have the lowest.

Table 7.4A. Current occupation by ancestry and generation: Men (row percentages).

	Salariat	Routine non-manual	Petty bourgeoisie	Skilled manual	Semi- and unskilled	Un-employed	N
Native German	28.1	8.3	7.8	33.1	16.4	6.2	172759
First generation							
Italian	4.7	1.8	11.2	20.4	51.0	10.9	1410
Greek	6.2	1.2	12.1	16.5	51.6	12.5	764
Yugoslav	4.8	0.8	3.7	30.2	46.0	14.6	2061
Iberian	6.7	1.6	1.4	25.4	55.6	9.3	442
Turkish	2.6	0.6	3.8	16.7	57.7	18.6	4001
W. European & US	42.5	5.7	8.0	18.3	19.4	6.2	1265
E. European	12.5	2.1	2.6	25.5	36.6	20.7	699
Other European	19.0	2.7	3.7	16.3	35.6	22.7	327
African	4.9	1.4	2.3	12.3	50.9	28.2	428
(Mid) Eastern	17.4	3.1	6.9	12.3	35.0	25.4	941
Other non-European	26.2	5.4	6.4	12.3	27.3	22.5	164
Second generation							
Italian	10.1	7.3	5.8	33.9	31.3	11.6	302
Greek	7.4	5.1	12.0	27.7	30.0	18.0	190
Yugoslav	6.6	9.9	2.7	46.3	23.6	11.0	293
Iberian	17.1	6.3	2.5	44.3	24.1	5.7	138
Turkish	3.2	4.3	3.4	38.3	35.0	15.8	956
W. European & US	27.0	10.0	11.0	28.0	14.0	10.0	263
All Other	14.4	1.8	2.7	21.6	33.3	26.1	97

While access to the salariat has only slightly improved intergenerationally, second-generation labour migrants find much better access to routine non-manual jobs (for women) and to the skilled manual sector (for men) than their parents. It is interesting to note that second-generation ex-Yugoslav, Iberian and Turkish men are most likely found in skilled manual work, even exceeding the German benchmark rate. The same holds true for second-generation ex-Yugoslav and Iberian women in the routine non-manual sector. As with educational qualifications, the occupational attainment of first-generation Africans is similar to that of first-generation labour migrants.

A different pattern emerges for migrants from Eastern Europe, other European countries and the East, however. Although these groups are also predominantly located in the semi- and unskilled sector, they also have much better access to the salariat than the labour migrants. The latter fact reflects the U-shaped pattern of selectivity with regard to educational qualifications we mentioned earlier. Note, however, that even for these groups the shares of those working in the salariat are still lower than

Table 7.4B. Current occupation, by ancestry and generation: Women (row percentages).

	Salariat	Routine non-manual	Petty bourgeoisie	Skilled manual	Semi- and unskilled	Un-employed	N
Native German	23.6	28.2	5.7	5.3	30.1	7.2	131547
First generation							
Italian	6.6	7.4	6.8	4.3	61.4	13.5	556
Greek	3.1	4.0	11.1	4.8	65.4	11.6	506
Yugoslav	7.8	6.0	2.9	5.3	64.6	13.4	1441
Iberian	6.1	6.1	3.2	4.6	69.7	10.4	303
Turkish	3.1	3.8	3.2	4.2	64.3	21.5	1691
W. European & US	33.0	24.0	6.8	5.2	23.5	7.6	828
E. European	16.1	10.3	2.9	4.8	38.6	27.3	635
Other European	24.8	8.9	2.9	4.5	39.0	19.9	215
African	7.1	10.2	3.2	2.4	49.6	27.6	111
(Mid) Eastern	18.2	10.5	4.6	4.8	40.1	21.9	424
Other non-European	20.0	18.1	5.8	5.2	34.8	16.1	136
Second generation							
Italian	8.0	28.8	4.0	10.2	38.1	11.1	198
Greek	13.2	27.9	3.9	7.0	37.2	10.9	113
Yugoslav	7.5	46.0	0.0	8.0	27.6	10.9	209
Iberian	14.6	36.4	0.9	13.6	26.4	8.2	96
Turkish	5.2	24.1	1.5	11.9	39.3	18.1	604
W. European & US	29.3	27.8	4.7	7.3	24.6	6.3	167
All Other	21.4	22.5	2.3	11.2	28.1	14.6	78

the share for the indigenous population. This already hints at the theory that their high qualifications might not be fully rewarded in the German labour market. In the next section, the precise role of educational qualifications in explaining the labour market disadvantages of minority groups in Germany will be analysed in detail.

Labour market success of minority groups in Germany

Unemployment

As shown in Tables 7.4A and 7.4B, nearly all minority groups in Germany exhibit considerably higher unemployment rates than the indigenous population. This section will now analyse the extent to which these observed disadvantages can be traced back to different human capital endowments and also address whether there are inequalities in terms of differential returns to human capital investments for different groups.

In order to address the first of these questions, two logistic regression models are estimated separately for both men and women. The first model regresses the binary variable 'unemployed' on age, age squared, marital status, year of survey and the ancestry-generation variable.[7] As in the other chapters in this volume, we model the avoidance of unemployment. A negative coefficient thus indicates that the odds of being employed rather than unemployed are poorer for the group concerned than for the reference group. The logit coefficients stemming from this model (full models are not reported in this text) are shown as grey bars in Figures 7.2A and 7.2B, reflecting the gross amount of disadvantage for the different ethnic groups as compared to native Germans after taking into account the age structure, marital situation and period effects.[8] For men, one finds that the first-generation Africans are the most disadvantaged group and that the situation is only slightly improved for most of the other 'new' immigrant groups. The labour-migrant groups (except for the Turks) do significantly better, especially in the second generation (except for the Greeks); however for all groups but second-generation Iberians, the risk of being unemployed is still notably higher than for the Germans. In the first generation, Western Europeans have nearly the same unemployment risk as Germans, although the second generation fares worse.

The results for women are very similar in general, although three differences can be seen. First, the relative risk of unemployment compared with German women is somewhat less pronounced. Second, the overall pattern for the labour-migrant groups shows no exceptions. Third, in contrast to men the second-generation Western European women do slightly better than their first-generation counterparts.

The second step in our analysis of unemployment is to include educational qualifications in addition to the other control variables. (Full models are shown in Table 7.A1 in the Appendix.) The logit coefficients from these models now represent the amount of ethnic disadvantage net of educational qualifications and are shown as black bars in Figures 7.2A amd 7.2B. One finds similar results for both men and women; however, before we turn to the net ethnic differences we will briefly examine the effects of the control variables. Most importantly, the coefficients for qualification indicate that the higher the educational level the lower the risk of unemployment. The estimates for age show the expected

---

[7] When analysing factors influencing the risk of unemployment we exclude all those who are economically inactive, i.e. those looking after the home, students and 'other inactive'.

[8] In all Figures category labels for immigrant groups are abbreviated. The order of groups is the same as, e.g., in Table 7.4B. The numbers 1 or 2 indicate the first or the second generation.

EDUCATIONAL HURDLES IN GERMANY

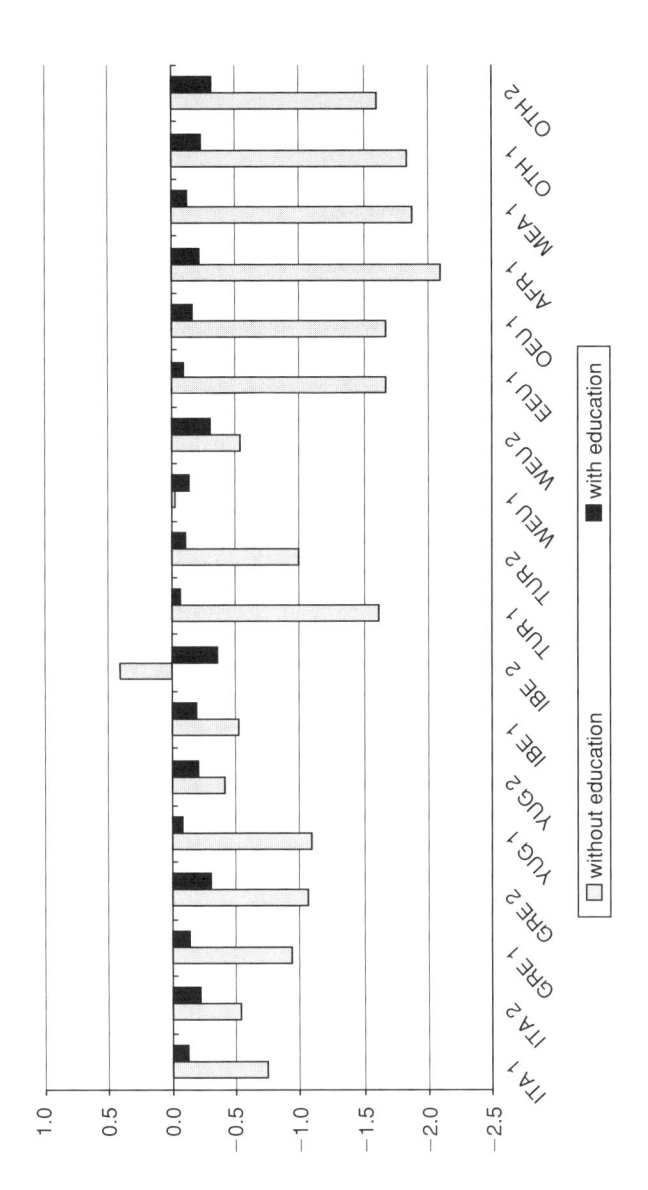

Figure 7.2A. Logit effects: Men, unemployed vs. employed.

Figure 7.2B. Logit effects: Women, unemployed vs. employed.

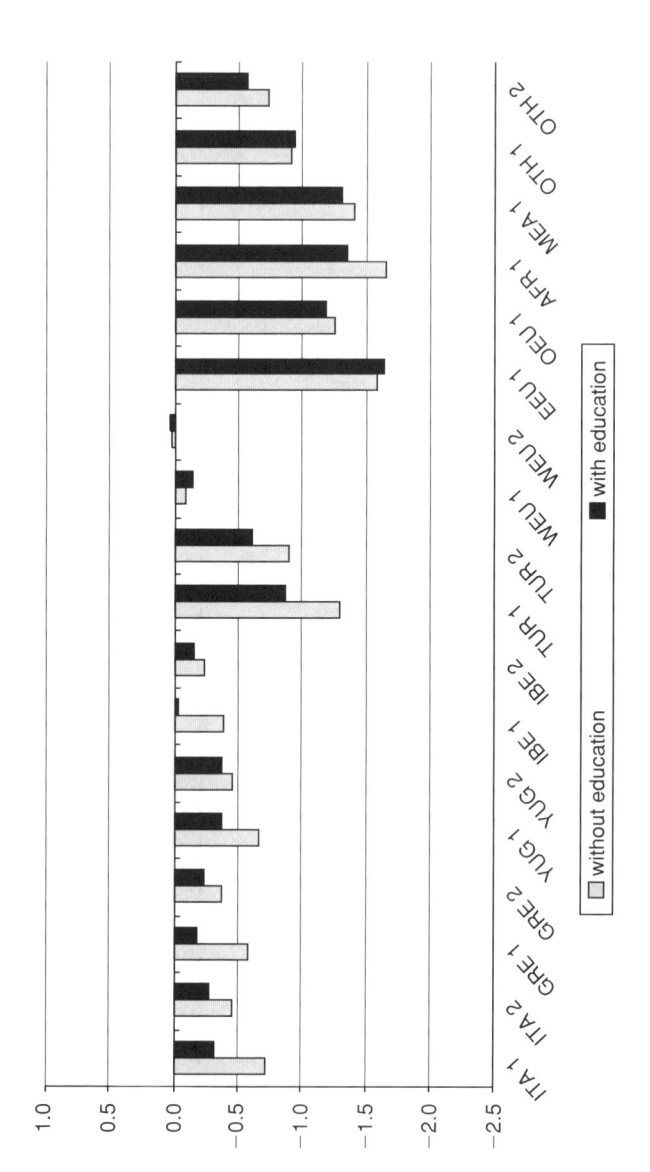

(non-linear) effect, with unemployment being highest among young people, declining with rising age and finally increasing for older respondents. With regard to marital status we find that married people suffer the lowest risk of unemployment.

Now we turn to ethnic differences. Leaving aside the (apparently) special case of Western European migrants, two distinct patterns arise. First, the risk of unemployment is clearly lower for the labour migrants after controlling for education, and for most groups the reduction tends to be considerable. For second-generation labour migrants ethnic disadvantages even disappear, as the respective effects are no longer significantly different from zero—with the exception of Greek and Turkish men, and Turkish women. This means that the higher unemployment risk among labour migrants can largely be explained by their lower educational qualifications. However, the 'new immigrant' groups show a different pattern as their ethnic disadvantages are only slightly reduced when educational qualifications are introduced into the model. Migrants from Western Europe have their own pattern. For first-generation men and both first- and second-generation women, the gross ethnic effect is already very close to zero and controlling for education does not change the picture much. However, second-generation West European men show an overall risk of unemployment that is comparable to that experienced by first-generation Iberians.

The impression these models leave us with—that for several groups education does not reduce the probability of unemployment—becomes more clear if interaction terms between education[9] and ethnicity are added into the models. These interaction terms are introduced to test whether returns to education in avoiding unemployment are similar for the different ethnic groups and the native Germans. The first columns in Table 7.A2A (men) and Table 7.A2B (women) (in the Appendix) show the coefficients for the interaction effects in the unemployment models. It turns out, for example, that the coefficient for first-generation Italian men is significantly negative, indicating that higher educational qualifications do not reduce the risk of unemployment to the same extent for first-generation Italian men as for native Germans. With the exception of Western Europeans, the interaction coefficients are negative for all other

---

[9] For the sake of simplicity the interaction variable was built by transforming education into a continuous variable $(-2,-1,0,1,2)$ while education was treated as categorical in the main effects (full models are not shown in this text, but interaction effects are given in Table 7.A2A and Table 7.A2B in the Appendix).

groups of first-generation men, and significant for seven. The results for the second-generation groups differ considerably from those for the first generation. Here—with only one exception—none of the effects is significantly different from zero, and some of the effects even show a positive sign. Note, however, that the interaction effect for second-generation Turks is significantly negative at a better than 95% confidence level—thus again representing an exceptional case within the male labour migrants in general. However, this negative interaction term is somewhat lower for second-generation Turks than for the first generation, again reflecting the general difference between first- and second-generation labour migrants.

In order to understand the exact pattern of these interactions, the main effects for the respective groups also need to be taken into account. For this purpose Figure 7.3A plots the predicted probabilities of unemployment resulting from the estimates of the full model for selected groups at different levels of education.[10] The figure illustrates clearly that in the reference group of German men the risk of unemployment monotonically declines as the level of education increases. While Western Europeans and second-generation Yugoslavs follow this general pattern—albeit from different starting points—the trend does not hold for the other ethnic groups shown in the figure.[11] The other groups (that is first- and second-generation Turks and first-generation Eastern Europeans and Yugoslavs) show the lowest probability of unemployment at the level of lower secondary education. Moreover, we can see very clearly that first-generation Eastern Europeans and Turks face the highest risk of unemployment among respondents with the lowest and highest levels of education (although the order is reversed for the highest educational level).

In the corresponding model for women, shown in Table 7.A2B, only three interactions turn out to be significantly different from zero (at the 99% confidence level), namely those for first-generation Yugoslavs, Turks and Africans. As the coefficients are negative, they indicate that the risk of unemployment for these groups is not reduced as much by educational advancement as it is for native German women. The resulting interaction patterns for these three and some other selected groups are plotted in

---

[10] Values are calculated for a married person of average age (39 years). The assumed point in time lies in the middle of the 3-year period between 1993 and 1996.

[11] Note, however, that due to the marginal distributions the interactions for most of the ethnic groups are dominated by the contrast between none or primary education and lower secondary education.

EDUCATIONAL HURDLES IN GERMANY 297

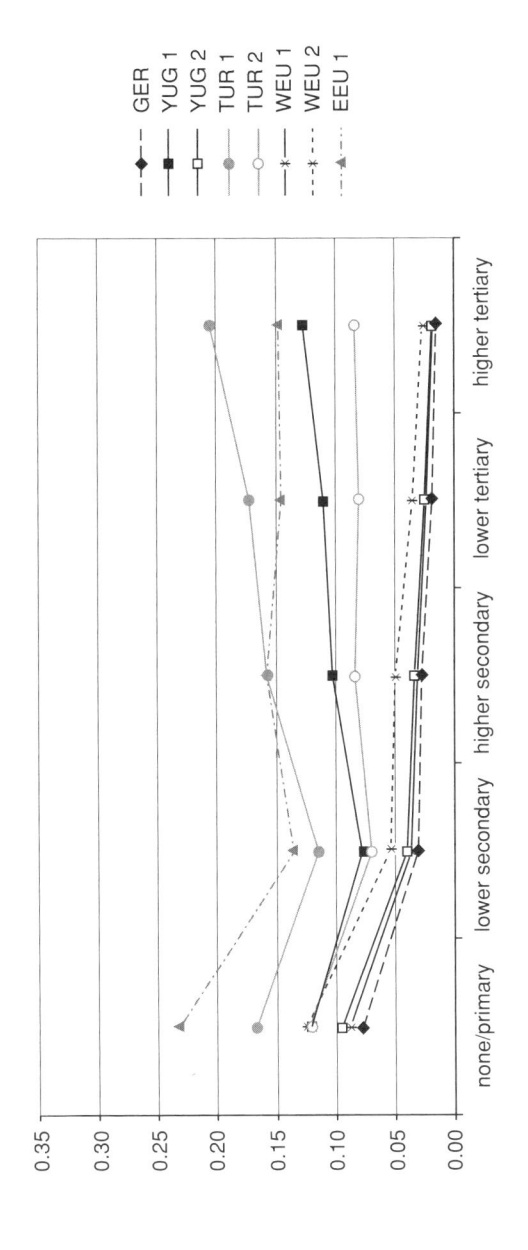

Figure 7.3A. Predicted probabilities of unemployment: Men.

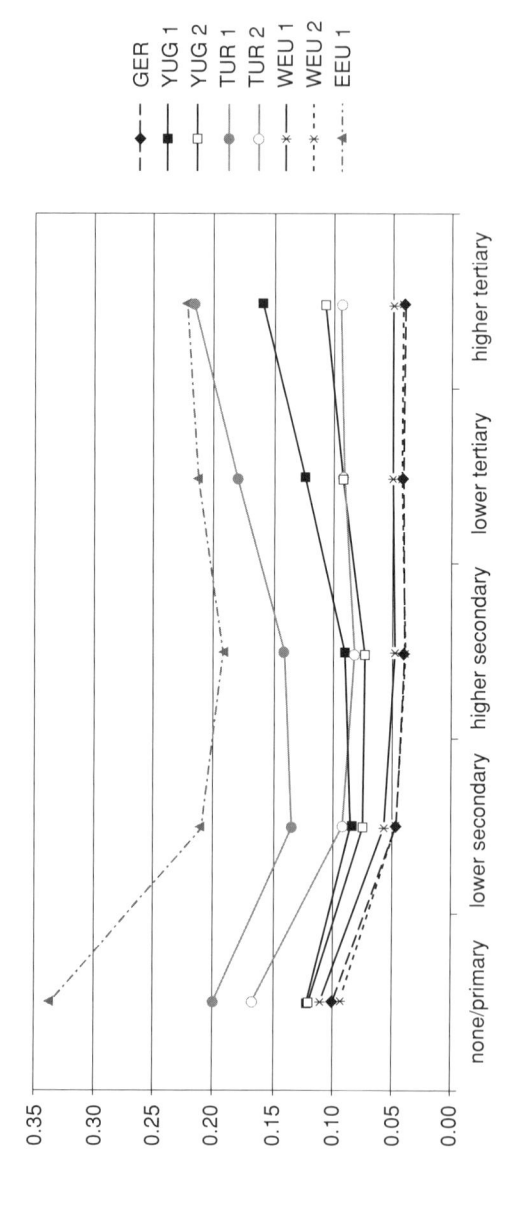

Figure 7.3B. Predicted probabilities of unemployment: women.

Figure 7.3B. Again, German and Western European women have the lowest probability of unemployment at all levels of education. Once more, first-generation Eastern European and Turkish women exhibit the highest probabilities of being unemployed amongst the unqualified and the highly qualified.

Overall, our analyses show that controlling for education reduces the magnitude of ethnic disadvantage. While there still is a significant ancestry effect for most first-generation migrant groups, most of the second-generation labour migrants face the same risk as similarly qualified native Germans. Another important finding is that returns to education are not equal for all groups, with most first-generation migrants being disadvantaged compared to native Germans. We will now turn our focus from comparing the chances of entering the labour market to the chances of high occupational attainment within the labour market.

Occupational attainment of employed minority groups

This section will now consider, for employed respondents, the probabilities of being in the occupational classes presented in Tables 7.4A and 7.4B—namely, the salariat, the routine non-manual class, the petty bourgeoisie, skilled manual work and semi- or unskilled work. By estimating multinomial logistic regression models, this section will compare the chances of working in one of the four higher classes with the chance of being employed in the semi- and unskilled sector.

Focusing on the chances of working in the salariat versus working in the lowest sector (semi- and unskilled work), Figures 7.4A and 7.4B show the logit coefficients for the different migrant groups (as compared to Germans).[12] The grey bars stem from a model that includes, in addition to ancestry, only the control demographic variables: age, age squared, marital status and year of survey. The black bars indicate amounts of ethnic disadvantage net of educational qualifications, as the coefficients are estimated in a model that controls for educational attainment in addition to demographics.

---

[12] If one distinguishes between higher salariat (EGP-class I) and lower salariat (EGP-class II), education, age, and marital status show significant effects on the contrast between both. Coefficients for ethnic group membership, however, are significant ($P<0.01$) only in few cases (men: first-generation Yugoslavs, first-generation Turks; women: first-generation Yugoslavs, first- and second-generation West Europeans). Therefore we group both categories to ease the interpretation of the whole model.

Table 7.5A. Logistic regression of occupational class: Men (parameter estimates, contrasts with semi- and unskilled class).

	Salariat		Routine non-manual		Petty bourgeoisie		Skilled manual	
Intercept	−0.62	(0.13)	1.94	(0.14)	−3.32	(0.16)	3.01	(0.10)
Ancestry								
Native German	0		0		0		0	
Italian 1	−2.03	(0.15)	−1.79	(0.19)	−0.30	(0.09)	−1.00	(0.07)
Greek 1	−2.29	(0.18)	−2.50	(0.32)	−0.41	(0.12)	−1.32	(0.11)
Yugoslav 1	−2.62	(0.13)	−3.09	(0.24)	−1.71	(0.12)	−0.94	(0.05)
Iberian 1	−1.74	(0.22)	−2.00	(0.37)	−2.59	(0.41)	−0.80	(0.12)
Turkish 1	−3.02	(0.12)	−3.14	(0.20)	−1.47	(0.09)	−1.45	(0.05)
West European & US 1	−0.34	(0.10)	−0.67	(0.14)	−0.30	(0.12)	−0.69	(0.09)
East European 1	−2.83	(0.17)	−2.41	(0.25)	−2.11	(0.24)	−1.12	(0.10)
Other European 1	−1.44	(0.22)	−1.62	(0.34)	−1.46	(0.31)	−1.27	(0.17)
African 1	−3.45	(0.30)	−2.66	(0.39)	−2.33	(0.34)	−1.71	(0.15)
(Mid) Eastern 1	−2.30	(0.15)	−1.74	(0.20)	−0.80	(0.14)	−1.41	(0.11)
Other non-European 1	−1.75	(0.38)	−1.09	(0.37)	−0.84	(0.36)	−1.36	(0.28)
Italian 2	−0.32	(0.25)	−0.43	(0.24)	0.04	(0.26)	−0.47	(0.14)
Greek 2	−1.22	(0.39)	−0.99	(0.35)	0.82	(0.25)	−0.77	(0.21)
Yugoslav 2	−0.12	(0.28)	0.00	(0.24)	−0.10	(0.36)	−0.13	(0.17)
Iberian 2	0.19	(0.29)	−0.55	(0.37)	−0.57	(0.53)	−0.10	(0.21)
Turkish 2	−1.25	(0.20)	−1.10	(0.18)	−0.26	(0.18)	−0.56	(0.09)
West European & US 2	0.30	(0.24)	0.30	(0.26)	0.86	(0.24)	0.08	(0.20)
All Other 2	−0.78	(0.43)	−1.99	(0.73)	−1.04	(0.64)	−1.11	(0.32)
Age/10	0.61	(0.07)	−0.91	(0.07)	1.14	(0.08)	−1.38	(0.05)
$(Age/10)^2$	−0.04	(0.01)	0.12	(0.01)	−0.09	(0.01)	0.16	(0.01)
Education								
None/primary	−4.18	(0.05)	−3.03	(0.05)	−1.92	(0.05)	−1.19	(0.03)
Lower secondary	−1.50	(0.03)	−0.88	(0.03)	−0.55	(0.04)	0.48	(0.03)
Higher secondary	0		0		0		0	
Lower tertiary	2.46	(0.07)	0.94	(0.08)	0.79	(0.09)	0.80	(0.08)
Higher tertiary	2.92	(0.07)	0.36	(0.09)	0.83	(0.08)	0.12	(0.09)

Marital status							
Single/cohabitating	0		0		0		0	
Married	**0.30**	**(0.02)**	**−0.10**	**(0.03)**	**0.19**	**(0.03)**	**0.28**	**(0.02)**
Other marital status	−0.08	(0.04)	**−0.18**	**(0.05)**	−0.01	(0.05)	−0.02	(0.04)
Year								
1993	0		0		0		0	
1996	**0.28**	**(0.02)**	**0.11**	**(0.02)**	**0.24**	**(0.02)**	**0.23**	**(0.01)**
N			182741					
Chi-square (D.F.)			55704.3 (108)					

Note: Standard errors given in parentheses; emboldened coefficients indicate significance at the $P<0.01$ level or better.

Table 7.5B. Logistic regression of occupational class: Women (parameter estimates, contrasts with semi- and unskilled class).

	Salariat		Routine non-manual		Petty bourgeoisie		Skilled manual	
Intercept	0.03	(0.12)	1.87	(0.10)	−4.66	(0.20)	1.22	(0.16)
Ancestry								
German	0		0		0		0	
Italian 1	−1.43	(0.26)	−1.20	(0.16)	−0.43	(0.17)	−0.40	(0.21)
Greek 1	−2.62	(0.33)	−1.91	(0.22)	−0.14	(0.15)	−0.34	(0.21)
Yugoslav 1	−1.22	(0.13)	−1.83	(0.11)	−1.34	(0.15)	−0.43	(0.12)
Iberian 1	−2.16	(0.35)	−1.83	(0.24)	−1.22	(0.31)	−0.69	(0.29)
Turkish 1	−1.56	(0.16)	−1.89	(0.13)	−1.06	(0.14)	−0.51	(0.12)
West European & US 1	−0.25	(0.13)	0.05	(0.10)	0.32	(0.15)	0.34	(0.16)
East European 1	−1.82	(0.17)	−1.65	(0.14)	−1.17	(0.24)	−0.55	(0.19)
Other European 1	−0.91	(0.27)	−1.41	(0.26)	−1.10	(0.42)	−0.52	(0.36)
African 1	−0.92	(0.39)	−0.90	(0.35)	−0.94	(0.60)	−2.03	(1.01)
(Mid) Eastern 1	−1.40	(0.24)	−1.22	(0.17)	−0.51	(0.24)	−0.45	(0.24)
Other non-European 1	−1.47	(0.34)	−0.57	(0.24)	−0.28	(0.38)	−0.09	(0.40)
Italian 2	−0.92	(0.30)	−0.32	(0.18)	0.25	(0.35)	−0.04	(0.24)
Greek 2	−0.54	(0.35)	−0.27	(0.25)	0.23	(0.48)	−0.17	(0.38)
Yugoslav 2	−0.73	(0.30)	0.22	(0.18)			−0.25	(0.28)
Iberian 2	−0.12	(0.37)	0.17	(0.27)	−0.91	(1.03)	0.55	(0.34)
Turkish 2	−0.88	(0.21)	−0.27	(0.12)	−0.58	(0.34)	0.16	(0.13)
West European & US 2	0.23	(0.23)	0.01	(0.22)	0.24	(0.39)	0.35	(0.31)
All Other 2	−0.10	(0.39)	−0.25	(0.34)	−0.28	(0.75)	0.48	(0.38)
Age/10	0.64	(0.07)	−0.42	(0.05)	1.34	(0.10)	−1.03	(0.09)
(Age/10)²	−0.08	(0.01)	0.04	(0.01)	−0.13	(0.01)	0.10	(0.01)
Education								
None/primary	−3.79	(0.05)	−2.46	(0.04)	−0.99	(0.06)	−1.05	(0.06)
Lower secondary	−1.42	(0.03)	−0.56	(0.03)	−0.61	(0.05)	−0.22	(0.05)
Higher secondary	0		0		0		0	
Lower tertiary	1.77	(0.07)	0.52	(0.08)	0.65	(0.11)	0.57	(0.12)
Higher tertiary	2.68	(0.06)	0.38	(0.07)	0.75	(0.10)	0.37	(0.13)

EDUCATIONAL HURDLES IN GERMANY

Marital status								
Single/cohabitating	0		0		0		0	
Married	−0.68	(0.02)	−0.44	(0.02)	0.50	(0.04)	−0.46	(0.03)
Other marital status	−0.45	(0.03)	−0.33	(0.03)	−0.01	(0.06)	−0.33	(0.05)
Year								
1993	0		0		0		0	
1996	0.30	(0.02)	0.28	(0.01)	0.01	(0.02)	0.13	(0.03)
N	134320							
Chi-square (D.F.)	34756.3 (107)							

Note: Standard errors given in parentheses; emboldened coefficients indicate significance at the $P < 0.01$ level or better.

Table 7.5A presents the multinomial results for males. The male labour-migrant groups show a very clear pattern: in the first generation the gross disadvantage is considerable, being strongest for Turks; however, controlling for education reduces this disadvantage substantially. Turning to second-generation labour migrants we find that their gross disadvantage is much smaller than for the first generation, and again controlling for educational attainment further diminishes the logit coefficients. Moreover, only two second-generation groups—Greeks and Turks—exhibit effects that are still significantly different from zero after controlling for education. Additionally, whereas first-generation Western Europeans exhibit a small (although significant) net disadvantage, the second generation is not significantly disadvantaged compared with native Germans. For all other groups, however, compared to the labour migrants we find a reversed pattern. For these groups, controlling for educational qualifications leads to an increase in ethnic disadvantage. This increase is very pronounced for Eastern Europeans, respondents from the East and from other non-European countries. Although first-generation Africans do not show the strongest increase, after controlling for education their net ethnic disadvantage is the largest among all migrant groups. The overall picture for women, shown in Table 7.5B, is very similar, although the level of disadvantage tends to be lower.

As with the previous models of unemployment, we also include interaction terms between education and ethnicity into the models. In these models, these interactions test whether educational attainments enhance the chances of reaching a position in the salariat to the same extent for the different migrant groups as for Germans. As the results in Table 7.A2A show, returns to education are lower for first-generation male Yugoslavs, Turks, Western Europeans, Eastern Europeans, respondents from the East and from 'other' countries. Among second-generation groups only Italian and Greek men have lower returns than the native Germans. Figure 7.5A shows the plotted probabilities of salariat access; as can be seen, the chance of working in the salariat rises with the level of education for all groups. This is a striking difference from the findings on unemployment, which showed that for some groups secondary education was more protective against the risks of unemployment than were tertiary qualifications. For first-generation male Yugoslavs, Turks and respondents from other European countries, Figure 7.5A also indicates that the chance of reaching a higher occupational position—although rising with educational qualifications—is clearly lower than for the other groups included.

EDUCATIONAL HURDLES IN GERMANY 305

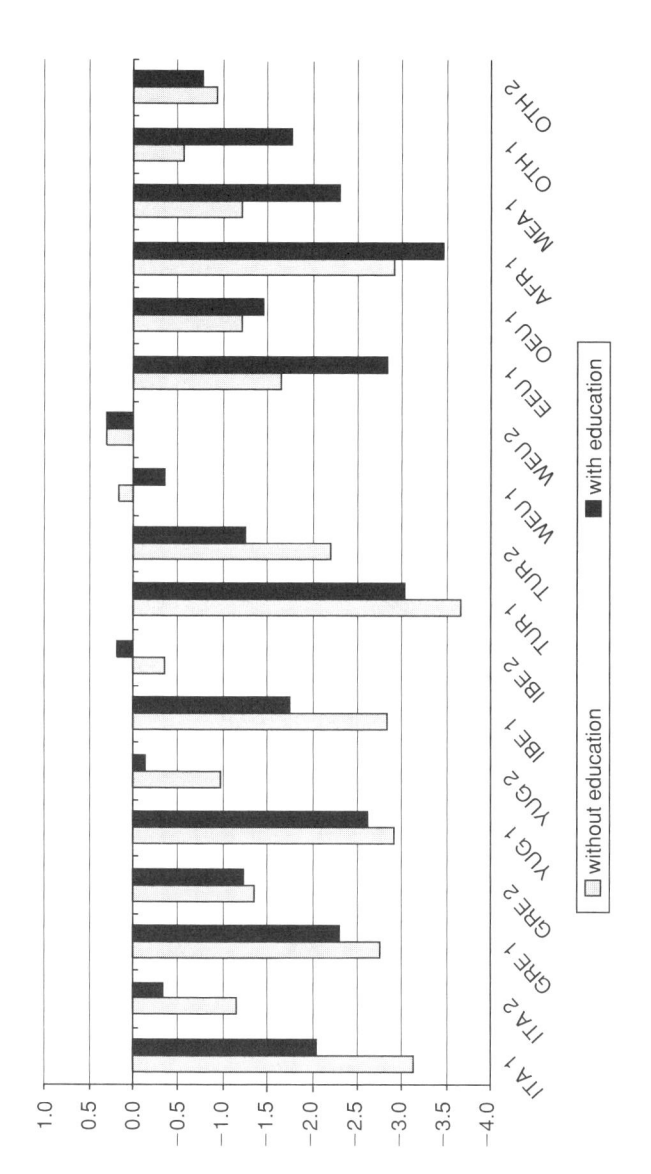

Figure 7.4A. Logit effects: Men, salariat vs. semi- or unskilled.

306 Frank Kalter & Nadia Granato

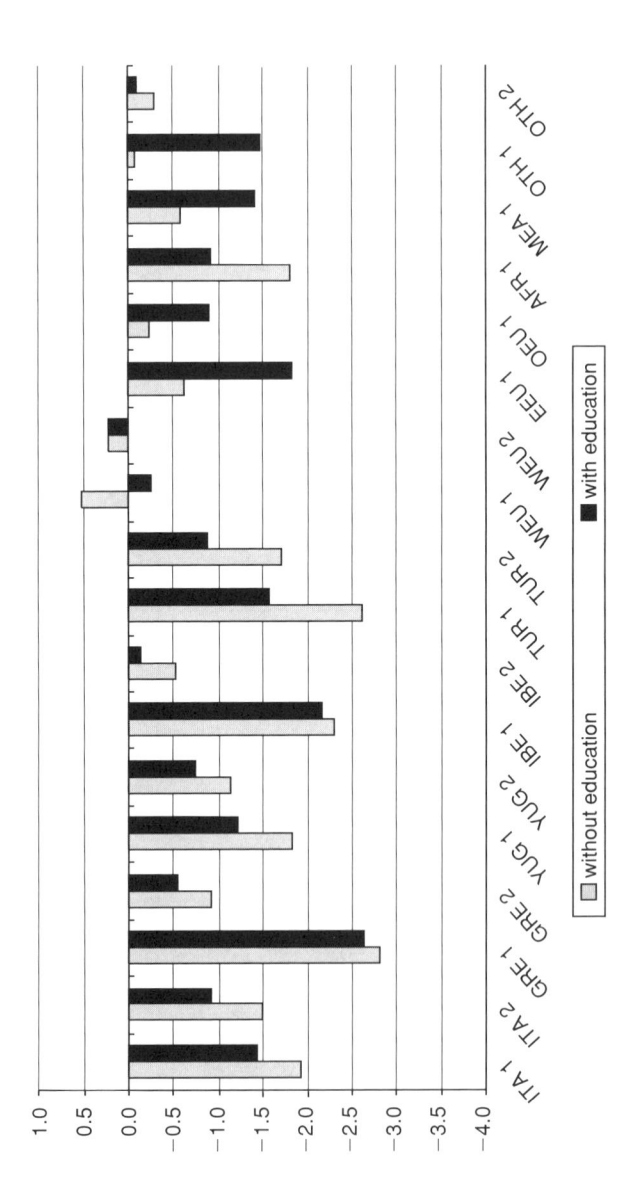

Figure 7.4B. Logit effects: Women, salariat vs. semi- or unskilled.

With respect to interaction terms (Table 7.A2B) and predicted probabilities (Figure 7.5B) the results for women are very similar. Nearly all of the same first-generation groups have significantly lower returns to education than German women and the probabilities of working in the salariat rise with the educational level for all groups. One difference from men that can be seen in the probability plot is that the chance of reaching a higher position varies much more between the minority groups for females than they do for males.

Tables 7.5A and 7.5B also show that, as with the salariat, educational qualification also has significant effects on the chances of accessing the other three occupational sectors for both men and women. Turning to ethnic disadvantage, we find the same pattern for gaining access to the routine non-manual sector and similar patterns concerning access to the petty bourgeoisie and skilled manual work as we did for the salariat. That is, all male first-generation groups are disadvantaged compared to Germans in accessing one of the four higher occupational destinations. For the second-generation, though, the picture is not as clear. Here Turkish men continue to be disadvantaged in accessing all sectors, as do Greeks (with the exception of accessing the petty bourgeoisie where their chance is higher than that of native Germans). Second-generation Italian

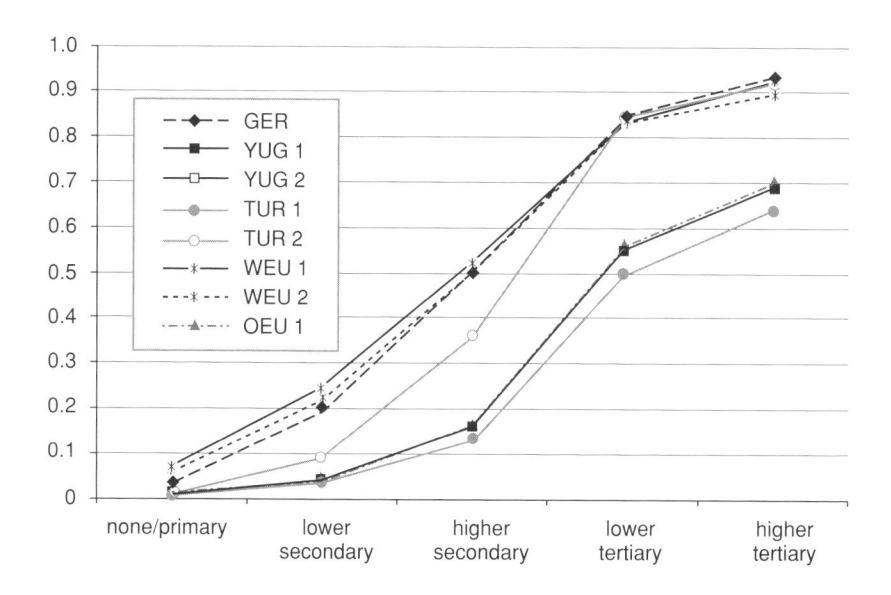

Figure 7.5A. Predicted probability of reaching the salariat: Men.

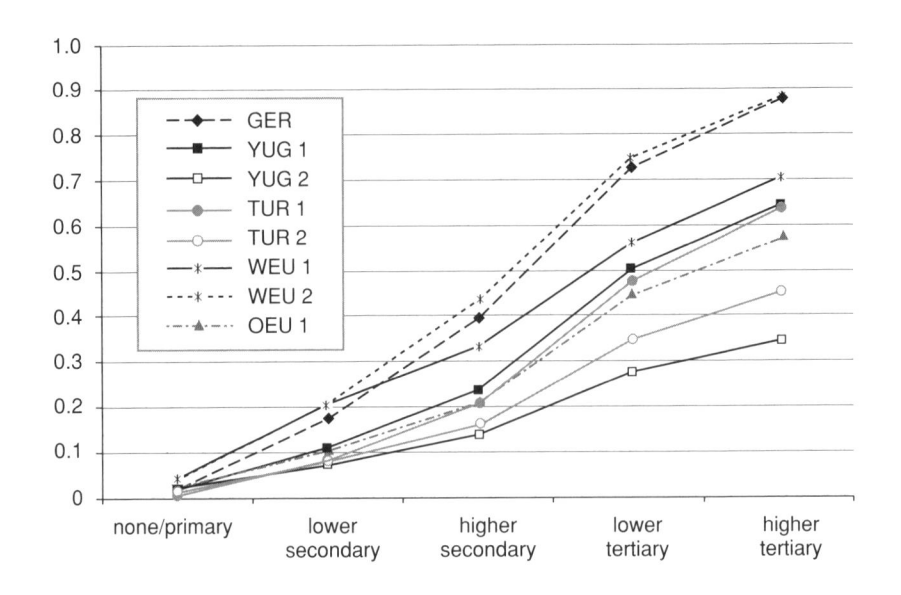

Figure 7.5B. Predicted probability of reaching the salariat: Women.

men only suffer disadvantage when accessing the skilled manual sector, while Yugoslav and Iberian men have the same chance as Germans of reaching a higher position as their respective ancestry coefficients are not significantly different from zero. Comparing first and second generations, it turns out that when a disadvantage remains for the second generation it tends to be smaller than for the respective first-generation group. All in all, second-generation men do much better in reaching higher occupational positions than do first-generation men.

The picture for women shown in Table 7.5B indicates that overall there is less ethnic disadvantage, particularly for the second generation. With regard to the first generation, the pattern is not as clear for women as it is for men. Yugoslav, Turkish and Eastern European women belong to groups that are disadvantaged in accessing all four higher classes. Italian and Iberian women have the same chance as Germans only in reaching the skilled manual sector; with respect to all other destinations their chance is lower. First-generation female respondents from Greece, 'other' European countries, the East, Africa and other non-European countries are disadvantaged accessing one or both of the two highest occupational classes (i.e., the salariat and/or routine non-manual sector). Finally, in contrast to Western European men, women have the same chance of reaching the occupational classes considered as do Germans. For second-generation women, however, there are just two distinct groups—Italian and Turkish—who are disadvantaged only with respect to the salariat. The coefficients for all other groups are not significantly different from zero, indicating that there are no ethnic disadvantages with respect to occupational destinations.

Examining returns from education (the interaction terms between national origins and educational qualifications from Tables 7.A2A and 7.A2B) we find almost no systematic disadvantages. With respect to men the exceptions are first-generation Western and Eastern European men, who receive lower returns from education than Germans with respect to all or nearly all occupational classes. Among the second generation, Turkish men receive lower returns except when competing for access to the salariat. For first-generation female respondents, no obvious patterns can be distinguished and among the second generation, Turkish women tend to receive lower returns from education, save when accessing the petty bourgeoisie.

Summary and discussion

Roughly, our analyses have revealed at least three distinct patterns of ethnic disadvantage which characterise the German labour market. The first applies to the first generation of labour migrants on which most research in this field, to-date, has focused. These groups were strongly negatively selected with respect to human capital resulting in clear ethnic stratification which is still highly visible today. Our analyses support this account, due to the fact that after controlling for educational qualifications the disadvantages faced by first-generation labour migrants clearly decrease. However, disparities in formal qualifications are by no means sufficient to explain the situation of these immigrants as even after controlling for them remarkable disadvantages are still apparent.

The pattern of ethnic disadvantage is quite different for other and more recent first-generation immigrants. For some groups selection with respect to human capital is U-shaped, meaning that they are over-represented at both ends of the educational qualification scale. Many highly educated immigrants face severe problems in gaining adequate labour market positions, which is indicated by the fact that the amount of ethnic disadvantage actually increases after controlling for formal qualifications. This turns out to be especially severe for immigrants from

Eastern Europe, but is also valid for immigrants from Africa, and the (mid) East. Recent research suggests that a similar pattern can also be found for the group of *Aussiedler* which cannot be identified within the data of the Microcensus. Using data from the German Socio-Economic Panel (GSOEP) Konietzka and Kreyenfeld (2001) show that—although formally acknowledged—their qualification certificates are *only* rewarded *within* the learned occupation. However, the vast majority of the *Aussiedler* fails to gain access to it.

A third distinct pattern of disadvantage can be found with respect to the second generation. In our case the 'second generation' predominantly refers to descendants of classical labour migrants, as the number of cases in other groups is too small for detailed analysis. What we find, firstly, is a clear trend towards structural assimilation over generations as for all the groups that we have been able to distinguish the second generation does markedly better than the first. Secondly, however, our analyses also clearly show that second-generation minority groups still do much worse than the indigenous population of comparable age. After examining the major causes of the existing gap, our results strongly support the view that this is largely due to immigrants' children still missing the relevant human capital. After controlling for formal qualifications, disadvantages are nearly absent for most groups. Thus for the second generation, the major obstacles to economic success seem to lie primarily in the educational system rather than in the labour market itself. Being a country of severe barriers to social mobility in general, it seems that the German educational system provides especially high hurdles for the descendants of the strongly negatively selected former labour migrants.

Against the background of these crude findings our analyses raise a number of open questions to be addressed in future research, and we want to emphasise at least two such questions. The first refers to understanding why the pattern of the more recent immigrants from Eastern Europe, including the *Aussiedler*, deviates from the pattern of the classical labour migrants. Here, as a first step, a more detailed description including further disaggregation of specific groups, trends over time, and most importantly trends of generations is necessary. The second question relates to how, in general, ethnic penalties remaining after controlling for educational qualifications can be explained, and specifically whether they might reflect labour market discrimination (in a narrower sense) or whether other mechanisms might be responsible. Given our data, this question is hard to answer as indicators connected to these alternative mechanisms are not contained in the Microcensus. Here again, the

GSOEP offers a promising complementary data source to address some of these questions since it provides some integration-related measures (e.g. for host country-specific capital), and also allows for longitudinal analyses. For example, recent research relying on the GSOEP shows that, above all, lacking proficiency in the German language (Dustmann and van Soest 2002) and labour market segmentation (Constant and Massey 2003) play a crucial role in understanding barriers to occupational attainment for the classical labour migrants of the first generation. With respect to second-generation labour migrants the situation of Greek men and Turks of both genders is most puzzling. With respect to the Greeks it is reasonable to assume that the existence of specific Greek schools in Germany contributes to explaining the observable penalties. They lead to high shares of higher secondary education (Kristen and Granato 2004; see also Tables 7.2A and 7.2B), however, the leaving certificates of Greek schools may be less valuable in the labour market— though a more severe empirical test of this obvious hypothesis is still lacking. With respect to Turkish youth recent analyses of the GSOEP data reveal that the especially large ethnic penalties seem to result from a lack of integration into social networks rather than from labour market discrimination (Kalter 2004).

So at least for the classical labour migrants in Germany it seems that many key processes of ethnic disadvantage precede entry into the labour market. It is access to relevant resources that largely accounts for ethnic inequality, most notably educational credentials, but also host country-specific resources like language proficiency or access to helpful networks. Therefore, future research should address exactly these processes more intensively in order to understand the intergenerational transmission and persistence of ethnic inequalities in the German labour market.

Appendix

This chapter utilises pooled data from the 1993 and 1996 waves of the German Microcensus (MZ). The German MZ is an annual survey of 1% of all (i.e. private and institutional) households in Germany. Containing detailed information on educational attainment as well as on a range of labour market variables it provides an adequate data source for the specific aims of comparative analysis. In addition, the sample size is large enough to obtain a sufficient number of immigrants and to allow distinction between several relevant subgroups. Moreover, being a compulsory survey with a response rate of 97%, the MZ delivers a largely unbiased picture of the immigrant population—another advantage compared to other available survey data. The

MZ is a random sample, with all households having the same probability of being selected. Technically spoken, it is a single-stage stratified cluster sample, where the clusters are geographic areas (Auswahlbezirke). Concerning survey mode, in most cases interviews are conducted face-to-face, but respondents can choose to complete the questionnaire themselves. All members of a selected household take part in the survey. Under certain circumstances proxy interviews about other members of the household are possible. For our analysis we use the so called scientific-use files from the MZ, each a 70% subsample of the included households ('ZUMA-file'). In order to insure data protection each subsample is randomly selected.

Unfortunately 1996 is the last year in which a construction of the class schema used in this volume is possible, an important requirement for the comparative analysis. Starting in 1997, the MZ no longer contains information on the precise position within a given firm. Therefore relevant information allowing distinction between 'skilled' and 'unskilled' jobs within given occupations is missing—an unfortunate oversight, as this distinction seems especially important when discussing ethnic inequalities.

Even though the MZ covers all households in Germany we exclude institutional households from our analysis, as complete information is only available for respondents in private households. Moreover, respondents are only included on two more conditions: they must be aged 18 to 59 and live in the Western part of Germany. The reason for excluding the Eastern part of Germany is that virtually no members of the group we refer to as classical labour migrants (and who are the focus of our analysis) live there.

As our analysis is constrained to respondents aged 18–59, pooling the 1993 and 1996 datasets leaves a total of 476,127 respondents, of which 31,852 (7.4%) can be defined as immigrants and their descendants. Pooling the years 1993 and 1996, however, leads to a certain problem. The MZ follows a rotating household panel design, i.e. every year one quarter of the selected households is renewed and as a consequence one household is included in four subsequent samples. Therefore combining data from the 1993 and 1996 waves leads to a possibility that one of every eight respondents in our combined data set could be contained twice—if drawn in both 70% subsamples—and the MZ scientific use files provide no way of identifying these cases. Thus, using the pooled data results in an underestimation of standard errors when running standard analyses. Our solution for this problem is to weight each case by 7/8 and use robust standard errors, ensuring that conservative estimations of standard errors and significance assessments are made. All tables and figures within this chapter are based on weighted numbers.

To measure educational qualifications we use a condensed form of the updated version of the CASMIN Classification (Brauns and Steinmann 1999). The first category (primary/none) combines CASMIN classes 1a and 1b and therefore includes respondents with inadequately completed general education or with general elementary education (Hauptschulabschluss ohne berufliche Ausbildung). The lower secondary category includes three CASMIN classes (1c, 2a and 2b), i.e. respondents with general elementary education and vocational qualification, or with intermediate general qualification (with or without vocational qualification). This corresponds to the German educational levels of Hauptschulabschluss mit beruflicher Ausbildung and Realschulabschluss mit oder ohne beruflicher Ausbildung. Higher secondary education comprises CASMIN 2c, i.e. general or vocational maturity certificate (Fachhochschulreife oder Abitur). Lower tertiary education corresponds to CASMIN 3a (Fachhochschulabschluss, Ingenieurschule) and higher tertiary education to CASMIN 3b (Hochschulabschluss).

With respect to labour force participation we distinguish between economically active (respondents in work and those actively looking for work), students, respondents looking after the home and others (retired, permanently sick and disabled, not looking for work, not classified elsewhere).

Current occupation is based on a condensed form of EGP. Salariat combines EGP I and II, routine non-manual corresponds to EGP IIIa, petty bourgeoisie includes EGP IV, skilled manual comprises EGP V and VI and semi- and unskilled EGP IIIb and VII. The category unemployment is added to these five occupational classes.

The variable marital status has three categories: single or cohabiting, married and other (divorced or widowed). Next to a variable indicating the year of the MZ wave (1993 or 1996) age and age squared are included in the multivariate analyses.

Table 7.A1. Logistic regression of avoidance of unemployment (parameter estimates, contrasts with unemployed).

	Men		Women	
Intercept	**1.74**	**(0.12)**	**1.08**	**(0.13)**
Ancestry				
Native German	0		0	
Italian 1	**−0.28**	**(0.09)**	**−0.31**	(0.12)
Greek 1	**−0.50**	**(0.11)**	−0.18	(0.14)
Yugoslav 1	**−0.81**	**(0.07)**	**−0.37**	**(0.08)**
Iberian 1	−0.05	(0.17)	−0.03	(0.19)
Turkish 1	**−1.11**	**(0.05)**	**−0.86**	**(0.06)**
W. European & US 1	−0.11	(0.12)	−0.13	(0.13)
East European 1	**−1.66**	**(0.10)**	**−1.63**	**(0.09)**
Other European 1	**−1.49**	**(0.14)**	**−1.19**	**(0.17)**
African 1	**−1.77**	**(0.12)**	**−1.35**	**(0.22)**
(Mid) Eastern 1	**−1.73**	**(0.09)**	**−1.30**	**(0.12)**
Other non-European 1	**−1.83**	**(0.20)**	**−0.93**	**(0.24)**
Italian 2	−0.30	(0.19)	−0.27	(0.23)
Greek 2	**−0.87**	**(0.19)**	−0.23	(0.31)
Yugoslav 2	−0.24	(0.18)	−0.37	(0.21)
Iberian 2	−0.56	(0.39)	−0.15	(0.35)
Turkish 2	**−0.69**	**(0.09)**	**−0.61**	**(0.11)**
W. European & US 2	**−0.52**	**(0.20)**	0.04	(0.30)
All Other 2	**−1.39**	**(0.24)**	−0.56	(0.32)
Age/10	**0.75**	**(0.06)**	**1.09**	**(0.07)**
(Age/10)^2	**−0.13**	**(0.01)**	**−0.14**	**(0.01)**
Education				
None/primary	**−0.90**	**(0.04)**	**−0.90**	**(0.04)**
Lower secondary	−0.07	(0.04)	**−0.20**	**(0.04)**
Higher secondary	0		0	
Lower tertiary	**0.37**	**(0.06)**	−0.04	(0.07)
Higher tertiary	**0.56**	**(0.05)**	−0.02	(0.06)
Marital status				
Single/cohabiting	0		0	
Married	**0.90**	**(0.03)**	**−0.15**	**(0.03)**
Other marital status	−0.07	(0.04)	**−0.61**	**(0.04)**
Year				
1993	0		0	
1996	**−0.27**	**(0.02)**	−0.02	(0.02)
N	196175		145389	
Chi-Square (D.F.)	7424.9 (27)		2984.6 (27)	

Note: Standard errors are given in brackets; emboldened coefficients indicate significance at $P<0.01$ level or better.

Table 7.A2A. Interactions between ancestry and qualifications: Men.

	Avoidance of unemployment		Occupational class					
			Salariat		Routine non-manual		Petty bourgeoisie		Skilled manual	
Italian 1	−0.35	**(0.11)**	−0.10	(0.16)	−0.13	(0.35)	−0.03	(0.13)	−0.18	(0.12)
Greek 1	−0.12	(0.11)	−0.14	(0.17)	−0.52	(0.43)	**−0.34**	**(0.14)**	−0.13	(0.14)
Yugoslav 1	**−0.43**	**(0.07)**	**−0.28**	**(0.11)**	−0.30	(0.41)	−0.22	(0.13)	−0.12	(0.09)
Iberian 1	**−0.34**	**(0.17)**	0.57	(0.48)	−0.27	(0.62)	0.81	(0.66)	−0.21	(0.21)
Turkish 1	**−0.48**	**(0.05)**	**−0.19**	**(0.10)**	0.11	(0.25)	−0.07	(0.09)	0.00	(0.07)
West European & US 1	0.01	(0.09)	**−0.42**	**(0.09)**	**−0.42**	**(0.14)**	**−0.27**	**(0.12)**	**−0.31**	**(0.12)**
East European 1	**−0.28**	**(0.08)**	**−0.31**	**(0.13)**	−0.02	(0.28)	**−0.56**	**(0.26)**	**−0.23**	**(0.12)**
Other European 1	−0.20	(0.11)	0.01	(0.22)	0.29	(0.33)	−0.11	(0.35)	−0.31	(0.24)
African 1	**−0.53**	**(0.09)**	−0.25	(0.21)	−0.15	(0.41)	−0.09	(0.29)	−0.19	(0.16)
(Mid) Eastern 1	**−0.24**	**(0.05)**	**−0.47**	**(0.10)**	−0.29	(0.22)	**−0.22**	**(0.11)**	−0.07	(0.09)
Other non-European 1	−0.26	(0.14)	**−0.94**	**(0.18)**	−0.38	(0.33)	−0.42	(0.24)	**−0.54**	**(0.26)**
Italian 2	0.26	(0.36)	**−0.67**	**(0.33)**	−0.61	(0.55)	−0.04	(0.40)	−0.06	(0.24)
Greek 2	−0.03	(0.22)	**−0.59**	**(0.29)**	−0.49	(0.34)	−0.32	(0.28)	**−0.78**	**(0.27)**
Yugoslav 2	0.02	(0.28)	−0.50	(0.36)	−0.50	(0.60)	−0.73	(0.81)	**−1.75**	**(0.28)**
Iberian 2	−0.26	(0.34)	0.60	(0.69)	0.30	(0.50)	0.33	(0.39)	0.45	(0.42)
Turkish 2	**−0.31**	**(0.13)**	−0.18	(0.31)	**−0.75**	**(0.34)**	**−0.73**	**(0.33)**	**−0.78**	**(0.14)**
West European & US 2	−0.01	(0.21)	−0.23	(0.24)	−0.49	(0.35)	0.02	(0.28)	−0.12	(0.26)
All Other 2	0.06	(0.23)	−0.20	(0.50)	0.67	(0.35)	−1.47	(0.75)	**−0.98**	**(0.49)**

Note: Standard errors given in parentheses; emboldened coefficients indicate significance at the $P<0.05$ level or better.

Table 7.A2B. Interactions between national origins and qualifications: Women.

	Avoidance of unemployment		Occupational class					
			Salariat		Routine non-manual		Petty bourgeoisie		Skilled manual	
Italian 1	−0.01	(0.14)	−0.19	(0.20)	0.27	(0.20)	**0.51**	**(0.17)**	−0.13	(0.24)
Greek 1	0.24	(0.15)	−0.01	(0.25)	**0.55**	**(0.25)**	0.09	(0.17)	0.28	(0.22)
Yugoslav 1	**0.31**	**(0.08)**	**−0.46**	**(0.12)**	−0.16	(0.19)	0.15	(0.14)	−0.07	(0.13)
Iberian 1	0.04	(0.22)	−0.22	(0.25)	0.23	(0.24)	0.08	(0.33)	−0.59	(0.41)
Turkish 1	**0.26**	**(0.08)**	−0.07	(0.17)	0.20	(0.18)	**0.53**	**(0.15)**	0.07	(0.19)
West European & US 1	0.03	(0.09)	**−0.36**	**(0.11)**	0.11	(0.11)	0.14	(0.13)	−0.18	(0.15)
East European 1	0.09	(0.07)	**−0.57**	**(0.11)**	0.01	(0.15)	−0.26	(0.15)	**−0.47**	**(0.18)**
Other European 1	0.19	(0.11)	**−0.56**	**(0.16)**	−0.33	(0.24)	0.07	(0.27)	−0.20	(0.33)
African 1	**0.56**	**(0.22)**	0.70	(0.63)	**−0.96**	**(0.41)**	−0.74	(0.99)	0.49	(0.30)
(Mid) Eastern 1	0.15	(0.08)	**−0.83**	**(0.11)**	0.11	(0.15)	−0.10	(0.17)	**−0.43**	**(0.18)**
Other non-European 1	0.13	(0.16)	−0.36	(0.25)	0.22	(0.23)	−0.22	(0.22)	0.08	(0.33)
Italian 2	0.28	(0.32)	0.25	(0.42)	0.64	(0.44)	0.69	(0.39)	0.48	(0.35)
Greek 2	0.38	(0.31)	−0.15	(0.42)	−0.42	(0.35)	−0.80	(0.70)	0.30	(0.74)
Yugoslav 2	0.20	(0.46)	−0.87	(0.51)	**−0.59**	**(0.29)**			−0.85	(0.73)
Iberian 2	−0.39	(0.64)	−0.41	(0.59)	−0.46	(0.52)			0.47	(0.62)
Turkish 2	0.07	(0.17)	**−0.81**	**(0.21)**	**−0.69**	**(0.18)**	−0.29	(0.47)	**−0.40**	**(0.20)**
West European & US 2	0.03	(0.18)	0.19	(0.35)	0.20	(0.41)	0.47	(0.34)	0.22	(0.36)
All Other 2	−0.46	(0.30)	**−0.53**	**(0.24)**	**−0.83**	**(0.36)**	−1.13	(0.83)	−0.35	(0.48)

Note: Standard errors given in parentheses; emboldened coefficients indicate significance at the $P<0.05$ level or better.

References

Aigner, D. J. and Cain, G. G. (1977), 'Statistical Theories of Discrimination in Labor Markets', *Industrial and Labor Relations Review*, 30, 175–87.

Alba, R. D., Handl, J., and Müller, W. (1994), 'Ethnische Ungleichheit im Deutschen Bildungssystem', *Kölner Zeitschrift für Soziologie und Sozialpsychologie*, 46, 209–37.

Arrow, K. J. (1972), 'Some Mathematical Models of Race Discrimination in the Labor Market'. In A. H. Pascal (ed.), *Racial Discrimination in Economic Life* (Lexington, MA: Heath), pp. 187–203.

Arrow, K. J. (1973), 'Higher Education as a Filter', *Journal of Public Economics*, 2, 193–216.

Arrow, K. J. (1998), 'What Has Economics to Say About Racial Discrimination?' *Journal of Economic Perspectives*, 12, 91–100.

Bade, K. J. (1992), 'Einheimische Ausländer: "Gastarbeiter"—Dauergäste—Einwanderer'. In K. J. Bade (ed.), *Deutsche im Ausland—Fremde in Deutschland: Migration in Geschichte und Gegenwart* (Munich: Beck), pp. 393–400.

Becker, G. S. (1971 [1957]), *The Economics of Discrimination*, 2nd edn. (Chicago: University of Chicago Press).

Bender, S. and Seifert, W. (1996), 'Zuwanderer auf dem Arbeitsmarkt: Nationalitäten- und geschlechtsspezifische Unterschiede', *Zeitschrift für Soziologie*, 25, 473–95.

Black, D. A. (1995), 'Discrimination in an Equilibrium Search Model', *Journal of Labor Economics*, 13, 309–34.

Bonacich, E. (1972), 'A Theory of Ethnic Antagonism: The Split Labor Market', *American Sociological Review*, 37, 547–59.

Borjas, G. J. (1987), 'Self-Selection and the Earnings of Immigrants', *The American Economic Review*, 77, 531–53.

Borjas, G. J. and Bronars, S. G. (1989), 'Consumer Discrimination and Self-Employment', *Journal of Political Economy*, 97, 581–605.

Brauns, H. and Steinmann, S. (1999), 'Educational Reform in France, West-Germany and the United Kingdom: Updating the CASMIN Educational Classification'. ZUMA Nachrichten 44/1999, pp. 7–44.

Breen, R. and Goldthorpe, J. H. (1997), 'Explaining Educational Differentials: Towards a Formal Rational Action Theory', *Rationality and Society*, 9, 275–306.

Chiswick, B. R. (1978), 'The Effect of Americanization on the Earnings of Foreign-born Men', *Journal of Political Economy*, 86, 897–921.

Chiswick, B. R. (1991), 'Speaking, Reading, and Earnings among Low-skilled Immigrants', *Journal of Labor Economics*, 9, 149–70.

Constant, A. and Massey, D. S. (2003), 'Labor Market Segmentation and the Earnings of German Guestworkers'. IZA Discussion Paper 774 (Bonn: Forschungsinstitut zur Zukunft der Arbeit).

Diehl, C. and Blohm, M. (2003), 'Rights or Identity? Naturalization Processes among Labor Migrants in Germany', *International Migration Review*, 37, 133–62.

Diekmann, A., Engelhardt, H., and Hartmann, P. (1993), 'Einkommensungleichheit in der Bundesrepublik Deutschland: Diskriminierung von Frauen und Ausländern?' *Mitteilungen aus der Arbeitsmarkt- und Berufsforschung*, 26, 386–98.

Dustmann, C. (1993), 'Earnings Adjustment of Temporary Migrants', *Journal of Population Economics*, 6, 153–68.
Dustmann, C. (2000), 'Temporary Migration and Economic Assimilation', *Swedish Economic Policy Review*, 7, 213–44.
Dustmann, C. and van Soest, A. (2002), 'Language and the Earnings of Immigrants', *Industrial and Labor Relations Review*, 55, 473–92.
England, P. (1992), *Comparable Worth: Theories and Evidence* (New York: de Gruyter).
Erikson, R. and Goldthorpe, J. H. (1992), *The Constant Flux: A Study of Class Mobility in Industrial Countries* (Oxford: Clarendon Press).
Erikson, R. and Jonsson, J. O. (1996), 'Introduction: Explaining Class Inequality in Education: The Swedish Test Case'. In R. Erikson and J. O. Jonsson (eds.), *Can Education Be Equalized? The Swedish Case in Comparative Perspective* (Boulder, CO: Westview Press), pp. 1–63.
Esser, H. (1999), 'Soziologie. Spezielle Grundlagen. Band 1: Situationslogik und Handeln' (Frankfurt a.M.: Campus).
Friedberg, R. M. (2000), 'You Can't Take It with You? Immigrant Assimilation and the Portability of Human Capital', *Journal of Labor Economics*, 18, 221–51.
Granato, N. (2003), 'Ethnische Ungleichheit auf dem deutschen Arbeitsmarkt'. Schriftenreihe des Bundesinstituts für Bevölkerungsforschung, Bd. 33, Opladen: Leske+Budrich.
Granato, N. and Kalter, F. (2001), 'Die Persistenz ethnischer Ungleichheit auf dem deutschen Arbeitsmarkt. Diskriminierung oder Unterinvestition in Humankapital?' *Kölner Zeitschrift für Soziologie und Sozialpsychologie*, 53, 497–520.
Heckmann, F. (1992), *Ethnische Minderheiten, Volk und Nation: Soziologie interethnischer Beziehungen* (Stuttgart: Enke).
Hoffmann-Nowotny, H.-J. (1973), *Soziologie des Fremdarbeiterproblems. Eine theoretische und empirische Analyse am Beispiel der Schweiz* (Stuttgart: Enke).
Kalter, F. (2003), *Chancen, Fouls und Abseitsfallen. Migranten im deutschen Ligenfußball* (Opladen: Westdeutscher Verlag).
Kalter, F. (2004), 'Occupational Attainment of Second-Generation Immigrants in Germany: Recent Trends and Possible Explanation for the Specific Role of Turks'. Paper presented at the Conference on 'The Next Generation', 29–30 Oct. 2004 at the Radcliffe Institute, Harvard University, Cambridge, MA.
Kalter, F. and Granato, N. (2002), 'Demographic Change, Educational Expansion, and Structural Assimilation of Immigrants: The Case of Germany'. *European Sociological Review*, 18, 199–216.
Konietzka, D. and Kreyenfeld, M. (2001), 'Die Verwertbarkeit ausländischer Bildungsabschlüsse: Das Beispiel der Aussiedler auf dem deutschen Arbeitsmarkt', *Zeitschrift für Soziologie*, 30, 267–82.
Konietzka, D. and Seibert, H. (2003), 'Deutsche und Ausländer an der "zweiten Schwelle": Eine vergleichende Analyse der Berufseinstiegskohorten 1976–1995 in Westdeutschland'. *Zeitschrift für Pädagogik*, 49, 567–90.
Kristen, C. and Granato, N. (2004), 'Bildungsinvestitionen in Migrantenfamilien'. In K. J. Bade and M. Bommes *Migration—Integration—Bildung: Grundfragen und Problembereiche*. IMIS-Beiträge 23/2004, pp. 123–41.

Lüttinger, P. and Riede, T. (1997), 'Der Mikrozensus. Amtliche Daten für die Sozialforschung'. ZUMA Nachrichten, 41, 19–43.

Madden, J. F. (1973), *The Economics of Sex Discrimination*. Lexington (MA: Heath).

Marsden, D. (1990), 'Institutions and Labour Mobility: Occupational and Internal Labour Markets in Britain, France, Italy, and West Germany'. In R. Brunetta and C. Dell'Aringa (eds.), *Labour Relations and Economic Performance* (London: Macmillan), pp. 414–38.

Müller, W. and Pollak, R. (2004), 'Social Mobility in West Germany: The Long Arms of History Discovered?' In R. Breen (ed.), *Social Mobility in Europe* (Oxford: Oxford University Press), pp. 77–113.

Müller, W., Lüttinger, P., König, W., and Karle, W. (1989), 'Class and Education in Industrial Nations', *International Journal of Sociology*, 19, 3–39.

Müller, W., Steinmann, S., and Ell, R. (1998), 'Education and Labour-Market Entry in Germany'. In Y. Shavit and W. Müller (eds.), *From School to Work* (Oxford: Clarendon Press), pp. 143–88.

Münz, R. (2002), '"Ethnos or Demos?" Migration and Citizenship in Germany'. In D. Levy and Y. Weiss (eds.), *Challenging Ethnic Citizenship: German and Israeli Perspectives on Immigration* (New York: Berghahn), pp. 15–35.

Münz, R., Seifert, W., and Ulrich, R. (1999), *Zuwanderung nach Deutschland. Strukturen, Wirkungen, Perspektiven* (Frankfurt a.M.: Campus).

Petersen, T. and Saporta, I. (2000), 'Offering a Job: Meritocracy and Social Networks', *American Journal of Sociology*, 106, 763–816.

Phelps, E. S. (1972), 'The Statistical Theory of Racism and Sexism', *The American Economic Review*, 62, 659–61.

Portes, A. and Rumbaut, R. G. (2001), *Legacies: The Story of the Immigrant Second Generation* (New York: Russell Sage Foundation).

Seifert, W. (1992), 'Die zweite Ausländergeneration in der Bundesrepublik. Längsschnittbeobachtungen in der Berufseinstiegsphase', *Kölner Zeitschrift für Soziologie und Sozialpsychologie*, 44, 677–96.

Szydlik, M. (1996), 'Ethnische Ungleichheit auf dem deutschen Arbeitsmarkt', *Kölner Zeitschrift für Soziologie und Sozialpsychologie*, 48, 658–76.

Velling, J. (1993), *Immigration to Germany in the Seventies and Eighties: The Role of Family Reunification*, ZEW-Discussion Paper No. 93–18 (Mannheim: Zentrum für Europäische Wirtschaftsforschung).

Velling, J. (1994), *Immigration und Arbeitsmarkt. Eine empirische Analyse für die Bundesrepublik Deutschland* (Baden-Baden: Nomos Verlagsgesellschaft).

8

Instant Absorption of Immigrants and Persistent Exclusion of Arab Citizens in Israel

YOSSI SHAVIT, NOAH LEWIN-EPSTEIN & IRIT ADLER

Summary: In contrast to most of the other countries presented in this volume, in Israel there is no 'host' group; all but a small fraction of the population are either immigrants, children of immigrants or members of an excluded indigenous minority. Moreover Israel is stratified not only along ethnonational lines dividing Jews from the indigenous Palestinian population but also between Ashkenazi (predominantly originating from Europe) and Sephardim (predominantly from North Africa and the Middle East). Regarding unemployment, our findings reveal that all male immigrant groups, as well as Palestinians, have higher probabilities than third-generation Jews of being unemployed. These results possibly reflect the advantage enjoyed by the founding generation and their offspring in terms of both residence in proximity to large labour markets and greater access to the more secure public sector jobs. This difficulty is reflected in the high odds of first-generation immigrants from the former USSR of being unemployed, while there is no generational difference in the likelihood of being unemployed for all other ethnic groups. The multivariate analyses revealed that, even after controlling for education and demographic attributes, Jews of Middle Eastern and North African origins had lower odds of attaining higher class positions than second-generation Israelis and Jewish immigrants of European descent. The odds of Palestinian men attaining such class positions were even lower. Similar patterns were found for the class position of women. The above patterns of differential ethnic advantage are further amplified by the greater sensitivity of the odds of obtaining higher class occupations to education, among Palestinians and to a lesser extent among Mizrahi Jews, compared with Jews of European origin. Put differently, Palestinians (and to some extent Mizrahim) must have higher education on average than their 'co-workers' of Jewish European origin to attain the same class positions.

Ethnic divides

ISRAELI SOCIETY IS SMALL (6.5 MILLION RESIDENTS) and ethnically diverse. Over the years numerous studies have documented the structure of ethnic stratification in Israel. Its central features include an acute divide along ethno-national lines separating Jews and Palestinians[1], and cultural as well as socio-economic distinctions based on ancestral origin within the Jewish population. With respect to the ethno-national divide, Palestinian Arabs are disadvantaged on every dimension of stratification. They have little political power, relatively low educational achievements, they are more likely to hold low status jobs, and have a standard of living that is substantially lower than that enjoyed by Jews (Al-Haj 1996; Lewin-Epstein and Semyonov 1993; Sa'di 1995). Within the Jewish population, ethnicity is an important stratifying factor as well. As an immigrant society the place from which one's family emigrated and the timing of migration have played a central role in determining the distribution of symbolic as well as material rewards among Jews, and life chances are strongly associated with one's ancestry (Cohen and Haberfeld 1998; Kraus and Hodge 1990; Lewin-Epstein and Semyonov 2000).

In order to comprehend the structure of inequality in Israel, and ethnic stratification in particular, it is necessary to bear in mind the historical processes that shaped Israeli society and its population composition during the second half of the twentieth century. The Jewish population, which numbered approximately 650,000 when the State of Israel was established in 1948, recently crossed the five million mark. The eight-fold increase was largely due to the continuous flow of immigrants. Indeed, immigration accounts for approximately 50% of the growth of the Jewish population.

---

[1] We use the term Palestinians, which is currently preferred by most Arab citizens of Israel. The reader should be aware, however, that our study does not include the Palestinian population residing in the West Bank and Gaza.

Jews migrated to Israel from practically every country on the globe. They were a diverse population in terms of their personal and family characteristics as well as the environments from which they emigrated (e.g., Semyonov and Lerenthal 1991; Khazzoom 1998). Modern Jewish migration to Israel (Palestine, at that time) began over a century ago. The first wave came mainly from East European countries, inspired by the Zionist vision of establishing a national home for the Jewish people in the Biblical Land of Israel. Additional waves followed in the early decades of the twentieth century consisting of Jews who feared the surge of anti-Semitism in Europe and hoping to build a Jewish society in the historic homeland. These immigrants established the pre-state political, economic and civil institutions, which were in place at the time of Israel's independence. Mass migration began only after the establishment of the State of Israel. European Jews—many Holocaust survivors—began arriving in 1947 and their numbers increased dramatically in 1948 and 1949.[2] Concomitant with the Jewish exodus from Europe, large numbers of immigrants arrived from Middle Eastern countries (primarily Iraq and Yemen) followed by immigrants from North Africa. This wave of mass migration was characterised by the uprooting and resettling of entire Jewish communities in Israel; most immigrants were refugees that arrived with only few belongings (Dominitz 1997; Semyonov and Lewin-Epstein 2002).

The decades following these mass movements were characterised by sporadic migration. The level of immigration depended mainly upon the degree of restrictions imposed upon Jewish emigration in source countries or upon various conditions that determined the desirability of Israel as a destination. In addition to political events in Israel itself, these included such developments as the Iranian revolution, unrest in South America, and the collapse of the Soviet Union which unleashed, by the end of the 1980s, the second major wave of Jewish immigration to Israel. During the last decade of the twentieth century over one million immigrants arrived in Israel, mostly from the former USSR, increasing its population by nearly 20%.

Although they came from diverse places, Jews residing in Israel have been categorised mostly according to their continent of origin— European Jews (and their descendants who arrived in Israel via the Americas); and Jews from Muslim countries. This division largely coincides

---

[2] For the annual numbers and origin distribution of immigrants since 1948, see <http://www.cbs.gov.il/shnaton53/dia04_01h.shtml>.

with a cultural distinction between the Ashkenazi and Sephardim religious traditions, which evolved over the centuries and was reinforced by the different environments in which Jews resided. Most European Jews are Ashkenazi and most Jews from Muslim countries, also referred to as Mizrahim (literally, Eastern), are Sephardim. From early settlement in Israel this categorisation of Jews has constituted a central fault line of Jewish Israeli society.

A combination of historical processes resulted in social and economic inequality and competition among the immigrant groups and their descendants. Due to the scope of this project we cannot discuss these in great detail. Nonetheless, it is essential to note the strong overlap between ethnic origin and class position. Ashkenazim had several advantages that gave them a head start. As a rule immigrants from Europe were relatively well educated, and were disproportionately represented in white-collar occupations. When they first arrived they established political, social and economic institutions that were modelled, for the most part, on (East) European societies. When additional waves of Ashkenazi immigrants arrived, these early immigrants used their dominant position in the political institutions and state bureaucracies to incorporate the newcomers into the evolving society. At the same time the policies they shaped and implemented upheld their advantages, often to the detriment of other groups such as immigrants from the Muslim countries and the indigenous Arab population (Segev 1991; Shohat 1988). Additionally, many immigrants from Europe received reparation payments from Germany after the Holocaust at a time when financial resources were scarce. Many of them used the funds they received to better their living conditions, establish small businesses and to ensure the material future of their offspring. As a consequence of the developments just described, Jews of European origins have dominated the social and economic order, and their advantaged position is still manifested in higher levels of education, occupational prestige and economic well being.

While most researchers of Israeli society used the dichotomous distinction between Ashkenazim and Mizrahim when studying the Jewish population, some studies have noted the heterogeneity of the Mizrahi category and underscored the need to distinguish between North African Jews who came primarily from Morocco, Algiers and Tunisia; and Middle Eastern Jews most of whom arrived from Iraq, Iran and Yemen (Nahon 1987; Elmelech and Lewin-Epstein 1998). Some students of Israeli ethnicity have also argued that the broad categories that coincide with continent of origin mask significant social differences that derive largely from the specific countries from which Jews emigrated. This is true for Jews who migrated from Europe as well as immigrants from the Middle East. These scholars argue that the use of a more refined classification of ethnic origin provides additional insight into the dynamic process of ethnic stratification in Israel (Semyonov and Lerenthal 1991; Khazzoom 1998). In a recent Ph.D. dissertation, Karin Amit (2002) evaluated the costs and benefits of using detailed rather than aggregate classifications of ethnicity in models of occupational attainment and earnings. Like Nahon (1987) before her, she found that during the 1970s and 1980s there was a convergence of the attainments of ethnic groups defined by country of origin within the two main blocks—Ashkenazim and Mizrahim. Among the sons and daughters of immigrants this crude classification of ethnicity captures nearly all of the variance between groups in occupation and earnings. However, using data collected in 1995 Amit then discovers the beginnings of a divergence of groups within the Mizrahi cluster during the 1990s. This result is consistent with findings reported by Shavit and his associates (Shavit *et al.* 1999) that the educational attainment of Middle Eastern Jews, but not that of North Africans, tends to converge with the educational attainment of Ashkenazim. As a group, Jews of North African origins have lower standing than those originating in the Middle East who, in turn, have lower education and socio-economic attainment than Ashkenazim. The present study employs data for the entire 1990s and one of our objectives will be to assess the degree of divergence in the occupational attainment of Mizrahim.

Immigration policy — ethinic inclusion and exclusion

Israel's immigration policy differs from that of other migrant societies (e.g., USA, Canada, and Australia) which control immigration through the establishment of priorities and preferences, quotas, and other means that limit immigrant entry. Israel defines itself as the State of the Jewish people and was established as a haven for all Jews, a place where they will be safe from persecution and discrimination. In accordance with this, the State of Israel views Jewish immigrants as a returning diaspora and sees the return to their historic homeland as the given right of all Jews. Consequently, ever since its establishment the state has practised an 'open door' policy accepting all Jews (but only Jews) who wanted to settle in Israel.

The centrepiece of Israel's ethnicity-based immigration policy is the Law of Return. The law, passed in 1950, states that every Jew has the right to settle in Israel, unless s/he has committed acts against the Jewish people or is liable to endanger public health and state security. Jews who immigrate to Israel acquire Israeli citizenship upon arrival and are entitled to all benefits conferred by this status (Horowitz 1996). Jewish identity of immigrants supersedes other considerations such as age, profession and financial status, or any other entrance requirements (Geva-May 1998; Dominitz 1997).[3] Throughout the years, Israeli governments have considered Jewish immigration a demographic imperative for the Jewish state in light of the rapid natural growth of the Arab population within Israel and around its borders. Hence, immigrant absorption is considered a fundamental responsibility of the state. Employment, language learning and social absorption are regarded as interwoven, and actions are undertaken by the government in these realms to facilitate absorption goals.

While Israel applies generous inclusionary practices to encourage the immigration of Jews from around the world, its policies toward non-Jews are generally exclusionary. There are no standard procedures for immigration to Israel for people who are non-Jewish. Indeed, it is all but impossible for non-Jews to gain permanent residence or Israeli citizenship. During the last decade of the twentieth century immigration policy was adapted to the needs of employers (especially in agriculture and construction) and thousands of migrant labourers entered the country. At present an estimated 250,000 foreigners reside in Israel as legal and illegal migrant workers. They have limited access to state and welfare institutions, are vulnerable to various forms of exploitation and are constantly under threat of expulsion. Most illegal migrant workers try to avoid surveyors and are not likely to be represented in the Labour Force Surveys employed in the study; thus we are unable to study them distinctly.[4] This is unfortunate because many other studies in this volume discuss in detail labour immigrants and their descendants.

While Israel's immigration policy has so far prevented large numbers of non-Jews from establishing a permanent home in Israel, Palestinian Arabs who were living in Israel at the time the State was established were

---

[3] *Halakha* (Jewish religious law) defines a Jew as any person born to a Jewish mother or converted to Judaism. Immigration to Israel determines eligibility for citizenship by means of an ascriptive, ethno-religious, criterion based on identification, which includes Jews, children and grandchildren of Jews and their nuclear families (even if the latter are not Jewish). Inclusion of non-Jewish spouses and descendants to the third generation was recognised by an amendment to the Law of Return passed in 1970 (Horowitz 1999; Shuval and Leshem 1998; Dominitz 1997).
[4] See Kemp *et al.* (2000) and Rozenhek (2000) for research on migrant workers in Israel.

granted citizenship and have been partially integrated into Israeli society. Of the 600,000 Palestinians who in 1947 resided in the territory that became the State of Israel, only 156,000 remained by 1949. The others fled or were driven out during the 1948 war and not permitted to return. Hence, the growth of this population, which now exceeds 1.2 million, represents natural growth.[5] The Arab residents that remained in Israel were mostly villagers, cut off from their political, intellectual and economic leadership that fled (or was driven out) during the war. Over the years the status of Arabs in Israel has been determined by a combination of factors. Most prominent among them are the Zionist definition of Israel as a Jewish homeland, the broader Arab-Israeli conflict and the security considerations it entails, and the democratic character of the state (Al-Haj 2002; Smooha 1990; Rouhana and Ghanem 1998). When these factors are in conflict it is the latter that most often gives way.

Then and now Arabs are highly segregated from the Jewish population and most Arabs still reside in over-grown and overcrowded villages that offer few employment opportunities. Most of these communities were under military rule until the mid-1960s and their development was hindered as a result of, on the one hand, constraints imposed by the State and, on the other, wilful neglect (Khalidi 1988; Lewin-Epstein and Semyonov 1993; Lustick 1980). The Arab population is not homogenous: 80% are Sunni Muslims, slightly over 10% are Christians (of several denominations), and less than 10% are Druse. Although the Arab population grew almost eight-fold during the fifty years following Israel's independence, they constituted approximately 17% of Israel's population throughout the period. The combination of spatial segregation and political and economic domination by the Jewish majority has marginalised the Arab population and rendered its communities to a socio-economic periphery (Al-Haj and Rosenfeld 1990; Sa'di 1995; Yiftachel 1997; Lustick 1980).

Research question

In this chapter we hope to meet several research objectives. The first is to provide descriptive data on differences in education, labour-force participation and occupational attainment between detailed ethnic groups and

---

[5] One sixth of this population (slightly over 200,000) reside in East Jerusalem which was annexed following the 1967 war.

generations of immigration. Second, we aim to estimate change across generations of immigration in ethnic differences in labour-force participation and occupational attainment. Our third objective is methodological: to evaluate the extent to which a detailed classification of ethnic groups adds to our understanding of ethnic stratification in Israel, above and beyond the use of the standard classification that distinguishes between Palestinians, Ashkenazim, North Africans and Middle Easterners.

Data and variables

We utilise a compiled file of Labour Force Surveys for the years 1992–2000. For the years 1992–4 we include all individuals aged 25–59 and for the years 1995–2000 all individuals aged 21–59 are included in the sample.[6] The advantages of the labour-force surveys are their large sample sizes, good quality data on labour-force participation and ethnic origins, and their continuous availability. The major drawback of these data is the absence of information on social background and their rather crude measures of education. The files include information on the duration of education in years and the type of school last attended but no information is available on whether or not respondents graduated.

Variables

The models presented in this chapter follow the guidelines laid out in the introductory chapter of this volume, with the following modifications.

Year: This variable represents the year of the LFS and ranges from 1992 to 2000. In preliminary analyses we coded year as a set of dummy variables but since their effects were quite linear and in the interest of parsimony, we present models that employ the continuous version

Ancestry: The following categories have been distinguished in the analyses, including respondents who were born (or whose parents were born) in the following areas:

---

[6] Since most young adults in Israel are subject to two to three years of compulsory military service at the age of 18, we decided on age 21 as the lower cut-off point for the study. Up to 1994, however, all persons aged 18–24 were grouped together in official statistics. Hence, for these years only people aged 25 or older are included in the data set.

- *Palestinians*: All Muslim, Christians and Druse who were born in Israel;
- *Third Generation Jews*: Native Jews whose parents were also born in Israel; this category will serve as the reference category in the majority of analyses;
- *Middle East*: Iran, Iraq, Turkey, Lebanon or Egypt;
- *North Africa*: Morocco, Algeria, Libya and Tunisia;
- *South Asia*: India and Pakistan;
- *East Europe*: Former East European Soviet Bloc countries;
- *West Europe*: Other European countries;
- *North America and Oceania*: USA, Canada and Oceania;
- *Latin America*: All Latin American countries.

Several very small groups were excluded from the analysis, including Ethiopians and respondents of mixed ethnic origins.[7] In earlier (unreported) analyses we attempted to include them but encountered problems in estimating some of their effects. In all, we excluded at this stage about 4% of the sample.

Finally, a dichotomous variable entitled 'generation' has also been included, with the purpose of identifying first-generation immigrants, or persons who immigrated to Israel after the age of six.[8]

Descriptive analysis

We already noted that Israel is a society of immigrants. This is seen in Table 8.1 which presents the distribution of the population by immigration generation for the years 1992 to 2000. About one-third of the population are first-generation, or immigrants who were older than six upon arrival; an additional 40% are second-generation immigrants, who are native children of immigrants or who immigrated themselves prior to age six. The proportion of the third-generation (i.e., the sons and daughters of native parents) is 20% to 30%, most of whom are Palestinians. Thus, and by contrast to the other countries presented in this volume, in Israel there is no 'host' group; all but a small fraction of the population are either immigrants, children of immigrants or members of an excluded

---

[7] The LFS files for 1992 through 1994 do not include information on mother's country of birth and immigration status. Therefore, for these years we cannot distinguish mixed origins.
[8] As in other chapters in this volume, we have excluded respondents whose parents were of different immigration generations.

Table 8.1. Generational composition of the Israeli Population, 1992–2000 (column percentages).

	1992	1993	1994	1995	1996	1997	1998	1999	2000
First generation	32.2	32.1	32.0	31.2	31.2	30.6	29.2	29.2	29.1
Second generation	45.9	46.1	45.9	40.9	41.3	41.1	41.7	40.5	40.3
Third-generation Jews	6.4	6.4	6.6	6.1	6.4	7.1	8.3	9.0	9.0
Palestinians	14.4	14.3	14.5	16.9	16.8	17.3	18.8	19.6	19.9
Unknown	1.2	1.0	1.0	5.0	4.3	4.0	1.9	1.7	1.6
N	54,361	53,007	57,580	57,376	58,214	56,893	60,530	60,385	59,632

Note: For surveys from 1992 to 1994, includes adult population aged 24 to 59; otherwise inclusive of ages 21 to 59.

indigenous minority. This configuration suggests that an analysis of ethnic stratification in Israel should not focus on the incorporation of ethnic and immigration groups into the host group but rather study change across time and generations of immigration in the pattern of association between group membership and position within social hierarchies.

The proportions of first- and second-generation immigrants in the year 2000 are shown by ethnicity in Table 8.2. As seen, the most recent arrivals are the East Europeans, most of whom arrived after 1989 from the former USSR, North Americans and Latin Americans. The latter two groups immigrated primarily during the late 1960s and 1970s.

Table 8.3 presents the distribution of ethnic origins in 2000. The largest groups, in the following order, are: East Europeans, third-generation

Table 8.2. Relative size of population in 2000, by area of origin (row percentages).

	Second generation	First generation	N
Middle East	84.1	15.9	8,906
South Asia	61.5	38.5	671
North Africa	78.1	21.9	8,496
Eastern Europe	31.3	68.7	16,222
Western Europe	64.3	35.7	2,591
North America and Oceania	23.7	76.3	1,046
Latin America	26.0	74.0	863
Middle East and North Africa	100.0	0.0	620
Middle East and Europe[a]	100.0	0.0	674
North Africa and Europe	100.0	0.0	444
Europe and Europe	100.0	0.0	967
Palestinian	100.0	0.0	2,776
Israel	100.0	0.0	14,690

Notes: Inclusive of adult population aged 21 to 59.
[a] Including Other developed and Latin America with Europe.

Table 8.3. Distribution of ethnic origins in Israel, 2000.

	Per cent
South Asian	1.18
Latin American	1.51
North American and Oceanic	1.83
West European	4.63
Palestinian	21.44
North African	15.09
Middle Eastern	15.84
Third-generation Jewish	9.7
East European	28.77

Jews, Middle Easterners, North Africans and Palestinians. The other groups are numerically quite small. This is significant because it suggests that the standard classification of ethnicity employed by most previous studies probably captures much of the variation between persons in social resources and achievements. As noted, the standard classification distinguishes between Ashkenazim (most of whom are of East European origins), North Africans, Middle Eastern Jews and Palestinians. Third-generation Jews are usually grouped together with Ashkenazim on the assumption that most of them are descendants of the Russian and Polish immigrants who arrived in the late nineteenth and early twentieth centuries.

Ethnic inequalities in education are shown in Tables 8.4A and 8.4B for men and women respectively. As can be seen, Palestinians and Jews of North African, Middle Eastern and South Asian origins attain lower levels of education than Europeans, third-generation Jews and the American groups. Interestingly, within most ethnic groups only small differences appear between the first and second generations. If anything, in the advantaged groups, the second-generation seems to attain lower educational levels than the immigrant generation. Evidently, immigration from developed countries to Israel entails a small 'educational penalty'. The educational aspirations of European Jews are said to be very high by comparison to both the general population in their countries of residence, and to non-European Jews. When living in developed countries they take advantage of the available educational opportunities and realise these aspirations. Where Jews are a small minority many of them can pursue professional careers through higher education. However, in Israel, where Jews are the majority, not all can find employment in the professions. In addition, the economy cannot sustain universal higher education. Therefore, immigration to Israel 'normalised' the educational

Table 8.4A. Highest education qualification, by ancestry: Males (row percentages).

	Primary or less	Lower secondary	Upper secondary	Some tertiary	Full tertiary	Unknown	N
First generation							
North African	23.3	27.7	19.1	11.9	11.3	6.6	1,567
Middle Eastern	25.3	20.5	18.9	11.8	14.2	9.2	1,283
South Asian	21.4	22.3	33.0	5.4	15.2	2.7	112
East European	7.2	12.3	16.2	21.8	39.9	2.7	5,925
West European	4.5	13.1	21.5	13.9	42.4	4.7	519
Latin American	3.3	10.6	17.2	21.5	46.4	1.1	414
North American and Oceanic	0.0	3.3	29.9	6.3	59.5	1.1	499
Second generation							
North African	11.6	39.5	21.4	10.6	12.2	4.7	4,144
Middle Eastern	11.2	37.0	20.2	11.1	16.3	4.2	5,231
South Asian	11.2	38.8	17.0	12.1	14.1	6.8	206
East European	4.5	20.2	15.8	14.8	40.8	4.0	3,827
West European	5.3	16.7	22.5	15.0	37.1	3.3	1,387
Latin American	0.0	15.7	16.5	15.7	46.3	5.8	121
North American and Oceanic	0.0	4.1	41.3	6.6	47.9	0.0	137
Third generation or indigenous							
Palestinian	42.8	8.3	26.2	6.0	10.9	5.8	6,185
Jewish	3.7	17.8	34.1	10.9	30.7	3.1	2,851

distribution of Ashkenazim in the sense that it is more similar to those of other populations in advanced societies than is their educational distribution pre-immigration. Among the Mizrahi (Middle Eastern and North African) groups differences between generations are not systematic.

Tables 8.5A and 8.5B present the distributions of economic activity for men and women respectively. The data reveal some expected patterns: among men, the labour-force participation rates of Latin Americans and Europeans are higher than among Palestinians and first-generation Mizrahim. A somewhat unexpected finding, however, is the high proportion of men of North American origins and third-generation Jews who are inactive. These are highly educated groups that do not suffer from discrimination or exclusion in the labour market; why are so many of them (over 20%) inactive? We hypothesise that the answer is related to the disproportionate concentration of ultra-orthodox Jews among immigrants originating in North America and among Jews who have lived in Israel and Palestine for several generations. Many ultra-orthodox Jewish men devote their life to religious study rather than gainful employment. They subsist on charity, family assistance and social security. Most survey

Table 8.4B. Highest education qualification, by ancestry: Females (row percentages).

	Primary or less	Lower secondary	Upper secondary	Some tertiary	Full tertiary	Unknown	N
First generation							
North African	34.5	18.5	25.3	10.6	8.0	3.1	1,777
Middle Eastern	6.3	33.3	26.1	12.1	13.5	8.7	1,305
South Asian	10.3	30.0	24.4	15.4	15.7	4.3	193
East European	3.7	5.1	15.6	25.7	42.1	7.7	7,039
West European	5.3	8.6	14.5	25.7	43.3	2.6	750
Latin American	1.9	7.8	14.6	23.3	51.5	1.0	465
North American and Oceanic	0.2	1.2	12.3	17.9	66.0	2.3	499
Second generation							
North African	32.8	13.9	27.8	10.5	8.3	6.7	3,798
Middle Eastern	12.2	27.6	24.2	13.8	17.4	4.6	5,161
South Asian	24.0	19.2	30.1	6.8	13.0	6.8	146
East European	2.1	12.0	22.8	17.7	42.8	2.6	750
West European	3.7	12.8	19.7	20.5	39.8	3.5	1,419
Latin American	2.2	6.0	19.2	20.0	50.7	1.9	125
North American and Oceanic	0.0	3.1	13.4	22.8	59.1	1.6	218
Third generation or indigenous							
Palestinian	58.8	1.7	25.1	6.3	5.9	2.2	6,174
Jewish	3.7	9.6	19.0	28.3	35.0	4.5	2,559

datasets do not include information on religious orthodoxy and do not permit the identification of the ultra-orthodox. However, one can employ an indirect crude measure to distinguish between orthodox and non-religious respondents. The Labour Force Survey requests respondents to identify the type of school last attended. One of the response categories to the question is 'Yeshiva', an institute of higher religious studies that is often attended by Orthodox Jews. Amongst North Americans and third-generation Jews nearly 8% and 6%, respectively, attended Yeshiva, in contrast to a rate of less than 2% amongst the total male sample. These figures lend some credence to our hypothesis that the low participation rates of North Americans and third-generation Jews are attributable to the high prevalence among them of ultra-orthodoxy. The hypothesis is also supported by the gender difference in labour-force participation rates in these groups: among women, who are not expected to devote many years to religious study, the labour-force participation rates for these groups are substantially higher than among men.

The class distributions of the ethnic and immigration groups are shown in Tables 8.6A and 8.6B. The distributions are consistent with

Table 8.5A. Economic activity in 2000, by ancestry: Males (row percentages).

	Economically active	Student	Other Inactive	N
First generation				
North African	68.7	2.0	29.2	883
Middle Eastern	68.7	1.3	30.0	703
South Asian	76.8	1.8	21.4	112
East European	82.2	2.1	15.7	5,121
West European	69.1	6.0	24.9	382
Latin American	85.4	3.6	10.9	274
North American and Oceanic	62.2	17.4	20.4	368
Second generation				
North African	75.0	4.6	20.3	3,321
Middle Eastern	79.1	4.6	16.3	3,692
South Asian	74.3	6.8	18.9	206
East European	82.6	4.2	13.2	2,511
West European	81.5	6.4	12.1	844
Latin American	76.0	14.9	9.1	121
North American and Oceanic	58.7	19.8	21.5	121
Third generation and indigenous				
Palestinian	68.4	3.2	28.4	5,917
Jewish	66.3	10.5	23.1	2,742

Note: Inclusive of adults aged 21 to 59.

those seen for education: for both men and women, the proportion in the salariat is higher in the European and American groups than among the Mizrahim and Palestinian groups.

Multivariate analysis

In the following sections we report the results of logistic analyses of unemployment and multivariate analyses of labour-force participation and occupational attainment. We analyse the same data set employed so far but exclude cases with missing values on any of the variables. To expedite the analysis we select a random sample of 15% of the remaining cases, resulting in sample sizes of 33,781 and 34,858 for men and women respectively.

Table 8.5B. Economic activity in 2000, by ancestry: Females (row percentages).

	Economically active	Student	Other Inactive	N
First generation				
North African	52.4	0.7	46.9	976
Middle Eastern	50.5	0.1	49.4	713
South Asian	63.0	1.4	35.6	146
East European	74.8	2.0	23.2	6,031
West European	64.2	2.8	33.1	544
Latin American	78.6	6.8	14.6	367
North American and Oceanic	64.4	4.2	31.4	430
Second generation				
North African	69.3	3.4	27.3	3,316
Middle Eastern	71.7	2.4	25.9	3,798
South Asian	75.8	1.4	22.7	207
East European	77.6	3.0	19.4	2,559
West European	78.0	2.6	19.5	821
Latin American	80.5	2.5	17.0	103
North American and Oceanic	70.9	6.3	22.8	127
Third generation and indigenous				
Palestinian	19.0	2.4	78.6	6,174
Jewish	74.1	7.3	18.6	2,700

Ethnicity, immigration generation and labour-force participation

In this section we model the relationship between ethnicity, immigration, demographic characteristics and labour-force participation. In line with the descriptive analysis, we do this separately for men and women. Labour-force participation—the dependent variable—comprises three categories: employed and those who are unemployed (the reference category), out of the labour force but in an educational institution, and not employed and not studying. The independent variables in the models are ethnicity (with third-generation Jews serving as the reference category), whether or not the respondent is a first-generation immigrant, educational attainment (with primary as the reference category), age and marital status. We also include survey year in order to control for changes over-time in the labour market.

We first estimate several competing multinomial models and, based on their goodness-of-fit statistics, we select the one that best balances fit and parsimony. We then report the coefficient estimates for the selected model and discuss the findings in light of the propositions put forward at

Table 8.6A. Occupational class in 2000, by ancestry: Males (row percentages).

	Salariat	Routine Non-manual	Petty Bourgeoisie	Skilled Manual	Semi- and Unskilled Manual	Unemployed	N
First generation							
North African	8.4	10.4	17.2	32.4	22.8	8.8	651
Middle Eastern	10.5	7.5	18.0	34.9	21.8	7.3	519
South Asian	7.3	11.0	12.2	38.9	27.9	2.7	111
East European	13.8	6.8	5.0	46.5	20.6	7.3	4,661
West European	32.9	13.6	10.9	21.9	17.5	3.1	351
Latin American	23.2	13.4	9.9	24.7	25.8	3.0	301
North American and Oceanic	35.4	6.8	8.5	30.3	15.2	3.8	237
Second generation							
North African	7.3	14.3	16.3	35.9	18.2	8.1	3,040
Middle Eastern	9.0	14.1	17.7	34.8	18.3	6.1	3,007
South Asian	4.7	12.9	14.8	33.1	29.0	5.5	201
East European	27.6	16.0	13.4	26.6	11.6	4.7	1,926
West European	26.1	15.6	16.4	23.5	14.3	4.0	650
Latin American	22.3	15.4	8.4	26.5	25.2	2.2	91
North American and Oceanic	41.9	14.2	4.3	19.3	9.0	11.4	88
Third generation and indigenous							
Palestinian	6.4	8.1	13.5	41.4	20.5	10.2	4,612
Jewish	17.0	16.5	12.9	26.9	20.8	6.0	1,819

Table 8.6B. Occupational class in 2000, by ancestry: Females (row percentages).

	Salariat	Routine Non-manual	Petty Bourgeoisie	Skilled Manual	Semi- and Unskilled Manual	Unemployed	N
First generation							
North African	8.4	10.4	17.1	32.3	22.7	9.1	560
Middle Eastern	10.5	7.5	18.0	34.9	21.8	7.4	363
South Asian	7.8	15.2	9.0	32.8	23.0	12.3	114
East European	13.6	6.7	4.9	45.8	20.2	8.8	4,904
West European	32.7	13.5	10.9	21.7	17.4	3.8	447
Latin American	22.7	13.1	9.7	24.2	25.2	5.2	307
North American and Oceanic	45.0	15.2	4.6	20.8	9.6	4.9	309
Second generation							
North African	7.1	14.0	15.9	35.0	17.8	10.2	2,640
Middle Eastern	9.4	29.3	6.8	12.0	33.5	8.9	2,528
South Asian	6.8	10.2	11.3	36.0	25.8	9.9	151
East European	32.3	12.7	11.1	23.9	13.2	6.8	1,918
West European	27.8	16.1	13.5	26.7	11.7	4.3	702
Latin American	21.4	14.7	8.1	25.4	24.1	6.3	80
North American and Oceanic	25.9	15.5	16.3	23.3	14.2	4.7	85
Third generation and indigenous							
Palestinian	4.5	12.3	14.2	31.6	27.7	9.8	1,117
Jewish	16.1	29.3	4.1	8.9	35.4	6.2	1,880

the outset of the chapter. Given the large samples employed we use the BIC statistic (Raftery 1986) as the criterion for selecting the preferred model[9]. Generally speaking the model to be preferred is the one with the lowest positive value of BIC (the largest distance from the null model).

Goodness-of-fit statistics for various models are presented in Table 8.7 The top panel presents models for men and the bottom panel presents models for women. The null model (listed as Model 0) serves as a baseline for the evaluation of subsequent models.

Model 1 includes the main effects of ethnicity and education, as well as the control variables—marital status, age and year. In this model we assume no difference between first and second-generation immigrants. When generation is added to the model (Model 2), the BIC statistic

Table 8.7. Goodness of fit statistics for models of labour-force participation.

Model	Variables (categories included in model)	Parameters	-2LogL	BIC
Men (n=33,781)				
0	Intercept only	2	46,837.1	46,858.0
1	Marital Status (2), Education (4), Age (1), Year (1), Ethnicity (8)	34	38,992.9	39,347.4
2	1+Generation (1)	36	38,960.2	39,335.6
3	2+Interactions of Generation with (Mid-East, N. Africa, E. Europe, W. Europe, N. America)	46	38,831.5	39,311.2
4	2+Interaction of Generation with (E. Europe)	38	38,857.9	39,254.2
5	4+Constraint: (Mid-East=N. Africa)	36	38,903.9	39,279.3
6	4−E. Europe=W. Europe=L. America=0	32	38,934.6	39,268.3
7	4+Interactions of Education with (Palestinians, Mizrahim, N. America)	44	38,573.5	39,032.3
Women (n=34,858)				
0	Intercept only	2	55,436.8	55,457.7
1	Marital Status (2), Education (4), Age (1), Year (1), Ethnicity (8)	34	42,531.8	42,887.4
2	1+Generation (1)	36	42,423.0	42,799.5
3	2+Interactions of Generation with (Mid-East, N. Africa, E. Europe, W. Europe, N. America)	46	42,352.5	42,833.6
4	2+Constraint: (Mid-East=N. Africa)	34	42,436.8	42,792.4
5	4−E. Europe=W. Europe=L. America=0	28	42,457.2	42,750.1
6	5+Interactions of Education with (Palestinians, Mizrahim, N. America)	34	42,204.0	42,559.1
7	5+Interactions of Education with (Palestinians, Mizrahim)	32	42,207.9	42,542.6

[9] With large samples the conventional tests of significance based on mean differences in deviance per degrees of freedom are often conservative, returning verdicts of significance for even the smallest of coefficients. The STATA formula for BIC is: $BIC = -2L^2 + (df)(\log n)$

declines a bit for men and considerably for women. In both cases Model 2, which assumes a generation effect, is preferable to Model 1. Model 3 evaluates the extent to which ethnic groups differ in their generation effects. It includes interactions of generation with each of the five large ethnic groups. The other origin groups are small and we could not test their specific interactions with Generation. The fit statistics reveal different patterns for men and women. Among men, Model 3 is preferable to model 2 indicating generational differences in the case of (at least) some ethnic groups. In the case of women, there are no significant interactions and Model 2 is preferred to Model 3. A closer examination of the coefficients in Model 3 for men (not shown) revealed that only one of the five interactions is significant—that between generation and East European origin. Hence, in Model 4 we re-estimate the model with only one interaction term and find, based on the fit statistics, that it is preferable to Model 3.

In general then there seem to be no generational differences in patterns of labour-force participation with the exception of East European men. The general absence of generation effects indicates that immigrants are quickly absorbed by the Israeli labour market. The exceptional group of East Europeans includes many recent immigrants from the former Soviet Union, who arrived within a decade of data collection and are still negotiating their way into the local labour market.

Models 5, 6 and 7 for men and Models 4 through 7 for women test the hypotheses that the ethnic blocks of Ashkenazi and Mizrahi are homogenous with respect to their association with labour-force participation. In Model 5 for men and Model 4 for women we impose an equality constraint on the effects of Middle Eastern and North African Jews. For men, the fit statistics reject this hypothesis; however for women it is sustained and Model 4 is preferred to previous models.

The specification of Model 6 for men and 5 for women is meant to test the proposition that the European groups and the Latin Americans are not significantly different from third-generation Jews with regard to labour-force participation. In other words, these models test for the homogeneity of the Ashkenazi groups. Note that the models allow North Americans to differ from other Ashkenazim—a result that we already noted in the descriptive part of the analysis. Once again, for men it appears that the model with full ethnic specification (Model 4) is preferable to Model 6. For women, the fit statistics confirm that the effects of ethnicity on labour-force participation is homogenous within broad ethnic blocks with one exception—immigrants from North America, who are distinct from other Ashkenazim (analysis not shown).

The final models (Model 7 for men and Models 6 and 7 for women) test the interaction effects of ethnicity and education on labour-force participation patterns. For men, the continuous measure of education[10] is interacted with each of the following groups: Palestinians, Mizrahim, and North Americans. For the sake of parsimony we assume that the effects of education do not vary for the distinct Mizrahi groups and for the European groups (including third-generation Jews). Including the interaction terms in the models for men improves the fit and we conclude that there are significant differences between groups in the effects of education. In the case of women, the preferred model (Model 7) allows education to interact with Palestinians and with Mizrahi but not with North Americans.

The parameter estimates of the two best models are shown in Tables 8.8A and 8.8B. Beginning with Table 8.8A we see that single men are more likely than ever-married men (married, divorced and widowed) to be out of the labour force (whether as students or otherwise). Older respondents are less likely to be students and are more likely to be out of the labour force than younger ones.

Turning to the effects of ethnicity, we find that most immigrant groups differ from third generation Jews in their labour-force participation patterns. Overall, ethnic differences in the left column of the table are larger than they are in the right-hand column. Palestinians, and to a lesser extent Mizrahim, are less likely to be students than Ashkenazim. Otherwise, among Jews there are small differences in labour-force participation, as indicated in the right-hand column. While first-generation immigrants are more likely than Israeli-born Jews to attend an educational institution, there is no generational difference in the likelihood of being out of the labour force except for the case of East Europeans where the recent immigrants (overwhelmingly from the republics of the former Soviet Union) are less likely to be in school or in the labour force. Finally, educated men are less likely than men with only primary education to be out of the labour force, and they are generally more likely to be students (except for men with some secondary education who exhibit a lower likelihood than the least educated to be in education).

---

[10] Based on the categorical measurement of CASMIN (scored -2, -1, 0, 1, 2 where 0 is full secondary). Thus, the categorical measure is independent of the continuous one.

Table 8.8A. Logistic regression of labour-force participation: Males (parameter estimates, contrasts with economically active).

	Student		Not Active	
Intercept	**2.77**	(0.21)	**−0.19**	(0.10)
Ancestry				
Third-generation Jewish	0.0		0.0	
Palestinian	**−1.87**	(0.12)	**−0.36**	(0.07)
Middle-Eastern	**−0.52**	(0.09)	**−0.37**	(0.07)
North African	−0.16	(0.08)	−0.08	(0.07)
South Asian	−1.26	(0.62)	0.21	(0.20)
West European	0.23	(0.11)	**−0.49**	(0.10)
East European	−0.17	(0.09)	**−0.56**	(0.08)
North American (and Oceanic)	**1.64**	(0.18)	**0.65**	(0.18)
Latin American	−0.47	(0.20)	**−0.61**	(0.17)
First Generation	**0.33**	(0.10)	0.01	(0.06)
Age	**−0.10**	(0.01)	**0.02**	(0.00)
Education				
Primary	0.0		0.0	
Some Secondary	−0.16	(0.15)	**−1.09**	(0.06)
Full Secondary	**1.25**	(0.15)	**−0.62**	(0.06)
Some Tertiary	0.06	(0.18)	−1.22	(0.08)
Full Tertiary	0.40	(0.17)	−1.57	(0.08)
Marital Status				
Single	0.0		0.0	
Married	**−1.48**	(0.06)	**−1.31**	(0.04)
Other	**−1.28**	(0.23)	**−0.42**	(0.08)
Year	**−0.24**	(0.01)	−0.01	(0.01)
Interaction of East European with				
First Generation	**−1.24**	(0.15)	**0.42**	(0.09)
Interactions of Ethnicity with				
Education				
Palestinian	**1.02**	(0.08)	**−0.10**	(0.04)
Mizrahim	**0.14**	(0.05)	0.03	(0.03)
North American (and Oceanic)	**−1.07**	(0.14)	**−0.53**	(0.12)

The interactions between ethnicity and education reveal a number of patterns. Better educated Palestinians are less likely than third-generation Jews with similar education to be out of the labour force and more likely to be in school. Education has a stronger positive effect on the likelihood of being in school (than in the labour force) for Mizrahim, but there are no differences in the effect of education on the likelihood of being out of the labour force. In the case of North American Jews the interaction terms are both negative and significant. Since education generally exerts a negative effect on the likelihood of being out of the labour force the negative interaction term for North-American immigrants can be interpreted to mean that their labour-force participation is more sensitive to level of education than that of third generation Israeli-born.

The results for women are presented in Table 8.8B. Since the best fitting model for women, as we saw in Table 8.7, is more parsimonious than the model for men, interpreting the coefficients is somewhat simpler. As is usually the case (and in contrast to men), married, divorced and widowed women are more likely than single women to be out of the labour force. They are also less likely than single women to be students. Evidently, many ever-married women are busy with home and family work.

The ethnic categorisation distinguishes Palestinian women, Mizrahi women, North American women versus all other women (overwhelmingly European immigrants and their offspring as well as other third-generation Israeli-born women). There are significant differences in labour-force behaviour between Palestinian women and the reference group. The former are more likely to be out of the labour force, but are

Table 8.8B. Logistic regression of labour-force participation: Females (parameter estimates, contrasts with economically active).

	Student		Not Active	
Intercept	**2.09**	(0.33)	−**0.61**	(0.09)
Ancestry				
Third-generation Jewish	0.0		0.0	
Palestinian	−**0.45**	(0.22)	**1.85**	(0.05)
Mizrahim	**0.66**	(0.10)	−0.01	(0.03)
South Asian	−0.30	(1.04)	−0.11	(0.16)
North American (and Oceanic)	0.48	(0.21)	**0.41**	(0.10)
First Generation	0.04	(0.093)	**0.35**	(0.03)
Age	−**0.13**	(0.01)	**0.01**	(0.00)
Education				
Primary	0.0		0.0	
Some Secondary	−0.49	(0.23)	−**0.78**	(0.05)
Full Secondary	0.07	(0.25)	−**0.72**	(0.06)
Some Tertiary	**0.78**	(0.27)	−**1.40**	(0.07)
Full Tertiary	**1.18**	(0.27)	−**1.84**	(0.07)
Marital Status				
Single	0.0		0.0	
Married	−**1.64**	(0.08)	**0.83**	(0.04)
Other	−**0.89**	(0.16)	**0.75**	(0.06)
Year	−**0.15**	(0.01)	−**0.06**	(0.01)
Interaction of East European with				
First Generation				
Interactions of Ethnicity with				
Education				
Palestinian	**0.74**	(0.13)	−**0.44**	(0.04)
Mizrahim	−**0.24**	(0.07)	−**0.12**	(0.03)
North American (and Oceanic)				

less likely to be students. This reflects the more traditional social position of Palestinian women as compared with Jews. Whereas Mizrahi men (immigrants from the Middle East and North Africa) are more likely to be in the labour force than the reference group, *Mizrahiot* do not differ from third-generation women in the odds of labour-force participation. But it is somewhat surprising that, other things being equal, the likelihood of being a student is higher for Mizrahi women than for the reference group.

The effect of immigration status differs for men and women. Whereas first-generation immigrant men did not differ from others in the likelihood of being out of the labour force, first-generation immigrant women are more likely to be out of the labour force, possibly reflecting the greater difficulty faced by women in entering the labour market. Contrary to the findings for men, recent immigrant women do not differ in this respect from other women.

As we found in the case of men, educated women are less likely than women with only primary education to be out of the labour force, and they are generally more likely to be students (except for women with some secondary education who exhibit a lower likelihood than the least educated to be in education). Age also makes a difference, with older women more likely to be out of the labour force and less likely to be in education.

As in the case for men, the interactions between education on the one hand and Palestinians and Mizrahim on the other are significant. The results indicate that among Palestinian women labour-force participation is more sensitive to education than is the case for Jewish women. As for educated Mizrahi women—they are less likely than other educated women to still be in school and are more likely to be in the labour force.

To summarise then, with regard to the particular interest of the present paper it would seem that the following findings are of special interest.

- First, among men most groups do not differ greatly in the odds of being out the labour force. There is one exception to this generalisation: North Americans' odds of labour-force participation are very low, probably reflecting wilful abstention that is made possible by the de-commodification of ultra-orthodox labour.[11]

---

[11] Israel's welfare state supports yeshiva students and enables them to subsist, albeit in poverty, through study rather than employment. The State is much less generous vis-à-vis other students. Although some members of all Jewish groups choose this path, they comprise a relatively high proportion only among those who emigrated from North America.

- Second, the Israeli labour market absorbs male immigrants rather quickly, as indicated by the null effect of the generation variable on the odds of labour-force participation. The exceptions are the very recent immigrants from the former USSR who still suffer from lower than average rates of labour-force participation. By 2001, 37.6% were still out of the civilian labour force (CBS 2003).
- Third, regarding women, conditional on not being in school, the main Jewish ethnic groups do not differ in their odds of labour-force participation.
- Fourth, Palestinian women show very low rates of both schooling and labour-force participation, both of which reflect constraints that are often imposed by families on Muslim women.
- Fifth, the labour-force participation rates of first-generation immigrant women are somewhat lower than those of second-generation immigrants and veterans and do not seem to vary by ethnic group. Evidently, the incorporation of immigrant women into the labour force is more difficult than that of men.

Ethnicity, generation and avoidance of unemployment

Our next objective is to model the relationship between ethnicity, generation of immigration, demographic characteristics and the avoidance of unemployment. The relevant population includes all persons in the labour force and the independent variables in the models are the same ones used in the analysis of labour-force participation. As in the previous analysis of labour-force participation, we first estimate several competing models of the association and, based on their goodness-of-fit statistics, select the one that best balances fit and parsimony. Goodness-of-fit statistics for various models are presented, for men and women in Table 8.9.

Model 8 is our preferred model for both sexes. For men, the model includes the control variables, generational effects and the interaction between generation and East European origin (the only interaction that was significant). The model also includes the main effects of ethnicity, except for those from East Europe, West Europe and Latin America. In a closer examination we found that these ethnic groups do not differ significantly from either one another or from third-generation Jews. Model 8 for men also interacts the continuous measure of education with North

Table 8.9. Goodness of fit statistics for models of unemployment.

Model	Variables (categories included in model)	Parameters	−2LogL	BIC
Men (n=26,204)				
0	Intercept only	1	12,920.9	12,931.1
1	Marital Status (2), Education (4), Age (1), Year (1), Ethnicity (8)	17	12,388.3	12,561.3
2	1+Generation (1)	18	12,361.3	12,544.4
3	2+Interactions of Generation with (Mid-East, N. Africa, E. Europe, W. Europe) (4)	22	12,307.1	12,530.9
4	3−Interactions of Generation with (Mid-East, N. Africa, W. Europe)	19	12,317.1	12,510.4
5	4−E. Europe, W. Europe, L. America	16	12,318.8	12,481.6
6	5+Constraint: (Mid-East=N. Africa)	15	12,329.4	12,482.0
7	5+Interactions of Education with (Ethnicity(8))	24	12,298.2	12,542.4
8	5+Interactions of Education with (N. Africa)	17	12,311.1	12,484.1
Women (n=21,027)				
0	Intercept only	1	12,711.8	12,721.8
1	Marital Status (2), Education (4), Age (1), Year (1), Ethnicity (8)	17	12,368.7	12,537.9
2	1+ Generation (1)	18	12,337.9	12,517.1
3	2+Interactions of Generation with (Mid-East, N. Africa, E. Europe, W Europe) (4)	22	12,280.9	12,499.8
4	3−Interactions of Generation with (Mid-East, N Africa, W Europe)	19	12,285.1	12,474.3
5	4−E. Europe, W. Europe, N. America, L. America	15	12,287.2	12,436.5
6	5+Constraint: (Mid-East=N. Africa)	14	12,303.9	12,443.2
8	5+Interactions of Education with (E. Europe)	16	12,243.8	12,403.1

African ethnicity.[12] In model 8 for women, the Ashkenazi groups do not differ significantly neither from one another nor from third-generation Jews, and thus the model allows education to interact only with East European ancestry. The parameter estimates for the preferred models (model 8) for both sexes are shown in Tables 8.10A and 8.10B.

Table 8.10A reveals that married men have a lower probability than single men or other unmarried men of being unemployed. Likewise, older respondents are less likely to be unemployed. (We also ran analyses including age squared but this term was not statistically significant.)

---

[12] Actually, according to BIC statistic Model 5 for men is the formally preferred model. Nevertheless, we will focus on Model 8 because the difference is very small and the interaction in Model 8 is significant.

Turning to the effects of ethnicity and generation, we find that most Jewish groups, as well as Palestinians, have higher probabilities than third-generation Jews[13] of being unemployed. These results most likely reflect the advantage enjoyed by the founding generation and their offspring in terms of both residence in proximity to large labour markets, and greater access to the more secure public sector jobs. No generational differences were observed in the likelihood of unemployment, except for first-generation immigrants from the former Soviet Union.[14] Evidently, these recent immigrants, most of whom arrived in the 1990s, have not yet been fully absorbed into the labour market, as evidenced by their relatively high unemployment rate.

Table 8.10A. Logistic regression of employment and unemployment: Males (parameter estimates, contrasts with unemployment).

Intercept	**1.71**	(0.15)
Ancestry		
Third-generation Jewish	0.0	
Palestinian	−**0.54**	(0.09)
Middle-Eastern	−**0.50**	(0.09)
North African	−**0.65**	(0.10)
South Asian	−**1.02**	(0.35)
West European	0.0	
East European	0.0	
North American (and Oceanic)	−**0.95**	(0.22)
Latin American	0.0	
First Generation	0.07	(0.10)
Age	**0.01**	(0.00)
Education		
Primary	0.0	
Some Secondary	**0.63**	(0.08)
Full Secondary	**0.41**	(0.08)
Some Tertiary	**0.75**	(0.10)
Full Tertiary	**1.01**	(0.09)
Marital Status		
Single	0.0	
Married	**0.78**	(0.07)
Other	0.03	(0.13)
Year	−0.01	(0.01)
Interaction of East European with First Generation	−**0.99**	(0.12)
Interactions of Ethnicity with Education		
North African	**0.17**	(0.06)

---

[13] As well as West European, East European and Latin American Jews whom we found to be no different from one another and from third Generation Jews.

[14] The major group of immigrants from East Europe (about 84%) is from the former Soviet Union (CBS 2003), and they comprise an even higher proportion among recent (post-1989) immigrants from East European countries.

The effects of education reveal that, as expected, educated men are less likely than men with only primary education to be unemployed. Finally, the interaction between North African ancestry and education reveals that better educated North Africans are less likely than third-generation Jews with similar education to be unemployed. The positive interaction term for North African immigrants can be interpreted to mean that their employment is more sensitive to the level of education than that of third-generation Israeli-born.

The results for women are presented in Table 8.10B. Similarly to men, when married women enter the labour force, they have better odds of being employed, compared with non-married women (divorced, widowed and singles). Educated women are less likely than women with only primary education to be unemployed (except for women with some secondary education who do not differ in their odds of unemployment from the least educated). Age also makes a difference, with older women more likely to be employed. (As with men, the parameter estimate for age squared was not statistically significant.)

The ethnic categorisation distinguishes Palestinian women, Middle Eastern, North African and South Asian women versus all other women (North Americans and overwhelmingly European immigrants and their offspring as well as other third generation Israeli-born women).

Surprisingly, Palestinian women do not differ statistically in their odds of being unemployed from Ashkenazi women and third-generation Jews. This might be explained by the particular features of Palestinian female employment which is very selective. Women who enter the labour force tend to be employed in the Arab labour market where they face little competition (Semyonov *et al.* 1999). As with Mizrahi men, Mizrahi women (Middle Eastern, North Africa and South Asian) are more likely to be unemployed compared with the Ashkenazi women bloc. Also, there is a significant difference between Middle Eastern and North African women in their odds of avoiding unemployment. The latter are significantly more likely to be unemployed than the former. We propose the following explanation for this result. About half of the North Africans live in 'development towns' (Adler, Lewin-Epstein and Shavit 2003), which are socially peripheral communities in which economic opportunities are rather scarce. Middle Easterners, by contrast, are more evenly spread among the different community types, including the large cities with their superior employment opportunities. Women, especially mothers of young children, seek employment in the immediate vicinity of the home and are confined by opportunities in local labour markets

Table 8.10B. Logistic regression of employment and unemployment: Females (parameter estimates, contrasts with unemployment).

Intercept	**1.04**	(0.16)
Ancestry		
Third-generation Jewsh	0.0	
Palestinian	−0.21	(0.12)
Middle-Eastern	**−0.29**	(0.08)
North African	**−0.59**	(0.08)
South Asian	**−1.04**	(0.28)
West European	0.0	
East European	0.0	
North American (and Oceanic)	0.0	
Latin America	0.0	
First Generation	0.10	(0.09)
Age	**0.03**	(0.00)
Education		
Primary	0.0	
Some Secondary	0.06	(0.10)
Full Secondary	0.26	(0.10)
Some Tertiary	**0.71**	(0.11)
Full Tertiary	**0.99**	(0.13)
Marital Status		
Single	0.0	
Married	**0.28**	(0.07)
Other	−0.13	(0.09)
Year	**0.03**	(0.01)
Interaction of East European with First Generation	**−0.84**	(0.11)
Interactions of Ethnicity with Education		
East European	**−0.26**	(0.04)

(Semyonov and Lewin-Epstein 1991). We suggest that the greater odds of unemployment seen for North African women reflect the confining effect of residence in development towns.

Similarly to men, first-generation immigrant women do not differ from others in the likelihood of being unemployed. The exception is immigrant women from the former USSR who have a higher probability of being unemployed, and their (un)employment is less sensitive to education, as indicated in the interaction with education. The results possibly reflect the greater difficulty faced by immigrant women when entering the labour market: they enter into lower occupational classes and face a higher risk of unemployment.

Ethnicity, generation and class

We now model the association between ethnicity, immigrant generation and class. For this analysis we focus on the employed population. Class is measured as a five-category variable, the distribution of which can be seen in Tables 8.6A and 8.6B. The independent variables in the models are the same as used in the prior analysis. As before, we first estimate several competing models of the association and, based on their goodness-of-fit statistics, select the one that best balances fit and parsimony. Goodness-of-fit statistics for various models are presented, for men and women in Table 8.11.

Model 8 is our preferred model for both sexes. It includes the control variables, generation, and the interaction between generation and East European origin. The model also includes the main effects of ethnicity, except that of East Europe, West Europe and Latin America, for men, and the whole Ashkenazi block for women. The model interacts the con-

Table 8.11. Goodness-of-fit statistics for models of models of occupational class.

Model	Variables (categories included in model)	Parameters	-2LogL	BIC
Men (n=24,441)				
0	Intercept only	4	72,743.1	72,783.5
1	Marital Status (2), Education (4), Age (1), Year (1), Ethnicity (8)	68	63,390.0	64,077.1
2	1+Generation (1)	72	62,622.0	63,349.5
3	2+Interactions of Generation with (Mid-East, N. Africa, E. Europe, W. Europe) (4)	88	62,096.6	62,985.8
4	3−Interactions of Generation with (Mid-East, N. Africa, W. Europe)	76	62,121.6	62,889.6
5	4−E. Europe, W. Europe, L. America	64	62,145.3	62,791.9
6	5+Constraint: (Mid-East=N. Africa)	60	66,728.4	67,334.7
7	5+Interactions of Education with (Palestinians, Mid-East, N. Africa, N. America)	80	61,913.2	62,739.5
8	7+ Constraint: Interactions of Education on Classes III and IV	72	61,955.9	62,683.4
Women (n=19,138)				
0	Intercept only	4	52,117.4	52,156.8
1	Marital Status (2), Education (4), Age (1), Year (1), Ethnicity (8)	68	44,720.7	45,391.1
2	1+ Generation (1)	72	44,020.7	44,730.6
3	2+Interactions of Generation with (Mid-East, N. Africa, E. Europe, W. Europe) (4)	88	43,726.8	44,594.4
4	3−Interactions of Generation with (Mid-East, N. Africa, W. Europe)	76	43,759.2	44,508.6
5	4−E. Europe, W. Europe, N. America, L. America	60	43,788.6	44,380.2
6	5+Constraint: (Mid-East=N. Africa)	56	46,304.5	46,856.6
7	5+Interactions of Education with (Palestinians)	64	43,737.6	44,368.7
8	7+Constraint: Interactions of Education on Class III	63	43,737.8	44,359.0

tinuous measure of education with Palestinians for women (constraining for the petty bourgeoisie), and also with Middle East, North Africans and North Americans, for men (constraining for the petty bourgeoisie and for unskilled workers).

The parameter estimates for the preferred models (model 8) for both sexes are shown in Tables 8.12A and 8.12B, for men and women respectively.[15] Turning first to Table 8.12A and inspecting the effects of ethnicity, we see the significant disadvantages of Mizrahim, South Asians and especially of Palestinians in the odds of gaining access to the salariat and petty bourgeoisie. Interestingly, net of education and the other control variables, these minorities enjoy a relative advantage in the odds of employment as skilled (the reference category) rather than unskilled workers. Jews of North American origin are more likely than all other groups to enter the salariat class and the petty bourgeoisie.

First-generation immigrants are at a handicap with regard to entry into higher-level classes. The handicap is much larger for recent immigrants from Eastern Europe who are less likely than other groups to enter the salariat, but also less likely, *ceteris paribus,* to enter the lower class (semi- and unskilled). Finally, the interactions between ethnicity and education indicate that for Palestinians to gain entry to the top two classes they are required to exhibit higher educational credentials than are third-generation Jews (the reference category). A similar but more modest pattern is seen for Mizrahim. Interestingly, North Americans enjoy an educational 'discount' and can access the salariat and routine non-manual classes with lower educational levels than other groups.

This educational 'discount' enjoyed by North Americans can be seen in more straightforward way in the plotted fitted probabilities for access to the salariat and to the routine non-manual classes[16] (Figures 8.1 and 8.2, respectively). The probabilities were computed for married male respondents of the (mean) age of 38.4 years, by different levels of education. In general, higher educational credentials are required for access to the upper classes. One exception is the odds of entry into the routine non-manual class where those with some tertiary education are at a disadvantage relative to those with general secondary education. As to ethnicity, North Americans are the advantaged group and they enjoy

---

[15] As before we have carried out supplementary analyses including a term for age squared. This proved to be statistically significant but did not affect the parameter estimates associated with the ethnicity variables in any material way.

[16] Compared with accessing the skilled class.

Table 8.12A. Logistic regression of occupational class: Males (parameter estimates, contrasts with skilled manual class).

	Salariat		Routine non-manual		Petty bourgeoisie		Semi- and unskilled manual	
Intercept	−3.18	(0.18)	−1.71	(0.21)	−2.46	(0.13)	**0.40**	(0.11)
Ancestry								
Third-generation Jewish	0.0		0.0		0.0		0.0	
Palestinian	−1.37	(0.09)	−0.90	(0.10)	−0.33	(0.07)	−0.40	(0.07)
Middle-Eastern	−0.66	(0.07)	−0.30	(0.08)	−0.20	(0.06)	−0.11	(0.06)
North African	−0.68	(0.07)	−0.50	(0.09)	−0.15	(0.07)	−0.22	(0.07)
South Asian	−2.34	(0.41)	−0.73	(0.36)	−1.52	(0.39)	−0.25	(0.24)
West European	0.0				0.0		0.0	
East European	0.0				0.0		0.0	
North American and Oceanic	**1.36**	(0.28)	0.60	(0.40)	**0.80**	(0.28)	0.34	(0.28)
Latin American First Generation	−0.20	(0.07)	−0.16	(0.09)	−0.26	(0.07)	0.15	(0.07)
Age	**0.03**	(0.00)	**0.01**	(0.00)	**0.04**	(0.00)	0.00	(0.00)
Education								
Primary	0.0		0.0		0.0		0.0	
Some Secondary	**0.91**	(0.14)	**0.65**	(0.15)	**0.19**	(0.07)	−0.57	(0.06)
Full Secondary	**1.73**	(0.14)	**1.29**	(0.16)	**0.43**	(0.07)	−0.15	(0.06)
Some Tertiary	**1.79**	(0.15)	**0.62**	(0.18)	−0.11	(0.09)	−0.97	(0.08)
Full Tertiary	**3.87**	(0.15)	**1.73**	(0.18)	**0.60**	(0.09)	−0.30	(0.07)
Marital Status								
Single	0.0		0.0		0.0		0.0	
Married	**0.50**	(0.07)	−0.07	(0.08)	**0.52**	(0.08)	−0.52	(0.05)
Other	**0.49**	(0.13)	−0.27	(0.20)	**0.62**	(0.14)	−0.09	(0.12)
Year	−0.03	(0.01)	−0.11	(0.01)	−0.04	(0.01)	−0.03	(0.01)
Interaction of East European with First Generation	−1.80	(0.09)	−1.66	(0.13)	−1.60	(0.10)	−0.43	(0.09)
Interactions of Ethnicity with Education								
Palestinian	**0.75**	(0.07)	**0.58**	(0.08)	—		—	
Middle-Eastern	**0.16**	(0.04)	**0.25**	(0.06)	—		—	
North African	**0.17**	(0.05)	**0.22**	(0.07)	—		—	
North American and Oceanic	−0.25	(0.13)	0.32	(0.21)	—		—	

higher probabilities of entry to both the salariat and the routine non-manual classes at every educational level. The figures also show the similarity between the Mizrahi groups (North Africans and Middle Easterners) and the disadvantage of the Palestinians. Nevertheless, it is worth noticing the relative advantage of the most educated Palestinians over the Mizrahi groups in entering both classes.

The results for women largely mirror those seen for men. Similar are the disadvantages of the Palestinians, Mizrahim and first-generation

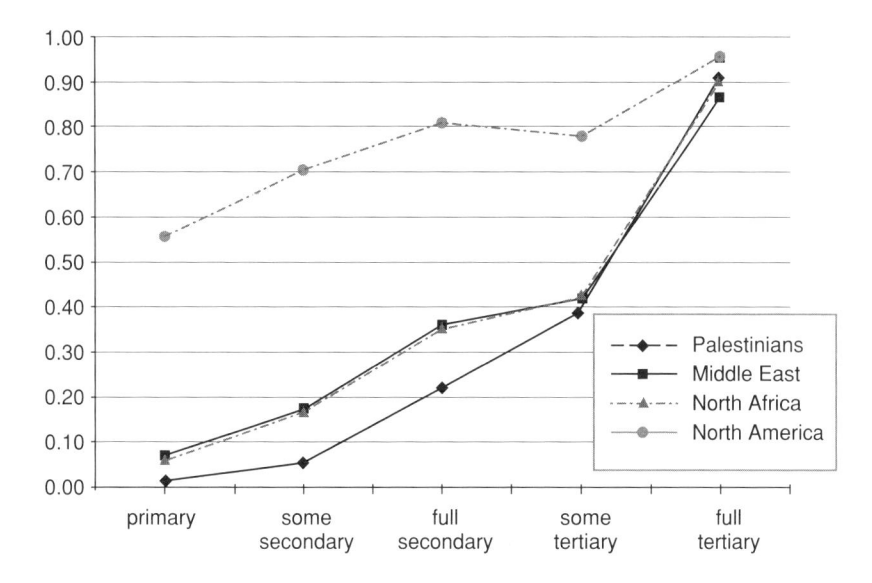

IMMIGRANT ABSORPTION: ARAB EXCLUSION IN ISRAEL 351

Figure 8.1. Probabilities of accessing the salariat, by ancestry: Men.

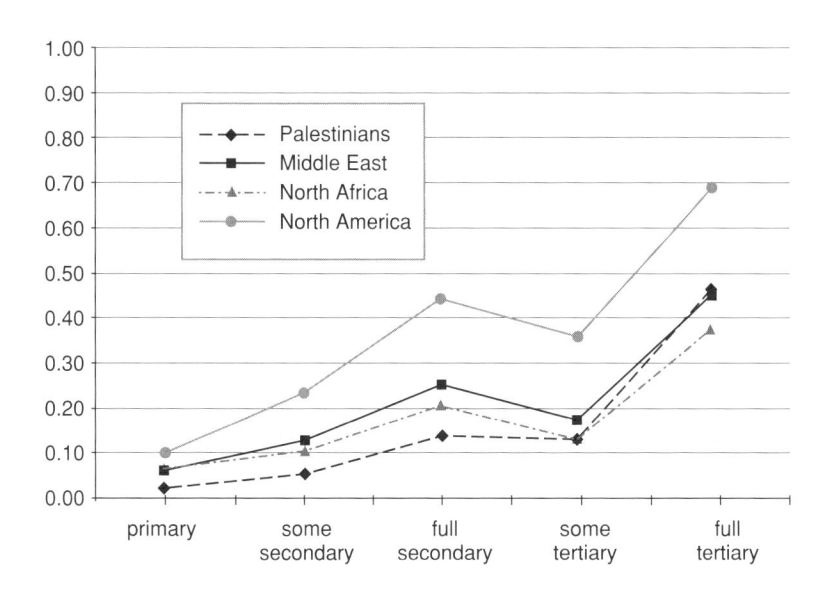

Figure 8.2. Probabilities of accessing the routine non-manual class, by ancestry: Men.

immigrants, especially among East Europeans. As in the case for men, the interactions between education and Palestinian ancestry are positive.

Summary and discussion

In line with the general question raised in this volume, regarding the 'ethnic penalties' experienced by immigrant groups in western advanced economies, this chapter set out to accomplish several objectives. First, it provided a detailed description of the ethnic composition of Israeli society in the last decade of the twentieth century and the educational and occupational position of the various groups. Second, it aimed to evaluate

Table 8.12B. Logistic regression of occupational class: Females (parameter estimates, contrasts with skilled manual class).

	Salariat		Routine non-manual		Petty bourgeoisie		Semi- and unskilled manual	
Intercept	−2.35	(0.26)	−1.85	(0.27)	−4.03	(0.31)	1.43	(0.18)
Ancestry								
Third-generation Jewish	0.0		0.0		0.0		0.0	
Palestinian	−0.49	(0.17)	−1.40	(0.19)	0.02	(0.19)	−0.96	(0.14)
Middle-Eastern	−0.32	(0.10)	−0.05	(0.11)	−0.53	(0.14)	0.05	(0.10)
North African	−0.30	(0.11)	−0.06	(0.11)	−0.13	(0.14)	0.21	(0.10)
South Asian	−1.77	(0.41)	−2.22	(0.51)	−2.44	(0.75)	−1.07	(0.26)
West European	0.0				0.0		0.0	
East European	0.0				0.0		0.0	
North American and Oceanic	0.0				0.0		0.0	
Latin American	0.0				0.0		0.0	
First Generation	−0.66	(0.11)	−0.39	(0.11)	−0.36	(0.14)	−0.30	(0.10)
Age	0.03	(0.01)	0.01	(0.00)	0.05	(0.01)	0.01	(0.00)
Education								
Primary	0.0		0.0		0.0		0.0	
Some Secondary	1.22	(0.22)	1.97	(0.21)	0.46	(0.21)	−0.10	(0.11)
Full Secondary	2.02	(0.21)	2.45	(0.21)	0.91	(0.18)	0.23	(0.11)
Some Tertiary	3.85	(0.21)	2.79	(0.22)	1.16	(0.17)	−0.28	(0.12)
Full Tertiary	4.60	(0.21)	2.74	(0.22)	1.28	(0.18)	−0.22	(0.11)
Marital Status								
Single	0.0		0.0		0.0		0.0	
Married	0.73	(0.09)	0.26	(0.09)	1.08	(0.17)	−0.05	(0.08)
Other	0.79	(0.12)	0.30	(0.14)	1.41	(0.21)	0.36	(0.12)
Year	−0.05	(0.01)	0.03	(0.01)	0.04	(0.02)	0.03	(0.01)
Interaction of East European with First Generation	−2.05	(0.12)	−1.25	(0.13)	−2.15	(0.17)	−0.86	(0.11)
Interactions of Ethnicity with Education								
Palestinian	0.56	(0.12)	0.97	(0.16)	—		0.34	(0.08)

the extent of convergence among ethnic groups as exemplified by differences in labour-market participation and occupational attainment between first and second generations of immigrants. More specifically in this regard, the analyses in this chapter examined the extent to which advantages or disadvantages associated with ethnicity are explained by recency of arrival in Israel (first- or second-generation) and the demographic and human capital characteristics of the groups.

Finally, and more specifically to the Israeli case, the chapter intended to evaluate the extent to which detailed vs. broad groupings of immigrant groups in the analyses lead to different conclusions regarding ethnic differences. The latter issue derives its importance from the fact that ethnicity is an emergent phenomenon and ethnic boundaries are constructed and reconstructed in social contexts. Certain ethnic groups have more in common than others and their boundaries may be quite blurred and fluid. Other groups may stand apart and preserve their particular attributes. Additionally, in many cases non-members may treat certain groups as indistinguishable, in effect 'lumping' them in one category. This is consequential to the experiences of different ethnic groups and to their position in society.

In the case of Israel, all Jewish groups share an ancestry and important components of their cultural traditions and identity. Yet, the diverse histories experienced by Jews in disparate locations where they resided for centuries resulted in unique cultural components and diversity of social organisation. The establishment of the state of Israel and the extraordinary ingathering of the diaspora that ensued had a dual effect on Jewish immigrant groups. At one level, inclusionary rhetoric and practices were used emphasising the Jewish heritage and the unity of the people while excluding the Palestinian citizens of Israel. At another level, distinctions were made and maintained, especially between Jews of European origin (who were dominant numerically and socio-economically at the time Israel gained independence) and all others. This distinction coincided in large part with the Ashkenazi and Sephardic religious traditions which developed historically in different parts of the world. This two-category classification of the Jewish population, combined with the category of Palestinians, was the basis of the tripartite ethnic division of Israeli society. Yet, this broad classification masks potentially meaningful differences within categories which were examined more closely in this chapter.

The first important point to stem from the findings regarding the ethnic composition of Israeli society is that unlike most/all other societies taking part in this project, there is no obvious group to serve as a 'bench-mark' to which immigrant ethnic groups might be compared. In view of the extremely high proportion of first- and second-generation Jews in Israel and the fact that the indigenous group consists of Palestinians who are politically and economically subordinate to the Jewish population, we emphasised inter-group comparisons rather than using a particular comparison to evaluate the 'ethnic penalty'.

In the multivariate analyses our strategy was to test the extent to which labour-force patterns, unemployment and class position of all ethnic groups differ from that of third-generation Jews. Our findings in this respect reveal complex patterns of ethnic advantages and disadvantages. With regard to labour-force participation of men we found that most groups do not differ greatly in the odds of being out of rather than in the labour force. There is one exception to this generalisation: North Americans' odds of labour-force participation are low, probably reflecting wilful abstention that is made possible by the de-commodification of ultra-orthodox labour. Israel's welfare state supports yeshiva students and enables them to subsist, albeit in poverty, through study rather than employment. The state is much less generous vis-à-vis other students.

We also found that the Israeli labour market absorbs male immigrants rather quickly as is indicated by the null effect of generation on the odds of labour-force participation. The exceptions are the very recent immigrants from the former USSR who still suffer from higher than national rates of unemployment. By 2001 their unemployment rate was still 10.3%, as compared to the national rates of 8.8% (CBS 2003).

The results were different for women. Conditional on not being in school, the main Jewish ethnic groups do not differ in their odds of labour-force participation. In addition, Palestinian women show very low rates of both schooling and labour-force participation, both of which reflect constraints that are often imposed by families on Muslim women. Finally, the labour-force participation rates of first-generation immigrant women are somewhat lower than those of second-generation immigrants and veterans and do not seem to vary by ethnic group. Evidently, the incorporation of immigrant women into the labour force is more difficult than that of men.

Regarding unemployment, our findings reveal that all male immigrant groups, as well as Palestinians, have higher probabilities than third-generation Jews[17] of being unemployed. These results possibly reflect the

---

[17] As well as West European, East European and Latin American Jews whom we found to be no different from one another and from third-Generation Jews.

advantage enjoyed by the founding generation and their offspring in terms of both residence in proximity to large labour markets and greater access to the more secure public sector jobs. This difficulty is reflected in the high odds of first-generation immigrants from the former USSR of being unemployed, while there is no generational difference in the likelihood of being unemployed for all other ethnic groups. Our findings also reveal that North African immigrants' employment is more sensitive to level of education than that of the third-generation Israeli-born.

The results for women show that ethnic categorisation distinguishes Palestinian women, Middle Eastern, North African and South Asian women versus all other women. Surprisingly, Palestinian women do not differ statistically in their odds of being unemployed from Ashkenazi women and the third generation. We explain this finding by the particular employment features of the Palestinian women. Palestinian female employment is very selective and women who enter the labour force tend to be employed in the Arab labour market where they face little ethnic competition and discrimination (Semyonov *et al.* 1999).

We also found that there is a significant difference between Middle Eastern and North African women in the odds of unemployment. The latter are significantly more likely to be unemployed than the former. We propose the following explanation for this result. About half of the North Africans live in development towns (Adler, Lewin-Epstein and Shavit 2003). These are socially peripheral communities in which economic opportunities are rather scarce. Middle Easterners, by contrast, are more evenly spread among the different community types, including the large cities with their superior employment opportunities. Women, especially mothers of young children, seek employment in the immediate vicinity of the home and are constrained by the opportunities in local labour markets (Semyonov and Lewin-Epstein 1991). We hypothesise that the greater odds of unemployment seen for North African women reflect the confining effect of residence in development towns.

Finally, we found that, similarly to men, first-generation immigrant women do not differ from others in the likelihood of being unemployed. The exception is immigrant women from the former USSR who have a higher probability of being unemployed, and their (un)employment is more sensitive to education, as indicated in the interaction with education. The results possibly reflect the greater difficulty faced by immigrant women in entering the labour market.

Turning now to the analysis of class allocation, rather similar patterns of relations between ethnicity and class emerged for both men and women. Specifically, models that did not group Jews of Middle Eastern and North African origins into one category of Mizrahim but did group most Jewish immigrants of European descent (except for immigrants from North America) fit the data as well or better than models that identified each of the groups separately. All analyses indicated that the Palestinians must be identified separately in order to achieve a good fit to the data.

The multivariate analyses revealed that even after controlling for education and demographic attributes, Jews of Middle Eastern and North African origins had lower odds of attaining higher class positions than second-generation Israelis and Jewish immigrants of European descent. The odds of Palestinian men attaining such class positions were even lower. While these findings in themselves do not demonstrate discrimination on the basis of ethnicity, they clearly underscore the pattern of advantages and disadvantages that various ethnic groups face.

Similar patterns were found for the class position of women. The above patterns of differential ethnic advantage are further amplified by the greater sensitivity of the odds of obtaining higher class occupations to education, among Palestinians and to a lesser extent among Mizrahi Jews, compared with Jews of European origin. Put differently, Palestinians (and to some extent Mizrahim) must have higher education on average than their 'co-workers' of Jewish European origin to attain the same class positions.

Finally, we found, for both men and women, that first-generation immigrants are heavily concentrated in the lower classes. When combined with the findings concerning generational differences in labour-force participation this result suggests that the Israeli labour market incorporates immigrants rather quickly, albeit at the bottom of the class structure. This pattern of results is reminiscent of a recent comparison of immigrant incorporation in the Israeli and Canadian labour markets in which it was found that in the former, new immigrants are quicker to find employment but in the latter they are quicker to attain an occupational status commensurate with their qualifications (Lewin-Epstein *et al.* 2003).

References

Adler, I., Lewin-Epstein, N., and Shavit, Y. (2003), 'Ethnic stratification and place of residence in Israel: a truism revisited', *Research in Social Stratification and Mobility (RSSM)*, 23: 157–92.

Al-Haj, M. (1996), *Arab Education in Israel: Control and Social Change* (Jerusalem: Magnes Press). (In Hebrew.)

Al-Haj, M. (2002), 'Multiculturalism in Deeply Divided Societies: The Israeli Case', *International Journal of Intercultural Relations*, 26, 169–83.

Al-Haj, M. and Rosenfeld, H. (1990), *Arab Local Government in Israel* (Boulder, CO: Westview).

Amit, K. (2000), *Mizrahim versus Ashkenazim: The dichotomous ethnic classification and the success of the first generation*. Ph.D. Dissertation, Tel Aviv University. (In Hebrew.)

Central Bureau of Statistics (CBS) (2003), *Statistical Abstract of Israel 2002, Table 12.23*. Available online at: <http://www.cbs.gov.il/shnaton54/st12_23.pdf>

Central Bureau of Statistics (CBS) (2003), *Statistical Abstract of Israel 2003, Table 4.4*. Available online at: <http://www1.cbs.gov.il/shnaton54/st04_04.pdf>

Cohen, Y. and Haberfeld, Y. (1998), 'Second-generation Jewish immigrants in Israel: Have the ethnic gaps in schooling and earnings declined?' *Ethnic and Racial Studies*, 21, 507–28.

Dominitz, Y. (1997), 'Israel's Immigration Policy and the Dropout Phenomenon'. In N. Lewin-Epstein, Y. Ro'I, and P. Ritterband (eds.), *Russian Jews on Three Continents: Migration and Resettlement* (London: Frank Cass), pp. 113–28.

Elmelech, Y. and Lewin-Epstein, N. (1998), 'Immigration and housing in Israel: Another look and ethnic inequality', *Megamot*, 39, 243–69. (In Hebrew.)

Geva-May, I. (1998), 'Immigration to Israel: Any Lessons for Canada?' *Research on Immigration and Integration in the Metropolis*. Working Paper Series, Number 3.

Horowitz, T. (1996), 'Value-Oriented Parameters in Migration Policies in the 1990s: The Israeli Experience', *International Migration*, 34, 513–37.

Horowitz, T. (1999), 'Integration or Separatism?' In T. Horowitz (ed.), *Children of Perestroika in Israel* (Washington, DC: University Press of America), pp. 1–21.

Kemp, A., Raijman, R., Resnik, J., and Schammah-Gesser, S. (2000), 'Contesting the Limits of Political Participation: Latinos and Black African Migrant Workers in Israel', *Ethnic and Racial Studies*, 23, 94–119.

Khalidi, R. (1988), *The Arab Economy in Israel: The Dynamics of a Region's Development* (London: Croom Helm).

Khazzoom, A. (1998), 'The origins of ethnic inequality among Jews in Israel'. Ph.D. Thesis, University of California at Berkeley.

Kraus, V. and Hodge, R.W. (1990), *Promises in the Promised Land: Mobility and Inequality in Israel* (New York: Greenwood).

Lewin-Epstein, N. and Semyonov, M. (1993), *The Arab Minority in Israel's Economy: Patterns of Ethnic Inequality* (Boulder, CO: Westview Press).

Lewin-Epstein, N. and Semyonov, M. (2000), 'Migration, ethnicity, and inequality: Homeownership in Israel', *Social Problems*, 47, 425–44.

Lewin-Epstein, N., Semyonov, M., Kogan, I., and Wanner, R. (2003), 'Institutional structure and immigrant integration: A comparative study of immigrants' labor market attainment in Canada and Israel', *International Migration Review*, 37, 389–420.

Lustick, I. (1980), *Arabs in the Jewish State* (Austin, TX: University of Texas Press).

Nahon, Y. (1987), *Patterns of Expansion of Education and Employment Opportunities: The Ethnic Dimension* (Jerusalem: Jerusalem Institute for Israeli Studies). (In Hebrew.)

Raftery, A. E. (1986), 'Choosing models for cross-classifications', *American Sociological Review*, 51, 145–6.

Rozenhek, Z. (2000), 'Migration Regimes, Intra-state Conflicts, and the Politics of Exclusion and Inclusion: Migrant Workers in the Israeli Welfare State', *Social Problems*, 47, 49–67.

Rouhana, N. and Ghanem, A. (1998), 'The crisis of minorities in ethnic states: The case of Palestinian citizens in Israel', *International Journal of Middle East Studies*, 30, 321–46.

Sa'di, A. (1995), 'Incorporation without integration: Palestinian citizens in Israel's labor market', *Sociology*, 29, 429–51.

Segev, T. (1991), *1949: The First Israelis* (Jerusalem: Domino Press).

Semyonov, M. and Lerenthal, T. (1991), 'Country of origin, gender, and the attainment of socioeconomic status: A study of stratification in the Jewish population of Israel', *Research in Stratification and Social Mobility*, 10, 327–45.

Semyonov, M. and Lewin-Epstein, N. (1991), 'Suburban labor markets, urban labor markets, and gender inequality in earnings', *The Sociological Quarterly*, 32, 611–20.

Semyonov, M. and Lewin-Epstein, N. (2002), 'Immigration and ethnicity in Israel: Returning Diaspora and nation-building'. In R. Munz and R. Ohliger (eds.), *Diaspora and Ethnic Migrants: Germany, Israel, and Post-Soviet Successor States in Comparative Perspective* (London: Frank Cass), pp. 327–37.

Semyonov, M., Lewin-Epstein, N., and Braham, I. (1999), 'Changing labour force participation and occupational status: Arab women in the Israeli labour force', *Work Employment and Society*, 13, 117–31.

Shavit, Y., Cohen, Y., Stier, H., and Bolotin, S. (1999), 'Ethnic Inequality in University Education in Israel', *Jewish Journal of Sociology*, 41, 5–23.

Shohat, E. (1988), 'Sephardim in Israel: Zionism from the standpoint of its Jewish victims', *Social Text*, 19/20, 1–35.

Shuval, J. T. and Leshem, E. (1998), 'The sociology of migration to Israel: A critical view'. In E. Leshem and J. T. Shuval (eds.), *Immigration to Israel: Sociological Perspectives* (New Brunswick, NJ: Transaction), pp. 3–50.

Smooha, S. (1990), 'Minority Status in an Ethnic Democracy: The Status of the Arab Minority in Israel', *Ethnic and Racial Studies*, 13, 389–413.

Yiftachel, O. (1997), 'Israel: Metropolitan integration or "fractured regions"? An alternative perspective', *Cities*, 14, 371–80.

9

Equal Opportunities or Social Closure in the Netherlands?

PAUL TESSER & JAAP DRONKERS

Summary. There are four major ethnic minority groups in the Netherlands—labour migrants from Turkey and Morocco together with migrants from former Dutch colonies in the Caribbean, namely Antilles and Surinam. Men from all four groups have lower labour-market participation and higher unemployment than the indigenous Dutch, and this holds for the second generation as well as for the first. For women the patterns of participation and unemployment are more complex. While first generation Turkish and Moroccan women participate at considerably lower levels than indigenous women, Surinamese and Antillean women participate at higher levels than their indigenous peers. Among second-generation women, however, these differences in participation have largely disappeared. The distribution of ethnic minorities across occupational classes also reveals a major change between generations. The first-generation experience substantial disadvantages but the second generation, after controlling for level of education, age and economic fluctuations, have similar chances of being in a particular occupational class as the indigenous Dutch population, with the exception of the salariat which remains more closed to ethnic minorities. This result holds for men as well as for women. Overall, processes of social closure appear to continue to operate within Dutch society. Equal opportunities have not yet been achieved.

Introduction

NOTWITHSTANDING A LONG HISTORY OF IMMIGRATION, the Netherlands were considered to be an almost mono-ethnic society far into the twentieth century. Since 1960, however, the picture has changed dramatically. After the post-war economic reconstruction, severe shortages of labour triggered succeeding immigration waves consisting of labour migrants, their families and inhabitants of the former Dutch colonies. Now the Netherlands have a substantial ethnic minority population.

The immigrants themselves, coming from largely agricultural societies, have to deal with a Dutch society that has been changing from an industrial to a post-industrial society. Our chapter analyses the accommodation of the immigrants and their children to this society in change. Our main question is whether the immigrants participate in the same stratification processes that hold for the indigenous Dutch population. More specifically, can (and will) they find the meritocratic path to social attainment by means of education that has become characteristic for the Dutch population in the twentieth century? Or alternatively, has increased immigration resulted in a splitting of the social structure and the elicitation of social closure, increasing the likelihood of the formation of an ethnic underclass?

To explore these questions we study labour-market position, occupational attainment and income for the main groups of immigrant ethnic minorities in the Netherlands. By relating labour-market success to educational attainment we analyse their acquisition of positions within the social strata. Comparing relations between educational qualifications, occupational attainment and income of ethnic minority groups with those of the indigenous population we try to address our main question. First, however, before analysing educational and occupational attainment we give some background information about immigration and ethnic minorities in the Netherlands and about some relevant social and economic developments in the Netherlands during recent decades.

Post-war immigration in the Netherlands

As seen in Figure 9.1, recent Dutch history has seen succeeding waves of immigration. As this figure begins in the 1960s, we skip the return in the early 1950s of around 300,000 Dutch nationals following the independence of the former Dutch colony of the East Indies (now Indonesia). Surprisingly these returning colonials were absorbed into the population in a short time. Although most of them had been living in the East Indies for several generations, their reintegration in a Dutch society that was recovering from the damaging effects of the Second World War was rather unproblematic.

The first wave of the more recent immigration started at the end of the 1950s. The post-war reconstruction of Dutch industry was finished and the domestic labour supply was insufficient for further expansion. The industries attracted semi-skilled and skilled workers from Spain, Italy, and Greece. Most of them settled only temporarily. Those who stayed, however, mixed with the Dutch population; about half of the men married Dutch wives. Their children have almost completely integrated in Dutch society. As a group they are by now, in fact, invisible.

The second wave of immigration soon followed in the early and mid 1960s. It consisted of unskilled, low-educated Turkish workers who were employed in semi- or unskilled jobs in the industrial sector. Most of them were recruited from the Turkish countryside. After the Turks, the Moroccans came. Their level of education was even more rudimentary. In addition to deliberate recruitment, many Turks and Moroccans also came on their own. The first of these newcomers returned after some years to their home countries. Those who came later did not return but gave rise to extensive family migration of close and far family members.

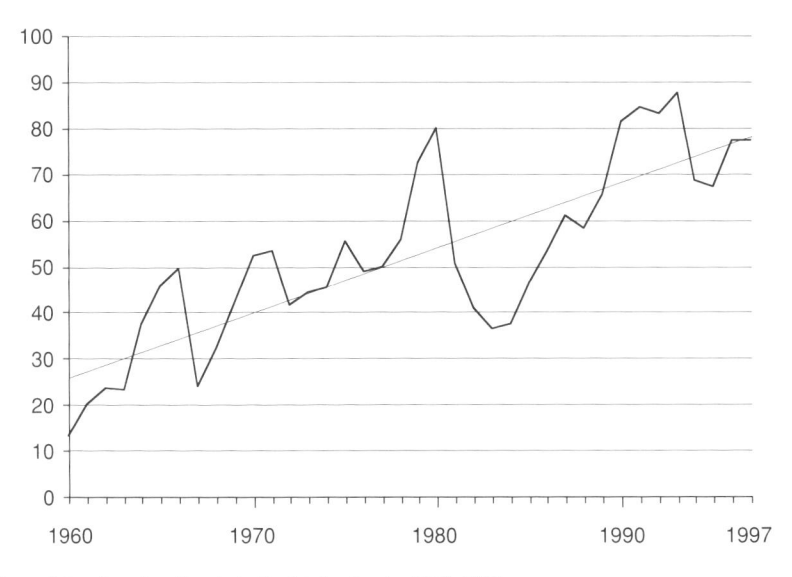

Figure 9.1. Immigration into the Netherlands, 1960–1997.
Source: Statistics Netherlands <http://www.cbs.nl/>.

It should be noted that the economic circumstances that gave rise to this second wave of immigration were different from those of the first wave. In the second-half of the 1960s Dutch industry had already passed its post-war peak levels of expansion. Nevertheless it had to cope with a shortage of labour at the unskilled level. The shortage was mainly a consequence of the rapid expansion of the service sector in the Dutch economy. Jobs in the service sector were more attractive to the young and better-educated Dutch entrants to the labour market than the 'dirtier' work of the industrial sector. The expansion of education and subsequent rising levels of education amongst Dutch youth reinforced this process; thus low-level jobs were left to the immigrants.

The next wave of immigration came from the former West Indian colonies: Suriname and the Antillean Islands, both situated in the Caribbean. In 1975, Suriname obtained independence, but the Antillean Islands are still an autonomous part of the Kingdom of the Netherlands. Suriname was, and still is, a very unstable society. So, in the years surrounding independence a large part of the Surinamese population decided to leave the country and to settle in the Netherlands. From 1974 to 1980 more than a 100,000 Surinamese moved from the Caribbean coasts to the coasts of the North Sea.

After the so-called 'oil crisis' of 1973 the Dutch economy deteriorated. Signs of social tension between the Dutch native population and the immigrants began to appear, accompanied by a decay of the inner-city neighbourhoods where many immigrants lived in very poor housing conditions. In response, the Dutch government tried to stop immigration and no longer allowed cheap labour migration from Turkey and Morocco. In 1980 the immigration of Surinamese people was also restricted. There are now also restrictions on cheap labour migration from the new East European members of the European Union. However, immigration figures began to rise again in the second-half of the 1980s as the economy recovered from the crisis.

More generally, in the long run the amount of immigration is mostly determined by four factors: (1) an autonomous growth trend reflecting the growth of communication and international trade; (2) the demand for labour in the immigrant country; (3) the high demand for marriage partners from migrant countries; and (4) incidental events (e.g., calamities, changed entrance regulations).

In 1973 the Dutch government introduced a ban on low-level labour migration from outside the EU, but settled immigrants still had a rather extended right of family reunification and this kept immigration levels relatively high. But what restrictive measures could not achieve, the economy and family could. The economic crisis of 1980 reduced the labour immigration surplus almost to zero, but the immigration caused by marriages of settled migrants with partners from their homeland continued to grow. Marrying partners from the homeland not only by first-generation migrants, but also by the second generation, became one of the major causes of continuing immigration, regardless of fluctuations in the demand for cheap labour by the Dutch economy. Since the mid-1990s, however, these extended rights of family reunification have become more restricted, and currently, there are proposals from governmental parties to restrict these rights further.

At the end of the 1980s the picture of immigration changed into a new and different wave of migration. Political instability, large differences in economic development and the almost complete closure of the borders for (legal) cheap labour migration from lesser developed countries caused a sharp increase in the influx of refugees and asylum seekers. In the 1990s, the average number of refugees and asylum seekers was about 40,000 people each year. New laws aimed at hindering this inflow of asylum seekers appear to have been rather successful, although it is debatable whether it was these new laws or the changing circumstances in the world that caused inflow to decline. Regardless, the Netherlands still have to solve the problem of those asylum seekers whose request to remain is denied but who do not (want to) leave the Netherlands.

Although reliable numbers are hard to come by, a non-trivial number of illegal migrants live and work in the Netherlands. Cheap and vulnerable illegal workers are important for some industrial and agrarian sectors of the Dutch economy, and also for domestic work in the more affluent Dutch households. The majority of these illegal migrants have entered the Netherlands legally—e.g., as tourists—and some try, with some success, to convert their illegal status into a legal one, for example through marriage, a general pardon or fraud.

As seen in Figure 9.2, these different waves of immigration have increased the number of ethnic minorities in Dutch society considerably. In 1970 the ethnic minority population counted slightly more than 200,000 people; it has since grown to surpass 1.5 million, or about 10% of the total population of 15 million, with further growth still forecast.

Most Surinamese and Antillean immigrants are Dutch citizens, due to the colonial past of the former and continuing colonial status of the latter. It is possible for citizens of non-EU countries to be naturalised as Dutch citizens after three to five years of legal residence, provided they

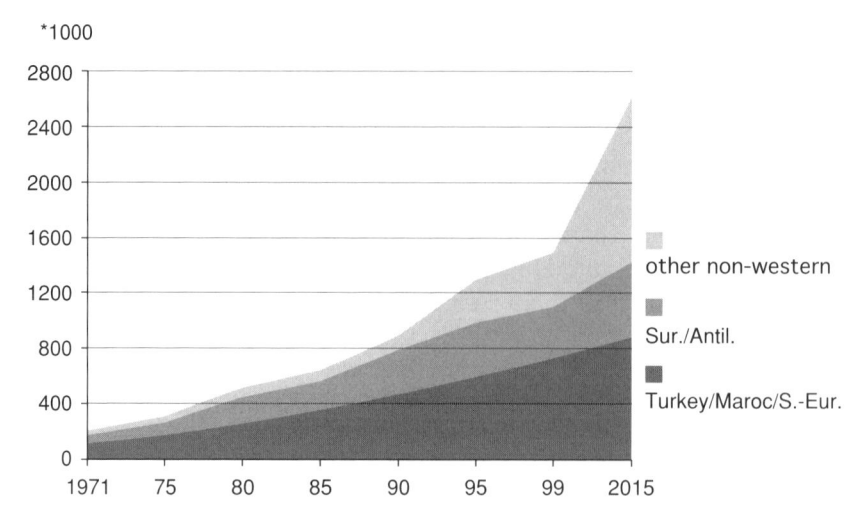

Figure 9.2. Population growth of the main categories of ethnic minorities, 1971–2015. Source: Statistics Netherlands <http://www.cbs.nl/>.

are sufficiently integrated into Dutch society, have some command of the Dutch language and sufficient economic resources. The law allows the retention of another citizenship, in addition to the Dutch, which explains the relatively large numbers of naturalized Turks and Moroccans. Recently, however, this has been changed, and now the combination of a Dutch citizenship with another is only allowed for asylum seekers, partners of Dutch citizens and for those foreign citizens who cannot relinquish their other citizenship (for instance, Moroccans).

Anti-discrimination legislation exists in the Netherlands, with both racial and sexual discrimination addressed even in the first article of the constitution, but the balance of this legislation with other rights—such as the freedom of religion and freedom of school choice—has still to be found and is sometimes contested. In general, though, ethnic minorities have more or less the same rights as the various indigenous religious groups receiving state grants for their organisations and schools (for example, Islamic schools).

Integration of immigrants into the labour market

This chapter could certainly discuss immigration and the demography of ethnic minorities in much more detail, but our interest is largely concerned with the integration of the immigrants into the Dutch social structure. Just as in most other western countries, in the second-half of the twentieth century the Dutch economy transformed from an industrial to a post-industrial economy. In 1965 the labour volume of the industrial sector reached its top level of nearly 1.9 million labour-years (De Beer 2001). Since then it has declined, to less than 1.4 million in 1990. While in 1965 the service sector was nearly as large as the industrial sector, from that year on the service sector has progressively outgrown the industrial sector. In 1990 the labour-volume of the service sector was about three times greater than the labour-volume of the industrial sector.

As previously mentioned, the growth of the service sector drained the supply of labour for low-level industrial jobs, triggering the second post-war immigration wave of Turkish and Moroccan workers. The low educational level of these groups was not much of problem up until about 1980. The economic crisis of 1980 was a turning point. The crisis meant the end of labour-intensive forms of industrial production, which had been prevalent in the foregoing decades. From then on only technology-driven forms of industrial production appeared to have a future in the service-dominated economy.

After the economic crisis of 1980 and the reconstruction of the economy in the years that followed, the labour-market position of immigrants drastically changed. The demanded level of qualification in the modernised industry was much higher than before the crisis, and also much higher than the qualifications that the Turkish and Moroccan workers could offer. They also lacked the qualifications demanded in the rapidly expanding service sector. Only a small part of the jobs in this sector—for example, in the cleaning services—remained open to them. As a consequence of this mismatch of supply and demand a considerable part of the minority workers lost their jobs and newcomers had little opportunity on the labour market.

In 1983, unemployment levels among Turkish and Moroccan men rose to one in three. Even this number, however, may have overestimated their true position on the labour market, as about half of those migrants over 40 were dependent on the National Insurance for disabled workers. However, these people are not counted in the unemployment figures.

Thanks to the reconstruction of the economy after 1983, unemployment in the native population declined quickly. As Figure 9.3 shows, in 1991 this rate was half the rate in 1983. During this same period, however, minority groups showed no improvement at all; this same pattern holds for the rest of the early 1990s.

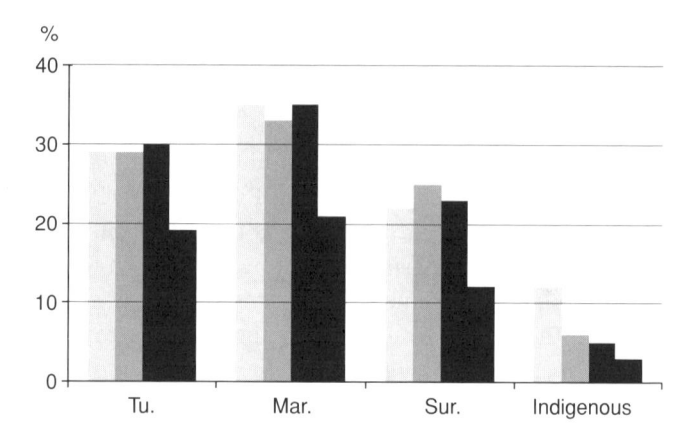

Figure 9.3. Unemployment, by ethnic group and year.
Source: Various labour surveys <http://www.cbs.nl/>.

Only in recent years have ethnic minorities benefited from the ongoing expansion of the labour market. Since 1994, unemployment among minorities has decreased considerably, by up to 15%. Notwithstanding this recent improvement, even in 1998 the risk of unemployment for members of ethnic minorities was between two and seven times larger than for the Dutch native labour force. In addition, recently there has been an increase in the public upheaval around 'family reunion' migration, asylum seekers, the religious values of some ethnic minorities, and Islamic schools within Dutch society. This upheaval has resulted in the rise of right-wing populist parties (with leaders like Pim Fortuyn) as coalition members in local and national government, as well as changes in the position of the established parties.

Theoretical framework

The description in the previous section of the position of immigrants in the Dutch labour market over the last several decades raises questions about the integration of the immigrants into the Dutch labour market and, more generally, their integration into the Dutch social structure. Why is it that unemployment among the native Dutch labour-market participants declined after 1983 while the labour-market position of the ethnic minorities apparently remained unchanged, at least until 1994? Is the position of ethnic minorities in the labour market governed by regularities other than the position of the indigenous-market participants? Has there been a process of ethnic closure in the 1980s, eventually leading to the formation of an ethnic underclass? If so, what accounts for the drop in the unemployment figures for minority groups in 1998?

In the absence of valid and reliable data, these questions can only be answered in a speculative or ad hoc way. Now, however, data on the labour-market position of immigrant minority groups are available. In this chapter, we analyse these data against a theoretical framework combining theories of stratification, immigration and the labour market. In this section we concentrate on the theoretical framework and on the subject of our analyses.

From a more general point of view, the questions about the fate of ethnic minorities on the labour market refer to the factors that determine success on the labour market, occupational attainment and ultimately social stratification. Two competing theoretical perspectives are offered to explain social stratification: functionalist modernisation theory (Blau and Duncan 1967) and class conflict theory (Wright 1985).

Modernisation theory states that in modern societies the position of individuals in the social structure depends on the weight of their contribution to societal production and reproduction. From the perspective of modernisation theory, stratification in a modern society is fluid and open. Positions are acquired, not ascribed. What counts is achievement realised by the employment of human capital. As human capital is built up by individual investment in education, modernisation theory stresses the importance of levels of education for processes of stratification. Modernisation presupposes an open educational system without any entrance barriers. Modernisation theory does not allow for any independent influence of an ascribed distinctive category—like ethnicity—on social attainment.

According to class conflict theory, however, it is precisely these distinctive ascribed features that could be the crystallisation points for social inclusion or exclusion. Ideas about these processes of inclusion and exclusion carry back to Max Weber (Parkin 1974; Murphy 1988) who stated that the correspondence of arbitrary features can bring individuals together in communities, through which mutual interests can develop. Power and property give status to these interest groups and provide them with 'class' characteristics.

Classes include some individuals, but exclude others. When competition for resources is sharpened, social closures may result in the marginalisation of individuals with specific characteristics, for example blacks or other ethnic groups or the low educated. Wilson (1987) offers a straightforward application of the idea of social closure in his analysis of the change in the position of the black population within the inner cities of the US in the early 1980s. According to Wilson, the transformation of the old industries in the northern cities of the US in the beginning of the 1980s moved employment out of the city centres. This diminished the demand for low-skilled workers, thereby driving the black workers into long-term unemployment and in that way fostered the development of a black 'ghetto' underclass.

Since its introduction in the US, the concept of the 'underclass' has been distorted to the point of becoming synonymous with criminal, marginalised and asocial individuals who reject mainstream American values (Gans 1990, Jencks 1992). Jencks argues that the concept of an underclass suggests more homogeneity among individuals than can be found in social reality. Not all blacks, of course, are unemployed inner-city school dropouts.

Criticism of the concept of the underclass, however, does not imply that the concept of social closure is of no use in the analysis of the social position of ethnic minorities. Indeed, Figure 9.3 suggests that, at least within the labour market, a form of social closure against ethnic minorities could be at work. Social closure against immigrant ethnic groups on the labour market implies 'independent' effects of ethnicity on labour-market success and social position, 'independent' in this sense meaning independent of achieved productive characteristics, especially level of education.

Here then we have two theoretical perspectives for analysing the position of immigrant ethnic groups on the labour market, leading to different expectations about the effects of minority membership on labour-market activity. According to modernisation theory, we should expect no ethnic minority effects on labour-market position, occupational attainment or income after controlling for levels of human capital. Class theory, on the other hand, would predict such an effect as ethnic minorities run the risk of being driven into an underclass position, especially in times of growing competition on the labour market.

Assuming levels of human capital are solely indicated by levels of education, we might even expect a positive effect of membership of an ethnic minority group, due to unmeasured effects of factors associated with migration, for example higher initiative, achievement orientation or open mindedness.

The two perspectives, although providing for specific expectations about the effects of minority membership, are too general to analyse the development of labour-market position over time. Their main shortcoming is that the dynamics of immigration, the labour market and social security schemas are not sufficiently taken into account.

The ethnic minority groups that are the subject of this study are also immigrant groups. The incorporation of immigrants into a society has its own regularities, some of which are relevant to understanding the social position of ethnic minorities. This holds especially for the development of ethnic and immigrant characteristics over generations. In most cases first-generation immigrants tend to conserve and stress their ethnic characteristics. They will do this even more so when there are movements toward closure in the surrounding society. Members of the second generation, on the contrary, are brought up in the immigration country, receive their education in the new country and come in close contact with their indigenous peers. Thus, if segregation is not too severe, they will likely lose at least a part of the ethnic characteristics which were distinctive for their parents.

This dynamic property of migration will have consequences especially when viewed from the perspective of social closure. It could be expected that the second generation, since exhibiting fewer of the ethnic characteristics of their parents, would be less affected by social closure; thus we might predict ethnic minority membership to have a smaller effect on the position of the second generation than on the first generation.

From the viewpoint of modernisation theory, differences in labour-market position between the first and second generation are expected as well, but these differences will be ascribed to an ameliorating effect of the human capital attained by the second generation, due to their education in the immigrant country.

The second missing link is the dynamics of the labour market. Positions of individuals on the labour market can be viewed as a result of decision processes on the part of the suppliers of labour. To begin with, there is the decision to participate or not to participate. Next there is the decision to invest in skill development, thereby postponing entrance onto the market. Other decisions pertain to the actions of the unemployed or the amount of effort exerted to obtain promotion. In these decisions economic fluctuations can play a decisive role. Although choice is relevant for labour-market participation as well as for unemployment, it is perhaps more relevant in the former case than in the latter (since unemployment will depend on the choices made by other actors such as potential employers).

Economic fluctuations will also influence the demand-side of the labour market. When there is a great supply of labour, there is room for exclusion of job seekers by means of (statistical) discrimination. Conversely, when supply is scarce, discrimination involves a risk for the demanders.

The third missing link is the dynamics of social security arrangements. A generous social security schema can help migrants to overcome economic hardship arising from the migration processes by offering economic benefits, and thus may promote integration into Dutch society. But the same social security arrangements might also create ethnic niches for the migrants, discouraging contact with the indigenous surroundings (either in- or outside the labour market) and thus may hinder integration into Dutch society.

The theoretical ideas presented in this section point to different patterns of influence on the position of ethnic minorities in relation to the labour market. To study these patterns we analyse relations between aspects of labour-market position and income as dependent variables and membership of minority groups, immigrant status, age, human capital and supply-and-demand fluctuations on the labour market as independent explanatory factors. One would also like to include the human capital of the parents of individuals in the analyses but unfortunately no data about this aspect are available. Gender differences also call for attention within our analysis, as from every relevant point of view gender plays a special role.

Data sources, variables and procedures

For the analyses of the labour-market position of ethnic minorities in the Netherlands, the Sociale Positie en Voorzieningengebruik van Allochtonen (Social Position and Facilities Use of Ethnic Minorities) (SPVA) data sets provide four surveys of samples of households from the four largest immigrant ethnic minority groups (Turks, Moroccans, Surinamese and Antilleans). SPVA surveys on these four immigrant groups have been conducted in 1988, 1991, 1994 and 1998.

Within these surveys, an individual is classified into a minority group if he or she was born in the respective country or if one of their parents was born there. Turkish and Moroccans whose parents had different countries of birth hardly exist. That is less true for Surinamese and Antillean parents, one of whom might not have been born in Suriname or Antilles; nonetheless a more restricted definition (e.g., both parents born in Suriname or Antilles) would misrepresent the mixed nature of these ethnic groups due to the long standing colonial relations between Suriname, the Antilles and the Netherlands (longer than the British relationship with India). As a consequence, the racial composition of Antillean and Surinamese ethnic minorities is relatively heterogeneous, reflecting the mixed racial composition of these societies (African, Indonesian, Hindu, Jewish, White), although a majority do belong to 'visible minorities' of various skin colours.

As the SPVA surveys cover four different ethnic groups and a sample of the indigenous population, a total of five ethnic groups are compared within the analyses: Turks, Moroccans, Surinamese, Antilleans, and the native Dutch population. Each of the minority groups are also classed as first- and second-generation. As a consequence of the Dutch migration history, however, there are many more first-generation minorities than second-generation amongst 18–59 year-olds. Moreover, as the members of the second generation are much younger, they have less labour-market experience. Additionally, they are concentrated in the 1994 and (especially) the 1998 surveys.

The analyses in this chapter utilise independent and dependent variables as laid out in the Introduction of this volume. Education is the sole exception, with only four categories utilised: (1) primary; (2) lower secondary; (3) higher secondary; and (4) tertiary. Labour-market position is considered in terms of (1) participation; (2) unemployment; and (3) occupational class.

With regard to labour-market participation, as in other chapters, individuals are divided into two groups: those who are working or actively looking for a job vs. those that are not working and not looking for work. In the Netherlands, among people aged 18–59 the main reasons for non-participation in the labour market are housekeeping and occupational disability. For many social security, covering the loss of income by occupational disability, is a better option than unemployment benefits. Occupational disability is therefore preferred and widely used both by employees and employers as an attractive alternative to unemployment.

In terms of unemployment, participants are counted as unemployed if they are on the labour market and actively looking for work. In 1992, Dutch authorities changed all of the definitions of the labour-market statistics. For the sake of comparability in most cases categories of the older definitions have been used. This implies, for example, that the cutting point for 'small jobs' is set on nineteen hours a week; thus people who work less than nineteen hours are not counted as working. This definition of 'working' has consequences for the classification of unemployment and labour-market participation, particularly as individuals looking for work for less than nineteen hours a week are not counted in the labour-market participation data.

Workers who work more than nineteen hours a week are classified according to their position in the occupational class structure—in these analyses, the five-class schema outlined in the Introduction. Income data in the SPVA are obtained by asking for net weekly or monthly income. Respondents could tell their exact income or could indicate it in categories. The categories have been recoded to their midpoints. Reported income includes not only income from work but also social security benefits (occupational disability; unemployment, etc.). As a consequence, persons without paid work could still report an income. Income is still measured in Dutch guilders (1 Euro=2.20 guilders), and is not corrected for inflation (since we already control for year of the survey). The natural log of income is used in our analyses.

These independent variables have been considered in this chapter through a two-step analysis. First, in the following section, a bivariate description of relations between the dependent variables and the explanatory factors are introduced. In the second section, various types of regression equations are employed to further elucidate the effects of minority membership on labour-market outcomes. Multivariate models are used to analyse effects of minority membership on labour-market position and income; a binary logistic regression is fitted in analyses of labour-market participation and unemployment; for the analysis of occupational class, a multinomial logistic model is estimated; and income is analysed via ordinary least squares (OLS) estimation.

Descriptive analyses

From previous sections it can be expected that there are large differences in labour-market characteristics related to ethnic minority group membership. The theoretical framework discussed above points to possible differences related to level of education, immigration status (first vs. second generation), year and gender.

Tables 9.1–9.3 present the basic bivariate information showing the education, economic activity and occupation of the different ethnic groups. We discuss each one in turn. When considering these descriptive tables, it should be kept in mind that the total sample is not representative of the total population of the Netherlands. Because of the sampling

Table 9.1A. Highest educational qualification, by ancestry and generation: Men (row percentages).

	Primary or none	Lower secondary	Higher secondary	Tertiary	N
Indigenous Dutch	23.4	24.9	25.9	25.8	2,915
First-generation					
Turkish	67.1	18.0	11.6	3.3	4,093
Moroccan	79.7	10.5	6.5	3.3	3,818
Surinamese	38.3	34.1	17.2	10.4	2,393
Antillean	35.5	31.4	20.5	12.6	1,432
Second-generation					
Turkish	40.7	31.0	22.9	5.4	297
Moroccan	57.2	24.2	15.2	3.4	178
Surinamese	35.6	27.4	25.6	11.4	457
Antillean	28.8	17.0	31.3	22.9	288

Table 9.1B. Highest educational qualification, by ancestry and generation: Women (row percentages).

	Primary or none	Lower secondary	Higher secondary	Tertiary	N
Indigenous Dutch	24.7	29.8	24.5	21.0	2,913
First-generation					
Turkish	81.3	9.9	7.6	1.2	3,428
Moroccan	89.1	5.6	4.2	1.1	2,649
Surinamese	41.4	30.9	18.4	9.3	2,925
Antillean	42.0	32.0	18.0	8.0	1,782
Second-generation					
Turkish	49.9	28.2	17.2	4.7	383
Moroccan	57.4	20.5	17.4	4.7	322
Surinamese	34.3	28.6	27.3	9.8	605
Antillean	34.1	22.9	26.8	16.2	414

design discussed above, the four minority groups are over represented by a factor of approximately thirteen.

We begin in Tables 9.1A and 9.1B with the highest education of the four ethnic groups compared with that of the indigenous Dutch population. In both generations we see that all four groups tend to have lower levels of education than the indigenous population, with the Turks and Moroccans heavily concentrated in the lowest educational level. This pattern is even more accentuated in the case of women. However, there is considerable progress between generations with the second generation of all four ethnic groups showing higher levels of education than the first, although still falling short of the indigenous population.

Tables 9.2A and 9.2B then present distributions of economic activity for both men and women. The most important source of variation in labour-market participation is of course gender. With respect to labour-market participation gender interacts with ethnic minority status. Among men differences in participation reach a maximum of 23 percentage points between second-generation Moroccan and indigenous men. Among women differences are much larger, up to a 44 percentage point difference between first-generation Moroccan and Surinamese women. Labour-market participation juxtaposes Moroccan and Turkish women to the other groups. It should also be noted that among the women participation of Surinamese women is higher than the participation rate of indigenous women.

There is also an interaction between gender and immigration status. Among men there is a small difference in participation between the first and the second generation (with the latter participation 6 percentage

Table 9.2A. Economic activity, by ancestry and generation: Men (row percentages).

	Economically active	Inactive and other	N
Indigenous Dutch	83.7	16.3	2,915
First-generation			
Turkish	77.5	22.5	4,093
Moroccan	70.6	29.4	3,818
Surinamese	82.3	17.7	2,393
Antillean	79.5	20.5	1,432
Second-generation			
Turkish	71.3	28.7	297
Moroccan	60.9	39.1	178
Surinamese	73.8	26.2	457
Antillean	71.3	28.7	288

Table 9.2B. Economic activity, by ancestry and generation: Women (row percentages).

	Economically active	Inactive and other	N
Indigenous Dutch	55.0	45.0	2,913
First-generation			
Turkish	31.0	69.0	3,428
Moroccan	18.5	18.5	2,649
Surinamese	62.4	37.6	2,925
Antillean	56.7	43.3	1,782
Second-generation			
Turkish	52.1	47.9	383
Moroccan	45.6	54.4	322
Surinamese	59.6	40.4	605
Antillean	61.3	38.7	414

points or more lower), in contrast to women where the second-generation participation rate for Turks and Moroccans tends to be considerably higher than in the first generation. The lower participation rate of the second-generation men can perhaps been explained by their relatively young age, with many of them still in full-time education.

Tables 9.3A and 9.3B present the distributions of current occupation and unemployment by ancestry. Compared to employment participation, the figures on unemployment reveal much more pronounced differences associated with ethnic minority membership. Unemployment among minorities is much higher than among the indigenous labour-market participants, but there are also clear differences between the minority groups. The Moroccans and Turks are decisively in the most unfavourable

Table 9.3A. Current occupation, by ancestry and generation: Men (row percentages).

	Salariat	Routine non-manual	Petty bourgeoisie	Manual supervisor/skilled manual	Semi- and unskilled	Unemployed	N
Indigenous Dutch	38.3	16.0	5.7	14.3	17.4	8.3	2,413
First-generation							
Turkish	4.5	4.1	3.7	14.3	41.4	32.1	3,134
Moroccan	5.6	5.2	2.7	11.0	40.4	35.2	2,654
Surinamese	17.2	17.6	3.7	17.1	23.8	20.6	1,950
Antillean	18.8	14.2	2.5	16.5	22.9	25.1	1,126
Second-generation							
Turkish	10.0	23.3	4.5	10.9	29.8	21.6	199
Moroccan	8.4	15.9	4.2	11.7	30.6	29.1	103
Surinamese	20.4	19.1	3.2	10.5	21.0	25.8	318
Antillean	21.6	16.3	2.8	19.0	26.4	13.8	189

Table 9.3B. Current occupation, by ancestry and generation: Women (row percentages).

	Salariat	Routine non-manual	Petty bourgeoisie	Manual supervisor/skilled manual	Semi- and unskilled	Unemployed	N
Indigenous Dutch	30.6	38.6	3.6	3.1	8.9	15.2	1,602
First-generation							
Turkish	4.7	11.0	3.0	11.0	46.7	23.7	1,038
Moroccan	4.4	16.2	1.4	2.3	21.1	54.6	476
Surinamese	15.5	36.7	1.1	3.2	14.8	28.7	1,806
Antillean	14.5	33.4	0.9	2.2	12.8	36.2	1,000
Second-generation							
Turkish	10.5	36.6	2.8	1.9	15.7	32.4	185
Moroccan	5.0	32.7	3.8	1.2	16.4	40.8	130
Surinamese	17.6	46.8	3.2	2.6	11.0	18.8	336
Antillean	18.5	35.0	2.4	4.1	18.0	22.0	209

position with both the first and second generations experiencing high levels of unemployment.

The bivariate distributions of class and minority group membership also take the expected form. Turks and Moroccans are concentrated in the categories of the manual workers. Surinamese and Antilleans have an intermediate position in these categories, while they concentrate also in the routine non-manual class. The indigenous workers have their highest representation in the salariat class. Again the pattern of first vs. second generation deserves attention. In the second generation there appears to be a considerable movement of ethnic minorities out of the manual working classes into the non-manual classes (but not into the petty bourgeoisie).

Gender plays its own special role in the distribution of workers between occupational classes. In the indigenous population there is the well known over-representation of women in the nonmanual occupations. We can see the same pattern among all the second-generation groups, but first-generation Turkish and Moroccan women are under-represented in nonmanual work and instead are concentrated in semi- and unskilled work.

The bivariate distributions discussed so far do not fail to have their consequences for the distribution of income over ethnic minority groups, migrant generation and of course gender. Income differences are as expected. All four ethnic groups have income substantially lower than the indigenous Dutch, but with the Turks and Moroccans again falling some way behind the Surinamese and Antilleans. The lower mean incomes of the second generation could be a consequence of their younger ages and continued educational participation.

The bivariate distributions tell us a great deal about the position of members of ethnic minority groups in the Dutch labour market and occu-

Table 9.4. Mean income, by ancestry and gender (Dutch Guilders).

	Men	N	Women	N
Indigenous Dutch	2,507	2,372	1,713	1,817
First-generation				
Turkish	1,829	3,473	1,329	1,097
Moroccan	1,724	3,145	1,344	556
Surinamese	2,038	1,885	1,633	2,044
Antillean	1,859	1,209	1,584	1,460
Second-generation				
Turkish	1,734	218	1,365	227
Moroccan	1,419	127	1,284	160
Surinamese	1,724	299	1,584	393
Antillean	2,039	232	1,533	259

pational structure. It is clear that their position is not nearly as strong as the position of the indigenous population. At the same time one can see that minority status is not a matter of all or nothing; Tables 9.1 through 9.3 show large differences between Turkish and Moroccan immigrants on one side, and Surinamese and Antillean immigrants on the other. Moreover there are differences associated with the immigrant generations suggesting that acculturation is a factor. The special role of gender is highlighted by the interactions with minority membership.

Being bivariate, the above tables do not give much of a clue about the meaning of the relations. Are minorities the targets of social closure or is it their lack of human capital that makes their position as unfavourable as the tables show? How can the differences between the ethnic groups be explained? What about the much better positions of the second generation? Is it their better education, are they more assimilated into Dutch culture, or do they exhibit fewer of the characteristics that trigger exclusion? What is the role of economic circumstances, in this case represented by the time factor? Are the answers to these questions the same for men and women? Only if we can answer these questions can we judge the validity of the theoretical perspectives we introduced earlier.

Models of labour-market position, occupational structure and income

The inconclusiveness of the descriptions above follows from the bivariate nature of analyses as presented. This bivariate analysis strategy does not allow us to determine the relative weight of the variables in explaining variance in the dependent variables. Another source of indeterminacy is caused by the covariation between the explanatory variables. Members of minority groups have lower levels of education than the indigenous population, so a bivariate analysis is inconclusive as to the effects of membership of minority groups. The same holds for immigrant status.

It is quite clear that the problem asks for a multivariate approach. Therefore a model of the variables under study is needed. The model should explain the position of individuals in the labour market, in the occupational class structure and in the income distribution. The model should be as parsimonious as possible, meaning that it should describe a maximum of variance in the dependent variables using a minimum of degrees of freedom. A model that includes all of the relevant variables best serves this objective.

Unfortunately there are some obstacles for the analysis of all the relevant variables in one model. A first obstacle is in the different levels of measurement that hold for the dependent variables. Some of them, i.e. participation on the labour market and unemployment are dichotomous. Occupational class is a polytomous nominal variable, and income is continuous.

Another obstacle is the selective nature of some of the explanatory variables. Unemployment, for example, is only defined for individuals who participate on the labour market. Occupational class is only defined for workers. Migrant generation is only relevant for members of minority groups.

A third obstacle is the special role of gender in processes of stratification. The bivariate analysis already shows that gender interacts in many ways with the other explanatory variables, so inclusion of gender in a model consumes many degrees of freedom. Therefore it seems wiser to analyse separate models for men and women.

Considering the obstacles for the analysis of a joint model for all of the variables, we have chosen the less ambitious strategy of analysing separate models for the four dependent variables. Thus, we have estimated logistic models for labour-market participation and unemployment, a multinomial model for class position and a linear model for income.

Constructing dummy variables for ethnic group membership and generation solves the problem of the selective nature of the migrant generation variable. We also use dummy variables for ethnic group membership and age to take into account the possible different consequences of labour-market experience for migrant generations and the indigenous population. Dummy variables for ethnic group membership and year measure the changing relation between the migrants and the Dutch society. Throughout the indigenous population is taken as the reference category.

Labour-market participation

Table 9.5 summarises the results for labour-market participation of men and women separately. The models for these aspects are logistic regression models. In Model 1, participation is regressed on the combinations of ethnic group membership, level of education, age, age-square and year. Model 2 adds significant interaction terms for the combinations of migrant generation and education, migrant generation and age, and migrant generation and measurement year. The addition of these terms improves the fit of the model.

Table 9.5. Logistic regression of labour-market participation (parameter estimates; contrasts with non-participation).

	Men				Women			
	Model 1		Model 2		Model 1		Model 2	
Intercept	**0.68**	(0.10)	**−0.41**	(0.12)	−0.07	(0.09)	−0.17	(0.10)
Ancestry								
Native Dutch	0.0		0.0		0.0		0.0	
Turkish 1	**−0.23**	(0.07)	**1.40**	(0.12)	**−0.49**	(0.06)	0.09	(0.12)
Moroccan 1	**−0.42**	(0.07)	**0.58**	(0.12)	**−1.18**	(0.08)	**−0.43**	(0.13)
Surinamese 1	**−0.16**	(0.08)	**0.61**	(0.15)	**0.54**	(0.06)	**0.52**	(0.06)
Antillean 1	−0.13	(0.10)	0.04	(0.10)	**0.28**	(0.07)	**−0.25**	(0.12)
Turkish 2	**−0.28**	(0.18)	**−0.68**	(0.56)	−0.08	(0.13)	−0.04	(0.14)
Moroccan 2	−0.28	(0.23)	−0.89	(0.65)	**−0.31**	(0.15)	**−0.91**	(0.36)
Surinamese 2	−0.18	(0.16)	−0.62	(0.32)	0.13	(0.11)	0.09	(0.12)
Antillean 2	**−0.61**	(0.18)	0.18	(0.24)	0.18	(0.14)	0.22	(0.14)
Age/10	**1.99**	(0.08)	**2.38**	(0.09)	**0.33**	(0.07)	**0.52**	(0.08)
$(Age/10)^2$	**−0.56**	(0.02)	**−0.54**	(0.02)	**−0.18**	(0.02)	**−0.20**	(0.02)
Education								
Primary	0.0		0.0		0.0		0.0	
Secondary lower	**0.63**	(0.06)	**0.78**	(0.08)	**0.71**	(0.05)	**0.68**	(0.06)
Sec higher	**0.17**	(0.07)	**0.63**	(0.11)	**1.12**	(0.05)	**1.09**	(0.07)
Tertiary	**1.01**	(0.11)	**1.53**	(0.16)	**1.93**	(0.09)	**1.86**	(0.09)
Year								
1988	**−0.58**	(0.06)	**−0.56**	(0.07)	**−0.84**	(0.06)	**−0.95**	(0.06)
1991	**−0.29**	(0.06)	**−0.29**	(0.07)	**−0.51**	(0.05)	**−0.58**	(0.06)
1994	**−0.70**	(0.06)	**−0.69**	(0.06)	**−0.54**	(0.05)	**−0.59**	(0.06)
1998	0.0		0.0		0.0		0.0	
Significant interactions								
Turkish 1 * education			**−0.46**	(0.08)				
Moroccan 1 * education			**−0.35**	(0.08)			**0.27**	(0.05)
Surinamese 1 * education			**−0.20**	(0.08)				
Antillean 1 * education			**−0.34**	(0.10)				
Turkish 1 * age			**−0.90**	(0.05)			**−0.24**	(0.05)
Turkish 1 * age			**−0.81**	(0.36)				
Moroccan 1 * age			**−0.55**	(0.05)			**−0.42**	(0.08)
Surinamese 1 * age			**−0.39**	(0.06)				
Antillean 1 * age							**0.31**	(0.06)
Turkish 1 * year							**−0.05**	(0.01)
Surinamese 2 * education			**−0.48**	(0.18)			**0.30**	(0.13)
Antillean 2 * education			**−0.67**	(0.20)				
Turkish 2 * year			**0.20**	(0.07)				
Moroccan 2 * year			**0.18**	(0.09)				
Surinamese 2 * year			**0.17**	(0.05)				
Chi-Square (D.F.)			1,866 (16)	2,232 (29)	3,424 (16)		3,581 (24)	
N			14,623	14,623	13,973		13,973	

Note: Standard errors are given in brackets; emboldened coefficients indicate significance at 0.05 level or higher.

The first thing that meets the eye when looking at the estimations for labour-market participation certainly is the outspoken differences between the models for men and women. The model for men fits the data only partly. It describes no more than approximately 12–14% of the 'variance' in the chances for participation. However, despite the small R^2, the estimates of the effects for men exhibit some definite patterns. First, in all cases but one (Antilleans) there are significant negative effects of first-generation ethnic group membership, while the effects of second-generation membership are not significant for all but one group (again, the Antilleans). Being a male member of a first-generation ethnic minority group reduces the labour-market participation to about 50% compared to that of the indigenous male population. However, this is only true if we do not take into account the smaller benefits of more than primary education for migrant men of the first generation. While more education boosts the odds for participation among all men, this is less true for the first (and partly the second) generation of males, given the negative interactions with education in Model 2. This does not mean that the better-educated migrant does not have more attractive prospects on the labour market than his lower-educated brother, but that his prospects are less bright than those of his equally educated indigenous neighbour. If we take this smaller yield of education for migrant males into account, the lower-educated migrants (especially the first generation Turks, Moroccans and Surinamese) have higher labour-market participation than equally low-educated indigenous men. The smaller yield of education for the higher-educated migrant generations indicates a certain degree of social exclusion from the Dutch labour market.

Age has a common effect on labour-market participation: the older one is, the higher the chances of being in the labour market. The age-square term also has its expected effect—beyond a certain age labour-market participation starts to decline due to occupational disability, long-term unemployment, early pension, etc. Interestingly, age has a weaker effect for Turks of both generations and for Moroccans and Surinamese as a mechanism for entering the labour market. This smaller yield of age for these migrant generations indicates also a certain degree of social exclusion from the Dutch labour market.

In the bivariate description we found hardly any difference in participation between the first and the second generation. Table 9.5 however reveals systematically smaller effects for men belonging to the second generation. Partly this can be explained by the inclusion of age into the equation, which takes account of the fact that a younger generation has yet to find its way into the labour market after finishing education. Moreover, after taking into account the lower yield of education and age for the second generation, the second-generation Turks, Moroccans and Surinamese have significantly lower labour-market participation than the first generations. This lower yield of education and age is however partly compensated by the interactions with migrant generation and year: the significant interaction shows that during the 1990s the second-generation migrants (Turks, Moroccans and Surinamese) improved their labour-market participation. The lower labour-market participation of the young second generation reflects their situation at the end of the 1980s, but during the 1990s their situation in the labour market improved.

The pattern of the parameter estimates over the years clearly reflects the economic circumstances of the time. The mini recession of 1994 and the economic boom of 1998 have their impact on the rates of participation. As it is easier to enter the labour market in times of economic growth, during such a period social closure will be less strong. Thus in 1998 there was a sharp rise in the likelihood of participation.

The interaction of ethnic group membership with year is significant for the second generation only. This implies that economic fluctuation affected the second-generation minority members less than comparable indigenous men, and that the integration of the second generation into the labour market is increasing as they become a longer-established component of Dutch society.

For women the model performs better than for men, and in particular the explained variance is higher. Education is a stronger predictor of participation among women and there is less oscillation over time along the linear growth trend. However, the pattern of significant parameters for the combinations of minority group membership and generation is more complex and contradictory among women than among men.

First, the likelihood of participation in the labour market is considerably smaller for Moroccan women of the first generation and also (to a lesser extent) for Turkish women. Contrarily, the odds for Surinamese and Antillean first-generation women are higher than the odds for indigenous women. The result for the second-generation minority women is strikingly different. The labour-market participation of the second-generation Turkish, Surinamese and Antillean females does not differ significantly from that of the comparable indigenous women. Only the second-generation Moroccan women still participate less than comparable indigenous women, although their shortfall is far smaller than the first-generation Moroccan woman with the same age and educational level.

Second, the impact of education is stronger for women than for men. Moreover, the yield of education for labour-market participation is larger for first-generation Moroccans and second-generation Surinamese than for comparable indigenous women, while for the analogous male migrants this age yield was smaller than for comparable indigenous men. Only the yield of education for Turkish first-generation women is significant smaller than that for indigenous women.

Thirdly, the age effects (both the linear and the squared) are also smaller for women than for men. This is not unexpected given the still dominant difference in roles for men and women as breadwinner and housewife. More interestingly, the age effect on labour-market participation is smaller for first-generation Turkish and Moroccans females, but is higher for first-generation Antillean women compared to analogous indigenous women. Lastly, over the years the only trend for women appears to be a growth of participation, a growth that was even larger for first-generation Turkish females.

The high participation of Surinamese and Antillean women deserves special attention. These levels may be due to instability of relations between men and women that characterises the Surinamese and Antillean communities in the Netherlands, no less than in their homelands. This instability may force the women of these groups not to rely on a husband or a male partner but to secure economic independence.

Unemployment

Labour-market participation can be conceived as the result of the active decisions of individuals. In unemployment, although one can expend more or less effort in looking for a job, an individual is much more the object of the decisions of others. Thus, when social closure of ethnic minorities is occurring, it should come to light in models of unemployment.

And indeed it does, as one can see in the Table 9.6. As in other chapters in this volume, we model the avoidance of unemployment and hence a negative parameter estimate indicates that the group in question has a greater risk of unemployment than the reference category of the native Dutch. With only two exceptions (second-generation Antillean males and Surinamese females) all combinations of minority membership and migrant generation result in considerably higher odds of unemployment than the indigenous population with the same age and educational level. This holds for men as well as for women, although the odds for men are worse. Lower levels of education or younger age struc-

Table 9.6. Logistic regression of employment (parameter estimates; contrasts with unemployment).

	Men				Women			
	Model 1		Model 2		Model 1		Model 2	
Intercept	−1.37	(0.12)	−1.07	(0.13)	0.69	(0.14)	0.63	(0.15)
Ancestry								
Native Dutch	0.0		0.0		0.0		0.0	
Turkish 1	−1.33	(0.09)	−0.85	(0.12)	−1.09	(0.10)	−0.64	(0.18)
Moroccan 1	−1.38	(0.09)	−1.42	(0.10)	−1.38	(0.13)	−1.02	(0.20)
Surinamese 1	−1.02	(0.10)	−1.37	(0.16)	−0.72	(0.09)	−0.75	(0.09)
Antillean 1	−1.26	(0.11)	−1.24	(0.11)	−1.04	(0.10)	−0.55	(0.16)
Turkish 2	−0.82	(0.20)	−0.72	(0.21)	−0.56	(0.20)	−0.56	(0.20)
Moroccan 2	−1.11	(0.26)	−0.65	(0.34)	−0.90	(0.23)	−0.91	(0.23)
Surinamese 2	−1.14	(0.16)	−1.09	(0.16)	−0.23	(0.17)	−0.04	(0.20)
Antillean 2	−0.41	(0.25)	−0.40	(0.25)	−0.42	(0.20)	−0.42	(0.20)
Age/10	0.88	(0.09)	0.99	(0.10)	0.60	(0.12)	0.72	(0.12)
(Age/10)^2	−0.19	(0.02)	−0.21	(0.02)	−0.12	(0.03)	−0.14	(0.03)
Education								
Primary	0.0		0.0		0.0		0.0	
Secondary lower	0.62	(0.06)	0.78	(0.07)	0.56	(0.08)	0.63	(0.08)
Secondary higher	0.69	(0.07)	0.96	(0.10)	1.11	(0.09)	1.24	(0.09)
Tertiary	0.89	(0.10)	1.19	(0.12)	1.33	(0.11)	1.46	(0.12)
Year								
1988	−0.25	(0.07)	−0.27	(0.07)	−0.44	(0.09)	−0.73	(0.11)
1991	−0.32	(0.06)	−0.33	(0.06)	−0.39	(0.08)	−0.60	(0.09)
1994	−0.60	(0.06)	−0.61	(0.06)	−0.52	(0.08)	−0.64	(0.08)
1998	0.0		0.0		0.0		0.0	
Significant interactions								
Turkish 1 * education			−0.32	(0.05)			−0.26	(0.09)
Moroccan 1 * education			−0.23	(0.07)				
Turkish 1 * age			0.33	(0.05)				
Turkish 1 * age							−0.18	(0.09)
Moroccan 1 * age							−0.27	(0.13)
Surinamese 1 * age			−0.23	(0.07)				
Turkish 1 * year							−0.06	(0.02)
Antillean 1 * year							−0.09	(0.02)
Moroccan 2 * education			1.03	(0.41)				
Surinamese 2 * education							−0.41	(0.16)
Chi-Square (D.F.)	1,079 (16)		1,176 (21)		853 (16)		894 (22)	
N	11,543		11,543		6,344		6,344	

tures of minority groups clearly are not sufficient to explain their higher risks of unemployment.

The pattern of effects of migrant generation status is irregular. The lower unemployment rate for the second generation seen in Table 9.3 does not hold for all ethnic groups. The odds of unemployment for Moroccan and Surinamese men belonging to the second generation are only slightly less than for the first generation, once one controls for age and education.

Among the women however the odds of unemployment for the second generation are consistently lower than for the first generation.

Education has its normal effect on the chances of unemployment: the higher the education, the greater the chance of avoiding unemployment. This is true for both men and women. But this yield of education is smaller for first-generation Turkish and Moroccan men, indicating a certain degree of exclusion of even higher-educated Turkish and Moroccan men, who migrated themselves, from the labour market. A possible mechanism explaining the closure might be the non-recognition of their educational qualifications. The same holds for first-generation Turkish and second-generation Surinamese females: they also have lower yields from their education for avoiding unemployment than comparable indigenous women. However, second-generation Moroccan men have a larger education yield than comparable indigenous men.

Getting older increases the chances of being unemployed more strongly for various migrant generations (first-generation Turkish males and females; first-generation Moroccan females) than for the comparable indigenous Dutch population. Again, there is an exception: getting older increases the chances of becoming unemployed less for first-generation Surinamese men than for comparable Dutch men.

The parameter for unemployment in 1994 indicates a sharp drop in unemployment between 1994 and 1998, another indicator of the improvement of Dutch economy during that period. But the unemployment of first-generation Turkish and Antillean women decreased during 1988–98 more strongly than for indigenous women, and this cannot be explained by their age. This can be interpreted as a modernisation effect for migrant women as the economically active first-generation women increasingly found jobs in an expanding labour-market. The absence of other interaction effects for males suggests that during 1988–98 the less favourable economic circumstances did not lead to further exclusion amongst minorities.

The results for unemployment clearly provide evidence for the closure perspective. Despite controls for level of education and age, unemployment for most minority generations is considerably higher than for the comparable indigenous population. Also age and education have a lower yield for avoiding unemployment for a number of migrant generations, indicating evidence of exclusion and closure processes.

Occupational position

The analysis of the position of minorities in the occupational class structure calls for a different type of analysis than that used to model labour-market participation and unemployment. Since occupational classes are represented as a nominal variable and most of the explanatory variables are categorical in nature, we use a multinomial logistic model for the analyses of the position of minorities in the occupational class structure. In this analysis a series of logistic regressions of the categories of occupational class on the explanatory variables is evaluated simultaneously (see Table 9.7A and 9.7B).

In the analysis the lowest class, unskilled manual worker, is treated as the reference category for the dependent variable. Thus the dependent variable represents the chances of being a member of each of the four higher classes relative to the chances of belonging to the unskilled manual class. The effects of the explanatory variables represent the chances of the categories of the explanatory variables relative to their reference categories.

The models' test parameters indicate that the two models provide a fairly good prediction of the position of men and women within the occupational class structure. We also searched for significant interaction terms in the models for men and women. We selected from these analyses those interaction terms that improved the fit of the model. These few significant interaction terms were introduced together into the equation. Only those interaction terms which significantly improved the fit of the model are included in Model 2. The explanatory variables cover approximately 30% of the 'variance' in the log-odds for the classes of males, and 20% for females.

The pattern of the parameters for the combinations of minority group membership and migrant generation is interesting. After controlling for level of education, migrant generation appears to be decisive for the position of minorities in the occupational class structure. For men and women of the first generation, many minority membership effects are significantly negative, indicating a lower chance of belonging to a given class relative to belonging in the unskilled manual class. These effects tend to be much closer to zero for the second generation.

Nonetheless, all second-generation males, with the exception of the Antilleans, have lower chances of belonging to the salariat class than comparable indigenous men. However, older second-generation Surinamese men have a higher chance of entering the salariat than comparable indigenous men, and as a consequence their final chances to enter the salariat

Table 9.7A. Logistic regression of occupational class: Men (parameter estimates; contrasts with semi- and unskilled manual).

	Salariat				Routine non-manual				Petty bourgeoisie				Skilled manual			
	1		2		1		2		1		2		1		2	
Intercept	2.55	(0.80)	1.29	(0.85)	1.03	(0.78)	0.34	(0.82)	0.82	(1.06)	0.47	(1.13)	0.12	(0.80)	−0.66	(0.84)
Ancestry																
Native Dutch	0.0		0.0		0.0		0.0		0.0		0.0		0.0		0.0	
Turkish 1	**−2.19**	(0.12)	**−2.17**	(0.12)	**−1.80**	(0.12)	**−1.78**	(0.12)	**−0.95**	(0.14)	**−0.94**	(0.14)	**−0.60**	(0.10)	**−0.58**	(0.10)
Moroccan 1	**−1.90**	(0.12)	**−1.46**	(0.18)	**−1.43**	(0.12)	**−1.15**	(0.16)	**−1.10**	(0.16)	**−0.77**	(0.22)	**−0.75**	(0.11)	**−0.41**	(0.14)
Surinamese 1	**−0.64**	(0.11)	**−0.64**	(0.11)	0.02	(0.11)	0.02	(0.11)	**−0.45**	(0.16)	**−0.45**	(0.16)	0.05	(0.11)	0.05	(0.11)
Antillean 1	**−0.78**	(0.13)	**−0.77**	(0.13)	**−0.31**	(0.13)	**−0.30**	(0.13)	**−0.58**	(0.20)	**−0.58**	(0.20)	−0.02	(0.12)	−0.02	(0.12)
Turkish 2	**−0.75**	(0.27)	**−0.64**	(0.28)	−0.32	(0.21)	0.05	(0.21)	−0.10	(0.32)	0.16	(0.32)	−0.16	(0.25)	−0.08	(0.26)
Moroccan 2	**−0.69**	(0.33)	−0.59	(0.34)	−0.25	(0.28)	−0.18	(0.28)	0.29	(0.36)	0.34	(0.36)	−0.04	(0.30)	0.04	(0.30)
Surinamese 2	**−0.40**	(0.20)	0.05	(0.25)	0.04	(0.19)	0.18	(0.22)	0.23	(0.26)	0.06	(0.34)	0.00	(0.21)	0.14	(0.25)
Antillean 2	−0.08	(0.23)	−0.03	(0.23)	0.06	(0.24)	0.10	(0.24)	**0.61**	(0.29)	**0.65**	(0.29)	0.27	(0.25)	0.32	(0.25)
Age-group																
18–30	**0.60**	(0.09)	**0.82**	(0.10)	−0.13	(0.09)	0.03	(0.10)	0.10	(0.12)	0.24	(0.14)	**0.26**	(0.08)	**0.43**	(0.09)
31–40	**0.18**	(0.09)	**0.28**	(0.09)	−0.02	(0.09)	0.06	(0.09)	0.01	(0.12)	0.09	(0.13)	0.10	(0.08)	0.19	(0.08)
41–60	0.0		0.0		0.0		0.0		0.0		0.0		0.0		0.0	
Education																
Primary	0.0		0.0		0.0		0.0		0.0		0.0		0.0		0.0	
Lower secondary	**0.34**	(0.10)	**0.33**	(0.10)	**0.54**	(0.09)	**0.54**	(0.09)	**0.48**	(0.12)	**0.46**	(0.12)	**0.62**	(0.08)	**0.62**	(0.08)
Higher secondary	**1.77**	(0.10)	**1.77**	(0.10)	**1.47**	(0.10)	**1.47**	(0.10)	**1.12**	(0.14)	**1.11**	(0.14)	**0.97**	(0.09)	**0.97**	(0.09)
Tertiary	**3.56**	(0.13)	**3.56**	(0.13)	**1.69**	(0.14)	**1.68**	(0.14)	**1.53**	(0.19)	**1.56**	(0.19)	**0.75**	(0.16)	**0.74**	(0.16)

	Model 1				Model 2			
Year								
1988	−0.92 (0.10)	−0.96 (0.10)	−0.09 (0.11)	−0.11 (0.11)	−1.29 (0.12)	−1.31 (0.12)	−1.20 (0.09)	−1.23 (0.09)
1991	−0.25 (0.10)	−0.28 (0.10)	−0.02 (0.09)	−0.03 (0.09)	0.05 (0.15)	0.04 (0.15)	−0.83 (0.08)	−0.85 (0.08)
1994	−0.34 (0.10)	−0.37 (0.10)	−0.33 (0.09)	−0.34 (0.09)	−0.52 (0.19)	−0.52 (0.19)	−0.48 (0.09)	−0.50 (0.09)
1998	0.0	0.0	0.0	0.0	0.0	0.0	0.0	0.0
Significant Interactions								
Moroccan 1 * age group	0.43 (0.13)		0.29 (0.12)		0.34 (0.16)		0.33 (0.09)	
Surinamese 2 * age group	0.71 (0.27)		0.23 (0.26)		−0.27 (0.32)		0.20 (0.28)	
Chi-square (D.F.)	Model 1: 1,229 (64)				Model 2: 1,197 (72)			
N	8851							

Note: Standard errors are given in brackets; emboldened coefficients indicate significance at the 0.05 level or higher.

Table 9.7B. Logistic regression of occupational class: Women (parameter estimates; contrasts with semi- and unskilled manual).

	Salariat		Routine non-manual		Petty bourgeoisie		Skilled manual	
	1	2	1	2	1	2	1	2
Intercept	2.13 (1.03)	2.97 (1.11)	2.54 (0.88)	3.86 (0.93)	−1.13 (1.40)	−0.78 (1.46)	−2.60 (1.41)	−2.69 (1.47)
Ancestry								
Native Dutch	0.0	0.0	0.0	0.0	0.0	0.0	0.0	0.0
Turkish 1	−2.42 (0.19)	−2.25 (0.38)	−2.54 (0.15)	−2.45 (0.31)	−1.03 (0.23)	−0.37 (0.37)	−0.08 (0.21)	0.72 (0.29)
Moroccan 1	−1.54 (0.24)	−1.56 (0.24)	−1.39 (0.18)	−1.48 (0.17)	−0.30 (0.29)	−0.38 (0.29)	0.03 (0.28)	−0.06 (0.28)
Surinamese 1	−0.77 (0.14)	−0.84 (0.16)	−0.39 (0.12)	−0.50 (0.12)	−0.93 (0.23)	−0.93 (0.25)	−0.18 (0.21)	−0.14 (0.21)
Antillean 1	−0.78 (0.16)	−0.80 (0.16)	−0.44 (0.14)	−0.47 (0.14)	−0.50 (0.25)	−0.54 (0.25)	−0.11 (0.24)	−0.15 (0.24)
Turkish 2	−0.78 (0.29)	−0.82 (0.29)	−0.64 (0.22)	−0.72 (0.22)	0.48 (0.34)	0.42 (0.34)	0.56 (0.36)	0.47 (0.36)
Moroccan 2	−1.11 (0.35)	−1.12 (0.35)	−0.82 (0.25)	−0.87 (0.25)	0.49 (0.38)	0.44 (0.37)	0.68 (0.41)	0.58 (0.40)
Surinamese 2	0.40 (0.22)	−0.41 (0.22)	−0.21 (0.19)	−0.25 (0.19)	**0.56** (0.28)	**0.52** (0.28)	**0.74** (0.30)	**0.67** (0.29)
Antillean 2	0.23 (0.25)	−0.23 (0.24)	−0.49 (0.22)	−0.50 (0.22)	0.55 (0.31)	0.54 (0.31)	**0.78** (0.31)	**0.77** (0.31)
Age-group								
18–30	**0.44** (0.13)	**0.50** (0.13)	−0.34 (0.11)	−0.32 (0.11)	**0.51** (0.18)	**0.56** (0.18)	**0.52** (0.16)	**0.58** (0.17)
31–40	0.15 (0.12)	0.16 (0.13)	−0.10 (0.11)	−0.10 (0.11)	0.21 (0.18)	0.20 (0.18)	0.33 (0.17)	0.33 (0.17)
41–60	0.0	0.0	0.0	0.0	0.0	0.0	0.0	0.0
Education								
Primary	0.0	0.0	0.0	0.0	0.0	0.0	0.0	0.0
Lower secondary	**0.54** (0.14)	**0.49** (0.15)	**0.98** (0.10)	**0.82** (0.11)	**0.38** (0.19)	0.24 (0.20)	0.18 (0.16)	0.08 (0.18)
Higher secondary	**1.93** (0.14)	**1.72** (0.16)	**1.53** (0.16)	**1.15** (0.13)	**1.20** (0.19)	**0.91** (0.21)	**0.70** (0.18)	**0.47** (0.21)
Tertiary	**3.55** (0.17)	**3.23** (0.20)	**1.30** (0.16)	**0.77** (0.19)	**1.90** (0.23)	**1.49** (0.26)	**1.42** (0.23)	**1.09** (0.27)

Year								
1988	**−1.27** (0.15)	**−1.15** (0.16)	**−0.36** (0.14)	−0.22 (0.15)	**−1.60** (0.20)	**−1.38** (0.22)	**−2.85** (0.18)	**−2.40** (0.20)
1991	−0.20 (0.13)	−0.21 (0.14)	0.30 (0.11)	0.31 (0.12)	−0.26 (0.21)	−0.17 (0.22)	**−0.92** (0.19)	**−0.67** (0.20)
1994	0.16 (0.12)	0.13 (0.13)	0.18 (0.10)	0.15 (0.10)	**−0.48** (0.17)	**−0.45** (0.18)	**−0.42** (0.19)	−0.31 (0.20)
1998	0.0	0.0	0.0	0.0	0.0	0.0	0.0	0.0
Significant Interactions								
Turkish 1 * education		**−0.38** (0.18)		**−0.58** (0.15)		**−0.37** (0.21)		−0.33 (0.19)
Surinamese 1 * education		**−0.48** (0.13)		**−0.63** (0.11)		**−0.48** (0.20)		**−0.36** (0.17)
Turkish 1 * year		0.03 (0.05)		0.02 (0.04)		0.10 (0.05)		**0.20** (0.05)
Chi-square (D.F.)		Model 1: 916 (64)						Model 2: 732 (76)
N		Model 1: 5,110						Model 2: 4,995

Note: Standard errors are given in brackets; emboldened coefficients indicate significance at the 0.05 level or higher.

become equal to those of indigenous men of the same age and educational qualifications. Apart from access to the salariat, second-generation men do not appear to be disadvantaged in gaining access to the other three classes compared to indigenous men. None of the other parameter estimates for the second generation men are statistically significant. The only exception is the higher chances of the second-generation male Antilleans of belonging to the petty bourgeoisie than indigenous men with the same age and education.

Turkish and Moroccan women of the second generation also have lower chances of belonging to the salariat or to the routine non-manual class than comparable indigenous women. But second-generation Antillean and Surinamese women have higher chances of belonging to the petty bourgeoisie or the skilled manual class than indigenous women with the same age and education. On the whole the inclusion of the active second generation of migrants into the Dutch class structure does not indicate strong exclusion. But the salariat class remains relatively more closed to this second generation and this closure cannot be explained by age or education.

The male first-generation migrants, whatever their origin, age and education, have higher chances of being members of the unskilled manual class than comparable indigenous men (although Surinamese are the exception for the routine non-manual and skilled classes and Antilleans for the skilled class). Given the labour-migration history of the Turks and Moroccans this is not surprising, but our results indicate that this low class position cannot be explained by their educational qualifications. The colonial-migration history of the first-generation Surinamese and Antilleans gave them more opportunities to enter classes above the unskilled manual classes, but prevented them from gaining entrance into the salariat.

The results for the first-generation females resemble that of the male migrants; the only exception is that for women there is in general no significant difference between entrance chances into the unskilled and skilled manual classes.

From the point of social closure against migrants by Dutch society, second-generation men have better chances of entering the higher classes of Dutch society than first-generation men, but there still appears to be closure of the salariat class. This is also true, albeit to a lesser degree, for second-generation female migrants.

Level of education has its expected effect on the chances of entering the various social classes—the greater the distance from the lowest class, the stronger the effects of education on the chances of belonging to a higher class. For migrant men, both first and second generation, there is no lower yield of education on entrance to the various classes. For Turkish and Surinamese women of the first generation, however, there are significantly lower yields of education on the chances to enter the petty bourgeoisie or higher classes than for equally educated indigenous women.

The results suggest that for active workers the mechanism for acquisition or ascription of occupational-class position might be different for the second generation as compared to the first. For the second generation the acquisition of an occupational-class position appears to follow the same path as it does for the indigenous workers. Occupational-class position for them depends mainly on human capital. This supports modernisation theory, although the highest classes are still a domain more closed to second-generation migrants than the modernisation theory would assume.

The modernisation viewpoint, however, applies little to the position of the male first generation. Controlling for education (and thus partly for the degree of fluency either in the Dutch or the English language) their chances of reaching higher-class levels in the occupational structure are much lower than the chances of the indigenous workers. Moreover the Antillean and Surinamese first-generation males (especially the higher educated) will have some fluency in the Dutch language, as the same language is also used in the Antilles and Suriname, but our results do not show chances equal to those of the comparable indigenous population. Thus this result supports the social closure viewpoint.

Does this conclusion mean that different theoretical frameworks are needed for the explanation of the position of the first and second generation minorities? This option is not very attractive. It could be argued that social exclusion holds for both the first and the second generation but that the second generation no longer has some of the minority characteristics (like low educational level or lack of fluency in the Dutch language) that trigger exclusion from the middle classes.

Income

Considering the results discussed so far it could be expected that the closure tendencies on the labour market and in the occupational structure will have their consequences for the incomes of members of minority groups, having the same age, educational level and class position. While overall income differences are associated with labour-market participation, unemployment, age, education and position in the class structure, if closure tendencies exist ethnic minorities should have lower incomes than comparable members of the indigenous population.

For the interpretation of the results of Table 9.8 it is important to remember three points: (1) the income measure is inclusive of social benefits, unemployment benefits, occupational disability benefits, etc. In short, income measures the available money of the individual; (2) the reference category in these analyses is an indigenous person with only primary education and without a job (but on benefits); (3) there are missing values for the income of a substantial number of male and female respondents. They are not included in our analyses.

The estimates for income in Table 9.8 show that minority membership has something of the expected effect on income. Controlling for class, education, age, age-square and year of measurement, incomes of men from the Moroccan, Surinamese and Antillean minority groups of the first generation are significantly lower than the incomes of the comparable indigenous male population. For the second generation this is only true for the Surinamese, as other second-generation male migrants have incomes equal to their indigenous counterparts within the same occupational class.

Yet there is a remarkable feature in the estimates for women: the coefficients for female migrants of both generations are positive and significant, indicating that they have a larger income than their indigenous equals. Considering income differences between men and women it should be kept in mind that women who do not participate in the labour market are not earning an independent income nor have substantial social benefit rights. Several explanations for the gender differences could be suggested. It could be possible that the overall lower rate of labour-market participation of all women as compared to men has a levelling influence on the differences between minority women and indigenous women. A second explanation is that income-generating minority women are a stronger positive selection from the total population of all minority women than income-generating women from indigenous population are compared to indigenous women as a whole.

Table 9.9 then includes the significant interactions between migrant generation group and class, education and age. (The main effects of the control variables are not shown as they do not alter appreciably.) A large number of significant negative interactions exist, of which all but three indicate that first-generation male and female migrants earn lower incomes from jobs in all classes, from the salariat down to the unskilled manual class. One might suggest that this is just a consequence of the gross classes used in the analyses and the apparently lower positions of

Table 9.8. Regression of logged income (parameter estimates).

	Men		Women	
Intercept	**6.77**	(0.02)	**6.72**	(0.03)
Ancestry				
Native Dutch	0.0		0.0	
Turkish 1	0.00	(0.01)	**0.06**	(0.02)
Moroccan 1	**−0.05**	(0.01)	**0.09**	(0.03)
Surinamese 1	**−0.09**	(0.01)	**0.15**	(0.02)
Antillean 1	**−0.12**	(0.01)	**0.15**	(0.02)
Turkish 2	0.04	(0.03)	**0.15**	(0.04)
Moroccan 2	0.01	(0.04)	0.05	(0.05)
Surinamese 2	**−0.12**	(0.02)	**0.10**	(0.03)
Antillean 2	−0.02	(0.03)	0.05	(0.03)
Age/10	**0.53**	(0.01)	**0.35**	(0.02)
(Age/10)²	**−0.09**	(0.00)	**−0.08**	(0.01)
Education				
Primary	0.0		0.0	
Secondary lower	**0.07**	(0.01)	0.03	(0.02)
Secondary higher	**0.04**	(0.01)	**0.09**	(0.02)
Tertiary	**0.18**	(0.01)	**0.25**	(0.02)
Year				
1988	**−0.25**	(0.01)	**−0.26**	(0.02)
1991	**−0.10**	(0.01)	**−0.11**	(0.02)
1994	**−0.09**	(0.01)	**−0.11**	(0.02)
1998	0.0		0.0	
Class				
Salariat	**0.60**	(0.01)	**0.48**	(0.02)
Routine non-manual	**0.45**	(0.01)	**0.30**	(0.02)
Petty bourgeoisie	**0.46**	(0.02)	**0.20**	(0.03)
Skilled manual	**0.44**	(0.01)	0.04	(0.03)
Unskilled manual	**0.37**	(0.01)	**0.11**	(0.02)
Unemployed	0.0		0.0	
Adjusted R squared	0.50		0.28	
N	12,196		7,368	

Note: Standard errors are given in brackets; emboldened coefficients indicate significance at the 0.05 level or higher.

migrants within each of these classes; but we believe that this is a misleading explanation of these negative interaction terms, as main effects of age and education are controlled for within the model, and these control variables should take care of these assumed lower positions of migrants within the classes.

Another plausible explanation for these negative interactions between migrant generation and class may be high social benefits obtained outside the labour market by first-generation migrant groups compared to their indigenous equals. The still-generous Dutch social welfare system,

Table 9.9. Regression of logged income: interaction effects (parameter estimates).

	Men		Women	
Main effects of Ancestry				
Native Dutch	0.0		0.0	
Turkish 1	**0.40**	(0.02)	**0.17**	(0.04)
Moroccan 1	**0.24**	(0.02)	**0.10**	(0.05)
Surinamese 1	**0.11**	(0.02)	**0.19**	(0.02)
Antillean 1	**0.06**	(0.03)	**0.20**	(0.02)
Turkish 2	−0.13	(0.09)	**0.19**	(0.04)
Moroccan 2	**0.13**	(0.04)	−0.14	(0.08)
Surinamese 2	**−0.15**	(0.04)	**0.13**	(0.03)
Antillean 2	0.05	(0.03)	**0.15**	(0.06)
Significant interactions between ancestry and class				
Turkish 1 * salariat	**−0.25**	(0.04)	−0.14	(0.10)
Moroccan 1 * salariat	**−0.32**	(0.04)	**−0.28**	(0.12)
Surinamese 1 * salariat	−0.05	(0.03)	**−0.13**	(0.04)
Antillean 1 * salariat			−0.08	(0.05)
Turkish 1 * non-manual	**−0.26**	(0.04)	**−0.19**	(0.06)
Moroccan 1 * non-manual	**−0.27**	(0.04)	**−0.20**	(0.07)
Turkish 1 * PB	**−0.22**	(0.05)		
Moroccan 1 * PB	**−0.24**	(0.06)		
Surinamese 1* PB	−0.07	(0.03)		
Antillean 1* PB	**−0.29**	(0.09)		
Turkish 1 * skilled	**−0.26**	(0.03)		
Moroccan 1* skilled	**−0.23**	(0.03)		
Turkish 1 * unskilled	**−0.13**	(0.02)		
Turkish 2 * unskilled	**0.11**	(0.06)		
Moroccan 1 * unskilled	**−0.15**	(0.02)		
Moroccan 2 * unskilled			**0.40**	(0.12)
Surinamese 2 * unskilled	0.08	(0.06)	−0.19	(0.09)
Significant interactions between ancestry and education				
Turkish 1 * education	**−0.05**	(0.01)	**−0.07**	(0.02)
Moroccan 1 * education	**−0.04**	(0.01)		
Moroccan 2 * education			**−0.10**	(0.05)
Surinamese 1 * education			**−0.05**	(0.02)
Antillean 1 * education			**−0.07**	(0.02)
Significant interactions between ancestry and age				
Turkish 1 * age	**−0.16**	(0.01)	**−0.07**	(0.02)
Moroccan 1 * age	**−0.10**	(0.01)		
Moroccan 2 * age			**0.23**	(0.07)
Surinamese 1 * age	**−0.09**	(0.01)		
Surinamese 2 * age	**0.09**	(0.03)		
Antillean 1 * age	**−0.08**	(0.01)		
Antillean 2 * age			**−0.08**	(0.04)
Turkish 1 * year			**0.01**	(0.00)
Turkish 2 * year	**0.03**	(0.01)		
Moroccan 1 * year	**0.004**	(0.002)	0.01	(0.01)
Adjusted R squared	0.52		0.29	
N	12,196		7,368	

Note: Standard errors are given in brackets; emboldened coefficients indicate significance at the 0.05 level or higher. PB stands for petty bourgeoisie.

combined with special social policies directed at migrants, might have led to higher incomes for lower-educated older migrants outside the labour market compared to their equally low-educated older indigenous neighbour. If this second explanation is (also) correct, it can explain the erosion among the working classes and social-democrat voters of their former support for generous policies towards labour-migration. Interestingly, some second-generation migrants in the unskilled classes have higher incomes than their indigenous equals. We do not have a good explanation for this result, next to the suggestion that they might have more sources for income than the indigenous equals (illegal work in family business perhaps).

The lower yields of education, particularly for women of the first generation, suggest that they had a weaker position than their indigenous peers in obtaining the same amount of money. But first-generation male Turks and Moroccans also have lower yields from their education for their income. This result underpins a closure tendency within the Dutch labour market.

The lower yield of ageing on income among the first-generation male migrants might reflect this closure tendency of Dutch society. However, another explanation might be that social benefits are generally independent of the age of the receiver and that thus the income of the first-generations migrants, who received mostly social security at a relatively young age, did not change with their age.

Conclusion

From the analyses of the position of ethnic minorities in the Dutch labour market, the following conclusions can be derived.

Among men, minority group membership has definite negative effects on labour-market participation and unemployment. Controlling for level of education, age and economic fluctuations, the chances of labour-market participation for ethnic minority men are consistently lower than for indigenous men and their risk of unemployment is consistently higher. This pattern is evident among both generations, but holds for the second generation less than for the first.

For women the patterns of participation and unemployment are more complex. There are differences between ethnic groups and differences associated with migrant generation. For the first generation, as far as participation is concerned, there is a sharp divide between, on one side, Turkish and Moroccan women and, on the other, Surinamese and Antillean women.

While Turkish and Moroccan women participate at considerably lower levels than indigenous women, Surinamese and Antillean women participate at higher levels than their indigenous peers. Among second-generation women, however, these differences in participation have disappeared (with the exception of Moroccan women). Second-generation women also have a smaller risk of unemployment than the first generation; however this risk remains higher than the risk for indigenous women, and differs somewhat by ethnic group.

The distribution of ethnic minorities across occupational classes reveals a consistent pattern. For the second generation, again controlling for level of education, age and economic fluctuation, the chances of being in a particular occupational class are the same as for the indigenous population, with the exception of the salariat which remains more closed to migrants. This result holds for men as well as for women. But the distribution of the first generation within occupational classes is strikingly different from the distribution of the second generation. In most cases the odds of first-generation migrants being in a class higher than manual worker are considerably lower than the odds for comparable indigenous workers.

After controlling for education, age, occupational class and year, first-generation migrants also have lower incomes than the indigenous population. A possible explanation for this finding could be the relatively high level of social benefits which lower-educated older migrants receive compared to their similarly low-educated older indigenous neighbours. The higher social benefits might be an unintended consequence of the Dutch social welfare system, which developed various special policies directed to migrant groups. Some second-generation ethnic groups who have an unskilled job have higher incomes than the comparable indigenous people. The lower yield of age and education for the male and female first generation suggests a closure tendency in the Dutch labour market, especially for the better educated.

To what extent are these results new? Compared with recent publications (Tesser, Merens and van Praag 1999; Dagevos 2001) using the same type of data, our results on labour-market participation and unemployment are not contradictory, although we make the distinction between first- and second-generation migrants (due to our combining the SPVA data), and thus can see the progress of the second generation in their labour-market participation. However, because these publications focus largely on the lower strata of the migrants, there is no comparable analysis of the SPVA data on the chances of entrance to the different occupational classes. In particular, the lower odds of entrance into the salariat of the second generation have not been studied before. The same holds for income—one will not find a section on income in these publications. This omission might be explained by the dominant definition of the migrant problem (low education and bad entrance to the labour market) and by the political incorrectness of comparing the amount of social security benefits obtained by various migrant groups to those obtained by the indigenous population.

What do the results tell us about the two theoretical perspectives on stratification: modernisation and social closure? At first sight the results are rather confusing. Results for men generally support the thesis of social closure for minorities, but there is one important exception: the equal participation chances of second-generation minority men in most of the higher occupational classes. However, one could maintain that the unequal access of the second generation to the salariat provides further evidence of a closure tendency, as the other classes are less accretive.

Aside from their lower odds of entrance to the salariat, our results could be interpreted as showing that men of the second generation are less likely to be affected by social closure, perhaps because they exhibit fewer ethnic characteristics (such as a lack of fluency in the Dutch language) that trigger exclusion than did first-generation men. However if this argument is valid, what explains the continued lower levels of labour-market participation among the second generation, or their increased risk of unemployment?

One possible explanation for these results might be that the second generation has survived a more severe selection at the entrance to the labour market than the indigenous workforce. One might assume that entrance selection follows the logic of social closure, hence the results on labour-market participation and unemployment support closure for the second generation as well as for the first. However, those second-generation migrants who survive the entrance selection are hired more or less according to the same rules as the indigenous workforce: occupational class is largely determined by human capital. By successfully entering the labour market, minority members have shown that they possess the necessary qualifications to compete with the indigenous workforce on an equal footing.

However, there is another possible interpretation of the same results. The more severe entrance selection of the second generation would normally have produced higher positions within the occupational class structure, compared to the less selective indigenous workforce. The absence of this positive effect of the more severe entrance selection for the second generation suggests the existence of social closure not only at the entrance but also *within* the labour market. In this interpretation the positive effect of a more severe selection balances the negative effect of social closure at the labour market.

Then the mirror question comes up regarding the first generation: why does the selection process not apply to their position in the occupational class structure? The main result from our analyses is that the two driving forces in advances within the labour market (age and education) pay off less for the first generation. This result might be caused by problems of recognition of educational and occupational qualifications, but might also be caused by closure, especially in the higher strata of society and thus within the labour market. Another argument is that in the first generation there is much less variance in various characteristics within ethnic groups; most variance, rather, is between groups. This between-group variance indeed has its effects on chances in the occupational structure as can be derived from the better odds for Surinamese and Antillean minorities vs. Turks and Moroccans in obtaining higher positions within the occupational structure.

The more severe selection argument could also serve to explain some of the deviating results among women. However, an unknown part of the entrance selection among women is that there is likely to be more self-selection. Thus women who decide to participate on the labour market, regardless of their ethnic background, have characteristics that distinguish them from the women who decide not to participate. Social closure may operate less among women because of the greater importance of self-selection. Not participating on the labour market for women is likely a more attractive alternative than for men. However, an alternative interpretation of the women's results could argue that the social closure for second-generation women is balanced by the positive effect of the more severe entrance selection, because they are an even more selective group at the entrance to the labour market than second-generation men.

Certainly the special position of Surinamese and Antillean women may have to do with cultural factors. In particular, marriage and partnership relations among Surinamese and Antillean men and women tend to be very unstable. Thus, many Surinamese women cannot trust that a man will take responsibility for the common household, and she subsequently orients herself to being economically independent.

Our findings do not therefore allow us an unambiguous answer to our question about equal opportunities or closure. While many of our results are consistent with modernisation theory, the continued high levels of unemployment among second-generation men, and their difficulties in gaining access to the salariat, suggest that social closure plays continues to play some role in Dutch society, although problems of selection prevent us from saying categorically how large that role is.

Appendix

SPVA data sets provide four surveys of samples of households from the four largest immigrant ethnic minority groups (Turks, Moroccans, Surinamese and Antilleans). SPVA surveys on these four immigrant groups have been conducted in 1988, 1991, 1994 and 1998, on behalf of the Social and Cultural Planning Office (an independent governmental agency monitoring social-cultural developments in Dutch society). Other ethnic minorities (like Chinese or West African) are not included in the SPVA samples as their position is not considered as problematic by Dutch authorities which have financed these samples. More information on the *Social and Cultural Planning Office* can be found at <http://www.scp.nl/miss/spva.htm>.

An individual is classified into a minority group if he or she was born in the respective country or if one of their parents was born there. Turks and Moroccans whose parents had different countries of birth hardly exist. This is less true for Surinamese and Antillean parents, one of whom might not have been born in Suriname or Antilles; nonetheless a more restricted definition (e.g., both parents born in Suriname or Antilles) would misrepresent the mixed nature of these ethnic groups due to the long-standing colonial relations between Suriname, the Antilles and the Netherlands (longer than the British relation with India). As a consequence, the racial composition of Antillean and Surinamese ethnic minorities is relatively heterogeneous, reflecting the mixed racial composition of these societies (African, Indonesian, Hindu, Jewish, White), although a majority do belong to 'visible minorities' of various skin colours.

The SPVA samples of the minority groups are two-stage samples: for reasons of efficiency the samples are drawn in a limited number of municipalities in which ethnic minorities are concentrated. First only those municipalities with high concentrations of these four ethnic groups were selected. The four largest municipalities (Amsterdam, Rotterdam, The Hague and Utrecht) are among the selected municipalities; 80% of these four ethnic groups live in these selected municipalities. Then a sample of the relevant households was drawn from the civic register of that municipality. The SPVA samples are representative of the four ethnic populations from which they are drawn; however, while the group samples are roughly of the same size, the total sample is not proportional to the total size of the four groups within the Dutch population. In each year the sample size of the subgroups is approximately the same, except for the last. In 1998 the sample size was augmented by a factor 1.5.

Each of the surveys contains a comparison group of households from the indigenous population. The comparison sample is drawn in the same municipalities as the minority samples. Therefore it is not representative of the whole indigenous population, because municipalities without minorities had no chance of entering the first stage of the SPVA samples. As a consequence of white flight to the latter municipalities, the richer and more highly educated sections of the indigenous population are under-represented. However, analyses have shown that this under-representation of municipalities with few migrants hardly affects the strength of the correlations.

Data have been obtained by interviewing the head of the sampled household. In the interview a standardised questionnaire is used. A shortened form of the questionnaire is presented to all other members of the household 12 years of age and older. To diminish extraneous influences on the relations under study, analyses are constrained to persons 18–59 years of age.

Response rates have averaged around 60% in 1988, 1991 and 1994 but were slightly lower in 1998, varying from 48% to 61% in the different municipalities.

Membership of minority groups

As mentioned, membership of minority groups is determined by country of birth of a person and/or his or her parents. Five groups are compared: Turks, Moroccans, Surinamese, Antilleans and the indigenous population.

Immigrant status

Immigrant status classifies members of minority groups into a first generation and a second generation. Minority group members who are born in their home country or who immigrated after six years of age are considered first generation, whilst minority group members either born in the Netherlands or who immigrated before six years of age are classified as second generation.

As a consequence of the Dutch migration history, there are many more first-generation members than second-generation among 18–59 year-olds. Moreover, as the members of the second generation are much younger, they have less labour-market experience. Additionally, they are concentrated in the 1994 and (especially) the 1998 surveys.

Human capital

Variation in human capital is represented by levels of educational attainment. The variable has four classes: (1) primary or less; (2) secondary lower; (3) secondary higher; (4) tertiary.

Demand and supply fluctuations on the labour market

The different years in which the data are collected are characterised by different levels of economic activity, accompanied by fluctuations in demand and supply on the labour market. The year variable is treated as a proxy for fluctuations of the economy.

Gender

A straightforward measure with two categories: men and women.

Age

Measured in years and taken into account because the two migrant generations differ in their age and deviate from the indigenous Dutch population as a consequence of the migration processes. The age-square term is added to the equations to account for the non-linear relation between age and labour market outcomes.

References

Blau, P. M. and Duncan, O. D. (1967), *The American Occupational Structure* (New York: Wiley).

Dagevos, J. M. (2001), *Rapportage Minderheden 2001. Deel II Meer werk* (The Hague: Sociaal en Cultureel Planbureau).

de Beer, P. T. (2001), *Over Werken in de Postindustriele Samenleving* (The Hague: SCP).

Gans, H. J. (1990), 'Deconstructing the underclass', *Journal of the American Planning Association*, 56, 271–7.

Jencks, C. (1992), *Rethinking Social Policy: Race, Poverty, and the Underclass* (New York: Harper-Perennial).

Murphy, R. (1988), *Social Closure, the Theory of Monopolization and Exclusion* (Oxford: Clarendon Press).

Parkin, F. (1974), 'Strategies of social closure in class formation'. In F. Parkin (ed.), *The Social Analysis of Class Structure* (London: Tavistock), pp. 1–18.

Tesser, P. T. M., Merens, J. G. F., and van Praag, C. S. (1999), *Rapportage Minderheden 1999. Positie in het Onderwijs en op de Arbeidsmarkt* (The Hague: SCP).

Wilson, W. J. (1987), *The Truly Disadvantaged: The Inner City, the Underclass, and Public Policy* (Chicago: University of Chicago Press).

Wright, E. O. (1985), *Classes* (London: Verso).

10

The Legacy of *Apartheid*: Racial Inequalities in the New South Africa

DONALD J. TREIMAN

Summary. The legacy of 350 years of *apartheid* practice and fifty years of concerted *apartheid* policy has been to create racial differences in socio-economic position larger than in any other nation in the world. Whites, who constitute 11% of the population, enjoy levels of education, occupational status, and income similar to and in many respects superior to those of the industrially developed nations of Europe and the British diaspora. Within the White population, however, there is a sharp distinction between the one-third of English origin and the two-thirds of Afrikaner origin. Despite *apartheid* policies explicitly designed to improve the lot of Afrikaners at the expense of non-Whites, the historical difference between the two groups continues to be seen in socio-economic differences at the end of the twentieth century. Still, the disadvantages of Afrikaners are modest compared to those of non-Whites, particularly Coloureds and Blacks, who bear the brunt of *apartheid* policies. Ethnic penalties are especially large for people with lower levels of education. For those with less than a tertiary education, there appears to be an occupational floor under Whites and an occupational ceiling over non-Whites. For the small minority of Blacks and Coloureds with tertiary education, the likelihood of being employed and the kinds of jobs available differ relatively little from the opportunities of Asians and Whites; but for the vast majority lacking tertiary education the ethnic penalty is very large, particularly for Blacks. Most are unable even to find work, with about 40% of Black men and more than half of Black women unemployed; and those who are employed are relegated largely to semi- and unskilled jobs. Although tertiary education minimises racial differences in occupational opportunities, it has little effect on racial differences in income, which are large even among the well educated and even among those working in similar occupations.

Introduction

SOUTH AFRICA, WITH A CURRENT POPULATION of about 45 million, is a country of unusual sociological interest, in large part because until 1994 it was the only remaining national society whose political system and state institutions were explicitly designed to secure the advantage of one ethnic group at the expense of the remainder of the population. In South Africa, a small minority, consisting of immigrants from Europe, dominated the majority from the seventeenth century until the 1994 transformation to a non-racial democracy. It is thus of great interest, on both theoretical and policy grounds, to understand how the system of racial domination was organised and what its consequences have been for the socio-economic opportunities and achievements of South Africa's component racial groups. This paper addresses the consequences—the racial inequalities left as a legacy of the *apartheid* system of racial domination in place from 1948 through 1994.

South Africa's four official racial groups ('Whites', 11% of the population in 1996; 'Asians', 3%; 'Coloureds', 9%; and 'Blacks', 77%)[1] differ substantially in their income and other socio-economic attributes. In 1996, non-White men, who together constituted 81% of the male labour force, on average earned 23% of what White men earned, up from 19% in 1991 and 15% in 1980 (Treiman, McKeever, and Fodor 1996: 112).[2] Thus, at the dawn of the new South African dispensation, racial

[1] Computations from the 1996 census. Although there are many ethnic distinctions within racial categories, almost all statistical tables published by the South African Central Statistical Service (now known as Statistics South Africa) are divided on the basis of race, using these four categories, a usage that has held from at least the 1904 census continuously through the 2001 census. For convenience, I refer to these groups without quotation marks.
[2] The increase in the non-White/White ratio is surely an under-estimate since the 1980 and 1991 ratios exclude the TVBC States, *bantustans* hived off from South Africa from the early 1970s until 1994 in an effort to increase the White fraction of the population and reduce the cost of providing for poor rural Blacks (Thompson 1990). About a quarter of the Black population of South Africa lived in the TVBC States, and they were disproportionately impoverished even relative to the Black population as a whole.

differences in South Africa were far larger than in other multi-ethnic countries. For example, in the US, Black males in 2000 earned, on average, about 67% of what non-Hispanic White males earned (US Bureau of the Census 2001). In Israel, Arabs in 1983 earned 63% of what Jews earned (Semyonov 1988). This paper extends previous work analysing racial differences in occupational status and income in South Africa in 1980 and 1991 (Treiman *et al.* 1996), using data from the most recent South African census available for scholarly use—that conducted in 1996.[3] Before describing these data, I briefly review the history and social structure of South Africa.

A (very brief) introduction to the social demography of South Africa[4]

The earliest known residents of what is now South Africa were hunters and herders known as the Khoi, who are genetically related to the present day San people ('Bushmen') of the Kalihari desert of Botswana. The influx of Bantu-speaking herders from Central Africa, starting in the fourth century AD, had driven the Khoi into a relatively small area near present-day Cape Town, which is where employees of the Dutch East India Company found them when they established a refuelling station in 1652. Unions between Dutch men and Khoi women resulted in what is now known as the 'Coloured' population, genetically enriched by later unions with slaves imported from elsewhere in Africa and from the Dutch East Indies, particularly Malaysia and Indonesia, and with people from the Indian subcontinent who arrived in the late nineteenth century.

Over the 200 years subsequent to first contact, the Dutch settlers, supplemented by French Huguenots and Germans, gradually spread east and then north, subsisting as semi-migratory cattle herders (*trekboers* in Afrikaans, literally 'wandering farmers') in much the same manner as the Bantu-speaking people who already occupied the areas into which the Afrikaners, as the European settlers came to be known, were moving. A series of clashes ensued, almost always won by the Afrikaners due

---

[3] A similar micro-data public use sample from the 2001 census is scheduled for imminent release but as of this writing is not yet available.
[4] This account draws heavily on Houghton (1976), McLaughlin (1981), Davenport (1987), and Thompson (1990).

to their superiority in fire arms. The Afrikaners remained a largely rural, ill-educated, and poor population until well into the twentieth century.

In 1820, after the acquisition of South Africa by Britain following the Napoleonic Wars, English settlers began to arrive. The English from the outset established themselves as an urban commercial class, and also as the governing class of South African society.

In 1867 diamonds were discovered, and seventeen years later gold, both discoveries fuelling a large influx of skilled miners and those seeking commercial opportunities from England and other parts of Europe, and creating the foundation for South Africa's industrial development. The technology required to exploit the gold reserves also had profound implications. Since the gold-bearing ore was of low grade, its profitable extraction required large capital outlays and low labour costs. The solution of the mining companies was to pay a small number of White miners high wages and a large army of Black labourers very low wages, but to force Blacks to take work in the mines (and on White farms) by instituting a hut tax, payable in money. Even the hut tax was not sufficient to induce Blacks to work on sugar cane plantations established by English commercial farmers in Natal, so indentured agricultural labourers were imported from the Indian subcontinent, starting in 1860 and continuing until 1911 (Thompson 1990:100).

An attempt in 1921 to substitute Black for White labour in the mines, and thereby further reduce the wage bill, led to a major strike on the part of the White workers—ironically, led by the communists—which ended in suppression by the army but achieved its intended effect in 1924 with the election of a Nationalist–Labour coalition government and enactment of the 'Civilized Labour Policy' establishing wage differentials based on race and the restriction of certain categories of employment to Whites. The following seventy years were marked by a variety of policies designed to ensure the continuing advantage of the White population, and particularly the upward mobility of the Afrikaner population. These policies cannot be detailed here, but their result has been to sharply reduce the difference in socio-economic status between the Afrikaners and English-speaking Whites. In 1948 the National Party gained a majority (only Whites and, in Cape Province, Coloured men with substantial property, could vote), and immediately began formalising customary racial distinctions and creating new ones. Every individual was officially classified by race; interracial marriage was made illegal; residential segregation was instituted, together with racial restrictions on where commercial property could be owned; jobs were reserved for people of specified race, and unemployment compensation for Blacks was abolished; a separate educational authority for Blacks was established; and, to consolidate White power, Coloureds were dropped from the electoral rolls and, under the pretext of the suppression of communism, the government was empowered to declare unlawful any organisation or publication it considered 'subversive'.

Two other policies were instituted to bolster the relative size of the White population. Early in the century, some 13% of the land area of South Africa—mainly the least productive land in the country—had been designated as Black 'homelands'. During the 1960s and 1970s, 3.5 million Blacks were 'removed' from the cities to their nominal 'homelands', often places where neither they nor their ancestors had lived (Platzky and Walker 1985; Davenport 1987). Then, in the 1970s, four of the ten homelands (the 'TVBC' States: Transkei, Venda, Bophutatswana, and Ceskei) were set up as puppet states, nominally independent from South Africa. As of 1991, the last date for which there are adequate data, some 38% of the Black population of (internationally recognised) South Africa lived in the six homelands still included within the 'South African' polity and 24% lived in the TVBC States. The rural areas of the homelands and TVBC States were—and no doubt still are—extremely economically marginal. The land was not productive and there were no non-agricultural jobs to speak of, which meant that residents either commuted extremely long distances to work in 'White' South Africa or became migrant labourers, leaving behind a population disproportionately consisting of women, children, and the elderly.

Second, selective immigration of Whites to South Africa was encouraged. Although White immigration (there was virtually no non-White immigration) was sharply curtailed in 1948 for fear that immigrants would dilute the Afrikaner majority, the situation soon changed: as neighbouring Southern African states acquired independence their White populations were welcomed to South Africa. This, of course, produced a selective migration of people uncomfortable with Black rule. In addition, immigration from Europe gradually began to be encouraged. This is not the place to recount the collapse of *apartheid*. Suffice it to say that a combination of the resources and energy necessary to sustain the domination by force of a huge majority by a small minority; increasing pressure from the business elite for more efficient use of labour, which required improving Black education; the increasing toll of the international boycott, which created both economic hardship and a strong sense of isolation; and an increasingly successful campaign of non-White resistance, led first to the gradual relaxation of racial restrictions, starting in the 1980s, and ultimately to a negotiated transition to a non-racial government in 1994.[5]

The analysis reported here, which is based on data from the 1996 census, conducted two and a half years after the April 1994 election, can thus be seen as a description of the extent and pattern of racial inequality at the point of transition, establishing a baseline against which attempts by the new government to reduce racial inequalities can be measured.

Data and racial/ethnic classification

This analysis is based on data from a 10% public use micro-data sample from the 1996 Census of South Africa (Statistics South Africa 1996). In keeping with the specifications for the comparative project of which this paper is a part, the analysis is restricted to people aged 18–59. Since there was some undercount of the population, all the analysis utilises 'person weights' designed to correct for differential undercount.[6]

Racial/ethnic classification

As noted above, South African statistics always distinguish four racial groups: Whites, Asians, Coloureds, and Blacks. Each of these groups can be further subdivided on the basis of the language spoken at home, religion, and national origin. It is already known that socio-economic differentiation within races is small relative to between-race differences (Treiman *et al.* 1996). However, to permit detailed cross-national comparisons, the authors of each chapter have been charged to present descriptive statistics for all of the major ethnic groups within each nation. Here I start by presenting basic statistics for a twenty-eight-category classification, designed to ensure at least 1,000 people in each category in the sample, or 10,000 in the population. The subsequent analysis is based on a reduced set of categories.

---

[5] For a fascinating account of the dynamics involved in the decision by the Nationalist Party leadership to voluntarily relinquish power, see Emery (2001).

[6] The undercount was quite substantial—10.7% of the population, as estimated from a post-enumeration survey—and was most substantial among young adult males, as it is in virtually all societies. Also, the undercount was greater for Blacks and Coloureds than for Whites, and greater for Whites than for Asians. See Statistics South Africa (1998: ch. 4) for details.

The twenty-eight-category classification, shown in Table 10.1, was created on the basis of information from four variables — race,[7] home language,[8] religion,[9] and place of birth[10]—which I combined using my best judgement as to what constitute meaningful ethnic groups in the South African context. Here are the details.

Whites. The primary division of Whites in South Africa, which has persisted for nearly two centuries and is still important today, is between Afrikaners and English-speaking Whites (Thompson 1990). As noted above, the Afrikaner population began as *trekboers* and then, as the mines developed and the cities grew, began to fill skilled manual jobs. As we will see, their lower socio-economic status, relative to English-speaking Whites, persists today, although in muted form. The English-speaking White population consists mainly of the descendants of those who came to South Africa in the nineteenth century, as an economic and political elite. However, there are important subgroups within the English-speaking population:[11] Jews, who began to arrive in the late nineteenth century and played an important role in the development of mining and other industries, and who remain a distinctive community[12] (Lever 1978, 1979); immigrants from Great Britain; and immigrants from other African nations, who fled Black rule after independence. In addition, I have formed a residual category of English-speaking Whites from other nations. Four other groups complete the White population: a visible Portuguese[13] community, consisting mainly of those who left Portuguese

---

[7] The census question was 'How would (the person) describe him-/herself?' The listed response categories were 'African/Black', 'Coloured', 'Indian/Asian', and 'White'.

[8] The census question was 'Which language does (the person) speak MOST OFTEN AT HOME? Write the language in the space provided.'

[9] The census question was 'What is (the person's) religion, denomination or belief? Please state the complete name or official abbreviation e.g. Apostolic Faith Mission; Catholic Church; Dutch Reformed Church; Hindu Faith; Muslim Faith; Zion Christian Church (ZCC). If no religion, write "none".'

[10] The census questions were 'Was (the person) born in South Africa? (Include the former Transkei, Bophuthatswana, Venda, Ciskei—TBVC states).' 'If "no", In what country was the person born? Write in the name of the country.'

[11] Those whose home language is neither English nor Afrikaans generally prefer to speak English, both because it is the elite language and because Afrikaans was regarded as the language of the oppressor. Many—including European immigrants, Asians, and upwardly mobile Coloureds and Blacks—adopt English as a new home language. Only among those whose home language is similar to Afrikaans (German and Dutch speakers) does any sizeable fraction become Afrikaans speakers.

[12] The Jewish category includes all Whites who identified as Jews on the religion question.

[13] The Portuguese category includes all Whites who either speak Portuguese at home or were born in Portugal or in former Portuguese territories.

Africa after independence, and who tended to become small shopkeepers in South Africa; Germans,[14] the largest among several European immigrant groups; and two residual categories of Whites speaking languages other than English or Afrikaans: those born in South Africa and those born abroad.

Asians. I divided Asians into three groups on the basis of religion: Muslims, Hindus, and those who practice other religions (mostly Christians). Historically, Muslims and Hindus have differed in socio-economic status because they differed at the outset—during the great immigration at the end of the nineteenth century, Muslims were much more likely than Hindus to have paid their own passage and to have arrived in South Africa with some capital (Pachai 1971: 7). The third group, those of other religion, are mainly converts from Hinduism (Oosthuizen 1979: 545), although this category also includes the descendants of the 60,000 Chinese imported during the first few years of the twentieth century to work in the mines (Richardson 1982), as well as a few foreign-born East Asians, mainly from Taiwan, living in South Africa for commercial reasons. Even combining all people of Chinese descent, the group is too small to treat separately.

Coloureds. The Coloured population, formed from unions between Afrikaners and various Black and Asian populations (see above), is culturally similar to the White Afrikaner population—they mainly are Afrikaans-speaking and members of the same Christian denominations. However, there are two distinctive small subgroups of Coloureds—Muslims (7% of Coloureds) and English-speakers (14% of Coloureds), although the latter group may reflect the consequences of upward mobility more than anything else (Patterson 1953: 167; Thomas 1982).

Blacks. Blacks are subdivided on the basis of home language, except that a separate category, foreign-born Blacks, is added (these are mostly migrant workers from neighbouring Southern African states), as is a residual category, 'Other Blacks'. There are two main groups of Blacks, Zulus (30% of the Black population) and Xhosas (22% of the Black population), but there are nine language groups in all, plus the two additional categories.

Race unspecified/Griqua. Finally, a small group of people who either failed to specify their race or who claimed to be 'Griquas' is treated as a

---

[14] The German category includes all Whites who either speak German at home or were born in Germany.

separate category. Griquas are mixed race people who in the nineteenth century were expelled from the Cape Town to the Northern Cape area and then were expelled again to what is now Transkei. The expectation of Statistics South Africa was that they would be counted as 'Coloured', but after protests they were allocated to the 'Other race' category (Christopher 2002: 406).

Socio-economic differentials by race/ethnicity

Table 10.1 provides a summary of the socio-economic characteristics of each of these twenty-eight groups, which are arrayed by race and within race by median income. (See Appendix 1 for details of the coding of education and income.) As would be expected from the *apartheid* history of South Africa, even the least advantaged White groups—Afrikaners and Portuguese—have far higher incomes than any non-White group, and on average Whites have about twice the incomes of Asians, nearly four times the incomes of Coloureds, and more than five times the incomes of Blacks. Whites are also far less likely to be unemployed, followed in order by Asians, Coloureds, and Blacks, among whom more than 40% are unemployed. Finally, there are substantial differences both between and within racial groups in the likelihood of working at high status occupations—non-manual jobs and also professional and managerial jobs (hereafter referred to as the 'salariat'). Interestingly, within-race differences in occupational distribution are not the simple consequence of within-race differences in educational attainment, which tend to be relatively small, although Whites enjoy a nearly two year advantage over Asians, who in turn have a two year advantage over Coloureds and a three year advantage over Blacks. There are several noteworthy distinctions between ethnic groups within each of the race categories.

Whites. First, Jews continue to be an elite group among South African Whites, enjoying the highest incomes together with immigrants from England and Germany, and also are disproportionately engaged in high-status occupations, with nearly 90% working in non-manual jobs and nearly two-thirds in the salariat. Second, Afrikaners have not yet achieved equality with English-speaking South-African-born Whites; although nearly equally well-educated, they have lower incomes and are less likely to work at non-manual jobs and, specifically at jobs in the salariat. Third, although—as noted above—the least advantaged Whites have substantially higher incomes than members of any other racial group, they are

Table 10.1. Socio-economic characteristics by race/ethnicity and nativity.

Race/Ethnicity (Country of birth in parentheses)[a]	Education (mean years)[c]	Econ. active (%)	Unemployed (%)[d]	Non-manual (%)[e]	Salariat (%)[e]	Median income (000s)[f]	% of Population
Whites							
English HL[b] (Gt. Britain)	12.2	80.2	2.9	80.8	56.7	51,481	0.36
Germans	12.9	66.4	3.2	75.8	57.6	50,172	0.10
Jews	12.9	76.2	2.8	87.2	63.8	49,898	0.15
English HL (Other)	12.3	57.5	3.4	79.9	56.3	49,093	0.38
Other Whites (FB)	12.1	67.2	5.0	72.2	54.5	44,293	0.07
English HL (Oth. Africa)	12.4	82.0	3.1	80.1	52.8	43,675	0.27
English HL (SA)	12.2	77.6	4.3	78.3	50.1	41,054	3.61
Portuguese	10.5	72.5	4.0	70.5	43.4	37,092	0.11
Afrikaans HL	11.9	70.4	4.6	68.7	37.5	34,338	7.12
Other Whites (SA)	11.0	62.7	8.3	61.9	35.8	27,356	0.21
Total	12.0	72.5	4.4	72.9	43.5	37,659	12.38
Asians							
Moslem	10.4	62.1	11.7	72.4	40.3	21,051	0.65
Hindu	10.3	66.0	11.6	60.3	31.4	19,217	1.52
Other religion	10.1	65.1	13.0	57.3	29.3	18,016	0.82
Total	10.2	64.9	12.0	62.2	32.8	19,240	2.99
Coloureds							
English HL (Other)	10.6	75.8	13.2	60.6	30.4	21,599	1.28
Moslem	9.4	69.5	18.5	42.2	19.2	15,075	0.63
Afrikaans HL (Other)	7.7	69.8	21.8	25.1	10.6	8,449	7.42
Total	8.2	70.6	20.3	31.7	14.2	10,580	9.33

Blacks							
Pedi/North Sotho	7.4	56.8	43.7	29.7	15.6	8,154	8.15
Venda	7.6	60.0	45.1	33.0	17.4	8,106	1.82
Tswana	7.3	65.8	39.7	27.9	13.7	7,903	8.21
Foreign born	5.2	86.4	14.2	10.1	5.6	7,846	1.64
Zulu	7.0	61.1	45.9	25.7	12.5	7,337	22.01
Xhosa	7.1	58.2	47.6	24.3	12.8	7,123	16.41
Ndebele	6.8	61.7	41.7	19.8	9.0	6,913	1.41
Shangaan	6.8	56.8	42.9	27.3	13.8	6,863	3.48
Other (SA)	7.6	68.9	20.4	25.8	13.7	6,819	1.45
Swazi	6.7	59.6	39.1	25.2	12.3	6,253	2.20
Sotho/South Sotho	7.6	67.4	39.1	23.0	10.8	6,180	7.70
Total	7.1	61.6	42.6	25.2	12.6	7,306	74.48
Race unspecified/Griqua	8.8	62.9	23.7	46.4	25.8	13,821	0.81
Total	7.9	63.9	33.8	36.9	19.8	10,614	99.99
N	1,777,064	1,864,017	1,191,431	704,206	704,206	759,978	1,864,017

[a] See text for details on how the race/ethnic classification was created.
[b] 'HL' means 'home language', the language spoken most often at home. See note 8.
[c] See Appendix 1 for details of the coding of education.
[d] Among those economically active.
[e] Among those employed and with a codable occupation. 'Non-manual' occupations are those in categories 1110–4223, 5111–13, and 5161–220 of the 1988 International Standard Classification of Occupations (ILO 1990): Legislators, Senior Officials and Managers; Professionals; Technicians and Associate Professionals; Clerks; and, within Service Workers and Shop and Market Sales Workers, subcategories 'Travel Attendants and Related Workers', 'Protective Services Workers', 'Fashion and Other Models', and 'Shop Salespersons and Demonstrators. The 'salariat' consists of EGP categories I and II (Erikson and Goldthorpe 1992: 35–47). See the discussion by Heath and Cheung in Chapter 1 of this volume.
[f] Among those employed. Annual income in South African Rand. See appendix 1 for details of the measure.

not much different from Asians and elite Coloureds in their likelihood of obtaining salariat positions. Thus, there is clear evidence (which will be documented below) of a racial penalty with respect to income, net of education and occupational status.

Asians. As expected, Muslims have somewhat higher status occupations than either Hindus or Asians of other religions. However, in these data the three groups are very similar with respect to income, in sharp contrast to the situation in 1980 and 1991 when Muslims had substantially higher incomes (Treiman *et al.* 1996: 115).

Coloureds. Note that with the exception of the small Muslim and English-speaking groups, the Coloured population has little more schooling than many of the Black groups, is no more likely to hold non-manual or salariat jobs, and at the median has incomes hardly larger. The higher status of Muslims probably reflects the similarity between their origins and those of Muslim Asians. Although the Coloured population includes some descendants of Malaysian and Indonesian slaves, these were very small populations and it is much more likely that some Muslims got arbitrarily classified as 'Coloured' during the rushed classification process resulting from passage of the Population Registration Act of 1950. The relatively high status of English-speaking Coloureds is perhaps misleading, and an argument could be made that they should not be distinguished from other Coloureds since their choice of language may well be a *consequence* rather than a *determinant* of their socio-economic status; successful Coloureds may switch from Afrikaans to English in an effort to consolidate their status gains. Unfortunately, I have no data with which to test this conjecture.

Blacks. Although, for reasons that are not at all clear, the Venda, who live in the far north of South Africa, have the highest percentages employed in non-manual jobs and in the salariat, and nearly the highest incomes, the remaining Black groups are, with one exception, relatively similar. The exception is the foreign born, who come mainly from other Southern African nations on short term labour contracts to staff the mines and to do other manual jobs. This recruitment source means that they are a distinctive group—less well-educated than the typical South African Black, much more likely to do manual work, and far less likely to be unemployed. They are mostly men, living apart from their families. They are in South Africa to work, and when there is no work they go, or are sent, home.

Immigration to South Africa

In keeping with the thrust of the comparative project, I carry out some analysis of immigration patterns before turning to the main story, which is one of racial distinctions among native South Africans. For this purpose, I distinguish English-speaking Whites, Afrikaans-speaking Whites, and 'other Whites'—those speaking a language other than English or Afrikaans at home.

Table 10.2 shows the distribution of the adult population (aged 18 to 59) by race and gender. In fact, there are no gender distinctions of note. For only a small fraction of the population is race unspecified. These people are dropped from further analysis. Among Whites, 3.3% speak a language other than English or Afrikaans at home; these 'other Whites', constituting only 0.4% of the population, are retained only for this and the following tables and are then dropped. Note that a majority of Whites (58%) are Afrikaans-speaking.

The only groups with substantial immigration from foreign countries are English-speaking Whites and the small fraction of 'other Whites'. Nonetheless, Table 10.3 lists, for all but Coloureds, for whom the percentage foreign-born is extremely small, the nations contributing at least 2% of the immigrant pool. From Table 10.3 it is evident that by far the largest group of foreign-born English speakers is from England and the bulk of the remainder are from Anglophone African nations, mainly Zimbabwe, which has always had close ties with South Africa (recall that Zimbabwe was formerly Southern Rhodesia).

Table 10.2. Distribution of the South African adult population by race/ethnicity and gender (table percentages).

	Male	Female	Total	Percent foreign-born
Whites: English home language	5.0	4.7	4.8	18.2
Whites: Afrikaans home language	7.3	6.9	7.1	2.1
Other Whites	0.4	0.4	0.4	38.0
Asians	3.0	2.9	3.0	2.3
Coloureds	9.4	9.3	9.3	0.3
Blacks	74.1	74.9	74.5	2.3
Race unspecified	0.8	0.8	0.8	3.2
Total	100.0	99.9	99.9	3.0
N	892,228	971,789	1,864,017	

Table 10.3. Main countries of origin of foreign-born South Africans.

Whites: English home language		Whites: Afrikaans home language		Other Whites		Asians		Blacks	
Country	%	Country	%	Country	%	Country	%	Country	%
England	42.1	Namibia	44.4	Portugal	17.2	India	39.6	Mozambique	46.4
Zimbabwe	20.5	Zimbabwe	14.3	Germany	15.4	Taiwan	15.2	Lesotho	29.2
Zambia	5.1	Netherlands	11.1	Italy	6.1	Pakistan	5.3	Zimbabwe	7.7
Germany	3.0	Zambia	5.6	Greece	5.1	Hong Kong	4.9	Swaziland	5.8
Portugal	2.8	England	4.1	Netherlands	5.0	China	4.8	Botswana	2.6
Netherlands	2.1	Germany	3.7	Madeira	4.8	Mauritius	2.8		
		Kenya	2.9	Poland	3.8	Mozambique	2.5		
				Mozambique	3.3				
				Namibia	3.2				
				Switzerland	2.3				
				England	2.2				
				France	2.1				
Percentage of total foreign-born included in list									
75.6		86.1		70.6		75.1		91.7	
Number of foreign born									
16,020		2,676		2,802		1,271		30,597	

Note: Includes countries of origin with 2% or more of immigrants in each race/ethnicity, but excludes residual categories, e.g., 'Rest of Africa'.

The largest group of 'foreign-born' Afrikaans-speaking Whites is not truly foreign, since Namibia, a German colony until the First World War, was ruled as a mandate and then annexed by South Africa after the Second World War, gaining its independence only in 1990. About 11% of foreign-born Afrikaans speakers were born in the Netherlands, which is not surprising given the predominantly Dutch origins of the Afrikaner population and the Afrikaans language.

The dominant group of Whites speaking other languages is from Portugal/Madeira or Mozambique, a former Portuguese colony sharing a border with South Africa. In addition, Europeans seeking economic opportunities, from Germany and from Southern Europe (Italy and Greece), have contributed to the small 'other White' population. Foreign-born Asians have mainly come from India, presumably regarding life in *apartheid* South Africa as preferable to life at home, and perhaps pulled by family connections. Interestingly, 15% of the Asian influx is from Taiwan, a country with which *apartheid* South Africa established economic ties in 1976. The Taiwanese-origin population presumably has diminished since 1997 when the new South African government cut diplomatic ties with Taiwan.

With limited exceptions, Blacks from other African nations have not been permitted to immigrate to South Africa. However, there is a long-standing pattern of temporary labour migration to staff the mines, primarily from Mozambique and from Lesotho, a small (fewer than 2 million population) mountainous nation entirely surrounded by South Africa. There also is a certain amount of illegal migration from other Southern African nations that share borders with South Africa.

Differentials within the native-born South African population

The remainder of the analysis is restricted to native-born South Africans, divided by race and, among Whites, into English-speaking and Afrikaans-speaking subgroups, with the small fraction of Whites speaking other languages (less than 2% of all Whites) dropped from further consideration. However, I show results separately for men and women.

Educational attainment

Tables 10.4A (for men) and 10.4B (for women) show the distribution of educational attainment by race/ethnicity. Each category includes those who have at least some education at that level.[15] With respect to education, gender differences are quite small, although among Whites and Asians women are somewhat less likely to have any tertiary education. By contrast, race differences are very large. For Whites the social minimum is at least some secondary schooling. But this is not the case for non-Whites. Blacks, in particular, suffer a severe educational penalty, with nearly 20% entirely without schooling and more than half with no more than primary schooling, below the social minimum for Whites. Similarly, whereas about 30% of Whites have some tertiary schooling, a fraction comparable to those in the US, Israel, Japan and Taiwan (Müller and Shavit 1998: 12), and more than 10% have a BA or better, only about 3% of Blacks have any tertiary education and less than 1% have a BA or better. These huge disparities reflect a concerted policy of minimising educational opportunities for non-Whites, especially Blacks, and subsidising White education (Robertson and Robertson 1977; Fedderke, de Kadt, and Luiz 2000). With respect to education, in common with all

---

[15] See Appendix for a discussion of how the education categories were created.

Table 10.4A. Educational attainment by race/ethnicity: Males (column percentages).

Highest level completed	Race/ethnicity					Total
	English	Afrikaner	Asian	Coloured	Black	
BA or more	15.4	11.8	5.0	1.4	0.7	2.3
Lower tertiary	23.7	21.3	9.1	5.5	3.0	5.6
Secondary	58.3	62.7	67.4	44.4	40.4	43.9
Primary	1.8	3.5	16.4	40.9	39.1	34.6
None	0.8	0.8	2.0	7.7	16.8	13.7
Total	100.0	100.1	99.9	99.9	100.0	100.1
N	29,523	55,703	24,189	76,497	590,278	776,191

Table 10.4B. Educational attainment by race/ethnicity: Females (column percentages).

Highest level completed	Race/ethnicity					Total
	English	Afrikaner	Asian	Coloured	Black	
BA or more	11.1	9.4	3.3	1.0	0.6	1.7
Lower tertiary	16.8	13.6	6.0	4.6	3.2	4.6
Secondary	69.3	73.0	59.6	43.2	39.8	44.0
Primary	2.0	3.2	25.9	43.8	37.5	34.2
None	0.8	0.7	5.1	7.4	18.9	15.5
Total	100.0	99.9	99.9	100.0	100.0	100.0
N	32,555	60,058	26,337	86,923	693,357	899,231

socio-economic characteristics, the ordering of the data reflects the racial hierarchy of South Africa: Whites, Asians, Coloureds, and Blacks. Asians and Coloureds do better than Blacks but not as well as Whites, and Asians do better than Coloureds. Finally, the table reveals a lingering disparity in the educational attainment of English-speaking Whites and Afrikaners. English-speaking Whites are somewhat more likely to get at least some tertiary education, and also to get a university degree. But these differences are small relative to those between the different races.

Economic activity

With regard to economic activity (shown in Tables 10.5A and 10.5B), also, racial differences are very large and differences between the two White groups are small. The most striking aspect of these tables is the extremely high unemployment rate among Blacks. More than half of the economically active women, and more than a third of the economically active men (defined as the sum of the 'employed' and the 'unemployed'), are unem-

Table 10.5A. Economic activity by race/ethnicity: Males (column percentages).

	Race/ethnicity					Total
	English	Afrikaner	Asian	Coloured	Black	
Employed	83.1	81.5	75.7	68.4	45.6	53.1
Unemployed	3.6	3.5	9.6	14.6	25.0	21.0
Homemaker	0.2	0.2	0.3	0.2	0.4	0.3
Student	6.8	5.3	6.0	5.3	16.4	13.7
Other non-active	6.3	9.5	8.4	11.4	12.6	11.9
Total	100.0	100.0	100.0	99.9	100.0	100.0
N	33,773	61,824	25,903	79,337	611,427	812,264

Table 10.5B. Economic activity by race/ethnicity: Females (column percentages).

	Race/ethnicity					Total
	English	Afrikaner	Asian	Coloured	Black	
Employed	65.8	56.4	40.5	48.3	26.3	32.5
Unemployed	3.0	3.2	6.5	14.8	29.0	24.2
Homemaker	18.9	26.8	37.9	21.8	13.0	15.8
Student	5.6	4.8	5.4	4.4	15.6	13.1
Other non-active	6.7	8.8	9.7	10.7	16.0	14.4
Total	100.0	100.0	100.0	100.0	99.9	100.0
N	35,908	64,762	27,748	89,577	712,939	930,933

ployed and looking for work, compared to less than 5% of Whites, with Asians and Coloureds again in between (see the bottom row of each panel of Tables 10.6A and 10.6B). There is a clear racial gradient in the propensity to be economically inactive for reasons other than going to school or keeping house, which probably reflects a combination of a 'discouraged worker' effect—after a while the chronically unemployed give up and withdraw from the active pursuit of employment—and racial differences in physical and mental disabilities that reflect differences in both economic and social status (Statistics South Africa 2004: ch. 5). Blacks are more likely than members of other groups to still be in school, a reflection of both late school starting ages for Blacks and a relatively high propensity to be required to repeat grades (Anderson, Case, and Lam 2001). Finally, as Table 10.5B shows, South African women tend to be economically active, with the exception of Asian women, nearly 40% of whom are homemakers.[16]

---

[16] Cheung and Heath, in their paper in this volume, show (Table 12.4B) that a much higher proportion of first-generation Pakistani/Bangladeshi women than women of any other group are

Table 10.6A. Current occupational class by race/ethnicity: Males.

	Race/ethnicity					Total
	English	Afrikaner	Asian	Coloured	Black	
Salariat	45.6	31.8	23.3	9.4	6.2	11.3
Routine non-manual	3.5	4.4	5.9	3.4	1.9	2.5
Petty bourgeoisie	8.7	9.1	5.2	3.7	3.2	4.1
Skilled manual	9.0	13.8	10.8	15.0	10.2	11.0
Semi- and unskilled manual	13.9	23.2	24.8	42.6	35.7	33.9
Unknown[a]	15.1	13.6	18.6	8.3	7.5	8.9
Unemployed	4.2	4.2	11.3	17.6	35.4	28.3
Total	100.0	100.1	99.9	100.0	100.1	100.0
N	29,311	52,628	22,113	65,902	432,109	602,064

[a] In some cases the informant did not know the occupations of others in the household. See the text for further discussion.

One implication of the racial differential in the propensity to be employed, highest among Whites and lowest among Blacks, is that employed Blacks are almost certainly more highly selected on the basis of unmeasured characteristics positively related to socio-economic outcomes than are employed Whites, with Asians and Coloureds, as always, falling in between. When employment is difficult to obtain, only the 'best and the brightest', those with the personal attributes that make them particularly likely to do well, are likely to be successful in finding jobs. The result of this kind of sample selection bias is to understate the 'ethnic penalty' in occupational status and income—that is, the true race difference that would emerge if we were able to control for the unmeasured characteristics that differentiate employed people in each race group.

---

homemakers, and that the percentages of homemakers among second-generation Pakistani/Bangladeshi and first-generation Indian women are also high. Among women from 'Asian' (Indian sub-continental) origins, I find a modestly greater propensity for Muslims to be homemakers than is true of Hindus or those who have adopted Western religions (the percentages are, respectively, 44, 37, and 34). Recall that I have restricted this portion of the analysis to the South African born, so that they correspond to Cheung and Heath's second generation.

Table 10.6B. Current occupational class by race/ethnicity: Females.

	Race/ethnicity					Total
	English	Afrikaner	Asian	Coloured	Black	
Salariat	36.5	30.2	21.7	11.3	7.1	11.0
Routine non-manual	28.8	32.4	20.0	10.2	3.3	7.8
Petty bourgeoisie	4.7	3.8	2.0	1.8	1.7	2.0
Skilled manual	1.0	1.4	3.7	3.4	2.1	2.2
Semi- and unskilled manual	12.6	16.9	24.5	43.5	29.8	29.4
Unknown[a]	11.9	9.9	14.4	6.3	3.5	4.9
Unemployed	4.4	5.4	13.8	23.5	52.4	42.7
Total	100.0	100.0	100.1	100.0	99.9	100.0
N	24,682	38,566	13,017	56,454	394,243	526,962

[a] In some cases the informant did not know the occupations of others in the household. See the text for further discussion.

Occupational class

Tables 10.6A and 10.6B show the distribution of the economically active population across occupational class categories, by race/ethnicity and gender. I have followed the specifications of the comparative project,[17] except that I have included the very small fractions of subsistence farmers (less than thirteen per 10,000 of any race group) with semi- and unskilled manual workers and have coded all other farmers in the petty bourgeoisie category even though many White-owned farms are quite large and employ many Black or Coloured farm labourers; unfortunately,

---

[17] See the discussion by Heath and Cheung in Chapter 1 of this volume. Mapping the categories of the 1996 South African Census occupation classification into EGP categories is relatively unproblematic, since the census classification is based on a 3-digit version of the 1988 International Standard Classification of Occupations (ILO 1990), which means that it was possible to use the ISCO-to-EGP algorithm provided by Ganzeboom and Treiman (1996). The one difficulty was in distinguishing between EGP categories IIIa (Routine non-manual workers, Higher grade) and IIIb (Routine non-manual workers, Lower grade), which were combined by Ganzeboom and Treiman into a single category but which had to be split here because in the specification for this volume, EGP category IIIb is combined with EGP categories VIIa and VIIb, to form a single 'semi- and unskilled manual worker' category. Unfortunately, no detailed coding manual has been published by the authors of the EGP scheme. However, on the basis of the discussion in Erikson and Goldthorpe (1992: 44), I treated the following South African census occupation categories as 'Routine non-manual workers, Lower grade', and hence ultimately as 'semi- and unskilled workers': 410, 414–19, 520, 522–30, 910–11.

the 1996 South African census does not include information on the number of employees, required to distinguish between small holders and large commercial farmers. I also have included a separate category for 'occupation unknown'. Since the census asked one member of each household to report on all persons in the household, there is a substantial amount of missing data—for about 9% of men and 5% of women. This category also includes a small number of people whose reported occupations were unclassifiable. There was also a substantial fraction of missing data on income, about 8% of the population (but less than 4% of the employed). There was little missing data for the remaining questions.

Comparing the corresponding rows, it is clear that for both men and women there is a very strong racial gradient. I have already noted the far higher unemployment rates among non-Whites, particularly Blacks, but there are also sharp racial distinctions with respect to the probability of being small employers (petty bourgeoisie). Although we might think of petty bourgeois activity as relatively unattractive to Whites, and more attractive to non-Whites, there were strong impediments in *apartheid* South Africa to non-White business ownership, most importantly restrictions on property ownership outside racially designated areas, but also restrictions on licensing, differential access to bank loans, etc.

The remainder of the tables surely reflect racial differences in educational attainment, although, as we will see shortly, the story actually is somewhat more complicated. Whites, particularly English-speaking Whites, are far more likely than members of other groups to be members of the salariat, and White women are far more likely than others to be higher-grade routine non-manual workers (recall that lower-grade routine non-manual workers are combined with semi- and unskilled workers; see note 17). Interestingly, there is little racial differentiation in the likelihood of doing skilled manual work, but there is a clear racial differential in the likelihood of doing semi-skilled or unskilled work, with Coloureds and Blacks disproportionately relegated to jobs in this sector.

Despite the limited differentiation between the two White groups with respect to education (Tables 10.4A and 10.4B), English-speaking White men are substantially more likely to be in the salariat and substantially less likely to do manual work, especially semi- and unskilled work, than are Afrikaners, which perhaps reflect the rural and working class origins of the Afrikaner population.

Income

Table 10.7A shows the cumulative distribution of monthly income by race, among men who were employed at the time of the census, and Table 10.7B shows the corresponding distributions for women. Although the South African census question refers to income from all sources, in South Africa, as elsewhere, most income is derived from employment. These tables document what we already have seen in Table 10.1—very large differences in income by race. Half of Black men and nearly 40% of Coloured men had incomes of less than R1,000 per month (the equivalent of British £140 or US $220), compared to about 7% of White men. Similarly, about 30% of English-speaking White men, 40% of Afrikaner men, 70% of Asian men, and 90% of Coloured and Black men had incomes of less than R3,500 per month. Interestingly, among employed men the income gap between English-speaking Whites and Afrikaners is at least as large as that between Coloureds and Blacks.[18] Again, we have

Table 10.7A. Current monthly income by race/ethnicity: employed males (cumulative percentage).

	Race/ethnicity					Total
	English	Afrikaner	Asian	Coloured	Black	
None	0.8	1.1	0.8	0.7	1.1	1.0
R1–R200	1.8	2.3	2.1	3.7	8.8	6.7
R201–R500	3.4	4.0	4.8	18.6	25.4	19.9
R501–R1,000	6.0	7.4	13.5	38.6	49.4	39.1
R1,001–R1,500	10.9	14.0	32.0	60.0	72.8	59.0
R1,501–R2,500	19.9	25.7	55.5	78.9	87.6	74.0
R2,501–R3,500	30.6	39.4	70.8	88.1	93.8	82.0
R3,501–R4,500	42.7	53.6	80.4	93.4	96.7	87.4
R4,501–R6,000	58.9	70.6	89.5	97.2	98.5	92.4
R6,001–R8,000	72.6	82.6	94.7	98.8	99.2	95.4
R8,001–R11,000	84.3	91.0	97.5	99.5	99.6	97.6
R11,001–R16,000	92.5	96.0	98.9	99.8	99.8	98.9
R16,001–R30,000	98.0	98.9	99.7	99.9	100.0	99.7
R30,000 or more	100.0	100.0	100.0	100.0	100.0	100.0
N	26,001	46,193	18,859	52,197	273,908	417,158

Note: Income from all sources, from 1 October 1995 to 30 September 1996, as solicited by the census question. In this and the following table, persons for whom income was unspecified (about 2% of Blacks, 4% of Asians and Coloureds, and 8% of Whites) were omitted.

[18] The evidence for this claim is that when the income categories are treated as ordinal categories, the odds that English-speaking Whites will be in a higher category than Afrikaners are 1.67:1, while the corresponding odds ratio for Coloureds and Blacks is 1.63.

Table 10.7B. Current monthly income by race/ethnicity: employed females (cumulative percentage).

	Race/ethnicity					Total
	English	Afrikaner	Asian	Coloured	Black	
None	1.5	1.6	1.3	0.9	1.5	1.4
R1–R200	3.9	3.9	3.6	8.7	18.6	13.8
R201–R500	7.3	7.3	8.8	29.6	47.1	35.6
R501–R1,000	12.4	13.9	25.3	49.2	68.7	53.8
R1,001–R1,500	21.1	25.9	51.2	70.8	81.4	67.8
R1,501–R2,500	39.7	49.1	71.7	85.6	89.7	80.0
R2,501–R3,500	59.4	69.2	84.1	92.8	94.8	88.5
R3,501–R4,500	74.3	82.4	91.3	96.8	97.6	93.7
R4,501–R6,000	87.2	92.7	96.7	99.0	99.1	97.4
R6,001–R8,000	93.5	96.6	98.4	99.6	99.6	98.7
R8,001–R11,000	96.8	98.4	99.3	99.8	99.8	99.4
R11,001–R16,000	98.8	99.4	99.7	99.9	99.9	99.8
R16,001–R30,000	99.7	99.8	99.9	100.0	100.0	99.9
R30,000 or more	100.0	100.0	100.0	100.0	100.0	100.0
N	21,930	33,028	10,773	41,511	183,848	291,689

evidence that Afrikaners have not quite caught up with English-speaking Whites.

Among women the story is quite similar (Table 10.7B), although in South Africa, as in most other nations (Treiman and Roos 1983; Nelson and Bridges 1999), women's incomes are substantially less than those of men; the median income for women is 59% of that of men and the odds that a man will be in a higher income category than a woman are 1.81:1. The gender income gap aside, however, racial differences in income attainment among women are quite similar to those for men. More than two-thirds of Black women have incomes of less than R1,000 per year, compared to only about half of Coloured Women, one-quarter of Asian women, and one-eighth of White women, and similar differences appear at virtually all levels of income. However, among women the Coloured–Black gap is larger than the English–Afrikaans gap. Whereas the odds that English-speaking Whites will be in a higher category than Afrikaners are 1.45:1, the corresponding odds ratio for Coloureds and Blacks is 2.03. It is unclear just why the English–Afrikaner difference is smaller for women than for men while the Coloured–Black difference is larger for women than for men.

Of course, the observed differences in income by race and sex are due, in large part, to race and sex differences in the average level of education, in the kind of jobs held, in the level of work experience, and in the number of hours worked. In a later section, I consider to what extent these differences explain the racial (and gender) penalties with respect to income.

Determinants of employment, occupational status and income

Thus far we have seen strong racial/ethnic differences with respect to education, employment, occupational status, and income. But these aspects of socio-economic status are not independent. It is well known that the driving force in occupational attainment is education and that, as was just noted, both occupational position and education are important determinants of income. Moreover, in most societies the likelihood of being employed, and also occupational standing and income, tend to increase with age, at least through most of the career cycle, although at some point both employment and income begin to decline as people shift to part-time or less demanding work or even become unable to work.[19] Thus, the obvious question is to what extent observed racial/ethnic differences in these outcomes simply reflect racial/ethnic differences in education—which, as I already have noted, are the direct consequence of *apartheid* policies—and also in age, since because of their relatively high fertility and also their poverty, which reduces longevity, non-Whites, and particularly Blacks, tend to be younger on average than Whites.[20]

Employment

We start by considering racial differences in unemployment. Table 10.8 shows coefficients for a simple binary logit model of whether economically active people are employed—that is, have avoided unemployment—

---

[19] In what follows, I interpret age differences as 'life cycle' effects. The alternative, of course, is that age differences reflect the experiences of different birth cohorts. Unfortunately, given that the data used here are cross-sectional and contain no information about past experience, it is impossible to distinguish between the two sorts of effects. However, some indication that life cycle effects dominate cohort effects can be found in the patterns of increasing socio-economic status with age, particularly for non-Whites, which is contrary to what we would expect if all change were due to improvement in the socio-economic circumstances of non-Whites as *apartheid* came to an end; in such a case the youngest cohorts would be most advantaged.

[20] Even within the restricted age range employed in this analysis, 18 through 59, the racial gradient in average age holds: the median ages for Whites, Asians, Coloureds, and Blacks are, respectively, 36, 34, 32, and 31.

Table 10.8. Logistic regression of employment (parameter estimates; contrasts with unemployment).

	Males		Females	
Intercept	**−0.18**	(0.05)	**1.50**	(0.05)
Race/ethnicity				
English	0		0	
Afrikaner	−0.05	(0.04)	**−0.13**	(0.04)
Asian	**−0.91**	(0.04)	**−0.96**	(0.05)
Coloured	**−1.19**	(0.04)	**−1.44**	(0.04)
Black	**−2.08**	(0.04)	**−2.98**	(0.04)
Age/10	**1.28**	(0.02)	**2.04**	(0.02)
(Age/10)^2	**−0.15**	(0.00)	**−0.20**	(0.00)
Marital status				
Single	0		0	
Currently married	**1.23**	(0.01)	**−0.07**	(0.01)
Formerly married	**0.40**	(0.02)	**0.35**	(0.01)
Educational attainment				
BA or higher	**1.19**	(0.11)	**1.15**	(0.14)
Some tertiary	**0.72**	(0.06)	**1.06**	(0.08)
Secondary	0		0	
Primary	−0.02	(0.06)	**0.43**	(0.08)
None	0.14	(0.12)	**0.92**	(0.15)
Interactions of race/ethnicity and education[a]				
English* education	0		0	
Afrikaner* education	**0.19**	(0.08)	0.17	(0.09)
Asian* education	**0.40**	(0.07)	**0.63**	(0.10)
Coloured* education	0.10	(0.06)	**0.76**	(0.08)
Black* education	**0.26**	(0.06)	**0.66**	(0.08)
N[b]	570,077		503,989	

Note: Emboldened coefficients indicate significance at the 0.05 level or better; standard errors are given in brackets.

[a] In keeping with the specifications for the comparative project, the education component of the interaction terms is expressed as a linear variable, coded −2 through +2 for the five levels of education, 'None' through 'BA or more'. This treatment of education holds for all the remaining models as well.

[b] Chi-square statistics for the improvement over the 'no effects' model are not shown here because the data are weighted. With weighted data, 'pseudo likelihoods' are estimated by Stata 8.0, the software used in this analysis. But changes in pseudo likelihoods are not meaningful—that is, cannot be interpreted as an indicator of model improvement. Thus, chi-square statistics are not shown in this or the remaining tables.

estimated separately for men and women. The coefficients are 'logits'. For continuous predictor variables they indicate the expected difference in the log odds of employment among those who differ by one unit with respect to the specified variable, holding constant all other predictors; for categorical predictor variables they indicate the expected difference in the log odds of employment between individuals in the specified category and individuals in the omitted or reference category, holding constant all other predictors. The variables included in the model are those agreed upon for the comparative project: race, educational attainment and their interaction; and also, as controls, age (divided by ten to ease interpretation) and its square, and marital status. As expected, the likelihood of employment increases with age for both men and women, but peaks at age 41 for men and at age 50 for women.[21] It is unclear why the two curves differ, but one possibility is that women tend to do less physically demanding work and hence their capabilities are less likely to depreciate with age. Net of all other factors, the odds of men age 41 being employed are more than twice as large as the corresponding odds for men age 18 (precisely 2.3) and even at age 59, the odds of men being employed are about 40% larger than at age 18. For women the age-employment curve is much steeper: the odds of being employed at age 50 are more than eight times the odds of being employed at age 18 and the odds of being employed at age 59 are nearly seven times as large as the odds of being employed at age 18. It may be that this is the result of unemployed older women dropping out of the labour force, an option not as readily available to men.

Not surprisingly, the effect of marital status differs by gender. Net of all other factors, the odds that currently married men are employed are more than three times the odds for never married men ($3.4 = e^{1.23}$) and the odds for formerly married men are about half again as large as the odds for never married men ($1.49 = e^{0.40}$).[22] However, currently married women are slightly less likely than never married women to be employed. Recall again that the analysis is restricted to economically active women and thus does not reflect the propensity for currently married women to be housewives. Perhaps currently married women are more restricted in their occupational opportunities because of their greater need to balance work and family responsibilities. Formerly married women are most likely to be employed, possibly because their circumstances force them to be less choosy about the kind of work they do.

---

[21] For a concave curve, the maximum value can be calculated as $-b_1/2b_2$ where b_1 is the coefficient associated with age and b_2 is the coefficient associated with age-squared.

[22] In this analysis, the 'currently married' include all cohabiting couples: those married in a civil or religious ceremony, those married in a traditional ceremony, and those who say they are 'living together'; the formerly married include both those who are separated or divorced and those who are widowed.

The central feature of Table 10.8 is, however, the combined effects of race and educational attainment. Because the model is constructed in such a way as to allow the effects of education to vary by race (or, what is the same thing, the effect of race to vary by education), direct interpretation of the coefficients is difficult; these effects are much more readily grasped in graphical form. Figures 10.1A (for men) and 10.1B (for women) show the expected percentage employed by race/ethnicity and education among married people of average age.[23]

The results are similar for men and women but are more dramatic for women. Among those lacking tertiary schooling there are very large racial differences in the probability of being employed. The model predicts that more than a quarter of married, mature, economically active Black men and nearly half of comparable Black women fail to secure

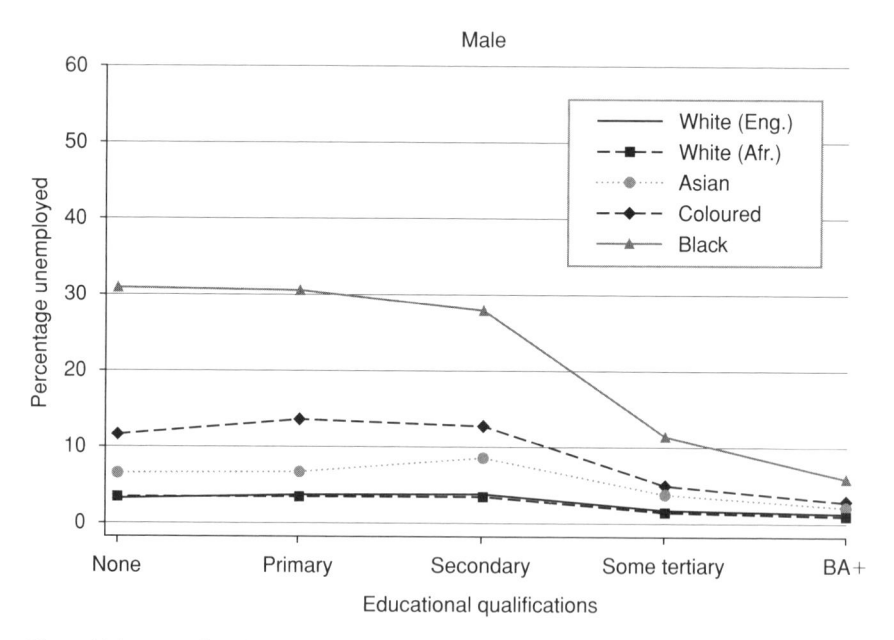

Figure 10.1A. Predicted percentage unemployed, by race/ethnicity and educational qualifications: males.
Note: Unless otherwise noted, all figures are for married, native-born South Africans of average age, 1996.

---

[23] Logits are converted to percentages by the formula $p = e^x/(1+e^x)$ where x is the expected log odds evaluated for specified values of the independent variables, here specific combinations of education and race/ethnicity with currently married = 1 and age and age-squared set at their sex-specific means.

THE LEGACY OF *APARTHEID* 429

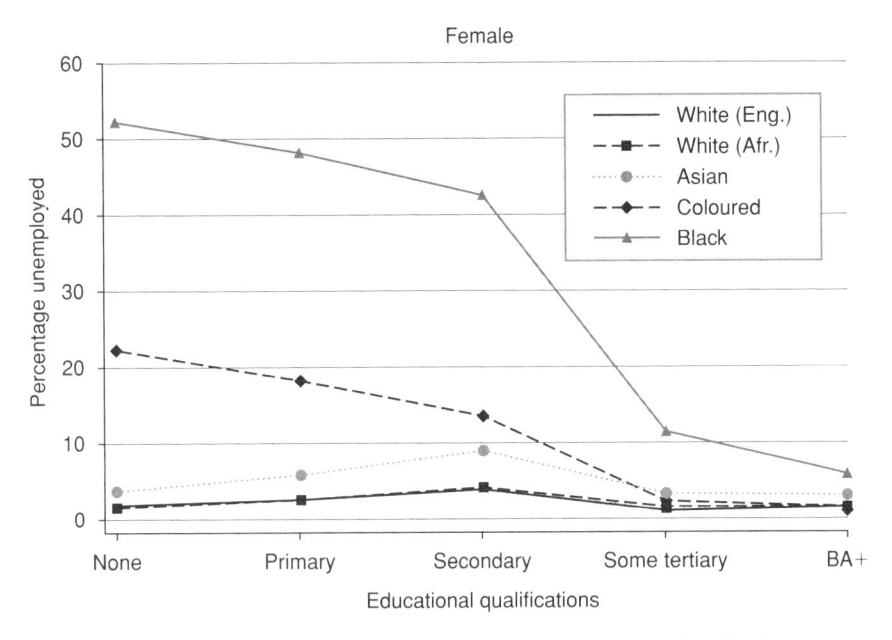

Figure 10.1B. Predicted percentage unemployed, by race/ethnicity and educational qualifications: females.

employment, and the percentages unemployed are also very high for Coloureds—above 10% for men and close to 20% for women—and are non-trivial for Asians. Tertiary education substantially reduces, but does not eliminate, the racial gap in unemployment, and completed university education reduces it still further. Recall the large racial differences in educational attainment shown in Tables 10.4A and 10.4B. What Figures 10.1A and 10.1B reveal is that tertiary education offers some protection against unemployment for the very small fractions of Coloureds and Blacks who are able to advance that far, while for Whites education is of little importance—virtually no Whites are unemployed regardless of how poorly educated they are. As is typical, Asians fall somewhere in between the other groups.

Occupational position

Tables 10.9A and 10.9B show coefficients for a simple multinomial logit model of the determinants of occupational attainment, for employed men and women, using the seven-category classification shown in Tables 10.6A and 10.6B (except, of course, that the unemployed are excluded). For ease of interpretation, semi-and unskilled work serves as the reference category of the dependent variable. As in Table 10.8, the coefficients shown in the tables are logits, contributions to the log odds of an individual being in the category shown as opposed to working at a semi-skilled or unskilled job, net of other factors included in the model. As before, age (divided by ten), and its square and marital status are included as controls, since occupational status tends to improve with age and among the currently married, at least for men, and, as noted, there are racial differences in average age. Marital status is a somewhat problematic control, since it could be argued that marriage is endogenous to occupational attainment—people marry when they secure good positions in life. But, in keeping with the specifications of the comparative project, I include it here.

Table 10.9A. Logistic regression of occupational class: Males.

	Salariat		Routine non-manual		Petty Bourgeoisie		Skilled manual		Occupation unknown	
Intercept	−1.62	(0.08)	−1.52	(0.12)	−3.74	(0.11)	−1.80	(0.07)	−1.20	(0.07)
Race/Ethnicity										
English	0		0		0		0		0	
Afrikaner	−0.90	(0.03)	−0.27	(0.05)	−0.39	(0.04)	−0.04	(0.04)	−0.52	(0.03)
Asian	−0.98	(0.03)	0.04	(0.05)	−0.83	(0.05)	−0.15	(0.04)	−0.13	(0.03)
Coloured	−1.90	(0.03)	−0.54	(0.05)	−1.37	(0.04)	−0.07	(0.04)	−1.13	(0.03)
Black	−2.12	(0.02)	−0.87	(0.04)	−1.64	(0.03)	−0.58	(0.03)	−1.22	(0.03)
Age/10	1.02	(0.04)	0.01	(0.06)	1.32	(0.06)	0.58	(0.04)	0.46	(0.04)
(Age/10)²	−0.11	(0.01)	0.01	(0.01)	−0.13	(0.01)	−0.07	(0.00)	−0.04	(0.01)
Marital status										
Single	0		0		0		0		0	
Currently married	0.02	(0.01)	−0.08	(0.02)	−0.03	(0.02)	−0.07	(0.01)	−0.12	(0.01)
Formerly married	−0.18	(0.03)	−0.05	(0.05)	0.04	(0.04)	−0.04	(0.03)	−0.25	(0.03)
Educational attainment										
BA or higher	2.04	(0.06)	0.43	(0.12)	0.78	(0.08)	−0.84	(0.12)	1.03	(0.07)
Some tertiary	1.06	(0.03)	−0.22	(0.06)	0.72	(0.05)	1.15	(0.05)	0.47	(0.04)
Secondary	0		0		0		0		0	
Primary	−0.26	(0.04)	−0.72	(0.07)	−0.24	(0.06)	−0.24	(0.06)	−0.19	(0.05)
None	0.50[a]	(0.07)	−0.47	(0.14)	−0.38	(0.11)	−0.84	(0.12)	−0.22	(0.09)
Interactions of race/ethnicity and education										
English* education	0		0		0		0		0	
Afrikaner* education	0.11	(0.03)	−0.03	(0.07)	−0.04	(0.05)	−0.04	(0.06)	−0.13	(0.04)
Asian* education	0.60	(0.04)	0.43	(0.08)	0.15	(0.07)	−0.26	(0.07)	0.13	(0.05)
Coloured* education	1.28	(0.04)	1.01	(0.07)	0.35	(0.06)	0.20	(0.06)	0.53	(0.05)
Black* education	1.18	(0.03)	0.99	(0.06)	−0.09	(0.05)	−0.39	(0.06)	0.15	(0.04)
N					406,562					

Note: Reference category is semi- and unskilled workers. Emboldened coefficients indicate significance at the 0.05 level or better; standard errors are given in brackets.

[a] Because of the way the interactions are constructed, this coefficient pertains to English-speaking Whites. Only 83 English-speaking Whites are coded as having no education, and 36 of these are coded as having salariat occupations. Although a large fraction of these are in managerial positions, for which education is not strictly required, the results may well reflect error in the coding of education or occupation or both.

Table 10.9B. Logistic regression of occupational class: Females.

	Salariat		Routine non-manual		Petty Bourgeoisie		Skilled manual		Occupation unknown	
Intercept	**−1.97**	(0.09)	**0.48**	(0.09)	**−2.90**	(0.15)	**−3.65**	(0.15)	**−0.91**	(0.10)
Race/ethnicity										
English	0		0		0		0		0	
Afrikaner	**−0.54**	(0.03)	**−0.21**	(0.03)	**−0.51**	(0.05)	−0.00	(0.09)	**−0.50**	(0.04)
Asian	**−0.80**	(0.04)	**−0.80**	(0.04)	**−1.30**	(0.08)	**0.59**	(0.09)	**−0.25**	(0.04)
Coloured	**−1.46**	(0.03)	**−1.54**	(0.03)	**−1.86**	(0.06)	**0.35**	(0.08)	**−1.28**	(0.04)
Black	**−1.65**	(0.03)	**−2.16**	(0.03)	**−1.59**	(0.05)	**0.27**	(0.08)	**−1.49**	(0.03)
Age/10	**1.10**	(0.05)	**0.13**	(0.05)	**0.77**	(0.08)	**0.76**	(0.08)	**0.36**	(0.06)
(Age/10)²	**−0.12**	(0.01)	**−0.02**	(0.01)	**−0.08**	(0.01)	**−0.12**	(0.01)	**−0.05**	(0.01)
Marital status										
Single	0		0		0		0		0	
Currently married	**0.21**	(0.02)	**0.20**	(0.02)	**0.12**	(0.02)	**0.07**	(0.02)	**0.05**	(0.02)
Formerly married	**0.09**	(0.02)	**0.18**	(0.02)	−0.05	(0.04)	0.06	(0.04)	**−0.08**	(0.03)
Educational attainment										
BA or higher	**1.96**	(0.07)	**−0.27**	(0.08)	**0.48**	(0.12)	0.01	(0.26)	**0.91**	(0.08)
Some tertiary	**1.61**	(0.04)	**0.30**	(0.05)	**0.63**	(0.07)	−0.08	(0.15)	**0.25**	(0.05)
Secondary	0		0		0		0		0	
Primary	**−0.65**	(0.05)	**−1.06**	(0.06)	−0.17	(0.09)	**−0.33**	(0.16)	−0.05	(0.06)
None	0.47[a]	(0.10)	**0.41**	(0.12)	0.01	(0.18)	**−0.67**	(0.32)	**0.69**	(0.12)
Interactions of race/ethnicity and education										
English* education	0		0		0		0		0	
Afrikaner* education	**0.20**	(0.04)	**0.16**	(0.05)	**0.23**	(0.07)	0.16	(0.15)	0.10	(0.05)
Asian* education	**0.93**	(0.06)	**0.88**	(0.07)	0.25	(0.13)	**−0.57**	(0.18)	**0.52**	(0.07)
Coloured* education	**1.51**	(0.05)	**1.45**	(0.06)	0.15	(0.10)	0.29	(0.16)	**0.94**	(0.06)
Black* education	**1.63**	(0.05)	**1.45**	(0.05)	0.08	(0.09)	0.12	(0.16)	**0.80**	(0.05)
N					294,658					

Note: Reference category is semi- and unskilled workers. Emboldened coefficients indicate significance at the 0.05 level or better; standard errors are given in brackets.

[a] See note *a* to Table 10.9A. Among White English-speaking women, 90 have no education; of these, 30 are in the salariat.

Consider first the results for men, shown in Table 10.9A. The effects of age are as we would expect. The odds of employment in the salariat or in petty bourgeoisie positions vs. employment in semi- or unskilled occupations increase sharply with age, and the odds of skilled employment also increase substantially, albeit not quite as rapidly. The coefficients for the squared term are negative for all three outcomes, suggesting that the odds of entering these types of occupations vs. semi- and unskilled positions increase sharply early in men's careers and then level off and reverse. In fact, they peak at age 49, 52, and 41, respectively, for salariat, petty bourgeois, and skilled positions. Routine non-manual work requires no particular comment since only very small fractions of men of any age or race are employed in such positions. For women—see Table 10.9B—a generally similar pattern holds, except that for both routine non-manual work and petty bourgeois positions, the odds of employment peak much earlier, at age 34 and 31 respectively. Marital status has relatively little impact on occupational attainment, especially for men. But currently married women are somewhat more likely to work at salariat or routine non-manual jobs, and formerly married women to work at routine non-manual jobs than are never-married women. However, the reasons for this are unclear.

To see the combined effect of education and race/ethnicity, we turn to graphs of the expected percentages in each occupational category for married employed persons of average age.[24] Figures 10.2A and 10.2B show the expected percentages in salariat occupations, separately for men and women. Consider men first. These results are striking in a number of ways. First, there is a pronounced racial and ethnic gradient among those with no more than secondary education. The racial difference is dramatic, with a large fraction of Whites, and a smaller but non-trivial fraction of Asians, able to secure salariat jobs even when they lack tertiary education. However, among Whites the English-speaking population is sharply advantaged relative to Afrikaners. Interestingly, there is no difference at all between Coloureds and Blacks. By 1996 the *apartheid*-era advantage of Coloureds over Blacks (Treiman *et al.* 1996) apparently had completely eroded. Second, the racial penalty narrows very substantially among those with some tertiary schooling and reverses among those with university degrees or more. That is, among those with university degrees, Black and Coloured men are somewhat more likely than Asians and English-speaking Whites and still more likely than Afrikaans-speaking Whites of the same age and marital status to attain salariat positions. Recall from Table 10.4A, however, that less than 1% of Blacks and only 1.4% of Coloureds managed to achieve this level of education, compared to 15% of English-speaking Whites, 12% of Afrikaans-speaking Whites, and 5% of Asians. Thus, university-educated Black and Coloured men are much more highly selected than men of other racial groups.

For women the story is essentially the same and even more orderly, with racial and ethnic differences somewhat smaller at lower levels of schooling than for men, but reversing among those with at least some

---

[24] Logits are converted to percentages by the formulas $p=1/(1+ \Sigma_{j=1-4,6}e^x)$ for the omitted category, 5, of the dependent variable and $p= e^x/(1+ \Sigma_{j=1-4,6}e^x)$ for the remaining categories, where x is the expected log odds evaluated for specified values of the independent variables, here specific combinations of education and race/ethnicity with currently married = 1 and age and age-squared set at their sex-specific means, and a specific category, j, of the dependent variable.

THE LEGACY OF *APARTHEID* 433

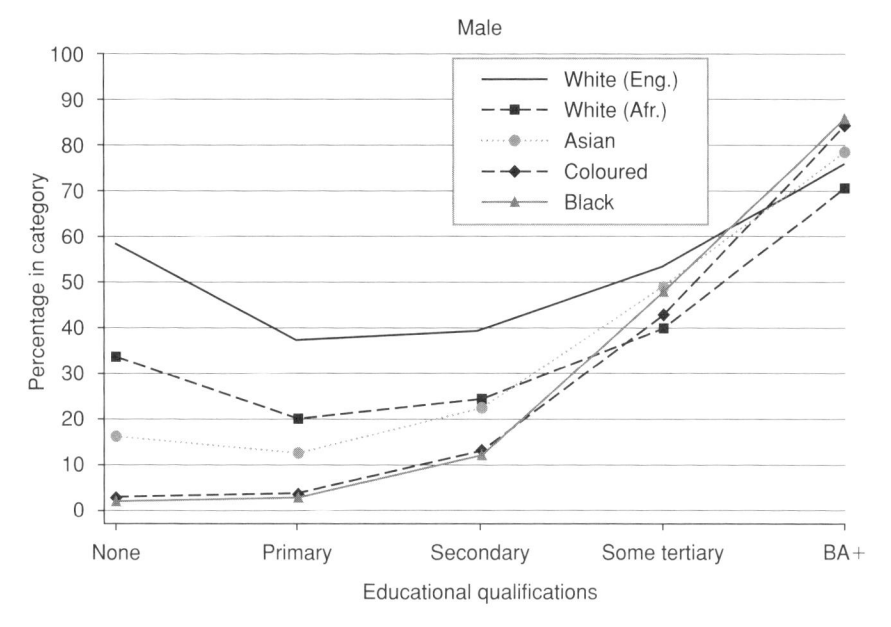

Figure 10.2A. Predicted percentage in salariat occupations, by race/ethnicity and educational qualifications: males.

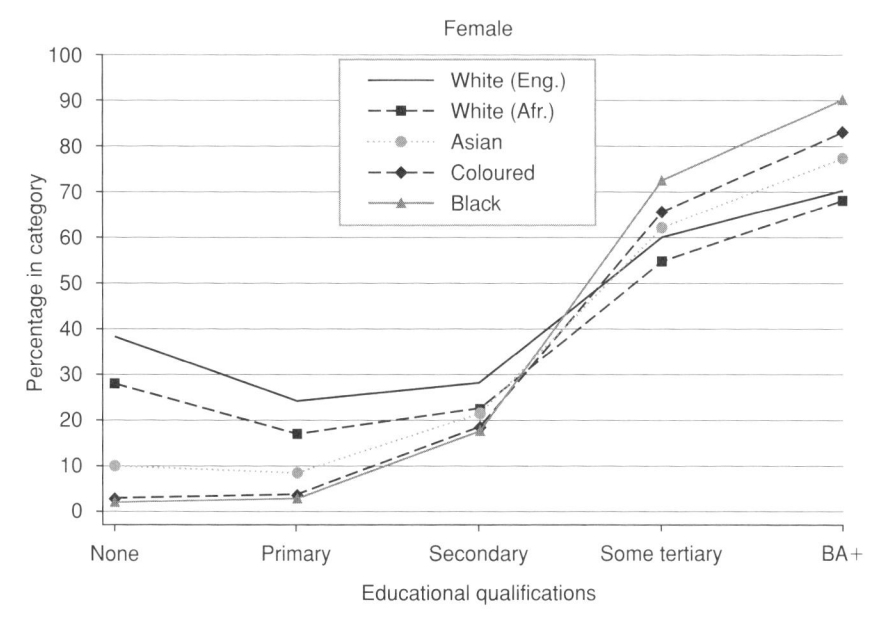

Figure 10.2B. Predicted percentage in salariat occupations, by race/ethnicity and educational qualifications: females.

tertiary schooling. A similar status reversal by race among well-educated women was observed thirty years ago in the US (Treiman and Terrell 1975). It is likely that tertiary-educated Black and Coloured women work as professionals and managers in segregated establishments, e.g., schools and hospitals, but my data do not permit me to investigate this. The same caveat as for men applies here as well—Black and Coloured women who achieve a university education are extremely highly selected, as we saw in Table 10.4B—much more highly selected than Asian and especially than White women.

Figure 10.3 shows the expected percentages in routine non-manual occupations for women. There is little point in showing the corresponding figure for men since when the coefficients in Table 10.9A are evaluated at the mean age for men, virtually no men would be predicted to work at routine non-manual occupations. For women the racial gap is unsurprising—among those lacking tertiary education White women are more likely than Asian women and Asian women are more likely than Coloured or Black women to work at routine non-manual occupations; but here Afrikaner women are a bit more likely than English-speaking White women to occupy such positions. The racial gap narrows substan-

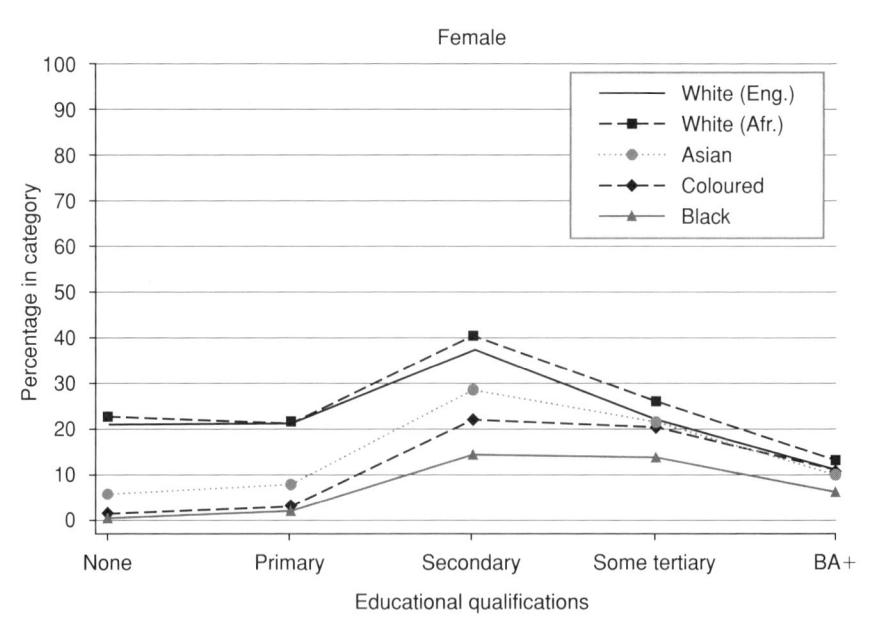

Figure 10.3. Predicted percentage in routine non-manual occupations, by race/ethnicity and educational qualifications: females.

tially among those with at least some tertiary schooling, with English-speaking White women, Asian women, and Coloured women all about equally likely to do routine non-manual work, Afrikaner women the most likely, and Black women the least likely.

Since very few people of any race or either gender occupy petty bourgeoisie positions, graphing race and sex differences is uninformative. Figure 10.4 shows the expected percentages in skilled manual occupations for men; the corresponding graph is not shown for women since very few women do skilled manual work. What is most striking about the graph is that among Afrikaner and Coloured men, the likelihood of doing skilled manual work increases with education up to some tertiary schooling. Only among those with a BA or more does the percentage sharply decline. This may reflect the historical working class tradition of both groups, which continues to be reflected in their current role as a labour aristocracy, filling skilled manual and supervisory jobs that today require technical tertiary education. By contrast, for Asians and Blacks the percentage doing skilled manual work declines with education, and English-speaking Whites are unlikely to do such work regardless of their level of education. All in all, however, racial differences are quite modest.

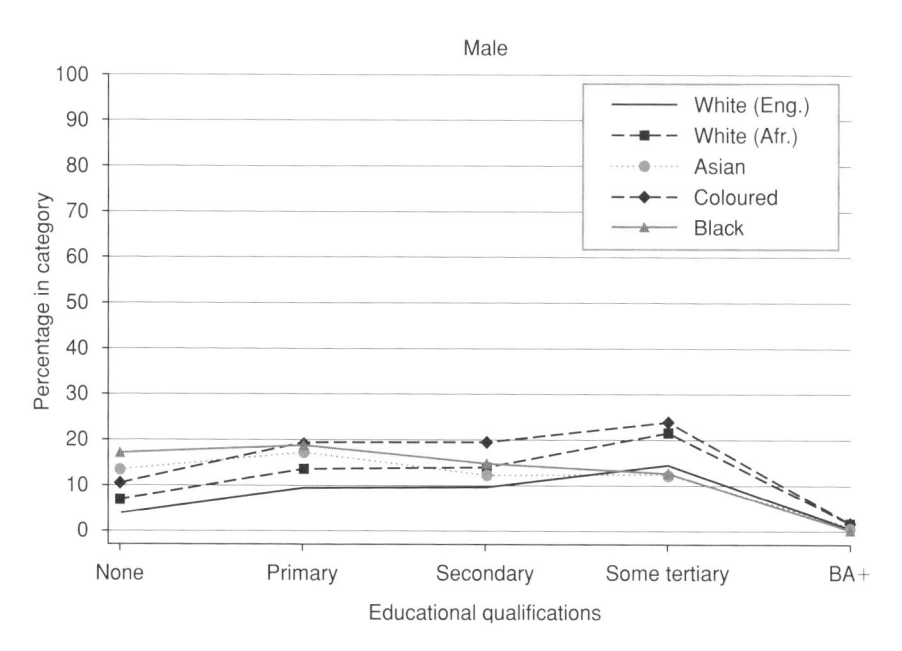

Figure 10.4. Predicted percentage in skilled manual occupations, by race/ethnicity and educational qualifications: males.

The contrast with semi- and unskilled work, shown in Figures 10.5A and 10.5B, is dramatic. Here racial differences are very large, for both men and women. More than 60% of Black and Coloured men and about 80% of Black and Coloured women who lack secondary schooling are relegated to semi- and unskilled jobs, compared to much smaller fractions of Asians and even smaller fractions of Whites. The racial gradient narrows somewhat among those with secondary schooling, and more or less disappears among those with at least some tertiary education, mainly because few men and almost no women with tertiary education do such work.

In sum, for a non-White person in South Africa the only way to achieve equality with Whites, at least with respect to occupational attainment, is to obtain at least some tertiary education—something that very few are able to do. Among those with tertiary schooling, racial differences in occupational outcomes are quite small. However, for those lacking tertiary education, they are very large, with Whites frequently able to achieve salariat positions and to avoid semi- and unskilled work but with non-Whites, and particularly Coloureds and Blacks, excluded from the salariat and relegated to semi- and unskilled jobs. That is, for those with

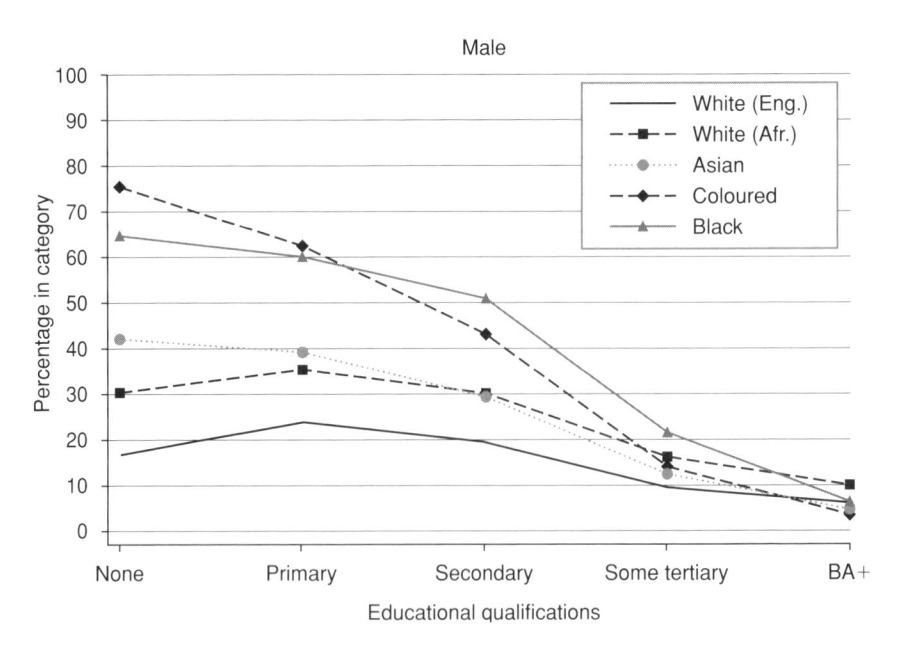

Figure 10.5A. Predicted percentage in semi- and unskilled occupations, by race/ethnicity and educational qualifications: males.

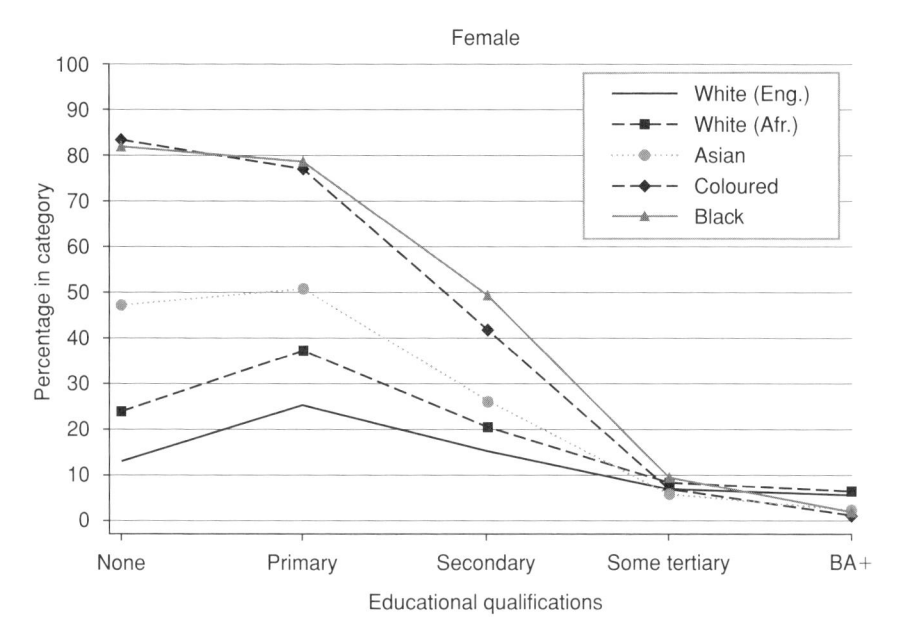

Figure 10.5B. Predicted percentage in semi- and unskilled occupations, by race/ethnicity and educational qualifications: females.

less than a tertiary education, there appears to be an occupational floor under Whites and an occupational ceiling over non-Whites. Whether this pattern extends to income is the concern of the next section.

Income

Recall from the note to Table 10.7A that the 1996 South African census solicited and reported income in intervals, with a bottom code of zero and a top code of Rand 360,000 per year. Given this specification of the income variable, I utilise interval regression (StataCorp 2003: Vol. 4, 255–60) to model the determinants of annual income. Since the census question refers to income from all sources, I first model the determinants of income for the entire population, excluding only those missing data on the income question, and utilising the same predictor variables as in the previous analyses of employment and occupational outcomes. These results are shown in Table 10.10 as Model 1, separately for men and women. Model 2 is restricted to the employed (about half of all men and about one-third of all women) and includes an indicator of full-time vs. part-time employment and also indicators of employment status

Table 10.10. Interval regression of annual income, by race/ethnicity and gender.

	Males				Females			
	Model 1		Model 2[a]		Model 1		Model 2[a]	
Intercept	−54,805	(610)	9,582	(748)	−56,184	(526)	3,278	(538)
Race/ethnicity								
English	0		0		0		0	
Afrikaner	**−11,813**	(451)	**−12,689**	(533)	**−9,415**	(288)	**−7,155**	(315)
Asian	**−29,419**	(458)	**−29,370**	(521)	**−19,046**	(331)	**−14,509**	(346)
Coloured	**−35,789**	(423)	**−35,926**	(487)	**−16,164**	(271)	**−18,233**	(284)
Black	**−49,062**	(416)	**−42,335**	(473)	**−29,353**	(266)	**−23,423**	(270)
Age/10	**50,142**	(308)	**20,585**	(339)	**38,825**	(268)	**12,772**	(264)
(Age/10)^2	**−5,880**	(39)	**−2,154**	(45)	**−4,446**	(33)	**−1,439**	(35)
Marital status								
Single	0		0		0		0	
Currently married	**15,211**	(100)	**3,966**	(94)	**−2,111**	(75)	**1,152**	(77)
Formerly married	**5,818**	(266)	**988**	(327)	**6,601**	(119)	**2,601**	(135)
Educational attainment								
BA or higher	**54,644**	(1,129)	**50,695**	(1,257)	**28,565**	(740)	**22,642**	(813)
Some tertiary	**19,198**	(553)	**13,998**	(621)	**18,068**	(379)	**8,536**	(407)
Secondary	0		0		0		0	
Primary	**−10,950**	(568)	**−12,463**	(644)	**2,087**	(386)	**−1,837**	(427)
None	**−17,903**	(1,128)	**−19,720**	(1,282)	**8,095**	(762)	**2,499**	(843)
Employed full-time			**7,566**	(129)			**7,275**	(97)
Employment status								
Self-employed without employees			0				0	
Employer			**11,253**	(504)			**3,854**	(433)
Employee			**−868**	(270)			**1,231**	(224)
Family worker			**−4,884**	(560)			**−2,544**	(444)
Interactions of race/ethnicity and education								
English* education	0		0		0		0	
Afrikaner* education	557	(641)	1,120	(724)	**2,115**	(426)	**1,109**	(472)
Asian* education	504	(665)	−641	(751)	**11,551**	(453)	**5,222**	(523)
Coloured* education	−540	(575)	194	(649)	**11,307**	(392)	**7,970**	(431)
Black* education	**−3,498**	(561)	**−3,716**	(636)	**8,353**	(378)	**6,160**	(418)
N	718,354		357,278		814,460		247,953	

Note: Emboldened coefficients indicate significance at the 0.05 level or better; standard errors are given in brackets.

[a] Employed persons.

(self-employed without employees, employers, employees, and family workers). Tables 10.11A and 10.11B replicate Model 2 for each occupation category, separately for men and women.

In both Models 1 and 2 the effects of age and marital status are similar to those we observed for employment and occupational outcomes: income increases with age and then declines. Currently married men have the highest incomes, followed by formerly married men, but formerly married women have the highest incomes, net of all other factors. The additional variables included in Model 2 also behave as expected: those

THE LEGACY OF *APARTHEID*

Table 10.11A. Interval regression of annual income, by race/ethnicity and occupational category: Males.

	Salariat		Routine non-manual		Petty Bourgeoisie		Skilled manual		Semi- and unskilled manual	
Intercept	−48,201	(3,067)	−15,303	(5,850)	6,917	(4,350)	7,665	(1,255)	12,628	(938)
Race/ethnicity										
English	0		0		0		0		0	
Afrikaner	−14,015	(1,016)	−7,044	(1,687)	−10,955	(2,244)	−2,472	(962)	−3,203	(839)
Asian	−34,179	(1,046)	−19,637	(1,649)	−29,102	(2,339)	−16,710	(947)	−18,985	(834)
Coloured	−38,744	(956)	−21,943	(1,603)	−40,613	(2,047)	−19,490	(880)	−24,438	(774)
Black	−49,729	(882)	−28,916	(1,578)	−46,958	(1,943)	−26,964	(859)	−28,231	(764)
Age/10	48,971	(1,695)	23,164	(1,701)	21,868	(2,203)	14,582	(545)	12,612	(283)
(Age/10)^2	−5,029	(223)	−2,311	(232)	−2,276	(285)	−1,633	(72)	−1,362	(37)
Marital status										
Single	0		0		0		0		0	
Currently married	7,108	(476)	4,206	(474)	5,738	(573)	3,256	(161)	2,751	(86)
Formerly married	1,519	(1,280)	1,832	(1,449)	1,082	(1,708)	1,544	(514)	857	(296)
Educational attainment										
BA or higher	41,149	(1,690)	32,667	(5,721)	30,048	(5,330)	34,272	(4,654)	34,933	(3,636)
Some tertiary	10,701	(903)	9,906	(2,732)	−1,819	(2,628)	13,374	(1,332)	10,042	(1,621)
Secondary	0		0		0		0		0	
Primary	−19,801	(1,074)	−13,709	(2,765)	−4,366	(3,049)	−7,859	(1,365)	−10,202	(1,669)
None	−23,519	(2,167)	−15,886	(5,618)	3,419	(6,016)	−13,669	(2,719)	−16,590	(3,338)
Employed full-time	16,562	(896)	8,395	(912)	10,058	(485)	4,937	(184)	5,513	(124)
Employment status										
Self-employed without employees	0		0		0		[b]		0	
Employer	20,604	(1,614)	8,670	(12,962)	6,280	(582)	[b]		9,798	(1,078)
Employee	−627	(1,046)	5,479	(4,939)	[a]		0[b]		448	(405)
Family worker	−6,394	(1,924)	226	(5,457)	[a]		−2,366	(835)	−1,741	(695)
Interactions of race/ethnicity and education										
English* education	0		0		0		0		0	
Afrikaner* education	705	(1,035)	2,859	(3,349)	4,132	(3,025)	−1,097	(1,506)	3,930	(1,872)
Asian* education	−413	(1,184)	−2,106	(3,115)	5,376	(3,416)	−303	(1,547)	−1,146	(1,766)
Coloured* education	−806	(1,035)	−1,385	(2,948)	8,816	(2,954)	72	(1,384)	−272	(1,667)
Black* education	−2,894	(915)	−3,576	(2,754)	4,071	(2,956)	−3,741	(1,358)	−3,132	(1,665)
N	55,305		12,705		21,968		54,897		172,570	

Note: Emboldened coefficients indicate significance at the 0.05 level or better; standard errors are given in brackets.

[a] Not defined for petty bourgeoisie.

[b] Not defined for skilled workers. The omitted category is employees.

Table 10.11B. Interval regression of annual income, by race/ethnicity and occupational category: Females.

	Salariat		Routine non-manual		Petty Bourgeoisie		Skilled manual	
Intercept	−20,533	(2,056)	−12,633	(3,151)	7,167	(3,414)	19,363	(3,831)
Race/ethnicity								
English	0		0		0		0	
Afrikaner	−10,186	(704)	−5,424	(396)	−6,298	(2,063)	−11,461	(4,288)
Asian	−14,574	(917)	−10,116	(506)	−12,004	(2,682)	−20,961	(3,994)
Coloured	−19,702	(648)	−11,240	(390)	−19,715	(1,903)	−22,394	(3,896)
Black	−25,700	(605)	−16,533	(369)	−25,004	(1,662)	−27,505	(3,925)
Age/10	23,380	(1,101)	16,778	(806)	10,795	(1,849)	7,035	(1,028)
(Age/10)^2	−2,670	(147)	−1,903	(109)	−1,241	(245)	−718	(141)
Marital status								
Single	0		0		0		0	
Currently married	660	(303)	1,271	(252)	1,289	(453)	814	(275)
Formerly married	4,663	(539)	4,268	(454)	4,705	(932)	646	(492)
Educational attainment								
BA or higher	20,107	(1,172)	11,469	(1,549)	19,369	(5,474)	15,618	(8,383)
Some tertiary	5,901	(624)	4,007	(690)	1,684	(2,468)	−1,530	(4,284)
Secondary	0		0		0		0	
Primary	−5,816	(824)	−5,157	(796)	−1,190	(2,842)	230	(4,260)
None	667	(1,531)	1,711	(1,701)	1,833	(5,590)	2,672	(8,532)
Employed full-time	17,831	(536)	10,619	(364)	7,709	(506)	4,116	(417)
Employment status								
Self-employed without employees	0		0		0		^{b}	
Employer	7,402	(1,391)	4,925	(3,768)	1,711	(518)	^{b}	
Employee	3,206	(798)	3,681	(2,843)	^{a}		0^b	
Family worker	−2,156	(1,576)	−1,339	(2,990)	^{a}		2,160	(2,888)
Interactions of race/ethnicity and education	0		0		0		0	
Afrikaner* education	2,249	(712)	−122	(827)	−1,426	(2,966)	5,340	(4,475)
Asian* education	2,824	(938)	1,884	(1,069)	11,489	(4,700)	3,555	(4,286)
Coloured* education	−5,737	(721)	3,691	(840)	7,792	(2,913)	4,244	(4,276)
Black* education	−4,554	(641)	4,154	(736)	4,687	(2,775)	3,552	(4,265)
N	46,955		34,354		9,516		9,696	

Note: Emboldened coefficients indicate significance at the 0.05 level or better; standard errors are given in brackets.
^{a} Not defined for petty bourgeoisie.
^{b} Not defined for skilled workers. The omitted category is employees.

who work full-time earn substantially more than those who work part time;[25] employers earn substantially more than those who are self-employed without employees; and family workers earn substantially less. Interestingly, among men employees do not do quite as well as the self-employed without employees while female employees earn more than

---

[25] Of course, there could well be racial differences in hours worked even among those who purport to work full time. However, data from a national probability sample survey of South African adults that I conducted in the early 1990s reveals only small racial differences in hours

women who are self-employed without employees. It may be that in South Africa women who are self-employed without employees are disproportionately small-scale vendors of foods or other self-made goods, but I have no data with which to check this conjecture.

As before, the best way to assess the joint effects of education and race is to graph them. Figure 10.6A shows incomes predicted from Models 1 (top panel) and Model 2 (bottom panel) for men and Figure 10.6B shows the corresponding predicted incomes for women. Inspecting Figure 10.6A first, the contrast with the employment and occupational outcome graphs is striking. With respect to income it turns out that there is virtually no interaction between race and education. At every level of education, there is a nearly identical racial gradient in income in Model 1: English-speaking Whites, Afrikaans-speaking Whites, Asians, Coloureds and Blacks; and nearly the same is true of Model 2, except that poorly educated Coloureds have incomes about the same as those of Blacks while well-educated Coloureds have incomes nearly as high as Asians. While tertiary education mitigates racial disparities in occupational outcomes, it does not reduce the income gap at all.

The story is rather different for women. Figure 10.6B shows that the racial gap in income is successively narrowed with increasing education. One reason for this is that for White women income hardly increases with education whereas the relationship between education and income for non-White women is substantially positive. Two other features of Figure 10.6B deserve comment. First, as I already noted in the discussion of Tables 10.7A and 10.7B, women's incomes are much lower than men's, even among the employed. Here we see that the relationship holds net of education and marital status and, in the graph for Model 2, net of full time vs. part time work and employment status as well. Second, note that in the graph for Model 1, the expected incomes of non-Whites with less than secondary schooling, and of Blacks with secondary schooling, are below zero. This is because the interval regression procedure yields estimates of a latent 'income propensity' rather than estimates of actual income. The implication is that non-White, and especially Black, women lacking secondary schooling are some distance from having positive incomes, and that Black women are far from having positive incomes even when they have secondary schooling. These outcomes no doubt reflect the

---

worked per week among all workers, full time and part time combined: for men, the means are 47.5, 42.6, 42.5, and 43.5, respectively, for Whites, Asians, Coloureds, and Blacks; for women they are 40.1, 40.9, 40.8, and 40.3.

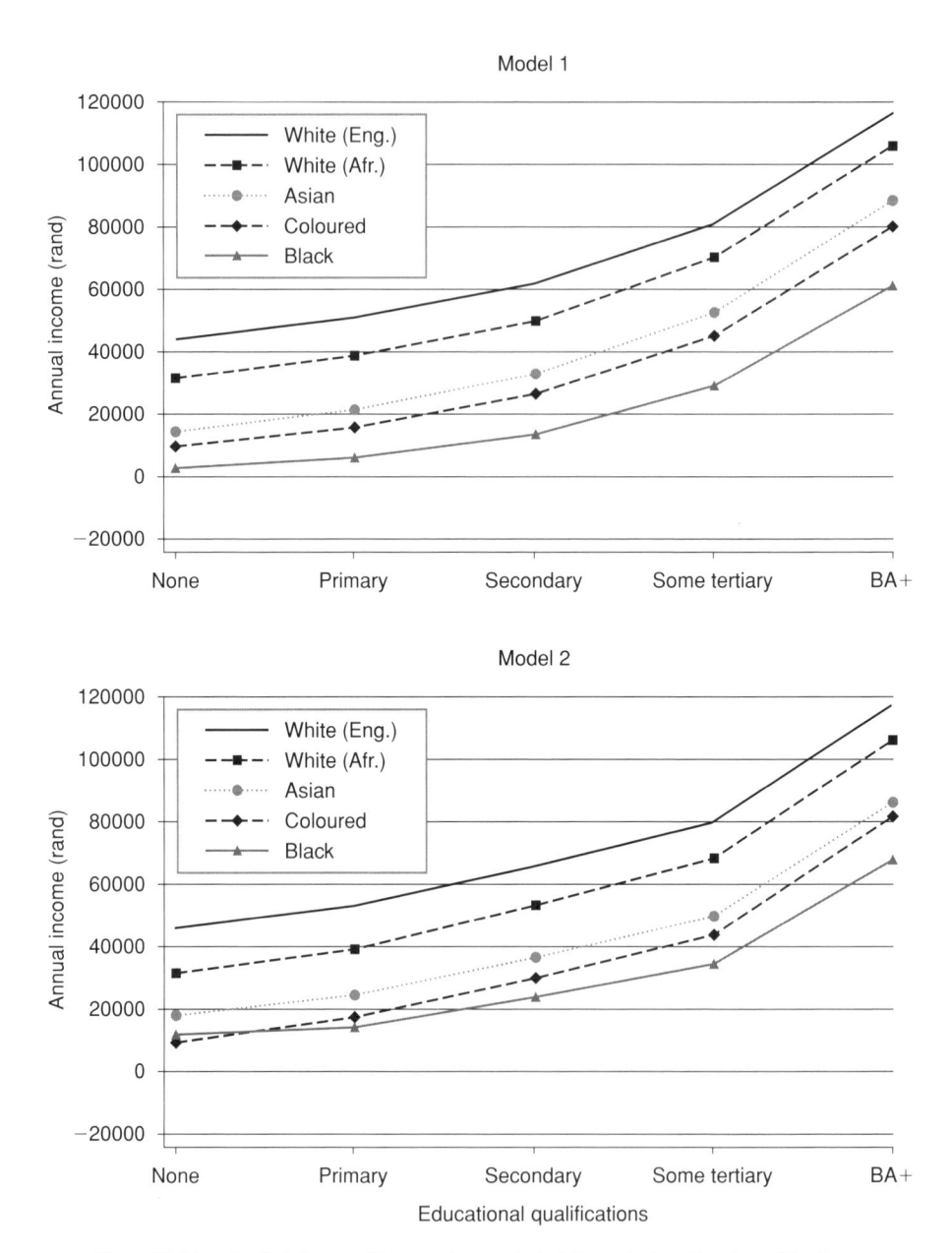

Figure 10.6A. Predicted annual income, by race/ethnicity and educational qualifications: males.
Note: Predictions based on Table 10.10 above. Model 1 is estimated for all men. Model 2 is estimated for employed men; the graphs are for full time employees.

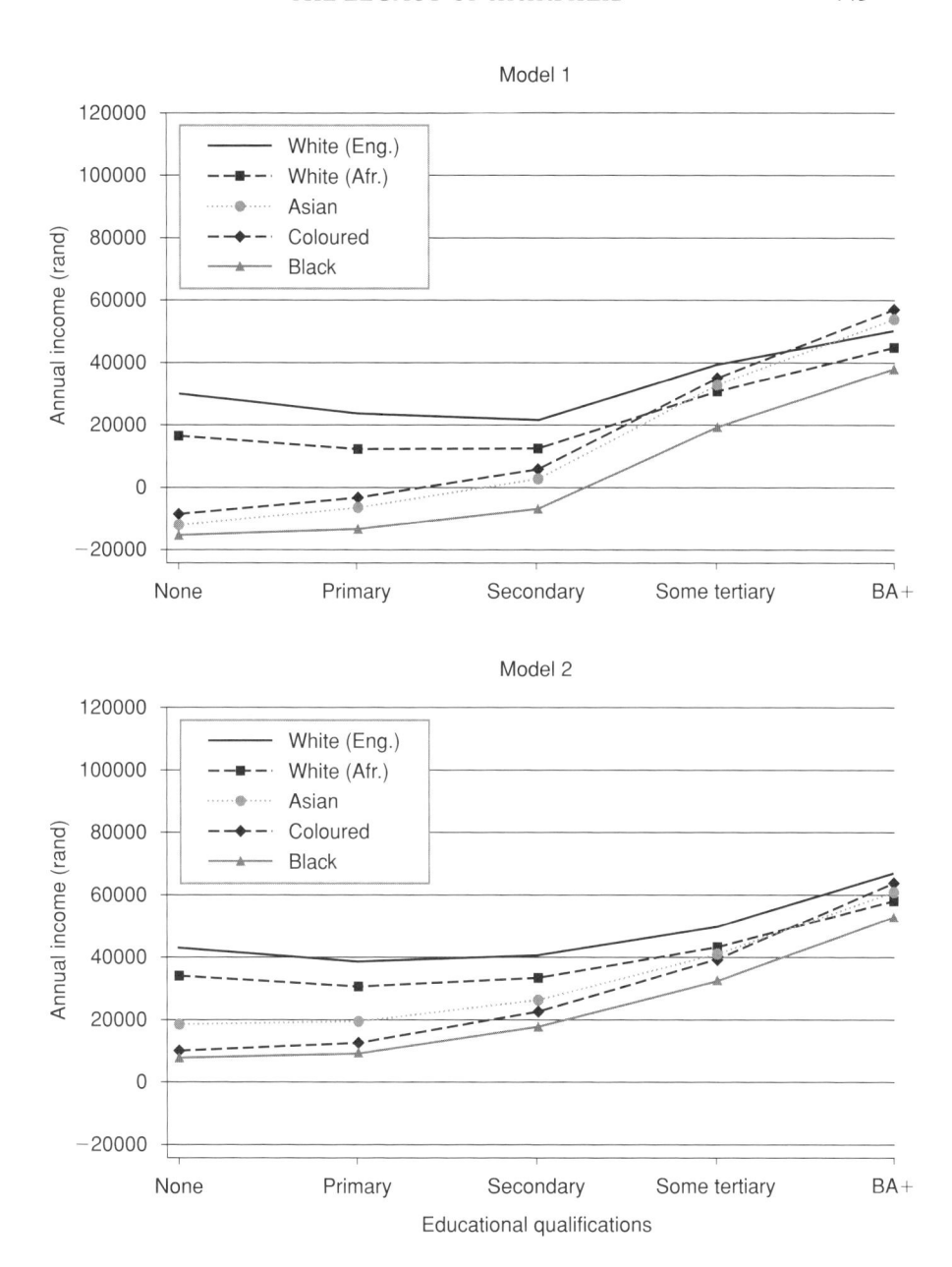

Figure 10.6B. Predicted annual income, by race/ethnicity and educational qualifications: females.
Note: Predictions based on Table 10.10 above. Model 1 is estimated for all women. Model 2 is estimated for employed women; the graphs are for full time employees.

very high unemployment rates of poorly educated non-White women observed in Figure 10.1, together with the substantial fractions of women occupied as housewives (recall Table 10.5B). These conditions result in large fractions of the population, especially the female population, having no income whatsoever: 32, 51, 44, and 66% of White, Asian, Coloured, and Black women, respectively (overall 60%), and 10, 18, 23, and 47% of men (overall 40%).

Figure 10.7 shows expected incomes for Model 2 estimated separately by gender and occupation category, except that the model for women in semi- and unskilled occupations is omitted because the estimation did not converge, probably because only a handful of White women engage in such occupations (the coefficients used to generate the graphs in Figures 10.7 are shown in Tables 10.11A and 10.11B). For men, the relationship between education and income is surprisingly constant across racial groups, with one exception: for non-university graduate English-speaking Whites in petty bourgeois occupations there appears to be no penalty for lack of education (although it is important to keep in mind that there are almost no White men with less than a secondary education). For women the story is one of minimal racial differences in incomes, especially among the well educated.

Conclusions

The legacy of 350 years of *apartheid* practice and fifty years of concerted *apartheid* policy has been to create racial differences in socio-economic position larger than in any other nation in the world. Whites, who constitute 11% of the population, enjoy levels of education, occupational status, and income similar to and in many respects superior to those of the industrially developed nations of Europe and the British diaspora. Almost all Whites attain at least secondary schooling and more than one-third of men and one-quarter of women secure at least some tertiary education. Few Whites are unemployed and more than one-third are members of the salariat, doing administrative and professional work. Whites also enjoy high incomes and comfortable lives. Although their incomes are low compared to other industrialised nations, so are the prices of local goods; and their incomes are very high by local standards, with the median income of White men equal to the 91st percentile of the entire male population, and the corresponding figure for White women the 93rd percentile.

THE LEGACY OF *APARTHEID* 445

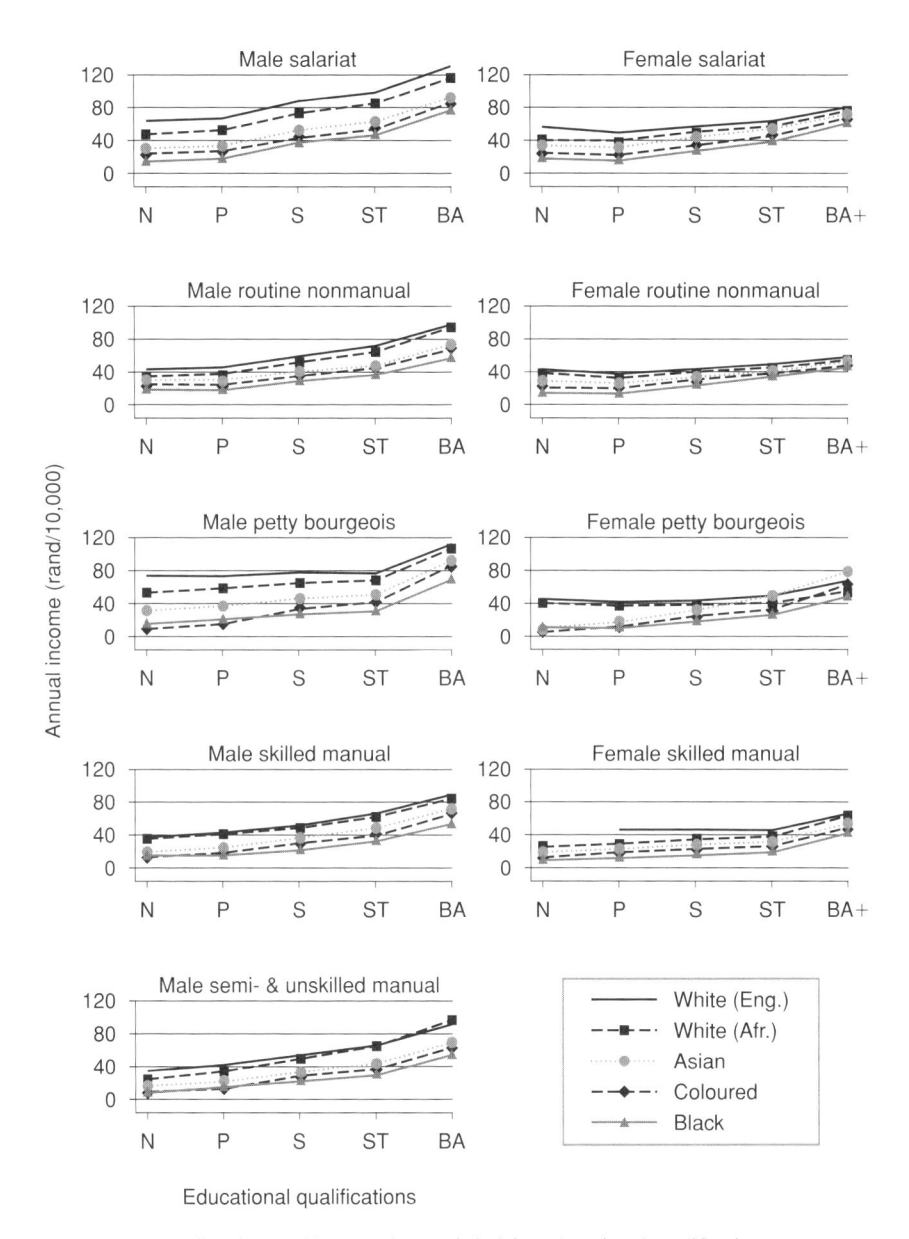

Figure 10.7. Predicted annual income, by race/ethnicity, educational qualifications, occupational class and gender.

Within the White population, however, there is a sharp distinction between the one-third of English origin and the two-thirds of Afrikaner origin. As was noted above, the English came to South Africa as an urban commercial and political elite while the Afrikaners began as *trekboers* and then moved into manual supervisory positions in the mines and factories as South Africa industrialised. Despite *apartheid* policies explicitly designed to improve the lot of Afrikaners at the expense of non-Whites, the historical difference between the two groups continues to be seen in socio-economic differences at the end of the twentieth century: modest differences in educational attainment; large difference in income; and, among men, a substantially greater likelihood that English speakers occupy salariat positions and a substantially smaller likelihood that they occupy manual positions.

Still, the disadvantages of Afrikaners are modest compared to those of non-Whites, particularly Coloureds and Blacks, who bear the brunt of *apartheid* policies. Whereas secondary education is a social minimum for Whites, it is a maximum for Coloureds and Blacks except in exceptional circumstances, with fewer than 10% of Coloureds and 5% of Blacks achieving any tertiary schooling. For the fortunate minority of Blacks and Coloureds with tertiary education, the likelihood of being employed and the kinds of jobs available differ relatively little from the opportunities of Asians and Whites, but for the vast majority lacking tertiary education the ethnic penalty is very large, particularly for Blacks. Most are unable even to find work, with about 35% of economically active Black men and more than half of economically active Black women unemployed, and those who are employed relegated largely to semi- and unskilled jobs. Although tertiary education minimises racial differences in occupational opportunities, it has little effect on income differences, which continue to be large even among the well educated and even within occupational categories, continuing a pattern documented earlier (Treiman *et al.* 1996). If stratification ultimately is about who has the money, racial and ethnic disparities remained extremely large in 1996 at the dawn of a new dispensation for South Africa. How quickly the balance will be altered remains an open question, but the 150 year post-emancipation history of racial disparities in the US does not offer much hope for optimism.

Appendix 1: Coding of variables

Education

A 'years of education completed' variable was created from the census variable, 'deducode', which combines responses to two questions: 'What is the highest school class/standard that this person has COMPLETED? (write in)' and 'Does (the person) have a technical or artisan certificate, a diploma or degree, completed at an educational institution? If "Yes", what is the highest qualification he/she has? (first part pre-coded, second part write in)'. The conversion of 'deducode' categories to years of schooling (and to education levels; see below) is based on my understanding of the South African education system. Several features are of note: (1) During the period studied, 'schooling' in South Africa consisted of two 'grades' followed by 10 'standards'. This yields twelve years of primary plus secondary schooling; (2) Some people obtain 'certificates' or 'diplomas' without completing secondary school. I have assigned thirteen years to these cases (secondary completion plus one year). This is based on inspection of a tabulation of 'field of qualification' by 'type of qualification' among those with 'qualifications' but less than Standard 10, which reveals no systematic pattern, although the bulk of qualifications are technical or unspecified; (3) In South Africa a bachelor's degree typically requires three years, and a bachelor's degree with honours typically requires four years. Here are the recodes:

deducode	edyrs	deducode	edyrs
01 No schooling	0	13 Standard 9	11
02 Grade 0	0.5	14 Less than Standard 10 + certificate/diploma	13
03 Grade 1	1	15 Standard 10 only	12
04 Grade 2	2	16 Standard 10 + certificate	13
05 Standard 1	3	17 Standard 10 + diploma	14
06 Standard 2	4	18 Standard 10 + Bachelor's degree	15
07 Standard 3	5	19 Standard 10 + Bachelor's + diploma	16
08 Standard 4	6	20 Standard 10 + Bachelor's + honours	16
09 Standard 5	7	21 Standard 10 + Master's degree	17
10 Standard 6	8	22 Standard 10 + Doctor's degree	20
11 Standard 7	9	23 Other	—
12 Standard 8	10	99 Unspecified	—

I then created five education categories: no schooling; primary (grade 0 through standard 6); secondary (standard 7 through standard 10, except category 14); some tertiary (categories 14, 16, and 17); and bachelors or more (categories 18–22). Categories 23 and 99 were treated as missing data.

Income

Respondents were asked to report into what category their current weekly, monthly, or annual income fell, with the correspondence between the three series based on the assumption of year-round employment. Thus weekly income = monthly income/4.35, and annual income = monthly income * 12. The exact wording of the question was: 'Please indicate each person's income category before tax. Answer this question by indicating each person's weekly, monthly or annual income. Include all sources of income, for example housing loan subsidies, bonuses, allowances such as car allowances and investment income. If the person receives a pension or disability grant, please include this amount.' Midpoints used by Statistics South Africa were assigned to each category but linear interpolation was used to calculate the medians. On 1 October 1996 (the date of the 1996 South African census), 1 Rand = £0.14 = $0.22.

References

Anderson, K. G., Case, A., and Lam, D. (2001), 'Causes and Consequences of Schooling Outcomes in South Africa: Evidence from Survey Data', *Social Dynamics: A Journal of the Faculty of Social Science, University of Cape Town*, 27, 37–59.

Christopher, A. J. (2002), '"To Define the Indefinable": Population Classification and the Census in South Africa', *Area*, 34, 401–8.

Davenport, T. R. H. (1987), *South Africa: A Modern History* (3rd edn.) (Johannesburg: Macmillan).

Emery, A. L. (2001), *Insurgency and Democratization in South Africa: The Community Mobilization of Ideological, Military, and Political Power*. Unpublished Ph.D. dissertation, Department of Sociology, UCLA.

Erikson, R. and Goldthorpe, J. H. (1992), *The Constant Flux: A Study of Class Mobility in Industrial Societies* (Oxford: Clarendon Press).

Fedderke, J. W., de Kadt, R., and Luiz, J. M. (2000), 'Uneducating South Africa: The Failure to Address the 1910–1993 Legacy', *International Review of Education*, 46, 257–81.

Ganzeboom, H. B. G. and Treiman, D. J. (1996), 'Internationally Comparable Measures of Occupational Status for the 1988 International Standard Classification of Occupations', *Social Science Research*, 25, 201–39.

Houghton, D. H. (1976), *The South African Economy* (4th edn.) (Cape Town: Oxford University Press).

International Labour Office (1990), *International standard classification of occupations: ISCO-88* (rev. edn.) (Geneva: International Labour Office).

Lever, H. (1978), *South African Society* (Johannesburg: Jonathan Ball).

Lever, H. (1979), 'The Jewish Voter in South Africa', *Ethnic and Racial Issues*, 2, 428–40.

McLaughlin, J. L. (1981), 'Historical Setting'. In H. D. Nelson (ed.), *South Africa: A Country Study* (Washington, DC: US Government Printing Office), pp. 1–62.

Müller, W. and Shavit, Y. (1998), 'The Institutional Imbeddedness of the Stratification Process: A Comparative Study of Qualifications and Occupations in Thirteen Countries'. In Y. Shavit and W. Müller (eds.), *From School to Work: A Comparative Study of Educational Qualifications and Occupational Destinations* (Oxford: Clarendon Press), pp. 1–48.

Nelson, R. L. and Bridges, W. P. (1999), *Legalizing Gender Inequality: Courts, Markets, and Unequal Pay for Women in America* (New York: Cambridge University Press).

Oosthuizen, G. C. (1979), 'Major Religions'. In B. Pachai (ed.), *South Africa's Indians: The Evolution of a Minority* (Washington, DC: University Press of America), pp. 517–77.

Pachai, B. (1971), *The Internal Aspect of the South African Indian Question, 1860–1971* (Cape Town: C. Struck).

Patterson, S. (1953), *Colour and Culture in South Africa: A Study of the Status of the Cape Coloured People within the Social Structure of the Union of South Africa* (London: Routledge and Kegan Paul).

Platzky, L. and Walker, C. (1985), *The Surplus People: Forced Removals in South Africa* (Johannesburg: Ravan Press).

Richardson, P. (1982), *Chinese Mine Labour in the Transvaal* (London: Macmillan).

Robertson, N. L. and Robertson, B. L. (1977), *Education in South Africa* (Fastback 90) Bloomington, IN: Phi Delta Kapppa Educational Foundation).

Semyonov, M. (1988), 'Bi-Ethnic Labor Markets, Mono-Ethnic Labor Markets, and Socioeconomic Inequality', *American Sociological Review*, 53, 256–66.

StataCorp (2003), *Stata Statistical Software: Release 8.0* (College Station, TX: Stata Corporation).

Statistics South Africa (1996), *Population Census of South Africa, 1996: 10% Sample* [Computer File]. Pretoria, South Africa: Statistics South Africa [Producer], 1996 (Pretoria, South Africa: South African Data Archive [Distributor]), 2002.

Statistics South Africa (1998), *The People of South Africa. Population Census, 1996. Calculating the Undercount in Census '96*. Report 03–01–18 (1996) (Pretoria: Statistics South Africa).

Statistics South Africa (2004), *Perceived Health and Other Health Indicators in South Africa* (Pretoria: Statistics South Africa).

Thomas, W. (1982), 'The Coloured People and the Limits of Separation'. In R. Schrire (ed.), *South Africa Public Policy Perspectives* (Cape Town: Juta), pp. 141–64.

Thompson, L. (1990), *A History of South Africa* (New Haven: Yale).

Treiman, D. J. and Roos, P. A. (1983), 'Sex and Earnings in Industrial Society: A Nine Nation Comparison', *American Journal of Sociology*, 89, 612–50.

Treiman, D. J. and Terrell, K. (1975), 'Sex and the Process of Status Attainment: A Comparison of Working Women and Men', *American Sociological Review*, 40, 174–201.

Treiman, D. J., McKeever, M., and Fodor, E. (1996), 'Racial Differences in Occupational Status and Income in South Africa, 1980 and 1991', *Demography*, 33, 111–32.

US Census Bureau (2001), Table 11 in Income 2000. Retrieved 15 Dec. 2003 from <http://www.census.gov/hhes/income/income00/tableindex.html>.

11

The Farther They Come, the Harder They Fall? First- and Second-Generation Immigrants in the Swedish Labour Market

JAN O. JONSSON[1]

Summary. Sweden has been an immigrant country since the Second World War, with a mix of labour (especially from neighbouring Nordic countries) and refugee immigration up to the early 1970s and a large inflow of refugees, especially from the Middle East, after that. In 2002 almost 13% of the Swedish population was born in another country, summing up to more than one million inhabitants out of a total nine million. Labour immigrants arriving before 1970 used to have a labour-market achievement on a par with native Swedes but in recent decades the first-generation immigrants, particularly those of non-European origin, have had relatively poor success in the labour market. This is counterbalanced by two facts: first, immigrants' labour-market attainment improves with years of residence in Sweden; second, there is considerable assimilation across generations. Sons and daughters of immigrants (born in Sweden, or who immigrated before starting school) do almost as well in the labour market as those with two Swedish-born parents. The remaining worry for this group is their relatively low employment rates. After controlling

---

[1] Financial support from the Swedish Council for Working Life and Social Research (FAS Dnr 2881/2001 and 2893/2002) is gratefully acknowledged. I have benefited from comments on a previous draft by the editor, other colleagues in the project, and from Lena Schröder. An additional thanks to Robert Erikson.

statistically for resources in the family of origin there is a gradient in the disadvantages faced by second-generation immigrants suggesting that the more visible the ethnic origin, the lower the probability of being employed (culminating with those of non-European origin). This result is not direct evidence of employer discrimination—which in this case should be limited to labour market entrance—but is certainly in line with such an interpretation.

Introduction

OVER THE LAST FEW DECADES, the issue of the labour market success of immigrants has aroused a great deal of interest. In Sweden, as in many European countries, this is partly due to the rapid growth of the immigrant population as well as their relatively poor labour-market attainment. Immigrants' disadvantage in the labour market is well documented, but is a rather recent phenomenon. Much in the same way as the American seminal contributions by Chiswick (1982) and Carliner (1980), early Swedish studies (Wadensjö 1973; Ohlsson 1975) found that immigrants' wages—after a while in the new country—reached the level of natives, and their labour-market participation was even higher than the Swedes'. And just as Borjas (e.g., 1985; 1995) found that more recent immigrants in the US did not have the qualifications and other resources to repeat the labour-market achievements of earlier immigrant cohorts, Swedish studies have shown immigrants' employment probabilities (Ekberg and Andersson 1995; Ekberg 1999; Bevelander and Nielsen 2001) and wage levels (Aguilar and Gustafsson 1991; 1994) declining over time relative to native Swedes. This unfortunate development, however, although running parallel with increased immigration from non-European countries, is not so easily interpreted in terms of a change towards less-skilled workers—as will be shown below, several of the most recently arrived immigrant groups are characterised by relatively high levels of formal qualifications.

The situation today in Sweden (as in many other Western countries) is that of diversity in the immigrant population. While some groups are very similar to native Swedes, others face disadvantages in the labour market, even after taking account of differences in educational qualifications, labour-market experience, family situation, place of residence and age (e.g., Rooth 1999; Bevelander and Nielsen 2001; Arai and Vilhelmsson

2002; Integrationsverket 2004 (employment opportunities), and le Grand and Szulkin 2002 (wage levels)). Interestingly, there appears to be a steady increase in such 'ethnic penalties' relative to the home country's distance from Sweden, and the worst off are systematically those of non-European origin—largely immigrants from Turkey, Iran, Iraq, Lebanon, and South America.

There may be various sources of ethnic penalties for first generation immigrants, such as low portability of human capital (or, as is the case for language for most immigrants to Sweden, no transferability at all), outright or statistical discrimination, and lack of social networks. However, sons and daughters of immigrants, especially if they were born in Sweden or arrived at a young age, are arguably in a much better position when it comes to resources such as language skills, educational qualifications, and networks. Through studying these second-generation immigrants we thus approach the question of whether there is employer discrimination on the grounds of ethnic origin in the Swedish labour market (though isolating discrimination effects is of course almost impossible). Studies of the second-generation are much rarer than those of first-generation immigrants as it is more difficult to find adequate data. The few Swedish studies that have been carried out suggest that unemployment risks for those born before 1970 were on par with those of natives with Swedish-born parents (Ekberg 1997) while those born later and whose parents come from non-Nordic European and non-European countries have greater difficulties of getting a job after leaving school (Vilhelmsson 2002). Similar results for unemployment were obtained for second-generation immigrants from Southern Europe and non-European countries in a more recent analysis of data from 1998 by Rooth and Ekberg (2003), who also found much the same pattern for wage levels amongst the employed.

Following on from this research, this chapter aims to study the first- and second-generation immigrants in the Swedish labour market in 1990. In addition to analysing employment, this chapter will provide analyses of occupational attainment amongst the employed, contributing to prior Swedish studies on ethnic penalties. The data set used in this chapter is based on the 1990 Census and matched register data, and consists of nearly 2.9 million people born between 1941 and 1964, thus allowing the most common countries of origin to be distinguished. This improves on previous Swedish studies in that more descriptive detail can be achieved. Also, it is possible to address, albeit indirectly, the question of labour-market discrimination due to visible minority status. In addition, the analysis of this chapter will show that the pessimistic view of the labour market attainment of second-generation immigrants partly depends on the fact that previous studies have not taken their social background into account.

Sweden as an immigration country

Like many European countries, for a long time Sweden had net emigration—from the mid-nineteenth century up to the second decade of the twentieth century nearly one million people, out of an initial three and a half million, moved to North America. However, by the 1930s emigration had virtually ceased and for the first time the country experienced a small immigration surplus; it was from the 1940s though that Sweden really became an immigrant society. The first big immigration wave, of, in particular, German and Baltic refugees, as well as immigrants from other Nordic countries, came after the Second World War, followed by people escaping oppression during the turmoil in Eastern Europe, notably from Hungary in 1956, Czechoslovakia in 1968, and Poland from the late 1960s. A free Nordic labour market was introduced in 1954 and in the 1960s labour immigration became of numerical importance, with immigrants arriving primarily from Finland, the other Nordic countries and the Mediterranean (especially Yugoslavia).[2] This was to a large extent an active labour market policy that had begun after the Second World War, but by the 1960s had intensified: Sweden's expanding industry and service sector needed people, and those who arrived were mostly workers with relatively low educational qualifications. The Swedish policy was also to avoid a guest worker system in favour of family immigration, resulting in a fairly even gender distribution within the immigrant population (see Table 11.3 below).

Labour immigration from non-Nordic countries was beginning to face limitations in 1967 when the government (influenced by demands from the trade unions) re-interpreted the Asylum Act of 1954 and introduced a requirement for jobs and residence before arrival. The economic recession following the oil crisis in 1973 effectively put an end to large-scale non-Nordic labour immigration, but immigration proceeded with a

---

[2] It should be noted that immigration from Finland had been noticeable since the sixteenth century. Immigration from Germany, Scotland, and Belgium also had historically been important, although not significant numerically.

new wave of refugees, this time coming from various non-European countries.³ War and persecution, especially in the Middle East and in Latin America, led to an immigration of around 100,000 people.⁴ Family reunion ('tied') immigration further boosted the number of immigrants from countries already represented in Sweden. In 2002, close relatives constituted 56% of the non-Nordic immigrants, refugees 24%, and labour immigrants 14%; the remainder were guest students (4.5%) and adopted children (2.3%) (Statistics Sweden 2004, table 97).⁵

Table 11.1 summarises Sweden's recent immigrant history. The proportion of people born in another country increased from 4% to almost 8% between 1960 and 1980, and in 2002 a good one million people out of almost nine million inhabitants were born in another country, i.e., nearly 12% (a figure of similar magnitude to the US, for example). These figures are much lower for the older part of the population, however, which can be seen indirectly from the figures from 1960 in Table 11.1. What is also worth noting in Table 11.1 is that the proportion of foreign citizens has not increased to the same extent as the immigration. From the 1970s onwards, this proportion is rather stable at around 5% to 6%. This is because Sweden (unlike, say, Germany) has had a liberal policy for immigrants becoming Swedish citizens.⁶

Immigrant countries and regions, 1970–2002

The numerical importance of different origin countries and regions in particular years is reflected in Table 11.2. In 2002, Finland is still the

---

[3] Sweden had a liberal interpretation of the 1954 Geneva Convention, with permanent residence given for humanitarian reasons and not only for 'traditional' political refugees. These practices were later included in the Aliens Act of 1989, when permanent visas were also given to those who had applied before 1988.

[4] Apart from these parts of the world, Sweden also received around 7,000 refugees from Eritrea and 6,000 from Vietnam/China. On the whole, however, immigrants in Sweden predominantly come from the Nordic countries, Eastern and South-eastern Europe, the Middle East and South America.

[5] Thus there remains some labour immigration to Sweden, mostly because of the EEA agreement (Sweden joined the EU in 1995). In addition, a good 10,000 immigrants in 2002 came from the other Nordic countries. As the greatest share of these no doubt came for labour-market reasons (though there will be relatives in this group too), it is possible that labour immigrants made up almost one-third of the total immigrant population in 2002.

[6] The demands during most of the period covered in this paper have been that the applicant had been living in Sweden for five years (two years for Nordic citizens), were at least 18 years of age, and had no criminal record. If they fulfilled these demands both the applicant and their children under 18, if any, could become Swedish citizens.

Table 11.1. Selected statistics on immigration to Sweden (1960–2002).

	1960	1970	1980	1990	2002
Population size (on 31 December)	7,497,967	8,081,229	8,317,937	8,590,630	8,940,788
Number of non-Swedish citizens	190,621	411,280	421,667	483,704	474,099
Percentage of non-Swedish citizens	2.5	5.1	5.1	5.6	5.3
Number not born in Sweden	299,879	537,585	626,953	790,445	1,053,463
Percentage not born in Sweden	4.0	6.7	7.5	9.2	11.8
Number of immigrants[a]	26,143	77,326	39,426	60,048	64,087
Immigration 'surplus'[a]	11,005	48,673	9,587	34,852	31,078

Source: Statistics Sweden.
[a] These figures refer to the number of immigrants and the number of immigrants minus the number of emigrants during the year in question.

most important immigration country—more than one-fifth of the immigrant population is of Finnish origin—although their proportion has decreased substantially since 1970 (from almost 44% to 18%). Norway and Denmark are also common origins, due to the geographical proximity as well as the long-standing free Nordic labour market. The change in relative size of the Nordic immigrants as a whole is quite dramatic—from 60% to 26% of the immigrants over forty years. The 'Other European immigrants' have maintained their relative share, mostly through a rising influx of immigrants from Poland and a sudden increase in the (already large) group from Yugoslavia. This increase is largely explained by Bosnians and ex-Yugoslavians coming for humanitarian reasons during the war—in 1994 alone amounting to 40,000.

Immigrants from (the former) Yugoslavia are hence a mix of an earlier labour immigration with a large inflow of refugees arriving in the 1990s. The labour-market success of the latter, and particularly the younger immigrants, will of course be very difficult to assess until well into the present decade—partly because many of those from the former Yugoslavia may not obtain permanent residency in Sweden if the political situation in their home countries improves (which is the case, for example, for Bosnians). It should be noted that as the data used in this chapter come from 1990, this latest wave of immigrants will not be included in the analyses below.

Table 11.2 also clearly shows the dramatic increase in the proportion of Asian immigrants, from 2% of the immigrant population in 1970 to almost 27% in 2002. Four Asian countries alone—Iraq, Iran, Turkey, and Lebanon—account for 16% of the immigrants residing in Sweden in 2002. It is evident that the immigrant population in Sweden has become not only much more Asian in character, but also much more diverse—the

Table 11.2. Relative size of immigrant populations, by country/region of birth (1970–2002) (column percentages).

Country of birth	1970	1980	1990	2002
Finland	43.8	40.1	27.5	18.2
Yugoslavia/Bosnia/Croatia	6.3	6.1	5.5	12.6
Iraq	—	0.2	1.2	6.0
Iran	0.1	0.5	5.1	5.0
Norway	8.3	6.8	6.7	4.2
Poland	2.0	3.2	4.5	3.9
Denmark	7.3	6.9	5.6	3.8
Germany	7.8	6.2	4.6	3.7
Turkey	0.7	2.3	3.2	3.1
Chile	0.0	1.3	3.5	2.6
Lebanon	0.0	0.3	2.0	1.9
Great Britain	1.0	1.3	1.4	1.5
U.S.A.	2.4	1.9	1.6	1.4
Hungary	2.0	2.1	1.9	1.3
Greece	2.2	2.4	1.7	1.0
Total from countries above	83.9	81.7	76.1	70.4
From other countries	16.1	18.3	23.9	29.6
By region				
Nordic	59.7	54.4	40.4	26.5
Europe, other	32.8	30.5	27.9	32.6
Africa	0.8	1.6	3.5	5.6
North America	2.9	2.3	2.4	2.4
South America	0.4	2.7	5.6	5.1
Asia	1.8	7.2	19.0	26.7
Soviet Union	1.3	1.1	0.9	0.7
Oceania	0.1	0.2	0.2	0.3
Total percentage	100.0	100.0	100.0	100.0
Total number	537,585	626,953	790,445	1,053,463

Source: Statistics Sweden.
Note: Before 2002, Yugoslavia was reported as one country. In the 2002 figures, Moldavia and Slovenia are not included (only a small fraction of immigrants come from these countries). The figure for Iraq in 1980 is estimated from the figure in 1982.

fifteen countries listed account for only around 70% of the immigrant group, as compared to 84% in 1970.

Immigration to Sweden: An international perspective

Comparative statistics indicate that immigrant populations as well as immigration (or integration) policies differ significantly among countries (OECD 2003; Integrationsverket 2004). In particular, characteristic of

Sweden's immigrant population are the large share of Nordic immigrants and the concentration of non-European immigrants coming from the Middle East; however, with substantial proportions of immigrants also coming from Eastern and Southern Europe, Africa, and from Latin America, perhaps the *diversity* amongst the sending countries is the most striking feature of Sweden's immigrant population. Additionally, Sweden hosts a comparatively large refugee population. Since the 1970s, Sweden has not (unlike many other countries) pursued quota immigration based on skills, education or other labour market-relevant assets. Only a very small proportion—probably around 10%—of immigrants comes from the same language area, not only because this area is small but also because Sweden has no (recent) colonial tradition.[7] Finally, overall Sweden has a relatively large proportion of its population born in a foreign country—a slightly larger proportion than in the US and about the same size as in Belgium, France, the Netherlands, and Austria. It is not surprising, given the characteristics of immigration to Sweden, that recent unemployment rates show the relative disadvantage of the immigrant group (as compared to native-born) to be among the highest in the OECD countries, together with precisely the four aforementioned countries (OECD 2004).

Previous studies on immigrants in the Swedish labour market

Although in the 1950s and 1960s many immigrants to Sweden undoubtedly faced problems in the labour market, for a long time such problems were relatively uncommon—in the 1970s the labour-force participation of immigrants was in fact higher than that of Swedes, particularly amongst women (Wadensjö 1973). From the 1970s and onwards, when immigration from non-European countries started to increase—and when the long-booming economy started to behave more erratically—immigrants' difficulties in the labour market increased. Ekberg (1999,

---

[7] The small proportion of immigrants who come from the same language area is in sharp contrast to countries such as Australia, United Kingdom, France and Portugal, where this proportion is 65% or higher, but rather similar to the other Nordic countries, Germany, Italy and the Netherlands (OECD 2003).

table A.3) estimates that in 1960 the labour-force participation of immigrant men was the same as for native-born Swedes, but that by the end of the 1970s it had declined to 95% of the latter's, and by 1991 stood at 84%; the corresponding figures for women were 10% 'plus' in 1960, a similar level by the end of the 1970s, and 83% in 1991.

These unfavourable figures must be seen against a backdrop of almost full employment during the 1980s, by the end of which there were, in practice, labour shortages in most sectors of the economy. Things would get worse—and much worse. When a sudden and exceptionally deep recession hit the Swedish economy in the period from 1991 to 1993, with a loss of around 550,000 jobs out of an initial 4.5 million (Statistics Sweden 2004, fig. 297), immigrants suffered most. Those who were employed lost their jobs to a higher degree than native Swedes, even controlling for human capital, establishment characteristics, and wage rate (Arai and Vilhelmsson 2002). Furthermore, the continuing flow of immigrants, especially those connected to the civil war in Yugoslavia, had very small chances of gaining a foothold in the labour market. By 1996, the employment rate among immigrants had fallen to below 75% that of native-born Swedes (Ekberg 1999), for whom the unemployment rate was still extremely high. Since the end of the 1990s the Swedish economy has improved, but the labour-market situation for immigrants remains precarious. The Swedish Integration Board (Integrationsverket 2004) has recently presented figures showing that the average employment rate of foreign-born in 2003 was 60%, compared with 76% for those born in Sweden (in 1990, the corresponding figures were 74% and 84%, respectively)—indicating that the relations between immigrants and Swedish-born at any rate had increased to 80% during the latter half of the 1990s (ibid., fig. 2). This average figure conceals the fact that among those who arrived during the 1990s, and especially from Asia and Africa, employment rates were as low as 17% to 45% in 2003 (ibid., figs. 8–9).

The story for wage differences is fairly similar to that for employment. Whereas early waves of immigrants reached salaries on a par with native Swedes (Wadensjö 1973), this has not been the fortune of more recent immigrants, especially, though not exclusively, those from non-European countries (Aguilar and Gustafsson 1994). Between 1992 and 1995, when unemployment was very high—suggesting a strong positive selection effect on immigrant employment—wage levels for non-European immigrants were 14% lower for men and 7% lower for women as compared to native-born Swedes with the same level of qualification (le Grand and Szulkin 2002, table 4).[8]

Why, then, are immigrants disadvantaged in the Swedish labour market? There are more theories than evidence on this issue. A common observation is that immigrants' qualifications are not immediately transferable to the Swedish labour market, either because they are not adequate (such as language and other country-specific human capital), or because employers do not know or trust them. An issue of some relevance in an international perspective is that the Swedish language takes quite a while to learn and very few immigrants—almost exclusively those from Norway and Denmark, and, to a much lesser extent, from Iceland and Finland—have even a rudimentary knowledge of it upon arrival.[9] This issue has led to a Swedish policy making language courses for newly arrived refugees (in practice) mandatory, something that in turn has delayed their entry into the labour market.

Another theory accounting for this disadvantage is, of course, discrimination. With the increasing problems of the non-native population during the 1980s and onwards, immigrants' opportunities have become a political issue of growing importance. In the governmental bill on integration policy in 1998, 'equal rights and opportunities of everyone, irrespective of ethnic and cultural background' were included as one of three aims (Proposition 1997/98: 16). An Ombudsman protecting the rights of those who were subject to ethnic discrimination was installed in 1986 and a new law against discrimination in the labour market that put the burden of proof on employers was passed in 1999 (Proposition 1997/98: 177). A common view is that these actions so far have had limited effect; there seems, for example, to be little chance of succeeding in a legal case against an employer who is accused of discrimination, and, contrary to what is the case, for example, in the US, penalties for violating discrimination laws are not severe.

---

[8] Controls were made for years of schooling, years of potential experience, and years of seniority. The estimates reported here concern employees with 11–20 years of residence.

[9] The case of Finland is complicated. Finnish is not even an Indo-European language (belonging to the same group as Estonian and Hungarian) and as such is very different from Swedish. On the other hand, given the historical relations between the two countries, for a long time Finns have had obligatory education in Swedish in school. Around 6% also belong to a Swedish minority in Finland (*Finlandssvenskar*), which was over-represented among post-1970 immigrants (Wadensjö 1973). Furthermore, in the remote north-eastern part of Sweden (*Tornedalen*), a particular type of Finnish is spoken.

Another explanation for immigrant disadvantage is that the Swedish labour market, with high minimum wages and strong employment security, provides an effective barrier against outsiders aiming to gain footing in the labour market (Lindbeck and Snower 1988). One long-term change in the labour market has also been, partly because of the compressed wage structure, that unqualified labour has declined while white-collar work in the service sector—normally requiring clearly defined professional qualifications and more often involving communicative skills—has grown. While in the mid-1970s more than 40% of those employed in the age range 25–64 were in unskilled (either manual or non-manual) jobs, this was the case for only 32% in 1990 and only 25% in 1999 (Jonsson 2004, fig. 9.1).[10] Entry into the labour market at low levels has thus become more complicated for immigrants who lack Swedish-specific skills.

While it is fairly easy to find plausible explanations for first-generation immigrant disadvantage in the labour market without assuming discrimination, it is more difficult to explain why second-generation immigrants—i.e., children to immigrants who were born and/or went to school in Sweden—still face disadvantages. Le Grand and Szulkin (2002) studied the wage level in 1995 of Swedish- and foreign-born who finished their upper secondary education in Sweden, controlling for human capital variables as well as average school grades. They found a remaining wage difference of 4% for men and 3.5% for women. Vilhelmsson (2002), in his study of unemployment in the Swedish youth labour market, found an excessive risk of being unemployed, out of the labour force, and in a labour market training programme for non-European immigrants in 1995, also controlling for grades in Swedish, human capital variables, parental education, place of residence, and time of immigration.[11] Rooth and Ekberg (2003) report even greater disadvantages for non-European

---

[10] The unskilled jobs are defined as those in which less than two years of schooling in addition to the compulsory nine years are necessary. During the same period, 1976 to 1999, the salariat (containing higher and medium level managers and administrators, as well as professionals and semi-professionals) has grown from 23% to 38%. In most jobs in these social classes, formal merits are needed, and foreign qualifications may be difficult to translate into merits that will have a value in the Swedish labour market.

[11] Relative risks are around three for labour-market programmes and out of the labour force, and around two for unemployment (relative to working in the regular labour market). Non-Nordic European immigrants (dominated by Yugoslavs) also have an excessive risk for unemployment (log-odds=1.7) and for being out of the labour force (log-odds=3.6). It should be mentioned that both the non-European immigrant groups also have higher odds of being in education (1.9). (All ratios compared with the reference category of Swedish-born with two Swedish-born parents.)

second-generation immigrants aged 20 to 45 in 1998, both concerning unemployment and wage level, controlling for human capital variables (although not for ability).[12] These studies all suggest that there may be employer discrimination, though few studies take parental resources into account (a notable exception being Vilhelmsson 2002)—it remains a viable hypothesis, at the heart of the sociological tradition, that differences in social, economic, and cultural resources in the family of origin may explain some of the disadvantages faced by second generation immigrants.

Data sources

The data used in this chapter come mainly from register information on country of birth, immigration age, and education, which has been linked with census data on occupation, income, and social class. By using the censuses it is possible to match parents and children to each other through a unique personal identifier and thus obtain information about social and ethnic origin; these matchings are entirely accurate and non-matched cases very few. The links are based on household connections in the census of 1960 and 1970[13] while the outcome variables—mainly occupational information—have been taken from the 1990 Census. As this linking demands that the respondent lives in the same household as the parent at least in 1960, it is unwise to include those born earlier than 1941 in the sample as a non-negligible fraction of them will have moved out at ages 19 and above. The data set also does not include people born later than 1964, so the analyses cover men and women aged (in 1990) 26 to 49. For the purpose at hand this is reasonable because social-class mobility is very low in Sweden after the age of 30–40 and because a noticeable proportion of those younger than 26 will still be in education. An important advantage is that the data set consists of all Swedish residents in 1990

---

[12] They also find that second-generation immigrants from Southern Europe are disadvantaged in terms of unemployment risks and men's wage levels. Because of differences in samples and model specifications, it is not possible to conclude that the disadvantages of second-generation immigrants have become worse between 1995 and 1998.

[13] For respondents immigrating later, we have information on their country of birth via registers, but for those who were born in Sweden there is no way of determining their 'second-generation' immigrant status except having access to the corresponding information for the parents. In Sweden there is no direct question about country of origin or ethnicity in the Censuses that could be used for this purpose.

born between 1941 and 1964, meaning that—after taking a small proportion of missing values into account—there are about 2.9 million people in the data set. This allows for quite a detailed account of ethnic origins and leads to precise estimates for many immigrant groups. The common problem in surveys of a high non-response rate within immigrant groups is also avoided. Through the connection between parents and children, it is also possible to identify both first- and second-generation immigrants in the same analysis (though few of the latter will of course be children to the former, given the rather narrow age differences).

Variables, definitions and the composition of the ethnic origin groups

What will be termed 'ethnic groups' or 'ethnic origins' are in Swedish registry data defined as the country of birth. To define 'pure' ethnic groups one would need to have additional information, primarily on language, life-style, religion, and skin colour (and information about the latter two characteristics would be considered ethically problematic to collect). This means that we cannot identify ethnic minorities within Sweden, such as indigenous groups.[14] Furthermore, we cannot distinguish different ethnic groups among immigrants.[15] The information on country of birth, along

---

[14] According to the EU convention on protecting national minorities, that Sweden ratified in 2000, there are five ethnic minorities and minority languages in Sweden (see Proposition 1998/99: 143): Finns (*Sverigefinnar*; their language is Finnish), Finns from Tornedalen (*Tornedalingar*; Meänkieli), Sami (*Samer*; Lappish), Romanies (*Romer*; Romany Chib), and Jews (*Judar*; Jiddisch), of which the three former are territorial minorities. The Finns are included in this study as immigrants while the other groups cannot be discerned. The minority that comes closest to an indigenous group is the Sami of which there are around 20,000 in Sweden at the beginning of the twenty-first century.

[15] A case in point is the Turks in Sweden. About 1990, when our data begin, there were around 20,000 Turks living in Sweden, but only approximately 8,000 of them were 'ethnic Turks' (mostly Kuluturks). Around 9,000 were Assyrians (belonging to the Syrian-Orthodox Church) and 3,000 Kurds. All of these groups are identified in the data as 'Turks' but this conceals important ethnic divisions within this group. Another indication of the lack of precision in the measure of national origin is that it is assumed that around 8,000 people living in Sweden by the end of the 1980s were Kurds, the additional 5,000 coming from neighbouring countries such as Iran and Iraq (estimates from Sveriges Nationalatlas 1991). On the other hand, there is hardly any theoretical reason to expect differences between these ethnic groups.

with year of immigration (available from 1968 and onwards)[16] as well as the year of Swedish citizenship, is regularly included in official records, meaning that these data are administrative and not based on survey questions.

A distinction which follows the one commonly made in the literature is between 'first'- and 'second'-generation immigrants (where the latter group more properly could be called 'second-generation Swedes'). 'First-generation immigrants' are defined as those who immigrated after the start of primary school, which takes place at age seven in Sweden.[17] 'Second-generation immigrants' are those who either were born in Sweden or moved there before the age of eight, *and* whose parents were *both* born in another country.[18] There is a theoretical reason for this distinction: the important dimension in socialisation should be to have access to Swedish-specific resources and characteristics, and it is most likely sufficient to have one parent who is Swedish-born for having Swedish spoken at home, acquaintance with the Swedish school system and labour market, and for 'knowing the way around' in Swedish society.[19] There is also a pragmatic reason, namely that the big divide in educational and labour-market attainment is between those who have no Swedish-born parent and those who have one (Similä 1994; Lundh *et al.* 2002). In the analyses of second-generation immigrants, the contrast is with Swedish-born with no foreign-born parent (i.e., who have either two Swedish-born parents, or, in the case of single parents, the custodial parent is of Swedish origin). This reference group is referred to as those with 'Swedish ancestry'. As a special category I distinguish those with 'mixed Swedish-foreign ancestry' (i.e., those who have two parents of which one was born in Sweden and the other in some other country).[20]

---

[16] The information concerns the most recent year of immigration, in case the person has immigrated more than once. Unfortunately, there is no way in the data to take multiple immigration histories into account.

[17] This chapter defines the age as eight because children start school in the autumn of the year they have their seventh birthday.

[18] If the respondent lived with a single parent in the year in which the household connection was done (mostly in 1960), we have no information on the other ('absent') parent. These cases (4.6% of the total number) are assigned the country of origin of the custodial parent.

[19] Classifying someone with a native-born parent as a 'second-generation immigrant' seems often to stem from an assumption that a foreign-born parent is like some sort of disease that may contaminate the child. Alternatively, having one foreign-born parent may lead to visible minority status, though this is true for small proportions of immigrants to Sweden.

[20] The Swedish-born parent in the category of mixed Swedish-foreign ancestry may still have foreign-born parents. In some cases there is mixed ancestry among immigrants because the

Table 11.3 shows the ethnic groups that were distinguished in the data for the bulk of the analyses, where '1' is used to indicate the first generation and '2' the second. It should be noted that the categorisation of countries is, like most groupings in previous research, not theoretically founded; thus, it aims more at descriptive detail than explanation. With that in mind, most country groupings are straightforward, but some classification decisions have been made. Those (few) from Iceland have been coded with the Norwegian and Danish immigrants; the category 'Western' includes Great Britain (the biggest group), Ireland, Belgium, the Netherlands, Luxembourg, France, Switzerland, Austria, Canada, the US, Australia, and New Zealand; 'Southern Europe' comprises Portugal, Spain, and Italy. Asian immigrants in Sweden are dominated by those from the Middle East. Immigrants from Latin America mostly come from Chile (a country of origin that is distinguished for first- but not second-generation immigrants). In further analyses of first-generation immigrants, I will use a more detailed classification, particularly for the African and Asian category (described in connection to Table 11.10, where numbers for these sub-categories also can be found).

Immigrants in Sweden have disincentives to work immediately upon arrival because they receive special 'arrival-support' that is intended to take them through the first transitory period, especially involving language courses. Furthermore, asylum seekers could not, during most of the time period under study, get a work permit during the first year. Because of this, and the fact that newly arrived immigrants already faced great structural barriers (such as language problems) in getting a job, I have excluded those who immigrated to Sweden in 1989 and 1990 in all analyses.

As can be seen from Table 11.3, some ethnic groups among second-generation immigrants are too small to be discerned—these cases are later excluded from the analyses in order to keep the other categories as comparable as possible. It may seem surprising to find such a discrepancy between the number of first- and second-generation immigrants, but it is likely because the youngest cohort included here were born in 1964 (and started school in 1971), before which immigration to Sweden was still limited. More recent data would have yielded more second-generation

---

mother and the father come from different, foreign countries. In these, rather few, mixed cases we let the father's country of origin determine the classification. This is reasonable because the household class position will most often be derived from the father who in general has the strongest connection to the labour market and more often the 'dominant' class position.

Table 11.3. Relative size of ethnic origin groups in 1990, by generation and gender.

	Men			Women		
	N	% of Total Population	% of Immigrant Population	N	% of Total Population	% of Immigrant Population
Swedish	1,181,350	81.9	—	1,126,988	81.6	—
Mixed (Swedish & Other)	48,074	3.3	—	45,241	3.3	—
Finnish 1	46,199	3.2	21.6	58,176	4.2	27.9
Finnish 2	17,527	1.2	8.2	16,870	1.2	8.1
Norwegian/Danish 1	12,786	0.9	6.0	14,752	1.1	7.1
Norwegian/Danish 2	14,611	1.0	6.8	13,671	1.0	6.6
Western 1	10,281	0.7	4.8	7,049	0.5	3.4
Western 2	5,295	0.4	2.5	5,037	0.4	2.4
German 1	5,743	0.4	2.7	4,492	0.3	2.2
German 2	5,635	0.4	2.6	5,264	0.4	2.5
Polish 1	5,605	0.4	2.6	11,729	0.8	5.6
Polish 2	1,504	0.1	0.7	1,400	0.1	0.7
Greek 1	4,347	0.3	2.0	2,727	0.2	1.3
Greek 2	307	0.0	0.1	278	0.0	0.1
Yugoslavian 1	11,076	0.8	5.2	10,701	0.8	5.1
Yugoslavian 2	1,285	0.1	0.6	1,225	0.1	0.6
East European 1	7,865	0.5	3.7	8,620	0.6	4.1
East European 2	6,884	0.5	3.2	6,801	0.5	3.3
South European 1	4,387	0.3	2.1	2,178	0.2	1.0
South European 2	1,239	0.1	0.6	1,127	0.1	0.5
African 1	7,957	0.6	3.7	3,837	0.3	1.8
African 2	372	0.0	0.2	373	0.0	0.2
Latin American 1	8,572	0.6	4.0	8,100	0.6	3.9
Latin American 2	346	0.0	0.2	333	0.0	0.2
Asian 1	14,538	1.0	6.8	11,527	0.8	5.5
Asian 2	2,075	0.1	1.0	1,987	0.1	1.0
Iranian 1	10,916	0.8	5.1	5,638	0.4	2.7
Turkish 1	6,293	0.4	2.9	4,781	0.3	2.3
Other 2	392	—	—	289	—	—
Total	1,443,461	100.0	100.0	1,381,191	100.0	100.0

Notes: Numbers shown are for respondents 26–49 years of age who were born or arrived in Sweden before 1989. Further divisions of certain groups can be seen in Table 11.11. The suffix 1 indicates first generation and the suffix 2 indicates second generation.

immigrants from non-European countries in particular, but also from Yugoslavia and Poland, for example.[21] One consequence of the different waves of immigration (and the resulting difference between the number of first and second generation immigrants) is that some ethnic groups consist of people who have been living in Sweden for many years, while

---

[21] Unfortunately, it is nearly impossible to replicate the analyses in this chapter on more recent data as Sweden abolished the censuses after 1990. This means that it is not (yet) possible to get register data on the population's occupational attainment of sufficient scope and quality after that.

others arrived very recently—a difference that of course will lead to corresponding differences in their labour-market outcomes. This heterogeneity will be handled in special analyses by controlling for year of immigration.

Social class is based on information on occupation and employment status, resulting in a standard classification used by Statistics Sweden (1982). This class schema is similar to the commonly used so-called 'EGP' class schema (Erikson and Goldthorpe 1992: 35–47). (For details of the way this schema has had to be modified for the Swedish data, see the technical appendix to this chapter.) The occupational title and employment status were reported by the respondents in the 1990 Census. Both parental education and social class origin will also be used as control variables. The definitions and data sources are the same as for the respondent and I have taken the higher of the father's and mother's education and class to indicate family characteristics. In addition, the analyses use single parenthood as a control as well to identify those who live with a single parent from those who live with two parents (whether biological or not).

It can be noted from Table 11.3 that some categories are rather small, while the number of first-generation Finns is very large—they dominate the immigrant group when it is defined as the total of first- and second-generation immigrants. Due to demographic reasons, such as age and immigration year, different countries are more and less represented in the two different generations of immigrants. For example, among the second generation the Nordic groups dominate (56%) while in the first generation only the Finns stand out, constituting 30% of men and 38% of women. Apart from these categories, however, there is a fairly even spread of ethnic groups, reflecting the wide variety of immigrants coming to Sweden in the post-Second World War period.

Educational qualifications are measured by a standard Swedish educational coding (SUN, see Statistics Sweden 1988) that has been recoded in order to be comparable with the CASMIN schema as developed by Müller and associates (Müller and Shavit 1998; see the description in the technical appendix to this chapter). The information comes primarily from a register on the education of the population which was complemented with a question on the highest educational qualification attained in the 1990 Census.[22]

---

[22] The existing code at the time of the census, derived from official registers of examined from secondary and tertiary level schools, was printed on the census form and the respondent was asked to correct it if wrong (in particular, vocational qualifications not taken in the public school

Information on economic activity and non-employment is unfortunately not available from the censuses. This means that we cannot with any certainty distinguish between those who are unemployed, students, home-workers or gainfully employed in 1990. However, the latter category should have an occupational code (few of the others would have such a code). As we can expect some non-response on the question of occupation in the census, especially among immigrants who arrived quite recently, estimating the number of non-employed from the occupational code alone is not feasible. Fortunately, the data include information on individual income for 1990 from tax records.[23] Thus I estimated a 'lowest bound' of income by cross-classifying the occupational code (missing versus other) against income bands, and choosing an income limit above which it seems unlikely that a respondent would be without a job. Those with income above that limit are all classified as employed, together with those below that limit with an occupational code. This strategy leads to estimates of non-employment of 6% for men and 9% for women. The group of non-employed, it must be added, is not the same as the unemployed. Especially among female immigrants there may be house workers in it (although those on parental leave who held a job prior to this will be counted as employed). There will also be those who are undergoing labour-market training, most of which is 'hidden unemployment'. There is also a certain number of university students among the non-employed. However, because those younger than 26 are not in the data set, this is not such a big problem (and when I experimented by raising the age-limit to 30 the changes in the proportion of non-employed were rather similar among different ethnic groups, i.e., also in the reference group of Swedish ancestry). While it is unwise to pay attention to the exact numbers or percentages of non-employed in the data, the relation between ethnic groups is likely to be a reliable estimate of the relative proportions that are out of the labour market, and therefore of which groups have a particularly vulnerable position.

---

system would have been under-reported in the register). For most immigrants there would not have been a code as they had their education from another country. In these cases, the educational information is based on the response to the census. The relatively large proportion of missing information indicates that some did not respond to this question, and in other cases the information gathered was not sufficient for assigning an educational code.

[23] As the income variable taps 'total income', which also includes benefits and allowances, it is not possible to use the criteria 'positive income' as a substitute for non-employment, as everyone has a positive value.

Educational and labour-market attainment of different ethnic groups

This section presents the actual differences in educational and labour-market attainment among the ethnic groups. Tables 11.4, 11.5, and 11.6 report outflow distributions of educational qualifications, gainful employment, and occupational class (among those estimated to be gainfully employed), for 26–49-year olds of different ethnic origins.

Tables 11.4A and 11.4B show the distribution of highest educational qualification for the different ethnic groups, for men and women respectively. The available information sums row-wise to 100%. The information is missing for only 1% or fewer of those groups that have their education in Sweden; however it is clear that classifying qualifications of immigrants involves a number of difficulties.[24] Because of the sizeable amount of non-classifiable educational qualifications, 'missing' is used as a separate category in the analyses below, and results are reported from models including the interaction between the missing value status and country of origin.

The immigrant groups differ markedly in their educational profiles.[25] In general, first-generation immigrants have relatively low qualifications, both compared with those of Swedish (and mixed) ancestry and with second-generation immigrants. Those from Greece, other Southern European countries, and Yugoslavia clearly have lower average levels of education than native-born Swedes, as do Finnish men and women from Asia (except Iran) and Africa. But the educational level of Turks, especially women, lags even further behind.[26] Immigrants from Eastern European countries (except Yugoslavia), on the other hand, have relatively high levels of education. Many intellectuals (politically active as well as from groups who were harassed in their home countries, such as Jews) came from these countries, mostly as political refugees. Immigrants

---

[24] Missing values range from almost 15% (men from 'other Western' nations) to around 5% (most European origins) or lower (for Nordic immigrants). For immigrants of Non-European origin around 10% have missing values on education. The problem is insignificant among the second-generation immigrants.

[25] The groups we compare have different distributions of birth cohorts which affect their average educational chances, in addition to their country of origin and in conjunction with the selectivity of emigration.

[26] It is interesting to note the overall quite large gender differences in the most educationally disadvantaged groups, with women having less education than men (although for those of Swedish ancestry, the distribution is fairly even between men and women).

from other Western countries also have relatively high educational qualifications.

In relation to the immigration history of Sweden it can be noted that many early immigrants (such as the Germans and those from the Baltic countries) have relatively high levels of education; that the immigrants of the 'mid-period' of the 1960s and 1970s show a mixed pattern, with refugees having high formal qualifications (e.g., Poles and Latin Americans) but labour-force immigrants (e.g., Greeks, Yugoslavs, and Finnish men) relatively low levels; while the most recent immigrants (with the important exception of the Turks) are comparatively well educated (e.g., those from Iran, and men from Africa and some countries in Asia).

Tables 11.4A and 11.4B also demonstrate that differences between second-generation immigrants and those with Swedish ancestry are substantially less than for first-generation immigrants. The increase in educational attainment across generations is particularly great for women from the more educationally disadvantaged countries of origin. Further analyses (e.g., Erikson and Jonsson 1993; Similä 1994; Jonsson 2002) show that once birth cohort, family structure, and the social and educational background of individuals are taken into account, the educational attainment of children of immigrant parents is, on average, not lower than that of children with Swedish ancestry. Some groups do markedly better (especially those from Eastern Europe, such as Poland) whereas some do worse (e.g., those from Nordic countries and Asia). A common pattern among second-generation immigrants, however, is polarisation: children of immigrant origin have higher chances of achieving a university degree but also stand greater risks of early school-leaving.[27]

Table 11.5 displays the proportion of non-employed for different ethnic groups. It should be recalled that the percentages are estimates and that we should concentrate on the differences between groups rather than on the absolute values. Generally, the proportion non-employed is much higher among first-generation immigrants, both in comparison with second-generation immigrants and with Swedes of native-born parents.[28] Overall, Table 11.5 paints a rather gloomy picture of weak labour-market attachment among several immigrant groups. Non-employment is

---

[27] This is the case for children whose parents immigrated from Latin America, Greece, Turkey, and Africa. For all immigrant groups except those from other Nordic countries the outstanding pattern is that they choose vocational branches of study at secondary school to a much lesser degree than those with Swedish-born parents (Jonsson 2002, tables 6–7).

[28] A peculiar exception is the pattern for Yugoslavs among whom second-generation immigrants have a higher non-employment rate than the first.

IMMIGRANTS IN THE SWEDISH LABOUR MARKET 471

Table 11.4A. Highest educational qualification by ancestry: Men (row percentages).

	Compulsory only	Basic vocational	Lower second	Full second	Lower tertiary	Full tertiary	Post-graduate	N
Swedish ancestry	26.1	30.0	11.1	7.7	12.7	11.4	1.1	1,181,350
Mixed (Swedish & Other)	21.7	32.5	10.5	8.7	13.5	12.1	1.1	48,074
First generation								
Finnish	42.1	32.8	9.3	4.4	6.3	4.7	0.4	46,199
Norwegian/ Danish	30.5	28.1	13.5	4.5	7.8	13.5	2.0	12,786
Western	17.8	18.7	14.9	9.2	14.0	20.7	4.6	10,281
German	15.7	27.1	23.2	7.3	11.4	12.7	2.6	5,743
Polish	11.0	28.0	12.7	8.3	14.5	22.6	2.9	5,605
Greek	40.7	24.7	9.1	5.2	8.1	10.4	1.9	4,347
Yugoslavian	35.7	35.5	14.8	4.8	5.8	3.1	0.2	11,076
East European	13.3	24.8	18.2	9.3	12.5	19.2	2.6	7,865
South European	37.8	28.0	10.4	5.5	8.0	8.6	1.7	4,387
African	22.9	34.0	9.3	6.5	11.1	13.4	2.8	7,957
Latin American	23.4	33.0	11.6	6.2	12.7	11.5	1.7	8,572
Asian	32.6	28.6	8.0	5.0	10.1	12.5	3.2	14,538
Iranian	13.0	23.4	14.1	19.7	13.8	14.6	1.3	10,916
Turkish	52.9	25.0	5.8	3.9	7.2	4.9	0.3	6,293
Second generation								
Finnish	20.7	43.7	8.8	7.3	12.0	6.9	0.6	17,527
Norwegian/ Danish	25.8	34.3	10.4	7.0	11.7	9.9	0.8	14,611
Western	18.0	24.9	10.4	11.3	16.7	16.8	1.9	5,295
German	16.0	28.5	10.4	11.6	16.9	15.1	1.7	5,635
Polish	18.3	25.0	10.1	8.3	15.9	19.6	2.8	1,504
Greek	15.5	36.3	12.2	13.5	12.5	8.9	1.0	307
Yugoslavian	18.0	42.0	8.4	10.9	13.1	7.5	0.2	1,285
East European	17.6	27.4	10.1	10.9	15.6	16.7	1.8	6,884
South European	20.0	29.2	11.8	10.9	14.3	12.3	1.6	1,239
African	14.9	24.0	9.4	11.6	16.6	20.7	2.8	372
Latin American	15.4	21.7	10.1	13.3	14.2	23.5	1.7	346
Asian	20.1	26.2	10.2	10.4	14.3	17.0	1.7	2,075
Total	26.3	30.2	11.1	7.6	12.4	11.3	1.1	1,443,069

Note: Includes respondents aged 26–49 who were born or arrived in Sweden before 1989.

generally very high among non-European immigrant categories, partly, as will be shown below, because they are relatively recent arrivers. Low employment rates are particularly evident for women.

Tables 11.6A and 11.6B show the distribution of occupational class positions among those who are classified as gainfully employed (which, as we have just seen, in some ethnic categories is a highly selective group). Naturally, the pattern of occupational attainment reflected in Tables 11.6 is to a large extent predictable from the educational distributions in Tables 11.4. Thus, starting from the disadvantaged class positions, we can note that persons who immigrated from most non-European countries as

Table 11.4B. Highest educational qualification by ancestry: Women (row percentages).

	Compulsory only	Basic vocational	Lower second	Full second	Lower tertiary	Full tertiary	Post-graduate	N
Swedish	20.5	32.6	11.3	7.3	19.2	8.8	0.3	1,126,988
Mixed (Swedish & Other)	17.5	32.0	12.0	9.3	19.0	9.9	0.3	45,241
First generation								
Finnish	32.5	31.3	8.9	6.2	13.6	7.2	0.2	58,176
Norwegian/ Danish	30.7	31.8	10.2	5.5	13.9	7.5	0.4	14,752
Western	16.7	19.3	10.4	9.1	20.2	21.5	2.8	7,049
German	18.0	30.1	14.6	8.0	17.6	10.8	1.0	4,492
Polish	13.6	29.1	12.1	11.5	16.9	15.9	0.9	11,729
Greek	61.4	15.7	5.7	4.2	8.0	4.5	0.6	2,727
Yugoslavian	50.9	24.9	9.3	5.5	6.6	2.7	0.1	10,701
East European	13.2	24.1	13.6	11.0	18.2	18.8	1.1	8,620
South European	39.5	23.9	7.1	7.1	12.1	8.9	1.5	2,178
African	44.8	25.1	7.3	5.0	10.3	6.6	0.8	3,837
Latin American	30.8	29.7	9.1	4.7	16.4	8.6	0.7	8,100
Asian	50.5	21.0	5.1	4.5	9.6	8.1	1.0	11,527
Iranian	20.2	22.3	11.8	18.2	18.0	9.1	0.4	5,638
Turkish	74.1	15.0	3.8	1.6	3.5	1.8	0.2	4,781
Second generation								
Finnish	19.1	37.4	12.1	9.6	15.4	6.2	0.2	16,870
Norwegian/ Danish	23.3	33.7	11.7	7.7	15.9	7.3	0.3	13,671
Western	15.0	26.3	12.2	11.7	21.2	13.3	0.4	5,037
German	14.0	27.0	12.4	13.2	20.1	12.8	0.5	5,264
Polish	14.0	28.2	12.4	12.2	18.8	13.8	0.7	1,400
Greek	25.7	21.5	11.7	15.5	10.9	14.3	0.4	278
Yugoslavian	18.5	33.1	13.6	15.0	12.5	7.2	0.2	1,225
East European	14.3	27.6	12.2	12.2	19.6	13.6	0.5	6,801
South European	17.1	28.9	13.3	16.5	15.4	8.4	0.4	1,127
African	17.0	20.3	10.0	11.4	24.2	15.3	1.7	373
Latin American	15.0	18.4	12.3	11.0	20.2	22.7	0.3	333
Asian	16.4	29.5	10.9	9.5	19.2	14.1	0.5	1,987
Total	21.6	32.0	11.2	7.5	18.5	8.8	0.3	1,380,902

Note: Includes respondents aged 26–49 who were born or arrived in Sweden before 1989.

well as from Greece and Yugoslavia more often have unqualified positions, in either manual or lower white-collar work. Immigrants from Turkey and Yugoslavia, and women from Greece, Africa, Latin America and Asia are rarely found in the salariat.[29] Finnish men—surprisingly similar across generations—are characterised by a large proportion of

---

[29] We should note that the Iranian immigrants pose an exception to the relatively poor achievements of other Asian groups. They are also relatively well educated (see Tables 11.4A and 11.4B); however they are characterised by high levels of non-employment (see Table 11.5).

Table 11.5. Estimated proportion non-employed, by ancestry, generation and gender.

	Men %	Women %
Swedish	4.9	8.0
Mixed (Swedish & Other)	7.2	9.8
First generation		
Finnish	10.2	9.0
Norwegian/Danish	11.6	13.5
Western	19.7	26.5
German	9.8	16.1
Polish	14.8	16.7
Greek	24.6	24.0
Yugoslavian	10.2	9.8
East European	14.0	16.0
South European	18.1	21.1
African	20.2	30.5
Latin American	18.0	23.4
Asian	23.2	32.2
Iranian	33.9	48.0
Turkish	20.8	34.6
Second generation		
Finnish	8.7	10.2
Norwegian/Danish	7.5	10.6
Western	8.8	10.9
German	8.6	10.9
Polish	8.0	11.1
Greek	23.1	25.2
Yugoslavian	15.9	16.2
East European	8.5	10.1
South European	13.6	14.5
African	16.9	20.9
Latin American	7.8	14.4
Asian	9.7	11.2
Total	6.4	9.2

Note: Includes respondents aged 26–49 who were born or arrived in Sweden before 1989. The Ns are the same as in Tables 11.4A and 11.4B.

skilled workers. Among Turkish men, to take another 'deviant' case, self-employment is remarkably common.

Some of the European first-generation immigrant groups actually have a more favourable class composition than our reference category, those of Swedish ancestry. This goes especially for second-generation immigrants from 'other Western' countries and from Germany (men) and Eastern Europe except Yugoslavia (women). If we turn to second-generation immigrants it is evident that more ethnicities join in the advantaged group, primarily those from Poland, Africa and Latin America (although the latter two are also characterised by small sample sizes and therefore less precise estimates).

Although the whole array of ethnic groups displays a fairly complex pattern, there is one clear message: Whether we measure non-employment or social class attainment, overall first-generation immigrants from non-European countries are worst off. Also, clearly among those disadvantaged are the traditional labour immigrants from Greece, Yugoslavia, and Finland (though the latter two groups are not doing as poorly when it comes to employment). It is worth noting also that even the Swedish-born children in these groups do relatively poorly.

Table 11.6A. Occupational class distribution, by ancestry and generation: Men (row percentages).

	Upper salariat	Lower salariat	Routine nonmanual	Petty bourgeoisie	Skilled manual	Semi- and unskilled	N
Swedish	16.2	19.5	8.1	8.4	22.9	24.9	1,024,489
Mixed (Swedish & Other)	15.7	19.6	8.1	7.0	23.0	26.5	39,435
First generation							
Finnish	7.7	14.0	4.7	5.4	34.1	34.0	35,325
Norwegian/Danish	18.5	16.1	6.0	8.5	23.2	27.7	9,472
Western	23.7	22.3	7.3	9.2	20.7	16.9	7,094
German	18.3	24.1	7.3	9.8	23.2	17.3	4,564
Polish	17.9	16.6	5.0	9.8	22.7	28.0	4,033
Greek	9.4	10.5	2.6	15.0	16.9	45.5	2,625
Yugoslavian	3.1	8.6	2.9	11.5	30.7	43.2	8,192
East European	19.9	18.4	6.1	7.7	24.1	23.8	5,771
South European	11.0	14.8	5.2	9.7	29.6	29.8	3,070
African	11.4	11.0	3.3	6.5	20.3	47.5	4,961
Latin American	9.5	11.8	3.4	2.5	23.4	49.5	6,017
Asian	10.7	10.8	3.3	10.8	23.3	41.2	9,038
Iranian	12.5	12.2	2.7	7.2	21.1	44.3	5,651
Turkish	4.5	9.4	1.7	28.1	15.9	40.4	4,175
Second generation							
Finnish	9.6	16.1	7.0	4.3	31.2	31.8	13,957
Norwegian/Danish	13.9	17.6	7.6	6.8	25.5	28.6	11,857
Western	21.3	22.0	9.7	6.6	19.7	20.7	4,246
German	19.6	22.0	9.4	5.7	21.0	22.3	4,496
Polish	23.5	24.1	9.1	6.0	18.7	18.6	1,219
Greek	12.1	13.5	10.1	8.2	19.8	36.2	207
Yugoslavian	9.8	18.0	7.8	5.7	26.5	32.2	907
East European	21.7	20.9	8.7	5.0	20.8	22.8	5,493
South European	16.5	18.8	12.2	6.1	20.8	25.7	938
African	29.3	21.4	9.8	5.3	11.3	22.9	266
Latin American	31.5	20.0	8.8	7.3	16.5	15.8	260
Asian	21.3	22.6	7.6	5.0	20.1	23.4	1,644
Total	15.7	19.0	7.7	8.2	23.4	25.9	1,219,402

Note: Includes gainfully employed men aged 26–49 who were born or arrived in Sweden before 1988.

Table 11.6B. Occupational class distribution, by ancestry and generation: Women (row percentages).

	Upper salariat	Lower salariat	Routine nonmanual	Petty bourgeoisie	Skilled manual	Semi- and unskilled	N
Swedish	9.7	22.6	13.6	3.9	11.7	38.6	964,901
Mixed (Swedish & Other)	10.1	22.1	14.4	3.4	12.5	37.4	37,181
First generation							
Finnish	7.1	17.5	10.1	2.7	14.4	48.2	47,160
Norwegian/Danish	8.4	17.0	9.5	5.3	12.4	47.4	11,235
Western	19.0	24.5	14.7	4.9	9.4	27.5	4,579
German	12.8	20.2	15.5	5.7	9.8	35.9	3,428
Polish	12.0	15.9	9.1	4.2	13.5	45.4	8,410
Greek	4.0	10.7	3.6	7.5	10.5	63.8	1,434
Yugoslavian	2.8	8.5	4.8	5.9	14.2	63.8	7,418
East European	16.3	20.2	11.3	4.4	11.5	36.3	6,402
South European	9.6	15.9	10.6	3.8	13.5	46.6	1,457
African	5.4	11.2	6.3	2.6	11.3	63.3	2,186
Latin American	6.6	14.5	5.6	1.3	16.2	55.8	5,416
Asian	5.7	10.5	5.0	5.0	16.6	57.2	6,619
Iranian	7.5	21.2	4.1	2.1	23.7	41.4	2,423
Turkish	3.3	7.0	2.1	6.0	17.8	63.7	2,401
Second generation							
Finnish	6.9	18.1	13.3	2.5	15.8	43.5	13,604
Norwegian/Danish	8.2	18.9	13.3	3.2	13.3	43.1	11,051
Western	14.1	24.5	14.9	3.9	10.8	31.8	4,083
German	13.3	23.0	16.1	3.0	11.4	33.1	4,192
Polish	13.6	21.4	15.7	3.6	10.7	35.1	1,118
Greek	12.2	16.9	13.4	7.0	18.0	32.6	172
Yugoslavian	7.4	14.2	16.9	4.5	14.1	43.0	894
East European	13.4	23.2	15.8	2.9	11.6	33.1	5,536
South European	10.8	18.7	17.8	2.1	12.6	37.9	839
African	18.6	30.5	11.2	5.9	10.0	23.8	269
Latin American	22.7	23.9	17.3	2.7	7.5	25.9	255
Asian	14.9	22.9	13.9	3.0	12.0	33.3	1,628
Total	9.6	21.9	13.2	3.9	12.0	39.5	1,156,291

Note: Includes gainfully employed women aged 26–49 who were born or arrived in Sweden before 1989.

Ethnic penalties

First- and second-generation immigrants: An overview

The next step is to estimate the degree of 'ethnic penalties', defined here as any remaining disadvantage among immigrant groups for labour-market outcomes—employment and occupational class attainment, respectively—after statistically controlling for educational qualification and age. It should be noted that 'ethnic penalties' is to be viewed as a metaphor, and is not to be equated with discrimination (although discrimination is one possible cause of such penalties). For example, in order to control fully for individuals' human capital, we would need to take into account their language skills and the labour-market value of foreign qualifications and labour-market experience.[30]

In the first step, shown in Table 11.7, logistic models are fitted of employment versus non-employment and of occupational class attainment (using the unqualified classes as the reference category). These models have ethnic origin as the main independent variable, using educational attainment, age and age-squared as control variables (although the coefficients for these controls are not shown). As in the other chapters in this volume, a negative parameter estimate indicates an ethnic penalty. This is an initial, general test, so the sample is divided into first- and second-generation immigrants, respectively.[31] Each of these groups is compared with the reference category of people born in Sweden to Swedish parents. Mixed Swedish–foreign origin is included as a benchmark. The results in this condensed analysis are clear in highlighting that:

- Ethnic penalties for employment are more than halved between first- and second-generation immigrants, but are still prevalent for men (whilst penalties for women are substantially minor);
- Among those holding a job, ethnic penalties in the achievement of an occupational class position (other than in an unqualified job) are strong among the first generation but weak or non-existent among the second generation, with the only exception being a lower level of self-employment among second-generation immigrant men;
- Ethnic penalties, in general, are somewhat less severe for women than for men; and
- Ethnic penalties exist for employment, but not for occupational class amongst those with mixed Swedish-foreign ancestry.

The results in Table 11.7 are much influenced by the pattern among the dominating immigrant categories, notably the Finns, and they conceal important differences between immigrant categories. The analyses in the following sections go into more detail, first by distinguishing more

---

[30] It should also be noted that some ethnic groups may have unfavourable educational outcomes (e.g., because of pre-labour market discrimination) which are concealed in the analyses of ethnic penalties here. As mentioned above, previous studies suggest that this is not such a big problem, as children of immigrants do as well or better than Swedish-born children once social background characteristics are controlled (Erikson and Jonsson 1993; Similä 1994).

[31] For purity rather than for practical reasons, origin countries for which there are too few people in the second-generation to analyse separately have also been excluded in the first-generation.

Table 11.7. Logistic regression of employment and occupational class (parameter estimates).

	Men		Women	
Employment vs Non-employment				
Native Swedish	0.00		0.00	
First-generation immigrants	**−1.06**	(0.01)	**−0.61**	(0.01)
Second-generation immigrants	**−0.40**	(0.02)	**−0.14**	(0.01)
Mixed (Swedish & Other)	**−0.31**	(0.02)	**−0.14**	(0.02)
−2LL	620,961.3		794,125.1	
N	1,441,753		1,379,560	
Occupational class (vs. class IIIb/VII)				
Upper salariat				
First-generation immigrants	**−1.02**	(0.01)	**−0.68**	(0.02)
Second-generation immigrants	−0.01	(0.02)	**0.06**	(0.02)
Mixed (Swedish & Other)	**−0.09**	(0.02)	−0.01	(0.03)
Lower salariat				
First-generation immigrants	**−0.76**	(0.01)	**−0.60**	(0.01)
Second-generation immigrants	−0.03	(0.02)	**−0.06**	(0.02)
Mixed (Swedish & Other)	**−0.04**	(0.02)	−0.04	(0.02)
Routine nonmanual				
First-generation immigrants	**−0.96**	(0.02)	**−0.60**	(0.01)
Second-generation immigrants	−0.02	(0.02)	**0.09**	(0.02)
Mixed (Swedish & Other)	**−0.04**	(0.02)	**0.08**	(0.02)
Petty bourgeoisie				
First-generation immigrants	**−0.39**	(0.01)	**−0.31**	(0.02)
Second-generation immigrants	**−0.21**	(0.02)	−0.04	(0.03)
Mixed (Swedish & Other)	**−0.10**	(0.02)	0.00	(0.03)
Skilled manual				
First-generation immigrants	**−0.16**	(0.01)	**0.10**	(0.01)
Second-generation immigrants	0.02	(0.01)	−0.01	(0.02)
Mixed (Swedish & Other)	**−0.06**	(0.01)	0.00	(0.02)
−2LL	29,905.9		21,800.9	
N	1,218,418		1,155,283	

Note: Ethnic groups for which there are insufficient numbers in the second generation are excluded. Emboldened coefficients indicate significance at the 0.05 level or better; standard errors are given in brackets.

origin countries and regions, and second by making separate analyses for first- and second-generation immigrants, respectively.

Employment

Table 11.8 makes use of a more detailed list of geographical units in analysing (as in the upper panel of Table 11.7) employment. We may note, first, that the control variables show the expected pattern: employment is less common among the younger (though the increasing propensity of employment with age levels off at older ages), and among those at the lowest level of education.[32]

All ethnic groups (except first-generation Yugoslavian women) have lower employment rates than the reference category, people born in Sweden with Swedish-born parents, after taking differences in age and education into account.[33] Some of these excessive risks of non-employment are very high, such as those for most first-generation non-European immigrant groups as well as male Greek immigrants; however, it is striking that employment rates are lower among first-generation immigrants regardless of origin.[34] What we cannot see from Table 11.8 is that the divergent employment pattern across immigrant groups is partly dependent on how long they have been in Sweden; neither do the results presented reveal the heterogeneity of non-European groups. These issues will be addressed below (Table 11.10).

We learned from Table 11.7 that employment propensities are on average higher for second-generation immigrants than for first-generation. We can see from Table 11.8 that this is an impressively systematic pattern. The only exception is the Yugoslavs, who show a remarkable worsening of employment rates across generations, and the Africans and Greeks

---

[32] It is noticeable, but not surprising, that those with lower vocational schooling have relatively high employment rates; their qualifications are more labour-market oriented than those of the reference category (having academically oriented upper-secondary schooling); although it is also possible that non-employment among the latter, to a greater extent, is because they are still in education.

[33] A remaining worry is that there is heterogeneity across countries in the category that have missing values on the educational qualification variable. For example, if Europeans with tertiary education have not been assigned a value whereas this goes for unqualified non-Europeans, the ethnic origin coefficients will be biased. Models were fitted both exclusive of those with missing values as well as models that included a set of interaction effects between missing values on education and country of origin to check for this eventuality. There is in fact some ground for this suspicion. As compared with men with compulsory schooling only, those with missing values have (as shown in Table 11.8) clearly lower employment propensities, and this difference is more pronounced among those with Swedish ancestry (the reference category) than among first-generation immigrants of non-European origin. The difference does not appear for women and is not so large for men either; for example, when taking country-differences in the relation between missing value and employment into account, the coefficient for African men decreases from -1.23 to -1.44, which is the biggest change (for the other four non-European immigrant categories the decrease in the log odds is between 0.13 and 0.15). Nonetheless, I will address this issue further in the analysis of first generation immigrants in Table 11.11.

[34] Apart from the first-generation female immigrants from Yugoslavia, the exceptions are Finnish females (first- and second-generation) who have employment rates on par with the reference category.

Table 11.8. Logistic regression of employment versus non-employment (parameter estimates).

	Men		Women	
Intercept	**2.85**	(0.01)	2.36	(0.01)
Ancestry				
Swedish	0.00		0.00	
Mixed (Swedish & Other)	**−0.32**	(0.02)	**−0.15**	(0.02)
Finnish 1	**−0.61**	(0.02)	−0.02	(0.02)
Norwegian/Danish 1	**−0.67**	(0.03)	**−0.42**	(0.03)
Western 1	**−1.09**	(0.03)	**−1.13**	(0.03)
German 1	**−0.76**	(0.05)	**−0.80**	(0.04)
Polish 1	**−1.09**	(0.04)	**−0.75**	(0.03)
Greek 1	**−1.57**	(0.04)	**−0.74**	(0.05)
Yugoslavian 1	**−0.63**	(0.03)	**0.16**	(0.03)
East European 1	**−1.13**	(0.04)	**−0.78**	(0.03)
South European 1	**−1.10**	(0.04)	**−0.72**	(0.06)
African 1	**−1.23**	(0.03)	**−0.99**	(0.04)
Latin American 1	**−1.16**	(0.03)	**−0.92**	(0.03)
Asian 1	**−1.35**	(0.02)	**−1.16**	(0.02)
Iranian 1	**−1.95**	(0.02)	**−2.08**	(0.03)
Turkish 1	**−1.19**	(0.03)	**−1.11**	(0.03)
Finnish 2	**−0.29**	(0.03)	0.01	(0.03)
Norwegian/Danish 2	**−0.32**	(0.03)	**−0.15**	(0.03)
Western 2	**−0.52**	(0.05)	**−0.29**	(0.05)
German 2	**−0.44**	(0.05)	**−0.22**	(0.05)
Polish 2	**−0.49**	(0.10)	**−0.35**	(0.09)
Greek 2	**−1.32**	(0.14)	**−0.82**	(0.15)
Yugoslavian 2	**−0.83**	(0.08)	**−0.39**	(0.08)
East European 2	**−0.46**	(0.04)	**−0.17**	(0.04)
South European 2	**−0.79**	(0.09)	**−0.40**	(0.09)
African 2	**−1.13**	(0.14)	**−0.90**	(0.14)
Latin American 2	−0.46	(0.20)	**−0.55**	(0.16)
Asian 2	**−0.62**	(0.08)	**−0.29**	(0.07)
Age/10	**0.43**	(0.01)	**0.35**	(0.00)
(Age/10)^2	**−0.20**	(0.01)	**−0.09**	(0.01)
Qualifications				
Missing	**−2.19**	(0.02)	**−2.27**	(0.02)
Compulsory	**−0.07**	(0.01)	**−0.46**	(0.01)
Lower vocational/				
Lower secondary	**0.49**	(0.01)	**0.32**	(0.01)
Upper secondary	0.00		0.00	
Lower tertiary	**0.60**	(0.02)	**0.68**	(0.01)
University degree	**0.58**	(0.02)	**0.66**	(0.02)
−2LL	618758.9		788764.0	
N	1,443,069		1,380,902	

Note: Includes respondents aged 26–49 who were born or arrived in Sweden before 1989. Emboldened coefficients indicate significance at the 0.05 level or better; standard errors are given in brackets.

who show no statistically significant difference between first- and second-generation immigrants.

It should be repeated that the measure of employment is imprecise, and that it is not possible to equate non-employment with unemployment. Nonetheless, there is little doubt that the pattern in Table 11.8 does reveal a marked difference in labour-market attachment between immigrants and those of Swedish ancestry, a difference that is likely to affect living standards and plausibly the educational chances of their offspring.

Occupational class attainment

When we consider only those who are gainfully employed, do some immigrant groups experience 'ethnic penalties' in the achievement of a privileged occupational class position? This question is addressed in Tables 11.9A (for men) and 11.9B (for women), where multi-nomial logistic regression models are fitted for class destination. Unqualified class positions are taken as the reference category. The estimates show the log-odds of an individual from a given ethnic group ending up in a given occupational class rather than in an unqualified position, relative to the corresponding log-odds of someone with Swedish ancestry, when we have taken into account the differences in the educational and age structures.

Beginning with the attainment of positions in the salariat it is evident that much of what was found in the descriptive analysis in Table 11.6 is replicated here. Even when restricting the analysis to those who have a job, immigrants from non-European groups do much worse than those of Swedish ancestry.[35] As before, we can add those of Yugoslavian, Greek, and Finnish origin to this disadvantaged group. Men from Southern European countries (other than Greece) and women from Norway/Denmark also experience disadvantage, although not as great. In addition, there are severe ethnic penalties for first-generation immigrants from Poland and other Eastern European countries. Their relatively high educational attainment led to a favourable class distribution in Tables 11.6A and 11.6B (on par with those of the reference category), but once their educational qualifications are taken into account, it turns out that their occupational class achievements are markedly less than those of Swedish ancestry.

---

[35] An exception is Turkish women in the upper salariat, but as we saw in Table 11.6B their estimate is based on a very small cell frequency (only 3.3% end up in this most privileged class).

Table 11.9A. Logistic regression of occupational class: Men (parameter estimates).

	Upper Salariat		Lower salariat		Routine nonmanual		Petty bourgeoisie		Skilled manual	
Intercept	**0.16**	(0.01)	**0.64**	(0.01)	**−0.17**	(0.01)	**−0.74**	(0.02)	**−0.78**	(0.01)
Ancestry										
Swedish	0.00		0.00		0.00		0.00		0.00	
Mixed (Swedish & Other)	**−0.09**	(0.02)	**−0.05**	(0.02)	**−0.05**	(0.02)	**−0.10**	(0.02)	**−0.06**	(0.01)
Finnish 1	**−0.69**	(0.03)	**−0.40**	(0.02)	**−0.72**	(0.03)	**−0.83**	(0.03)	**0.11**	(0.01)
Norwegian/Danish 1	**−0.09**	(0.04)	**−0.24**	(0.04)	**−0.36**	(0.05)	**−0.18**	(0.04)	**−0.09**	(0.03)
Western 1	0.01	(0.05)	**0.14**	(0.04)	0.06	(0.05)	**0.37**	(0.05)	**0.31**	(0.04)
German 1	0.00	(0.06)	**0.22**	(0.05)	0.05	(0.07)	**0.26**	(0.06)	**0.30**	(0.05)
Polish 1	**−1.62**	(0.06)	**−1.21**	(0.06)	**−1.19**	(0.08)	**−0.23**	(0.06)	**−0.12**	(0.05)
Greek 1	**−1.42**	(0.09)	**−1.21**	(0.08)	**−1.70**	(0.13)	−0.04	(0.06)	**−0.85**	(0.06)
Yugoslavian 1	**−2.15**	(0.07)	**−1.38**	(0.05)	**−1.58**	(0.07)	**−0.34**	(0.04)	**−0.27**	(0.03)
East European 1	**−1.00**	(0.05)	**−0.76**	(0.05)	**−0.70**	(0.06)	**−0.32**	(0.06)	0.06	(0.04)
South European 1	**−0.57**	(0.08)	**−0.36**	(0.06)	**−0.56**	(0.09)	−0.11	(0.07)	**0.12**	(0.05)
African 1	**−2.00**	(0.06)	**−1.72**	(0.05)	**−1.84**	(0.08)	**−0.98**	(0.06)	**−0.74**	(0.04)
Latin American 1	**−2.07**	(0.06)	**−1.68**	(0.05)	**−1.82**	(0.07)	**−1.97**	(0.08)	**−0.65**	(0.03)
Asian 1	**−1.65**	(0.05)	**−1.38**	(0.04)	**−1.54**	(0.06)	**−0.22**	(0.04)	**−0.43**	(0.03)
Iranian 1	**−1.95**	(0.05)	**−1.73**	(0.05)	**−2.15**	(0.08)	**−0.71**	(0.05)	**−0.54**	(0.04)
Turkish 1	**−1.35**	(0.09)	**−0.79**	(0.06)	**−1.77**	(0.12)	**0.95**	(0.04)	**−0.76**	(0.05)
Finnish 2	**−0.27**	(0.04)	**−0.16**	(0.03)	**−0.21**	(0.04)	**−0.43**	(0.04)	**0.05**	(0.02)
Norwegian/Danish 2	**−0.09**	(0.04)	**−0.10**	(0.03)	**−0.10**	(0.04)	**−0.17**	(0.04)	−0.04	(0.03)
Western 2	**0.19**	(0.06)	**0.13**	(0.05)	**0.25**	(0.06)	0.06	(0.07)	0.05	(0.05)
German 2	**0.23**	(0.06)	**0.18**	(0.05)	**0.22**	(0.06)	−0.02	(0.07)	0.04	(0.05)
Polish 2	**0.27**	(0.11)	**0.31**	(0.10)	**0.30**	(0.12)	0.01	(0.14)	0.10	(0.09)
Greek 2	−0.21	(0.29)	**−0.53**	(0.24)	−0.02	(0.25)	0.29	(0.27)	**−0.52**	(0.20)
Yugoslavian 2	−0.07	(0.15)	0.01	(0.11)	−0.07	(0.14)	0.10	(0.15)	−0.11	(0.09)
East European 2	**0.21**	(0.05)	0.07	(0.05)	**0.11**	(0.06)	**−0.24**	(0.07)	0.01	(0.04)
South European 2	0.20	(0.13)	0.07	(0.11)	**0.47**	(0.12)	0.09	(0.15)	−0.11	(0.10)
African 2	0.29	(0.23)	0.02	(0.21)	0.18	(0.24)	−0.16	(0.30)	**−0.60**	(0.22)
Latin American 2	**0.72**	(0.24)	0.31	(0.23)	0.43	(0.27)	0.42	(0.28)	0.19	(0.22)
Asian 2	0.04	(0.10)	0.07	(0.08)	−0.08	(0.11)	**−0.36**	(0.12)	−0.05	(0.08)
Age/10	**0.91**	(0.01)	**0.64**	(0.00)	**0.39**	(0.01)	**0.61**	(0.01)	**0.04**	(0.00)
(Age/10)^2	**−0.08**	(0.01)	**−0.02**	(0.01)	**−0.06**	(0.01)	**−0.31**	(0.01)	**−0.03**	(0.01)
Qualifications										
Missing	**−1.25**	(0.09)	**−1.25**	(0.07)	**−0.99**	(0.09)	−0.08	(0.07)	**0.47**	(0.05)
Compulsory	**−3.17**	(0.02)	**−2.55**	(0.01)	**−1.67**	(0.01)	**−0.38**	(0.02)	**0.50**	(0.01)
Lower vocational/secondary	**−1.80**	(0.01)	**−1.25**	(0.01)	**−1.07**	(0.01)	**−0.27**	(0.02)	**0.95**	(0.01)
Upper secondary	0.00		0.00		0.00		0.00		0.00	
Lower tertiary	**1.19**	(0.02)	**1.45**	(0.01)	**0.74**	(0.02)	**0.49**	(0.02)	**0.51**	(0.02)
University degree	**3.22**	(0.02)	**1.53**	(0.02)	**0.88**	(0.02)	**0.87**	(0.03)	**−0.19**	(0.03)
−2LL					71,287.6					
N					1,219,402					

Note: Includes gainfully employed respondents aged 26–49 who were born or arrived in Sweden before 1989. Reference category is the semi- and unskilled working class. Emboldened coefficients indicate significance at the 0.05 level or better; standard errors are given in brackets.

Table 11.9B. Logistic regression of occupational class: Women (parameter estimates).

	Upper Salariat		Lower salariat		Routine nonmanual		Petty bourgeoisie		Skilled manual	
Intercept	−1.19	(0.01)	−0.31	(0.01)	**0.13**	(0.01)	−1.93	(0.02)	−1.57	(0.02)
Ancestry										
Swedish	0.00		0.00		0.00		0.00		0.00	
Mixed (Swedish & Other)	−0.02	(0.03)	−0.04	(0.02)	**0.08**	(0.02)	0.00	(0.03)	0.00	(0.02)
Finnish 1	−0.52	(0.03)	−0.34	(0.02)	−0.44	(0.02)	−0.64	(0.03)	**0.15**	(0.01)
Norwegian/Danish 1	−0.33	(0.05)	−0.37	(0.04)	−0.48	(0.03)	0.07	(0.04)	−0.02	(0.03)
Western 1	−0.02	(0.06)	−0.09	(0.05)	**0.24**	(0.05)	**0.42**	(0.07)	**0.20**	(0.06)
German 1	0.06	(0.08)	−0.15	(0.06)	0.08	(0.05)	**0.29**	(0.08)	−0.04	(0.06)
Polish 1	−1.35	(0.05)	−1.37	(0.04)	−1.00	(0.04)	−**0.40**	(0.06)	−**0.08**	(0.03)
Greek 1	−1.17	(0.18)	−0.82	(0.12)	−1.42	(0.15)	**0.29**	(0.10)	−**0.18**	(0.09)
Yugoslavian 1	−1.27	(0.09)	−1.01	(0.05)	−1.28	(0.06)	−0.04	(0.05)	−0.01	(0.04)
East European 1	−0.62	(0.05)	−0.72	(0.05)	−0.50	(0.04)	−0.11	(0.06)	0.05	(0.04)
South European 1	−0.24	(0.13)	−0.31	(0.10)	−0.24	(0.09)	−0.20	(0.14)	**0.25**	(0.08)
African 1	−1.26	(0.13)	−1.12	(0.09)	−1.04	(0.09)	−0.74	(0.14)	−**0.37**	(0.07)
Latin American 1	−1.38	(0.08)	−1.26	(0.06)	−1.28	(0.06)	−1.53	(0.12)	0.05	(0.04)
Asian 1	−1.45	(0.07)	−1.21	(0.06)	−1.17	(0.06)	−0.06	(0.06)	**0.25**	(0.04)
Iranian 1	−1.10	(0.10)	−0.71	(0.07)	−1.54	(0.11)	−0.70	(0.14)	**0.63**	(0.05)
Turkish 1	−0.43	(0.15)	−0.56	(0.10)	−1.64	(0.14)	**0.29**	(0.09)	**0.38**	(0.06)
Finnish 2	−0.11	(0.05)	−0.10	(0.03)	0.01	(0.03)	−0.15	(0.06)	0.00	(0.03)
Norwegian/Danish 2	−0.08	(0.05)	−0.13	(0.04)	−0.04	(0.03)	−0.14	(0.06)	−0.04	(0.03)
Western 2	**0.29**	(0.07)	0.10	(0.06)	**0.21**	(0.05)	**0.27**	(0.08)	0.03	(0.06)
German 2	**0.25**	(0.07)	0.04	(0.06)	**0.27**	(0.05)	0.09	(0.09)	0.00	(0.05)
Polish 2	0.07	(0.13)	−0.17	(0.11)	0.10	(0.10)	0.01	(0.17)	−0.10	(0.11)
Greek 2	0.21	(0.35)	0.14	(0.30)	0.35	(0.26)	**1.34**	(0.32)	**0.60**	(0.23)
Yugoslavian 2	−0.20	(0.17)	−**0.35**	(0.13)	**0.25**	(0.10)	**0.65**	(0.17)	−0.12	(0.10)
East European 2	**0.20**	(0.06)	0.04	(0.05)	**0.24**	(0.04)	−0.03	(0.08)	0.02	(0.05)
South European 2	**0.52**	(0.16)	0.06	(0.13)	**0.35**	(0.10)	−0.21	(0.24)	−0.03	(0.11)
African 2	**0.66**	(0.26)	**0.50**	(0.22)	0.23	(0.23)	**1.05**	(0.28)	0.30	(0.23)
Latin American 2	**0.64**	(0.26)	0.22	(0.24)	**0.59**	(0.21)	0.12	(0.40)	−0.05	(0.27)
Asian 2	**0.26**	(0.11)	0.02	(0.09)	0.11	(0.08)	−0.07	(0.15)	0.10	(0.09)
Age/10	**0.53**	(0.01)	**0.33**	(0.01)	**0.26**	(0.00)	**0.50**	(0.01)	−**0.23**	(0.00)
(Age/10)^2	**0.03**	(0.01)	−**0.13**	(0.01)	−**0.12**	(0.01)	−**0.30**	(0.01)	−**0.08**	(0.01)
Qualifications										
Missing	−**0.28**	(0.11)	−**0.45**	(0.08)	−1.23	(0.09)	0.02	(0.11)	−0.06	(0.08)
Compulsory	−3.16	(0.03)	−2.54	(0.02)	−2.29	(0.01)	−**0.56**	(0.02)	−**0.62**	(0.02)
Lower vocational/secondary	−1.96	(0.02)	−1.49	(0.01)	−1.12	(0.01)	−**0.34**	(0.02)	**0.77**	(0.02)
Upper secondary	0.00		0.00		0.00		0.00		0.00	
Lower tertiary	**1.63**	(0.02)	**2.80**	(0.01)	**0.23**	(0.01)	**0.94**	(0.03)	**0.23**	(0.02)
University degree	**4.23**	(0.02)	**2.56**	(0.02)	**0.68**	(0.02)	**1.48**	(0.03)	**0.28**	(0.04)
−2LL					58,179.7					
N					1,156,291					

Note: Includes gainfully employed respondents aged 26–49 who were born or arrived in Sweden before 1989. Reference category is the semi- and unskilled working class. Emboldened coefficients indicate significance at the 0.05 level or better; standard errors are given in brackets.

Before turning to the propensities for self-employment it should be noted that there have been diverging views on the prestige or benefits of self-employment. Politicians often hold self-employment in high regard and it is assumed by many to be a way of getting ahead in a country to which one is emigrating. Others have come to question the virtues of self-employment, arguing that it is really marginal labour-market positions that may stand in for 'real' jobs for those who through lack of qualifications or because of discrimination have difficulties in gaining secure footing in the labour market (e.g., Moore 1983; Bögenhold and Staber 1991).

Our data show that in Sweden, at least in 1990, it is the case—perhaps surprisingly—that the same disadvantages that characterise some ethnic groups when it comes to gaining positions in the salariat also apply to gaining positions in self-employment. Again, then, those of non-European origin are less likely to be found in self-employment rather than unskilled work as compared with native Swedes, and the same goes for those who immigrated from Finland and, to a lesser extent, Poland. Men from Yugoslavia and other Eastern European countries are also relatively rarely found in self-employment relative to unskilled work.[36] There is however an exception of some magnitude: Turkish men are self-employed to a very large degree (as we saw from Table 11.6A, almost 30% of those estimated to be in gainful employment were self-employed in 1990). Self-employment also appears to be relatively high in some Asian groups. It is quite possible that these forms of self-employment—mostly involving people who lack educational qualifications—is best understood as offering rather marginal jobs in ethnic enclaves within the service sector (particularly small-scale restaurant business).[37] Among women, for whom

---

[36] It should be recalled from Table 11.6A that among men in some immigrant groups (such as the Greek) self-employment rates are on par with, or even higher, than the figures for native Swedes. Thus, self-employment is on average not less important for immigrant men (see, for example, Hammarstedt 2001). Instead, the results reported in Table 11.9A are driven very much by the excessive risks immigrants have to end up in unskilled work.

[37] Even though ethnic residential concentration in Sweden is relatively high—42% of the immigrant population live in areas in which the share of the ethnic group is at least twice that of the share in the population in 1997, according to calculations reported by Edin, Fredriksson and Åslund (2003)—it is only for a few groups that the size and the concentration make it reasonable to talk about ethnic enclaves, or clusters (Andersson 1998). One of them is Turks in Botkyrka, Stockholm. Such ethnic clusters can function by providing marginal jobs in self-employment and unskilled labour, for example. Recent evidence using a natural experiment in Sweden (Edin et al. 2003) suggests that living in ethnic enclaves leads to a 13% wage increase for those with low levels of education, but has no effect for those with higher qualifications.

self-employment is rare, several ethnic groups are more prone than those of Swedish ancestry to go into such work.

One caveat, however, is that things may well have changed in Sweden since 1990. The deep recession during the first half of the decade may well have led more immigrants into self-employment or other kinds of marginal employment (although the greatest effect no doubt was to increase their unemployment rates).

Positions in the routine non-manual class and in the skilled working class are on average preferable to unskilled positions and therefore the log odds of ending up in the former rather than the latter is of some importance for employees. As can be seen in Table 9 routine non-manual work is hardly an escape for immigrants from outside Europe who could not make it to the salariat. The estimates for the disadvantaged categories—in addition to non-European, also those from Greece, Yugoslavia, Poland, and other Eastern European countries—are strongly negative. Access to skilled manual work is more equal among women—the Asian groups compensate some of their previous disadvantage by having relatively high propensities of ending up in skilled manual work rather than in an unskilled job. Among men, however, the results mostly reinforce the pattern we have now got used to: Men from non-European countries and from Greece are substantially less likely to end up at the skilled end of the occupational distribution. The main exception is that Finnish men do have a slight advantage in getting skilled, rather than unskilled working class positions.

One noteworthy result from Tables 11.9A and 11.9B is that second-generation immigrants are systematically better off than their parents. In most cases the ethnic penalties experienced by first-generation immigrants are eradicated for the second generation (although for Turks and Iranians we have no second-generation comparison category). Only children of the traditional labour market immigrants—the Finns, men from Greece and women from Norway, Denmark, and Yugoslavia—seem to suffer continuing disadvantage in the second generation. Second-generation immigrants from Poland and other Eastern European, as well as from Germany and other Western countries are, on the other hand, doing slightly better than those of Swedish ancestry. More surprisingly, this is also the case for African and Latin American second-generation immigrants.

Thus, in 1990, second-generation immigrants—if they had a footing in the labour market—were more or less assimilated in terms of their occupational attainment. This result supports the idea that two of the barriers faced by first-generation immigrants are the non-transferability of their educational qualifications and previous labour market experience as well as non-fluency in the Swedish language.

Are ethnic penalties more severe for those with higher education?

The discussion about the non-portability of human capital has centred on those with professional education—in Sweden typically those with a university degree. Recent research has shown that many academically educated immigrants have had great difficulties in obtaining an appropriate job (see, for example, Ekberg and Rooth 2004). As is evident from Tables 11.8 and 11.9, a degree leads to a substantial increase in the chances of getting a job in general, and avoiding unskilled labour in particular. Does this hold for first- and second-generation immigrants to the same extent as for those of Swedish ancestry?

Figure 11.1 compares the labour market-related ethnic penalties of degree-holders with those of people with compulsory schooling only (those with missing values are omitted). As those of Swedish ancestry remain the reference category, the advantage of having a degree over having compulsory schooling among first- and second-generation immigrants, respectively, is related to the same advantage in the reference category. Hence, what is at issue is whether the 'employment and occupational pay-off' of higher education is higher or lower among immigrants when compared with native Swedes of Swedish parents.[38] Though there are differences among immigrant categories, the overall negative coefficients in Figure 11.1 support the expectation that the advantage of having a degree is less for immigrant groups than for native Swedes.[39] Among second-generation immigrants the pay-off of higher education is overall on par with the pay-off for the reference category. There are some

---

[38] Figure 11.1 shows the interaction effect between university education (rather than compulsory schooling) and country of origin (relative to those of Swedish ancestry) on employment (rather than non-employment) and on gaining access to a position in the salariat (rather than having an unskilled position). This interaction effect is generated in models including three categories for education and in the latter case three destination classes. I do not display interaction effects that are not statistically significant at the 5%-level or better. I have also omitted the interactions between education and salariat position for second-generation Greeks as they are far out (log odds = −15–16), although significant (the outlier status of these coefficients probably depend on the fact that no one of Greek origin with compulsory education reaches the salariat).

[39] Some part of the disadvantages appears to arise because first-generation immigrants more often have followed academic programmes that are in less demand in the Swedish labour market (e.g., in the humanities) (Ekberg and Rooth 2004).

exceptions, especially for those of South-European ancestry, but also for women whose parents come from Finland, Poland, or Yugoslavia and for male and female offspring of other East European immigrants. It is not unlikely also that second-generation immigrants from non-European countries would have shown a similar pattern if there had been enough cases to analyse; as it stands, the standard errors are very large.

The findings displayed in Figure 11.1 support the idea of non-portability of human capital, because this idea assumes that labour-market problems should be large for first-generation but low for second-generation immigrants with academic qualifications. However, it should be noted, although it is not reflected in Figure 11.1, that there are also considerable labour-market disadvantages among first-generation immigrants with only compulsory schooling, as well as among those with secondary and lower tertiary level education. Thus, Figure 11.1 does not suggest that the disadvantages for first-generation immigrants fall only on those with higher qualifications, only that they fall a bit more so.

First-generation immigrants: the importance of years since immigration

The results reported in the analyses of employment (Table 11.8) and occupational class attainment (Table 11.9) strongly suggest that the immigrant categories that face the greatest problems in the labour market are those of non-European origin. However, as described in the introduction, non-European immigration is also a more recent phenomenon in Sweden than much of the labour-market immigration from the Nordic and other European countries. This means that we may mix up disadvantages due to, for example, discrimination and lack of qualification transferability with the negative effects of a short job-search period. It is a consistent finding in the literature that the time spent in a new country is strongly related to labour market success (for a recent account, see Integrationsverket 2004); we may however also believe that this positive effect of time in Sweden levels off after some years. Furthermore, it is plausible that the time of arrival (period) is of importance—for example, it may be an advantage to arrive during a period of economic growth rather than during a recession.

Fortunately, for those who arrived in Sweden later than 1967 there is information on year of immigration, making it possible to construct variables on time of residence in Sweden (and time in Sweden squared to

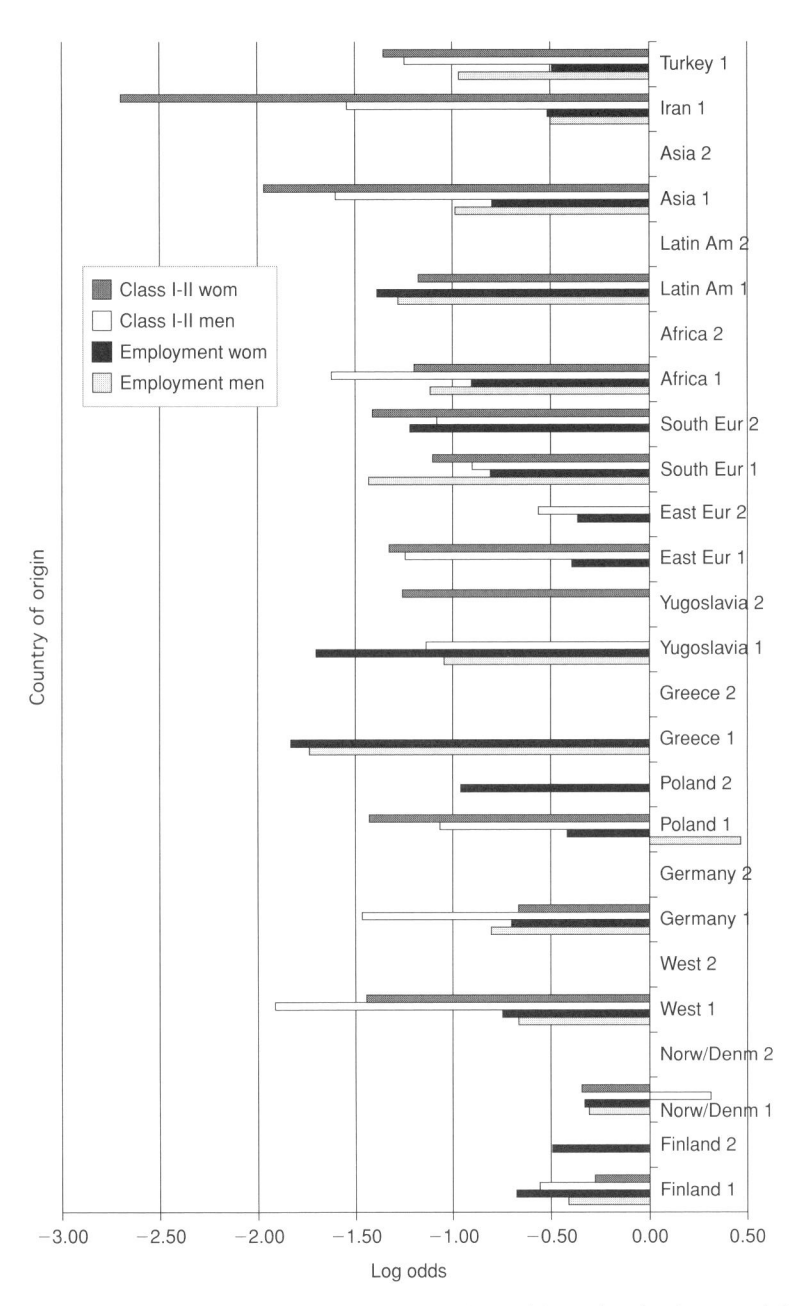

Figure 11.1. Differences in ethnic penalties between those with a university degree and those with compulsory schooling for immigrants relative to those of Swedish ancestry. Men and women 26–49 year of age in 1990.

test for leveling-off tendencies) as well as labour-market-related macro-level variables tapping period effects. In Table 11.10 I have run the same analysis as in Table 11.8—that is, a logistic regression of employment (versus non-employment) in 1990, controlling for age and education—on first-generation immigrants who arrived in Sweden in the period 1968 to 1988. As the sample is now more restricted, Table 11.10 shows both a model that is identical to that shown in Table 11.8 (A) and one further model (B) adding number of years spent in Sweden and its square term as covariates.[40] Immigrants from Finland, who are the ones that are most similar to the 'Swedes' in the analysis in Table 11.8, are chosen as the reference category in this analysis.

As we now are analysing only first-generation immigrants, it is possible to go into more detail in the classification of immigration groups, especially the non-European. Lacking a theory of how ethnic penalties vary with country of origin, I have mostly used geographical principles in creating big groups (some of which must also be a conglomerate of different countries). Chile, an important sending country, is distinguished from the rest of Latin America. North Africans are distinguished from Sub-Saharan Africans, and the relatively large group of immigrants formally coming from Ethiopia (in practice, most being Eritrean refugees) forms a separate category.[41]

Asia is divided into six groups. As before, Iranians and Turks are made into separate categories, and the other countries in the Middle East (numerically dominated by Iraq and Lebanon) constitute a third category. Furthermore, Bangladesh, Pakistan, India and Sri Lanka are merged into one category (India being the biggest sending country). Mainland China is a separate category, while a number of 'modern' Far Eastern countries

---

[40] I also fitted a model including the macro (period) variables 'number of jobs' and 'unemployment rate', respectively, at the year of arrival. These variables had inconsistent and not very large effects. The unemployment rate turned out, contrary to what one could have expected, to be positively associated with employment and with reaching the salariat. As the former effect reached statistical significance for women only and the latter for men only, it is probably unwise to pay too much attention to them.

[41] There seem to be different views on the definition of North Africa and Sub-Saharan Africa, the main issue being where to put the 'real Saharan' countries (primarily Mauritania, Mali, Niger, Chad, Sudan, and Eritrea). I have Eritrea as a separate category (though indistinguishable from Ethiopia as Eritrea did not exist as a separate country at the time most immigrants arrived in Sweden) and the rest of the border countries are defined as Sub-Saharan (where these are put is of no importance for the results as there are few immigrants from these countries). This means that North Africa is defined as Egypt, Libya, Tunisia, Algeria, Morocco (and Western Sahara); Eritrea is a separate category; all other countries are defined as Sub-Saharan.

Table 11.10. Logistic regression of employment among first-generation immigrants: the role of years since immigration (parameter estimates).

| | Men | | | | Women | | | | N | |
	Model A		Model B		Model A		Model B		Men	Women
Intercept	**2.12**	(0.04)	**1.38**	(0.05)	**2.30**	(0.03)	**0.97**	(0.05)		
Ancestry										
Finnish	0.00		0.00		0.00		0.00		29,462	36,874
Norwegian/Danish	0.00	(0.04)	**0.17**	(0.04)	**−0.50**	(0.03)	**−0.28**	(0.03)	8,569	9,813
Western	**−0.46**	(0.04)	**−0.28**	(0.04)	**−1.23**	(0.04)	**−0.97**	(0.04)	7,369	5,054
German	**−0.21**	(0.06)	−0.10	(0.06)	**−1.03**	(0.06)	**−0.81**	(0.06)	2,430	1,917
Polish	**−0.23**	(0.04)	−0.07	(0.05)	**−0.65**	(0.03)	**−0.37**	(0.03)	5,242	11,316
Greek	**−0.86**	(0.04)	**−0.84**	(0.04)	**−0.86**	(0.05)	**−0.86**	(0.05)	3,715	2,231
Yugoslavian	**0.11**	(0.04)	**0.12**	(0.04)	**0.09**	(0.04)	**0.11**	(0.04)	7,886	7,888
East European	**−0.37**	(0.04)	**−0.20**	(0.04)	**−0.73**	(0.04)	**−0.41**	(0.04)	5,768	6,518
South European	**−0.49**	(0.05)	**−0.37**	(0.05)	**−0.87**	(0.06)	**−0.68**	(0.06)	3,300	1,595
North African	**−0.50**	(0.05)	**−0.35**	(0.05)	**−1.19**	(0.07)	**−0.90**	(0.07)	3,112	1,042
Eritrean/ Ethiopian	**−0.39**	(0.06)	−0.10	(0.06)	**−0.98**	(0.07)	**−0.53**	(0.07)	1,904	1,156
Sub-Saharan African	**−0.50**	(0.06)	**−0.28**	(0.06)	**−0.96**	(0.06)	**−0.60**	(0.07)	2,410	1,424
Latin American	**−0.79**	(0.05)	**−0.59**	(0.05)	**−1.18**	(0.04)	**−0.85**	(0.05)	3,463	3,359
Chilean	0.01	(0.05)	**0.29**	(0.05)	**−0.66**	(0.04)	**−0.19**	(0.04)	4,825	4,501
Middle Eastern	**−0.74**	(0.03)	**−0.47**	(0.03)	**−1.63**	(0.04)	**−1.25**	(0.04)	8,005	3,671
Indian/Pakistani/ Bangladeshi	**−0.24**	(0.06)	−0.06	(0.06)	**−0.95**	(0.06)	**−0.64**	(0.06)	2,479	1,851
Japanese, Taiwanese etc.	**−0.86**	(0.09)	**−0.67**	(0.10)	**−1.66**	(0.07)	**−1.34**	(0.07)	670	1,025
Chinese	**−1.16**	(0.09)	**−0.88**	(0.09)	**−1.05**	(0.09)	**−0.61**	(0.10)	633	618
Iranian	**−1.15**	(0.03)	**−0.80**	(0.03)	**−1.96**	(0.03)	**−1.26**	(0.04)	10,648	5,480
Turkish	**−0.52**	(0.04)	**−0.43**	(0.04)	**−1.21**	(0.04)	**−1.10**	(0.04)	5,859	4,538
South-East Asian	**−0.22**	(0.06)	−0.02	(0.06)	**−0.69**	(0.04)	**−0.30**	(0.04)	2,085	3,937
Age/10	**−0.12**	(0.02)	**0.13**	(0.01)	**0.28**	(0.01)	**0.09**	(0.02)		
(Age/10)^2	**0.28**	(0.01)	**−0.10**	(0.02)	**−0.16**	(0.02)	**−0.08**	(0.02)		
Qualifications										
Missing	**−1.88**	(0.04)	**−1.76**	(0.04)	**−1.73**	(0.04)	**−1.59**	(0.04)		
Compulsory	0.03	(0.04)	0.05	(0.04)	**−0.28**	(0.03)	**−0.26**	(0.03)		
Lower vocational/ secondary	**0.16**	(0.03)	**0.14**	(0.03)	**0.26**	(0.03)	**0.23**	(0.03)		
Upper secondary	0.00		0.00		0.00		0.00			
Lower tertiary	**0.15**	(0.04)	**0.16**	(0.04)	**0.30**	(0.04)	**0.33**	(0.04)		
University degree	**0.12**	(0.04)	**0.14**	(0.04)	**0.28**	(0.04)	**0.35**	(0.04)		
Years since immigration			**0.06**	(0.01)			**0.14**	(0.01)		
(Years since immigration)^2			**−0.07**	(0.03)			**−0.33**	(0.03)		
−2LL	103,120.8		102,238.0		101,144.9		99,070.3			
N			119,834				115,808			

Note: Includes respondents aged 26–49 who immigrated to Sweden in the period 1968–88. Emboldened coefficients indicate significance at the 0.05 level or better; standard errors are given in brackets.

(Hong Kong, Singapore, Taiwan, South Korea, and the numerically most important country in the group, Japan) are also merged. The 'rest' of Asia, predominantly the south-east (with Thailand, the Philippines, and the two Vietnams as the most important immigrant countries), constitutes the last category.

Models B in Table 11.10 show, as expected, that time since immigration has a positive effect on employment propensities. The negative effect of the square term tells us, also as expected, that this positive effect of years in Sweden levels off. When controlling for these variables we can see that the advantage of early arrivers in Sweden's post-War immigration history over the more recent immigrant groups is partly accounted for by the fact that the former have been in Sweden longer than the latter. In Models B, for example, men from Germany and Poland no longer appear to have a more privileged situation than the Finns (the reference group); and for women their advantage is clearly reduced. Also, and importantly, the disadvantages of the non-European groups shrink in Models B (and, in the case of immigrants from Chile, are turned into an advantage over the Finns). In general, between 20% and 40% of the ethnic penalty coefficients of non-European immigrants, as compared with the Finns, are due to differences in the number of years they have been staying in Sweden.

The situation for the non-European immigrants is thus not as bad as it previously looked. However, even controlling for time in Sweden, most of the non-European immigrant groups display noticeable disadvantages, though they part company with immigrants from Greece (and to a lesser extent from other Southern European countries) and also with women from Germany and 'other Western' countries. It should be noted that the overall stronger effects for women reflect the fact that Finnish women—like Yugoslavian women—are much less disadvantaged relative to their Swedish counterparts than is the case for Finnish men (as was evident from Table 11.8).

While there are overall substantial disadvantages for non-European immigrants remaining after controlling for time in Sweden, there are also some groups for whom ethnic penalties are not particularly great. Immigrant men from Chile, India, Eritrea, and South East Asia have relatively high employment rates. The former two cannot, in fact, be distinguished from Finns, the reference category, and are thus doing better than most immigrant men from Europe. Somewhat unexpectedly, the (mostly Japanese) 'modern Far East' subgroup appears to be worst off, together with Iran (and China, among men; Turkey, among women). It should be noted, however, that the coefficients for the non-European countries are slightly underestimated and thus gives a rosier picture than the actual employment situation. This is because, as was mentioned in relation to Table 11.8, several of these categories have a relatively large number of missing values on the educational qualification variable, and on average these subjects do better than European immigrants with missing values. Correcting for this (again by including dummy variables interacting the missing category with country of origin) returns ethnic penalties which for most non-European immigrant groups are somewhat higher than those displayed in Table 11.10—for example, for the African categories the coefficients become −0.51, −0.30, and −0.43 (instead of −0.35, −0.10, and −0.28). The changes are smaller, but still noticeable for men from Iran, Middle East, and Turkey. For other immigrant men, and for women generally, the differences are both substantially and statistically insignificant.

Turning to occupational class attainment, Tables 11.11A (men) and 11.11B (women) show the contrast between being found in an unskilled job rather than in the salariat and in self-employment, respectively (dismissing for simplicity the other classes). Although Finns are kept as the reference category, it should be noted that they lag far behind immigrants from Germany and other Western countries (and among men, from the other Nordic countries). The results in Tables 11.11 echo much of those in Table 11.10. When we control for time in Sweden (Models B) the disadvantages experienced by non-European immigrants become less severe, though this reduction is not as compelling as the one for non-employment in Table 11.10. Even so, for immigrants from Eritrea, Sub-Saharan Africa, Chile, India, and South East Asia, the chances of reaching the salariat are clearly lower than for Finns—and even further below those of other European origins, except for the Greek, Polish, and Yugoslavian. For self-employment there is a systematic increase in the effects as we control for years since immigration, reflecting the fact that the Finns have, on average, been in Sweden a long time in combination with having comparatively low odds of being self-employed rather than found in an unskilled occupation. In fact, only immigrants from Eritrea and Chile (and men from Sub-Saharan Africa and Latin America) have lower propensities of being self-employed than the Finns.[42]

---

[42] The models in Tables 11.11 were also fitted using the dummy variables for the interaction between missing value on education and country of origin, but the estimates from these models are virtually identical with the ones presented.

Table 11.11A. Logistic regression of access to the salariat and self-employment among first-generation immigrant men: the role of years since migration (parameter estimates).

	Access to the salariat				Access to self-employment				N
	Model A		Model B		Model A		Model B		
Intercept	0.01	(0.05)	−1.12	(0.07)	−1.90	(0.07)	−4.03	(0.10)	
Ancestry									
Finnish	0.00		0.00		0.00		0.00		21,482
Norwegian/Danish	**0.47**	(0.05)	**0.62**	(0.05)	**0.76**	(0.06)	**0.89**	(0.06)	6,000
Western	**0.75**	(0.05)	**0.94**	(0.05)	**1.34**	(0.07)	**1.52**	(0.07)	4,795
German	**1.04**	(0.08)	**1.15**	(0.08)	**1.51**	(0.10)	**1.63**	(0.10)	1,794
Polish	**−0.42**	(0.05)	**−0.23**	(0.06)	**0.85**	(0.07)	**1.07**	(0.07)	3,748
Greek	**−0.57**	(0.07)	**−0.55**	(0.07)	**0.92**	(0.07)	**0.92**	(0.07)	2,219
Yugoslavian	**−1.02**	(0.06)	**−0.98**	(0.06)	**0.63**	(0.06)	**0.69**	(0.06)	5,710
East European	**−0.15**	(0.05)	0.06	(0.05)	**0.75**	(0.07)	**1.04**	(0.07)	4,063
South European	0.14	(0.07)	**0.27**	(0.07)	**0.76**	(0.09)	**0.86**	(0.09)	2,188
North African	**−0.63**	(0.08)	**−0.47**	(0.08)	**0.77**	(0.08)	**0.88**	(0.09)	1,905
Eritrean/Ethiopian	**−1.24**	(0.10)	**−0.97**	(0.10)	**−1.61**	(0.25)	**−1.23**	(0.25)	1,176
Sub-Saharan African	**−1.23**	(0.08)	**−1.02**	(0.08)	**−0.75**	(0.15)	**−0.56**	(0.15)	1,505
Latin American	**−0.45**	(0.07)	**−0.25**	(0.07)	**−0.51**	(0.13)	**−0.34**	(0.13)	2,141
Chilean	**−1.31**	(0.06)	**−1.03**	(0.06)	**−1.31**	(0.12)	**−0.96**	(0.13)	3,662
Middle Eastern	**−0.60**	(0.05)	**−0.28**	(0.06)	**0.89**	(0.06)	**1.27**	(0.06)	4,615
Indian/Pakistani/Bangladeshi	**−1.18**	(0.08)	**−1.00**	(0.08)	**0.49**	(0.09)	**0.63**	(0.09)	1,709
Japanese, Taiwanese etc.	0.16	(0.17)	0.33	(0.17)	**1.76**	(0.18)	**1.89**	(0.18)	393
Chinese	**1.40**	(0.22)	**1.64**	(0.22)	**2.45**	(0.21)	**2.62**	(0.22)	351
Iranian	**−0.91**	(0.05)	**−0.49**	(0.05)	**0.29**	(0.07)	**0.92**	(0.07)	5,515
Turkish	**−0.32**	(0.06)	**−0.24**	(0.06)	**1.91**	(0.05)	**1.90**	(0.05)	3,888
South-East Asian	**−1.00**	(0.10)	**−0.82**	(0.11)	−0.07	(0.12)	0.06	(0.13)	1,486
Age/10	**0.27**	(0.02)	0.09	(0.02)	**0.33**	(0.02)	**0.13**	(0.03)	
(Age/10)²	**−0.19**	(0.03)	**−0.12**	(0.03)	**−0.45**	(0.04)	**−0.27**	(0.04)	
Qualifications									
Missing	**−0.79**	(0.08)	**−0.68**	(0.08)	0.00	(0.10)	0.15	(0.10)	
Compulsory	**−2.00**	(0.05)	**−2.02**	(0.05)	**−0.18**	(0.06)	**−0.19**	(0.06)	
Lower vocational/secondary	**−0.70**	(0.04)	**−0.74**	(0.04)	0.10	(0.06)	0.05	(0.06)	
Upper secondary	0.00		0.00		0.00		0.00		
Lower tertiary	**1.31**	(0.05)	**1.31**	(0.05)	**0.28**	(0.08)	**0.28**	(0.08)	
University degree	**2.28**	(0.05)	**2.32**	(0.05)	**0.44**	(0.08)	**0.48**	(0.08)	
Years since immigration			**0.13**	(0.01)			**0.31**	(0.01)	
(Years since immigration)²			**−0.34**	(0.03)			**−1.02**	(0.05)	
−2LL	25,926.8		91,596.6		25,926.8		91,596.6		
N					80,345				

Notes: The category of 'unqualified jobs' (class IIIb–VII) serves as the reference category. Emboldened coefficients indicate significance at the 0.05 level or better; standard errors are given in brackets. Model fit information comes from a model in which class IIIb–VII is reference category, and which also includes class IIIa–VI, excluded from presentation here.

Table 11.11B. Logistic regression of access to the salariat and self-employment among first-generation immigrant women: the role of years since migration (parameter estimates).

	Access to the salariat				Access to self-employment				N
	Model A		Model B		Model A		Model B		
Intercept	−0.51	(0.04)	−1.67	(0.07)	−2.75	(0.08)	−4.28	(0.14)	
Ancestry									
Finnish	0.00		0.00		0.00		0.00		29,327
Norwegian/Danish	0.06	(0.04)	**0.16**	(0.04)	**0.86**	(0.07)	**0.94**	(0.07)	7,119
Western	**0.47**	(0.06)	**0.60**	(0.06)	**1.27**	(0.10)	**1.39**	(0.10)	2,998
German	**0.54**	(0.09)	**0.65**	(0.09)	**1.34**	(0.13)	**1.45**	(0.13)	1,296
Polish	**−0.70**	(0.04)	**−0.56**	(0.04)	**0.38**	(0.07)	**0.51**	(0.07)	8,082
Greek	**−0.38**	(0.12)	**−0.39**	(0.12)	**1.07**	(0.13)	**1.07**	(0.13)	1,154
Yugoslavian	**−0.69**	(0.06)	**−0.68**	(0.06)	**0.74**	(0.07)	**0.76**	(0.07)	5,438
East European	**−0.24**	(0.05)	−0.06	(0.05)	**0.60**	(0.09)	**0.80**	(0.09)	4,665
South European	0.13	(0.11)	**0.22**	(0.11)	**0.43**	(0.19)	**0.51**	(0.19)	1,016
North African	−0.25	(0.16)	−0.10	(0.16)	**0.83**	(0.21)	**0.98**	(0.21)	527
Eritrean/Ethiopian	**−0.95**	(0.15)	**−0.78**	(0.16)	**−1.28**	(0.45)	**−1.02**	(0.45)	660
Sub-Saharan African	**−0.86**	(0.13)	**−0.69**	(0.13)	−0.16	(0.23)	0.03	(0.23)	848
Latin American	**−0.28**	(0.07)	−0.10	(0.07)	−0.27	(0.17)	−0.08	(0.17)	2,053
Chilean	**−0.99**	(0.07)	**−0.76**	(0.07)	**−1.25**	(0.20)	**−0.97**	(0.20)	3,172
Middle Eastern	**0.39**	(0.09)	**0.57**	(0.09)	**1.31**	(0.11)	**1.50**	(0.11)	1,701
Indian/Pakistani/Bangladeshi	**−1.21**	(0.12)	**−1.04**	(0.12)	**0.69**	(0.15)	**0.84**	(0.15)	1,057
Japanese, Taiwanese etc.	**−0.41**	(0.14)	**−0.29**	(0.14)	**1.33**	(0.17)	**1.44**	(0.18)	541
Chinese	−0.16	(0.19)	0.10	(0.19)	**1.83**	(0.18)	**2.06**	(0.18)	370
Iranian	−0.16	(0.07)	**0.35**	(0.07)	0.05	(0.15)	**0.70**	(0.16)	2,357
Turkish	−0.15	(0.09)	−0.14	(0.09)	**1.07**	(0.10)	**1.06**	(0.10)	2,272
South-East Asian	**−1.46**	(0.09)	**−1.23**	(0.09)	−0.14	(0.13)	0.09	(0.14)	2,650
Age/10	**0.14**	(0.02)	0.01	(0.02)	**0.26**	(0.03)	**0.14**	(0.04)	
(Age/10)^2	**−0.20**	(0.03)	**−0.10**	(0.03)	**−0.30**	(0.05)	**−0.18**	(0.05)	
Qualifications									
Missing	**−0.38**	(0.09)	**−0.30**	(0.09)	−0.10	(0.15)	0.00	(0.15)	
Compulsory	**−2.41**	(0.05)	**−2.43**	(0.05)	**−0.65**	(0.08)	**−0.66**	(0.08)	
Lower vocational/secondary	**−1.02**	(0.04)	**−1.04**	(0.04)	−0.12	(0.08)	−0.14	(0.08)	
Upper secondary	0.00		0.00		0.00		0.00		
Lower tertiary	**2.30**	(0.04)	**2.33**	(0.05)	**0.83**	(0.09)	**0.87**	(0.09)	
University degree	**2.86**	(0.05)	**2.92**	(0.05)	**0.98**	(0.10)	**1.06**	(0.11)	
Years since immigration			**0.15**	(0.01)			**0.21**	(0.02)	
(Years since immigration)^2			**−0.45**	(0.04)			**−0.68**	(0.07)	
−2LL	21,552.6		73,230.8		21,552.6		73,230.8		
N					79,303				

Notes: The category of 'unqualified jobs' (class IIIb–VII) serves as the reference category. Emboldened coefficients indicate significance at the 0.05 level or better; standard errors are given in brackets. Model fit information comes from a model in which class IIIb–VII is reference category, and which also includes class IIIa–VI, excluded from presentation here.

All in all, the time since arrival does matter for immigrants' labour market attainment[43] whereas the labour market situation upon arrival does not seem to be of much importance. We are not in the position to explain exactly why time in Sweden has positive effects, but several causes are likely: early arrivers have had longer time to search for jobs, to build up networks, to acclimatise to the Swedish labour market and culture and also more time to learn the language. We cannot rule out that different cohorts of immigrants have different skills or ambition, that there is what Borjas (1985) call a decreasing 'quality' of immigrants across cohorts; although given the advantageous distribution of formal qualifications of more recently arrived (mostly refugee) immigrants as compared to traditional labour-force immigrants (see Table 11.4), this is unlikely.[44]

We also learned that some of the particularly strong disadvantages experienced by non-European immigrants could be accounted for by the fact that they arrived relatively recently in Sweden. Even controlling for time since arrival, however, immigrants from several non-European origins have very low employment rates—especially those from China, Japan, Iran, Turkey, other Middle East countries, and Latin America (save Chile). However, we cannot conclude that immigrants from these countries are the most disadvantaged. This is because several of these categories show a much more advantageous situation when it came to occupational class attainment. For example, whereas immigrant men from China are, to a large degree, non-employed, those who have a job are much more likely than other immigrants to be found in the salariat. Those from Chile and Yugoslavia, on the other hand, have high employment propensities but very small chances of reaching the salariat. A reasonable interpretation of such a disparate pattern of labour-market success is that there is population heterogeneity within immigrant groups on some individual characteristic which we do not observe, but which is important for labour-market performance; for example, this characteristic could be ambition or skills that are not measured by educational qualifications. If there is a barrier to labour-market entrance for some immigrant groups (say, the Chinese) based on these unobserved charac-

---

[43] Arai, Regnér and Schröder (2000) and Bevelander and Nielsen (2001) found a similar importance of time in Sweden for unemployment risks and employment propensities, as did Ekberg and Rooth (2004) for occupational attainment. The assimilation when it comes to wage levels seems not to be so impressive (le Grand and Szulkin 2002).

[44] There is however a possibility that the incentives for employment is less among later arrivers because these to a large extent consist of relatives. As the age-range in this data set is 26–49 this is probably not a great problem in the analyses above.

teristics, those who make it into the labour market may be positively selected, i.e., they may be very highly motivated or possess certain marketable skills. If the labour market-entry barrier does not exist for other groups (say, the Chileans) the employed group will on average be less competitive. The question, then, is why entry barriers might differ between immigrant groups. One tentative answer could refer to the notion of ethnic enclaves: if some immigrant groups have a long history in Sweden, and/or if they are relatively 'tight' (geographically, socially, or economically), they may provide an entry port to the Swedish labour market that does not exist for other groups, be it only in the form of unqualified jobs. As we lack information to test this, it must remain a hypothesis (and the pattern in Tables 11.10 and 11.11 does not easily fit into such an explanation).

This section must be concluded with a word of caution. This chapter has, like most others analysing the socio-economic attainment of ethnic minorities, treated immigrants as a permanent group. In reality, many immigrants move home again. Return migration has been common especially among labour-force immigrants in Sweden: for example, of the Nordic immigrants arriving in 1970 and 1980, respectively, 60% and 65% had moved home again by 1990 (Klinthäll 2003, fig. 2.2). The corresponding figures for Greek immigrants were between 40% and 60%, and for Yugoslavs between 20% and 35% (ibid., figs. 2.8–2.9). Among political refugees, return migration has been less common up to 1990. As the cross-sectional sample used in my analyses consists of the sub-group of immigrants who have not returned home by 1990 a crucial question is whether they are special in any way that may affect the results presented above; if the more successful Greeks move home again, to take one example, this may explain the poor situation for Greek immigrants still living in Sweden. The results by Klinthäll (2003) tend at least partly to support this view: return migrants from Greece and Yugoslavia have relatively high incomes over a number of years (suggesting a target-saving behaviour). Given the complex results in Klinthäll's and other studies, it may well be that both relatively successful and unsuccessful immigrants return, making it difficult to estimate what effect return migration might have for our cross-sectional estimates of ethnic penalties.[45] As the return migration

---

[45] The results from Klinthäll's and others' (e.g., Edin *et al.* 2000; Nekby 2004) analyses are not easy to interpret: return migration in the cross-sectional view is more likely if an immigrant is unemployed and has a low income, but there is also a positive effect of the sum of incomes over a number of preceding years. Klinthäll argues that the former results may come about because

among refugees to poorer countries generally is low (even though it is unknown for several of the countries in Tables 11.10 and 11.11 because they are not included in existing studies of return migration), the major concern is with Greece and Yugoslavia. For the time being, the best advice is to interpret their estimates with caution.

Second-generation immigrants: discrimination against visible minorities?

It is not possible with the data at hand to explain why some ethnic groups—particularly those of non-European origin—are doing worse than others in the labour market. As mentioned, the fact that first-generation immigrants, to a larger extent than the second generation, are out of employment may be due to incompatibility of their human capital with demands in the Swedish labour market. The result that first-generation immigrants from non-European countries on average face greater ethnic penalties than most European immigrant groups may be due to discrimination based on visible characteristics. Skin colour is not such a relevant marker among the biggest immigrant groups in Sweden. However, hair and eye colour will normally be different between those of Swedish ancestry, on the one hand, and those from Southern and Eastern Europe, and particularly from non-European countries, on the other. In addition, their names will most often differ. One way of addressing the question of whether visible minorities fare less well in the labour market—which could indicate employer discrimination—is by studying second-generation immigrants, i.e., those with foreign-born parents who either were born in Sweden or arrived there before school started. Their education is Swedish and we assume that their proficiency in the Swedish language is by-and-large comparable with those with Swedish parents.

The strategy followed in the analysis below is to rank national origins according to how similar (we assume that) they are to those of Swedish ancestry. Norwegians and Danes are ranked as most similar—their mother tongue is closely related to Swedish (spoken, this is the case

---

the remigration decision has already been taken at the cross-section data point and the migrant-to-be therefore stopped working (or reduced working hours), or even because the person has already left Sweden (without being registered as an emigrant yet). Those who have emigrated but not notified the authorities, pose a potential problem for the analysis of employment as well, as they will be registered as non-employed in our data.

especially for Norwegian), they are not possible to distinguish visually, and many names are similar too. Next we rank Finns—most are distinct from Swedes when it comes to language and names, but they would be very difficult to point out in the street. In addition, there is a minority with Swedish names and Swedish as their mother tongue. The third group is people of 'other Western' origins. The fourth consists of those from Eastern and Southern Europe, who on average are more easily distinguished from the reference group than those of German and Anglo-Saxon origin (who dominate the Western category). The fifth group, finally, is made up of those of non-Western and non-European origins. This group is arguably closest to a 'visible minority' in Sweden.

In order to introduce even finer distinctions into this analysis separate categories are also made out of those who have one parent from each of these five groups and one parent who was born in Sweden, i.e., a 'mixed-origin' category. Table 11.12 reports the results of logistic regressions on employment for these categories, contrasted with those of Swedish ancestry. It is for employment probabilities that we expect discrimination to occur, given the results in Tables 11.7 and 11.9, showing that second-generation immigrants hardly experience any ethnic penalty in occupational attainment. If visible characteristics were important we would expect not only to see a ranking in the estimates among second-generation immigrants along the lines outlined above, but also that ethnic penalties among those with mixed origins would be somewhere in between the second-generation immigrants and the reference group, also increasing as we move towards groups defined as 'more visible' minorities.

With the exception of the ordering of Finns and Danish/Norwegian, the results in Models A in Table 11.12 support the hypothesis of visible minority discrimination: the estimates become more negative as minorities become more easily discernable. For men, but not for women, the estimates for the mixed origin categories follow the expected pattern as well. It is of course not possible to conclude that discrimination drives these results. One very plausible source of heterogeneity among the groups analysed is differences in resources in the family of origin, resources that may help children to find employment. To account for some of this, in Models B in Table 11.12 we add three additional variables: the higher of the parents' levels of education, the higher of their class positions, and an indicator of single parent household. The results show that these resources have the expected impact on employment probabilities, and that controlling for them reduces the negative effects of having immigrant parents (the coefficients decrease on average 20% for

Table 11.12. Logistic regression of Employment versus non-employment among the second-generation, by ancestry and gender (parameter estimates)

	Men				Women			
	Model A		Model B		Model A		Model B	
Intercept	**2.85**	(0.01)	**2.23**	(0.03)	**2.36**	(0.01)	**1.94**	(0.02)
Ancestry								
Swedish	0.00		0.00		0.00		0.00	
Norwegian/Danish	**−0.31**	(0.03)	**−0.29**	(0.03)	**−0.15**	(0.03)	**−0.14**	(0.03)
Norwegian/Danish & Swedish mix	**−0.26**	(0.04)	**−0.29**	(0.04)	**−0.17**	(0.03)	**−0.18**	(0.03)
Finnish	**−0.27**	(0.03)	**−0.28**	(0.03)	0.01	(0.03)	−0.01	(0.03)
Finnish & Swede mix	**−0.30**	(0.03)	**−0.34**	(0.03)	**−0.08**	(0.03)	**−0.10**	(0.03)
Western	**−0.48**	(0.04)	**−0.34**	(0.04)	**−0.26**	(0.03)	**−0.17**	(0.03)
Western & Swedish mix	**−0.34**	(0.04)	**−0.24**	(0.04)	**−0.24**	(0.04)	**−0.18**	(0.04)
East/South European	**−0.60**	(0.03)	**−0.54**	(0.03)	**−0.28**	(0.03)	**−0.25**	(0.03)
East/South European & Swedish mix	**−0.41**	(0.06)	**−0.36**	(0.06)	**−0.19**	(0.06)	**−0.15**	(0.06)
Non-European	**−0.81**	(0.06)	**−0.61**	(0.06)	**−0.56**	(0.05)	**−0.44**	(0.05)
Non-European & Swedish mix	**−0.55**	(0.10)	**−0.42**	(0.10)	−0.15	(0.10)	−0.06	(0.10)
Age/10	**0.44**	(0.01)	**0.43**	(0.01)	**0.36**	(0.01)	**0.36**	(0.01)
(Age/10)^2	**−0.26**	(0.01)	**−0.20**	(0.01)	**−0.08**	(0.01)	**−0.05**	(0.01)
Qualifications								
Missing	**−2.71**	(0.03)	**−2.84**	(0.03)	**−3.09**	(0.04)	**−3.14**	(0.04)
Compulsory	**−0.08**	(0.01)	**−0.30**	(0.02)	**−0.50**	(0.01)	**−0.61**	(0.01)
Lower vocational/ secondary	**0.58**	(0.01)	**0.40**	(0.01)	**0.33**	(0.01)	**0.24**	(0.01)
Upper secondary	0.00		0.00		0.00		0.00	
Lower tertiary	**0.70**	(0.02)	**0.67**	(0.02)	**0.74**	(0.01)	**0.75**	(0.01)
University degree	**0.74**	(0.02)	**0.87**	(0.02)	**0.76**	(0.02)	**0.87**	(0.02)
Child of single parent			**−0.34**	(0.02)			**−0.17**	(0.02)
−2LL	495,369.2		490,977.2		663,807.0		660,990.4	
N		1,286,778				1,226,789		

Notes: First generation immigrants are excluded from the analysis. The ethnic group reference category consists of Swedish-born with *no* immigrant parent. Model B includes controls for parents' level of education (six levels) and parents' occupational class (seven levels), although those parameters are not presented here. Emboldened coefficients indicate significance at the 0.05 level or better; standard errors are shown in brackets.

the non-Nordic groups). However, the ranking of the groups according to visibility of immigrant status remains after controls.

Considering the extensive controls for family origin resources and for personal educational attainment, it is worth noting that the negative effects on employment of having parents born in a foreign country are by no means small. There is, of course, probably some remaining unobserved heterogeneity in the data. For example, ethnic minorities more often live in segregated areas where job opportunities, as well as information about such opportunities, are fewer (though ethnic enclaves may have a counterbalancing effect). Also, there may be some effects of 'cultural distance' that are not captured in observed variables.[46] Nonetheless, it appears to be a plausible interpretation of the pattern found in Table 11.12 that visible minority status is a disadvantage in the job-search process.

Conclusion and discussion

Sweden has been an immigrant country since the Second World War, with a mix of labour and refugee immigration up to the early 1970s and a large inflow of refugees, especially from the Middle East, after that. In 2002 almost 13% of the Swedish population was born in another country, totalling more than one million inhabitants out of a total nine million. Labour immigrants arriving before 1970 used to have a labour-market achievement on par with native Swedes. These traditional groups—the Finnish, Yugoslavian, and Greek immigrants—are more disadvantaged in 1990 (and, as more recent data show, their disadvantage has carried on into the 1990s). Their employment rates are not so much lower than those of native-born Swedes, but their chances of reaching the most privileged class positions are substantially poorer. The situation for more recently arrived immigrants (mostly refugees), predominantly for those of non-European origin, is more problematic. Non-employment figures are very high and if employed, these immigrants are mostly stuck in unskilled work. Although a university degree provides some protection against poor labour-market outcomes for first-generation immigrants, the advantage of having a degree is substantially less for most groups than for native Swedes.

The poor (and worsening) labour-market situation of immigrants notwithstanding, economic assimilation does exist and has shown to be important. This is evident from two types of results. First, the time since arrival has a positive effect for labour-market outcomes, though there seems to be little hope that assimilation alone would lead non-European immigrants to catch up with native-born Swedes (an expected labour shortage in Sweden due to demographic changes may improve their chances

---

[46] 'Cultural' factors are often invoked to explain remaining differences among immigrant groups (and their distance from the indigenous population) but are, just as discrimination, notoriously difficult to support by empirical evidence. One, admittedly indirect, result that seems to question a cultural explanation is that the disadvantages of immigrant groups are greater for men that for women, despite the fact that it is likely that women in sending countries are more bound to traditional role models than men compared to their Swedish-born counterparts.

somewhat). Second, the rather pessimistic view of first-generation immigrants is counterbalanced by the fact that there is considerable assimilation across generations. Sons and daughters of immigrants (born in Sweden, or immigrated before starting school) do almost as well in the labour market as those with two Swedish-born parents.

The remaining worry for the second-generation immigrants is that their employment rates are relatively low. After controlling statistically for resources in the family of origin there is a gradient in the disadvantages faced by second-generation immigrants suggesting that the more visible the ethnic origin, the lower the probability of being employed (culminating with those of non-European origin). This result is not evidence of employer discrimination—which in this case should be limited to labour market entrance—but is certainly in line with such an interpretation. An interesting result, not easily reconciled with the one just mentioned, however, is that once in the labour market second-generation immigrants do not face any ethnic penalties in gaining access to the most advantaged class positions. It is possible that the tougher first hurdle means that those who clear it are then positively selected (on a variable that we do not observe, such as social network, ability, or aspiration); however in the absence of more direct evidence this must, as the discrimination interpretation, remain a speculation.[47]

This study has benefited from a large register-based data-set that enables the analysis of many single countries of origin, which is particularly valuable in Sweden which is home to immigrants from a fairly broad spectrum of ethnic origins. Most other studies group countries on some geographical/regional dimension following an underlying, but rarely explicit, idea of the impact of 'distance'; because the US and Australia, for example, typically are counted as Western countries (and thus close to Sweden), the real assumption seems to be one of 'cultural' distance. And though there seems to be, by and large, falling employment rates according to such 'cultural distance' (whatever the causal mechanism), the pattern at a fine-graded level is more complex than what the usual aggregation of countries would suggest.

---

[47] One possibility is that the academic labour market is relatively meritocratic. Previous Swedish studies have shown, for example, that among those with tertiary level education there is no remaining association between social origin and class position (Erikson and Jonsson 1998). However, the results of the interaction between education and country of origin on labour-market outcomes (reported in Fig. 11.1) show that some academically educated second-generation immigrant categories have difficulties in getting a job that corresponds to their qualifications.

For example, first-generation immigrants from Chile do better than other immigrants from remote and poor countries when it comes to employment (although to a large extent they end up in unfavourable occupations). The traditional European labour market immigrants face disadvantages in general, but while first-generation Finns and Yugoslavs have high employment rates this is not the case for Greek immigrants. On the other hand, the improvement across generations is not so great for the former groups—in fact, even the reverse for Yugoslavs—so their higher employment propensities in previous generations do not seem to have favourable consequences for their children (although we have not, strictly speaking, studied parents and children). Another example is the Turks who overall show poor achievements even considering their exceptionally low educational level, but who have a very high propensity of self-employment.

To explain single-country deviations from the general ethnic penalty pattern is beyond the scope of this chapter, but characteristics of the immigrant groups, of the sending countries, and of the social networks in Sweden are no doubt important. One possible lead in the search for the heterogeneous fate of immigrants is the marriage patterns of different groups. It is rarely noted that in many immigrant groups the most common pattern is to marry someone who was born in the country of destination, thereby creating a more favourable social network. Children in these groups will also have a situation that is similar to that of children born to two native-born parents. Other ethnic groups, such as the Turks and the Yugoslavs in Sweden, will have greater difficulties in eradicating their disadvantages in the filial generation because of very high within-group marriage (which is partly a function of the demographic pattern at immigration). Another factor that should be considered more often is the potential selectivity on return migration, which for some immigrant categories has been very high in Sweden (Klinthäll 2003).

Finally, as noted in the introduction, the substantial inflow of refugees to Sweden in the 1990s have created a new situation for first-generation immigrants, and it is far from certain that the results in these analyses (stemming from 1990) are still valid. We know, for example, that the employment opportunities are much worse now, in general and especially among immigrants. Nor can we be certain that the economic assimilation of second-generation immigrants will occur for those who arrived in Sweden in the 1980s and 1990s (of whom many come from 'new' immigrant countries). What we can say, however, is that for younger cohorts—born at the beginning of the 1980s—the educational achievements are not lagging behind in general (Dryler 2001). However, children who are first-generation immigrants do have lower grade point averages, a problem that is amplified by residential segregation (Szulkin and Jonsson 2004). The labour-market opportunities for non-European first- and second-generation immigrants in particular will be an important topic to study at the beginning of the 2010s.

Appendix

Swedish data have been fitted into the EGP class schema as follows:

I   Higher-grade professionals and administrators, and officials in the public sector.
II Lower-grade professionals, higher-grade technicians, lower-grade administrators and officials, managers in small firms and services.
IIIa Routine non-manual employees in administration and commerce and supervisors of both non-manual and manual employees.
IIIb Routine non-manual workers in services, without qualifications.
IV Proprietors and artisans with or without employees and self-employed farmers.
V   Not used
VI Skilled manual workers and technicians.
VII Unskilled workers including agricultural labourers and lower-grade service workers.

Unlike the EGP class schema, all employers are in class IV (i.e., also the few with more than twenty employees). Foremen, supervisors of manual workers, and lower grade technicians do not form a separate class (Class V in the EGP schema). Some qualified supervisors go into Class II while foremen in general are classified in Class IIIa. Blue-collar technicians (relatively uncommon in Sweden) go mostly into Class VI. Occupations normally organised in the manual workers' trade union in Sweden (LO) are classified into Class VI and VII. In the latter class are included some occupations that in the EGP coding schema are found in the unqualified strata of the non-manual classes (IIIb). Among these are lower grade salespersons and shop-assistants as well as lower grade service workers (employed, *inter alia*, in hotels, restaurants, and in offices) and nurses' aids. However, in the analyses above, Class IIIb and Class VII are merged, so these differences will not have any bearing on comparability of results.

Swedish education has been fitted into the CASMIN educational schema in the following manner:

1ab This is the social minimum of education, in Sweden corresponding to *folkskola* or *grundskola*.
1c Basic vocational training above and beyond compulsory schooling, including vocational courses of at least one year's duration (also 2-year programmes at upper secondary school).
2ab Advanced vocational training or secondary programmes in which general intermediate schooling is combined with vocational training (2a) plus academic or general

tracks at the secondary intermediate level (2b) (in Sweden *realskola* and vocational training on top of that, or equivalent).

2c Full maturity certificates (e.g. the *Abitur*, Matriculation, *Baccalaureat*, A-levels; in Sweden *Studentexamen* or 3-year Academic programmes at upper secondary school (*teoretiskt gymnasium*).

3a Lower-level tertiary degrees, generally of shorter duration and with a vocational orientation (e.g. technical college diplomas, or non-university teaching certificates; in Sweden 1–2 years of education beyond upper secondary school).

3b The completion of a traditional, academically-oriented university education.

3c Post-graduate exam

In the logistic regressions, educational qualification is used as a control variable that merges some categories: The five groups are 1ab, 1c+2ab, 2c, 3a, and 3bc (with 2c as the reference category).

References

Aguilar, R. and Gustafsson, B. (1991), 'The Earnings Assimilation of Immigrants', *Labour,* 5, 37–51.

Aguilar, R. and Gustafsson, B. (1994), 'Immigrants in Sweden's labour market during the 1980s', *Scandinavian Journal of Social Welfare*, 3, 139–47.

Andersson, R. (1998), 'Socio-spatial Dynamics: Ethnic Divisions of Mobility and Housing in post-Palme Sweden', *Urban Studies*, 35, 397–428.

Arai, M., Regnér, H., and Schröder, L. (2000), *Invandrare på den svenska arbetsmarknaden — vistelsetidens betydelse*. Appendix 3, The Diversity Project (Stockholm: Näringsdepartementet).

Arai, M. and Vilhelmsson, R. (2002), 'Unemployment-Risk Differentials Between Immigrant and Native Workers in Sweden', Paper III in R. Vilhelmsson, *Wages and Unemployment of Immigrants and Natives in Sweden*. Dissertation No. 56 (Stockholm: Swedish Institute for Social Research).

Bevelander, P. and Nielsen, H. S. (2001), 'Declining employment success of immigrant males in Sweden: Observed and unobserved characteristics?', *Journal of Population Economics*, 14, 455–71.

Bögenhold, D. and Staber, U. (1991), 'The Decline and Rise of Self-Employment', *Work, Employment, and Society*, 5, 223–39.

Borjas, G. J. (1985), 'Assimilation, Changes in Cohort Quality and the Earnings of Immigrants', *Journal of Labor Economics*, 3, 463–89.

Borjas, G. J. (1995), 'Assimilation and Changes in Cohort Quality Revisited: What Happened to Immigrant Earnings in the 1980s?', *Journal of Labor Economics*, 13, 201–45.

Carliner, G. (1980), 'Wages, Earnings and Hours of First, Second and Third Generation American Males', *Economic Inquiry*, 18, 87–102.

Chiswick, B. (1982), *The Employment of Immigrants in the United States* (Washington DC: American Enterprise Institute).

Dryler, H. (2001), 'Etnisk segregering i skolan—effekter på ungdomars betyg och övergång till gymnasieskolan', in J. Fritzell and J. Palme (eds.), *Välfärdens finansiering och fördelning* (SOU 2001:57) (Stockholm: Fritzes), pp. 319–56.

Edin, P.-A., LaLonde, R., and Åslund, O. (2000), 'Emigration of Immigrants and Measures of Immigrant Assimilation: Evidence from Sweden', *Swedish Economic Policy Review*, 7, 163–204.

Edin, P.-A., Fredriksson, P., and Åslund, O. (2003), 'Ethnic enclaves and the economic success of immigrants—evidence from a natural experiment', *Quarterly Journal of Economics*, 118, 329–57.

Ekberg, J. (1997), 'Hur är arbetsmarknaden för andra generationens invandrare?', *Arbetsmarknad och arbetsliv*, 3, 5–16.

Ekberg, J. (1999), 'Immigration and the public sector: Income effects for the native population in Sweden', *Journal of Population Economics*, 12, 411–30.

Ekberg, J. and Andersson, L. (1995), *Invandring, sysselsättning och ekonomiska effekter*. Ds 1995:68 (Stockholm: Finansdepartementet).

Ekberg, J. and Rooth, D.-O. (2004), 'Yrke och utbildning på 2000-talets arbetsmarknad—skillnader mellan inrikes och utrikes födda personer'. Appendix to *Rapport integration 2003* (Stockholm: Integrationsverket).

Erikson, R. and Goldthorpe, J. H. (1992), *The Constant Flux: A Study of Class Mobility in Industrial Societies* (Oxford: Clarendon Press).

Erikson, R. and Jonsson, J. O. (1993), *Ursprung och utbildning*. SOU 1993:85 (Stockholm: Fritzes).

Erikson, R. and Jonsson, J. O. (1998), 'Qualifications and the Allocation Process of Young Men and Women in the Swedish Labour Market'. In Y. Shavit and W. Müller (eds.), *From School to Work. A Comparative Study of Educational Qualifications and Occupational Destinations* (Oxford: Oxford University Press), pp. 369–406.

le Grand, C. and Szulkin, R. (2002), 'Permanent Disadvantage of Gradual Integration: Explaining the Immigrant-Native Earnings Gap in Sweden', *Labour*, 16, 37–64.

Hammarstedt, M. (2001), 'Immigrant self-employment in Sweden—its variation and some possible determinants', *Entrepreneurship & Regional Development*, 13, 147–61.

Integrationsverket (2004), *Rapport integration 2003* (Stockholm: Integrationsverket).

Jonsson, J. O. (2002), 'The educational and labour market attainment in Sweden of immigrants and native-born Swedes', Paper presented at the ISA RC28 Conference in Oxford, April 2002.

Jonsson, J. O. (2004), 'Equality at a Halt? Social mobility in Sweden, 1976–1999'. In Breen, R. (ed.), *Social Mobility in Europe* (Oxford: Oxford University Press), pp. 225–50.

Klinthäll, M. (2003), *Return Migration from Sweden 1968–1996*. Lund Studies in Economic History 21 (Lund: Dept of Economic History).

Lindbeck, A. and Snower, D. (1988), *The Insider-Outsider Theory of Employment and Unemployment* (Cambridge, MA: MIT Press).

Lundh, C., Bennich-Björkman L., Ohlsson R., Pedersen P. J., and Rooth, D.-O. (2002), *Arbete? Var god dröj? Invandrare i välfärdssamhället*. Välfärdspolitiska rådets rapport 2002 (Stockholm: SNS Förlag).

Moore, R. L. (1983), 'Employer discrimination: evidence from self-employed workers', *The Review of Income and Statistics*, 65, 496–501.

Müller, W. and Shavit, Y. (1998), 'The institutional embeddedness of the stratification process: A comparative study of qualifications and occupations in thirteen countries'. In Y. Shavit and W. Müller (eds.), *From School to Work* (Oxford: Oxford University Press), pp. 1–48.

Nekby, L. (2004), 'Inte bara invandring. Utvandring av utrikes födda från Sverige'. Appendix to *Rapport integration 2003* (Stockholm: Integrationsverket).

OECD (2003), *Trends in International Migration*. SOPEMI 2002 (Paris: OECD).

OECD (2004), *Trends in International Migration*. SOPEMI 2003 (Paris: OECD).

Ohlsson, R. (1975), *Invandrarna på arbetsmarknaden*. Dissertation No. 16 (University of Lund: Department of Economic History).

Proposition (Governmental Bill) 1997/98:16.

Proposition (Governmental Bill) 1997/98:177.

Proposition (Governmental Bill) 1998/99:143.

Rooth, D.-O. (1999), *Refugee Immigrants in Sweden: Educational Investments and Labour Market Integration*. Lund Economic Studies, No. 84 (University of Lund).

Rooth, D.-O. and Ekberg, J. (2003), 'Unemployment and earnings for second generation immigrants in Sweden. Ethnic background and parent composition', *Journal of Population Economics*, 16, 787–814.

Similä, M. (1994), 'Andra generationens invandrare i den svenska skolan'. In R. Erikson and J. O. Jonsson (eds.), *Sorteringen i skolan* (Stockholm: Carlssons), pp. 226–63.

Statistics Sweden (1982), *Socio-ekonomisk indelning* (SEI). MiS 1982:4. (Swedish Socioeconomic Classification) (Stockholm: Statistics Sweden).

Statistics Sweden (1988), *Svensk utbildningsnomenklatur (SUN). Del 1. Systematisk version* (Swedish standard classification of education. Part 1. Numerical order). Reports on Statistical Co-ordination, 1988:4 (Stockholm: Statistics Sweden).

Statistics Sweden (2004), *Statistisk Årsbok 2004* (Statistic Yearbook 2004) (Stockholm: SCB).

Sveriges Nationalatlas (1991), *Befolkningen* (Höganäs: Bokförlaget Bra Böcker).

Szulkin, R. and Jonsson, J. O. (2004), 'Ethnic segregation and educational outcomes in Swedish comprehensive schools: A multilevel analysis' (Swedish Institute for Social Research and Dept of Sociology, Stockholm University).

Vilhelmsson, R. (2002), 'Ethnic Differences in the Swedish Youth Labor Market'. Paper I in R. Vilhelmsson, *Wages and Unemployment of Immigrants and Natives in Sweden* (Stockholm University: Swedish Institute for Social Research).

Wadensjö, E. (1973), *Immigration och samhällsekonomi*, Lund Economic Studies No. 8 (University of Lund).

12

Nice Work if You can Get it: Ethnic Penalties in Great Britain

SIN YI CHEUNG & ANTHONY HEATH[1]

Summary. Britain has long been home to migrants from Ireland (which until 1921 had been part of the United Kingdom). More recently it has seen major inflows from a number of less-developed countries such as Jamaica, India, Pakistan, Nigeria, Kenya and Hong Kong that had formerly been part of the British Empire. Indeed, under the 1948 British Nationality Act, rights of entry were given to 800 million citizens of the British Commonwealth. While there is some reason to believe that the Irish experienced some discrimination in Britain in the first half of the twentieth century or before, our evidence suggests that the Irish, both first and second generation, now compete on equal terms with the indigenous British. The ethnic penalties experienced by the visible minorities from the less-developed members of the Commonwealth have declined markedly in the second generation, but all the major visible minorities still find it more difficult to obtain jobs commensurate with their qualifications than do the various white groups, even in the second generation. However, when they do obtain jobs, they tend to be of similar standing and with similar rates of pay to those gained by the indigenous white British. Continuing discrimination against visible minorities is likely to be a major part of the explanation for the difficulty in gaining employment.

---

[1] Acknowledgement: We thank the UK Data Archive for giving us permission to use the General Household Survey data and Jane Roberts for preparing the datasets for us.

Introduction

BRITAIN, LIKE MOST OF THE OTHER developed countries of Western Europe, experienced a major influx of immigrants in the last decades of the twentieth century. Many of these migrants were members of what can be termed 'visible minorities' (Black Caribbeans, Indians and Pakistanis), coming from the British commonwealth, although there was also a sizeable influx of white migrants from Ireland and Europe too. Early research on the experiences of the first migrants suggested that, on arrival in Britain, they experienced considerable discrimination in employment and housing and faced considerable disadvantages in securing employment appropriate to their qualifications and skills (Daniel 1968; Castles and Kosack 1973. See also Prandy 1979; Chiswick 1980; McNabb and Psacharopoulos 1981; Heath and Ridge 1983; Stewart 1983; and Heath and Yu 2005 for research on the first generation of post-war migrants to Britain).

Forty years on, the children of these first arrivals are now in the labour market. There are many reasons for hoping that the experience of the British-born, the second generation, will be a great deal more favourable than that of the first generation. The lack of human capital— skills, fluency in the English language, and qualifications—that hampered the first generation should have much reduced impact on the second generation. The second generation will have acquired British qualifications and know-how about the operation of the British labour market. Anti-discrimination legislation and the efforts of the Commission for Racial Equality might be expected to have reduced direct discrimination, and prejudice among the white population may have declined, particularly among younger generations of British-born whites who have themselves been brought up in a multicultural Britain (Rothon and Heath 2003). Our key research question, therefore, is whether these second-generation ethnic minorities have had better fortune in finding jobs or securing jobs appropriate to their qualifications than their parents' generation did. Have they achieved parity in the British labour market with white people of British ancestry? Furthermore, how do the fortunes of the different ethnic minorities compare? Do visible minorities fare as well as white ethnic minorities such as the Irish?

Patterns of immigration

For much of the last four hundred years Britain was a country of emigration rather than of immigration. Beginning in the seventeenth century large numbers of Britons left, first to Ireland which has sometimes been regarded as Britain's first experiment in colonisation, and then to North America, Australia and New Zealand, South Africa and in smaller numbers to other parts of the growing British Empire. While movements have never been solely one-way the balance began to shift during the twentieth century, particularly after the Second World War as Britain's low rate of fertility and the gradually improving economy produced labour shortages. By the last decades of the twentieth century Britain had become a country of net immigration.

The composition of the migrants coming to Britain also changed over the course of the century. In the first half of the century migrants had been of three main sorts: first local regional labour market migration especially from Ireland. (It should be noted that the whole of Ireland was, at the beginning of the century, part of the United Kingdom. Southern Ireland secured *de facto* independence with the creation of the Irish Free State in 1921.) Second, there were refugees, especially European Jews, both from Eastern Europe before the First World War and then from Germany during the interwar period. Third, there were returning white British from the Empire (later redesignated the Commonwealth). (The existence of a substantial amount of return migration from the Commonwealth makes for some important measurement problems which we discuss later.)

After the Second World War, there continued to be an influx of white migrants but these were outnumbered for the first time by 'visible' ethnic minorities, particularly from the Caribbean and from South Asia. The main white groups over this period continued to be the Irish, the level of net migration from Ireland tending to reflect the relative states of the Irish and British economies. There was always substantial return migration, too, to Ireland from Britain, particularly after the improvement in the Irish economy in the last quarter of the century. In addition to the Irish, there was a considerable influx of Polish migrants immediately after the Second World War and there was a continuing stream of white migrants to Britain from the Old Commonwealth (that is from Canada, Australia and New Zealand) and most recently, following Britain's entry into the European Union, from Western Europe. Many of these white migrants from Europe and the Old Commonwealth were highly educated and with skills that were in demand in the labour market.

Outnumbering these white migrants were a growing number of Black and Asian migrants. Immediately after the war there had been direct recruitment of Black Caribbeans, particularly in order to fill vacancies for nurses in the newly formed National Health Service and for public-sector employment, for example London Transport. Black migrants in Britain's major conurbations such as London, Birmingham and Manchester became increasingly a part of urban Britain. These migrants (with the important exception of nurses for the NHS) tended to enter less-skilled work and to be concentrated in the run-down inner city areas where cheap housing was available. By the 1960s there was a substantial population of Black Caribbeans in some inner cities and this was accompanied by considerable ethnic tension and conflict, such as the so-called Notting Hill race riots in London in 1958.

The next major groups to arrive were South Asians, both from India and Pakistan, and later from Bangladesh (a state which had originally been a part of Pakistan after independence from Britain and partition from India). As with the Black Caribbeans, these migrants tended to concentrate in the major conurbations, but more of the South Asians became established in northern cities where they were particularly associated with the once-strong (but now declining) textile industry. While many of these South Asian migrants were labour migrants entering unskilled work, there were also important groups of highly skilled South Asian migrants, most famously Indian doctors (as with the Caribbean nurses recruited to fill shortages in the NHS).

There were also important groups of African Indians who came as refugees from East Africa. There had been an Indian diaspora to many of Britain's colonies in the nineteenth and early twentieth centuries, with large groups of Indians to be found in Fiji, Guyana, South Africa and particularly in East African countries such as Kenya and Uganda. Many of these Indian migrants had secured positions in government service and in business and had become dominant economically. After Britain's Sub-Saharan African colonies secured independence in the 1960s, a number undertook policies of Africanisation and there was a major exodus, some forced and some in anticipation of forcible expulsion, of these East African Indians. These groups of refugees tended to be highly skilled and to speak fluent English, unlike many of the less-skilled migrants from rural areas of South Asia, especially from Bangladesh, who had little education and little knowledge of English.

Another major group of migrants to Britain were Black Africans, again largely from commonwealth countries in Sub-Saharan Africa, especially Nigeria. Whereas the Black migrants from the Caribbean had been what might be termed 'migrant workers' with relatively low levels of skill and human capital, many of the Africans came to acquire British educational qualifications and then remained in Britain. As we shall see later in this chapter, they were one of the most educated groups of migrants to Britain. Another group of recent arrivals were the Chinese who came predominantly from Britain's dependency of Hong Kong, although some also arrived from Singapore and Malaysia. (As with Indians, there had been a Chinese diaspora to other countries of the British Empire such as Malaysia and South Africa where many worked as indentured labourers.) Small numbers of Chinese had long been established in Britain, filling particular niches in the catering and laundry sectors. However, there was an added impetus to this migration late in the twentieth century when negotiations with China over the return of Hong Kong began. These later Chinese migrants tended to be highly skilled and educated.

Most migration to Britain, therefore, has been from the countries of the New and Old Commonwealth and from Ireland—countries with which Britain has had especial ties from her period of Empire. Ethnic minorities have thus become a growing feature of British society. The trends over time in the size of the ethnic minority population are shown in Table 12.1. (Table 12.1 like all our results in this chapter is based on analysis of the pooled General Household Surveys for 1991–2001. For details see below.) As we can see, the ethnic minority population (including both white and visible ethnic minorities) has grown from around 3% of the adult population in 1951 to 8% in 2001. It is set to increase further over the next few decades as the age profile of ethnic minorities is substantially younger than that of the charter population.

The arrival of substantial groups from Ireland in the first half of the twentieth century, from the Caribbean immediately after the Second World War, and from South Asia more recently also means that Britain now has a substantial second- (or indeed third-) generation ethnic minority population. The second generation now amounts to over one-third of the total ethnic minority population. In addition the 2001 Census indicates that there are a growing number of people of mixed ancestry in Britain, amounting to 1.2%, and again this group can be expected to increase both in absolute and in relative size.

Table 12.1. The growth of Britain's ethnic minority population, 1951–2001 (column percentages).

	1951	1961	1973	1981	1991	2001
First generation	2.3	3.4	4.5	5.0	4.5	5.2
Second generation	0.6	0.6	0.6	1.3	2.0	3.5
Total ethnic minority	2.9	4.0	5.1	6.3	6.5	8.3
British ancestry	97.1	96.0	94.9	93.8	93.5	91.3
N	NA*	NA*	18,376	17,238	15,474	11,898

* Figures for 1951 and 1961 are estimates derived from information on country of birth and age of arrival.
Source: GHS 1973, 1981, 1991, 2001.

The context of reception

In post-war Britain, initial immigration legislation had been very liberal. The 1948 British Nationality Act created the concepts of citizenship of the United Kingdom and Colonies and of citizens of Independent Commonwealth Countries. Individuals falling into either of these two main categories were allowed to enter the UK freely and to secure employment. The Act thus gave an unrestricted right to settle and work in Britain to 800,000,000 people (Hansen 2000).

As the number of immigrants grew, so did the political concerns. There was direct evidence of discrimination against visible ethnic minorities in the housing and labour markets. A famous piece of research carried out in the 1960s using actors (Hungarian, Black and Cypriot) to apply for advertised jobs demonstrated clear evidence of discrimination against Blacks (Daniel 1968). There was also evidence of widespread white hostility to recent arrivals from the New Commonwealth, given symbolic expression by the (then) Conservative politician Enoch Powell in his notorious 'river of blood' speech, in which he predicted mounting racial conflict.[2] There was some evidence that this fear of immigrants affected the parties' political fortunes in the 1970 general election, and there was undeniable evidence from the ballot box that the racist National Front increased its electoral support in the two general elections of 1974. Survey evidence showed that there was widespread public support for restrictions on immigration (Studlar 1978).

---

[2] Powell did not himself use the phrase 'river of blood' although that is how his speech is usually remembered. He actually said 'As I look ahead, I am filled with foreboding. Like the Roman, I seem to see "the River Tiber foaming with much blood"' (speech at Birmingham, 20 April 1968).

The main political parties reacted to these concerns with a series of measures. While the rhetoric of some Conservative politicians (such as Margaret Thatcher) was relatively hostile towards immigration and Labour rhetoric more multicultural and liberal, broadly speaking the two main parties followed a bipartisan policy of attempting to limit immigration but to legislate for equal treatment for those already in Britain.

The immigration legislation thus became increasingly restrictive. The 1962 Commonwealth Immigration Act attempted to control immigration and established a voucher system for intending immigrants. This seems to have had little effect on numbers entering as vouchers seemed to have been issued rather liberally (Layton-Henry 1985). New legislation in 1965 restricted the number of vouchers to 8,500 per year. However, under the 1965 Immigration Act, the voucher-holders retained the right to bring their partner and children as well. Further legislation was enacted in 1968 to counter the influx of Asian immigrants who were being driven out from the Africanising Commonwealth countries, notably Kenya, at this time (Spencer 1997). The 1968 Act for the first time limited the right of UK passport-holders to enter Britain. It also required all citizens of the UK and colonies with no substantial connection to the UK (through birth or descent) to obtain an entry voucher before arriving.

The Immigration Act of 1971 followed this up with the introduction of the concept of 'patriality': broadly speaking to establish a right of abode it was necessary to have at least one parent or grandparent born in Britain. The concept of patriality was removed by the 1981 British Nationality Act, which finally introduced the notion of British citizenship (as opposed to the citizenship of the United Kingdom and Colonies which had existed ever since the 1948 Act). In practice the 1981 Act gave British citizenship to all those who had previously held a right of abode through patriality. The Act also created the concepts of British Dependent Territories Citizenship and British Overseas Citizenship, but neither of these categories of citizenship gave a right to enter the United Kingdom (Hansen, 2000). In effect the 1981 Act brought the citizenship legislation into line with the immigration legislation. However, none of this legislation affected the rights of citizens of the Republic of Ireland to enter Britain, and more recently there has also been freedom of movement within the European Union.

While successive British governments, both Labour and Conservative, became increasingly restrictive towards immigration over this period, they coupled this with increasingly serious efforts to secure fair treatment for minorities in Britain. There were three major pieces of legislation, beginning with the 1965 Race Relations Act. This act excluded employment and housing and made discrimination in public places (such as pubs, restaurants and cinemas) unlawful. This was superseded by the 1968 Race Relations Act that made it unlawful to 'discriminate on grounds of colour, race, or ethnic or national origins in recruitment, training, promotion, dismissals, and terms and conditions of employment' (Layton-Henry 1985). These first two acts were then replaced by the 1976 Race Relations Act which extended the definition of discrimination to include indirect discrimination. Indirect discrimination can be thought of as any case where, even in the absence of a deliberate intention to discriminate, practices and procedures applying to everyone have the effect of putting a particular minority group at a disadvantage. Now 'any unjustifiable practices and procedures that have the effect of putting people of a particular racial group at a disadvantage' were outlawed (Layton-Henry, 1985). The Act also established a new monitoring authority, the Commission for Racial Equality (CRE). Perhaps the most important of the CRE's roles is that of supporting people who claim racial discrimination at industrial tribunals. These Acts were backed up with some official encouragement of a multicultural Britain (such as the Swann Report on the education of ethnic minority children). Most recently the Race Relations (Amendment) Act 2000 extended further the 1976 Act in relation to public authorities, particularly to the police, outlawing race discrimination in functions not previously covered. It also placed a duty on specified public authorities to work towards the elimination of unlawful discrimination and promote equality of opportunity and good relations between persons of different racial groups.

These two trends may well have had some consequences for the experiences of ethnic minorities within the British labour market. On the one hand, the increasingly restrictive immigration legislation, although doing little to restrict the actual numbers arriving, might have influenced the characteristics of migrants entering Britain. We might expect that more recent migrants would be rather better-endowed with human capital than were the earlier migrants. On the other hand, we would expect to find that the increasingly tough anti-discrimination legislation would have improved the fortunes of all those ethnic minorities in Britain, both earlier and later entrants and both human-capital rich and poor (see however Heath and Yu 2005 which shows that the first generation have failed to close the gap with the white population over time).

Data and measures

There are a variety of sources that can be used for investigating the labour market experiences of ethnic minorities in Britain, notably the Census, the Labour Force Surveys and the General Household Surveys, as well as some specific surveys of ethnic minorities such as the four National Surveys of Ethnic Minorities. The main difficulty with most of these sources is that they used the standard government measure of self-assigned ethnicity, focused largely on the visible ethnic minorities and thus pooling all white groups into a single category of 'White'. The classification thus confuses ethnicity with race, and also makes it impossible to distinguish the different ethnic groups within the 'White' category. The 2001 Census remedied this problem to some extent by adding a category for Irish to the other categories for the visible minorities, as well as including a category for 'mixed origin'. However, other white groups cannot be distinguished from those of British ancestry. Instead of using the standard government classification of self-assigned ethnicity, therefore, we have constructed a measure of ancestry that can also be applied to white groups such as the Irish. To do this we have used measures of own country of birth and parents' country of birth. (In practice we find that, for the visible minorities, our results using ancestry are very close to those using the official classification of self-assigned ethnicity. See Table 12.A1 in the Appendix to this chapter.)

The one large-scale dataset that includes the information we require on parents' country of birth is the General Household Survey. The GHS is a nationally representative continuous survey conducted by the Office for National Statistics. However, it is relatively small, and therefore in order to obtain sufficiently large samples of ethnic minorities we have pooled the data from a number of years. Specifically we pool the years 1991 to 2001, with the exception of 1997 and 1999 when no GHS was carried out.[3]

We construct ethnic groups as follows: groups are defined according to the country or area of birth of their two parents and their own country of birth. For example, if both parents were born in India, the respondent is counted as having Indian ancestry. We then distinguish between the first and second generation according to the respondent's own area or country of birth. The first generation consists of those who were born

---

[3] Additional checks have also been carried out as to whether our findings are stable across the years that we have pooled.

overseas in the same country or area as their parents and arrived in Britain after the age of six; the second generation are those who were born in Britain or came to Britain at or before the age of six (thus receiving virtually all their education in Britain). With the exception of the East African Indians we exclude the small numbers whose parents were born in one country or area and were themselves born in another country other than Britain.

There are sufficiently large sample sizes in the pooled GHS surveys for us to distinguish the following ancestries:

Caribbean: This covers respondents whose parents were born in the Caribbean commonwealth, including Barbados, Belize, Guyana, Jamaica and Trinidad and Tobago. This group is overwhelmingly Black although it also includes a few people of other ancestries, such as Indian.

Indian: This covers respondents whose parents were born in India. It also includes, in the first generation, respondents born in the East African commonwealth with at least one parent born in India. This group will be predominantly Hindu but will also include some Muslims and Christians and members of other religions. A few of the respondents classified as Indian by our measure identify themselves as Pakistani (see Table 12.A1 in the Appendix). This may be because their parents were born before partition in what is now Pakistan or because, as Muslims, they identify with Pakistan rather than with India.

Pakistani/Bangladeshi: This covers respondents whose parents were born in Pakistan or Bangladesh. Ideally one would distinguish people of Pakistani from those of Bangladeshi ancestry but there are too few Bangladeshis in our sample for this to be practicable. Moreover, before 1967 these two countries were in fact a single state and so many parents would have been born in a united Pakistan. This group is predominantly Muslim.

Irish: This covers respondents whose parents were born in the Republic of Ireland but does not include those born in Northern Ireland. This group will be predominantly Catholic but may include a small number of Irish Protestants (descendants of the Anglo-Irish Protestant ascendancy.)

Sub-Saharan African: This covers respondents whose parents were born in the African commonwealth, including Botswana, Swaziland, Lesotho, The Gambia, Ghana, Nigeria, Sierra Leone and Zimbabwe. (We exclude those with East African ancestry because of the difficulty of distinguishing them from East African Indians.) This group is predominantly Black but may include a few people of white British ancestry returning from Zimbabwe. The largest single group is likely to be the Nigerian.

Western European: This covers the EU countries Belgium, Denmark, France, Germany, Italy, Netherlands, Luxembourg, Greece, Portugal and Spain. This is an overwhelmingly white group although of course in many other respects it is highly diverse ethnically.

We have checked our classification based on ancestry against the self-assigned measure of ethnicity used in the GHS (See Table 12.A1 in the Appendix). This provides a reassuring picture that our measure of ancestry tallies well with self-reported ethnic identifications. The main point to note is the proportions who self-identify as mixed or as belonging to other ethnicities. This is especially true for the second-generation Caribbeans, many of whom define themselves as Black British rather than as Black Caribbean.

Table 12.2 gives us the cross-tabulation of ancestry by generation. We should note that there is a large residual unidentifiable group consisting largely of people whose parents were born in different countries or areas. This would include respondents who had one parent born, for example, in India and one born in Britain. It might be tempting to regard these respondents as having mixed ancestry but as Table 12.A1 shows this would not, in fact, be a safe interpretation. Only one-quarter of the first-generation 'unidentifiables' (and less than one-tenth of the second generation) described themselves as having mixed ancestry. In practice we find that these two groups look very like the white British in their

Table 12.2. Britain's population from different origins, by generation (table percentages).

	First generation	Second generation	All
British ancestry	0.2*	84.1	84.3
African commonwealth	0.2	0.1	0.3
Caribbean	0.5	0.5	1.0
Indian	1.1	0.4	1.5
Pakistani/Bangladeshi	0.7	0.3	1.0
Irish	0.7	0.8	1.5
West European	0.7	0.3	1.0
Other	1.0	0.2	1.2
Unidentifiable	1.6	6.7	8.3
N	7,870	111,457	119,327

* First generation people of British national origin cover respondents with British-born parents but themselves born outside the UK.
Source: Pooled GHS 1991–2001.

characteristics and labour-market fortunes, but because of the ambiguity involved we exclude them from our subsequent analyses. We also exclude a number of the smaller groups where sample sizes are not sufficient for reliable estimation.

Profiling the first and second generations

We begin by examining briefly the education of our main ethnic groups, their patterns of economic activity, and their occupational outcomes before turning to an analysis of ethnic penalties. Tables 12.3A and 12.3B show the highest educational qualifications of our principal groups.

People of British ancestry prove to be middling in their educational qualifications. Among the men, the most educated group proves to be the first generation from the African Commonwealth followed by second-generation Indians. Both these groups have higher proportions with tertiary qualifications and lower proportions with primary (or no) qualifications than people of British ancestry. The high level of qualifications of these groups will partly reflect their relative youth, as in general their average ages are lower than those of the British ancestry group, and (as is well known) most countries have seen considerable increases in educational levels among younger cohorts. These higher levels will also reflect, to some extent, selective processes of migration. For example, some of the migrants from Africa came to Britain from relatively affluent backgrounds in order to enrol in higher education (Daley 1996).

Table 12.3A. Highest educational qualification, by ancestry and generation: Men (row percentages).

	Primary or none	Lower secondary	Higher secondary	Lower tertiary	Higher tertiary	N
British ancestry	30.8	22.6	18.0	13.6	14.9	39,722
First generation						
African	8.9	20.5	18.8	17.9	33.9	112
Caribbean	55.7	21.1	7.6	8.1	7.6	185
Indian	37.2	28.9	9.5	5.9	18.5	529
Irish	51.5	25.2	8.5	5.6	9.2	305
Pakistani/Bangladeshi	50.9	29.7	8.8	4.8	5.9	273
West European	34.8	31.3	4.5	11.2	17.3	224
Second generation						
Caribbean	26.2	30.0	24.0	9.0	10.7	233
Indian	14.0	19.2	24.2	13.6	29.1	265
Irish	23.4	24.6	20.8	14.0	17.3	394
Pakistani/Bangladeshi	24.3	28.0	28.0	3.7	15.9	107

Table 12.3B. Highest educational qualification, by ancestry and generation: Women (row percentages).

	Primary or none	Lower secondary	Higher secondary	Lower tertiary	Higher tertiary	N
British ancestry	37.3	27.3	14.7	10.5	10.2	44,521
First generation						
African	18.8	31.6	15.8	24.8	9.0	133
Caribbean	46.6	15.4	7.2	21.9	9.0	279
Indian	51.3	26.1	7.3	6.1	9.2	509
Irish	47.2	20.6	8.1	15.2	8.9	394
Pakistani/Bangladeshi	63.8	26.1	5.3	2.9	1.9	207
West European	35.1	29.6	5.3	11.3	18.7	379
Second generation						
Caribbean	20.7	33.9	24.7	9.9	10.9	304
Indian	18.7	29.9	24.3	9.7	17.5	268
Irish	31.1	30.4	15.1	9.8	13.5	437
Pakistani/Bangladeshi	21.7	29.4	32.2	10.5	6.3	143

We then have a group of origins that are clearly less educated than people of British ancestry. The least qualified are the first-generation Caribbeans, Irish, Pakistani/Bangladeshis and Indians. Again these groups will all tend to be somewhat older, but they also came from less developed countries with fewer educational opportunities than Britain.

Very similar patterns hold among the women. Overall the women have lower levels of tertiary education than the men and higher proportions with no or low qualifications. In the first generation there is a substantial gender gap in educational qualifications with female migrants tending to be less qualified than the men. The main discrepancy from this picture is the Caribbean women, who tend to be more educated than the Caribbean men. We should also note that in the case of the first-generation South Asians (both Indian and Pakistani/Bangladeshi) the gender gap is even larger than elsewhere. This will tend to reflect both the gender inequalities in the countries of origin and the patterns of selective migration. Many of the women from South Asia will have come as family members to join husbands who were the main breadwinners, while as noted earlier many of the Caribbean women were directly recruited for employment in the NHS.

We next turn to economic activity, shown in Tables 12.4A and 12.4B. As might be expected, all the male groups show fairly high levels of economic activity, although in general the ethnic minority rates are slightly below the rates for men of British ancestry. In several cases, particularly those of the second-generation Caribbean, Indian and Pakistani/

Table 12.4A. Economic activity, by ancestry and generation: Men (row percentages).

	Economically active	Other inactive	Looking after home	Full-time student	N
British ancestry	90.4	7.1	0.8	1.8	45,182
First generation					
African	92.2	2.3	0.0	5.5	128
Caribbean	84.7	12.1	3.3	0.0	215
Indian	87.9	9.7	1.0	1.5	610
Irish	86.2	12.7	0.6	0.6	354
Pakistani/Bangladeshi	77.4	15.4	3.0	4.3	371
West European	82.8	8.4	0.8	8.0	265
Second generation					
Caribbean	88.4	5.5	0.7	5.5	275
Indian	85.8	2.0	0.3	11.9	295
Irish	91.1	6.3	1.1	1.5	460
Pakistani/Bangladeshi	69.0	12.4	0.0	18.6	145

Table 12.4B. Economic activity, by ancestry and generation: Women (row percentages).

	Economically active	Other inactive	Looking after home	Full-time student	N
British ancestry	73.1	7.0	18.2	1.7	47,313
First generation					
African	72.5	3.3	17.6	6.5	153
Caribbean	80.9	8.6	9.2	1.3	304
Indian	59.3	7.3	32.8	0.6	629
Irish	71.3	9.8	16.4	2.6	428
Pakistani/Bangladeshi	16.1	6.1	75.2	2.6	391
West European	69.1	5.3	19.3	6.3	414
Second generation					
Caribbean	79.3	2.7	13.8	4.2	334
Indian	69.2	2.4	17.6	10.8	295
Irish	72.8	4.4	20.5	2.3	478
Pakistani/Bangladeshi	47.0	3.0	32.9	17.1	164

Bangladeshi men, a relatively large proportion are students. As in the profiles of educational levels, this will partly reflect the fact that these are relatively young groups of people. However, it is probably not a simple matter of age differences: the explanation may have something to do with the difficulties that these men have in securing employment. In other words, discrimination in the labour market may make further education a more attractive option than it would otherwise have been (Leslie and Drinkwater 1999). A further implication of this is that our later evidence on ethnic penalties in the labour market for these groups may actually be an underestimate of what might be termed 'economic exclusion'.

The other important point to note from Table 12.4A is that there are unusually high rates of economic inactivity (the 'other inactive' category) among the first-generation Caribbeans, Indians, Pakistani/Bangladeshi and Irish. A likely explanation for this is that these are 'discouraged workers' who have taken early retirement or secured sickness benefit consequent on difficulties in obtaining paid work. As with the high proportions of students, this may well mean that our later measures of ethnic penalties in the labour market underestimate the true scale of the problem for ethnic minorities.

Table 12.4B shows the corresponding picture for women. In several respects the patterns are similar to those for men, with higher proportions of students among some of the second-generation groups than among women of British ancestry, and higher proportions of 'other inactive' respondents among some of the first-generation groups. However, there are some additional important findings with regard to the proportions looking after the home. First we observe that Caribbean women, both in the first and second generations, have lower rates of looking after the home than do women of British ancestry. This pattern may well have its origins in the migration of Caribbean women for work, rather than as family dependants, to which we have already referred. It may also be connected with the prevalence of female-headed households among the Caribbean community.

Second, and in complete contrast, Table 12.4B also shows that first-generation women from India and most strikingly from Pakistan and Bangladesh have much higher proportions looking after the home than is found among women of British ancestry. In the case of the first-generation Pakistani and Bangladeshi women this proportion reaches three-quarters. The second-generation Pakistani and Bangladeshi women also display a high proportion looking after the home.

There are two main explanations for these striking exceptions to the general pattern. One is the role of cultural traditions based partly on religion, although here it is important to note that this is not purely a Muslim pattern: Sikh and Hindu women also have high proportions that are economically inactive. The second explanation is lack of fluency in the English language. The Fourth National Survey of Ethnic Minorities has shown that first-generation South Asian women tend to have the lowest levels of fluency in English, and this is clearly a major factor in making entry into the labour market (other than at the lowest level) very difficult (Modood *et al.* 1997; see also Holdsworth and Dale 1997).

We should note that these patterns of economic inactivity mean that there will be very substantial selection biases in the characteristics of women from these groups who are economically active. This has important implications for our subsequent analysis of women's fortunes in the labour market.

We now come to the occupational outcomes. The picture here is well known with ethnic minority men tending to have rates of unemployment often twice those of comparable men of British ancestry (Karn 1997). Table 12.5A shows that the visible minorities, especially in the second generation, tend to have much higher rates of unemployment, reaching 25% and above for Caribbeans and Pakistanis/Bangladeshis. We can also see that, if they do secure employment, these groups are also more likely

Table 12.5A. Current occupation, by ancestry and generation: Men (row percentages).

	Salariat	Routine non-manual	Petty bourgeoisie	Skilled manual	Semi- and unskilled	Unemployed	N
British ancestry	35.4	7.2	12.1	22.7	13.5	9.1	40,118
First generation							
African	36.8	6.1	12.3	12.3	17.5	14.9	114
Caribbean	21.1	2.8	8.9	28.9	21.1	17.2	180
Indian	29.0	5.5	22.2	16.1	16.5	10.6	527
Irish	31.6	5.0	20.9	16.9	15.0	10.6	301
Pakistani/Bangladeshi	10.9	3.9	18.3	12.0	29.2	25.7	284
West European	42.8	4.3	16.8	12.5	16.8	6.7	208
Second generation							
Caribbean	24.1	6.8	8.0	21.5	15.2	24.5	237
Indian	44.7	11.8	10.6	11.8	8.1	13.0	246
Irish	40.6	7.1	11.7	18.7	10.2	11.7	411
Pakistani/Bangladeshi	18.8	12.5	11.5	11.5	15.6	30.2	96

Table 12.5B. Current occupation, by ancestry and generation: Women (row percentages).

	Salariat	Routine non-manual	Petty bourgeoisie	Skilled manual	Semi- and unskilled	Unemployed	N
British ancestry	33.0	30.3	5.1	3.9	22.0	5.7	33972
First generation							
African	25.2	24.3	0	3.7	33.6	13.1	107
Caribbean	41.0	15.2	2.9	2.9	27.5	10.7	244
Indian	23.5	19.2	8.1	5.4	38.9	4.9	370
Irish	45.5	19.9	3.4	2.7	23.2	5.4	297
West European	39.4	16.9	7.0	3.3	25.0	8.5	284
Second generation							
Caribbean	38.2	32.3	0.8	1.6	12.4	14.7	251
Indian	28.3	35.9	4.3	2.2	13.6	15.8	184
Irish	41.1	29.9	3.3	3.3	16.9	5.6	338

Note: Pakistani and Bangladeshi women are excluded because of the low numbers of economically active and the major selection biases involved.

to be found in semi- and unskilled manual work than are men of British ancestry. Thus first- and second-generation Caribbean and Pakistani/Bangladeshi men, together with first-generation African and Indian men have higher rates both of unemployment and of semi- and unskilled-manual work than do those of British ancestry. Here, then, there is strong evidence of economic exclusion. At the other extreme, we find that men from second-generation Indian and Irish origins have overtaken men of British ancestry in gaining access to the salariat.

The other notable feature of Table 12.5A is the over-representation of certain ethnic minorities in the petty bourgeoisie. The most striking examples are the first-generation Indian men, but the first-generation Irish and Pakistani/Bangladeshi are also significantly over-represented in the petty bourgeoisie. This is a phenomenon more evident in the first generation than in the second. It may well be that self-employment, like higher education, is a strategy that people follow when they are likely to experience discrimination in the labour market (Clark and Drinkwater 1998).

Turning to the women, we again see higher rates of unemployment among the visible minorities than among women of British ancestry. We also see a particular concentration of first-generation Indian women in semi- and unskilled work (probably much of it in the textile industry), although here we need to remember the important selection biases mentioned earlier: it may well be the case that higher caste and college-educated Indian women in the first generation chose not to work and that those who did seek employment were less skilled and of lower social status. Once again, Caribbean women also stand out in a contrasting way from the South Asian women, with high proportions of first- and second-generation Caribbean women in the salariat. Whereas on this criterion the Indian men were the most successful group and the Caribbean men one of the least successful, it is the other way round for women.

One has to be very careful in the interpretation of the results from Tables 12.3, 12.4 and 12.5, since the age and educational levels of the different groups vary considerably. However, these tables are important in indicating the likelihood of major selection biases, particularly although not exclusively affecting women. These selection biases could be important when considering the ethnic penalties, to which we now turn.

Ethnic penalties in the labour market

As we described in the introductory chapter to this volume, ethnic penalties are estimates of the extent to which ethnic minorities are disadvantaged in comparison with people belonging to the charter population who have the same age, educational qualifications and marital status (Heath and McMahon 1997; Berthoud 2000; Carmichael and Woods 2000). As we also described in the introduction, there are a range of other factors, such as lack of fluency in the English language, possession of foreign qualifications, and lack of experience in the destination labour market, that may also affect the occupational outcomes of the first-generation groups (Dustmann and Fabbri 2000; Friedberg 2000). These are all important sources of disadvantage but are not included in our data source of the GHS. We cannot therefore take them into account when calculating our measures of ethnic penalties and we should therefore remember that these omitted variables could provide substantial parts of the explanation for the penalties experienced by the first generation.

To calculate the ethnic penalties we carry out logistic regressions controlling for education, age and marital status. Since we have a pooled dataset of the GHS, spanning a decade, we also control for the year of the survey (and we have also checked whether the relationships are stable across years). We begin by looking at the ethnic penalties in avoiding unemployment. That is to say, we consider the factors influencing whether people were in paid employment or were unemployed. (We exclude all those who were economically inactive, that is those who were looking after the home, were students, or were 'other inactive'.) In effect, we look at processes of economic exclusion. We then turn to those people who were in employment and consider their likelihood of being in the different occupational classes, that is in the salariat, routine non-manual class, petty bourgeoisie, skilled manual or semi and unskilled work. In this second analysis, then, we are in effect considering processes of economic inclusion.

Avoidance of unemployment

Table 12.6, then, shows the results of our analysis of unemployment. We have coded our dependent variable with '1' representing employment and '0' representing unemployment. Negative parameters thus indicate that members of the group concerned were less likely to be employed than were people in the reference category. In the case of ancestry this means that we can think of negative parameters as indicating ethnic penalties relative to people of British ancestry. However, before turning to the ethnic penalties, we should consider the estimates for the control variables. As expected we see a curvilinear effect of age: unemployment tends to be highest among young people, declines initially among older people but then increases once again as people approach the age of retirement. We also find that educational qualifications increase one's likelihood of avoiding unemployment, people with no qualifications being particularly at risk of unemployment. As has been shown in other research, married people are less likely to be unemployed than the single or divorced/separated.

We also include year of survey as one of our control variables. In general, the earlier years had higher unemployment rates than our reference year of 2001.[4] However, one issue that has sometimes been raised is that ethnic minority unemployment is hyper-cyclical; that is to say, when national unemployment rates rise, ethnic minority rates rise even faster. We checked this by including interaction terms between ethnicity and year. However, while some of the interaction terms proved to be statistically significant, no clear evidence of a hyper-cyclical pattern emerged from this analysis.

Our primary focus is on the estimates associated with the different ethnic groups. The headline story is that the first-generation visible minority men (African, Caribbean, Indian and Pakistani/Bangladeshi) had poorer chances of avoiding unemployment than did men of British ancestry of the same age and marital status and with similar educational qualifications. In contrast neither of the white groupings (Irish and West European) experienced a significant ethnic penalty.

The other striking finding is that there is no significant difference in the ethnic penalties experienced by the first and the second generation. Thus for the Caribbeans the estimates are -0.78 and -0.80 for the first and second generations respectively; for the Indians the estimates are -0.54 and -0.39 and for the Pakistanis and Bangladeshis -1.27 and -1.11. (If we pool the generations and include a general term for generation, we find that the parameter estimate for generation is effectively zero.) This result is also replicated in analyses using the Labour Force Survey (see Table 12.A2 in the Appendix to this chapter).

[4] Unemployment rose from 8.4% in 1991 to a peak of 10.5% in 1993 before falling steadily to 4.9% in 2001.

Table 12.6. Binary logistic regression of avoidance of unemployment (parameter estimates (contrasts with unemployed)).

	Men				Women			
	I		II		I		II	
Intercept	**3.08**	(0.11)	**3.09**	(0.11)	**3.62**	(0.14)	**3.62**	(0.14)
Ancestry								
British	0.00		0.00		0.00		0.00	
African 1	**−1.21**	(0.29)	**−1.08**	(0.30)	**−0.98**	(0.31)	**−0.98**	(0.31)
Caribbean 1	**−0.78**	(0.21)	**−0.77**	(0.21)	**−0.90**	(0.22)	**−0.90**	(0.22)
Pakistani/Bangladeshi 1	**−1.27**	(0.17)	**−1.27**	(0.17)	—		—	
Indian 1	**−0.54**	(0.15)	**−0.54**	(0.15)	−0.04	(0.26)	−0.04	(0.26)
Irish 1	−0.16	(0.20)	−0.15	(0.20)	−0.06	(0.26)	−0.06	(0.26)
West European 1	0.32	(0.31)	0.32	(0.31)	**−0.48**	(0.23)	**−0.69**	(0.24)
Caribbean 2	**−0.80**	(0.18)	**−0.80**	(0.18)	**−0.74**	(0.19)	**−0.74**	(0.19)
Indian 2	−0.39	(0.21)	−0.43	(0.21)	**−0.86**	(0.21)	**−0.86**	(0.21)
Irish 2	−0.30	(0.17)	−0.30	(0.17)	0.11	(0.25)	0.11	(0.25)
Pakistani/Bangladeshi 2	**−1.11**	(0.28)	**−1.11**	(0.28)	—		—	
Age /10	**0.17**	(0.02)	**0.17**	(0.02)	**0.37**	(0.03)	**0.37**	(0.03)
(Age/10)^2	**−0.13**	(0.02)	**−0.13**	(0.02)	**−0.07**	(0.02)	**−0.07**	(0.02)
Marital Status								
Married/cohabiting	**0.89**	(0.05)	**0.89**	(0.05)	**0.67**	(0.07)	**0.67**	(0.07)
Divorced/separated	**−0.20**	(0.07)	**−0.20**	(0.07)	**−0.35**	(0.09)	**−0.35**	(0.09)
Single	0.00		0.00		0.00		0.00	
Qualification								
Higher tertiary	**0.38**	(0.08)	**0.41**	(0.08)	0.03	(0.10)	0.05	(0.10)
Lower tertiary	**0.30**	(0.08)	**0.30**	(0.08)	0.13	(0.11)	0.14	(0.11)
Higher secondary	0.00		0.00		0.00		0.00	
Lower secondary	**−0.32**	(0.06)	**−0.32**	(0.06)	**−0.18**	(0.08)	**−0.18**	(0.08)
No qualification	**−0.89**	(0.06)	**−0.89**	(0.06)	**−0.77**	(0.08)	**−0.78**	(0.08)
Year								
1991	**−0.85**	(0.11)	**−0.85**	(0.11)	**−1.02**	(0.13)	**−1.02**	(0.13)
1992	**−0.95**	(0.11)	**−0.96**	(0.11)	**−0.85**	(0.13)	**−0.86**	(0.13)
1993	**−1.13**	(0.11)	**−1.14**	(0.11)	**−0.82**	(0.13)	**−0.83**	(0.13)
1994	**−1.01**	(0.11)	**−1.02**	(0.11)	**−0.76**	(0.13)	**−0.76**	(0.13)
1995	**−0.88**	(0.11)	**−0.89**	(0.11)	**−0.76**	(0.13)	**−0.76**	(0.13)
1996	**−0.81**	(0.11)	**−0.81**	(0.11)	**−0.61**	(0.14)	**−0.62**	(0.14)
1998	**−0.35**	(0.12)	**−0.35**	(0.12)	**−0.41**	(0.14)	**−0.40**	(0.14)
2000	−0.14	(0.12)	−0.15	(0.12)	−0.19	(0.15)	−0.19	(0.15)
2001	0.00		0.00		0.00		0.00	
Significant interactions between ancestry and qualifications								
African 1			**−0.40**	(0.20)				
West European 1							**−0.27**	(0.14)
Indian 2			**−0.37**	(0.16)				
Chi-square (D.F.)	2,297 (26)		2,285 (28)		1,088 (24)		1,092 (25)	
N	38,145		38,145		34,492		34,492	

Note: Emboldened coefficients indicate significance at the 0.05 level or better; standard errors are given in brackets.

The results for women are very similar. The magnitude of the ethnic penalties is comparable to that for men. Visible minorities tend to have significant ethnic penalties while white minorities do not. One exception here is that the first-generation Indian women do not have a significant ethnic penalty—possibly because of the selection bias discussed earlier (although the LFS data suggest that they do experience a significant penalty). Additionally, as with men, there is no general tendency for these ethnic penalties to become smaller in the second generation.

The models which form the basis of Table 12.6 assume that higher educational qualifications bring the same benefits to ethnic minorities as they do to the people of British ancestry (who constitute the great bulk of the sample and who therefore 'drive' the results). However, it has frequently been suggested that ethnic minorities, and especially the first generation with overseas qualifications, may receive lower returns on their educational investments than do the native born. While for the population of British ancestry, secondary or higher qualifications increase the chances of finding employment, this may not necessarily be true for first-generation ethnic minorities. Technically this means that there will be an interaction between qualifications, ancestry and employment. To investigate this we add interaction terms to the models reported in Table 12.6. In order to provide a parsimonious treatment we treat education as a continuous variable in the interaction term, thus giving a single parameter estimate.

In practice only two of the interactions prove to be significant for men (for first-generation Africans and second-generation Indians) and one for women (for first-generation West Europeans). In all three cases these interaction terms are negative, indicating that these three groups receive lower returns on their educational investments, at least as far as avoiding unemployment is concerned, than do people of British ancestry. (Replication using the LFS confirms a significantly lower return for first-generation African men but also suggests that there may be lower returns for first-generation Indian and 'Other' men, and for first-generation Caribbean women. However, the LFS fails to confirm the lower returns for second-generation Indian men.)

To ease the interpretation of these interactions, we calculate the predicted probabilities of unemployment. The predicted probabilities are derived from the logistic regressions reported in model 2 of Table 12.6. They give us an indication of both the substantive size of the ethnic penalties and of the impact of the interaction terms. We show the probabilities of unemployment faced by men in Figure 12.1A and by women in

528   *Sin Yi Cheung & Anthony Heath*

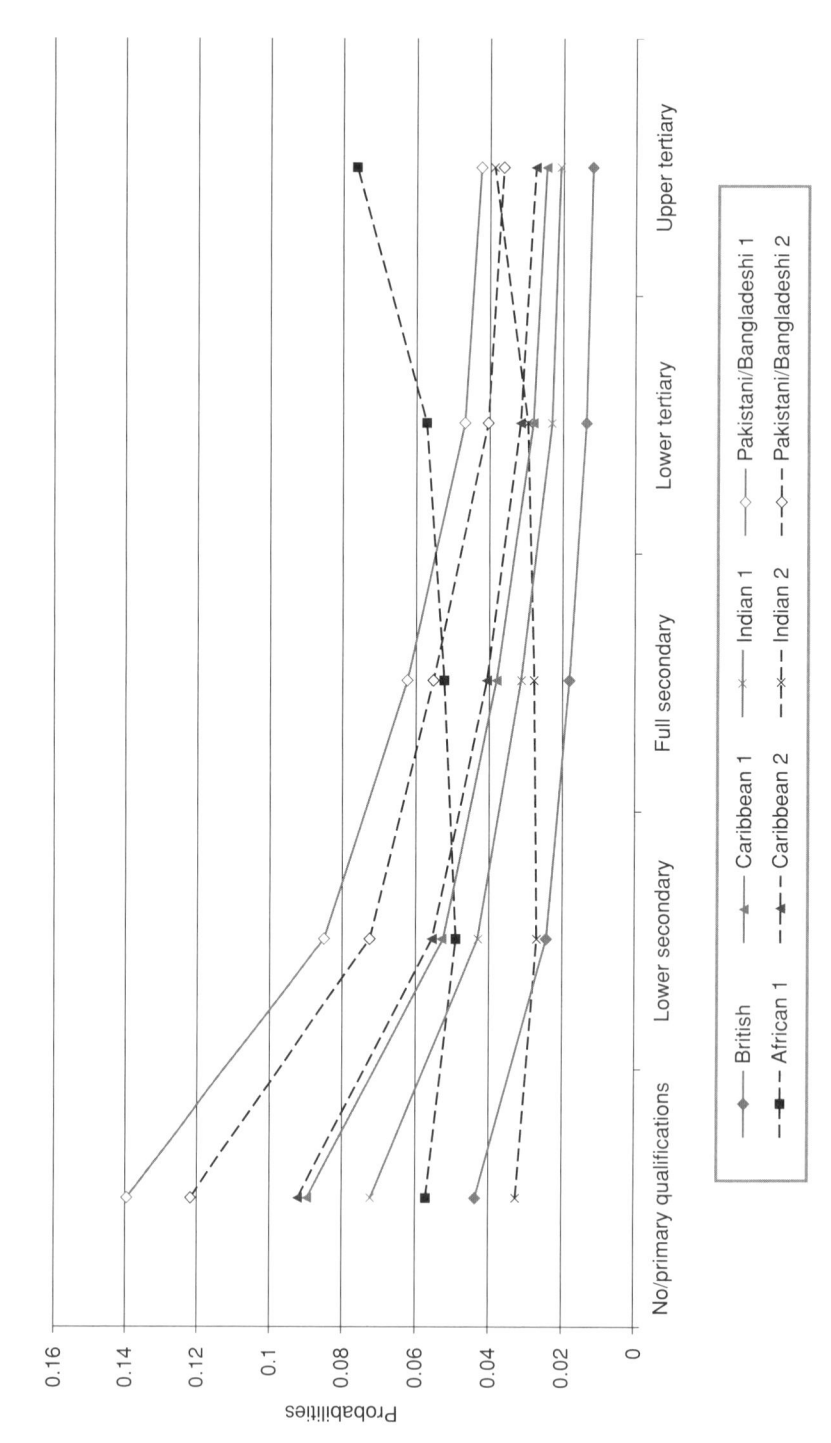

Figure 12.1A. Predicted probabilities of unemployment: males.

ETHNIC PENALTIES IN GREAT BRITAIN 529

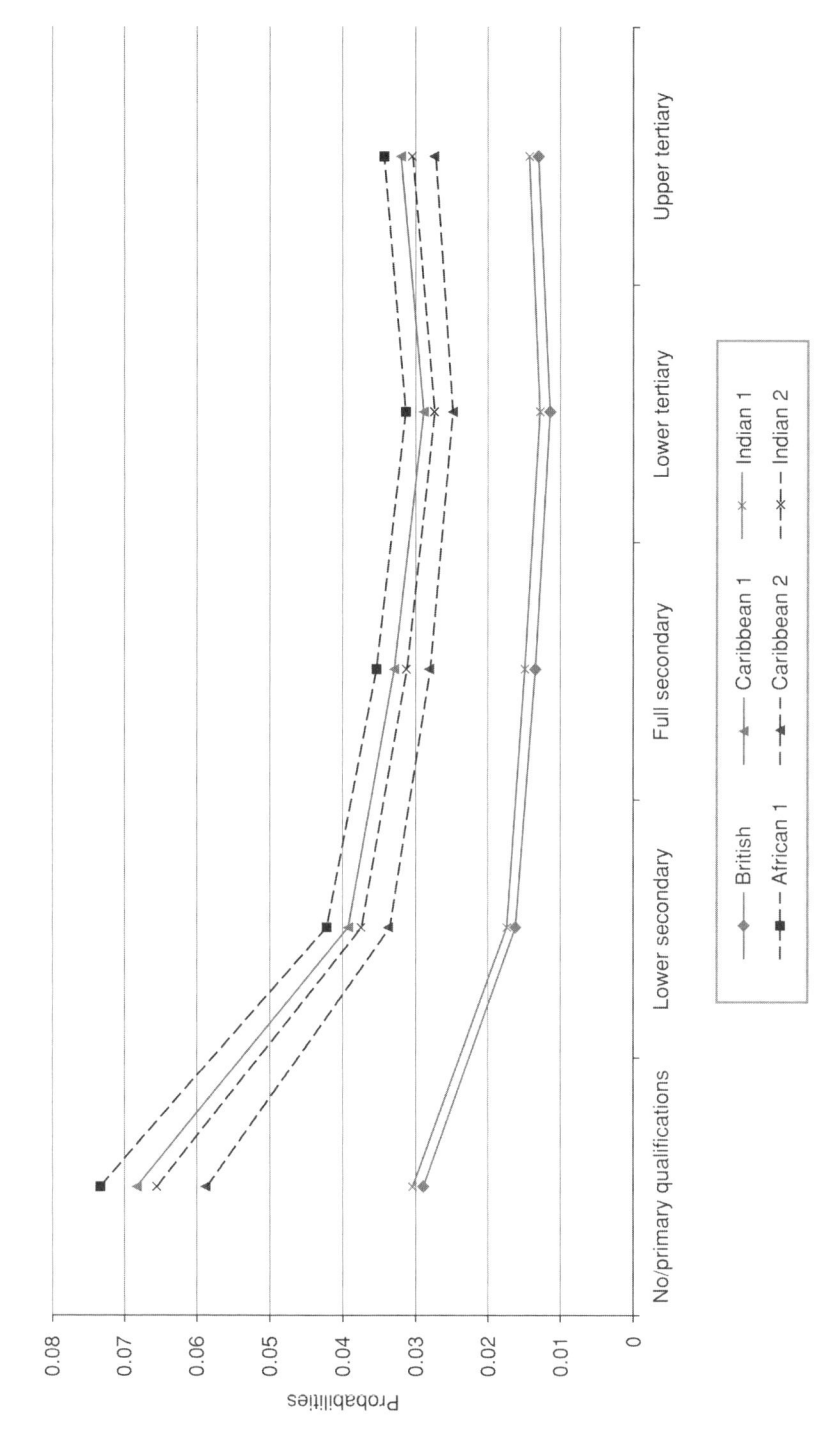

Figure 12.1B. Predicted probabilities of unemployment: females.

Figure 12.1B. In these two figures we compare the picture for the visible ethnic minorities with that for the charter population—people of British ancestry. (The predicted probabilities are those for married people of average age in 2001.)

As we can see very clearly, at all levels of education the visible minorities had much higher probabilities of being unemployed than the charter population. Thus among respondents with the lowest level of education, the first-generation Pakistani and Bangladeshi men could expect an unemployment rate of 14%, over three times the expected rate for men of British ancestry. Among respondents with the highest level of education, unemployment rates were much lower with Pakistani and Bangladeshi men having an unemployment rate of around 4%, but this was still three times as high as that of the charter population's unemployment rate of 1.2%.

Figure 12.1A also brings out clearly the distinctive patterns for the first-generation Africans and the second-generation Indians. In both cases higher qualifications fail to protect against unemployment in the way that they do for other groups. Most strikingly, the highly qualified Africans have an unemployment rate of nearly 8%, around twice as high as that of the other ethnic minorities.

Figure 12.1B shows the picture for women. Again we see that qualifications tend to protect their holders against unemployment, but that at all levels of education both first- and second-generation visible minorities have unemployment rates over twice those of women of British ancestry. The West European women, however, exhibit a rather different pattern, the unqualified having much the same risks of unemployment as women of British ancestry but the highly qualified having much higher rates of unemployment (see Table 12.6).

It is not immediately clear why first-generation African men, second-generation Indian men and first-generation West European women show these deviant patterns with higher qualifications failing to protect against unemployment. This is clearly not to be explained by foreign qualifications since many other groups with foreign qualifications have similar returns to education as people of British ancestry. It may however be linked to the fact that all these three groups are very highly educated. We saw in Table 12.3A that first-generation African men and second-generation Indian men were two of the most highly educated groups, while Table 12.3B shows that first-generation West European women are the most qualified of all the female groups. Why might high group levels of tertiary education influence graduates' rates of unemployment? One possibility is that the marginal graduates from these groups may have lower (unmeasured) skills than do the marginal graduates from other groups. Another possibility is that the ambition and drive that lead the members of these groups to acquire such high levels of education also leads them to have what economists call higher 'reservation wages'; that is, they may not be willing to take work which they feel is incommensurate with their qualifications. The available evidence does not, however, enable us to discriminate between these alternative explanations. Perhaps the more important finding is that in general ethnic minorities in Britain, both first and second generation, tend to reduce their risks of unemployment by increasing their educational investments in just the same way as do members of the charter population. Their problem is that at all levels of education their risks of unemployment are greater.

Occupational class

We now turn to consider the case of those respondents who were fortunate enough to have avoided unemployment and to have found paid work of some kind. We focus on the kinds of jobs that they achieved— were they successful in reaching the well-paid and secure professional and managerial jobs of the salariat, in reaching skilled white-collar or manual work? Did they become self-employed joining the small shop-keepers, restaurateurs or own-account workers of the petty bourgeoisie? Or did they take jobs in semi- and unskilled work with its low wages and high risks of unemployment?

To answer these questions we carry out a multinomial logistic regression, comparing chances of reaching the four higher classes with those of being found in the lowest class of semi- and unskilled work. Broadly speaking we find that similar patterns, although of varying strengths, apply to the salariat, routine non-manual class and the skilled manual class, while a somewhat different pattern applies to the petty bourgeoisie.

The patterns for the control variables (age, education, marital status and year) follow the expected lines. The most notable effect is that of education on access to the salariat. As with other countries, educational qualifications are the single most important factor influencing one's chances of reaching the professional and managerial jobs of the salariat in Britain. Education also has large and significant effects on access to the other three class destinations, albeit of much smaller magnitude than in the case of the salariat.

Table 12.7A. Multinomial logit models of occupational destinations: Men (parameter estimates (contrasts with semi- and unskilled work)).

	Salariat		Routine Non-manual		Petty bourgeoisie		Manual Supervisor or Skilled Manual	
Intercept	**1.16**	(0.09)	0.03	(0.11)	0.02	(0.11)	**0.84**	(0.09)
Ancestry								
British	0.00		0.00		0.00		0.00	
African 1	**−1.62**	(0.35)	**−0.97**	(0.49)	−0.62	(0.39)	**−1.19**	(0.39)
Caribbean 1	**−0.66**	(0.28)	**−1.10**	(0.54)	**−0.85**	(0.32)	−0.32	(0.24)
Indian 1	**−0.52**	(0.18)	−0.26	(0.25)	0.30	(0.16)	**−0.50**	(0.17)
Irish 1	**0.47**	(0.22)	−0.18	(0.37)	**0.60**	(0.23)	−0.24	(0.24)
Pakistani/Bangladeshi 1	**−1.62**	(0.28)	**−0.94**	(0.35)	−0.40	(0.23)	**−1.50**	(0.25)
West European 1	0.11	(0.25)	−0.50	(0.41)	0.10	(0.27)	**−0.86**	(0.29)
Caribbean 2	−0.11	(0.27)	−0.24	(0.35)	0.02	(0.32)	0.07	(0.25)
Indian 2	**0.67**	(0.29)	**0.87**	(0.31)	0.57	(0.34)	−0.14	(0.32)
Irish 2	0.24	(0.21)	0.29	(0.26)	0.30	(0.24)	−0.00	(0.22)
Pakistani/Bangladeshi 2	−0.17	(0.49)	0.18	(0.49)	0.51	(0.50)	−0.62	(0.49)
Age /10	**0.46**	(0.02)	**−0.02**	(0.03)	**0.42**	(0.03)	**0.12**	(0.02)
$(Age/10)^2$	**−0.22**	(0.02)	**0.03**	(0.02)	**−0.20**	(0.02)	**−0.10**	(0.02)
Marital Status								
Married/cohabiting	**0.52**	(0.06)	0.01	(0.07)	**0.58**	(0.07)	**0.45**	(0.05)
Divorced/separated	0.03	(0.09)	−0.08	(0.13)	**0.45**	(0.10)	**0.26**	(0.09)
Single	0.00		0.00		0.00		0.00	
Qualification								
Higher tertiary	**2.61**	(0.12)	**0.99**	(0.14)	**0.38**	(0.14)	**−0.57**	(0.15)
Lower tertiary	**0.55**	(0.08)	**−0.15**	(0.10)	0.14	(0.09)	**0.23**	(0.08)
Higher secondary	0.00		0.00		0.00		0.00	
Lower secondary	**−0.94**	(0.06)	**−0.57**	(0.07)	**−0.45**	(0.07)	**−0.39**	(0.06)
No qualification	**−2.47**	(0.06)	**−1.85**	(0.08)	**−1.01**	(0.07)	**−0.78**	(0.06)
Year								
1991	**0.53**	(0.09)	0.11	(0.11)	**0.37**	(0.10)	0.11	(0.09)
1992	**0.49**	(0.09)	0.21	(0.11)	**0.34**	(0.10)	0.08	(0.09)
1993	**0.35**	(0.09)	0.06	(0.11)	**0.27**	(0.10)	−0.05	(0.09)
1994	**0.42**	(0.09)	0.22	(0.11)	**0.33**	(0.11)	0.00	(0.09)
1995	**0.20**	(0.09)	0.00	(0.11)	**0.26**	(0.10)	−0.08	(0.09)
1996	0.10	(0.09)	0.03	(0.11)	−0.07	(0.11)	**−0.20**	(0.09)
1998	0.11	(0.09)	0.11	(0.11)	−0.13	(0.11)	**−0.24**	(0.09)
2000	−0.11	(0.09)	0.06	(0.11)	−0.17	(0.11)	**−0.19**	(0.09)
2001	0.00		0.00		0.00		0.00	
Chi-square (D.F.)			13,563 (104)					
N			33,823					

Note: Emboldened coefficients indicate significance at the 0.05 level or better; standard errors are given in brackets.

Turning to the ethnic penalties, the picture for occupational destinations shown in Tables 12.7A and 12.7B has some similarities but also some notable differences from the results for unemployment. Among first-generation men we find that the visible minorities all suffer ethnic penalties in gaining access to the salariat, routine non-manual work and

Table 12.7B. Multinomial logit models of occupational destinations: Women (parameter estimates (contrasts with semi- and unskilled work)).

	Salariat		Routine Non-manual		Petty bourgeoisie		Manual Supervisor or Skilled Manual	
Intercept	**0.75**	(0.09)	**0.95**	(0.08)	**−1.16**	(0.15)	**−0.72**	(0.14)
Ancestry								
British	0.00		0.00		0.00		0.00	
African 1	**−1.54**	(0.32)	**−0.83**	(0.28)	—		−0.58	(0.54)
Caribbean 1	−0.06	(0.21)	**−0.68**	(0.22)	−0.66	(0.41)	−0.44	(0.43)
Indian 1	**−0.74**	(0.18)	**−0.79**	(0.16)	−0.10	(0.22)	−0.32	(0.29)
Irish 1	**0.47**	(0.18)	−0.28	(0.19)	−0.45	(0.36)	−0.37	(0.40)
West European 1	0.02	(0.20)	**−0.61**	(0.20)	0.28	(0.28)	−0.44	(0.40)
Caribbean 2	**0.62**	(0.25)	**0.59**	(0.24)	−0.91	(0.74)	−0.56	(0.61)
Indian 2	0.00	(0.30)	**0.55**	(0.26)	0.51	(0.45)	−0.11	(0.55)
Irish 2	**0.45**	(0.19)	0.16	(0.18)	−0.15	(0.35)	0.14	(0.34)
Age /10	**0.32**	(0.02)	**0.08**	(0.02)	**0.46**	(0.04)	−0.05	(0.04)
(Age/10)²	**−0.20**	(0.02)	−0.02	(0.01)	**−0.25**	(0.03)	**−0.11**	(0.03)
Marital Status								
Married/cohabiting	**−0.16**	(0.06)	−0.06	(0.05)	**0.36**	(0.11)	−0.13	(0.10)
Divorced/separated	**−0.22**	(0.08)	**−0.32**	(0.07)	−0.05	(0.14)	−0.12	(0.13)
Single	0.00		0.00		0.00		0.00	
Qualification								
Higher tertiary	**2.78**	(0.11)	**0.55**	(0.12)	**1.09**	(0.16)	0.38	(0.22)
Lower tertiary	**1.27**	(0.07)	**−0.34**	(0.08)	0.11	(0.12)	0.08	(0.16)
Higher secondary	0.00		0.00		0.00		0.00	
Lower secondary	**−0.66**	(0.06)	**−0.18**	(0.05)	**−0.41**	(0.09)	0.03	(0.11)
No qualification	**−2.20**	(0.06)	**−1.34**	(0.05)	**−1.40**	(0.09)	−0.10	(0.11)
Year								
1991	**0.73**	(0.08)	0.14	(0.08)	**0.54**	(0.13)	**−0.76**	(0.13)
1992	**0.78**	(0.08)	**0.25**	(0.08)	**0.50**	(0.13)	**−0.77**	(0.14)
1993	**0.69**	(0.08)	**0.27**	(0.08)	**0.54**	(0.13)	**−0.75**	(0.14)
1994	**0.62**	(0.08)	**0.17**	(0.08)	**0.46**	(0.13)	**−0.76**	(0.14)
1995	**0.58**	(0.08)	**0.17**	(0.08)	**0.47**	(0.13)	**−0.93**	(0.14)
1996	**0.42**	(0.08)	0.15	(0.08)	**0.32**	(0.14)	**−0.70**	(0.14)
1998	**0.52**	(0.08)	0.06	(0.08)	0.14	(0.14)	**−0.90**	(0.14)
2000	**0.16**	(0.08)	0.02	(0.08)	−0.01	(0.14)	**−0.95**	(0.14)
2001	0.00		0.00		0.00		0.00	
Chi-square (D.F.)				11,360 (96)				
N				3,1820				

Note: Emboldened coefficients indicate significance at the 0.05 level or better; standard errors are given in brackets.

to skilled manual work. This means that the first generation are significantly more restricted to semi and unskilled manual work than would have been expected given their age, education and marital status (exactly as had been argued by scholars such as Castles and Kosack (1973) who studied the first arrivals). The Pakistanis and Bangladeshis experience the largest ethnic penalties, quite probably because of their lack of English language skills in the first generation. The white minorities of Irish and

West Europeans in contrast fare at least as well as men of British ancestry, even in the first generation.

Similar patterns obtain for women with the one important exception of first-generation Caribbean women, who do not suffer any ethnic penalty in gaining access to the salariat (although they do suffer an ethnic penalty with respect to routine non-manual work).

However, in the second generation there is a quite different story. None of our three visible minorities—Caribbeans, Indians and Pakistanis/Bangladeshis—experience a significant ethnic penalty in access to the higher classes. Once again, the same pattern holds true for women. And in the case of both men and women the patterns are replicated using the Labour Force Surveys (see Tables 12.A3A and 12.A3B in the Appendix).

In the case of the Indians, Caribbeans and Pakistanis, then, we see a substantial intergenerational improvement in relative chances of gaining access to the salariat or routine non-manual classes (relative to their chances of being found in the reference category of semi- and unskilled manual work). In effect this means that these two minorities are much less restricted to low-skilled work in the second generation than they had been in the first. In contrast with the picture for unemployment, neither Indian nor Caribbean men and women experience significant ethnic penalties in the second generation in gaining access to the salariat or the other major class destinations. For those who have gained access to employment, their experiences seem to be broadly comparable with those of members of the charter population with the same age, qualifications and civil status. These results are very similar to those of other researchers using different datasets (Model 1999; Leslie *et al.* 1998) and we believe that they are therefore robust and reliable.

Table 12.8 shows that there are few systematic differences in the returns to education experienced by the various ethnic groups in competing for jobs in the salariat. For men, none of the interactions with qualifications is significant although the interaction for first-generation Africans is quite close to significance.

A few of the interactions with respect to other classes are significant, but we should not place too much reliance on a few significant estimates that lack any clear pattern. Since we are testing for a large number of interaction effects, some might by chance alone achieve 'significance' at the 0.05 level. The safest overall conclusion is that, for those respondents fortunate enough to have secured paid employment, the process of stratification operates in much the same way for migrants and for visible ethnic minorities as it does for the charter population.

Table 12.8. Occupational attainment and differential returns to education, by gender (parameter estimates).

	Salariat		Routine Non-manual		Petty bourgeoisie		Manual Supervisor or Skilled Manual	
Men								
Main effects of ancestry								
British	0.00		0.00		0.00		0.00	
African 1	**−1.45**	(0.37)	**−1.16**	(0.56)	−0.67	(0.39)	**−1.44**	**(0.45)**
Significant interactions between ancestry and qualifications								
African 1	**−0.51**	(0.27)	−0.12	(0.40)	−0.30	(0.30)	**−0.91**	**(0.36)**
Women								
Main effects of ancestry								
British	0.00		0.00		0.00		0.00	
Indian 1	**−0.74**	(0.18)	**−0.67**	(0.25)	−0.77	(0.45)	−0.56	(0.58)
West European 1	0.30	(0.33)	−0.09	(0.35)	0.15	(0.50)	0.25	(0.53)
Significant Interaction between ancestry and qualifications								
Indian 1	0.07	(0.16)	0.14	(0.16)	**−0.55**	(0.27)	−0.17	(0.34)
West European 1	0.09	(0.20)	**0.53**	(0.21)	−0.18	(0.30)	0.56	(0.32)

Note: Emboldened coefficients indicate significance at the 0.05 level or better; standard errors are given in brackets.

To give us a clearer idea of what the results of these logistic regressions mean in practice, we show in Figures 12.2A and 12.2B the predicted probabilities of gaining access to the salariat. (These predicted probabilities are calculated for married people of average age in 2001.) These figures show clearly the progress made by the second generations of visible minorities. For example, in the case of men with full secondary education we see that 39% of Pakistanis and Bangladeshis are predicted to gain access to the salariat compared with only 24% in the first generation. Among Indian men 52% of the second generation are predicted to reach the salariat, substantially more than among the first generation (33%) and indeed than among white British (42%).

While the second generation ethnic minorities appear to have similar chances to the charter population of gaining access to the higher classes, it may well be that they have poorer promotion prospects and lower earnings within these broad classes—that they are in effect limited to the lower levels of, say, the salariat. While suitably qualified ethnic minority individuals may be able to secure jobs in teaching or nursing (where there are chronic shortages in Britain), they may fail to win the promotions to senior posts that equally qualified people of British ancestry win. We can check this with data on average earnings within each class. The results are shown in Figures 12.3A and 12.3B.

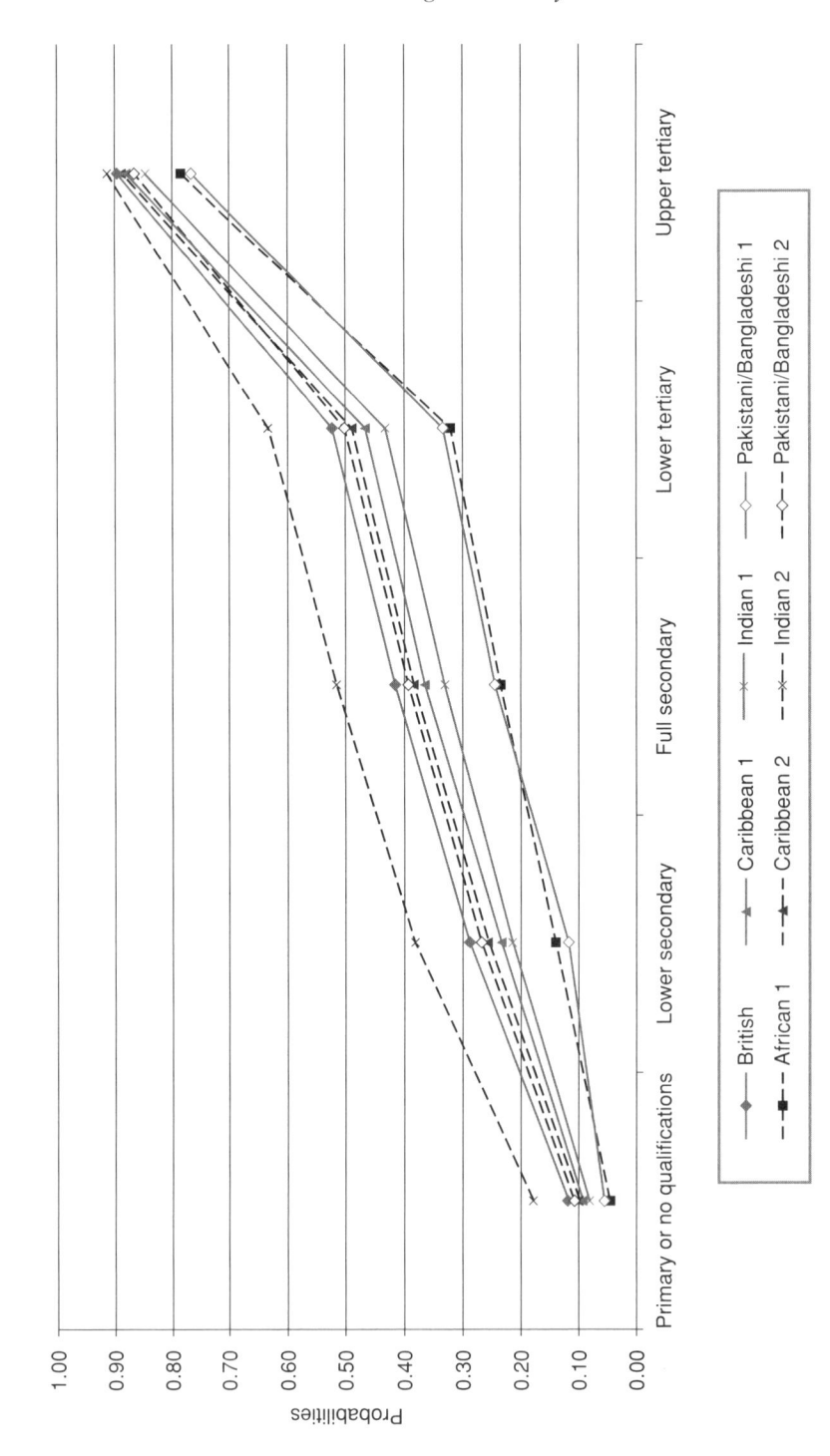

Figure 12.2A. Predicted probabilities of access to the salariat: males.

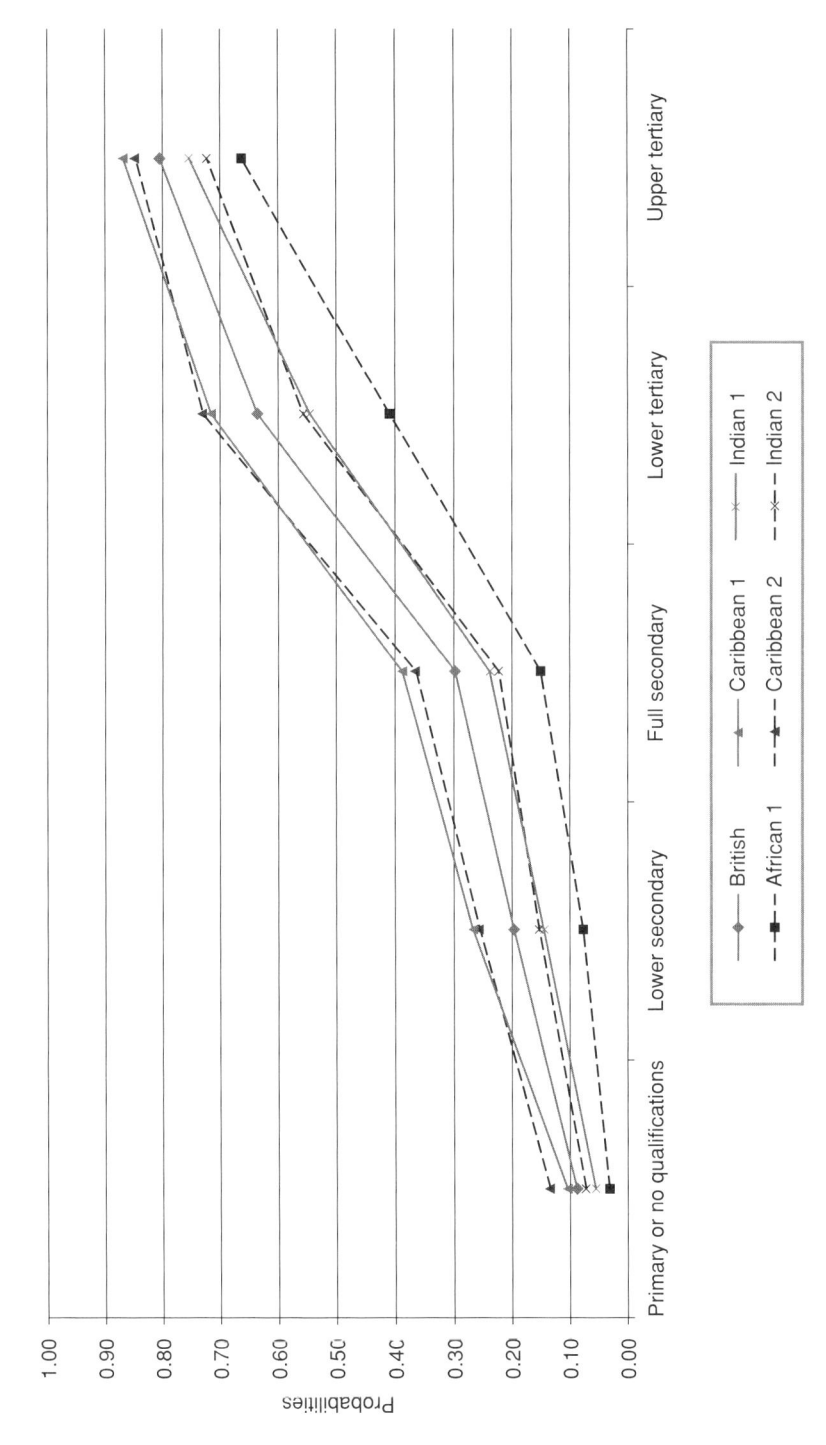

Figure 12.2B. Predicted probabilities of access to the salariat: females.

Figures 12.3A and 12.3B show the predicted hourly earnings of men and women from the different ethnic groupings within each of our five classes. The predictions are obtained from a set of linear regression equations, one for each class, in which log hourly earnings is regressed on ethnicity and our usual control variables. Since the 'typical' member of the salariat will be much more qualified than the 'typical' member of the unskilled class, we show the predicted earnings for different educational categories in each class. Thus we calculate the predicted hourly earnings of, for example, first-generation African men with full tertiary qualifications in the salariat, first-generation African men with full secondary qualifications in the skilled manual class, and of first-generation African men with no qualifications in the semi-and unskilled manual class.

What Figures 12.3A and 12.3B show is that, although there are possibly some disadvantages in the first generation, ethnic minority men and women in the second generation earn similar amounts to the men and women of British ancestry holding similar qualifications and in the same class. There are to be sure some variations, but most of these are within the bounds of sampling error. For example, the predicted figure for graduate men from the charter population in the salariat is £10.75 per hour but first-generation African, Caribbean and Indian male graduates in the salariat are all predicted to earn somewhat less than this. However, none of these shortfalls is statistically significant, and we can also see that the second-generation Caribbeans and Indians earn almost exactly the same as men of British ancestry.

As expected, earnings are substantially lower in the skilled manual class and lower still in the unskilled class, but the same pattern is in evidence: the first-generation visible minorities tend to earn somewhat less—significantly so in the case of Pakistani and Bangladeshi men—but the second generation have similar earnings to their peers with British ancestry. We can thus conclude that the results of our analyses of occupational class tend to underestimate the disadvantages experienced by the first generation of visible minorities but do not give a misleadingly optimistic picture of the parity achieved by the second generation, or at least by those members who have succeeded in gaining work. The one major qualification to this is that Indians and Pakistanis in the petty bourgeoisie do earn significantly less than people of British ancestry. This may reflect the fact that the Indians and Pakistanis have tended to find self-employment as shopkeepers or restaurateurs whereas the British might be found in a broader spectrum of more lucrative niches in the market. In turn this might reflect the differing processes that lead ethnic

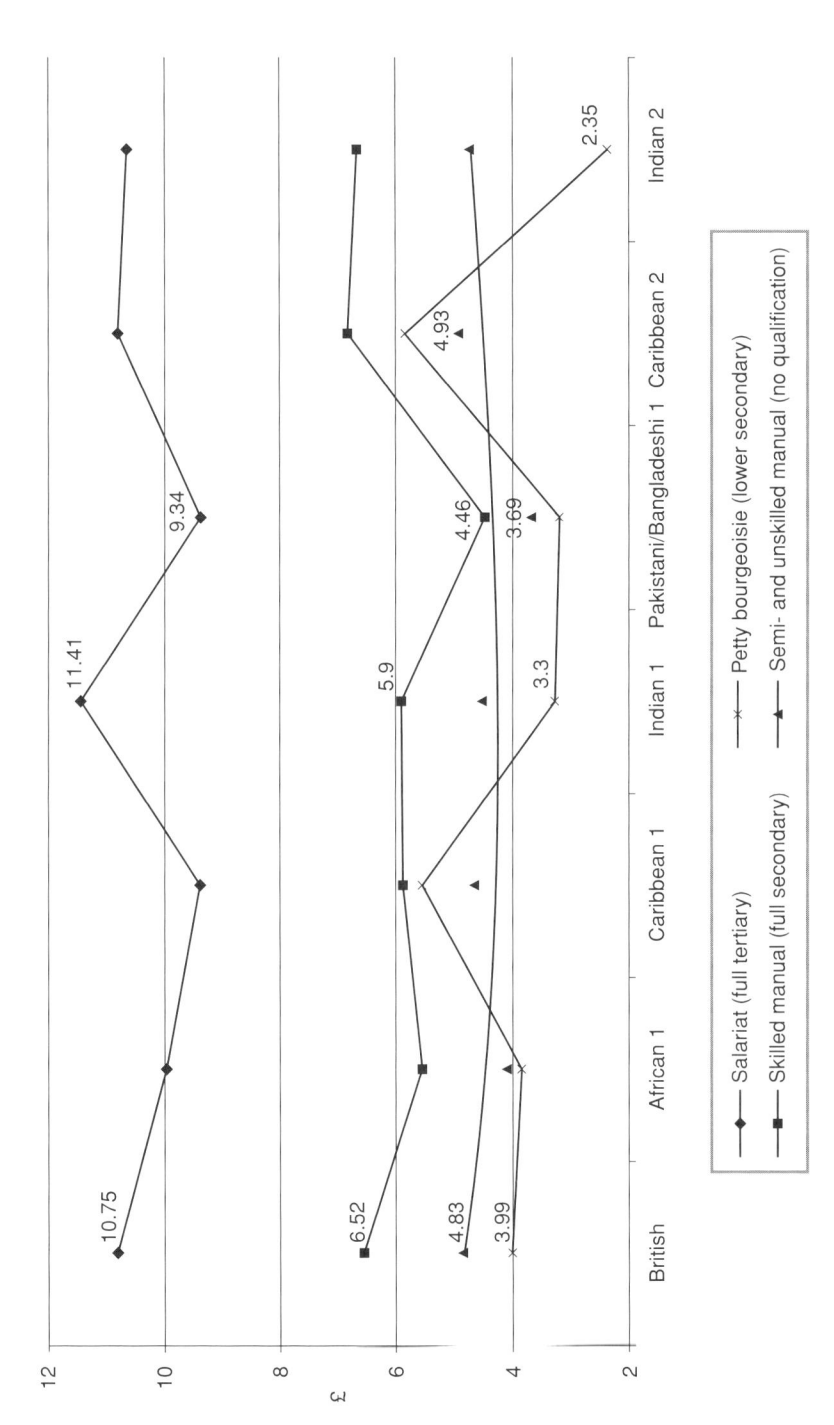

Figure 12.3A. Predicted net hourly earning by social classes: males.

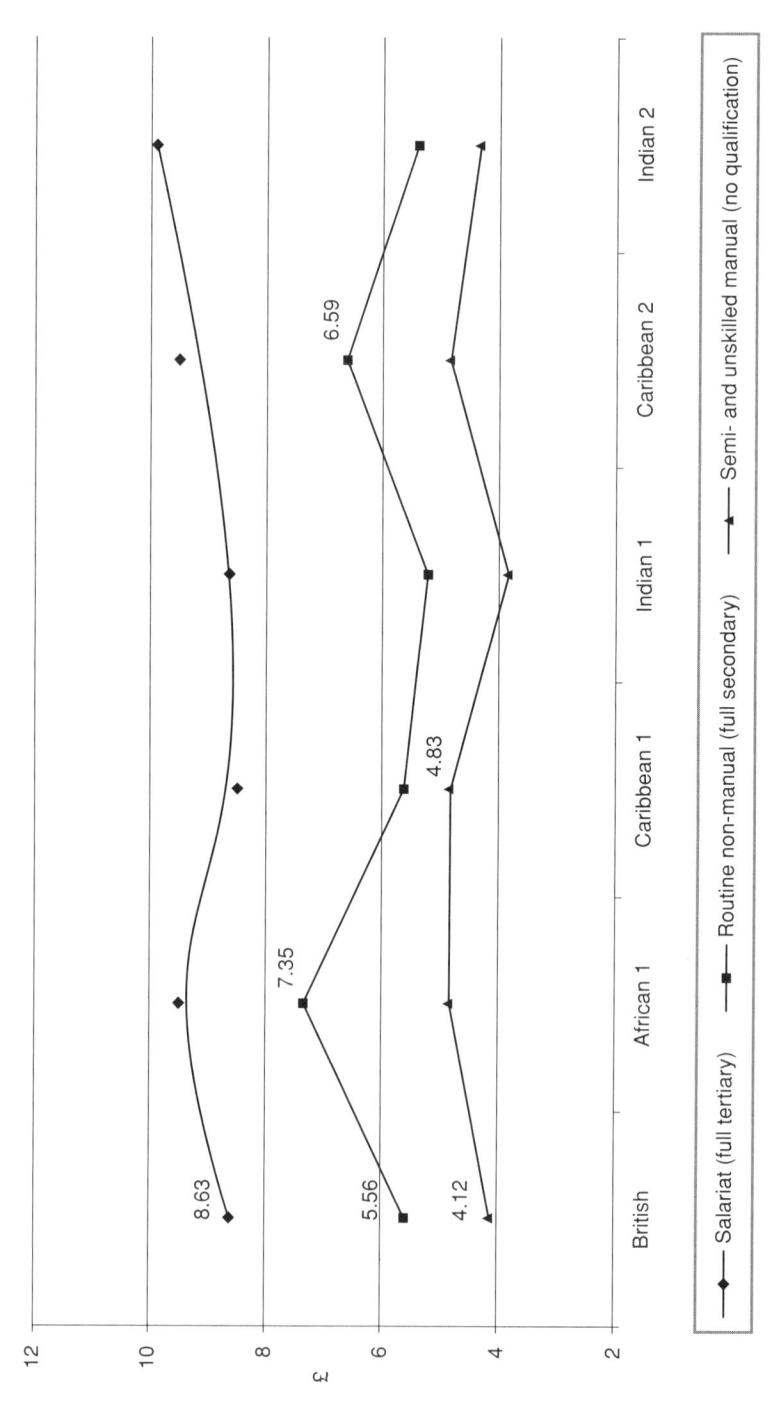

Figure 12.2B. Predicted net hourly earning by social classes: females.

minorities and the charter population into self-employment, the Indians and Pakistanis more often turning to self-employment as an alternative to unemployment.

Discussion and conclusion

We have five main conclusions:

- First-generation members of visible minorities (Black Caribbeans, Indians and Pakistanis/Bangladeshis) experienced significant ethnic penalties, both with respect to unemployment and with respect to access to salariat or nonmanual work.
- First-generation white minorities from Ireland and other countries of Western Europe appear to compete on equal terms with people of British ancestry.
- Second-generation members of visible minorities (Black Caribbeans and Indians) continue to experience disadvantages in gaining employment, but those who have gained employment appear to obtain the same kinds of jobs as people of British ancestry with the same qualifications.
- Within occupational classes, second-generation ethnic minorities obtain comparable earnings to their similarly qualified peers of British ancestry.
- With a few exceptions, the process of stratification appears to work in much the same way for visible ethnic minorities as it does for whites. In some cases ethnic minorities obtain lower returns on their educational investments but this is not a general phenomenon, and is not restricted to visible minorities.

We also have two important caveats. In the case of the first generation there are a number of important control variables which are not available in our dataset, such as lack of fluency in the English language, which could well explain some of the ethnic penalties experienced by members of visible minorities. In addition there are some important selection biases in patterns of economic activity that suggest our conclusions could be overly optimistic. In particular, second-generation visible minorities are likely to stay on in education rather than entering the labour market, perhaps because they expect to have difficulty in finding jobs. We also found evidence, especially in the first generation, of 'discouraged workers'.

Broadly speaking our results have confirmed other British research that has found clear differences between ethnic groups (Berthoud 2000; Carmichael and Woods 2000; Heath and McMahon 1997) and between the generations. However, the explanation for these patterns is less certain.

The contrasting experience of the generations with respect to economic inclusion and exclusion is a major puzzle. How can we explain the continuing presence of ethnic penalties in unemployment but their disappearance with respect to the salariat? In the first generation factors such as lack of fluency in the English language, lack of British qualifications and lack of British labour-market experience may all contribute to the disadvantages experienced—although lack of language fluency cannot account for the disadvantages experienced by the Caribbeans, and lack of British qualifications and labour-market experience does not seem to have hindered groups such as the Irish or West Europeans. Nevertheless, linguistic fluency must have been a very important factor for some first-generation groups in gaining access to salaried and skilled jobs. And the second generation undoubtedly have made very substantial gains in English fluency (Modood *et al.* 1997).

As we emphasised in the introductory chapter, the mere presence of ethnic penalties does not enable one to infer that discrimination is the sole cause of the disadvantage. There are other possible contributory factors. There is some evidence, for example, that some visible minorities are disadvantaged by their geographical concentration in areas of high unemployment. It is likely that this is a small component of the second-generation ethnic penalty but that it far from explains the entirety of the penalty (Fieldhouse and Gould 1998; Fieldhouse 1999). Other explanations, in terms of social or cultural capital, are also possible but there is little evidence as yet on these mechanisms. Discrimination, however, must clearly be a rather likely explanation for the disadvantages experienced by the visible minorities in the second generation. Over the years there has been a great deal of hard evidence from field experiments showing discrimination against visible minorities (for example Daniel 1968; Brown and Gay 1985; CRE 1996; Wrench and Modood 2000). The fact that ethnic penalties with respect to unemployment are not present for any of the white ethnic groups is also suggestive of racial discrimination as a major explanatory factor.

Why then do we find ethnic penalties for the second generation with respect to unemployment but not with respect to the salariat? One possible explanation is that, in the second generation, ethnic minorities have come to share the same conceptions as indigenous white British about what constitutes an appropriate job for, say, a graduate. Hence they apply for the same jobs as the white British graduates—as professionals, managers, and so on—but are more likely to get turned down than are the white British graduates. They may also have come to have the same kind of conception of their 'reservation wages' as do their white British peers. So when they get jobs, they are the same kinds and with the same remuneration as their white British peers get, but at all levels of qualification they are simply less likely to get a job. In contrast, in the first generation there is some ethnographic evidence that Indian graduates were willing to take lower-level jobs. This may have been because their frames of reference were different from those of the indigenous white British. They were partly oriented to their countries of origin; perhaps in their desire to be able to send some remittances home to their families they were willing to take any job, however low status. The first, migrant, generation then may well have had a frame of reference that was more oriented to their countries of origin whereas in the second generation they have developed a frame of reference that is similar to that of other native-born British. They have come to expect the same kinds of jobs as their peers of British ancestry but are not given equal access to them.

Appendix

Source

The source is the pooled General Household Surveys (GHS) for the period 1991–2001 inclusive (but excluding 1997 and 1999).[5] The GHS is a continuous government survey conducted by the Office for National Statistics. The survey covers persons living in private households in Great Britain (and excludes Northern Ireland). The sampling unit is the household and the sampling frame is the Postcode Address File. Within each household interviews are attempted with all household members aged sixteen or over. The sample is stratified by region, proportion of households with no car, proportion of households in SEG 1–5, or SEG 13, and proportion of people who were pensioners. The survey is conducted face to face, and from 1994 moved to computer-assisted personal interviewing (CAPI). Response rates tend to be high, around 75% for the most recent surveys. For further details see <www.statistics.gov.uk/statbase>.

Measures

Age:
Age is measured in years but is centred on the average age for the full sample, namely 38 years. In presenting the parameter estimates for age in the logistic regressions we multiply the estimate by 10.

---

[5] For the surveys which we use, the GHS year is the financial year running from April to March.

Highest educational qualification:
Higher tertiary qualifications include degrees or equivalent qualifications.
Lower tertiary includes post-school qualifications such as nursing, teaching and other higher professional and vocational qualifications.
Higher secondary qualifications include Advanced Level GCE examinations (the school-leaving examination taken at age 18) and their equivalents such as Scottish Highers.
Lower secondary qualifications include Ordinary Level GCE examinations (taken at age 16) and their equivalents such as a grade 1 pass at CSE, and foreign qualifications.
Primary or none includes lower level qualifications such as CSE with grades below 1.
When fitting the interaction terms between education and ethnicity shown in Tables 6 and 12.8, we treat educational qualifications as a continuous variable coded -2 (primary or none), -1 (lower secondary), 0 (full secondary), 1 (some tertiary), 2 (full tertiary).

Economic activity:
Economically active respondents cover those in paid work or looking for paid work although currently unemployed.
Other inactive cover those who are retired or permanently sick or disabled.
Student includes those in full-time education.
Looking after the home is the final category.

Unemployment
Unemployment is measured using the ILO definition and thus refers to people who are both looking and available for work.

Occupational class:
This variable is constructed from the government Socio-Economic Group (SEG) classification used in the GHS. We construct our categories as follows:
Salariat: professional, managerial and administrative work included in SEGs 1.1, 1.2, 2.2, 3, 4, 5.1 and 5.2.
Routine non-manual: clerical and secretarial work included in SEG 6.
Petty bourgeoisie: small employers and own account workers (other than professional but including farmers) included in SEGs 2.1, 12, 13, 14.
Skilled manual: manual foremen, technicians and skilled manual workers included in SEGs 8 and 9.
Semi and unskilled: less skilled jobs, both manual and non-manual, included in SEGs 7, 10, 11 and 15.
We exclude members of the armed forces, SEG 16.

Earnings
We calculate the natural logarithm of hourly earnings (before tax and deductions).
Since we control for year in our regressions, we do not adjust the earnings for inflation. Percentage of the adult population aged 18–59 (column percentages).

Table 12.A1. Ancestry and self-assigned ethnicity, by generation (row percentages).

Ancestry based on birthplace	Self-reported ethnicity									
	White	Black Caribbean	Black African	Black other (1998 only)	Indian	Pakistani	Bangladeshi	Chinese	Mixed, other	N
British ancestry	99.5	0.1							0.2	164,306
African 1	4.3		93.1	0.7					1.8	276
Caribbean 1	1.9	92.6	0.6	0.3	0.9				3.9	701
Caribbean 2	0.3	79.8	1.6	2.7	0.7				15.0	769
Pakistani/Bangladeshi 1	0.0				0.9	68.6	29.9		0.6	796
Pakistani/Bangladeshi 2	0.0				0.4	70.7	24.0		4.2	1,128
Indian 1	1.2		0.1		91.3	3.1	0.1	0.1	4.2	1,442
Indian 2	1.9		1.3		88.6	3.1	0.1	0.1	5.0	1,347
Irish 1	100.0									1,258
Irish 2	99.6					0.2			0.2	1,119
W European 1	99.0	0.1							0.9	909
W European 2	98.9								1.1	262
Others 1	76.9	0.4	0.1	0.1	0.4			6.2	15.9	1,456
Others 2	72.8							10.2	17.0	657
Unidentifiables 1	39.4	1.5	9.6	0.4	8.4	5.4	1.2	10.1	24.0	2,083
Unidentifiables 2	82.5	2.1	1.3	0.3	2.5	1.9	0.2	0.8	8.3	12,496

Table 12.A2. Binary logistic regression of avoidance of unemployment (LFS data) (parameter estimates (contrasts with unemployed)).

	Men				Women			
	I		II		I		II	
Intercept	**2.78**	(0.04)	**2.78**	(0.04)	**3.21**	(0.05)	**3.21**	(0.05)
Ancestry								
White	0.00		0.00		0.00		0.00	
African 1	**−1.27**	(0.10)	**−1.33**	(0.10)	**−1.19**	(0.11)	**−1.19**	(0.11)
Bangladeshi 1	**−1.61**	(0.12)	**−1.61**	(0.12)	**−1.55**	(0.27)	**−1.55**	(0.27)
Caribbean 1	**−0.90**	(0.11)	**−0.90**	(0.11)	**−0.56**	(0.13)	**−0.78**	(0.15)
Chinese 1	−0.09	(0.21)	−0.09	(0.21)	−0.21	(0.24)	−0.21	(0.24)
Indian 1	**−0.24**	(0.09)	**−0.37**	(0.10)	**−0.57**	(0.09)	**−0.57**	(0.09)
Pakistani 1	**−1.01**	(0.08)	**−1.01**	(0.08)	**−1.51**	(0.14)	**−1.51**	(0.14)
Other 1	**−0.93**	(0.11)	**−1.07**	(0.11)	**−0.58**	(0.14)	**−0.58**	(0.14)
Mixed-Black 1	—		—		—		—	
Mixed-Other 1	**−0.69**	(0.22)	**−0.69**	(0.22)	.05	(0.32)	0.05	(0.32)
African 2	**−0.87**	(0.26)	**−0.87**	(0.26)	**−1.78**	(0.22)	**−1.78**	(0.22)
Caribbean 2	**−0.90**	(0.11)	**−0.90**	(0.11)	**−1.01**	(0.10)	**−1.01**	(0.10)
Indian 2	**−0.53**	(0.13)	**−0.53**	(0.13)	**−0.53**	(0.15)	**−0.53**	(0.15)
Pakistani 2	**−1.11**	(0.16)	**−1.11**	(0.16)	**−1.13**	(0.21)	**−1.13**	(0.21)
Other 2	**−1.26**	(0.16)	**−1.26**	(0.16)	**−0.65**	(0.19)	**−0.65**	(0.19)
Mixed-Black 2	**−0.45**	(0.24)	**−0.45**	(0.24)	**−1.32**	(0.18)	**−1.32**	(0.18)
Mixed-Other 2	**−0.76**	(0.23)	**−0.76**	(0.23)	**−0.69**	(0.27)	**−0.69**	(0.27)
Age /10	**0.07**	(0.01)	**0.07**	(0.01)	**0.32**	(0.01)	**0.32**	(0.01)
(Age/10)^2	**−0.12**	(0.01)	**−0.12**	(0.01)	**−0.04**	(0.01)	**−0.04**	(0.01)
Marital Status								
Married/cohabiting	**0.95**	(0.03)	**0.95**	(0.03)	**0.70**	(0.03)	**0.70**	(0.03)
Divorced/separated	**−0.17**	(0.04)	**−0.17**	(0.04)	**−0.33**	(0.04)	**−0.33**	(0.04)
Single	0.00		0.00		0.00		0.00	
Qualification								
Higher tertiary	**0.43**	(0.04)	**0.43**	(0.04)	0.10	(0.05)	0.10	(0.05)
Lower tertiary	**0.31**	(0.05)	**0.31**	(0.05)	**0.42**	(0.06)	**0.42**	(0.06)
Higher secondary	0.00		0.00		0.00		0.00	
Lower secondary	**−0.19**	(0.03)	**−0.19**	(0.03)	**−0.24**	(0.04)	**−0.24**	(0.04)
No qualification	**−0.84**	(0.02)	**−0.84**	(0.02)	**−0.84**	(0.04)	**−0.84**	(0.04)
Year								
1994	**−0.66**	(0.04)	**−0.66**	(0.04)	**−0.43**	(0.04)	**−0.43**	(0.04)
1995	**−0.55**	(0.04)	**−0.55**	(0.04)	**−0.37**	(0.04)	**−0.37**	(0.04)
1996	**−0.46**	(0.04)	**−0.46**	(0.04)	**−0.29**	(0.05)	**−0.29**	(0.05)
1997	**−0.26**	(0.04)	**−0.26**	(0.04)	**−0.17**	(0.05)	**−0.17**	(0.05)
1998	**−0.15**	(0.04)	**−0.15**	(0.04)	−0.05	(0.05)	−0.05	(0.05)
1999	**−0.12**	(0.04)	**−0.12**	(0.04)	−0.11	(0.05)	−0.11	(0.05)
2000	0.00		0.00		0.00		0.00	
Significant interactions between ancestry and qualifications								
African 1			**−0.13**	(0.06)			—	
Caribbean 1			—				**−0.22**	(0.09)
Indian 1			**−0.13**	(0.06)			—	
Other 1			**−0.20**	(0.06)				
Chi-square (D.F.)	8,406 (32)		4,552 (32)		8,426 (35)		4,558 (33)	
N	182,538		160,814		182,538		160,814	

Source: pooled LFS 1994–2000.
Notes: Emboldened coefficients indicate significance at the 0.05 level or better; standard errors are given in brackets. The measurement of ethnicity is based on a self-report measure which offered respondents a fixed set of options such as white, Black Caribbean, Indian etc. Smaller groups where numbers are less than 100 have been omitted. The first generation are defined as those born abroad and the second generation as those born in the UK, irrespective of the year of arrival.

Table 12.A3A. Multinomial logit models of occupational destinations: Men (LFS data) (parameter estimates (contrasts with semi and unskilled work)).

	Salariat		Routine Non-manual		Petty bourgeoisie		Manual Supervisor or Skilled Manual	
Intercept	**0.82**	(0.04)	**0.40**	(0.04)	**0.13**	(0.04)	**0.84**	(0.03)
Ancestry								
White	0.00		0.00		0.00		0.00	
African 1	−**0.75**	(0.15)	−0.14	(0.19)	−**0.93**	(0.19)	−**0.73**	(0.15)
Bangladeshi 1	−0.35	(0.18)	−0.44	(0.27)	−0.42	(0.20)	−**1.60**	(0.23)
Caribbean 1	−**0.89**	(0.14)	−0.28	(0.19)	−**0.82**	(0.16)	−0.10	(0.12)
Chinese 1	−0.24	(0.18)	−**1.13**	(0.38)	**0.61**	(0.17)	−**1.29**	(0.24)
Indian 1	−**0.28**	(0.08)	**0.23**	(0.10)	−0.02	(0.08)	−**0.41**	(0.08)
Pakistani 1	−**0.68**	(0.12)	0.21	(0.14)	**0.61**	(0.10)	−**0.51**	(0.11)
Other 1	**0.55**	(0.13)	**0.49**	(0.18)	−0.13	(0.17)	−**0.52**	(0.16)
Mixed-Other 1	−0.12	(0.24)	0.09	(0.33)	−0.43	(0.29)	−**0.65**	(0.27)
African 2	−0.28	(0.34)	0.12	(0.36)	−0.46	(0.48)	−**0.75**	(0.39)
Caribbean 2	−0.28	(0.14)	−0.05	(0.16)	−**0.72**	(0.21)	−0.28	(0.14)
Indian 2	−0.07	(0.15)	**0.35**	(0.15)	0.04	(0.19)	−**0.86**	(0.18)
Pakistani 2	−0.20	(0.26)	0.48	(0.25)	**0.84**	(0.26)	−0.30	(0.26)
Other 2	−0.01	(0.27)	**0.93**	(0.26)	−0.30	(0.36)	0.00	(0.27)
Mixed Black 2	−0.26	(0.28)	0.36	(0.28)	−**1.13**	(0.49)	−0.35	(0.27)
Mixed Other 2	−0.15	(0.28)	0.01	(0.33)	−0.63	(0.41)	−**0.70**	(0.32)
Age /10	**0.28**	(0.01)	−**0.12**	(0.01)	**0.40**	(0.01)	**0.04**	(0.01)
$(Age/10)^2$	−**0.26**	(0.01)	0.03	(0.01)	−**0.26**	(0.01)	−**0.11**	(0.01)
Marital Status								
Married/cohabiting	**0.65**	(0.02)	**0.06**	(0.03)	**0.61**	(0.03)	**0.54**	(0.02)
Divorced/separated	**0.19**	(0.04)	−0.12	(0.06)	**0.28**	(0.03)	**0.31**	(0.04)
Single	0.00		0.00		0.00		0.00	
Qualification								
Higher tertiary	**3.06**	(0.05)	**1.49**	(0.06)	**0.42**	(0.06)	−**0.75**	(0.06)
Lower tertiary	**1.71**	(0.04)	**0.84**	(0.05)	**0.15**	(0.05)	−0.10	(0.05)
Higher secondary	0.00		0.00		0.00		0.00	
Lower secondary	−**0.26**	(0.02)	−0.05	(0.03)	−**0.76**	(0.03)	−**0.80**	(0.02)
No qualification	−**1.71**	(0.02)	−**1.38**	(0.03)	−**1.17**	(0.02)	−**0.99**	(0.02)
Year								
1994	**0.14**	(0.03)	0.06	(0.04)	**0.33**	(0.04)	0.03	(0.03)
1995	**0.13**	(0.03)	0.04	(0.04)	**0.32**	(0.04)	0.04	(0.03)
1996	**0.08**	(0.03)	0.00	(0.04)	**0.23**	(0.04)	0.01	(0.03)
1997	**0.08**	(0.03)	0.04	(0.04)	**0.18**	(0.04)	0.05	(0.03)
1998	−0.01	(0.03)	−0.08	(0.04)	−**0.09**	(0.04)	−0.05	(0.03)
1999	−0.05	(0.03)	−0.03	(0.04)	0.05	(0.04)	−0.03	(0.03)
2000	0.00		0.00		0.00		0.00	

Chi-square (D.F.) 69,141 (116)
N 167,894

Note: Emboldened coefficients indicate significance at the 0.05 level or better; standard errors are given in brackets.

Table 12.A3B. Multinomial logit models of occupational destinations: Women (LFS data) (parameter estimates (contrasts with semi and unskilled work)).

	Salariat		Routine Non-manual		Petty bourgeoisie		Manual Supervisor or Skilled Manual	
Intercept	**0.77**	(0.04)	**0.61**	**(0.04)** (0.04)	−1.26	(0.07)	−**0.98**	(0.06)
Ancestry								
White	0.00		0.00		0.00		0.00	
African 1	−**0.82**	(0.13)	−**1.07**	(0.14)	−**1.00**	(0.27)	−**0.55**	(0.21)
Bangladeshi 1	0.24	(0.38)	−0.17	(0.37)	**1.00**	(0.51)	−0.78	(0.82)
Caribbean 1	−**0.40**	(0.10)	−**0.92**	(0.12)	−**1.63**	(0.31)	−0.34	(0.16)
Chinese 1	0.09	(0.19)	−0.12	(0.19)	**1.12**	(0.21)	−0.51	(0.37)
Indian 1	−**0.42**	(0.08)	−**0.30**	(0.07)	0.0	(0.11)	−0.11	(0.11)
Pakistani 1	−0.04	(0.18)	−0.36	(0.19)	**0.76**	(0.23)	−0.58	(0.35)
Other 1	−0.10	(0.12)	−**0.39**	(0.12)	−0.02	(0.19)	−**0.55**	(0.21)
Mixed-Other 1	**0.78**	(0.23)	**0.78**	(0.22)	0.25	(0.38)	0.42	(0.35)
African 2	0.04	(0.42)	0.42	(0.39)	−1.03	(1.32)	−0.13	(0.75)
Caribbean 2	0.19	(0.13)	0.22	(0.13)	−0.69	(0.38)	−0.07	(0.23)
Indian 2	**0.48**	(0.18)	**0.83**	(0.16)	0.50	(0.35)	0.07	(0.31)
Pakistani 2	−0.15	(0.27)	0.01	(0.24)	−0.01	(0.49)	−0.28	(0.46)
Other 2	**0.48**	(0.24)	**0.89**	(0.22)	0.25	(0.47)	0.26	(0.39)
Mixed Black 2	−0.07	(0.26)	0.20	(0.23)	−0.14	(0.54)	−0.35	(0.27)
Mixed Other 2	0.20	(0.30)	−0.01	(0.29)	−0.02	(0.59)	−0.42	(0.48)
Age /10	**0.25**	(0.01)	**0.06**	(0.01)	**0.54**	(0.02)	**0.07**	(0.01)
(Age/10)²	−**0.21**	(0.01)	−0.01	(0.01)	−**0.27**	(0.01)	−**0.08**	(0.01)
Marital Status								
Married/cohabiting	0.00	(0.02)	0.03	(0.02)	**0.53**	(0.05)	**0.10**	(0.04)
Divorced/separated	−**0.12**	(0.03)	−**0.19**	(0.03)	0.03	(0.07)	0.08	(0.05)
Single	0.00		0.00		0.00		0.00	
Qualification								
Higher tertiary	**2.88**	(0.05)	**0.80**	(0.05)	**1.02**	(0.07)	−0.14	(0.10)
Lower tertiary	**1.77**	(0.04)	**0.14**	(0.04)	**0.20**	(0.06)	0.06	(0.07)
Higher secondary	0.00		0.00		0.00		0.00	
Lower secondary	−**0.27**	(0.02)	**0.20**	(0.02)	−**0.38**	(0.04)	−**0.24**	(0.04)
No qualification	−**1.60**	(0.02)	−**0.95**	(0.02)	−**1.31**	(0.04)	−**0.44**	(0.05)
Year								
1994	**0.26**	(0.03)	**0.08**	(0.03)	**0.32**	(0.05)	0.09	(0.05)
1995	**0.22**	(0.03)	**0.08**	(0.03)	**0.27**	(0.05)	0.08	(0.05)
1996	**0.15**	(0.03)	0.03	(0.03)	**0.22**	(0.05)	0.06	(0.05)
1997	**0.11**	(0.03)	0.03	(0.03)	**0.25**	(0.05)	0.00	(0.05)
1998	**0.08**	(0.03)	0.02	(0.03)	**0.20**	(0.05)	0.07	(0.05)
1999	**0.09**	(0.03)	0.02	(0.03)	0.09	(0.05)	0.01	(0.05)
2000	0.00		0.00		0.00		0.00	
Chi-square (D.F.)				50,983 (116)				
N				150,811				

Note: Emboldened coefficients indicate significance at the 0.05 level or better; standard errors are given in brackets.

References

Berthoud, R. (2000), 'Ethnic employment penalties in Britain', *Journal of Ethnic and Migration Studies*, 26, 389–416.
Brown, C. and Gay, P. (1985), *Racial Discrimination 17 Years after the Act* (London: Policy Studies Institute).
Carmichael, F. and Woods, R. (2000), 'Ethnic penalties in unemployment and occupational attainment: evidence for Britain', *International Review of Applied Economics*, 14, 71–98.
Castles, S. and Kosack, G. (1973), *Immigrant Workers and Class Structures in Western Europe* (Oxford: Oxford University Press).
Chiswick, B. R. (1980), 'The earnings of white and coloured male immigrants in Britain', *Economica*, 47, 81–7.
Clark, K. and Drinkwater, S. (1998), 'Ethnicity and self-employment in Britain', *Oxford Bulletin of Economics and Statistics*, 60, 383–407.
CRE (1996), *We regret to inform you: Testing for racial discrimination in youth employment in the North of England and Scotland* (London: Commission for Racial Equality).
Daley, P. (1996), 'Black-African: students who stayed'. In C. Peach (ed.), *Ethnicity in the 1991 Census*, volume 2. London: HMSO, pp. 44–65.
Daniel, W. W. (1968), *Racial Discrimination in England* (London: Penguin).
Dustmann, C. and Fabbri, F. (2000), 'Language proficiency and labour market performance of immigrants in the UK'. Discussion Paper No. 156, IZA Bonn.
Fieldhouse, E. A. (1999), 'Ethnic minority unemployment and spatial mismatch: the case of London', *Urban Studies*, 36, 1569–96.
Fieldhouse, E. A. and Gould, M. I. (1998), 'Ethnic minority unemployment and local labour market conditions in Great Britain', *Environment and Planning*, 30, 833–53.
Friedberg, R. M. (2000), 'You can't take it with you: Immigrant assimilation and the portability of human capital', *Journal of Labor Economics* 18, 221–51.
Hansen, R. (2000), *Citizenship and Immigration in Post-War Britain: The Institutional Origins of a Multicultural Nation* (Oxford: Oxford University Press).
Heath, A. F. and McMahon, D. (1997), 'Education and occupational attainments: the impact of ethnic origins'. In V. Karn (ed.), *Ethnicity in the 1991 Census, vol 4: Education, Employment and Housing* (London: HMSO), pp. 91–113.
Heath, A. F. and Ridge, J. M. (1983), 'Social mobility of ethnic minorities', *Journal of Biosocial Science*, Supplement no. 8, 169–84.
Heath, A. F. and Yu, S. (2005), 'The puzzle of ethnic minority disadvantage'. In A. F. Heath, J. Ermisch and D. Gallie (eds.), *Understanding Social Change: Proceedings of the British Academy* (Oxford: Oxford University Press), pp. 187–224.
Holdsworth, C. and Dale, A. (1997), 'Ethnic differences in women's employment', *Work, Employment and Society*, 11, 435–57.
Karn, V. (ed.) (1997), *Ethnicity in the 1991 Census, Volume 4: Employment, education and housing among the ethnic minority populations of Britain* (London: The Stationery Office).
Layton-Henry, Z. (1985), 'Great Britain'. In T. Hammar (ed.), *European Immigration Policy: A Comparative Study* (Cambridge: Cambridge University Press), pp. 89–126.

Leslie, D. and Drinkwater, S. (1999), 'Staying on in full-time education: reasons for higher participation rates among ethnic minority males and females', *Economica*, 66, 63–77.

Leslie, D., Drinkwater, S., and O'Leary, N. (1998), 'Unemployment and earnings among Britain's ethnic minorities: some signs for optimism', *Journal of Ethnic and Migration Studies*, 24, 489–506.

McNabb, R. and Psacharopoulos, G. (1981), 'Racial earnings differentials in the UK', *Oxford Economic Papers*, 33, 413–25.

Model, S. (1999), 'Ethnic inequality in England: an analysis based on the 1991 Census', *Ethnic and Racial Studies*, 22, 966–90.

Modood, T., Berthoud, R., Lakey, J., Nazroo, J., Smith, P., Virdee, S., and Beishon, S. (1997), *Ethnic Minorities in Britain: Diversity and Disadvantage* (London: Policy Studies Institute).

Prandy, K. (1979), 'Ethnic discrimination in employment and housing: evidence from the 1966 British Census', *Ethnic and Racial Studies*, 2, 66–79.

Rothon, C. and Heath, A. (2003), 'Trends in racial prejudice'. In A. Park *et al.* (eds.), *British Social Attitudes, the 20th Report: Continuity and change over two decades* (London: Sage), pp. 189–213.

Spencer, I. R. G. (1997), *British Immigration Policy since 1939: The Making of Multi-Racial Britain* (Routledge: London).

Stewart, M. (1983), 'Racial discrimination and occupational attainment in Britain', *The Economic Journal*, 93, 521–41.

Studlar, D. T. (1978), 'Policy voting in Britain: The coloured immigration issue in the 1964, 1966 and 1970 general elections', *American Political Science Review*, 72, 46–64.

Wrench, J. and Modood, T. (2000), 'The effectiveness of employment equality policies in relation to immigrants and ethnic minorities in the UK'. Report commissioned by the International Labour Office, Geneva. International Migration Papers 38. <http://www.ilo.org/public/english/protection/migrant/publ/imp-list.htm>.

13

Progress in Reducing Catholic Disadvantage in Northern Ireland

YAOJUN LI & RICHARD O'LEARY[1]

Summary: In this chapter on Northern Ireland our focus is not on ethnic minorities of recent immigrant origin but rather on the indigenous Catholic and Protestant populations who can be viewed as ethno-religious groups. The historically disadvantaged position of the Catholic population continued after the partition of Ireland and the establishment of Northern Ireland in 1921 and the differences with respect to their position in the labour market, especially unemployment rates, have long been a symbol of contention and a matter of political importance. Comparing data from the Continuous Household Surveys in 1985/6 and 2002/3 we find substantial improvement for Catholic men in terms of avoidance of unemployment. This is consistent with the positive impact of the improving economy and the British government's fair employment legislation (Acts of 1976, 1989 and 1998). The class situations of Catholic women have also improved over the period covered. However, we find that Catholic men are still disadvantaged in accessing the salariat and in their labour-market earnings. While there is an increase in the absolute numbers of Catholic males working in the professional and managerial posts that make up the salariat in Northern Ireland, relative to Protestant males they are still not achieving a comparable degree of success in gaining access to the salariat.

---

[1] Acknowledgement. We would like to thank Sin Yi Cheung, Bernie Hayes, Anthony Heath and Robert Miller for their suggestions on an earlier version of this chapter, and the UK Data Archive for giving us permission to use the Continuous Household Survey data. We alone are responsible for the views expressed, and any errors that might exist in this chapter.

Introduction

IN THIS CHAPTER ON NORTHERN IRELAND our focus is not on ethnic minorities of recent immigrant origin[2] but rather on the indigenous Catholic and Protestant populations. The Catholic and Protestant populations may be viewed as ethno-religious groups in the way defined by Anthony Smith (1993), that is, as ethnic groups comprising a named population with a myth of common ancestry, shared culture and group solidarity, and a link with a historic territory or homeland.

The differences between Protestants and Catholics in Northern Ireland with respect to their position in the labour market have long been a matter of political importance. According to Smith and Chambers (1991), the unemployment rates between the two groups were a symbol of contention. A much reported (and apparently enduring) feature was the finding that Catholic men were about two and a half times as likely as Protestant men to be unemployed. Such was the importance of the issue of equality in the labour market that in each of the last three decades the British government has introduced religious equality legislation (Acts of 1976, 1989 and 1998). Bew, Patterson and Teague (1997) comment on the political tensions between the groups on the issue of equality in the labour market with Catholics insisting that more effort be made to address the matter while Protestants feared that affirmative action meant that they were losing out.

Although there has been much previous research and comment on this topic, our chapter can extend the research in the following ways. First, we examine the most recent Continuous Household Survey (2002/2003) data on labour-market performance. We compare it with earlier data (1985/1986) to examine change over time. This is of considerable interest given the economic and political changes Northern Ireland has experienced in this period. The improved economic situation generally, including the sharp fall in the rate of unemployment in recent years, might be expected to assist more balance in the ethno-religious situation in the labour market. In addition, the stronger fair employment legislation implemented by the British government in the 1990s, and the major political changes such as the paramilitary ceasefires begun in 1994 and the communal peace deal of 1998 (known as the 'Good Friday' or 'Belfast Agreement'), would give us a reasonable expectation for improvement by

---

[2] It is estimated that they account for less than 1% of the population (Irwin and Dunn, 1997). The 2001 SAR shows that they account for 0.74% of the population (authors' analysis).

2002/2003 as regards the differences between Catholics and Protestants in the labour market.

A second contribution of this chapter is that we move beyond the sole focus on unemployment which characterised most of the previous research on Northern Ireland. Undoubtedly, unemployment is important and it has been stubbornly higher in Northern Ireland than in the rest of the UK. However, it is not only that Catholics are more likely to be unemployed but—even when employed—they are also less likely to be found in the higher occupations. Therefore, we extend our interest to include the additional question of occupational attainment. This combined focus is particularly appropriate given the relatively big fluctuations from year to year in the overall rate of unemployment at the societal levels *vis-à-vis* the relative stability of different social groups in the occupancy in the class structures. As we shall soon see, the unemployment rate has fallen substantially in the period covered such that it now affects a much smaller proportion of people, both Catholic and Protestant, than it did nearly two decades ago. Furthermore, the occupational structure has been much improved in Northern Ireland as in the rest of the UK, with a much bigger salariat and a much contracted working class. In this context of substantial improvement in the labour market, it would be of both academic and policy importance to see whether Catholics have caught up with Protestants in terms of both participation in the labour market and of relative positions in the class structure.

Third, this study is designed within the framework of a cross-national comparison. While the requirements of standardisation may limit our research design in some respects, the benefit is that readers will be able to view the Northern Ireland experience with an international perspective where they can assess whether the Catholic experience in Northern Ireland is similar to that of minorities in the other countries, and thereby make some inferences on the effects of national government policies and of macro socio-economic changes.

The historical distinction between the people in Northern Ireland who make up the Catholic and Protestant populations can be traced back to the seventeenth century. At that time the English government planted with loyal Protestant settlers from Scotland and England lands held by the Gaelic Catholic Irish. The political conflict over land and government between the two groups was given an added intensity because of the religious differences. The disadvantaged position of the Catholic population continued after the partition of Ireland and the establishment of Northern Ireland in 1921. Protestant advantage was evident in the labour market and Protestants were especially over-represented in sectors such as the security forces and the higher levels of the public service, as well as among the skilled labour.

The Protestant population in Northern Ireland is itself made up of numerous denominations. The largest is the Presbyterian Church in Ireland, followed by the Church of Ireland (Anglican) and the Methodists. We have in this chapter put the Protestant denominations into one single religious group. This is justified not only on operational grounds (for the ease of presentation) but on historical grounds. In the last two centuries the political and social divide between the Catholic and the Protestant populations overshadowed any intra-Protestant differences. An illustration of the primacy of the binary distinction is that, in contemporary Northern Ireland, Protestants from the largest Protestant denominations do not refer to marriage between their denominations as intermarriage: they only make that distinction for marriage with Catholics. Persons in Northern Ireland invariably categorise themselves, and are categorised by others, as belonging to the Catholic or the Protestant groups and are treated as such in much of public policy.

Apart from the Catholic and the Protestant distinction in Northern Ireland, there also exists a sizeable, and growing, proportion of the population who would not identify themselves as belonging to any religion or religious denomination. These people are conventionally called 'religious non-identifiers' or 'Nones' for short. This group is often omitted in the analysis of occupational or educational attainment (Cormack *et al.* 1993; Compton 1995; Gallagher *et al.* 1995; Power and Shuttleworth 1997; Anderson and Shuttleworth 1998; Breen 2003). However, given their distinct characteristics from Catholic and Protestant identifiers (Li 2004), we have decided to include them in the present analysis.[3]

This chapter will focus on the Catholic and the Protestant experience in the labour market between 1985/1986 and 2002/2003 based on the Northern Ireland Continuous Household Survey.[4] The earlier time points

---

[3] A question that has remained unanswered is whether Protestants or Catholics are more likely to report 'Not Stated/None' in the census returns or social surveys. So far, no data exist to allow such an analysis. The 2001 Census for Northern Ireland contains information on religious denomination and religious background. However, in the newly released 2001 Individual SAR, the variable for community background ('combgn') is defined as 'a person's current religious group, if any, or the religious group brought up in for people who do not regard themselves as belonging to any religion' <http://www.ccsr.ac.uk/sars/2001/indiv/resources/01ukind-codebook.pdf>. This definition precludes an effective analysis.

[4] See Technical Appendix for more detail on the CHS.

are chosen not only because they provided the earliest available CHS surveys to be compared with the most current ones, but also as they were a time point in the middle of a thirty-year-long conflict. Politically, it marked the introduction of the Anglo-Irish Agreement, a political agreement between the British and Irish governments which heralded a greater focus on equality issues for Catholics within Northern Ireland. It was followed four years later with greatly strengthened labour-market equality legislation (the Fair Employment Act, 1989). Methodologically, using the best available government data almost twenty years apart as contained in the CHS ensures comparability in terms of research design, sampling procedure and question wording, which will help us gain a good understanding of the mechanisms for the discrepancies in labour-market outcomes between Catholics and Protestants.

Existing research and policy initiatives

Existing research has found that the labour-force participation rate of Catholics tends to be lower than that of Protestants, for both men and women. A striking historical characteristic of the Northern Ireland labour market has been the high rate of unemployment as compared with the UK average. Furthermore, the unemployment rate for Catholics has been consistently much higher than for Protestants, especially for men. Catholic men have, in recent decades, typically experienced an unemployment rate almost two and a half times that of Protestant men.

The more detailed occupational profiles and sectors of employment of the two groups exhibit some sharp differences. For example, about 20% of males from a Catholic background are employed in the construction industry compared to 12% of Protestants (Northern Ireland Census 2001 Standard Tables, S337). Twelve percent of Protestant males work in the public administration, defence and social security sector compared to 7% of Catholics (Census 2001 Standard Tables, S337). A striking occupational difference between the religious groups is evident in the security sector, which in 1990 accounted for one in four of all Protestant male public sector workers compared to one in twenty for Catholics (Russell 2004). This sector expanded greatly with the onset of violent conflict.

It is not just in terms of unemployment that Catholics are disadvantaged. Historically Protestants have been better represented than Catholics among the higher social classes. Catholic men are less likely to be found in the professional and managerial classes and more likely to be in the non-skilled classes (Breen and Whelan 1999). Protestants are especially over-represented in higher levels of the civil service and the police (Sheehan and Tomlinson 1999: 146).

Existing research has also established a number of significant changes in the labour market over the past few decades. The number of persons entering the job market has increased in line with Northern Ireland's growing population. The participation of women in the active labour force has greatly increased. The population of working age grew by 9% between 1990 and 2000 (NISRA 2001). Northern Ireland has responded to this with strong growth (13%) in employment in the 1990s (McCrudden, Ford and Heath 2004).

In the economy the heavy industries (e.g., shipbuilding) and traditional manufacturing have declined. These were sectors where Protestants were especially over-represented. On the other hand, the service sector has grown. The sharp growth in public sector employment in the 1970s slowed down in the 1980s and the 1990s.

Coulter (1999) highlights that, prior to the outbreak of the 'Troubles' in 1969, the Catholic middle class was relatively small, but since the 1970s the Catholic middle class has grown remarkably, aided by greater participation in higher education and the expansion of public sector employment. Breen and Whelan (1999) have found some convergence in the class distributions between Catholic and Protestant men although Catholics are still less likely to be found in the professional and managerial classes and are disadvantaged compared to Protestants as regards long-range social mobility. They found convergence in the class distributions for Catholic and Protestant women.

Notwithstanding the fact that Catholics are still more likely to be unemployed than Protestants, it is generally accepted that there has been substantial improvement in the employment profile of Catholics. Indeed, a more recent observation has been that there are now emerging some areas of employment where Protestants are under-represented, such as the health and education sectors and some local government councils (Russell 2004).

Accounting for differences between Catholics and Protestants in Northern Ireland as regards unemployment or class attainment is both complex and controversial. It is complex because of the range of factors that can be introduced as part of the explanation. These factors include the political structure and its historical legacy, with an emphasis on the macro-level role of the state and intergroup power relations. Other structural factors include the match between the geographical distributions of workers and the available jobs, differences between groups in qualifications, age structure, migration patterns and the traditional higher fertility of Catholic women. Workers or potential workers may experience discrimination or firms may have an associated 'chill factor' which discourages job applications from a particular religious group. Still other factors may include social networks which may serve as 'channels of communication' providing the necessary information to job-seekers about potential job openings (Granovetter 1973, 1995; Portes and Zhou 1993; Portes 1998).

Among the relevant studies examining change over time a declining direct effect of religion has been proposed (Miller 1979, 2004; Miller *et al.* 1991). Miller (2004) notes the contrast in the findings from his studies of males from the 1970s and the 1990s. Miller (2004: 52) concluded after his analysis of the 1973/4 data that once the other variables in his model had been taken into account, religion continued to have a statistically significant, though weak, direct effect upon occupational status, with Protestants being somewhat more likely to have a higher status occupation. He suggested that this could be interpreted as indirect evidence of religious discrimination affecting Catholics. For the 1996/7 data he reported (2004: 54) that religion did not have a direct statistically significant effect on present occupation once the effects of first job had been taken into account, although it had indirect effects via father's occupation and first job status.

Consistent with the general approach of the international studies in this volume, the approach we adopt here is one that is set within the econometric tradition. Among previous studies which have adopted this approach are studies by Smith and Chambers (1991) and Murphy and Armstrong (1994). We examine the probability that an individual will be found unemployed or situated in a particular class position after taking into account his/her ethno-religious designation and some personal socio-demographic characteristics. A key interest is whether ethno-religious disadvantages remain even after the socio-demographic characteristics are controlled for.

Different approaches tend to reach different conclusions, in part reflecting the factors included in the research design.[5] Econometric approaches have been criticised for not including some variables.[6]

---

[5] See, for instance, Murphy and Armstrong (1994); Gudgin and Breen (1996).
[6] For example, Smith and Chambers (1991) were criticised for not including a variable for the occupational category of the security forces.

Econometric approaches are always open to this kind of criticism, as indeed is our study given the requirements in this volume for the cross-national standardisation of key explanatory variables and the limits of data at our disposal. We remind the reader that an ethno-religious penalty in our study is an estimate of the extent to which Catholics are disadvantaged relative to Protestants with the same age, marital status and educational qualifications. Our inclusion of age and education allows us to investigate two of the main explanations that have been offered to account for differences in ethno-religious outcomes in the labour market: demographic explanations and human capital explanations.

Demography

The demographic explanations tend to focus on population size and age structure. In this regard the Protestants have been numerically larger than Catholics in Northern Ireland. Table 13.1 shows the religious affiliation as reported in the censuses of population between the establishment of Northern Ireland in 1921 and the most recent census in 2001. At the time of the establishment of Northern Ireland, the Catholics comprised about one-third of the population. This proportion has grown in recent decades, although this is less obvious from the 1971 and especially the 1981 censuses of population when there was under-reporting of the Catholic population.[7] The most useful contrast is between 1961 and 1991 where the declared Catholic population increased from 34.9% to 38.4% while the declared Protestant population (approximated in Table 13.1 by the 'Other Denomination' category) declined from 63.2% to 50.6%. The most recent census, that for 2001, has the added advantage of allowing us to allocate people by religious background, including the 'not stated' and 'none' categories. On this basis the Census Office reports that Catholics account for 43.7% of the population, Protestants and other Christians 53.1%, with 0.4% 'Other Religions' and 2.7% 'None' (Northern Ireland Census 2001: Key Statistics).

Therefore, the Catholic proportion of the total population has grown over time. Catholics as a group are not only gaining in size, but are younger than Protestants. Twenty-five percent of people with a Catholic background are under the age of 15 as compared with 18% of persons of a Protestant background. On the other hand, only 10% of Catholics are

---

[7] In 1981 there was an organised boycott of the census.

Table 13.1. Proportions of Catholics and Protestants in Northern Ireland (1911–2001) (column percentages).

	1911	1926	1937	1951	1961	1971[b]	1981[b]	1991	2001[c]
Catholic	34.4	33.5	33.5	34.4	34.9	31.4	28.0	38.4	40.2
Other Denomination[a]	65.4	66.3	66.3	65.2	63.2	59.2	53.5	50.6	45.9
None	—	—	—	—	—	—	—	3.7	13.9
Not stated	0.2	0.2	0.2	0.4	1.9	9.4	18.5	7.3	
%	100.0	100.0	100.0	100.0	100.0	100.0	100.0	100.0	100.0

[a] The 'Other Denomination' category is overwhelmingly Protestant, and we take it as such, but it includes some unspecified Christians and a tiny number of persons of other religions. Other religions amounted to 0.3% in 2001.

[b] The 1971 and especially the 1981 Censuses were affected by substantial non-response, especially for Catholics.

[c] The 2001 Census also inquired about religious background. On that basis the Census Office reports that Catholics account for 43.7% of the population and Protestants and other Christians 53.1%, with 0.4% 'Other religions' and 2.72% 'None'.

Sources: The Northern Ireland Census 1991: Religion Report; The Northern Ireland Census 2001: Key Statistics.

aged 65 or over, as compared with 17% of Protestants (Northern Ireland Census: 2001 Standard Tables, S306). This demographic information has two main implications for the study of the labour market. First, it highlights that the growing Catholic population is giving rise to an increased demand for employment by Catholics. Second, demographic change can itself raise tensions within society about the ethno-religious balance.

The Catholics thus have a younger age profile and young people are generally more prone to unemployment. Furthermore, Catholic parents have on average a larger number of children than Protestants. Larger numbers of dependent children have tended to depress participation in employment, especially for women (O'Leary 1998). Overall, with regards to demographic explanations it should also be noted that Catholic disadvantage is a historical feature which predates their recent population growth.

Education

The key role of education has been highlighted among studies conducted on religious group differences (see Osborne 2004; Osborne et al. 1987; Miller et al. 1991). Historically there were differences in the levels of educational attainment of Catholics and Protestants, with Protestants more likely to hold a degree and less likely to leave school without any qualifications. Persons with lesser or no educational qualifications are far more likely to become unemployed or attain low social class positions. Therefore, ethno-religious differences in the level of education could contribute to higher rates of Catholic unemployment and less success in achieving advantaged class positions. Of course, this would still leave open the question as to how those educational differences were produced in the first place. In recent years Catholic educational attainment has been converging with that of Protestants. Furthermore, it has been noted that, even among the higher-educated, there is a higher rate of unemployment among Catholics than Protestants (Osborne 2004: 85).

However, it is not just the level but also the type of education that has been the subject of research. It has been suggested that some of the Catholic disadvantage in the labour market might be due to the type of education which they receive. Education in Northern Ireland is largely segregated on religious lines with the great majority of Catholics attending Catholic-managed schools while Protestants attend schools in the state system with an overwhelming Protestant pupil composition. It had been noted that, traditionally, the Protestant pupils in their state schools were more likely than Catholics in their Catholic schools to specialise in scientific and technical subjects. This lesser participation in science-related subjects was noted in the 1970s (Osborne and Murray 1978) and was still observed thirty years later (Osborne and Shuttleworth 2003). This could give Protestants an advantage in the labour market; however, as Bew, Patterson and Teague (1997: 127) point out, any such differences should be increasingly irrelevant in the contemporary Northern Ireland labour market where the traditional manufacturing sector has declined.

The level of education is thus widely accepted as a key explanatory variable in labour market outcomes. Apart from the main effects of education, we should also be alert for possible interaction effects between particular ethno-religious groups and levels of education—to show, for instance, whether Catholics receive lower returns on their educational qualifications.

The demographic and education factors should also be viewed in the context of educational expansion and population migration. In recent decades there has been a preference for Protestant students to leave Northern Ireland to obtain university education in Britain. Protestants form the majority of those university students migrating from Northern Ireland (Osborne *et al.* 1987). Research has indicated that most of the migrating students are not returning to Northern Ireland upon completion of their education, thereby reducing the competition from Protestant graduates for jobs there (Miller *et al.* 1991).

Turning now to the issue of class, the lower class profile of Catholics could also make them more vulnerable to unemployment. However, other researchers have noted that even among professional or managerial workers, Catholic men are more likely to be unemployed than Protestants (Smith and Chambers 1991: 166). For some specific occupational categories, unemployment can be particularly high, as was the case in the 1980s for construction workers, an industry in which Catholics are traditionally over-represented (Smith and Chambers 1991).

Previous research has concentrated on the relative disadvantage of Catholic men compared to Protestant men, commenting that the gap appears much smaller for women and noting that fewer women are active in the labour market than men. Our study includes an examination of the labour-market position of women. Women's work careers have been more disrupted by breaks due to childrearing responsibilities than has been the case for men and Catholic women tend to have more children. There is also a tendency for women to under-report their unemployment (McLaughlin 1993). As we shall see, there has been a growth in the economic activity of women in the recent decades, and this has been related particularly to the public service sector (Coulter 1999). Catholic and Protestant women are usually found in different occupational categories and sectors with Catholic women disproportionately employed in the health and social services.

In sum, higher levels of unemployment among Catholics compared to Protestants have been a persistent feature of the Northern Ireland labour market, especially for men. These have not been convincingly accounted for by the demographic, educational or occupational characteristics of the Catholic population. A key plank of the British government's response to the ethno-religious penalty has, since 1976, been the introduction of fair employment legislation and monitoring aimed at equal labour-market outcomes for the two groups. The next section gives a brief account of these state-sponsored initiatives.

Policy Initiatives

The Fair Employment (Northern Ireland) Act 1976 outlawed discrimination in employment on grounds of religious or political beliefs. A Fair Employment Agency was set up to promote fair employment practices. It had advisory and limited investigative and enforcement functions (Bew, Patterson and Teague 1997). However, the 1976 Act and the Agency were criticised for being ineffective and in the 1980s pressure mounted on the British government to introduce stronger legislation.

The Fair Employment (Northern Ireland) Act 1989 extended the number of workplaces which had to register with the new Fair Employment Commission (FEC). It required all private companies with more than ten employees who work more than sixteen hours a week to register. All public sector employers were already required to be registered. The registered employers were required to report annually to the FEC the religious composition of their workforce. It increased the level of monitoring in that all the public sector employers and those in the private sector who had more than 250 employees had to report to the FEC on the ethno-religious backgrounds of the job applicants and those appointed. In support of the legislation, government departments were to ensure that they only awarded contracts to firms which complied with the FEC requirements. A new Fair Employment Tribunal was established to adjudicate on individual claims of discrimination.

The FEC expected employers to make progress over time in matching the ethno-religious composition of their workforce with that of the relevant employment catchment area. Voluntary affirmative action measures were encouraged but employers could also be directed by the Commission to undertake affirmative action. The type of affirmative action set out often involved the setting of goals and timetables to measure progress but did not include setting down quotas (Bew, Patterson and Teague 1997).

In 1999, in the aftermath of the Good Friday Agreement, the Equality Commission for Northern Ireland replaced the FEC, with an enhanced remit. The Fair Employment Monitoring Regulations (NI) 1999 extended monitoring to internal applications and appointments and more significantly for the first time has sought employer returns on promotees (for employers of 251 or more persons). Given these strengthened fair employment measures it is reasonable to expect some improvements as regards the ethno-religious balance in the labour market.

Labour-market situation of Catholics and Protestants (1985/1986–2002/2003)

We now turn to the heart of our analysis: comparing the labour-market situations of Catholics and Protestants over two decades. We analyse labour-market situations in terms of participation rates, unemployment risks and class positions, and we do this for men and for women separately. As noted earlier, the data sources used are the Northern Ireland Continuous Household Survey (CHS), the equivalent of the General Household Survey for Britain (used by Cheung and Heath in this volume). It is noted here that even though the CHS is the standard government survey and the best possible data source for our present purposes, the sample sizes for individual years are still insufficient for the analysis at hand, due chiefly to the constraints imposed in this volume for international compatibilities (e.g., including only individuals aged 18–59). We thus combined the data for 1985 and 1986 and the data for 2002 and 2003.[8]

Labour-market participation

Before we proceed to the thrust of our analysis, we need to examine briefly changing educational profiles of Catholics and Protestants. We observed earlier that Catholics historically tended to have lower levels of educational qualifications and that these qualifications were also less rewarding in terms of labour-market attainments. It is thus of importance to examine how their profiles of educational qualifications have changed over the period of interest and what implications that might have for labour-market situations.

The data in Tables 13.2A and 13.2B show a very important feature of convergence between Catholics and Protestants in terms of educational attainment. Over the past two decades, the differences between the two groups have been sharply reduced, especially for men. In the earlier period, Protestant men were almost twice as likely as Catholic men to have higher tertiary (first degree or above) qualification (6.9% and 3.7% respectively), and the former were also more likely than the latter to have lower tertiary (professional qualifications below degree, such as teaching and nursing) qualifications (17.7% and 12.6% respectively). Combining the two tertiary figures, we can see that nearly a quarter of the Protestant men (24.6%) had tertiary education, 8.3 percentage points higher than the Catholic men. If we look under the column for 'Primary/None', we find that well over half (58.7%) of the Catholic men had only primary or no formal educational qualifications, a figure 12 percentage points higher

---

[8] See Appendix for more detail.

Table 13.2A. Highest educational qualification, by religion and period: Males (row percentages).

	Higher tertiary	Lower tertiary	Higher secondary	Lower secondary	Primary/ none	N
1985/1986						
Protestant	6.9	17.7	17.8	10.9	46.6	2,068
Catholic	3.7	12.6	13.8	11.3	58.7	1,422
None	15.2	20.7	16.5	17.7	29.9	164
2002/2003						
Protestant	12.6	13.2	14.7	33.7	25.8	2,138
Catholic	12.4	10.8	15.0	35.5	26.2	1,224
None	27.7	16.1	17.5	24.1	14.6	137

Sources: The Northern Ireland Continuous Household Survey (CHS) for 1985/6 and 2002/3 for this and the other tables in this chapter.

Table 13.2B. Highest educational qualification, by religion and period: Females (row percentages).

	Higher tertiary	Lower tertiary	Higher secondary	Lower secondary	Primary/ none	N
1985/1986						
Protestant	4.8	11.7	22.9	12.4	48.1	2,586
Catholic	3.2	10.4	17.5	12.8	56.2	1,771
None	13.3	16.4	21.9	16.4	32.0	128
2002/2003						
Protestant	12.2	11.0	12.2	40.5	24.2	2,179
Catholic	12.3	11.7	12.0	38.9	25.0	1,653
None	25.8	12.9	15.1	31.2	15.1	93

than that for the Protestant men. However, looking at the data for 2002/2003, we see that the Protestant lead has been largely reduced; Catholic men have caught up with their Protestant counterparts at almost every level of education.

The differences between Catholic and Protestant women were not as polarised as those between Catholic and Protestant men, even in the earlier period. In fact, we find very little difference between Catholic and Protestant women in terms of higher and lower tertiary qualifications in the 1985/1986 period. The differences were mainly in the higher secondary (A-Levels or equivalent) and the 'Primary/None' categories. The Protestant women were more likely to have higher secondary and less likely to have no qualifications than Catholic women in the earlier period. Yet by 2002/2003, the religious group differences are barely discernible at each of the five levels. It is also noteworthy that the 'Nones' were quite highly educated.

Given their respective educational profiles, we may expect marked differences in the labour-market outcomes between Catholics and Protestants in the earlier period—for men in particular. The data would also suggest, however, that no such differences will persist in the later period. With this in mind, we now turn to our main analysis. Our samples are restricted to men and women aged 18 to 59 and resident in Northern Ireland at the time of interview. We start with the economic activity rates among the targeted populations, then move to the labour-market positions among the economically active, and finally come to the class positions among the employed. At the each level of our analysis, we shall explore where differences lie and what possible factors could account for the differences.

The data in Tables 13.3A and 13.3B show the labour-market participation rates for Catholic and Protestant men (13.3A) and women (13.3B) in 1985/1986 and 2002/2003. Here we get our first glimpse of the Catholic disadvantage. For both sexes alike, and at both time points, Catholics were less likely to be economically active than Protestants. For instance, in 1985/1986 Catholic men were 4.4 percentage points behind Protestant

Table 13.3A. Economic activity, by religion and period: Males (row percentages).

	Active	Other inactive	Looking after home	Student	N
1985/1986					
Protestant	92.1	5.5	0.2	2.2	2,190
Catholic	87.7	8.2	0.3	3.9	1,532
None	87.9	4.9	1.2	6.1	165
2002/2003					
Protestant	86.0	10.7	1.0	2.3	2,166
Catholic	81.0	13.3	2.4	3.2	1,233
None	78.8	11.7	0.7	8.8	137

Table 13.3B. Economic activity, by religion and period: Females (row percentages).

	Active	Other inactive	Looking after home	Student	N
1985/1986					
Protestant	58.0	4.2	35.4	2.4	2,647
Catholic	47.1	4.5	46.1	2.4	1,817
None	62.3	3.1	2.7	6.9	130
2002/2003					
Protestant	67.8	9.1	19.3	3.7	2,198
Catholic	60.4	10.7	24.9	4.0	1,653
None	55.2	14.6	25.0	5.2	96

men in terms of active labour-market participation, and in 2002/2003, the figure is even higher at 5 points. The differences for women are much bigger. In the earlier period, Catholic women were 11 points behind their Protestant counterparts; in the later period, the figure has decreased somewhat but remains high at 7.4 points. It is also notable in the context that the 'Nones' were, as compared with the other two groups, more likely to be students.

If Catholic disadvantage is exemplified in lower participation rates, a related question is, then, where do the main differences among the economically non-active lie? Here we remind the reader that we are dealing with a population of working age (18 to 59). A closer look at Table 13.3A shows that, among men, Catholics were more likely to be found in the 'other inactive' group. Since these respondents were not of a legal retirement age, the most probable situations in this group are the disabled, long-term sick or discouraged workers who had opted for early retirement. Amongst women we do not find much difference between the two main groups with regard to their membership in the 'other inactive' category; rather the main difference lies in the category of 'looking after home'. As we noted earlier, Catholics, by tradition and culture, tend to have more children and hence larger families (especially true in the 1985/1986 period). Here we find that nearly half (46%) of Catholic women were 'looking after home' in 1985/1986, compared with 35% of Protestant women, a difference of 11 percentage points. In this regard, the difference was halved in the later period (to 5.6 points), reflecting the fact that both Catholics and Protestants now have smaller families than some twenty years ago as well as that more women are now economically active even when they have children.

Labour-market situations of the economically active

Looking at the differences in the participation rates is only a first, albeit very important, step. There are pronounced differences among the economically active as well, to which we shall pay particular attention in the following analysis. We shall first look at the differences among the economically active (i.e., among those who are working or seeking work) and then look at the class positions among those who are working (i.e., omitting those who are unemployed). It is thus the case that at each further step in our analysis we are narrowing down our focus by including a smaller sample. The aim of this procedure is to highlight the patterns and the trends of social differences between Catholics and Protestants in the most important aspects of their labour-market situations, and to explore the mechanisms whereby such differences are brought about.

The data in Tables 13.4A and 13.4B show the occupational and unemployment distribution positions among the economically active. In both tables, we find marked disadvantages for Catholics in the earlier period and much reduced differences between the two groups in the later period. For instance, in the earlier period a staggering 36.4% of the Catholic men were unemployed, roughly two and half times as many as amongst Protestant men (15.3%). Although the difference is less than amongst men, Catholic women were also more likely to be unemployed than Protestant women (14.5% vs. 10.3%). In 2002/2003, the general economic situation was much improved and the overall unemployment rate was much lower than in 1985/1986. However, we still find Catholics more likely to be unemployed than Protestants, around 2 points for men and 1.4 points for women. This data thus suggests that Catholics bore the brunt of economic hardship when unemployment ran rampant in society

Table 13.4A. Current occupational class, by religion and period: Males (row percentages).

	Salariat	Routine non-manual	Petty bourgeoisie	Manual supervisor/ skilled manual	Semi- and unskilled	Unemployed	N
1985/1986							
Protestant	24.3	9.7	11.0	26.0	13.8	15.3	2,008
Catholic	14.5	4.5	10.2	21.3	13.1	36.4	1,342
None	34.7	11.8	6.3	19.4	7.6	20.1	144
2002/2003							
Protestant	33.2	9.5	10.9	25.4	15.0	6.0	1,812
Catholic	30.5	7.0	11.3	25.5	17.6	8.1	967
None	47.6	8.6	6.7	19.1	9.5	8.6	105

Table 13.4B. Current occupational class, by religion and period: Females (row percentages).

	Salariat	Routine non-manual	Petty bourgeoisie	Manual supervisor/ skilled manual	Semi- and unskilled	Unemployed	N
1985/1986							
Protestant	22.3	29.7	2.3	2.8	32.6	10.3	1,532
Catholic	20.5	26.0	1.5	1.2	36.3	14.5	854
None	40.7	25.9	2.5	1.2	17.3	12.4	81
2002/2003							
Protestant	34.8	31.3	3.5	4.7	22.3	3.4	1,456
Catholic	38.9	25.6	1.7	4.5	24.4	4.8	976
None	46.2	19.2	1.9	3.9	21.2	7.7	52

and that the social inequality still remains even in a much ameliorated socio-economic context. It is, however, also the case that the enduring theme of '2.5 times' in terms of unemployment, as was much commented upon in the earlier research, is not found in the most recent data. It is also the case that in the earlier period, Protestant men were much more likely to be in the 'white-collar' (salariat or routine non-manual) or supervisory positions than Catholic men.

As Table 13.4 also shows, with regard to class positions we again find that the Catholics have been disadvantaged, although this disadvantage has been reduced over time. At the earlier time point, the Catholic disadvantage was mainly found in their higher likelihood of working within semi- or unskilled manual jobs (if we re-percentage in order to exclude the unemployed the figures are 20.6% vs. 16.3% for men and 42.5% vs. 36.3% for women). Catholic men were also less likely to have professional or managerial jobs (22.8% vs. 28.6% for Protestant men when re-percentaged). In 2002/2003, the differences in terms of access to the salariat and the semi- and unskilled manual working class were, while still visible, much reduced. As the data show, by this later time period, Catholic women were actually more likely to be found in the salariat than Protestant women.

A final comment in this section relates to self-employment. It has been suggested that ethnic minorities tend to seek self-employment as a strategy to avoid discrimination in the charter labour market (Clark and Drinkwater 1998). We find few signs of such strategy, either in Tables 13.4A and 13.4B or in our modelling tables (Appendix Table 13.1A). At neither time point were Catholic men more likely to be self-employed than Protestant men, nor Catholic women more so than Protestant women.[9]

Unemployment: ethno-religious penalties in accessing the labour market

Having discussed the patterns and trends at the descriptive level, we now turn to statistical modeling. The descriptive data give us the broad profile of Catholic disadvantage, but not the net effects due to ethno-religious statuses after controlling for age, education and marital status, all of

---

[9] One possible explanation for the difference between our finding and that by Clark and Drinkwater is that Catholics in Northern Ireland do not see themselves as 'ethnic minorities' in the same way or to the same extent as, say, Indians or Chinese do in Britain, and hence do not seek self-employment as an economic enclave as actively as do ethnic minorities in other societies.

which are likely to affect labour-market outcomes between different social groups. As with other chapters in this volume, we measure ethno-religious penalties by the extent to which ethno-religious minorities (in this case Catholics) are disadvantaged in comparison with the majority group (in this case Protestants) of the same age, educational qualification and marital status. There are other variables which have been included in other studies and which we could control for but have not, as our analysis is shaped by considerations of cross-national comparison. For example, type of industry, geographic areas, number of children and social networks could all be expected to impact on labour-market situations in Northern Ireland but are not included in the analyses below.[10]

Specifically our analysis focuses on two aspects of labour-market outcomes: avoidance of unemployment and access to the salariat (as opposed to semi- or unskilled manual working class). These two aspects can be seen as referring to 'economic exclusion' and 'economic inclusion' respectively. To see the patterns and trends more clearly, we shall present the data for the two periods separately, and also in a combined form ('pooled data') which will help us analyse the trends. Separate analyses are presented for men and women. In Tables 13.5A and 13.5B, we present results for three sets of data: (1) data for the earlier period (1985/1985), (2) for the later period (2002/2003) and (3) the pooled data (all four years). In each set, we conduct two models. In Model 1, we control for age, ethno-religious status, education and marital status. In Model 2, we add interaction effects with education, to test whether Catholics obtain similar returns to their educational qualifications. In the pooled data, we also control for the interaction effects of Catholics in the later as opposed to the earlier period, to check for change over time.

Data in Tables 13.5A and 13.5B show the results of logistic regression on the avoidance of unemployment for men and women respectively, with negative coefficients indicating a higher likelihood of unemployment. Let us first look at the data for men in Table 13.5A. In 1985/1986, we find significant effects for age, education and marital status, mostly in the expected directions.[11] With regard to age, there is also a significant curvilinear relationship,

---

[10] However, it is noted that Smith and Chambers argue that type of industry and locational factors 'do very little to explain the difference in the unemployment rate between Protestant and Catholic men' (1991: 175).

[11] We find an unexpected feature here in that men with lower secondary qualifications were significantly more likely to be in employment than those with higher secondary qualifications. Further analysis shows that of the 335 Protestant men with higher secondary qualifications, 49 (14.6%) were unemployed, as compared with 9.4% of Protestant men with lower secondary

570 Yaojun Li & Richard O'Leary

Table 13.5A. Logistic regression of the avoidance of unemployment: Men (parameter estimates, contrast with unemployed).

	1985/1986				2002/2003				Pooled data			
	Model 1		Model 2		Model 1		Model 2		Model 1		Model 2	
Intercept	−0.48	(0.51)	−0.46	(0.51)	0.28	(0.82)	0.19	(0.82)	0.64	(0.44)	0.30	(0.45)
Religion												
Catholic	**−1.07**	**(0.09)**	**−1.10**	**(0.13)**	−0.27	(0.16)	−0.03	(0.22)	**−0.87**	**(0.08)**	**−1.03**	**(0.12)**
None	**−0.55**	**(0.23)**	**−0.55**	**(0.23)**	−0.41	(0.38)	−0.36	(0.38)	**−0.49**	**(0.20)**	**−0.49**	**(0.20)**
Protestant	0.00		0.00		0.00		0.00		0.00		0.00	
Age/10	**0.94**	**(0.29)**	**0.94**	**(0.30)**	**1.15**	**(0.47)**	**1.14**	**(0.47)**	**0.92**	**(0.25)**	**0.96**	**(0.25)**
(Age/10)²	**−0.08**	**(0.04)**	**−0.08**	**(0.04)**	**−0.14**	**(0.06)**	**−0.14**	**(0.06)**	**−0.08**	**(0.03)**	**−0.09**	**(0.03)**
Education												
Higher tertiary	**1.85**	**(0.41)**	**1.87**	**(0.41)**	0.49	(0.37)	0.36	(0.37)	**1.27**	**(0.26)**	**1.24**	**(0.26)**
Lower tertiary	**0.65**	**(0.18)**	**0.66**	**(0.18)**	0.45	(0.38)	0.39	(0.38)	**0.58**	**(0.16)**	**0.57**	**(0.16)**
Higher secondary	0.00		0.00		0.00		0.00		0.00		0.00	
Lower secondary	**0.54**	**(0.19)**	**0.52**	**(0.19)**	−0.20	(0.25)	−0.11	(0.26)	**0.29**	**(0.14)**	**0.30**	**(0.15)**
Primary/none	**−0.68**	**(0.13)**	**−0.70**	**(0.15)**	**−1.29**	**(0.26)**	**−1.10**	**(0.28)**	**−0.84**	(0.13)	**−0.79**	**(0.13)**
Marital Status												
Married/cohabiting	0.22	(0.12)	0.22	(0.12)	**1.45**	**(0.22)**	**1.46**	**(0.22)**	**0.49**	**(0.10)**	**0.49**	**(0.10)**
Divorced/separated	**−0.92**	**(0.23)**	**−0.92**	**(0.23)**	0.40	(0.34)	0.40	(0.34)	**−0.55**	**(0.19)**	**−0.55**	**(0.19)**
Single	0.00		0.00		0.00		0.00		0.00		0.00	
Period												
1985/1986									**−1.16**	**(0.09)**	**−0.81**	**(0.12)**
2002/2003									0.00		0.00	
Interaction effects												
Catholic* qualifications			−0.02	(0.08)			0.24	(0.15)			0.03	(0.07)
Catholics* 2002/2003											**0.77**	**(0.18)**
Chi-square (D.F.)	471(10)		471(11)		177(10)		180(11)		949(11)		968(13)	
N		3,314				2,939				6,253		

Note: Standard errors are given in parentheses; emboldened coefficients are significant at the 0.05 level or lower.

suggesting that unemployment tends to be high amongst the young, declines as people reach occupational maturity, and starts to increase again as people approach retirement. Education, as expected, helps people find and stay in employment. Married people are also more likely to be in jobs than the single or the divorced/separated. Yet, controlling for the effects

---

qualifications. No such 'anomalies' are found for Catholic men in 1985/1986, or for women at either time point.

Table 13.5B. Logistic regression of the avoidance of unemployment: Women (parameter estimates, contrast with unemployed).

	1985/1986				2002/2003				Pooled data			
	Model 1		Model 2		Model 1		Model 2		Model 1		Model 2	
Intercept	−0.01	(0.73)	−0.07	(0.73)	−0.06	(1.11)	−0.08	(1.12)	0.63	(0.64)	0.61	(0.64)
Religion												
Catholic	−0.22	(0.14)	−0.09	(0.17)	**−0.35**	**(0.22)**	−0.31	(0.24)	**−0.25**	**(0.12)**	−0.10	(0.16)
None	−0.15	(0.38)	−0.13	(0.38)	**−1.40**	**(0.57)**	**−1.37**	**(0.58)**	−0.43	(0.32)	−0.40	(0.32)
Protestant	0.00		0.00		0.00		0.00		0.00		0.00	
Age/10	0.77	(0.46)	0.78	(0.46)	**1.50**	**(0.67)**	**1.51**	**(0.67)**	**0.99**	**(0.38)**	**1.02**	**(0.38)**
(Age/10)^2	−0.04	(0.06)	−0.04	(0.06)	−0.17	(0.09)	−0.17	(0.08)	−0.07	(0.05)	−0.08	(0.05)
Education												
Higher tertiary	0.50	(0.36)	0.41	(0.37)	0.28	(0.41)	0.20	(0.43)	0.39	(0.26)	0.29	(0.27)
Lower tertiary	0.24	(0.25)	0.18	(0.25)	0.52	(0.50)	0.48	(0.51)	0.31	(0.22)	0.25	(0.23)
Higher secondary	0.00		0.00		0.00		0.00		0.00		0.00	
Lower secondary	−0.27	(0.21)	−0.22	(0.21)	−0.15	(0.31)	−0.11	(0.32)	−0.18	(0.17)	−0.13	(0.17)
Primary/none	**−0.61**	**(0.18)**	**−0.51**	**(0.19)**	**−0.83**	**(0.37)**	−0.76	(0.41)	**−0.66**	**(0.16)**	**−0.56**	**(0.18)**
Marital Status												
Married/cohabiting	**0.54**	**(0.17)**	**0.54**	**(0.17)**	**1.76**	**(0.35)**	**1.76**	**(0.35)**	**0.77**	**(0.15)**	**0.77**	**(0.15)**
Divorced/separated	**−0.54**	**(0.26)**	**−0.55**	**(0.26)**	−0.32	(0.34)	−0.32	(0.34)	**−0.52**	**(0.21)**	**−0.52**	**(0.21)**
Single	0.00		0.00		0.00		0.00		0.00		0.00	
Period												
1985/1986									**−1.03**	**(0.14)**	**−1.09**	**(0.18)**
2002/2003									0.00		0.00	
Interaction effects												
Catholic* qualifications			0.13	(0.11)			0.08	(0.17)			0.12	(0.09)
Catholic* 2002/2003											−0.14	(0.25)
Chi-square (D.F.)	142 (10)		144 (11)		111 (10)		111 (11)		341 (11)		343 (13)	
N		2,393				2,521				4,914		

of age, education and marital status, Catholics were still found to be significantly less likely to be in employment than Protestants.

As we noted earlier, existing research (Osborne 2004) shows that Catholics are more likely to be unemployed than Protestants, even when highly educated. Our initial results corroborated this finding when three-way tables were analysed.[12] However, as Model 2 shows, when age and

---

[12] Data not presented, but available on request.

marital status are included in the models as covariates, we find no significant interaction effects between Catholics and education. Thus, as indicated in the main effects, Catholic men are, at each level of education, less likely than Protestant men to avoid unemployment. Judging by the magnitude of the coefficients, education and ethno-religious status have the more pronounced effects.

In the 2002/2003 data, no significant differences were found between the two groups after age, education and marital status were taken into consideration, even though further analysis did show that Catholics were still significantly more likely to be unemployed than Protestants when no other factors were taken into account.[13] These analyses indicate that age, marital status and the lack of educational qualifications largely account for employment status. Finally, the pooled data show that Catholic men were on the whole disadvantaged as compared to Protestant men, that the overall employment situation had significantly improved by 2002/2003, and that the Catholics (as well as Protestants) benefited from this improvement.

The patterns in Table 13.5B show that, among economically active women, it is educational qualifications and marital status that mainly account for differences in avoidance of unemployment. At neither time point were there any significant differences between the Catholic and Protestant probabilities when the other variables were included in the model.[14] In the analysis of the pooled data, we find that Catholic women were disadvantaged to some extent (significantly in Model 1 where no interaction effects were included[15]). Comparing the patterns for men and for women, we find that education and age play a more important role for men whilst marital status plays a more important role for women.

---

[13] The Catholic men had log-odds of −0.31 in terms of avoidance of unemployment in 2002/3 as compared with Protestants, which is significant at the 0.05 level. It is noted here that the coefficient for the interaction effect of 'Catholic qualifications' was quite strong (at 0.24), which is significant at the 0.10 level.

[14] Further analysis shows that when no other variables are included, Catholic women were significantly less likely than Protestant women to have a job at the 0.01 and 0.10 levels respectively at the two time points.

[15] With large samples, it is easy to detect even relatively small differences. However, we notice that the coefficients for Catholic women in all the models in the table were negative, suggesting that Catholic women were on the whole disadvantaged as compared with Protestant women with regard to employment opportunities.

Occupational class: ethno-religious penalties in the labour market

Turning now to occupational class positions among the employed (Tables 13.6A and 13.6B), we report results from multinomial logit regression models where each of the other class categories (as shown in Tables 13.4A and 13.4B) is contrasted with the semi- and unskilled working class. Four such contrasts are obtained. However, for the ease of presentation and in terms of theoretical importance,[16] we only report the results comparing access to the salariat with access to the semi- and unskilled working class. The data on the other contrasts are shown in Appendix Table 13.1A.

The data for men in Table 13.6A show that, in the competition for access to the most advantaged professional and managerial positions (salariat) and for avoidance of the least advantaged positions of semi- and unskilled working class, Catholics were disadvantaged compared to Protestants at both time points. In 1985/1986, Catholics were significantly less likely to be in the salariat than Protestants.[17] The data also make evident that educational qualifications were of crucial importance in helping people gain access to the salariat and, as Tables 13.2A and 13.2B showed, Protestants were on the whole better qualified than Catholics. Model 2, however, shows that even similarly qualified Catholics do not fare equally well in the competition for salariat positions. Compared with Protestant men of the same age, educational qualification and marital status, Catholic men in 1985/1986 were estimated to have only slightly better than a 50% chance of being in the salariat rather than in the semi- and unskilled working class.[18]

We might have expected from Tables 13.2A and 13.2B and 13.4A and 13.4B that, as a result of the convergence in educational attainment, the class disparities between the two groups would have levelled off by 2002/2003. However, the data for 2002/2003 show that Catholic men

---

[16] Insofar as social equality is concerned, it can be argued that it is the competition in this regard rather than that in gaining access to routine non-manual, petty bourgeoisie, foremen and manual supervisors, or skilled working class versus semi/unskilled working class positions that has much greater impact on people's life chances and life choices (Goldthorpe 1987; Heath 1981).

[17] With no other factors controlled for, Catholic men are less likely than Protestant men to be in salariat. The log odds are -0.46 and -0.25 at the two time points respectively, which are significant at the 0.001 and 0.05 levels. It is also noted that as no male graduates were found in the semi- and unskilled working class in the earlier period, we randomly added one such case for Protestant and one such case for Catholic in the dataset so as to reduce the effects of full tertiary education on the salariat versus unskilled contrast.

[18] Calculated as $e^{-0.56} = 0.57$.

Table 13.6A. Logistic regression of access to the salariat: Men (parameter estimates, contrast with semi- and unskilled class).

	1985/1986				2002/2003				Pooled data			
	Model 1		Model 2		Model 1		Model 2		Model 1		Model 2	
Intercept	−6.57	(0.97)	−6.49	(0.97)	−4.01	(0.92)	−4.02	(0.92)	−5.44	(0.67)	−5.36	(0.67)
Religion												
Catholic	−0.25	(0.15)	−0.56	(0.21)	−0.36	(0.14)	−0.42	(0.17)	−0.30	(0.10)	−0.44	(0.18)
None	0.44	(0.39)	0.42	(0.39)	0.33	(0.40)	0.31	(0.42)	0.40	(0.28)	0.38	(0.28)
Protestant	0.00		0.00		0.00		0.00		0.00		0.00	
Age/10	3.79	(0.53)	3.82	(0.53)	2.02	(0.50)	1.99	(0.49)	2.84	(0.36)	2.84	(0.36)
$(Age/10)^2$	−0.41	(0.07)	−0.41	(0.07)	−0.18	(0.06)	−0.19	(0.06)	−0.29	(0.04)	−0.29	(0.04)
Qualification												
Higher tertiary	3.03	(0.75)	3.18	(0.77)	3.02	(0.40)	3.09	(0.42)	3.00	(0.35)	3.13	(0.36)
Lower tertiary	0.41	(0.29)	0.48	(0.30)	0.79	(0.26)	0.82	(0.26)	0.67	(0.19)	0.72	(0.19)
Higher secondary	0.00		0.00		0.00		0.00		0.00		0.00	
Lower secondary	−1.10	(0.29)	−1.17	(0.30)	−0.79	(0.19)	−0.82	(0.20)	−0.88	(0.16)	−0.94	(0.17)
Primary/none	−2.69	(0.25)	−2.82	(0.27)	−2.34	(0.23)	−2.40	(0.25)	−2.42	(0.16)	−2.53	(0.17)
Marital Status												
Married/cohabiting	0.33	(0.21)	0.33	(0.21)	0.64	(0.19)	0.64	(0.19)	0.50	(0.14)	0.50	(0.14)
Divorced/separated	−0.89	(0.55)	−0.88	(0.55)	0.40	(0.35)	0.40	(0.35)	0.02	(0.28)	0.02	(0.28)
Single	0.00		0.00		0.00		0.00		0.00		0.00	
Period												
1985/1986									0.28	(0.11)	0.26	(0.13)
2002/2003									0.00		0.00	
Interaction effects												
Catholic*qualifications			−0.16	(0.13)			−0.09	(0.13)			−0.13	(0.09)
Catholic*2002/2003											−0.05	(0.21)
Chi-square (D.F.)	1103	(40)	1109	(44)	1176	(40)	1187	(44)	2170	(44)	2185	(52)
N	2,523		2,523		2,659		2,659		5,182		5,182	

remained significantly less likely than their Protestant counterparts to gain access to salariat positions, and this feature obtains whether or not we control for the interaction effects of Catholic education. For instance, the log coefficients for Catholic men were −0.36 and −0.42 under the two models, both significantly different from zero. The evidence from the combined dataset also suggests that Catholic men were still lagging behind their Protestant counterparts in 2002/2003. However, we should also note that the Catholic ethno-religious penalty did decrease from

Table 13.6B. Logistic regression of access to the salariat: Women (parameter estimates, contrast with semi- and unskilled class).

	1985/1986				2002/2003				Pooled data			
	Model 1		Model 2		Model 1		Model 2		Model 1		Model 2	
Intercept	−6.35	(1.03)	−6.39	(1.01)	−3.22	(0.90)	−3.40	(0.91)	−4.22	(0.66)	−4.33	(0.67)
Religion												
Catholic	−0.21	(0.16)	−0.15	(0.18)	−0.11	(0.13)	0.14	(0.17)	−0.16	(0.10)	−0.04	(0.17)
None	0.73	(0.45)	0.73	(0.44)	0.09	(0.48)	−0.05	(0.48)	0.48	(0.32)	0.49	(0.32)
Protestant	0.00		0.00		0.00		0.00		0.00		0.00	
Age/10	3.57	(0.58)	3.58	(0.58)	1.87	(0.50)	1.91	(0.50)	2.50	(0.37)	2.51	(0.37)
(Age/10)^2	−0.43	(0.07)	−0.43	(0.07)	−0.19	(0.06)	−0.19	(0.06)	−0.28	(0.05)	−0.29	(0.05)
Qualification												
Higher tertiary	3.16	(0.49)	3.07	(0.49)	2.92	(0.38)	2.72	(0.39)	3.02	(0.30)	2.88	(0.30)
Lower tertiary	1.57	(0.23)	1.51	(0.23)	1.30	(0.27)	1.18	(0.27)	1.41	(0.17)	1.32	(0.17)
Higher secondary	0.00		0.00		0.00		0.00		0.00		0.00	
Lower secondary	−0.77	(0.27)	−0.71	(0.27)	−1.22	(0.21)	−1.08	(0.21)	−1.03	(0.15)	−0.94	(0.16)
Primary/none	−2.86	(0.23)	−2.76	(0.24)	−2.93	(0.27)	−2.68	(0.29)	−2.89	(0.17)	−2.75	(0.18)
Marital Status												
Married/cohabiting	−0.38	(0.22)	−0.38	(0.22)	0.05	(0.19)	0.04	(0.19)	−0.13	(0.14)	−0.13	(0.14)
Divorced/separated	−0.17	(0.36)	−0.18	(0.36)	−0.21	(0.27)	−0.21	(0.27)	−0.20	(0.21)	−0.20	(0.21)
Single	0.00		0.00		0.00		0.00		0.00		0.00	
Period												
1985/1986									−0.37	(0.11)	−0.34	(0.13)
2002/2003									0.00		0.00	
Interaction effects												
Catholic qualifications			0.16	(0.14)			0.32	(0.14)			0.22	(0.09)
Catholics in 2002/2003											0.08	(0.21)
Chi-square (D.F.)	1525	(40)	1533	(44)	1098	(40)	1107	(44)	2659	(44)	2677	(52)
N	2,107		2,107		2,365		2,365		4,472		4,472	

−0.56 in the earlier period to −0.42 in the later period, suggesting that some progress may have been made.

The models for employed women, in Table 13.6B, show three main features. First, no significant differences between Catholics and Protestants existed as regards salariat attainment rather than semi- and unskilled manual positions. This is the case whether we look at the data for the earlier or the later period, or for the pooled data. Second, at both time points (in contrast to men) higher educational qualifications have disproportionately helped Catholic women, Catholic women obtaining higher returns on their educational investments than did Protestant women. In the later period, the effects were even significantly so. Third, the patterns in the pooled data show no sign of improvement for Catholic women in 2002/2003 (the interaction term between period and religion falling well short of statistical significance).

In order to understand the patterns more clearly, we show the fitted probabilities of access to the salariat for men and women, by educational levels, for both time periods in Figures 13.1A and 13.1B. Three features emerge. First, at both time points, Protestant men were somewhat more likely than Catholic men to be in the salariat, especially with full secondary and lower tertiary levels of education. For women, however, ethnic differences were barely visible. This feature seems to suggest some level of ethnic penalty for Catholic men. Second, it is also the case that the greatest determinant of access to the salariat (by far) was education and not ethno-religious group. Thus Catholic men with degrees were much more likely to be in the salariat than Protestant men without degrees. Third, as women salariat members are usually found in the lower rather than the higher grades (Heath and McMahon 1997; Li 2002), lower tertiary education has a much stronger effect on women in their access to the salariat than on men.

Finally this section will conclude with a brief look at earnings differentials between the two groups. Earnings data are collected in the CHS[19] just as in the GHS. In this chapter, we shall use predicted values of total annual gross earnings from the labour market as our dependent variable, controlling for class, education, religion, age, age square and marital status. Like Cheung and Heath (Chapter 12 of this volume), we calculate the earnings profiles of certain class/educational groups, such as salariat with full tertiary education, skilled workers with full secondary education, petty bourgeoisie with lower secondary education and semi- and unskilled working class with only primary or no formal education. The findings are shown in Figures 13.2A and 13.2B.

The earnings of the Protestant salariat were set as 100% and all other groups were compared with them. For men and women alike at both time points, salariat with full tertiary education had, as expected, higher earnings than did less educated groups in lower social classes. The differentials are more noticeable in the later period (2002/2003) than the earlier period (1985/1986). As our main focus is upon the differences between the

---

[19] See Appendix for more detail.

CATHOLIC DISADVANTAGE IN NORTHERN IRELAND   577

Predicted probabilities of being in Salariat: for men

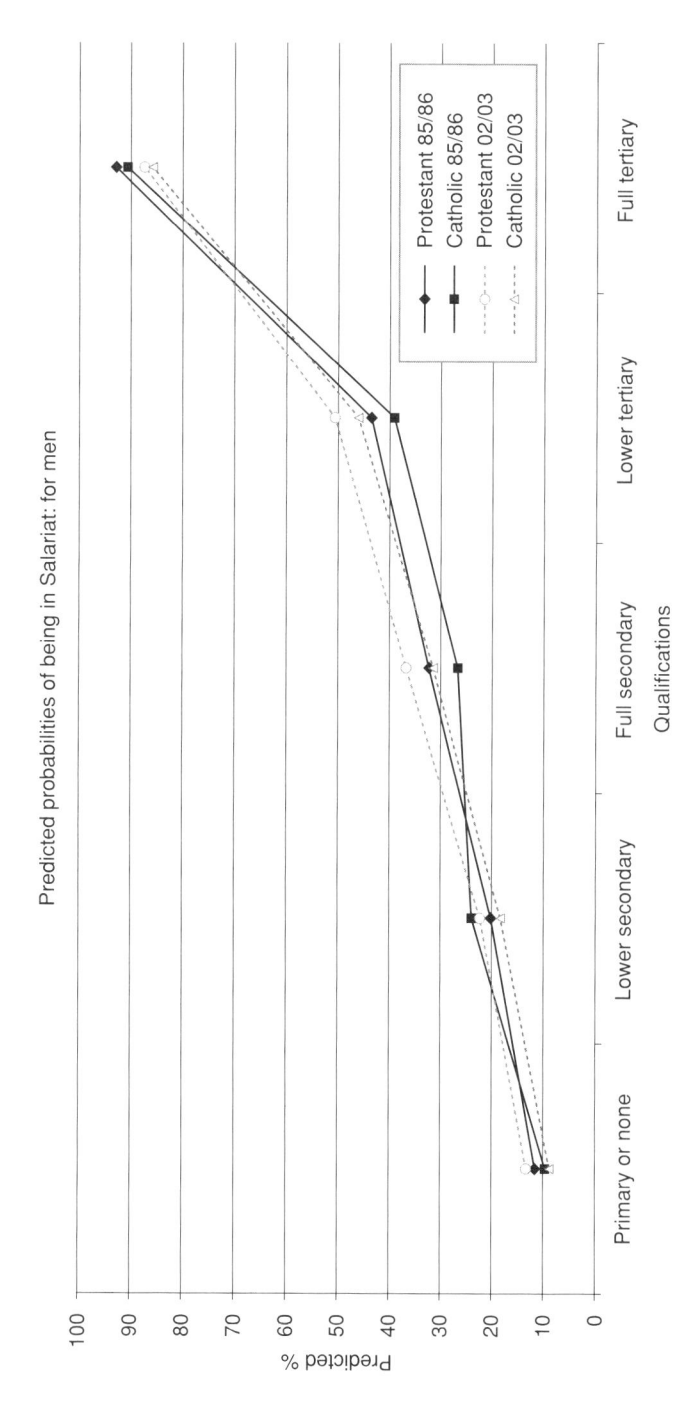

Figure 13.1A. Predicted probabilities of access to the salariat, by educational level: males.

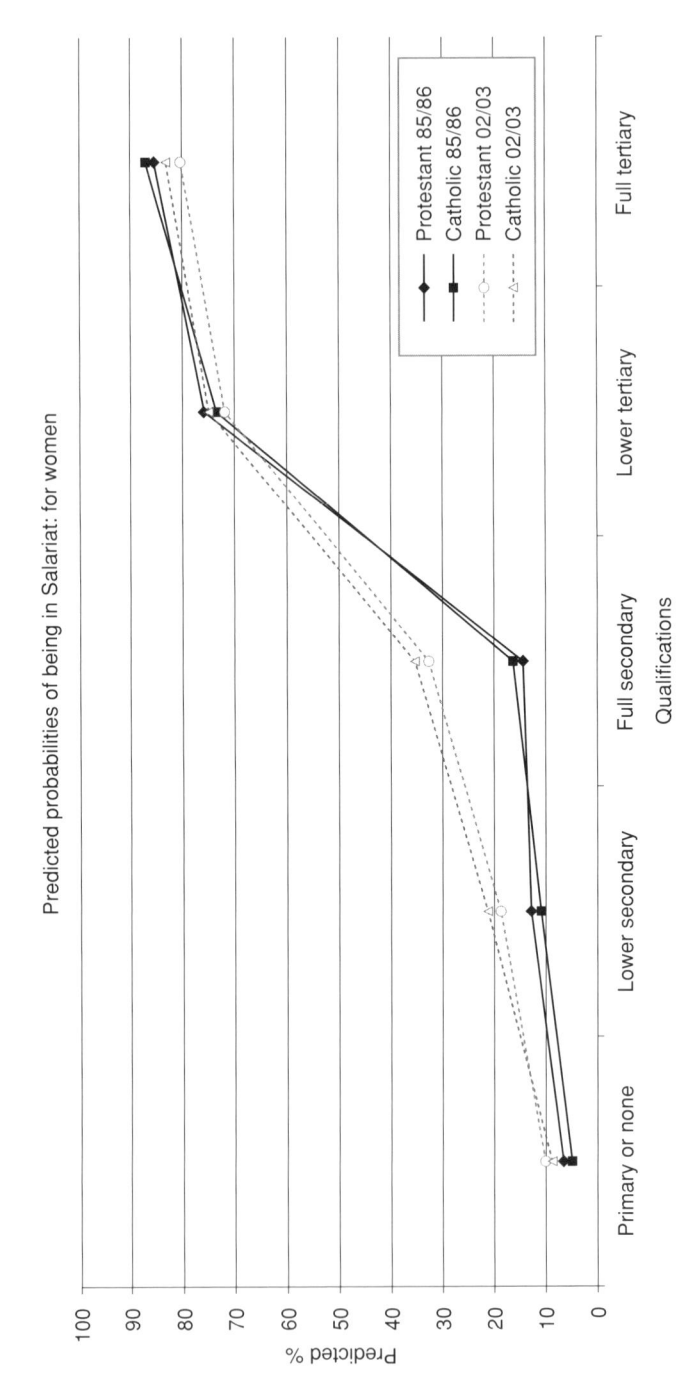

Figure 13.1B. Predicted probabilities of access to the salariat, by educational level: females.

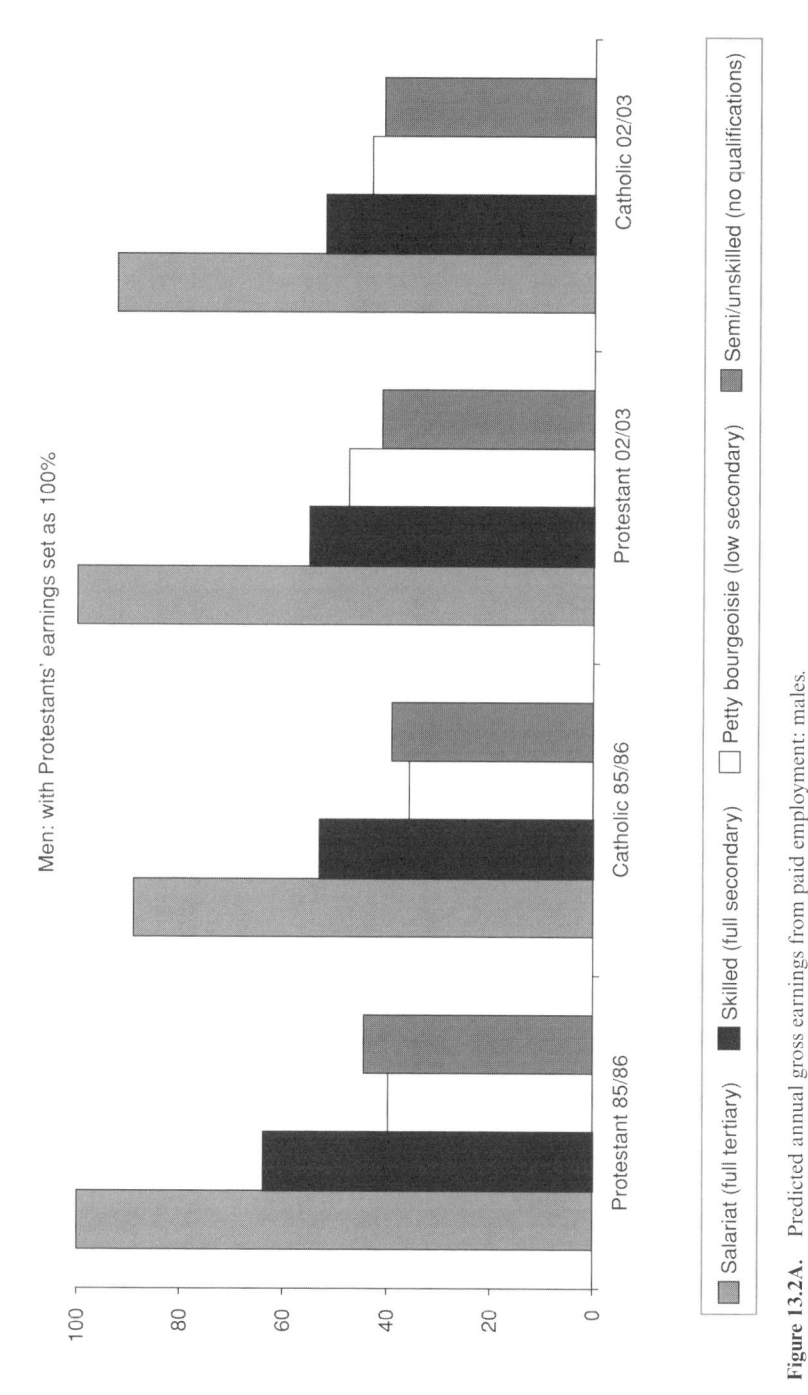

CATHOLIC DISADVANTAGE IN NORTHERN IRELAND 579

Figure 13.2A. Predicted annual gross earnings from paid employment: males.
Note: Based on predicted values controlling for class, education, religion, age, age squared and marital status.
Source: the income files from the CHS 1985, 1986, 2002 and 2003.

Figure 13.2B. Predicted annual gross earnings from paid employment: females.
Note: Based on predicted values controlling for class, education, religion, age, age squared and marital status.
Source: The income files from the CHS 1985, 1986, 2002 and 2003.

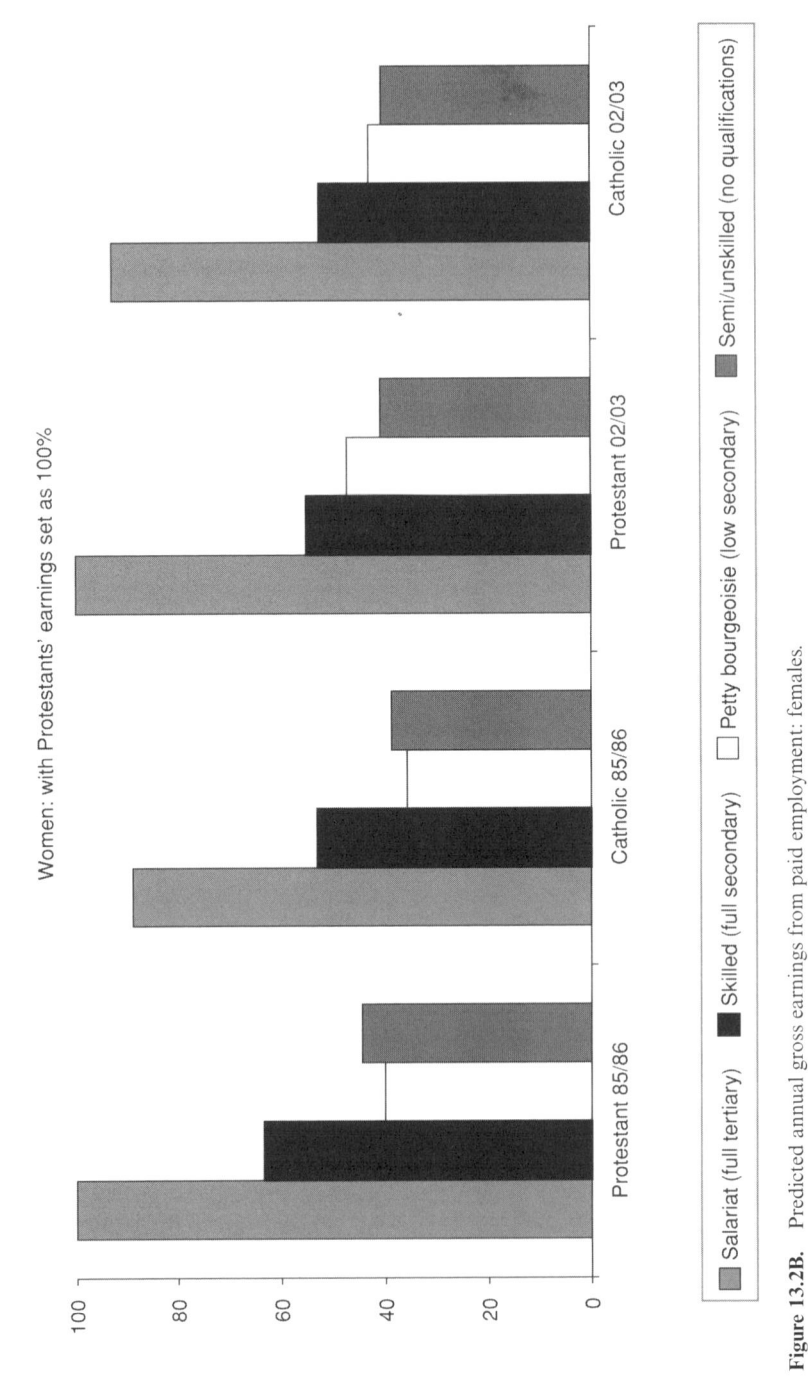

Protestants and the Catholics, we find that for men in the lower social positions and for women, there is hardly any difference between the two groups. Yet for men in the salariat with degrees, Catholic disadvantages are quite clear. In the earlier period, a Protestant man in the salariat and with a degree was predicted to earn £1,268 per annum more than his Catholic counterpart of the same age and marital status.[20] In the later period, the differential was £2,021.[21] In other words, a Catholic man in the salariat and with a degree was earning 89.2% (in 1985/1986) and 92.5% (2002/2003) of what his Protestant counterpart earned. A Catholic woman in the salariat and with a degree earned less (95.5%) in the earlier period than her Protestant counterpart, but slightly more (103.4%) in the later period. Thus in earnings, as in access to the salariat, disadvantages remained for Catholic men.

One caveat regarding this analysis: We should point out that our earnings data do not necessarily show that Catholic men in the same job grades and with the same work experience were paid less than their Protestant colleagues. The salariat as a class is a broad group and, owing to data limitations, our analysis did not differentiate between, for example, the higher and the lower grades within the class (see Goldthorpe 1987; Savage et al. 1992; Li 1997, 2002; and Breen 2003 for further discussion).[22] It could well be that Catholics are employed in lower-level jobs within the salariat and have yet to penetrate the higher echelons to the same extent as Protestants. Further research with more complete data sets may be needed to address the issue of equal pay more completely.

Discussion and conclusion

This chapter has used the Continuous Household Survey (CHS) to analyse patterns and trends of labour market activity for Catholics and Protestants aged 18 to 59 in Northern Ireland. This is a solid data source and our variables are all standardised. We shall give a brief summary of our findings here.

---

[20] Calculated as £11,732−£10,464.
[21] Calculated as £26,921−£24,900.
[22] Using the newly released samples of anonymised records from the 2001 Census for Northern Ireland, we find that Catholic men, but not women, are still behind Protestant men in gaining access to the higher grades of the salariat (6.7% and 8.2% respectively). Even among the highly educated (qualification level 5), Catholic men are 5 percentage points behind their Protestant counterparts (30.7% and 35.6% respectively) in being found in Class I of the salariat.

At the broadest level, Catholic disadvantage is shown in their lower rates of participation. The patterns were nearly constant between 1985/1986 and 2002/2003: Catholic men were less likely to be economically active and more likely to be inactive at both time points, whilst Catholic women were more likely to be in home duties, especially in the earlier period.

At each further level, we find Catholic men and women more likely to be unemployed, to be in the semi- and unskilled working class, and less likely to be in the salariat. However, we also find that the longstanding and widely reported feature of '2.5 times' difference in unemployment rates of Catholics and Protestants is present for men only in the earlier, but not the later, period. Therefore, we find significant improvement for Catholic men in terms of avoidance of unemployment from 1985/1986 to 2002/2003. However, this is a recent development and, as such, we do not know if it marks a permanent shift or one which might be undermined by any economic downturn and the operation of 'last in/first out' redundancy policies. Nevertheless, it is an important development, which may be due to a combination of factors, including the improved economic environment and the operation of fair employment legislation. Our analysis points to the fact that unemployment rates may fluctuate from year to year, frequently beyond the control of individual firms (or even the government), and hence may not be effectively used as a 'golden rule' of fairness and equality. The relative position within the class structure is, in our view, a more effective indicator of social equality. Indeed, the fall in the overall level of unemployment and the reduced educational difference between the religious groups may herald a revised policy focus. Our own results suggest what that focus could be—Catholic male disadvantage as regards attaining high social class positions.

Even though we find significant improvement for Catholics in terms of avoidance of unemployment (for men) and class situations (for women) over the period covered, we still find that Catholic men are substantially disadvantaged in accessing the salariat and in their labour market earnings. This occurs in spite of the overall improved class structure in Northern Ireland and improvements in their educational attainment, now almost parallel to that achieved by Protestant men. While there may be an increase in the absolute numbers of Catholic males working in the professional and managerial posts that make up the salariat in Northern Ireland, relative to Protestant males they are still not achieving a comparable degree of success in gaining access to the salariat, and in particular to the higher grades of the salariat.

However, it is also important to take note in this context that, in spite of the disadvantages experienced by the Catholic men in the period as covered by our data, our analysis does show that progress has been made, both in accessing the salariat and in their annual earnings from the labour market. Whilst equality is still a goal to strive for, these achievements cannot be dismissed. Another important point to note here is that as our analysis in this chapter is geared towards international comparison, our selection of explanatory variables may well be different from that in other studies and, as such, our results may be different from those of other scholars concerned with similar issues.

How, then, do we explain these findings and what are the policy implications? It may be that improvement as regards exiting unemployment can be affected in a shorter time period than accessing the salariat. Furthermore, more Catholics in employment may bring to their careers the disadvantage of a labour-market history marked by earlier periods of unemployment. However, we return to the policy matter of the operation of fair employment legislation.

An examination of the fair employment legislation and monitoring procedures in Northern Ireland shows that they have been designed for redressing religious group differences in unemployment. For most of the period covered in our study, the Fair Employment Commission has been active in monitoring and advising on fair recruitment. Indeed a review by the Standing Advisory Commission on Human Rights (SACHR 1997) on the impact of the 1989 legislation even concluded that for the monitored workforce there is 'no evidence that either community is experiencing systematic discrimination at the point of selection'. Another study of the fair employment agreements adopted by employers concluded that they effected an improvement in fair employment (McCrudden, Ford and Heath 2004: 123 n. 2).

However, it is only in the aftermath of the 1998 Good Friday Agreement that the Fair Employment Monitoring Regulations (NI) 1999 extended monitoring to internal applications and appointments and more significantly for the first time has sought employer returns on promotees (for employers of 251 or more persons). Information on promotees is provided for the year 2001 and subsequent years. Given our results on access to the salariat, this would seem to be a timely development. It may also be part of the explanation for the discrepancy in our findings regarding the different levels of progress on unemployment and class attainment.

It is sometimes difficult to resist the temptation to regard Northern Ireland as a place where little ever changes. Differences between the religious groups in their relative chances of unemployment have been a long-standing and contentious feature of Northern Ireland society. However, our results uncover a significant change in that substantial progress has been made between 1985/1986 and 2002/2003 as regards religious differences in avoidance of unemployment. We also confirm the growth in the size of the Catholic middle class. Our attention is instead directed to a somewhat less publicly visible outcome, namely, access to the salariat and earnings from the labour market where Catholic male disadvantage still exists even though some progress has been observed. This disadvantage will pose a challenge to the society generally and to the fair employment body in particular. At the societal level, the young, educated, Catholic population is continuing to increase in a political environment where their expectations of equality are affirmed by the Good Friday Agreement. This is at a time when Protestants are reported as starting to have concerns about their position in the workplace (Equality Focus 2004). The success of affirmative action agreements in reducing religious segregation within firms has been noted, yet these less segregated firms will be the sites for increased competition for promotion between the religious groups. If the fair employment legislation is effective, and many commentators conclude that it is, then in time it may also have an impact on improving the access by Catholic males to the salariat.

Appendix

The Continuous Household Survey (CHS) began in 1983 and samples approximately 1% of households in Northern Ireland each year. It is designed primarily to meet the information needs of government departments in Northern Ireland by providing accurate information on housing, employment, health, education, income and social services etc. The core questions are asked each year but additional modules could change from year to year. The structure of the survey is very much the same as that of the General Household Survey (GHS) used by Cheung and Heath in this volume. We use the CHS 1985/1986 and 2002/2003 as the data for 1985 are the earliest, and that for 2003 the most recent, available from the Data Archive at the time of research for this chapter.

We have conducted careful analysis of whether the overall patterns in 1985 and 1986, and 2002 and 2003, were close enough for us to combine them. The analysis shows that, in terms of both economic activity and class position, the distributions in 1985 were very close to those in 1986, as were the distributions in 2002 and 2003. Detailed data are not presented here but are available from the authors. It is also noted here that there are many respondents in the age range whose religious affiliations are not recorded. For respondents whose own religion is missing but for whom both parents' religions are recorded (both Catholic, or both Protestant, but not otherwise), or who has only one parent with known religion, we have thus coded personal religion as appropriate for the respondent. For respondents with missing religion who do not fall into these two categories, no recoding is done. We feel that this procedure is appropriate in the Northern Ireland context.

The earnings data refer to the total annual gross earnings before deductions from all forms of paid employment. It is noted here that, in the income file for the 1985, no such variable is readily available and considerable time was spent on checking all the available information in the file in order to construct such a variable. The procedure is too complex to report here but all details are available on request. For 1986, 2002 and 2003, the variables (i1b, work, work) are measured as income bands and midpoint values were calculated from the bands. Incremental values for four out of the five last (highest) bands were calculated, the mean of which was used for the increment of the highest band where no upper limit is recorded. The constructed earnings variables were put into natural log forms to ensure stability in the modeling procedure. The predicted values from the models were then exponentiated and the figures for the Protestant salariat were set as 100%, as shown in Figures 13.2A and 13.2B. We would like to thank Professor Anthony Heath for encouraging us to conduct the analysis on earnings and for suggesting that we use the Protestant salariat's earnings as the basis upon which to make the comparison.

Table 13A.1. Multinomial logistic regression of occupational class (parameter estimates, contrasts with semi- and unskilled class).

	Men						Women					
	Routine non-manual		Petty bourgeoisie		Manual supervisor/ skilled manual		Routine non-manual		Petty bourgeoisie		Manual supervisor/ skilled manual	
Intercept	−0.27	(0.70)	**−4.91**	**(0.70)**	0.34	(0.52)	**1.46**	**(0.51)**	**−5.03**	**(1.37)**	**−2.79**	**(1.08)**
Age/10	0.34	(0.39)	**2.27**	**(0.37)**	0.32	(0.29)	−0.03	(0.29)	**1.72**	**(0.75)**	0.80	(0.61)
(Age/10)^2	−0.05	(0.05)	**−0.23**	**(0.05)**	−0.03	(0.04)	−0.01	(0.04)	**−0.18**	**(0.09)**	−0.11	(0.08)
Religion												
Catholic	**−0.74**	**(0.22)**	−0.22	(0.21)	**−0.39**	**(0.17)**	−0.11	(0.31)	−0.52	(0.42)	−0.46	(0.41)
None	0.35	(0.31)	−0.06	(0.34)	0.08	(0.27)	0.05	(0.32)	0.15	(0.63)	−0.03	(0.62)
Protestant	0.00		0.00		0.00		0.00		0.00		0.00	
Qualification												
Higher tertiary	**1.32**	**(0.43)**	0.89	(0.48)	−0.36	(0.47)	0.16	(0.32)	**1.12**	**(0.52)**	0.19	(0.61)
Lower tertiary	−0.35	(0.23)	0.27	(0.24)	0.26	(0.19)	**−1.34**	**(0.19)**	−0.39	(0.42)	−0.04	(0.38)
Higher secondary	0.00		0.00		0.00		0.00		0.00		0.00	
Lower secondary	**−0.56**	**(0.18)**	**−0.44**	**(0.19)**	**−0.68**	**(0.16)**	**−0.63**	**(0.13)**	**−0.67**	**(0.32)**	−0.03	(0.29)
Primary/none	**−1.89**	**(0.19)**	**−0.70**	**(0.19)**	**−1.40**	**(0.16)**	**−2.39**	**(0.14)**	**−1.51**	**(0.32)**	−0.43	(0.31)
Marital Status												
Married/cohabiting	0.15	(0.16)	0.01	(0.15)	0.24	(0.12)	−0.07	(0.12)	0.19	(0.31)	0.09	(0.26)
Divorced/separated	−0.10	(0.36)	−0.34	(0.29)	0.25	(0.24)	−0.05	(0.18)	−0.06	(0.43)	0.52	(0.33)
Single	0.00		0.00		0.00		0.00		0.00		0.00	
Period												
1985/1986	**0.46**	**(0.15)**	0.26	(0.14)	**0.29**	**(0.12)**	−0.04	(0.11)	**−0.56**	**(0.25)**	**−0.76**	**(0.22)**
2002/2003	0.00		0.00		0.00		0.00		0.00		0.00	
Interaction effects												
Catholic qualifications	0.06	(0.12)	**−0.21**	**(0.11)**	**−0.25**	**(0.09)**	0.22	(0.09)	−0.15	(0.21)	**0.42**	**(0.17)**
Catholics in 2002/2003	0.12	(0.26)	−0.09	(0.22)	−0.02	(0.18)	−0.07	(0.18)	−0.36	(0.45)	0.64	(0.42)
Chi-square (D.F.)	2195 (52)						2677 (52)					
N	5180						4472					

References

Anderson, J. and Shuttleworth, I. (1998), 'Sectarian demography, territoriality and political development in Northern Ireland', *Political Geography*, 17, 187–208.
Bew, P., Patterson, H., and Teague, P. (1997), *Between War and Peace* (London: Lawrence and Wishart).
Breen, R. (2003), 'Is Northern Ireland an Educational Meritocracy?', *Sociology*, 37, 657–75.
Breen, R. and Whelan, C. (1999), 'Social Mobility in Ireland: A comparative analysis'. In A. Heath, R. Breen and C. Whelan (eds.), *Ireland North and South* (Oxford: Oxford University Press), pp. 319–39.
Clark, K. and Drinkwater, S. (1998), 'Ethnicity and self-employment in Britain', *Oxford Bulletin of Economics and Statistics*, 60, 383–407.
Cormack, R. and Osborne, R. (eds.) (1983), *Religion, Education and Employment: Aspects of Equality of Opportunity in Northern Ireland* (Belfast: Appletree).
Cormack, R. J., Gallagher, A. M., and Osborne, R. D. (1993), *Fair Enough? Religion and the 1991 Population Census* (Belfast: Fair Employment Commission for Northern Ireland).
Compton, P. (1995), *Demographic Review Northern Ireland* (Belfast: Northern Ireland Economic Development Office).
Coulter, C. (1999), *Contemporary Northern Irish Society* (London: Pluto).
Equality Focus (2004), Issue 2, Autumn (Belfast: Equality Commission).
Gallagher, A. M., Osborne, R. D., and Cormack, R. J. (1995), *Fair shares? Religion and the 1991 Population Census* (Belfast: Fair Employment Commission for Northern Ireland).
Goldthorpe, J. H. (with Llewellyn, C. and Payne, C.) (1987), *Social Mobility and Class Structure in Modern Britain* (Oxford: Clarendon Press).
Granovetter, M. S. (1973), 'The strength of weak ties'. *American Journal of Sociology*, 78, 1360–80.
Granovetter, M. S. (1995), *Getting a Job: A Study of Contacts and Careers*, 2nd edn. (Cambridge, MA: The University of Chicago Press).
Gudgin, G. and Breen, B. (1996), *Evaluation of the ratio of unemployment rates as an indicator of fair employment* (Queens University of Belfast: Central Community Relations Unit).
Heath, A. F. (1981), *Social Mobility* (London: Fontana).
Heath, A. F. and McMahon, D. (1997), 'Education and occupational attainments: the impact of ethnic origins'. In V. Karn (ed.), *Ethnicity in the 1991 Census* (London: The Stationery Office), pp. 91–113.
Irwin, G. and Dunn, S. (1997), *Ethnic Minorities in Northern Ireland* (Coleraine: Centre for the Study of Conflict, University of Ulster).
Li, Y. (1997), *The Service Class: Theoretical Debate and Sociological Value*, D.Phil. Thesis, University of Oxford.
Li, Y. (2002), 'Falling off the ladder? Professional and managerial careers', *European Sociological Review*, 18, 253–70.
Li, Y. (2004), 'Samples of Anonymised Records (SARs) from the UK Censuses: A Unique Source for Social Science Research', *Sociology*, 38, 553–72.
McCrudden, C., Ford, R., and Heath, A. (2004), *The Impact of Affirmative Action*

Agreements. In B. Osborne and I. Shuttleworth (eds.), *Fair Employment in Northern Ireland: A Generation on* (Belfast: Blackstaff Press), pp. 122–51.

McLaughlin, E. (1993), 'Unemployment'. In J. Kremer and P. Montgomery (eds.), *Women's Working Lives* (Belfast: HMSO).

Miller, R. (1979), *The Occupational Mobility of Protestants and Catholics in Northern Ireland* (Belfast: Fair Employment Agency).

Miller, R. (2004), 'Social Mobility in Northern Ireland: Patterns by Religion and Gender'. In B. Osborne and I. Shuttleworth (eds.), *Fair Employment in Northern Ireland: A Generation On* (Belfast: Blackstaff Press), pp. 49–64.

Miller, R., Curry C., Cormack R., and Osborne, R. (1991), *The Labour Market Experiences of an Educational Elite: A Continuous Time Analysis of Recent Higher Education Graduates* (Coleraine: University of Ulster).

Murphy, A. with Armstrong, D. (1994), *A Picture of the Catholic and Protestant Male Unemployed* (Belfast: Central Community Relations Unit).

Northern Ireland Census 2001: Standard Tables. (2003), Norwich: TSO.

Northern Ireland Census 2001: Key Statistics. (2002), Belfast Stationery Office.

Northern Ireland Continuous Household Survey (CHS) for 1985, 1986, 2002 and 2003. <http://www.data-archive.ac.uk/findingData/ghsTitles.asp> (last accessed 14/9/05).

O'Leary, R. (1998), 'Female Workers on long-term sickness benefit in the Republic of Ireland: The relevance of their relationship with the labour market', *Social Policy and Administration*, 32, 245–62.

Osborne, R. (2004), 'Education and the Labour Market', In B. Osborne and I. Shuttleworth (eds.), *Fair Employment in Northern Ireland: A Generation On* (Belfast: Blackstaff Press), pp. 65–87.

Osborne, R. and Murray, R. (1978), *Educational Qualifications and Religious Affiliation in Northern Ireland* (Belfast: Fair Employment Agency).

Osborne, R. and Shuttleworth, I. (2003), *Potential Skills Shortages in the Northern Ireland IT and Electronic Engineering Sectors—and Inequalities in Educational Uptake* (Belfast: Department for Employment and Learning).

Osborne, R., Miller R., Cormack R., and Williamson, A. (1987), 'Graduates: Geographical Mobility and Incomes'. In R. Osborne, R. Miller and R. Cormack, (eds.), *Education and Policy in Northern Ireland* (Belfast: Policy Research Institute).

Portes, A. (1998), 'Social capital: its origins and applications in modern sociology'. *Annual Review of Sociology*, 24, 1–24.

Portes, A. and Zhou, M. (1993), 'The New Second Generation: Segmented Assimilation and Its Variants Among Post-1965 Immigrant Youth', *Annals of the American Academy of Political and Social Science*, 530, 74–96.

Power, J. and Shuttleworth, I. (1997), 'Intercensal Population Change in the Belfast Urban Area 1971–91: The Correlates of Population Increase and Decrease in a Divided Society', *International Journal of Population Geography*, 3, 91–108.

Russell, R. (2004), 'Employment Profiles of Protestants and Catholics: A Decade of Monitoring'. In B. Osborne and I. Shuttleworth (eds.), *Fair Employment in Northern Ireland: A Generation on* (Belfast: Blackstaff Press), pp. 24–48.

Savage, M., Barlow, J., Dickens, P., and Fielding, T. (1992), *Property, Bureaucracy and Culture: Middle-class Formation in Contemporary Britain* (London: Routledge).

Sheehan, M. and Tomlinson, M. (1999), *The Unequal Unemployed: Discrimination, Unemployment and State Policy in Northern Ireland* (Aldershot: Ashgate).

Smith, A. (1993), 'The Ethnic Sources of Nationalism'. In M. E. Brown (ed.), *Ethnic Conflict and International Security* (Princeton: Princeton University Press).

Smith, D. and Chambers, G. (1991), *Inequality in Northern Ireland* (Oxford: Oxford University Press).

Standing Advisory Commission on Human Rights (1997), *Employment Equality: Building for the Future* (London: HMSO).

14

The New Second Generation at the Turn of the New Century: Europeans and non-Europeans in the US labour market

SUZANNE MODEL & GENE A. FISHER

Summary. At the turn of the twenty-first century, more immigrants resided in the US than at any time in the nation's history. Whereas in the past, most immigrants came from Europe, for the last several decades Asia and Latin America have provided the bulk of the influx. This chapter finds that the addition of non-Europeans to the American melting pot has wrought some changes in the traditional 'assimilation tale'. Ceteris paribus, at the turn of the new century, first-generation non-Europeans do not do as well as their European counterparts. On the other hand, most second-generation non-European groups do as well as native-born white people. Of the three economic outcomes studied, most ethnic minorities are vulnerable to unemployment, some face hardships in occupational attainment and a few incur earnings deficits within occupational categories. In general, women fare better than men, and the second generation better than both the first and the third. The one second-generation group in difficulty is Mexicans, but there is an important gender difference here. Both second- and third-generation Mexican women encounter fewer labour-market difficulties than their male counterparts. Within genders, Black women also do better than Black men, but the disparity is less pervasive. Among third generation groups, Asians do best, Puerto Ricans rank in the middle, while the other non-white backgrounds (Mexicans, African Americans and American Indians) incur substantial penalties.

Introduction

AT THE TURN OF THE twenty-first century, more immigrants resided in the US than at any time in the nation's history: 31,108,000. Although the proportion of the foreign born in America (11.1%) is smaller than the proportion in the other two 'classic immigrant receiving countries', Canada (17.0%) and Australia (22.5%), in real numbers, no country currently houses a larger non-native born population than the United States (U.S. Bureau of the Census 2000). Nor do we expect this trend to decline any time soon. Not only are American politicians beholden to interests that favour cheap labour, but immigrants themselves now represent a formidable voting block. Thus, most efforts at 'immigration reform' have actually increased the number of persons eligible for permanent settlement.

Within this context, questions regarding the socio-economic assimilation of immigrants and their children are especially timely. Some argue that America's politicians are creating a new, dependent population that is undermining the nation's prosperity (Borjas 1999). This assessment is often linked to the source of the immigration. Whereas in the past, most immigrants came from Europe, for the last several decades Africa, Asia, and especially Latin America have provided the bulk of the influx. This situation is a consequence of the 1965 Hart–Celler Act, which required that immigration officials cease favouring applicants from north-western Europe. Since the number of north-western Europeans eager to immigrate to America was far fewer than the number of Latin Americans, Asians and Africans, the consequences of the 1965 Act were enormous (Heer 1996).

To be sure, the US is not the only nation with large numbers of immigrants from less-developed countries (LDCs). This is a trend in Canada and Australia, as well as in Western Europe. But in most of these countries, labour-market demand has played a key role in the formulation of immigration policy, whereas in the US pride of place has gone to humanitarian considerations such as family reunion, political asylum, and the diversification of source countries. The Hart–Celler act introduced a 'preference system' which grants visas to more immigrants on familial than on occupational grounds. Furthermore, immediate relatives of US citizens—spouses, unmarried minor children and parents—can settle 'at will'; that is, they are exempt from limitations. In 1997, 40.4% of immigrants to the US fell in this category (U.S. Immigration and Naturalization Service 1999). America's willingness to accept very large numbers of newcomers, irrespective of their employment prospects is one of several ways in which the US differs from other host societies.

Another unusual aspect of US immigration is its large undocumented component. Obviously, exact numbers are unavailable. Demographer Robert Warren offers the figure of 3.379 million for October 1992—about 16% of the US foreign born population as estimated for that year (U.S. Immigration and Naturalization Service 1999). To be sure, illegal flows have increased everywhere, but the US is the only highly industrialised country to share a lengthy land-border with an LDC. This is relevant because about 54% of the 1996 undocumented population was born in Mexico (U.S. Immigration and Naturalization Service 1999). Other major sources included El Salvador, Guatemala, Canada, Poland and the Philippines (Heer 1996). As might be expected, research on the characteristics of the undocumented indicates that they have lower human capital—education and language skills, for instance—than documented immigrants do.

Another way in which the US differs from some immigrant-receiving countries is in the large number of migrants it receives from its 'modern colony', Puerto Rico. The term 'modern colony' refers to former colonies whose residents now hold metropolitan citizenship, enjoy unencumbered access to the motherland, 'and receive large transfers in the form of welfare, loans or credits' (Grosfoguel 1997). Other examples of 'modern colonies' are Martinique and Aruba. Shortly after the Second World War, meaningful numbers of Puerto Ricans began arriving on the mainland. About one-fifth to one-quarter of persons born in 'modern colonies' usually live in their respective metropoles. In the case of Puerto Rico, the figure is 25.4%. If mainland-born Puerto Ricans are added to the tally, then nearly half the world's Puerto Ricans live in 'the States'. Yet, Puerto Rico was never as thoroughly colonised as Martinique or Aruba. For instance, English never successfully replaced Spanish in Puerto Rico's schools (Spring 1997). This means that 'assimilation' is more difficult for Puerto Ricans than for other 'modern colonial' migrants.

Of course, Puerto Ricans are not the only non-Europeans with a relatively long tenure in the U.S. Longest resident are indigenous native Americans and those of Mexican origin whose forebears lived in the Southwest before its conquest. Less well recognised, the ancestors of most African Americans arrived before 1808, when the importation of slaves became illegal. By the mid-1860s, Chinese labourers began to arrive, followed a few decades later by residents of Mexico, Japan, and, after the First World War, of the British West Indies. Thus, non-Europeans have a long history in America, though they have usually fared less well than their European counterparts (Chan 1990). In the early 1960s, thanks to the Civil Rights movement, the US government initiated an affirmative action program to facilitate minority access to schools and jobs. Initially only individuals of African origin were targeted, but eligibility was later extended to women, Native Americans and Hispanics. Assessments of the policy, however, generally conclude that the major beneficiaries have been African Americans (Smith and Welch 1994). More recently, federal support has declined. Yet, affirmative action may still send a message to American employers about the importance of treating non-Europeans and women fairly.

To recapitulate, the US differs in a number of ways from the other host societies included in this volume. Every year about a million newcomers are legally admitted, most irrespective of their educational or occupational qualifications. Several thousand more enter annually without benefit of papers. More than a quarter of all entrants come from Mexico, the Hispanic Caribbean, or Central America. Finally, non-European groups have a longer history in the US than most observers recognise.

The research question

This chapter utilises data from four recent US Current Population Surveys to examine the labour-market outcomes of first-, second- and 'third- and later-generation' Americans (the latter hereafter called simply 'third-generation' Americans). Our substantive focus is the second generation, defined here as native-born persons with two foreign-born parents or foreign-born persons who arrived in the US at or under the age of six. We choose this cut-off because persons arriving at or under six complete all of their education in their new home and rarely have an accent (Lippi-Green 1997). The economic attainment of the second generation has greater theoretical and political significance than the attainment of the first because the foreign-born face greater problems than their children do. Immigrants' problems may include human capital shortfalls, such as an accent, foreign educational credentials and foreign work experience, as well as psychological handicaps, like evaluating their wages relative to wages in the sending society. To be sure, the children of immigrants also face difficulties. Their parents may not speak English; they may have been raised in segregated neighbourhoods; members of the dominant group may denigrate their cultural or religious heritage. Still, the shortfalls of the second generation should be smaller than the first.

To date, research is scant on the economic attainment of America's 'new second generation', as the children of the post-1965 immigrants are now called (Card *et al.* 1999; Farley and Alba 2002). This is partly because the vast majority are too young to have much exposure to the labour market, and partly because few data sets contain enough cases to study the children of immigrants by national origin. This is a problem because labour-market outcomes vary significantly by parents' nativity and 1970 was the last year in which the US Census inquired about parents' birthplace. Thus, scholarship on the second generation must rely on the few surveys that contain this question. The largest of these is the Current Population Survey, but it only supports the study of the bigger national origin groups. This includes some substantively interesting groups, for instance, Mexicans and Filipinos, but excludes others, such as the children of persons born in El Salvador or India.

In all, we are able to identify twelve second-generation national origin groups, two of which are composites. For comparative purposes we also report on the economic attainment of their first-generation counterparts and of five third-generation groups. Members of these groups are compared, separately by generation and gender, to native-born non-Hispanic White people of native born parentage, hereafter called native White people. We begin with some descriptive statistics: group size, educational qualifications, etc. Then, we offer a multivariate analysis of three dependent variables: unemployment, occupational class, and logged hourly earnings. In an effort better to understand the sources of second-generation shortfalls, we duplicate the strategy of other inquiries in this volume by adding some interactions to our models.

Theoretical expectations

With respect to the economic attainment of America's second generation, scholars are divided. There are optimists, pessimists and segmentationists (Alba and Nee 2003; Borjas 1999; Portes and Rumbaut 2001). Moreover, researchers don't always use the same measures; for instance, some emphasise gross outcomes, others make adjustments for individual characteristics, some focus on labour-force participation, some on earnings, and so on (Landale *et al.* 1998).

As one might expect, pessimists anticipate that most second-generation backgrounds will fare poorly on most dependent variables. There are several rationales for this expectation. The most simplistic is that some non-European immigrants are so physically and culturally different from 'mainstream Americans' that they will never blend in. For instance, journalist Peter Brimelow writes that today's 'immigrants come from completely different, and arguably incompatible, cultural traditions' (1995: 56). There are two sides to this coin. One is that some non-European cultures produce individuals with undesirable traits; for instance, a culture of poverty or low intelligence; the other is that native white employers have an (unfounded) low opinion of non-Europeans. Either way, cultural disparities are assumed to translate into difficulties in the labour market.

A more sophisticated pessimism comes from economist George Borjas (1994, 1999) who claims that residents of less-developed countries who settle in more-developed countries are 'negatively selected'. By this he means that they are less talented and diligent than those who stay at home. According to Borjas, immigrants are positively selected if the income distribution in their homelands is less unequal than the income distribution at destination and negatively selected if the income distribution in their homelands is more unequal than the income distribution at destination. Perceptive, talented, diligent residents of LDCs remain at home because their scarce skills offer them relatively high rewards. Their less-able counterparts relocate to first-world countries in order to profit from those nations' more equitable income distributions and more generous welfare benefits. The implication of this logic is that, in the absence of skill requirements for admission, most immigrants from the Third World to the First World are negatively selected. Furthermore, examination of the economic success of earlier waves of immigrants to America leads him to conclude that gaps between natives and newcomers do not soon disappear. He finds that groups that incur deficits relative to native-born White Americans continue to register shortfalls not only into the second but often into the third generation. What's more, these deficits are substantially larger today than in the past, a discovery that impels Borjas to urge the US to restrict immigration.

As for the optimists, they begin by noting that, a century ago, most Anglos considered several European ethnics as culturally and racially distinct. Over time, however, members of these groups became 'White or Euro-Americans'. Thus, they expect most non-European groups to travel the same road. In other words, the optimists are assimilationists. While they concede the salience of the black–white distinction in social life, the optimists note that intermarriage is already eroding the boundaries between Hispanics and 'Whites' and between Asians and 'Whites'.

In a different vein, they claim that the educational attainment of Third World migrants is bipolar. Some are very skilled; some are not. However, with higher education increasingly accessible to all, the optimists predict that most second-generation Americans will get the schooling they need to compete successfully in an increasingly credential-conscious post-industrial economy. Taken together, these trends lead optimists to conclude that second-generation Hispanics and Asians are likely to reach economic parity with Whites. However, with respect to the attainment of second and later generation black immigrants, even the optimists are less sanguine because of the stigma that black skin has traditionally carried in America (Alba and Nee 2003; Perlmann and Waldinger 1997).

Finally, segmentationists distinguish three potential trajectories, or segments, for the children of immigrants: two ultimately favourable, one not (Portes and Zhou 1993). First, they concur with optimists that some immigrants enter with strong skills. Most of the children of these 'human capital' migrants are expected to remain in school long enough to qualify for good jobs. But they dispute the contention that weak skills necessarily constrain immigrants to low paying jobs or welfare subsidies. Some immigrant groups have constructed an alternative to that pessimistic trajectory: a dynamic ethnic economy. Through self-employment or working for a co-ethnic, members of entrepreneurial groups secure the economic advantages of the mainstream economy. Their children are likely either to carry on the family business or to pursue a professional career. Yet, segmentationists concur with pessimists that a subset of immigrant offspring are at risk for faring poorly. The subset consists of non-white second-generation youth whose pan-ethnic acquaintances have responded to white racism with an 'adversarial subculture' (Ogbu 1978). The term 'pan-ethnic' refers to umbrella-like categories, such as African American, Asian American or Latino (Espiritu 1992). The term 'adversarial subculture' refers to adaptations that challenge the dominant ideology that success in school promotes success in the labour market. According to segmentationists, second-generation youth who live amongst adversarially oriented co-pan-ethnics—in particular, African Americans, Mexicans and Puerto Ricans—will face strong peer pressure to reject mainstream American values in favour of 'the code of the street' (Anderson 1990). Yielding to such pressures means dropping out of school in favour of the informal economy of crime, hustling, out-of-wedlock parenthood and government subsidies.

Previous empirical findings

As explained earlier, if the 'new second generation' is defined as persons born in the last third of the twentieth century, several studies of educational attainment have appeared but relatively few have focused on labour-market outcomes. But if the term refers to earlier cohorts, there are countless studies. A few have drawn upon survey research but most have utilised the US Census, which, prior to 1980, included questions about parents' birthplace (Alba *et al.* 2001; Hirschman and Kraly 1990; Laumann 1973; Levene and Rhodes 1981).

A few studies focused only on the effect of generation, irrespective of national origin. These inquiries revealed that the second generation has higher net earnings than the first or the third. The authors of these studies hypothesise that the first generation initially have difficulty translating their human capital into labour-market rewards; hence, for the first decade or more after their arrival, the foreign-born register a shortfall relative to native Whites (Chiswick 1979). The third and later generations, on the other hand, tend to merge into the mainstream. Perhaps the causal process is assimilation; perhaps it is 'regression toward the mean'. In any event, as a group, children of immigrants tend to out-earn their parents or their own children (Carliner 1980; Chiswick 1977). These observations make study of the second generation particularly intriguing.

However, studies that disaggregate generation by parents' birthplace reveal a more nuanced picture. The children of most European immigrant groups reported gross and net occupational status and earnings quite similar to native White people. A few backgrounds, Jews for instance, had more favourable outcomes; in some studies northern European groups did too. Occasionally Italians and Slavs had less favourable outcomes, but these shortfalls diminished as the century progressed. The story for non-Europeans was different. Chinese and Japanese men usually registered a gross occupational or earnings advantage which disappeared with the addition of controls. Their greater educational attainment and region of residence were the main reasons; controlling for these, East Asian men fared about as well as native White people. Filipinos, Mexicans and Puerto Ricans, on the other hand, consistently registered a gross occupational and earnings deficit which rarely disappeared with the addition of controls. Finally, second-generation West Indian blacks had consistently lower outcomes than native White people, though on occupation and earnings they occasionally outperformed African Americans (Chiswick

1977, 1983; Featherman and Hauser 1978; Hirschman and Kraly 1990; Model 1995).

Taken together, these findings on earlier cohorts are closer to the expectations of segmentationists than optimists or pessimists. Evidently some—but not all—Third World groups experience enduring deficits. However, we are not persuaded that the source of those deficits is assimilation to the norms of a native born pan-co-ethnic underclass. During the decade immediately prior to the 1970 census, the social problems in black and Latino American neighbourhoods were not nearly as severe as they later became. Thus, other sources of difficulty merit consideration. Perhaps these immigrants bring problematic cultural adaptations with them; perhaps they are subject to greater labour-market discrimination than other immigrant groups; perhaps they come from less prosperous family backgrounds (Nee and Sanders 2001; Wilson 1987). Interestingly, on at least one survey research study, US employers ranked Asian workers above native Whites (Lim 1999). Drawing on this and other findings by previous scholars, we hypothesise that second-generation Europeans and Asians will incur few if any gross or net labour-market deficits, while immigrants from Latin America, Africa, the Philippines and the Caribbean will have poorer outcomes than native White people.

Data and methods

The data for this survey are taken from four waves of the U.S. March Current Population Survey (CPS). National origin groups are identified by a combination of replies to questions about birthplace, parents' birthplace, race and Hispanic descent. The first generation consists of the foreign-born, save those who arrived in the United States at or under the age of six. Additionally, both parents of a first-generation person and the person him- or herself had to report the same country of origin. The second generation consists of native-born persons, both of whose parents were born in the same foreign country. Also included in the second generation are foreign-born persons who arrived in the United States at or before the age of six and who had two foreign-born parents born in the same country. The third generation consists of all native-born persons with native-born parents who, on the basis of their replies to questions on race and Hispanic descent, were either non-white, Hispanic or both. These questions support the creation of five third-generation groups: Mexicans,

Puerto Ricans, Blacks, Asians or Pacific Islanders and American Indians or Aleutian Eskimos.

In general, within each generation, a separate dummy was created for any national origin group for which there were 100 or more second-generation persons in the male or female sample. However, due to a shortage of cases, we created two composite groups: East Asians and Blacks. The East Asians come from the following origins: Korea, China, Hong Kong, Taiwan and Japan. Blacks include non-Hispanic persons who identified on race as black, with parents born in any country outside the United States; however, most of these Blacks have roots in the British Caribbean or Haiti. The remaining backgrounds large enough to merit inclusion are Canadians, Irish, Germans, Italians, Poles, Filipinos, Cubans, Dominicans, Mexicans, and, finally, Puerto Ricans—who are, of course, citizens of the US.

The multivariate portion of the analysis predicts three labour-market outcomes: unemployment, occupational class and hourly earnings. The unemployed are defined as persons currently seeking and available for work (using the International Labour Organization (ILO) definition). In coding this variable, we follow the convention established for this volume, which is to assign a 0 to the unemployed and a 1 to those with jobs. Individuals not in the labour force are missing on this variable. Occupational class is operationalised following the Shavit and Müller (1998) modification of Erickson and Goldthorpe's (1992) class schema. The eleven occupational classes are combined into five. The combined occupational classes are (1) the salariat (I and II), (2) routine non-manual (IIIa), (3) the petty bourgeoisie (IV), (4) skilled manual (V and VI) and (5) semi and unskilled manual (IIIb and VII). Translation of US occupational codings to the occupational classes follows Cheng (1994). Hourly earnings are calculated by dividing earned income by the product of hours worked per week and the number of weeks worked in the past year. Persons with zero hours or negative earnings were dropped from the analysis of hourly earnings. Information on the selection and coding of the independent variables appears in the Technical Appendix.

Results

Paralleling other chapters in this volume, we begin with a descriptive analysis. It provides estimates of the three generations by national origin, education, economic activity, and occupational status. Although sample Ns are shown in the tables, percentages refer to the population, not the sample. The CPS is a multi-stage cluster sample. Accordingly, estimations of population percentages are calculated from data weighted by the probability of sample selection.

Table 14.1 shows the relative size of the population by national origin and generation. Observe that our benchmark group, native born non-Hispanic Whites of native-born parents (hereafter called native White people) comprise nearly two-thirds (64.8%) of persons aged 18 to 59. Because the first two generations of East Asians and Blacks are 'composite groups', they contain persons born in different locales. This is one reason why they are relatively large. Other important trends include that, within the first and second generations, Mexicans are the largest group; within the third generation, Blacks (e.g., African Americans) are largest.

Tables 14.2A and 14.2B show how the national origin and generation groups differ in terms of educational attainment. The first and penultimate columns are the most intriguing. Table 14.2A presents these numbers for

Table 14.1. US population (aged 18–59), by origin and generation (percentage of total population[a]).

	First generation	Second generation	Third generation	All
Native born, non-Hispanic				
Whites	0.0	0.0	64.85	64.85
Canadian	0.15	0.11	—	0.26
German	0.12	0.11	—	0.23
Irish	0.06	0.07	—	0.13
Italian	0.10	0.21	—	0.31
Polish	0.16	0.07	—	0.23
Black	0.86	0.18	11.03	12.07
Filipino	0.52	0.13	—	0.65
East Asian	0.92	0.17	0.34	1.43
Puerto Rican	0.38	0.38	0.12	0.88
Mexican	3.34	0.97	1.99	6.30
Cuban	0.26	0.11	—	0.38
Dominican	0.22	0.05	—	0.28
American Indian	—	—	0.72	0.72
All other	5.21	2.12	3.95	11.28
Sample N	43,290	16,397	246,921	306,608

[a] Percentages are weighted to provide population estimates.
[b] In the first and second generations, 'East Asian' refers to persons who have known roots in East Asia. In the third generation, 'East Asian' denotes only people who identify themselves in the survey as 'Asian'.

men. Most Hispanic groups are educationally deprived. The Mexican-born have the lowest educational qualifications: 56.8% have completed no more than primary school. Also registering minimal education are a goodly proportion of men born in the Dominican Republic (33.6%) and Puerto Rico (29.4%). To be sure, these deficits are smaller for second- and third-generation Hispanics. Nevertheless Hispanics stand out as educationally disadvantaged. For instance, 8.7% of third-generation Mexicans and 7.8% of third-generation Puerto Ricans have no more than primary school, compared to 3.1% of native White men. However, at the other end of the scale, many national origin/generation groups have higher proportions with a university degree or more than native White males (27.2%) do. Interestingly, both first-generation East Asians (53.0%) and first-generation Filipinos (40.0%) have higher educations than their second-generation counterparts. We attribute this to the relatively young age of the second generation. Indeed, when interpreting these numbers it is important to keep in mind that many young adults are still in school— a fact that Tables 14.3A and 14.3B will better elucidate. Other backgrounds that Table 14.2A reveals to be highly educated include first- and second-generation Germans, second-generation Poles, and first- and second-generation Irish. Finally, the very strong educational outcomes of all generations of Asians are exceptional.

The women's results (Table 14.2B) generally parallel those of their male counterparts. With respect to primary school or less, with only a few exceptions, men are more likely than women to have very limited educations. Italians constitute one such exception: 26.2% of Italian women have completed only primary school or less, versus 16.0% of Italian men. As for college degrees or more, controlling for national origin/generation, men are generally more likely to be highly educated than women. But there are exceptions. For instance, within the first generation, Filipino women have higher proportions of college graduates (49.0%) than first generation Filipino men (40.0%). Over half (50.1%) of second-generation East Asian women have at least a bachelor's degree, compared to 42.5% of second-generation East Asian men. Finally, women outrank men on college degrees by at least 5% among second-generation Poles and second-generation Blacks.

Tables 14.3A and 14.3B report how group members spend most of their time: in economic activities, as homemakers or as students. The economically active include both the employed and those actively seeking jobs. The 'student' category pertains only to those in full-time study. Table 14.3A reports the men's results. Looking first at the economically active,

Table 14.2A. Highest educational qualification, by ancestry and generation: Men (row percentages).

	Primary or none	Lower secondary	Higher secondary	Lower tertiary	Higher tertiary	N
Native-born, non-Hispanic white	3.1	7.3	33.2	29.1	27.2	94,886
First generation						
Canadian	3.8	5.9	26.3	25.1	39.0	206
German	4.7	5.8	14.8	19.2	55.5	110
Irish	3.9	9.0	27.9	19.0	38.5	81
Italian	16.0	3.5	40.7	17.1	22.6	155
Polish	5.1	7.9	36.4	24.8	25.9	206
Black	10.0	9.4	28.7	26.5	25.4	1,091
Filipino	3.5	3.7	17.7	35.2	40.0	668
East Asian	6.0	4.5	18.5	18.1	53.0	1,152
Puerto Rican	29.4	16.4	27.1	17.3	9.8	774
Mexican	56.8	11.9	19.6	8.0	3.7	7,306
Cuban	19.4	9.1	31.3	23.4	16.8	560
Dominican	33.6	17.3	29.1	14.6	5.4	419
Second generation						
Canadian	4.1	1.8	30.6	31.5	32.0	202
German	0.9	1.7	23.7	26.5	47.2	157
Irish	0.9	3.6	20.5	37.3	37.7	114
Italian	1.5	3.8	33.9	29.0	31.8	327
Polish	0.6	5.5	25.3	28.4	40.2	106
Black	1.5	12.2	26.4	36.2	23.7	202
Filipino	0.0	6.6	14.8	53.7	24.9	197
East Asian	0.0	6.6	11.1	39.9	42.5	222
Puerto Rican	10.3	20.6	36.1	24.0	9.0	794
Mexican	13.1	20.8	32.1	27.5	6.6	1,869
Cuban	2.1	7.4	31.7	27.1	31.7	254
Dominican	6.6	27.8	26.0	29.3	10.3	116
Third generation						
Black	5.5	14.8	41.4	27.0	11.4	10,792
Asian	1.3	6.3	11.1	39.9	42.5	727
Puerto Rican	7.8	12.2	33.3	32.1	14.7	261
Mexican	8.7	16.2	37.3	27.5	10.3	3,810
American Indian	6.8	16.2	38.9	27.9	10.2	1,615

Note: percentages are weighted to provide population estimates.

several groups have higher rates of economic activity than the 88.9% reported by native White men. Among first-generation groups, the Irish (94.0%) and the Poles (94.1%) stand out; among the second generation, Canadians (93.7%) and Germans (93.4%) are the highest ranking. Interestingly, all third-generation groups have lower rates of economic activity than men with US national origins. But the lowest rates of all occur within two second-generation groups: Blacks (64.0%) and Dominicans (65.4%).

However, because Americans attend school for a relatively long time, the 'other inactive' column in Table 14.3A is a very important complement to the economic activity column. Because employment and education are 'legitimate' undertakings for prime age men, the small proportions in the 'looking after home' column are normative but large proportions

Table 14.2B. Highest educational qualification, by ancestry and generation: Women (row percentages).

	Primary or none	Lower secondary	Higher secondary	Lower tertiary	Higher tertiary	N
Native-born, non-Hispanic white	2.5	6.1	33.9	31.8	25.7	98,593
First generation						
Canadian	3.1	5.4	24.5	30.6	36.4	260
German	2.6	2.0	41.4	29.1	24.9	261
Irish	3.0	6.0	32.6	23.4	35.0	88
Italian	26.2	6.0	38.6	17.7	11.5	138
Polish	4.7	7.1	34.8	28.7	24.7	252
Black	9.8	10.3	32.0	27.7	20.2	1,093
Filipino	5.5	3.5	17.4	24.7	49.0	924
East Asian	7.7	3.6	27.1	19.5	42.2	1,441
Puerto Rican	28.4	12.8	29.4	19.4	10.0	1,046
Mexican	58.3	10.6	19.1	8.4	3.7	6,149
Cuban	17.6	7.0	35.8	20.5	19.2	559
Dominican	32.6	15.6	23.8	20.8	7.2	719
Second generation						
Canadian	1.0	2.9	33.8	38.0	24.3	187
German	1.2	3.6	26.8	32.6	35.8	159
Irish	2.8	5.3	25.9	26.5	39.5	110
Italian	2.3	4.0	43.2	21.2	29.3	291
Polish	0.6	5.7	25.0	21.0	47.8	92
Black	0.6	11.6	18.4	40.7	28.9	208
Filipino	0.0	5.9	13.5	54.9	25.8	187
East Asian	0.7	3.5	10.0	35.7	50.1	232
Puerto Rican	9.1	18.9	32.0	29.8	10.3	1,058
Mexican	13.0	17.8	31.9	30.2	7.1	2,028
Cuban	2.7	7.0	26.1	37.2	27.0	272
Dominican	3.8	25.8	20.9	36.5	13.0	121
Third generation						
Black	3.8	14.3	36.4	32.0	13.4	14,786
Asian	0.7	4.0	25.6	34.6	35.1	814
Puerto Rican	6.8	18.1	30.4	26.6	18.2	323
Mexican	10.6	14.9	36.7	28.7	9.1	4,405
American Indian	8.1	14.0	36.5	32.5	9.0	1,814

Note: percentages are weighted to provide population estimates.

Table 14.3A. Economic activity, by ancestry and generation: Men (row percentages).

	Economically active	Other inactive	Looking after home	Full-time student	N
Native-born, non-Hispanic white	88.9	8.0	0.3	2.8	91,234
First generation					
Canadian	88.0	8.4	1.0	2.7	198
German	85.0	9.8	1.8	3.5	108
Irish	94.0	4.8	0.0	1.2	79
Italian	87.1	11.1	0.0	1.8	153
Polish	94.1	3.6	0.4	1.9	196
Black	83.4	11.3	1.2	4.1	1,024
Filipino	92.0	5.7	1.1	1.3	620
East Asian	82.7	11.7	0.4	5.3	1,120
Puerto Rican	78.1	21.1	0.4	0.4	730
Mexican	91.6	6.8	0.6	1.1	7,011
Cuban	86.8	11.7	0.3	1.2	533
Dominican	78.4	17.6	1.5	2.6	395
Second generation					
Canadian	93.7	4.3	1.2	0.7	200
German	93.4	6.6	0.0	0.0	151
Irish	87.4	10.1	0.9	1.5	110
Italian	87.5	8.1	0.3	4.1	319
Polish	88.2	5.8	0.9	5.0	104
Black	64.0	15.4	0.6	20.0	187
Filipino	80.8	6.3	1.1	11.8	183
East Asian	70.4	4.0	0.9	24.7	216
Puerto Rican	73.7	21.9	1.0	3.3	718
Mexican	84.3	9.4	0.1	6.2	1,731
Cuban	87.6	5.5	0.0	6.9	247
Dominican	65.4	15.7	0.0	18.9	105
Third generation					
Black	75.5	19.1	1.0	4.4	9,877
Asian	86.3	8.1	0.9	24.7	693
Puerto Rican	75.3	13.9	1.7	9.1	240
Mexican	86.6	10.0	0.5	2.9	3,580
American Indian	76.3	19.2	1.2	3.3	1,476

Note: percentages are weighted to provide population estimates.

in the 'other inactive' column are potentially worrisome. Among native White men, 8.0% are economically inactive. Groups with substantially higher percentages include: in the first generation, Puerto Ricans (21.1%) and Dominicans (17.6%); in the second generation, Blacks (15.4%), Puerto Ricans (21.9%) and Dominicans (15.7%); and in the third generation, Blacks (19.1%) and American Indians (19.2%). Interestingly, third-generation Puerto Rican men have fewer economically inactive men (13.9%) than their more recently arrived compatriots. The rates of

Table 14.3B. Economic activity, by ancestry and generation: Women (row percentages).

	Economically active	Other inactive	Looking after home	Full-time student	N
Native-born, non-Hispanic white	76.3	10.9	10.5	2.4	96,313
First generation					
Canadian	70.5	10.5	18.4	0.7	254
German	63.9	18.5	17.2	0.4	254
Irish	79.8	8.8	11.3	0.0	88
Italian	59.5	17.0	22.1	1.4	134
Polish	66.5	12.3	17.0	4.3	245
Black	72.7	12.3	11.1	3.9	1,023
Filipino	82.3	8.2	8.8	0.7	908
East Asian	61.8	13.6	20.0	4.5	1,417
Puerto Rican	49.8	25.8	23.5	1.0	1,004
Mexican	48.1	13.3	37.7	0.9	5,890
Cuban	67.2	16.2	16.2	0.4	543
Dominican	53.6	20.0	24.7	1.7	657
Second generation					
Canadian	74.1	14.2	11.3	0.4	182
German	78.7	6.0	14.1	1.2	155
Irish	78.4	14.2	7.4	0.0	107
Italian	73.9	10.6	14.6	0.9	286
Polish	71.5	9.0	14.0	5.5	89
Black	74.5	8.9	4.6	12.0	191
Filipino	80.0	5.9	3.6	10.5	181
East Asian	66.1	7.1	9.1	17.7	230
Puerto Rican	64.7	13.7	17.8	3.8	1,002
Mexican	65.6	11.9	15.2	7.3	1,906
Cuban	78.4	6.9	7.0	7.7	265
Dominican	59.9	11.4	5.9	22.8	112
Third generation					
Black	72.0	16.5	7.8	3.7	13,913
Asian	76.7	12.1	6.8	4.4	794
Puerto Rican	63.3	14.7	15.2	6.9	311
Mexican	70.2	13.3	13.7	2.9	4,220
American Indian	64.7	20.2	11.2	3.9	1,702

Note: percentages are weighted to provide population estimates.

inactivity among second-generation Blacks, Puerto Ricans and Dominicans are consonant with the predictions of 'segmentation theory', but those of second-generation Mexicans are not.

Table 14.3B reports the analogous outcomes for women. Beginning with economic activity, the high rate among native White women (76.3%) is striking. The only groups that surpass this figure are first- and second-generation Irish, first- and second-generation Filipinos and second-generation Cubans. These Cubans excepted, Hispanic females tend to have relatively low rates of economic activity; for instance, first-generation Mexicans and first-generation Puerto Ricans both have rates slightly below 50%. Not surprisingly, the second generation exhibits rates roughly 15% higher. However, the Dominican pattern is quite different. Just over half (53.6%) of the first generation are economically active and only slightly more of the second generation (59.9%). Attention to the 'student' column reveals the reason for the small generational increment: 22.8% of Dominican women are full-time students—the highest proportion of any female group. Table 14.3B also provides an explanation for the finding in Table 14.2B that higher percentages of second-generation East Asian and second-generation Black women hold at least a college degree than do their male compatriots. The reason is that, in both groups, many more men than women are currently full-time students. Therefore, at later ages, higher proportions of males than females are likely to hold at least a college degree.

The 'looking after home' category in Table 14.3B is also informative because this activity has declining legitimacy among native White women (10.5%) but remains normative in some cultural traditions. Note that the highest proportion of women so engaged are first-generation Mexicans (37.7%), followed by first-generation Puerto Ricans (23.5%) and first-generation Italians (22.1%). These rates decline across generations, with the biggest drop occurring between the first and second generations. A glance at the 'other inactive' column conveys the proportions of women not engaged in any 'legitimate' undertaking. While 10.9% of native White women fit this description, groups with substantially higher percentages include first-generation Puerto Ricans (25.8%), first-generation Dominicans (20.0%) and American Indians (20.2%).

Our last descriptive efforts appear in Tables 14.4A and 14.4B, which present the four categories we use to operationalise occupational class as well the percentages that are unemployed. Again, in the interest of space, we focus on the extremes. Looking first at men (Table 14.4A), we see that, with respect to the salariat (professionals and managers), the following first-generation groups have higher proportions than native White men (34.2%): Germans (53.0%), Irish (43.6%), Canadians (44.9%) and East Asians (46.3%). At the same time, several groups with modest showings in the first generation surpass the benchmark group in the second: Poles (50.7%), Filipinos (41.3%), Cubans (39.8%), and Italians (39.0%). Also noteworthy is the relatively poor showing of all third-generation groups; only Asians surpass native White men.

At the other end of the scale is joblessness. Interestingly, although the overall male unemployment rate was low during the years of our study (native White males 3.1%), most of the groups in Table 14.4A have rates higher than this benchmark. Some are substantially higher; for example, in the first generation, Dominicans (7.7%), Blacks (6.2%), Cubans (5.9%) and Filipinos (5.2%); in the second, Dominicans (13.8%), Blacks (11.9%), Puerto Ricans (11.1%). In the third, only Asians (5.0%) have a rate less than twice that of the benchmark group.

Table 14.4B reports the same outcomes for women. As some other scholars have found, the percentage of women in the salariat is higher

Table 14.4A. Current occupation, by ancestry and generation: Men (row percentages).

	Salariat	Routine non-manual	Petty bourgeoisie	Skilled manual	Semi- and unskilled manual	Unemployed	N
Native-born, non-Hispanic white	34.2	8.5	11.4	20.3	22.6	3.1	84,780
First generation							
Canadian	44.9	5.7	17.6	16.6	12.6	2.6	182
German	53.0	3.5	14.7	16.6	9.7	2.5	97
Irish	43.6	2.7	13.6	17.7	20.6	1.8	75
Italian	23.6	3.5	28.1	22.7	20.4	1.7	136
Polish	20.6	3.9	14.0	25.9	30.6	5.0	194
Black	23.7	9.2	5.9	17.8	37.1	6.2	925
Filipino	30.3	9.8	5.0	14.1	35.7	5.2	599
East Asian	46.5	6.8	17.3	12.7	13.8	3.0	959
Puerto Rican	14.7	6.2	2.7	22.7	48.8	4.9	601
Mexican	4.1	2.4	4.9	28.7	55.3	4.6	6,763
Cuban	17.2	9.7	15.0	20.2	32.1	5.9	499
Dominican	9.3	8.1	9.0	13.4	52.6	7.7	344
Second generation							
Canadian	40.7	7.1	11.5	19.2	20.8	0.6	188
German	42.9	11.2	14.2	14.1	13.9	3.7	145
Irish	43.7	5.3	9.1	23.9	14.0	4.1	101
Italian	39.0	6.8	15.1	17.6	18.5	3.2	291
Polish	50.7	7.1	5.2	16.8	18.3	1.9	95
Black	28.0	19.3	3.1	11.4	26.3	11.9	137
Filipino	41.3	21.4	4.0	8.2	19.7	5.4	157
East Asian	49.3	15.1	7.3	2.6	23.6	2.2	163
Puerto Rican	21.5	7.2	3.9	22.6	33.7	11.1	615
Mexican	16.2	10.8	4.0	21.0	39.8	8.3	1,600
Cuban	39.8	13.4	8.2	14.4	21.0	3.3	228
Dominican	24.0	15.6	1.1	12.0	33.5	13.8	77
Third generation							
Black	18.6	8.1	4.3	19.6	40.0	9.4	8,384
Asian	39.5	9.9	10.6	16.3	18.8	5.0	635
Puerto Rican	28.0	14.6	6.0	17.7	23.4	10.3	205
Mexican	20.5	8.6	5.1	24.0	35.4	6.6	3,300
American Indian	20.0	5.2	7.0	26.4	33.3	8.1	1,234

Note: percentages are weighted to provide population estimates.

Table 14.4B. Current occupation, by ancestry and generation: Women (row percentages).

	Salariat	Routine non-manual	Petty bourgeoisie	Skilled manual	Semi- and unskilled manual	Unemployed	N
Native-born, non-Hispanic whites	39.6	26.3	7.1	4.6	19.5	2.9	77,107
First generation							
Canadian	50.9	17.3	7.3	2.9	17.8	3.8	190
German	39.5	16.2	12.0	5.9	23.6	2.9	176
Irish	48.1	15.8	11.3	17.9	23.0	0.0	68
Italian	23.1	23.9	13.5	14.6	19.5	5.4	88
Polish	22.6	19.6	9.6	5.2	38.9	4.1	167
Black	24.0	17.9	3.7	4.1	42.1	8.2	822
Filipino	41.2	19.1	2.9	4.3	30.8	1.8	762
East Asian	35.8	14.0	13.9	6.2	27.5	2.7	900
Puerto Rican	20.0	19.9	2.7	7.1	43.5	6.8	544
Mexican	6.3	9.7	4.1	11.1	60.4	8.5	3,119
Cuban	25.4	23.0	6.6	8.2	32.1	4.6	387
Dominican	10.7	17.9	3.9	5.2	51.5	10.9	405
Second generation							
Canadian	51.8	21.7	9.2	2.2	12.7	2.4	143
German	48.5	26.2	4.4	4.1	13.5	3.2	126
Irish	47.5	34.8	5.8	0.6	7.8	3.5	90
Italian	35.1	40.0	7.2	4.0	11.9	1.9	219
Polish	44.1	29.9	4.4	2.4	15.1	4.0	68
Black	41.9	28.0	1.9	1.8	15.7	10.6	159
Filipino	42.7	31.7	1.0	3.2	17.7	3.7	156
East Asian	47.4	30.2	5.6	2.8	13.1	1.1	160
Puerto Rican	27.1	35.3	1.9	4.1	24.7	6.9	707
Mexican	22.7	30.7	3.2	4.3	30.2	9.0	1,405
Cuban	38.8	44.1	1.7	2.9	9.8	2.7	221
Dominican	25.3	26.0	2.4	3.7	28.8	13.8	78
Third generation							
Black	26.5	24.7	2.5	6.5	32.0	7.9	10,889
Asian	43.5	28.3	4.9	3.8	15.9	3.7	658
Puerto Rican	40.6	24.8	2.1	5.1	22.5	4.8	213
Mexican	27.6	30.2	3.5	6.5	26.3	6.0	3,154
American Indian	26.0	24.0	4.3	7.5	29.1	9.2	1,218

Note: percentages are weighted to provide population estimates.

than the percentage of men. Nor are the national origin/generation patterns always identical to men's. For instance, Filipino women (but not men) have slightly higher representation in the salariat (41.2%) than the benchmark group (39.6%). In the second generation, the attainment of Blacks is noteworthy (41.9%); in the third, that of Puerto Ricans (40.6%) and Asians (43.5%) is likewise striking.

The last descriptive finding we review is women's unemployment. Interestingly, although the rate for native White women is even lower (2.9%) than for men, for some groups, especially the foreign born, female joblessness is higher than that of their male counterparts. More specifically, in the first generation, all female Hispanic groups (save Cubans) report more unemployment than their male compatriots. First-generation Black women are also more likely to be unemployed than first-generation Black men. However, in the second and third generations, Puerto Rican women have substantially lower unemployment rates than their male counterparts. An unexpected finding is that second-generation Dominican men and women have identical rates (13.8%), the highest rates in the table.

Taken together, Tables 14.2 through 14.4 reveal substantial variation within generations, and amongst origin groups. In general, Europeans fare best, Cubans, Asians and Blacks fall in the middle, and the remaining Hispanics register large shortfalls. An additional finding is that the second generation tends to have more favourable outcomes than the first or third. As already mentioned, third-generation Blacks and Asians are defined differently from their second-generation counterparts, so this conclusion must be viewed with caution. But the finding is consonant with both theory and previous work; hence, it should not be viewed as frivolous. Finally, some of the results for second-generation Blacks and Hispanics are consistent with segmented assimilation theory, which predicts that these groups will have higher rates of school drop out and economic inactivity than immigrants. But this description fits men better than women and Puerto Ricans better than other Hispanics. Furthermore, second-generation Black and Dominican men have both high rates of school attendance and high rates of economic inactivity. Thus, it is perhaps more accurate to describe these groups' trajectories as bipolar than as a wholesale rejection of mainstream values.

We move now to the multivariate analysis of avoiding unemployment; Table 14.5 communicates these results. The first and third columns of coefficients report the results, separately by sex, of Model 1, an additive model; the second and fourth columns report the results, again separately by sex, of Model 2, an equation to which interactions between ethnicity and education have been added. Recall that unemployment is coded 0; that is to say, positive coefficients convey effects that foster employment. Turning first to Model 1, note that the control variables operate largely as expected. Age has a curvilinear effect and more education is consistently associated with a better chance of holding a job, as is being married or cohabiting. Interestingly women (but not men) who are divorced or separated are less likely to be employed than never-married women. Perhaps this reflects difficulties associated with labour-market re-entry after some time as homemakers. Finally, joblessness was more of a problem in the early years of our survey (1995, 1997) than later on.

EUROPEANS AND NON-EUROPEANS IN US LABOUR MARKET 611

Table 14.5. Logistic regression of employment (parameter estimates; contrasts with employment).

	Men				Women			
	Model 1		Model 2		Model 1		Model 2	
Intercept	**0.83**	(0.16)	**0.82**	(0.16)	**1.64**	(0.17)	**1.68**	(0.17)
Ancestry								
Native born, non-Hispanic whites	0		0		0		0	
Canadian 1	−0.35	(0.42)	−0.36	(0.42)	−0.36	(0.42)	−0.36	(0.42)
German 1	0.00	(0.72)	−0.02	(0.72)	−0.71	(0.39)	−0.72	(0.39)
Irish 1	0.16	(0.72)	0.16	(0.72)	*		*	
Italian 1	0.57	(0.71)	0.57	(0.71)	−0.53	(0.52)	−0.48	(0.52)
Polish 1	−0.62	(0.33)	−0.62	(0.33)	−0.41	(0.39)	−0.41	(0.39)
Black 1	**−0.72**	(0.14)	**−0.71**	(0.14)	**−1.00**	(0.13)	**−0.98**	(0.13)
Filipino 1	**−0.61**	(0.20)	**−0.61**	(0.20)	0.19	(0.27)	0.20	(0.27)
East Asian 1	−0.29	(0.19)	−0.30	(0.19)	−0.11	(0.21)	0.81	(0.41)
Puerto Rican 1	−0.29	(0.19)	−0.28	(0.19)	**−0.83**	(0.17)	**−0.78**	(0.17)
Mexican 1	0.14	(0.07)	**0.48**	(0.11)	**−0.57**	(0.08)	**−0.72**	(0.10)
Cuban 1	**−0.53**	(0.21)	**−0.53**	(0.21)	−0.42	(0.26)	−0.39	(0.26)
Dominican 1	**−0.57**	(0.22)	**−0.55**	(0.22)	**−1.03**	(0.17)	**−0.97**	(0.17)
Canadian 2	1.64	(1.00)	1.64	(1.00)	−0.37	(0.46)	−0.37	(0.46)
German 2	−0.43	(0.46)	−0.44	(0.46)	−0.31	(0.51)	−0.32	(0.51)
Irish 2	−0.09	(0.59)	−0.10	(0.59)	−0.36	(0.59)	−0.37	(0.59)
Italian 2	−0.01	(0.36)	−0.01	(0.36)	0.24	(0.46)	0.24	(0.46)
Polish 2	0.36	(0.72)	0.35	(0.72)	−0.54	(0.60)	−0.55	(0.60)
Black 2	**−0.84**	(0.30)	**−0.83**	(0.30)	**−1.11**	(0.26)	**−1.11**	(0.26)
Filipino 2	−0.41	(0.33)	−0.40	(0.33)	−0.03	(0.42)	−0.03	(0.42)
East Asian 2	0.39	(0.51)	0.39	(0.51)	0.87	(0.71)	0.85	(0.71)
Puerto Rican 2	**−1.08**	(0.14)	**−1.07**	(0.14)	**−0.77**	(0.14)	**−0.76**	(0.14)
Mexican 2	**−0.39**	(0.10)	**−0.37**	(0.10)	**−0.65**	(0.10)	**−0.62**	(0.10)
Cuban 2	0.19	(0.42)	0.19	(0.42)	0.02	(0.39)	0.02	(0.39)
Dominican 2	−0.67	(0.37)	−0.66	(0.37)	**−0.91**	(0.36)	**−0.91**	(0.36)
Asian 3	**−0.40**	(0.08)	**−0.40**	(0.20)	−0.09	(0.23)	−0.10	(0.23)
Puerto Rican 3	**−0.92**	(0.25)	**−0.91**	(0.25)	−0.35	(0.31)	−0.34	(0.31)
Mexican 3	**−0.44**	(0.08)	**−0.40**	(0.08)	**−0.44**	(0.08)	**−0.40**	(0.08)
African American	**−0.91**	(0.05)	**−0.91**	(0.05)	**−0.83**	(0.04)	**−0.82**	(0.04)
American Indian	**−1.07**	(0.10)	**−1.06**	(0.10)	**−0.99**	(0.10)	**−0.98**	(0.11)
Age /10	**1.14**	(0.09)	**1.13**	(0.09)	**0.64**	(0.10)	**0.61**	(0.10)
Age/10^2	**−0.13**	(0.01)	**−0.13**	(0.01)	**−0.04**	(0.01)	**−0.04**	(0.01)
Qualifications								
Higher tertiary	**0.55**	(0.05)	**0.58**	(0.05)	**0.72**	(0.05)	**0.78**	(0.05)
Lower tertiary	**0.28**	(0.04)	**0.27**	(0.04)	**0.35**	(0.04)	**0.36**	(0.04)
Higher secondary	0		0		0		0	
Lower secondary	**−0.58**	(0.04)	**−0.57**	(0.05)	**−0.64**	(0.05)	**−0.65**	(0.05)
No qualification	**−0.58**	(0.06)	**−0.63**	(0.06)	**−0.57**	(0.06)	**−0.73**	(0.07)
Marital Status								
Married/cohabiting	**0.73**	(0.04)	**0.73**	(0.04)	**0.27**	(0.04)	**0.27**	(0.04)
Divorced/separated	0.07	(0.05)	0.07	(0.05)	**−0.24**	(0.05)	**−0.23**	(0.05)

Table 14.5. Logistic regression of employment (parameter estimates; contrasts with employment) (*cont.*).

	Men				Women			
	Model 1		Model 2		Model 1		Model 2	
Single	0		0		0		0	
Year								
1995	−0.29	(0.04)	−0.29	(0.04)	−0.28	(0.04)	−0.27	(0.04)
1997	−0.18	(0.04)	−0.18	(0.04)	−0.27	(0.04)	−0.27	(0.04)
1999	0.06	(0.04)	0.06	(0.04)	−0.08	(0.05)	−0.08	(0.05)
2001	0		0		0		0	
Significant interactions with education								
East Asian 1							−0.93	(0.25)
Mexican 1							−0.21	(0.06)
African American			**0.13**	(0.04)				
Mexican 3			**0.13**	(0.07)			**0.15**	(0.08)
Significant interactions with years since arrival								
Mexican 1			−0.27	(0.07)				
Chi-square (D.F.)	3217.0 (43)		3287.5 (48)		2870.5 (42)		2935.9 (48)	
N	130,208		130,205		118,346		118,346	

Note: standard errors are given in brackets; emboldened coefficients indicate significance at the 0.05 level or higher.
* All first-generation Irish women in the sample (N=68) were employed.

The group membership effects are disturbing. Looking first at men, many non-white groups face deficits. In the first generation, this includes Blacks, Filipinos, Cubans and Dominicans and in the second, Blacks, Puerto Ricans and Mexicans. Actually, the magnitude of the second-generation Dominican coefficient (−0.67) is greater than the first (−0.57), but the differences between them are not significant. In the third generation, all the groups are non-white and all are disadvantaged.

The women's story is not identical but the message is the same. Filipina women, many of whom immigrate specifically to work in the health care industry, have no difficulty finding jobs. But both first- and second-generation Blacks, Puerto Ricans, Mexicans and Dominicans do have difficulty. In the third generation, the disadvantaged female groups are African Americans, Mexicans and American Indians. As pointed out above, third-generation Asians consist of both Asians and Pacific Islanders. Though the CPS does not distinguish between them, a plurality of Pacific Islanders lives in Hawaii (though a goodly number of Asians do as well). Because we hypothesise that economic attainment is stronger among Asians than Pacific Islanders, we added an interaction between third-generation Asians and Hawaiians in all our models. Though Pacific

Islanders in Hawaii appear less able to gain employment than Asian Americans living in the continental United States, the difference was not significant.

Model 2 reports all the coefficients of a model to which two types of interactions with group membership have been added. First, like the other authors in this volume, we tested for interactions between group membership and education. And, again following our colleagues, we use a series of dummy variables to capture the main effects of education but a continuous variable for the interaction. This means that the coefficients of ethnicity convey the effect of group membership for those with a high school education and that, with increasing education, the gap between the ethnic group and native Whites increases or decreases depending on the sign of the interaction. Very few of these interactions attained significance, which means that, for most ethnic minorities, each level of education has the same effect on employment as for native White people. However, there is a positive interaction for both third-generation African American and Mexican men. To illustrate using third-generation Mexican men, for high school graduates the employment gap between third-generation Mexicans and native Whites is −0.40 (the group membership coefficient in the interactive model), but for those with a lower tertiary education, the gap diminishes to −0.27.[1] Those with higher tertiary education fare even better, with the gap diminishing to −0.14.[2] Conversely the employment differential between native Whites and third-generation Mexican men increases for high school drop outs, to −0.53.[3]

It is tempting to attribute this result to affirmative action, but the women's interactions belie that interpretation. Among women, African Americans—the group some believe have profited most from affirmative action—receive the same returns on education as White people. The female groups with significant education interactions include first-generation East Asians and Mexicans, both of which are negative; and third-generation Mexicans, who exhibit a positive interaction. The interpretation for third-generation Mexican females is very similar to that of third-generation Mexican males, so to illustrate we take up the larger negative interaction, that of first-generation East Asian females. This group membership coefficient, which conveys the employment effect for those with a high school diploma, is +0.81. First-generation East Asian women

---

[1] Computed as: $-0.40 + 1*.13 = -0.27$.
[2] Computed as: $-0.40 + 2*.13 = -0.14$.
[3] Computed as: $-0.40 + -1*.13 = -0.53$.

with lower tertiary schooling, however, incur a small ethnic penalty of −0.12;[4] those with higher tertiary education incur a substantial one— −1.05.[5] Since 42.2% of first-generation East Asian women have higher tertiary degrees (see Table 14.2B), this is a disturbing state of affairs.

Next we wondered whether immigrants' employment probabilities would increase with longer residence in the US. Because, like age, length of residence is assumed to have a curvilinear relationship with economic outcomes, we tested this hypothesis by interacting two variables—years since migration and its square—with each first-generation group. In no case was this interaction significant. We then tested if merely a linear interaction obtained, and this specification proved significant for one group: Mexican men. The first-generation Mexican male group membership coefficient tells us that, upon arrival, they are somewhat more likely to be employed than native White men (0.48). However, the interaction is unexpectedly negative. Two decades years after arrival, Mexican immigrant males' employment advantage has become a slight disadvantage, −0.06.[6] Perhaps Mexicans, more than other backgrounds, have jobs lined up already before they depart, and perhaps they are less able to secure jobs late in life because they work predominantly as manual labourers (55.3% have semi or unskilled manual jobs—see Table 14.4A).

In the main, however, we conclude that the interactions are a relatively unimportant part of the employment story because they do not display any clear pattern. Far more important is the discovery that most non-whites face a substantially greater risk of joblessness than their equally qualified white counterparts. Most disturbing, the analysis indicates that this difficulty persists into the second and third generations. To be sure, the grandchildren of the first generation will be very different people from today's third generation. But there are at least two reasons to expect that their employment shortfalls will persist. First, there are theoretical reasons for believing that earlier arrivals from a given locale are more positively selected—that is more diligent and talented—than later arrivals (Lee 1966). Second, government commitment to equal opportunity peaked in the 1980s and has since declined.

Following the mandate of this volume, our primary concern is to predict occupational class. These results appear in Tables 14.6A and 14.6B. The reference category is semi- and unskilled manual work. As expected,

---

[4] Computed as: $0.81 + 1*-0.93 = -0.12$.
[5] Computed as: $0.81 + 2*-0.93 = -1.05$.
[6] Computed as: $0.48 + 2*-0.27 = -0.06$.

EUROPEANS AND NON-EUROPEANS IN US LABOUR MARKET 615

most of the control variables (age, education, etc.) are significant in the manner theory predicts. Therefore, our discussion emphasises the group membership coefficients, especially with respect to entrance to the salariat. For some groups, self-employment is also an important economic strategy; thus we likewise pay some attention to entrance to the petty bourgeoisie.

Table 14.6A. Logistic regression of occupational class: Men (parameter estimates; contrasts with unskilled manual).

	Salariat		Routine non-manual		Petty bourgeoisie		Manual supervisor or skilled manual	
Intercept	−3.55	(0.12)	−0.95	(0.14)	−6.43	(.16)	−2.11	(0.10)
Ancestry								
Native-born, non-Hispanic white	0		0		0		0	
Canadian 1	0.29	(0.25)	−0.37	(0.41)	0.51	(0.27)	0.03	(0.27)
German 1	0.55	(0.40)	0.45	(0.68)	0.68	(0.42)	0.57	(0.42)
Irish 1	0.33	(0.37)	−0.57	(0.64)	0.19	(0.42)	−0.04	(0.39)
Italian 1	−0.27	(0.30)	−0.52	(0.49)	**0.68**	(0.25)	0.16	(0.25)
Polish 1	**−1.11**	(0.24)	**−1.20**	(0.40)	−0.39	(0.25)	−0.11	(0.19)
Black 1	**−1.09**	(0.11)	**−0.52**	(0.13)	**−1.28**	(0.15)	**−0.58**	(0.09)
Filipino 1	**−1.41**	(0.12)	**−0.85**	(0.16)	**−1.85**	(0.20)	**−0.98**	(0.13)
East Asian 1	0.11	(0.12)	0.01	(0.16)	**0.42**	(0.12)	0.02	(0.12)
Puerto Rican 1	**−0.99**	(0.15)	**−0.48**	(0.17)	**−2.00**	(0.24)	**−0.59**	(0.11)
Mexican 1	**−1.68**	(0.07)	**−1.17**	(0.83)	**−1.12**	(0.06)	**−0.34**	(0.04)
Cuban 1	**−0.68**	(0.15)	0.10	(0.17)	0.12	(0.14)	**−0.35**	(0.13)
Dominican 1	−1.28	(0.22)	−0.23	(0.21)	**−0.81**	(0.20)	**−1.10**	(0.16)
Canadian 2	0.02	(0.22)	0.04	(0.30)	−0.26	(0.27)	−0.21	(0.23)
German 2	0.11	(0.28)	0.44	(0.34)	0.25	(0.32)	0.05	(0.30)
Irish 2	**0.69**	(0.35)	−0.35	(0.58)	0.20	(0.43)	0.59	(0.36)
Italian 2	0.18	(0.19)	−0.13	(0.27)	0.27	(0.21)	0.09	(0.20)
Polish 2	0.43	(0.34)	0.17	(0.44)	−0.45	(0.49)	0.25	(0.35)
Black 2	−0.15	(0.27)	**0.55**	(0.26)	−0.43	(0.43)	**−0.64**	(0.32)
Filipino 2	0.27	(0.24)	**0.56**	(0.25)	−0.52	(0.45)	**−0.62**	(0.31)
East Asian 2	−0.06	(0.24)	0.09	(0.28)	−0.40	(0.36)	−0.14	(0.41)
Puerto Rican 2	−0.19	(0.13)	−0.17	(0.17)	**−1.17**	(0.22)	−0.21	(0.11)
Mexican 2	**−0.33**	(0.09)	0.03	(0.09)	**−0.86**	(0.13)	**−0.27**	(0.07)
Cuban 2	**0.52**	(0.21)	**0.65**	(0.25)	0.20	(0.29)	−0.08	(0.24)
Dominican 2	0.29	(0.36)	0.40	(0.37)	−1.48	(1.03)	−0.64	(0.39)
Asians outside Hawaii 3	0.46	(0.24)	**0.71**	(0.28)	0.33	(0.29)	0.10	(0.27)
Asians in Hawaii 3	**−0.45**	(0.15)	−0.32	(0.20)	**−0.48**	(0.19)	−0.15	(0.14)
Puerto Rican 3	0.28	(0.22)	**0.58**	(0.25)	−0.52	(0.35)	0.01	(0.21)
Mexican 3	**−0.37**	(0.06)	**−0.17**	(0.07)	**−0.93**	(0.08)	**−0.20**	(0.05)
African American	**−0.77**	(0.04)	**−0.42**	(0.05)	**−1.40**	(0.06)	**−0.54**	(0.03)
American Indian	**−0.35**	(0.09)	**−0.57**	(0.14)	**−0.60**	(0.12)	**−0.15**	(0.08)
Age /10	1.20	(0.06)	−0.29	(0.08)	2.19	(0.08)	**0.93**	(0.06)
Age/10^2	**−0.14**	(0.01)	**0.03**	(0.01)	−0.22	(0.01)	**−0.12**	(0.01)

Table 14.6A. Logistic regression of occupational class: Men (parameter estimates; contrasts with unskilled manual) (*cont.*).

	Salariat		Routine non-manual		Petty bourgeoisie		Manual supervisor or skilled manual	
Qualification								
Higher tertiary	**3.52**	(0.03)	**2.05**	(0.04)	**1.66**	(0.03)	**0.16**	(0.04)
Lower tertiary	**1.23**	(0.02)	**0.86**	(0.03)	**0.41**	(0.03)	**0.24**	(0.02)
Higher secondary	0		0		0		0	
Lower secondary	**−0.96**	(0.05)	**−0.56**	(0.05)	**−0.23**	(0.04)	**−0.16**	(0.03)
No qualification	**−1.54**	(0.07)	**−1.07**	(0.08)	**−0.47**	(0.05)	**−0.33**	(0.03)
Marital Status								
Married/cohabiting	**0.51**	(0.03)	**0.08**	(0.03)	**0.53**	(0.03)	**0.46**	(0.02)
Divorced/separated	**0.13**	(0.04)	−0.09	(0.05)	**0.20**	(0.04)	**0.33**	(0.03)
Single	0		0		0		0	
Year								
1995	**−0.11**	(0.02)	−0.02	(0.03)	**0.13**	(0.03)	**−0.08**	(0.02)
1997	**−0.07**	(0.03)	−0.02	(0.03)	**0.12**	(0.03)	**−0.06**	(0.02)
1999	−0.02	(0.03)	0.01	(0.03)	0.05	(0.03)	−0.02	(0.02)
2001	0		0		0		0	
Chi-square (D.F.)			56,311.6 (176)					
N			125,200					

Note: standard errors are given in brackets; emboldened coefficients indicate significance at the 0.05 level or higher.

Looking first at men, note the overwhelming tendency for improvement across generations. The largest number of deficits occurs in the first generation, with Mexican immigrants incurring the highest penalty of any entry in the table ($\beta = -1.68$). Other first-generation groups with a significant handicap include Poles, Blacks, Filipinos, Puerto Ricans, Cubans and Dominicans. Put another way, the only first-generation non-European group to access the salariat in the same proportion as the benchmark group is East Asians. The second generation displays marked improvement: only Mexicans still have a significant penalty, though in some cases the group membership coefficient is negative. But the majority are positive (eight out of twelve), and two significantly so: second-generation Irish and second-generation Cubans. In the third generation, there is considerable variation. The highest penalty obtains for African Americans ($\beta = -0.77$), followed by Asians in Hawaii. Given that the coefficient for Asians outside Hawaii is insignificantly positive, the shortfall associated with Hawaiian residence probably reflects the difficulties faced by the Pacific Islander component of the Asian category. A final difference concerns third-generation Puerto Ricans and third-generation

Table 14.6B. Logistic regression of occupational class: Women (parameter estimates; contrasts with unskilled manual).

	Salariat		Routine non-manual		Petty bourgeoisie		Manual supervisor/ skilled manual	
Intercept	−3.78	(0.12)	−0.58	(0.10)	−6.16	(.20)	−2.63	(0.17)
Ancestry								
Native-born, non-Hispanic white	0		0		0		0	
Canadian 1	0.34	(0.24)	−0.19	(0.26)	0.19	(0.31)	0.11	(0.40)
German 1	−0.22	(0.23)	−0.56	(0.25)	0.19	(0.27)	0.19	(0.35)
Irish 1	−0.13	(0.35)	−0.75	(0.39)	0.02	(0.46)	−0.73	(0.75)
Italian 1	−0.11	(0.37)	0.13	(0.34)	0.68	(0.36)	**0.90**	(0.37)
Polish 1	**−1.74**	(0.24)	**−1.12**	(0.22)	−0.68	(0.29)	−0.71	(0.37)
Black 1	**−1.34**	(0.11)	**−1.07**	(0.10)	**−1.59**	(0.21)	**−1.09**	(0.19)
Filipino 1	**−1.48**	(0.11)	**−1.11**	(0.11)	**−1.95**	(0.22)	−0.45	(0.17)
East Asian 1	**−0.96**	(0.10)	**−0.97**	(0.11)	−0.03	(0.12)	−0.18	(0.15)
Puerto Rican 1	**−1.25**	(0.14)	**−0.77**	(0.12)	**−1.47**	(0.26)	**−0.42**	(0.18)
Mexican 1	**−1.68**	(0.09)	**−1.22**	(0.07)	**−0.97**	(0.10)	**−0.22**	(0.07)
Cuban 1	**−0.77**	(0.16)	−0.35	(0.15)	−0.58	(0.22)	0.10	(0.20)
Dominican 1	**−1.53**	(0.19)	**−1.09**	(0.15)	**−1.03**	(0.25)	**−0.82**	(0.22)
Canadian 2	0.50	(0.27)	0.05	(0.28)	0.58	(0.33)	−0.60	(0.62)
German 2	0.39	(0.30)	0.33	(0.30)	−0.45	(0.51)	0.35	(0.48)
Irish 2	**1.03**	(0.44)	**1.14**	(0.43)	0.55	(0.59)	−0.50	(1.07)
Italian 2	0.44	(0.25)	**1.03**	(0.23)	0.57	(0.33)	0.27	(0.41)
Polish 2	−0.26	(0.41)	0.28	(0.38)	−1.03	(0.78)	−0.26	(0.77)
Black 2	0.37	(0.27)	0.39	(0.26)	−0.16	(0.55)	−0.24	(0.54)
Filipino 2	0.16	(0.25)	0.19	(0.24)	−1.15	(0.74)	−0.21	(0.48)
East Asian 2	−0.03	(0.27)	0.25	(0.26)	−0.14	(0.47)	−0.15	(0.54)
Puerto Rican 2	0.04	(0.12)	**0.40**	(0.12)	−1.08	(0.29)	−0.30	(0.21)
Mexican 2	−0.02	(0.09)	0.07	(0.07)	−0.48	(0.16)	**−0.31**	(0.13)
Cuban 2	**0.86**	(0.27)	**1.27**	(0.25)	−0.30	(0.55)	0.39	(0.44)
Dominican 2	−0.32	(0.38)	−0.00	(0.31)	−0.46	(0.75)	−0.15	(0.54)
Asians 3	0.03	(0.13)	0.21	(0.12)	−0.14	(0.20)	0.21	(0.20)
Puerto Rican 3	0.14	(0.21)	0.08	(0.20)	−0.80	(0.48)	−0.12	(0.35)
Mexican 3	−0.04	(0.06)	0.07	(0.05)	**−0.57**	(0.10)	0.03	(0.08)
African American	**−0.59**	(0.03)	**−0.43**	(0.03)	**−1.26**	(0.07)	**−0.16**	(0.05)
American Indian	**−0.25**	(0.09)	**−0.27**	(0.08)	**−0.69**	(0.15)	0.09	(0.12)
Age /10	**1.54**	(0.06)	**0.20**	(0.06)	**1.67**	(0.11)	**0.60**	(0.10)
Age/10^2	**−0.17**	(0.01)	−0.02	(0.01)	−0.16	(0.01)	**−0.07**	(0.01)
Qualification								
Higher tertiary	3.29	(0.03)	0.99	(0.03)	1.59	(0.04)	−0.05	(0.06)
Lower tertiary	1.19	(0.02)	0.64	(0.02)	0.66	(0.03)	−0.05	(0.04)
Higher secondary	0		0		0		0	
Lower secondary	−1.09	(0.05)	−0.99	(0.04)	−0.47	(0.06)	−0.08	(0.05)
No qualification	−1.87	(0.08)	−1.84	(0.06)	−0.75	(0.07)	−0.20	(0.06)
Marital Status								
Married/cohabiting	**0.35**	(0.03)	**0.28**	(0.03)	**1.12**	(0.05)	**0.08**	(0.04)
Divorced/separated	0.05	(0.03)	0.00	(0.03)	**0.27**	(0.06)	0.02	(0.05)
Single	0		0		0		0	

Table 14.6B. Logistic regression of occupational class: Women (parameter estimates; contrasts with unskilled manual) (*cont.*).

	Salariat		Routine non-manual		Petty bourgeoisie		Manual supervisor/ skilled manual	
Year								
1995	−**0.13**	(0.03)	0.00	(0.02)	**0.13**	(0.04)	−0.05	(0.04)
1997	−**0.08**	(0.03)	0.00	(0.03)	**0.08**	(0.04)	−0.03	(0.04)
1999	−0.04	(0.03)	0.02	(0.03)	0.04	(0.04)	−0.01	(0.04)
2001	0		0		0		0	
Chi-square (D.F.)				45,582.2 (172)				
N				113,684				

Note: standard errors are given in brackets; emboldened coefficients indicate significance at the 0.05 level or higher.

Mexicans. The coefficient for the former is insignificantly positive; for the latter significantly negative. We hypothesised that the second result might reflect long-standing discrimination against Mexican-Americans in the Southwest. Thus, we created an interaction term that distinguished third-generation Mexicans who resided in the Southwest; however the interaction term failed to attain significance ($p = 0.09$).

Turning briefly to the petty bourgeoisie, two immigrant groups are represented at significantly higher rates than native Whites: first-generation Italians and first-generation East Asians. This accords well with both stereotypes and scholarship. Interestingly, by the second generation neither of these two backgrounds is over-represented in this type of work. There are also several immigrant groups that are significantly less likely to be members of the petty bourgeoisie than native White people: first-generation Blacks, first-generation Filipinos, Puerto Ricans, first-generation Mexicans and first-generation Dominicans. The trend is clearly one of Hispanic under-involvement. Interestingly, the often emphasised proclivity of Cuban immigrants to be self-employed appears not confirmed ($\beta = 0.12$, $p = 0.14$) in this analysis. However, the coefficients in Table 14.6A do not fully take into account years since migration. This matter will be pursued in more detail shortly.

The results of the additive model for women appear in Table 14.6B. Again, the controls behave largely as expected; however, for only one occupational class (the petty bourgeoisie) do divorced/separated woman have significantly greater access than single women. This result is of interest because, in the case of men, for three out of four occupational classes, divorced/separated men have significantly greater access than single men. Recall that Table 14.5 showed that divorced/separated women (but not men) also faced an employment penalty. As stated earlier, these patterns may reflect unmeasured shortfalls in these women's characteristics, but they may also reflect discrimination against formerly married females.

With respect to the effect of group membership on women's access to the salariat, the results for the first and second generations are quite similar to those for men. Only one European group (Poles) registers a shortfall, but all first-generation non-European groups do. Again paralleling males, first-generation Mexican women incur the highest penalty in the table ($\beta = -1.68$). But unlike their male counterparts, East Asian women also suffer a significant shortfall ($\beta = -0.96$). Second-generation improvement is again the central theme. All the women's groups, at minimum, attain parity with native Whites; second-generation Irish and second-generation Cubans surpass it. Finally, third-generation disadvantages appear but not as ubiquitously as for men. The handicapped groups are African Americans and American Indians. Note that the table makes no mention of Asians in Hawaii. That is because, on occupational class, there were no significant differences on this parameter for Asian women.

Our next step was to estimate an interactive model of occupational class. Tables 14.7A and 14.7B report these results: the top panel contains the group membership coefficients, the middle panel the coefficients for the interaction of group membership with education and the third panel the coefficients for the interaction of first-generation group membership with years since migration and with its square. Ancestry groups that had significant interactions with education or years since migration are included in the main effects portion of the table. Interaction coefficients are included only when a Wald test showed that adding the interactions significantly improved the fit of the model. One consequence of this decision is that some of the interactions shown in Tables 14.7A and 14.7B are insignificant; indeed, for one group, first-generation Cubans in Table 14.7A, all the interactions of group membership with years since migration and its square are insignificant. However, tests of the interactions of years and years squared taken together are highly significant ($p = 0.000$ and $p = 0.011$) in two occupational classes (the salariat and the petty bourgeoisie). The discussion to follow focuses on significant interactions associated with accessing the salariat and the petty bourgeoisie.

As the middle panel of Table 14.7A indicates, with only one exception, the significant interactions with educational qualifications are negative. That is to say, if the returns to education of an ethnic minority male

Table 14.7A. Differential returns to education and years in the US: Men (parameter estimates; contrasts with semi- and unskilled manual).

	Salariat		Routine non-manual		Petty bourgeoisie		Manual supervisor/ skilled manual	
Main effects of ancestry								
German 1	0.27	(0.64)	0.47	(0.68)	0.78	(0.49)	0.46	(0.49)
Italian 1	−0.17	(0.40)	−0.12	(0.53)	**0.87**	(0.28)	0.33	(0.28)
Black 1	**−1.73**	(0.33)	−0.47	(0.34)	**−1.82**	(0.46)	**−0.87**	(0.25)
East Asian 1	0.21	(0.32)	**0.80**	(0.36)	**−1.16**	(0.41)	0.17	(0.31)
Puerto Rican 1	**−0.78**	(0.15)	**−0.37**	(0.17)	**−2.05**	(0.24)	**−0.54**	(0.11)
Mexican 1	**−2.32**	(0.20)	**−2.07**	(0.23)	**−1.97**	(0.20)	**−0.49**	(0.08)
Cuban 1	**−2.11**	(0.50)	−0.16	(0.42)	**−1.19**	(0.43)	−0.26	(0.30)
Dominican 1	−0.36	(0.58)	−1.20	(0.77)	**−1.46**	(0.70)	**−1.00**	(0.46)
German 2	−0.41	(0.54)	0.67	(0.51)	0.65	(0.39)	0.41	(0.35)
Black 2	0.45	(0.35)	**0.81**	(0.33)	−0.64	(0.66)	−0.67	(0.39)
Puerto Rican 2	−0.12	(0.14)	0.01	(0.17)	**−1.26**	(0.24)	**−0.22**	(0.11)
African American	**−0.75**	(0.05)	**−0.38**	(0.06)	**−1.36**	(0.06)	**−0.54**	(0.03)
American Indian	**−0.29**	(0.11)	**−0.42**	(0.14)	**−0.58**	(0.12)	**−0.16**	(0.08)
Significant interactions between ancestry and qualifications								
German 1	0.14	(0.45)	**−1.25**	(0.59)	−0.11	(0.39)	0.14	(0.42)
Italian 1	0.44	(0.32)	0.04	(0.45)	0.36	(0.23)	**0.64**	(0.25)
Black 1	**−0.28**	(0.11)	**−0.42**	(0.12)	−0.10	(0.12)	**−0.19**	(0.08)
East Asian 1	0.14	(0.12)	**−0.32**	(0.14)	0.10	(0.11)	−0.16	(0.10)
Puerto Rican 1	**−0.36**	(0.11)	**−0.43**	(0.14)	0.09	(0.17)	0.11	(0.09)
Mexican 1	**−0.25**	(0.05)	**−0.48**	(0.07)	−0.03	(0.05)	−0.03	(0.03)
Cuban 1	**−0.41**	(0.15)	**−0.47**	(0.15)	**−0.45**	(0.11)	−0.11	(0.11)
German 2	0.13	(0.39)	−0.38	(0.42)	−0.57	(0.35)	**−0.88**	(0.39)
Black 2	**−0.66**	(0.28)	−0.44	(0.29)	0.02	(0.48)	0.00	(0.36)
Puerto Rican 2	−0.15	(0.14)	**−0.49**	(0.17)	0.15	(0.22)	0.09	(0.12)
African American	−0.05	(0.04)	−0.07	(0.05)	**−0.13**	(0.06)	−0.02	(0.04)
American Indian	−0.16	(0.11)	**−0.39**	(0.15)	−0.17	(0.12)	−0.03	(0.09)
Significant interactions between first-generation ancestry and years (decades) in the United States								
East Asians								
Years in US/10	−0.72	(0.42)	−0.95	(0.50)	**1.73**	(0.52)	−0.35	(0.44)
(Years in US/10)^2	**0.24**	(0.12)	**0.31**	(0.14)	**−0.36**	(0.15)	0.14	(0.13)
Mexicans								
Years in US/10	**0.61**	(0.24)	**1.12**	(0.32)	**0.80**	(0.23)	0.28	(0.11)
(Years in US/10)^2	−0.07	(0.07)	**−0.27**	(0.10)	**−0.15**	(0.06)	**−0.09**	(0.03)
Cubans								
Years in US/10	0.98	(0.53)	0.00	(0.01)	0.91	(0.50)	−0.12	(0.43)
(Years in US/10)^2	0.06	(0.13)	0.05	(0.14)	−0.13	(0.13)	0.02	(0.12)
Dominicans								
Years in US/10	−1.82	(0.78)	2.19	(1.23)	0.47	(0.87)	−0.15	(0.68)
(Years in US/10)^2	**0.59**	(0.22)	−0.84	(0.44)	−0.02	(0.24)	0.05	(0.21)
Blacks								
Years in US/10	**0.80**	(0.40)	0.26	(0.49)	0.35	(0.55)	0.27	(0.36)
(Years in US/10)^2	−0.10	(0.11)	−0.05	(0.15)	0.01	(0.15)	−0.02	(0.11)
Chi-square (D.F.)	56,799.8 (284)							
N	125,197							

Note: standard errors are given in brackets; emboldened coefficients indicate significance at the 0.05 level or higher.

Table 14.7B. Differential returns to education and years in the US: Women (parameter estimates; contrasts with semi- and unskilled manual).

	Salariat		Routine non-manual		Petty bourgeoisie		Manual supervisor/ skilled manual	
Main effects of ancestry								
Black 1	−2.43	(0.40)	−1.64	(0.33)	−1.02	(0.56)	−0.61	(0.49)
Filipino 1	−1.19	(0.19)	−1.32	(0.17)	−2.07	(0.37)	−0.38	(0.18)
East Asian 1	−1.76	(0.32)	−1.82	(0.32)	−1.82	(0.43)	−0.44	(0.39)
Puerto Rican 1	−1.31	(0.19)	−0.71	(0.12)	−1.49	(0.26)	−0.44	(0.19)
Mexican 1	−1.88	(0.25)	−1.89	(0.20)	−0.69	(0.26)	0.12	(0.16)
Cuban 1	−2.21	(0.48)	−1.58	(0.42)	−1.93	(0.77)	0.41	(0.44)
Dominican 1	−3.25	(0.63)	−1.60	(0.41)	−2.15	(0.82)	−0.27	(0.50)
Italian 2	0.57	(0.30)	1.19	(0.24)	0.60	(0.37)	0.30	(0.42)
African American	−0.67	(0.04)	−0.52	(0.03)	−1.30	(0.08)	−0.16	(0.05)
Significant interactions between ancestry and qualifications								
Black 1	0.14	(0.13)	0.29	(0.12)	−0.02	(0.20)	−0.07	(0.19)
Filipino 1	−0.18	(0.12)	0.18	(0.12)	0.08	(0.23)	−0.31	(0.14)
East Asian 1	0.39	(0.13)	0.52	(0.13)	0.15	(0.11)	−0.02	(0.13)
Puerto Rican 1	−0.04	(0.14)	−0.27	(0.11)	−0.06	(0.21)	−0.07	(0.15)
Mexican 1	−0.07	(0.07)	−0.09	(0.06)	−0.15	(0.08)	0.03	(0.06)
Italian 2	−0.42	(0.24)	−0.51	(0.23)	−0.28	(0.32)	−0.13	(0.41)
African American	0.19	(0.04)	0.24	(0.04)	0.16	(0.08)	0.01	(0.05)
Significant interactions between first-generation ancestry and years (decades) in the United States								
East Asians								
Years in US/10	0.63	(0.38)	0.81	(0.41)	2.32	(0.51)	0.34	(0.53)
(Years in US/10)^2	−0.13	(0.11)	0.21	(0.12)	−0.55	(0.14)	−0.07	(0.15)
Mexicans								
Years in US/10	−0.19	(0.29)	0.38	(0.23)	−0.62	(0.30)	−0.43	(0.21)
(Years in US/10)^2	0.15	(0.07)	0.02	(0.06)	0.19	(0.08)	−0.12	(0.06)
Cubans								
Years in US/10	1.05	(0.56)	1.17	(0.50)	1.46	(0.84)	−0.63	(0.61)
(Years in US/10)^2	−0.12	(0.14)	−0.20	(0.13)	−0.29	(0.21)	0.18	(0.16)
Dominicans								
Years in US/10	2.11	(0.07)	0.57	(0.54)	1.29	(0.95)	−0.84	(0.76)
(Years in US/10)^2	−0.47	(0.19)	−0.10	(0.15)	−0.26	(0.24)	0.21	(0.21)
Blacks								
Years in US/10	1.05	(0.47)	0.53	(0.44)	−0.77	(0.75)	−1.14	(0.66)
(Years in US/10)^2	−0.19	(0.13)	0.13	(0.13)	0.21	(0.21)	0.39	(0.18)
Chi-square (D.F.)			45,967.7 (256)					
N			113,681					

Note: standard errors are given in brackets; emboldened coefficients indicate significance at the 0.05 level or higher.

differ significantly from the returns to education of a native White male, the difference works to the detriment of the minority. As will be seen in Table 14.7B, this generalisation does not hold for women.

With respect to the salariat, the education of several first-generation groups is significantly undervalued: Blacks, Puerto Ricans, Mexicans and Cubans. This is perhaps not surprising given that most first-generation persons completed much of their education before migration. Therefore, American employers may have difficulty assessing the meaning of their foreign educational credentials and their education may not fit the needs of the US labour market as closely as the education of the native born. For these reasons, some scholars might ask why there are so few first-generation interactions. By the second generation, only Blacks still carry an educational handicap. However, as will shortly become clear, this interaction does not always work to their disadvantage. Note too that the education interaction for African American access to the salariat fails to attain significance.

One way of conveying the effect of an interaction on the dependent variable is to graph the relationship of the interacting variable to the probability of membership in the salariat and in the petty bourgeoisie. Figure 14.1 graphs the adjusted probability of accessing the salariat for males by education for native Whites and the ethnic groups with significant interactions. Adjusted probabilities are predicted probabilities calculated by giving ethnic minorities the same means on the independent variables as White people. Figure 14.1 shows rising levels of access with education. The greatest differences occur at the lowest level of schooling. Most unqualified ethnic minorities have lower probabilities of accessing the salariat than Whites. Unqualified second-generation Blacks actually have a better chance than unqualified White people. Unqualified first-generation Blacks, Mexicans, and Cubans incur the largest penalty. As schooling increases, these penalties converge, primarily because the magnitude of the shortfall tends to decline as education increases. Still, first-generation college-educated Cuban men are only half as likely to enter the salariat as comparably educated native Whites (33% versus 72%).

The lower panel of Table 14.7A reports significant interactions for time spent in the US for first-generation men. Human capital theory expects time spent in the US to have a curvilinear effect on the probability of an immigrant entering one of the more desirable occupational classes. More specifically, upon arrival, his or her chances should fall below those of comparable natives; over time those chances should improve but at a diminishing rate. After two or three decades the likeli-

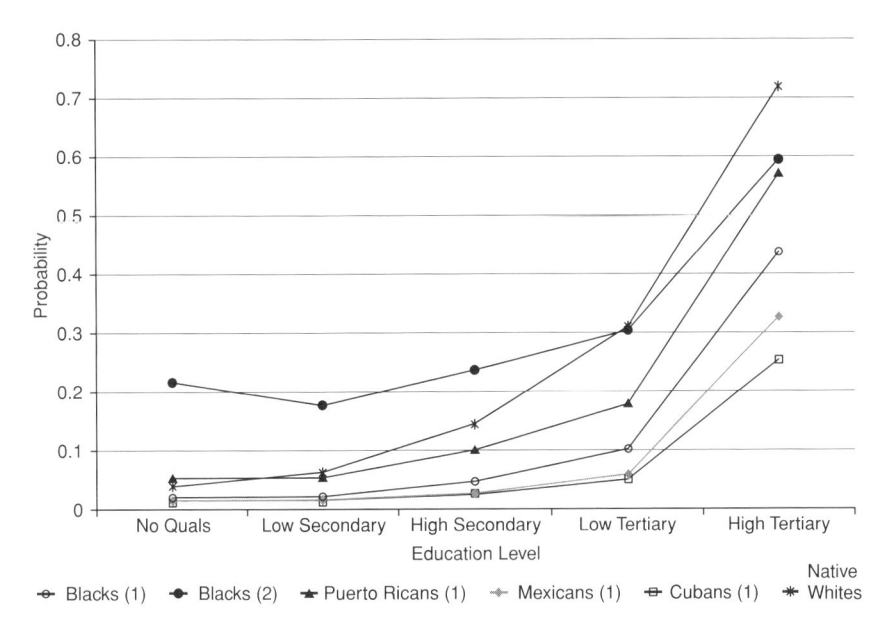

Figure 14.1. Adjusted probability of access to the salariat, by education level: Men.

hood of entering a favourable class should level off, or perhaps even diminish.

All five first-generation groups exhibit significant differences in accessing the salariat by years in the US. Figure 14.2 illustrates these trends. Three immigrant groups, Mexicans, Cubans and Blacks, display the expected convex pattern; but, even after forty years, Mexicans and Blacks have not attained parity with native Whites. Cubans who have been in the US twenty-six years or more do better than Whites. The other two groups, East Asians and Dominicans, exhibit a concave pattern. Upon arrival, they are about as likely to enter the salariat as native Whites, but as time goes by their chances first dip, and then improve. Not until after some thirty years, however, do they surpass native Whites' probability of entering the salariat—Dominicans by quite a bit, East Asians by no more than 7%.

A final result in Table 14.7A worthy of graphing is the relationship between years in the US and access to the petty bourgeoisie. Interestingly, this is the only outcome for which all groups display the expected convex pattern. However, two groups' interactions fail to attain statistical significance: Dominicans and Blacks. These are not included in Figure 14.3. As Figure 14.3 shows, East Asians are most likely to enter this occupational

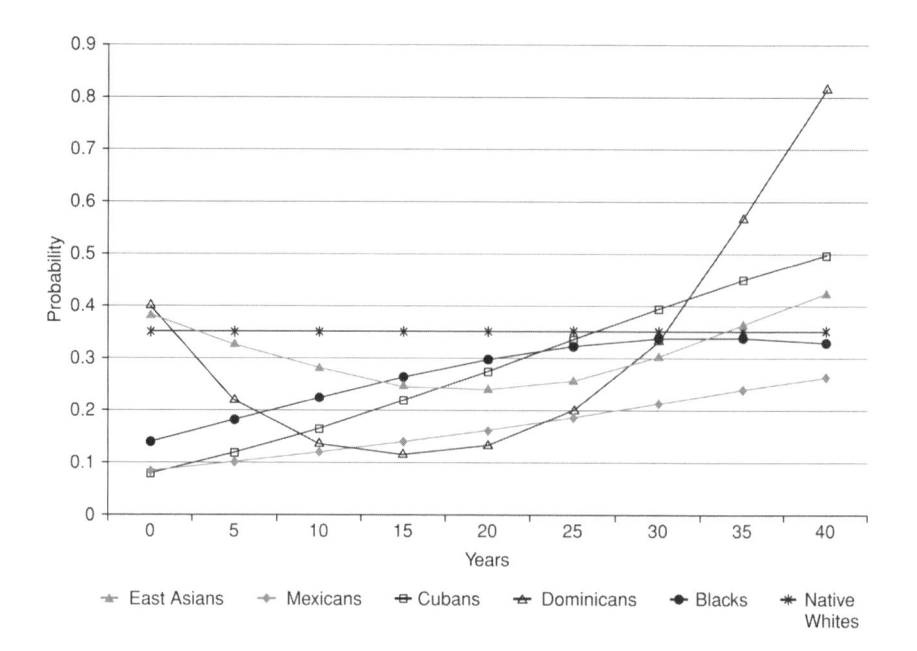

Figure 14.2. Adjusted probability of access to the salariat, by years in US: First-generation men.

class when they have lived in the US between eight and thirty-five years. Their greatest chances are at twenty years, at which point they are nearly twice as likely to belong to the petty bourgeoisie as native Whites. Cubans show a pattern similar to East Asians, but not as strong. They peak at between fifteen and thirty years, during which time the probability of their belonging to the petty bourgeoisie is 30% greater than for Whites. Mexican immigrants greatest chances are in the twenty-five to thirty year range, but even then Mexicans remain significantly (nearly 30%) less likely than native Whites. These results accord with public opinion and scholarly research—East Asian and Cuban immigrants are more entrepreneurial and Mexicans are as less so (Cheng 1994; Portes and Bach 1985).

The interactive models for women appear in Table 14.7B. It is configured in an analogous fashion to Table 14.7A. Looking first at the education interactions in the middle panel, observe that five of the seven included groups are first generation; one is second (Italians) and one is third (African Americans). Six of the ten significant education interactions are positive. In these cases, ethnic minority women translate their education into occupational class more favourably than native women.

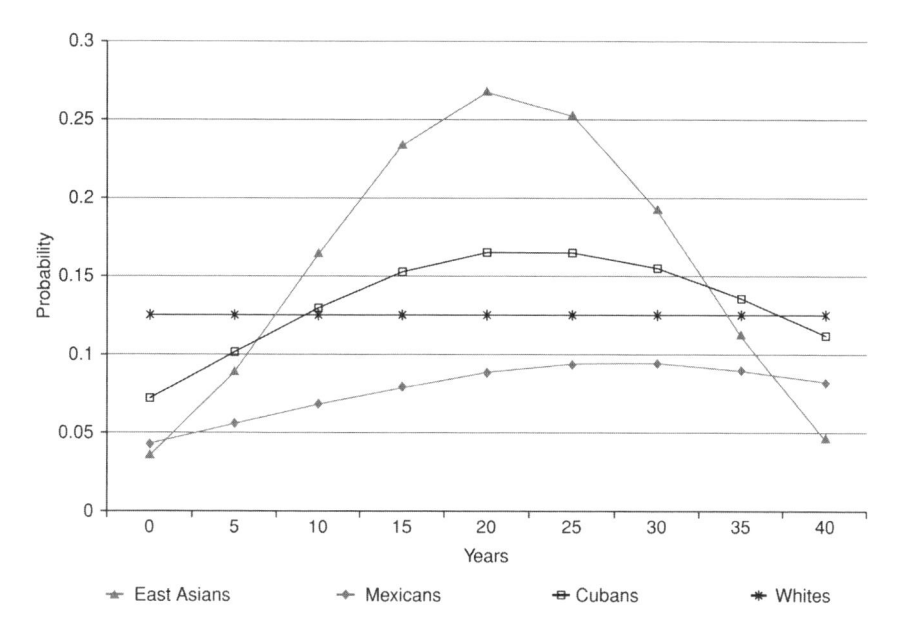

Figure 14.3. Adjusted probability of access to the petty bourgeoisie, by years in the US: First-generation men.

However, given the magnitude of the main effects—that is, of the effects of group membership at the higher secondary level—most ethnic minorities remain disadvantaged, even at high educational levels.

Figure 14.4, which presents the significant interactions between group membership and education in accessing the salariat, makes this point graphically. In the case of first-generation East Asian females, because the interaction is positive, their adjusted probability of entering the salariat climbs faster than that of White women. However, even at full tertiary education they do not get *quite* the same returns to schooling as native White females (predicted probability = 0.71 versus 0.76). At every level of education, African American women are closer to White women than are Asians. Because the interaction coefficient is positive, college-educated African American women have virtually the same access to the salariat as Whites (predicted probability = 0.75 versus 0.76). In sum, first-generation East Asian women are significantly disadvantaged in accessing the salariat, despite their higher returns to education; African American women, because of higher returns to education, are able to reach parity with White women, even though their higher returns to education are less than those of East Asian women.

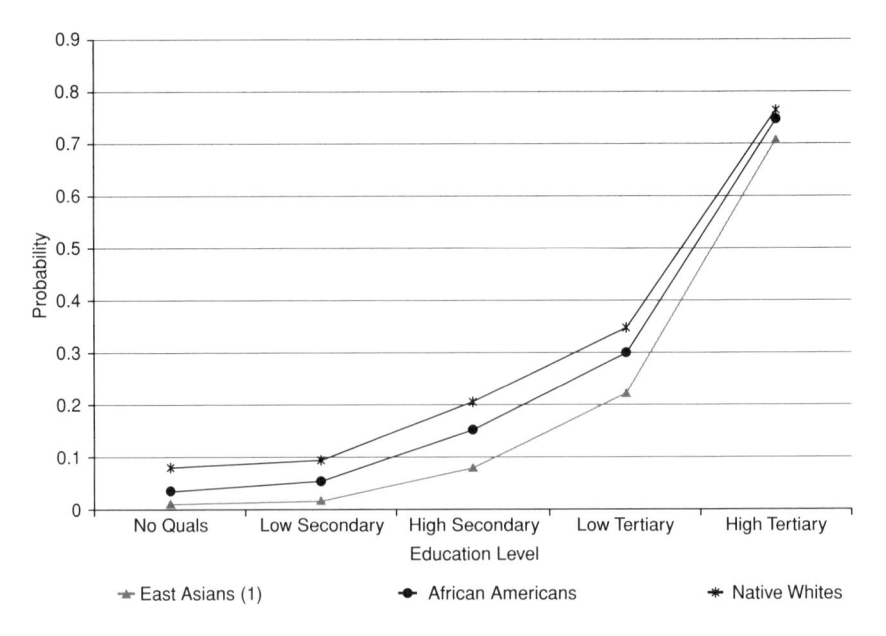

Figure 14.4. Adjusted probability of access to the salariat, by education level: Women.

The bottom panel of Table 14.7B conveys the significant interactions for years in the US (in decades) for immigrant women. Exactly the same groups appear as in the men's results, but the signs of the analogous coefficients are often different. Within the salariat, significant interactions are found for four groups—Cubans, Dominicans, Mexicans, and Blacks. These results appear graphically in Figure 14.5. As expected from the coefficients, the curves for three groups—Cubans, Dominicans and Blacks—have a convex shape; the fourth, Mexicans, generate a very slightly concave curve. The shape of the Dominican curve is the most dramatic. These immigrant women's chances of accessing the salariat at the extremes; e.g. both early and late in their American careers, are low indeed. On the other hand, in the intermediate range of ten to twenty-five years, Dominican immigrant women experience about the same chances of entering the salariat as Black immigrant women do. In fact, in this range of post-arrival years, both Dominican and Black women's probabilities are higher than those of Mexican women. Still, looked at in a more comprehensive fashion, no matter how long they have lived in America, only one female immigrant group, Cubans, has the same chance of entering the salariat as native-born White women, and that chance comes only to Cuban women who have been in the US at least thirty-five years.

Because CPS data include information on earnings, we add an analysis of this outcome to this chapter. Given the theoretical importance of occupational class to this volume, we estimate five separate earnings regressions for each gender: one for each class. This approach controls for class while revealing how the income determination process varies within each class. Another way that these equations differ from the previous ones is that they include controls for region and for size of place. The resulting group membership coefficients appear in Tables 14.8A and 14.8B.

Looking first at the male results, a few general comments are in order. First, in about half the cases, when a group membership coefficient is significant in one equation, it is significant in several more. Groups registering earnings shortfalls within at least four occupational classes include, in the first generation, Blacks, Mexicans, Cubans and Dominicans; in the third generation, African Americans. Another result that parallels previous findings is that the second generation incurs fewer penalties than the first or the third. Contrasting the occupational and earnings results, we find that the disadvantage of a few groups—first-generation Poles and

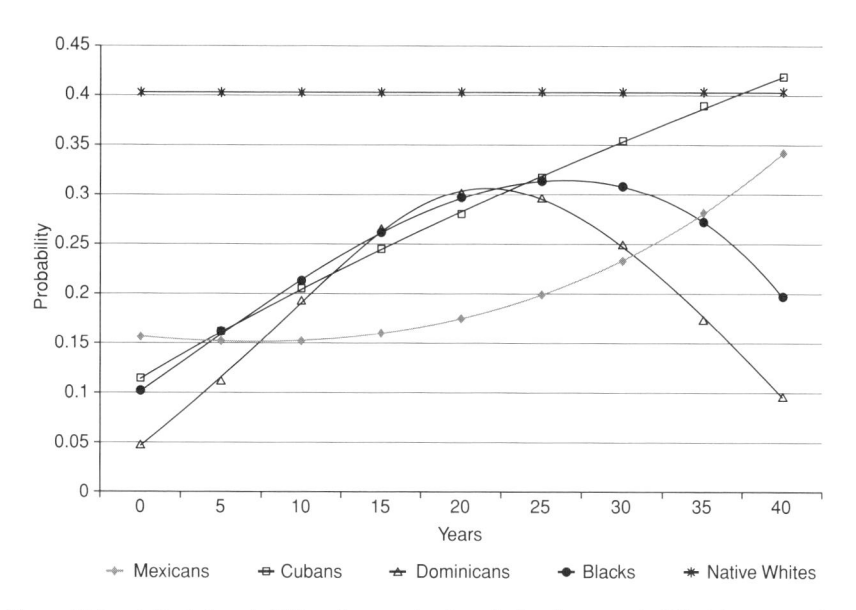

Figure 14.5. Adjusted probability of access to the salariat, by years in US: First-generation women.

Table 14.8A. Effects of ancestry on logged hourly earnings,[a] across occupational destinations: Men (parameter estimates).

	Salariat		Routine non-manual		Petty bourgeoisie		Manual supervisor/ skilled manual		Semi- and unskilled manual	
Effects of ancestry										
Canadian 1	**0.25**	(0.10)	0.01	(0.35)	0.13	(0.18)	0.14	(0.19)	−0.12	(0.19)
German 1	−0.09	(0.14)	0.04	(0.50)	0.01	(0.26)	−0.07	(0.25)	−0.16	(0.35)
Irish 1	0.11	(0.18)	−0.29	(0.58)	−0.22	(0.32)	0.07	(0.28)	0.07	(0.24)
Italian 1	−0.28	(0.19)	−0.15	(0.45)	0.10	(0.17)	−0.07	(0.17)	0.05	(0.19)
Polish 1	−**0.32**	(0.16)	−0.25	(0.38)	0.01	(0.20)	−0.07	(0.14)	−0.08	(0.13)
Black 1	−**0.20**	(0.07)	−**0.25**	(0.11)	−**0.34**	(0.14)	−**0.15**	(0.08)	−**0.25**	(0.05)
Filipino 1	−0.13	(0.08)	−0.16	(0.14)	−0.35	(0.20)	−0.12	(0.11)	0.00	(0.07)
East Asian 1	−0.01	(0.05)	−0.19	(0.13)	−**0.26**	(0.08)	−**0.44**	(0.09)	−**0.24**	(0.09)
Puerto Rican 1	−**0.31**	(0.11)	−0.19	(0.16)	−0.40	(0.26)	−0.04	(0.09)	−**0.18**	(0.06)
Mexican 1	−**0.18**	(0.06)	−**0.22**	(0.09)	−**0.20**	(0.06)	−**0.29**	(0.03)	−**0.22**	(0.02)
Cuban 1	−0.13	(0.10)	−**0.37**	(0.14)	−**0.28**	(0.12)	−**0.28**	(0.10)	−**0.31**	(0.08)
Dominican 1	−**0.37**	(0.18)	−**0.42**	(0.19)	−**0.46**	(0.19)	−**0.26**	(0.13)	−0.10	(0.08)
Canadian 2	0.13	(0.12)	0.21	(0.25)	**0.57**	(0.22)	−0.13	(0.17)	0.03	(0.15)
German 2	0.07	(0.13)	−0.02	(0.26)	0.14	(0.22)	−0.06	(0.21)	−0.01	(0.23)
Irish 2	−0.06	(0.14)	−0.17	(0.50)	0.09	(0.32)	0.29	(0.21)	0.30	(0.30)
Italian 2	0.09	(0.09)	0.03	(0.23)	0.26	(0.16)	0.05	(0.14)	0.06	(0.14)
Polish 2	0.13	(0.15)	0.03	(0.35)	−0.09	(0.41)	−0.01	(0.24)	0.04	(0.24)
Black 2	−0.13	(0.16)	−0.03	(0.19)	−0.72	(0.41)	0.22	(0.27)	0.03	(0.16)
Filipino 2	0.01	(0.13)	0.04	(0.19)	−0.19	(0.41)	−0.07	(0.25)	−0.01	(0.16)
East Asian 2	0.00	(0.11)	0.21	(0.22)	0.16	(0.34)	−0.18	(0.38)	−0.12	(0.17)
Puerto Rican 2	−0.10	(0.09)	−0.23	(0.14)	−0.14	(0.22)	0.03	(0.08)	−0.10	(0.07)
Mexican 2	−**0.14**	(0.06)	0.03	(0.08)	−0.15	(0.13)	−0.09	(0.05)	−**0.13**	(0.04)
Cuban 2	−0.00	(0.10)	−0.14	(0.18)	−0.18	(0.24)	−0.08	(0.17)	−0.17	(0.16)
Dominican 2	−0.13	(0.23)	0.04	(0.30)	−0.15	(0.71)	−0.07	(0.35)	−0.10	(0.18)
Asian 3	−0.08	(0.07)	−0.01	(0.13)	0.06	(0.13)	0.12	(0.09)	−0.02	(0.08)
Puerto Rican 3	0.05	(0.13)	0.21	(0.20)	0.19	(0.41)	0.01	(0.16)	−0.13	(0.13)
Mexican 3	−0.06	(0.04)	−0.06	(0.06)	−0.00	(0.08)	−**0.12**	(0.04)	−**0.13**	(0.03)

	(1)	(2)	(3)	(4)	(5)
African American	**−0.14** (0.02)	**−0.13** (0.04)	**−0.12** (0.06)	**−0.08** (0.03)	**−0.08** (0.02)
American Indian	0.01 (0.06)	−0.09 (0.13)	−0.07 (0.11)	−0.11 (0.06)	**−0.10** (0.05)
Chi-Square (D.F.)	27,001.9 (40,029)	72,94.3 (10,290)	17,599.6 (12,843)	13,369.6 (27,114)	41,491 (33,507)
R-square[b]	0.250	0.285	0.119	0.269	0.190
N	40,080	10,341	12,894	27,165	35,558

Note: standard errors are given in brackets; emboldened coefficients indicate significance at the 0.05 level or higher.

[a] Parameter estimates were achieved by regressing hourly earnings, assumed to have a gamma distribution, on the covariates using the generalised linear model (GLM) with the log of hourly earnings as the link function.

[b] R-square is the squared correlation of predicted with observed log hourly earnings.

Table 14.8A. Effects of ancestry on logged hourly earnings,[a] across occupational destinations: Men (parameter estimates).

	Salariat		Routine non-manual		Petty bourgeoisie		Manual supervisor/ skilled manual		Semi- and unskilled manual	
Effects of ancestry										
Canadian 1	**0.30**	(0.10)	0.19	(0.18)	0.34	(0.28)	−0.05	(0.38)	−0.00	(0.19)
German 1	−0.06	(0.12)	0.08	(0.18)	−0.34	(0.24)	0.03	(0.29)	−0.28	(0.16)
Irish 1	0.06	(0.18)	0.09	(0.30)	−0.62	(0.45)	0.18	(0.71)	0.19	(0.24)
Italian 1	−0.02	(0.23)	0.18	(0.24)	0.11	(0.29)	0.19	(0.29)	−0.19	(0.22)
Polish 1	−0.08	(0.17)	0.33	(0.17)	0.00	(0.27)	−0.42	(0.38)	−0.09	(0.12)
Black 1	−0.09	(0.07)	−0.09	(0.08)	−**0.57**	(0.21)	−0.19	(0.19)	−0.03	(0.05)
Filipino 1	0.04	(0.06)	−0.10	(0.09)	0.23	(0.23)	−0.02	(0.17)	−0.06	(0.06)
East Asian 1	0.03	(0.06)	−0.05	(0.09)	−**0.26**	(0.10)	−0.03	(0.14)	−**0.21**	(0.07)
Puerto Rican 1	−0.03	(0.10)	−0.14	(0.10)	−0.45	(0.26)	−0.08	(0.16)	−**0.13**	(0.07)
Mexican 1	−0.12	(0.07)	−**0.23**	(0.06)	−0.17	(0.10)	**0.26**	(0.07)	−**0.16**	(0.03)
Cuban 1	−0.06	(0.10)	−**0.20**	(0.10)	−0.31	(0.22)	−0.25	(0.18)	−0.07	(0.09)
Dominican 1	−0.21	(0.15)	0.10	(0.13)	−0.38	(0.25)	−0.34	(0.21)	−**0.20**	(0.07)
Canadian 2	0.22	(0.12)	0.11	(0.17)	0.04	(0.29)	−0.22	(0.71)	−0.03	(0.21)
German 2	−0.05	(0.13)	−0.10	(0.17)	0.21	(0.45)	−0.04	(0.41)	−0.47	(0.25)
Irish 2	0.14	(0.15)	0.02	(0.18)	−0.22	(0.45)	−0.05	(0.10)	−0.18	(0.41)
Italian 2	−0.16	(0.12)	0.01	(0.11)	−0.07	(0.26)	−0.02	(0.36)	0.18	(0.19)
Polish 2	0.07	(0.19)	−0.21	(0.22)	0.00	(0.71)	0.11	(0.71)	0.23	(0.29)
Black 2	−0.13	(0.13)	0.07	(0.15)	−0.55	(0.50)	−0.33	(0.45)	−0.11	(0.19)
Filipino 2	0.09	(0.13)	−0.08	(0.14)	0.78	(0.71)	0.11	(0.45)	−0.11	(0.19)
East Asian 2	−0.01	(0.11)	0.12	(0.15)	**1.11**	(0.50)	0.41	(0.45)	−0.00	(0.24)
Puerto Rican 2	−0.01	(0.07)	−0.04	(0.06)	−0.13	(0.30)	0.20	(0.18)	−0.03	(0.08)
Mexican 2	−0.01	(0.06)	0.01	(0.05)	0.10	(0.17)	0.04	(0.13)	−**0.09**	(0.05)
Cuban 2	0.03	(0.11)	0.11	(0.10)	−0.61	(0.50)	−0.22	(0.38)	−0.04	(0.22)
Dominican 2	−0.22	(0.22)	−0.10	(0.22)	−1.19	(0.71)	0.11	(0.50)	−0.20	(0.20)
Asian 3	−0.03	(0.06)	−0.05	(0.07)	−0.04	(0.18)	0.12	(0.18)	**0.19**	(0.10)
Puerto Rican 3	−0.09	(0.11)	0.23	(0.13)	0.02	(0.45)	−0.09	(0.27)	**0.33**	(0.14)
Mexican 3	−0.06	(0.03)	−**0.07**	(0.03)	−**0.22**	(0.10)	−0.01	(0.07)	0.01	(0.04)

African American	0.01	(0.02)	−0.00	(0.02)	−0.05	(0.07)	−0.01	(0.04)	0.00	(0.02)
American Indian	0.05	(0.06)	−0.03	(0.06)	0.07	(0.18)	−0.00	(0.10)	−0.09	(0.05)
Chi-Square (D.F.)	26,486.0 (41,883)		22,044.2 (29,921)		12,616.4 (6,444)		4,828.0 (6,066)		37,996 (28,020)	
R-square[b]	0.202		0.153		0.085		0.142		0.099	
N	41,934		29,972		6,495		6,117		28,071	

Note: standard errors are given in brackets; emboldened coefficients indicate significance at the 0.05 level or higher.
[a] Parameter estimates were achieved by regressing hourly earnings, assumed to have a gamma distribution, on the covariates using the generalised linear model (GLM) with the log of hourly earnings as the link function.
[b] R-square is the squared correlation of predicted with observed log hourly earnings.

Filipinos, second-generation Mexicans and American Indians—operates primarily by limiting group members' ability to access desirable occupational classes rather than by denying them earnings parity with other members of their respective class. A final generalisation concerns within-class variations. Compared to the upper three occupational classes, members of the lowest two classes are more often significantly penalised; that is to say, the lower the occupational class, the more disadvantage minority group members suffer.

Turning more specifically to the group membership effects within the salariat in Table 14.8A, five first-generation groups face ethnic penalties. Put in a more interesting way, once in the salariat, foreign-born Filipino, East Asian and Cuban males earn as much as native-born White males. The same as true for all second-generation men save one: Mexicans. And, only one third-generation group experiences a penalty within the salariat: African Americans.

The women's results appear in Table 14.8B. The finding vis-à-vis the salariat is striking: not a single group membership coefficient attains statistical significance. Indeed, within every class, there are far fewer significant group membership coefficients than in Table 14.8A. This gender disparity means that ethnic women's disadvantage—even more than men's—is mediated by class membership. For instance, although every first-generation non-white women's group faced a significant disadvantage in accessing the salariat, not one women's group, first or later generation, incurs an earning penalty within the salariat. Another difference from the male pattern is that a significant coefficient in one equation rarely implies a significant coefficient in another. The main exception to this generalisation is first-generation Mexican women, who earn significantly less than native White women in three out of five occupational classes. Note, too, that while African American men earned less within every class, African American women registered no shortfalls whatsoever. There is but one similarity between women and men—second-generation Mexican women and men employed in manual, unskilled occupations both earn significantly less than the benchmark group. Recalling the earnings shortfall of second-generation Mexican men within the salariat, we conclude that, with the exception of Mexicans, a key finding of this study is that second-generation Americans are quite successful in the labour market.

Conclusion

To begin, a brief methodological caveat: though we have used the best available data for quantitative analysis of the second generation, the CPS has several deficiencies that compromise our results. First, an important indicator of immigrants' human capital—language skill—is not available. Controlling for English ability might change the results, particularly among Hispanic immigrants, many of whom have relatively weak English skills. Second, an insufficiency of cases forced us to create two composite groups: Blacks and East Asians. Clearly, analysing composite groups is not an ideal strategy; however, at least we had some information about the respective heritages of our composite groups. In the case of the third generation, it is not possible to distinguish the ethnic backgrounds of Blacks or Asians. Though the great majority of third-generation Blacks are African American, third-generation Asians are a heterogeneous group that includes Pacific Islanders. In short, intergenerational comparisons must be done with care.

Turning to matters of substance, we find that the addition of non-Europeans to the American melting pot has wrought some changes in the traditional 'assimilation tale'. Ceteris paribus, at the turn of the new century, first-generation non-Europeans do not fare as well as their European counterparts. On the other hand, most second-generation non-European groups do as well as native-born White people. This is truer for women than men, and truer of earnings and access to the salariat than of unemployment, but the generalisation holds all the same. The one second-generation group in serious difficulty is Mexicans. But, as Waldinger and Feliciano (2004) also have noted, there is a gender difference here. Both second- and third-generation Mexican women encounter fewer labour-market difficulties than their male counterparts. A gender interaction also surfaces for Blacks, though it is weaker than for Mexicans. Still, looking across our many dependent variables, Black women incur fewer penalties within every generation than their male counterparts. This trend suggests a point that has been made many times: segmented assimilation theory needs to take gender into account (Waters 1996; Waldinger and Feliciano 2004).

A more unexpected gender interaction occurred among first-generation East Asians. Here women—but not men—have difficulty, first in finding employment, then, for those with less than a college degree, in accessing the salariat. The main causal mechanism seems to be an undervaluing of their education. In Zeng and Xic's (2004) analysis of Asian American men's earnings, they uncover a shortfall in educational returns between persons educated in Asia and persons educated in America. Since it is unlikely that foreign-born Asian women and men differ much in the geography of their education, why US employers evaluate the two genders' schooling differently remains a mystery.

Another theoretically informative result concerns first-generation Puerto Ricans. Puerto Ricans fare no worse than other first-generation groups, better than Mexicans, and, occasionally better than Cubans as well. This result is unexpected because, according to classic theories of immigrant selectivity, the easier relocation becomes, the less skilled and diligent is the immigrant. Because Puerto Ricans are US citizens and can enter (or leave) the mainland at will, scholars have generally assumed that they are 'less positively selected' than immigrants who must either satisfy immigration regulations or enter the US clandestinely (Borjas 1994). Our results call into question the assumption that legal obstacles play a major role in the economic outcomes of (im)migrants. These 'former colonials' fare at least as well in their 'metropole' as other immigrants do.

We turn finally to the third generation. Contrary to the expectations of assimilationists, third-generation Americans face more economic handicaps than second-generation Americans. At least, that is the conclusion suggested by a superficial reading of our results. However, for Blacks and Asians, no intergenerational implications can be drawn because the first and second generations are defined differently from the third. American Indians, of course, have no generational antecedents. And their economic difficulties are well known. Indeed, only the Puerto Rican and Mexican experiences can be compared across three generations. Looking first at Puerto Ricans, the overall picture is optimistic: each generation does somewhat better than the previous one. To be sure, Puerto Ricans overall are not very prosperous. But this is primarily due to their characteristics—especially low education—not to their ability to translate those characteristics into economic rewards. To be sure, their educational disadvantage may also reflect an ethnic penalty of some kind. The Mexican case is different, especially as it involves both low education and, for men, difficulty translating their characteristics into economic rewards. Only Mexican women exhibit intergenerational progress. One factor that might contribute to the Puerto Rican–Mexican difference is that an unknown portion of third-generation Mexicans are not the descendants of immigrants, but of conquered peoples native to the Southwest. The economic trajectory of the descendants of immigrants and the descendants of conquered peoples should be very different. However, to the extent that this distinction is captured by a dummy for Southwestern residence, it is not confirmed in our analysis; nor can it account for the gender interaction.

Thus, our third-generation results have few implications for the vast majority of groups in this study. To be sure, in the case of the European groups, other research findings provide a template from which to predict that the Europeans examined here will merge indistinguishably into the American mainstream, if they have not already. In the case of the non-Europeans, more is known about the later generations of groups with a long history in the US, such as the Chinese, than about the later generations of groups with a short history in the US, such as Dominicans. But, even when there is a 'paper trail', predicting the future on the basis of the past is risky. Moreover, before developing projections about a 'non-European immigrant third generation', we would do well to remember that today's second-generation non-Europeans are still a young group. Studies of other economically disadvantaged groups—women, for instance—show that the older they are, the more handicaps they encounter. The average age of our non-European second generation is 29.2 years. Thus, whether or not the results reported here obtain one or two decades from now is a question that only future scholars can address.

Technical appendix

The Current Population Survey is a nationwide survey of the civilian, non-institutionalised population age 15 and above, residing in all fifty states of the US. It is a multi-stage cluster sample; accordingly, in this chapter, estimates of population percentages are calculated from data weighted by the probability of sample selection. Details about the sampling strategy and construction of the variables can be found at <http://www.bls.census.gov/cps/cpsmain.htm>. Several archives offer these data; we obtained them from the Inter-university Consortium for Political and Social Research at the University of Michigan (<http://www.icpsr.umich.edu/>). As with most data collected by the US government, some subgroups are inadequately represented; for instance, African Americans, especially young adult males, and undocumented immigrants (Passel and Fix 2001; Robinson and Adlakha 2002). In addition, institutionalised persons are omitted altogether. In the US, both African Americans and some Hispanic groups are disproportionately incarcerated (Kennedy 2001). These considerations mean that the results pertaining to these groups contain an upward bias; that is to say, a more accurate sample would have produced less favourable results. However, there is no remedy for this problem, save its acknowledgement.

The interviewing strategy presents an additional but surmountable challenge. Beginning in January, respondents are interviewed for four consecutive months and then, eight months later, interviewed for another four months. Thus, those surveyed in March of one year are surveyed again in March of the following year. Each March, therefore, the survey sample contains one half of the respondents from the previous year's survey and one half of the respondents from the present year's survey. In order to avoid this 50% inter-year duplication, we extracted the data for this study in alternate years. Responses from four years—1995, 1997, 1999, and 2001—were pooled, yielding a total of 158,361 men and 148,247 women. Like other studies in this volume, the sample is restricted to persons aged 18 to 59.

Gender is controlled for by estimating models for men and women separately. Each model controls for age and the square of age. Following the guidelines for this volume, we divided education into five ordered categories: (1) less than tenth grade (labelled hereafter as 'primary or none'); (2) completion of tenth, eleventh or twelfth grade but no diploma ('lower secondary'); (3) high school diploma ('higher secondary'); (4) some post-high school study ('some tertiary'); and (5) a bachelor's degree or higher ('full tertiary'). In the additive, multivariate analyses, dummy variables represent these five categories, with elementary education as the contrast category. When interactions are included, however, education level was treated as a single, continuous variable centred at the third category, higher secondary, and coded as $-2, -1, 0, 1, 2$ years of schooling completed. Marital status was measured by two dummy variables indicating whether the person was (1) married with spouse present or (2) separated or divorced. Single/never married was the omitted contrast category. We also included dummy variables to indicate the year of the survey—1995, 1997, 1999, and 2001—and to adjust for the effects of inflation and the business cycle on our measures of economic outcomes. The year 2001 was used as the contrast category. In the supplementary analyses, we added four dummy variables to control for regional effects: Northeast, Midwest, South, and West. The last served as the omitted category. For foreign-born persons we included years in the US since migrating and the square of years; native born persons were given a value of zero on this variable.

References

Alba, R. and Nee, V. (2003), *Rethinking the American Mainstream* (Cambridge, MA: Harvard University Press).

Alba, R., Lutz, A., and Vesselinov, E. (2001), 'How Enduring Were the Inequalities Among European Immigrant Groups in the United States?', *Demography*, 3, 49–56.

Anderson, E. (1990), *Streetwise* (Chicago: University of Chicago Press).

Borjas, G. J. (1994), 'The Economics of Immigration', *Journal of Economic Literature*, 32, 1667–1717.

Borjas, G. J. (1999), *Heaven's Door: Immigration Policy and the American Economy* (Princeton, NJ: Princeton University Press).

Brimelow, P. (1995), *Alien Nation* (New York: Random House).

Card, D., DiNardo, J., and Estes, E. (1999), 'The More Things Change: Immigrants and the Children of Immigrants in the 1940s, the 1970s and the 1990s'. In G. J. Borjas (ed.) *Issues in the Economics of Immigration* (Chicago: University of Chicago Press), pp. 227–69.

Carliner, G. (1980), 'Wages, Earnings and Hours of First, Second and Third Generation American Males', *Economic Inquiry*, 18, 87–102.

Chan, S. (1990), 'European and Asian Immigration into the United States in Comparative Perspective, 1820s to 1920s'. In V. Yans-McLaughlin (ed.), *Immigration Reconsidered* (New York: Oxford University Press), pp. 37–75.

Cheng, Y. (1994), *Education and Class: Chinese in Britain and the U.S.* (Aldershot: Avebury).

Chiswick, B. R. (1977), 'Sons of Immigrants: Are They at an Earnings Disadvantage?', *The American Economic Review, Papers and Proceedings of the 89th Annual Meeting of the American Economic Association*, 67, 376–80.

Chiswick, B. R. (1979), 'The Economic Progress of Immigrants: Some Apparently Universal Patterns'. In W. Fellner (ed.), *Contemporary Economic Problems 1979* (Washington, DC: American Enterprise Institute), pp. 357–99.

Chiswick, B. R. (1983), 'An Analysis of the Earnings and Employment of Asian-American Men', *Journal of Labor Economics*, 1, 197–214.

Erickson, R. and Goldthorpe, J. H. (1992), *The Constant Flux* (Oxford: Clarendon Press).

Espiritu, Y. L. (1992), *Asian American Panethnicity* (Philadelphia: Temple University Press).

Farley, R. and Alba, R. (2002), 'The New Second Generation in the United States', *International Migration Review*, 36, 669–701.

Featherman, D. L. and Hauser, R. M. (1978), *Opportunity and Change* (New York: Academic Press).

Grosfoguel, R. (1997), 'Colonial Caribbean Migrations to France, the Netherlands, Great Britain and the United States', *Ethnic and Racial Studies*, 20, 594–612.

Heer, D. M. (1996), *Immigration in America's Future* (Boulder, CO: Westview).

Hirschman, C. and Kraly, E. P. (1990), 'Racial and Ethnic Inequality in the United States, 1940 and 1950: the Impact of Geographic Location and Human Capital', *International Migration Review*, 24, 4–33.

Kennedy, R. (2001), 'Racial Trends in the Administration of Criminal Justice'. In N. J. Smelser, W. J. Wilson and F. Mitchell (eds.), *America Becoming: Racial Trends and their Consequences*, Vol. 2 (Washington, DC: National Research Council), pp. 1–20.

Landale, N. S., Oropesa, R. S., and Llanes, D. (1998), 'Schooling, Work and Idleness Among Mexican and Non-Latino Adolescents', *Social Science Research*, 27, 457–80.

Laumann, E. O. (1973), *Bonds of Pluralism* (New York: John Wiley & Sons).

Lee, E. S. (1966), 'A Theory of Migration', *Demography*, 3, 47–57.

Levene, G. and Rhodes, C. (1981), *The Japanese American Community; A Three Generation Study* (New York: Praeger).

Lim, N. (1999), 'Employers' Ratings of Work Related Qualities of Racial and Ethnic Groups', unpub. MS (Department of Sociology, University of California at Los Angeles).

Lippi-Green, R. (1997), *English with an Accent* (New York: Routledge).

Model, S. (1995), 'West Indian Prosperity: Fact or Fiction?', *Social Problems*, 42, 501–19.

Nee, V. and Sanders, J. (2001), 'Understanding the Diversity of Immigrant Incorporation', *Ethnic and Racial Studies*, 24, 386–411.
Ogbu, J. U. (1978), *Minority Education and Caste: The American System in Cross-Cultural Perspective*, New York: Academic Press.
Passel, J. and Fix, M. (2001), U.S. Immigration at the Beginning of the 21st Century: Testimony Prepared for the Subcommittee on Immigration and Claims. Hearing on the U.S. Population and Immigration. Committee on the Judiciary. House of Representatives. Urban Institute. August 2, 2001.
Perlmann, J. and Waldinger, R. (1997), 'Second Generation Decline? Immigrant Children Past and Present—a Reconsideration', *International Migration Review*, 31, 893–922.
Portes, A. and Bach, R. L. (1985), *Latin Journey* (Berkeley: University of California).
Portes, A. and Rumbaut, R. G. (2001), *Legacies* (Berkeley: University of California Press).
Portes, A. and Zhou, M. (1993), 'The New Second Generation: Segmented Assimilation and Its Variants', *Annals of the American Academy of Political and Social Science*, 530, 74–96.
Robinson, J. G. and Adlakha, A. (2002), 'Comparison of A.C.E. Revision II Results with Demographic Analysis'. U.S. Bureau of the Census. DSSD A.C.E. Revision II Estimates Memorandum Series. Series PP-41. December 31, 2002. <http://www.census.gov/www/pdf/pp-41r.pdf>.
Shavit, Y. and Müller, W. (eds.) (1998), *From School to Work* (Oxford: Clarendon Press).
Smith, J. P. and Welch, F. R. (1994), 'Black Economic Progress After Myrdal'. In P. Burstein (ed.), *Equal Employment Opportunity* (New York: Aldine de Gruyter), pp. 155–82.
Spring, J. (1997), *Deculturalization and the Struggle for Equality: A Brief History of the Education of Dominated Cultures in the United States*, 2nd edn. (New York: McGraw-Hill).
U.S. Bureau of the Census (1994, 2000), *Statistical Abstract of the United States: 1994* and *2000* (Washington, DC: GPO).
U.S. Immigration and Naturalization Service (1999), *Statistical Yearbook of the Immigration and Naturalization Service, 1997* (Washington, D.C.: U.S. Government Printing Office).
Waldinger, R. and Feliciano, C. (2004), 'Will the Second Generation Experience Downward Assimilation? Segmented Assimilation Re-Assessed', *Ethnic and Racial Studies*, 27, 376–402.
Waters, M. C. (1996), 'The Intersection of Gender, Race and Ethnicity in the Identity Development of Caribbean American Teens'. In B. J. R. Leadbeater and N. Way (eds.), *Urban Girls* (New York: New York University Press), pp. 65–81.
Wilson, W. J. (1987), *The Truly Disadvantaged* (Chicago: University of Chicago Press).
Zeng, Z. and Xie, Y. (2004), 'Asian Americans' Earnings Disadvantage Re-examined: The Role of Place of Education', *American Journal of Sociology*, 109, 1075–1108.

15

Crossnational Patterns and Processes of Ethnic Disadvantage

ANTHONY HEATH

Introduction

OUR CENTRAL RESEARCH QUESTION IS WHETHER the disadvantages that have been well-documented for first-generation migrants to the developed countries of Europe and North America also hold for the second and later generations who have been brought up and educated in the countries of destination and thus do not have the handicaps such as lack of fluency in the destination language that would have held back the first, migrant, generation. As we argued in the introductory chapter, the experience of the second generation gives us a clearer idea of whether these liberal developed countries do actually provide equality of opportunity to all their citizens, irrespective of their ethnic or national origin. Our particular interest has been in the experience of the newer migrant groups from non-European origins. Will they have the same favourable outcomes that characterised the earlier waves of migrants from Europe to the New World in the nineteenth and early twentieth centuries? Or will they experience continuing legacies of their initial disadvantages in much the same way that African Americans appear to in the USA?

In this chapter we first try to bring together the evidence from the individual country chapters and to see whether they on balance support the more optimistic scenario, which expects gradual reduction in disadvantage across the generations, or whether a more pessimistic scenario of continuing disadvantage is in prospect. We shall then, in the second part of the chapter, explore some of the possible explanations that we reviewed in Chapter 1, focusing on the relationship between patterns of ethnic disadvantage and the nature of each country's economy, its patterns of social fluidity, its conception of nationhood, racism and xenophobia, and the relevant government policies.

As we explained in the introductory chapter, it is useful to distinguish between the gross disadvantages that ethnic minorities typically experience in the labour market and the net disadvantages (or ethnic penalties) after controlling for individual characteristics, especially for educational level and age. We begin by reviewing briefly the gross differences between groups. This shows the overall extent of ethnic stratification in each society and the nature of the vertical mosaic. We then turn to consider the process of stratification before turning to the pattern of ethnic penalties.

Patterns of ethnic stratification

Our chapter authors have documented continuing patterns of ethnic stratification along much the same lines, although often of reduced magnitude, in the second generation as in the first generation. The nature of the ethnic hierarchy is very similar across countries too. Several expected but important features stand out. First, in all countries there is clear ethnic stratification. Moreover, within each country the hierarchy is broadly similar, with groups from North-West European origins being at the top followed by those from other European origins and those from non-European origins tending to come at the bottom of the ethnic hierarchy. Secondly, both the rank order and the size of the disadvantages is broadly similar for women as for men. If we take unemployment rates as our yardstick we find a consistent pattern with

- groups of North-West European ancestry (e.g. British, Dutch, German and Irish) generally having similar (if not more favourable) unemployment rates as the charter populations in all the countries where we can distinguish them: Australia, Canada, Israel and the USA.
- South Europeans are not far behind but have more varied fortunes. While second-generation Italians do well in Canada, Australia and the US and South Europeans have low unemployment rates in France, Italians have unemployment rates twice those of the charter population in Belgium and Germany even in the second generation. Greeks and Maltese have low unemployment rates in Australia but in Germany Greek rates of unemployment are twice those of the charter population.
- East Europeans experience considerable disadvantages in the first generation, possibly because of language difficulties, but in the

second generation they too rank close to the South Europeans. Second-generation East Europeans (for example Poles) fare well in Canada, the USA, France and Israel but second-generation ex-Yugoslavs have unemployment rates around twice those of the charter population in Austria and Germany.
- Among groups of non-European ancestry Chinese and Indians have relatively low unemployment rates. Almost all the other second-generation groups of non-European ancestry have higher unemployment rates than the charter population, and generally they are higher than those of any of the European groups. Caribbeans in Canada, Britain, France, Netherlands and the US have unemployment rates two to three times as high as those of the charter populations as do Mexicans and Puerto Ricans in the USA and Lebanese in Australia.
- In the European countries of Austria, Belgium, France, Germany and the Netherlands Turks and Moroccans tend to have even higher unemployment rates and come at the bottom of their ethnic hierarchies. In France for example second-generation Maghrebins have unemployment rates three times those of the charter population. In Belgium the unemployment rates for second-generation men of Turkish and Moroccan ancestry are almost six times those of the charter population.
- Indigenous and involuntary minorities tend invariably to come at the bottom of the ethnic hierarchy in their respective countries. Native Americans in Canada and the US and aboriginals in Australia all have unemployment rates twice or more those of their charter populations but worst off are Blacks in South Africa with unemployment rates nearly ten times those of White South Africans.

This pattern of ethnic stratification is not especially surprising. European groups tend to be more highly educated than those of non-European ancestry, reflecting patterns of class reproduction. The children of migrant worker groups recruited as guestworkers to fill less-skilled jobs in Austria, Belgium, France and Germany will have disadvantaged class origins and on that account alone could be expected to have low educational and occupational attainment themselves. Our key question is whether these patterns of gross disadvantage are mirrored when we turn to net disadvantage (the ethnic penalties) after controlling for educational attainment. Educational inequalities can be expected to explain a considerable part of these gross inequalities in the labour market. We turn next, therefore, to the process of stratification and the role of education.

The process of stratification

As we suggested in the introduction to this volume, it is conventional to conceptualise the process of stratification in terms of the OED linkages, where O represents origins, E represents education, and D represents class destinations. In our case, we consider ethnic origins rather than class origins and our chapter authors have shown that there is a strong link between ethnic origins and educational attainment. Groups that were at the bottom of the occupational hierarchy in the first generation also tend to be at the bottom of the educational hierarchy in the second generation. This almost certainly reflects, at least in part, processes of social reproduction familiar from studies of class inequalities in education. As emphasised by all our chapter authors, we must not equate the first generation with the parents of the second generation, since the first generation will also include young recent arrivals. Only in the case of the French data can we unambiguously identify the parental generation. These French data show major educational advances made by the second generation in comparison with their parents (even larger in fact than those found in a comparison of the second generation with the current first generation) but the French data also confirm that there is ethnic stratification in education among the second generation that parallels the ethnic stratification in occupational class among the parental generation.

More generally, we find that groups which have broadly achieved economic parity with the charter population have also achieved educational parity, while economically disadvantaged groups also tend to be educationally disadvantaged. Broadly speaking, our chapter authors have shown that:

- Most ethnic groups in most countries have made substantial educational progress across generations.
- In the second generation gender inequalities in education have tended to decline, especially in the case of groups (such as South Asians) where gender differences were rather marked in the first generation.

- But many of the second generation whose parents were from non-European origins still lag considerably behind the charter population in educational terms.
- Indigenous groups have fared particularly badly in gaining access to education.

The next linkage in the general sociological model is that between education and occupational class. As we have seen in the individual chapters, in all our thirteen countries there is a strong association between educational level and labour-market success, less so with respect to unemployment and much more strongly with respect to the more privileged positions in the salariat. These are more or less universal features of developed societies (and quite probably of less developed ones too.)

There are, however, considerable differences between our societies in the strength of this ED association. This in turn may well be important for explaining cross-national differences in ethnic disadvantage. If education has only a weak link with occupational success, then educational disadvantage is unlikely to explain why an ethnic minority is occupationally disadvantaged. Table 15.1 shows the strength of the relationship between education and the two outcomes of avoidance of unemployment and access to the salariat. These estimates represent the main effects of education in the logistic regressions carried out in the country chapters[1] and in most countries will largely be driven by the processes that affect the numerically dominant charter populations.

While we have to be very cautious because of the methodological difficulties[2] in making cross-national comparisons of this sort, there do

---

[1] The parameter estimates shown in Table 15.1 show the full tertiary/social minimum contrast. In most of the individual country chapters the authors take full secondary education as the reference category. So for example in Australia we find, for male unemployment, a parameter estimate of +0.65 for tertiary education and an estimate of −0.67 for incomplete secondary education. To obtain the tertiary/social minimum contrast we therefore subtract the incomplete secondary estimate from the tertiary estimate. Thus in the Australian case 0.65− (−0.67) yields the figure of 1.32 in Table 15.1.

[2] In particular our classification of educational levels may not be equally suited to all the countries included in our study. For example, in many European countries there are important distinctions between academic and vocational tracks that are quite consequential for labour-market success but which are not distinguished in our classification. This means that the effect of education is likely to be underestimated in countries such as Austria, Belgium, France, Germany and the Netherlands. These academic/vocational distinctions are possibly less important in countries that have comprehensive systems of education such as Australia, Canada, Britain, Sweden and the USA. In addition we should note that some countries such as Austria and Belgium were unable to distinguish lower tertiary qualifications, and this may mean that our measure underestimates the effects of education in these countries.

Table 15.1. Crossnational differences in the effects of education on the avoidance of unemployment and access to the salariat (parameter estimates[a]).

	Avoidance of Unemployment		Access to the Salariat	
	Men	Women	Men	Women
Australia	1.32	1.35	4.04	3.96
Austria	1.45	1.09	7.75	7.93
Belgium	1.46	1.99	4.98	6.23
Canada	1.31	1.13	5.04	5.21
France	1.02	1.23	6.29	6.36
Germany	1.46	0.88	7.10	6.47
Israel	1.01	0.99	3.87	4.60
Netherlands	0.89	1.33	3.56	3.55
South Africa[b]	0.57	−0.31	0.87	0.53
Sweden[c]	0.65	1.12	4.08	5.10
UK—GB	1.27	0.74	5.08	4.98
UK—NI[d]	2.53	1.11	5.72	6.02
USA	1.13	1.29	5.06	5.17

Source: Chapters in this volume.

[a] The parameter estimates shown are those for the highest (full tertiary) versus lowest (primary or social minimum) contrast.

[b] The figures for South Africa are for the English-speaking whites.

[c] The Swedish figures are for employment versus non-employment and for access to the lower salariat.

[d] The Northern Ireland figures are for 1985/6.

appear to be some major differences between countries in the strength of the association. Leaving aside South Africa, which is a remarkable outlier to which we return shortly, we find that Austria, France and Germany exhibit very strong associations between education and labour-market success while Australia, Israel, the Netherlands and Sweden exhibit much weaker associations. Belgium, Britain, Canada, Northern Ireland and the USA lie somewhere in between. It is beyond the scope of this chapter to explore the reasons for these cross-national differences in the strength of the ED link, although it should be noted that Austria and Germany have highly selective systems of education where relatively few people complete tertiary education; those who do complete tertiary education may therefore be a particularly select group and this may well account for their relative success in the labour market.

Perhaps more crucial for a study of ethnic disadvantage is whether these educational processes operate in the same way for the second-generation ethnic minorities as they do for the charter populations.[3] As we suggested in the introduction, there are a number of theoretical reasons, such as employers' unwillingness to treat foreign qualifications as equivalent to domestic ones, that would lead us to expect that migrants will have poorer returns to education than the charter population. However, this line of argument suggests that the second generation, who will have domestic qualifications, will obtain the same returns on their qualifications as do the charter population.

Do second-generation ethnic minorities therefore get the same returns on their educational investments as the charter populations? The answer is that, in most countries and for most groups they do. As Model and Fisher comment in their chapter on the USA 'differential returns are not a major part of the story'. As expected, differential returns appear to be rather more common in the first generation, but for most second-generation groups the stratification process works in a similar way for ethnic minorities as for the charter population. This also holds true for most of our countries just as it does for the USA.[4] (See Table 15.A1 in the appendix to this chapter for details of all the statistically significant ethnicity*education interactions in the second generation.)

When testing for a very large numbers of interactions, we should expect to find some 'statistically significant' ones solely by chance. Rather than focusing on particular interactions, it makes more sense to look at the overall pattern. In most countries there are relatively few significant interactions in the second generation but a tendency for interactions, when they do occur, to be negative. In other words the ethnic groups concerned tend to obtain poorer returns on their educational investments. In Israel and even more so in South Africa, however, we find a very different pattern with a predominance of positive interactions. In particular for

---

[3] Moreover, from a technical point of view, if educational processes operate differently for ethnic minorities than for the charter populations, then our calculations of the ethnic penalties based on the assumption that processes are the same will be misleading. Since our reference category for education is full secondary, the parameter estimates for ethnicity in a model including education*ethnicity interactions will simply give the 'ethnic penalty' for respondents with full secondary education. The ethnic penalties for respondents at other educational levels will be different.

[4] We must remember that our ability to find statistically significant interactions will depend crucially on the size of the sample for that particular ethnic group. For some small groups we simply will not have the statistical power to detect interactions, while for some large groups in countries with large samples (e.g. South Africa), even substantively small interactions may be statistically significant. We should therefore pay attention to the size of the interaction and not simply its level of significance.

Palestinians in Israel and for Asians, Coloureds and Blacks in South Africa we find highly significant and substantively large positive interactions between ethnicity and education.

Why do we tend to find lower returns in most Western countries but higher returns in Israel and South Africa? One possibility, as Treiman suggested in his chapter on South Africa, is that Blacks with tertiary education are an especially highly selected group since so few Blacks are able to gain access to tertiary education. The ones that do have degrees are likely to be unusually talented or motivated and it is this that may account for their unusual success. This explanation could also apply to Palestinians in Israel, where very few Palestinians obtain degrees. However, there are some other ethnic groups, as we have seen, whose members rarely obtain degrees—for example Turks in Germany or Austria and Aboriginals in Australia or Canada. The selection argument ought to apply to these groups too but in fact we find negative interactions for these groups. So we doubt if selection is the whole story.

Another possibility is that there were specific mechanisms at work in South Africa (and perhaps Israel) that prevented members of the dominant groups from falling into lower-level jobs. The striking feature about South Africa is how weak the main effects of education are for the comparison group of English-speaking Whites. While we can describe this as indicating low returns to education, it is perhaps more helpful to think of it as indicating a floor which prevents White English-speakers from falling into low-skilled jobs or into unemployment. One might be tempted to term this the operation of a caste society, but that would be misleading because some members of the subordinate ethnic groups do appear to be able to access high-status occupations. These occupations are not reserved for the dominant group in the way that they are in a caste system. Instead we would suggest that South Africa represents the operation of what might be termed a 'British Raj' society (after the operation of the British Raj in India rather than of the indigenous caste system) or more generally a colonial system. That is to say, highly educated members of subordinate groups such as native Indians (most famously Gandhi and Nehru), might be allowed to become lawyers or to join other professions and up to a point to join the elite, largely because of the British Raj's strategy of using educated indigenous peoples to help manage the conquered, subordinate groups. However, corresponding downward mobility by members of the White elite was unthinkable. In practice, then, there was an asymmetry with a great range of low-skilled jobs for which only members of the subordinate ethnic groups were eligible and a limited number of elite jobs for which selected members of subordinate groups might be eligible.[5]

This raises important points about the operation of social stratification processes in different kinds of society. While South Africa is clearly an outlier in our study, it exhibits (or hopefully in the past tense 'exhibited') a colonial system of stratification. Possibly the relation between Jews and Palestinians in Israel also approximates to this colonial system. We would hypothesise that historically the same system would have applied in Northern Ireland and perhaps the Southern States of the USA although not in Australia and Canada, where the absence of large indigenous populations to fill the less-skilled jobs meant that other White settlers of European ancestry had to fill these roles.

What is also important is that this colonial system does not appear to operate in any of our other countries. For most second-generation groups in Western societies, the process of stratification operates in a broadly similar way for minorities as for the charter populations in the sense that minorities obtain much the same payoffs from their educational investments as do members of the charter population. It follows therefore that in most cases where an ethnic minority is disadvantaged, the disadvantages are present at all educational levels alike.

Cross-national differences in ethnic penalties

We turn now to consider the ethnic penalties themselves, that is the estimates for the OD link in our standard model of the stratification system, focusing particularly on the cross-national differences in the extent of 'inequality of opportunity' that they reveal. As we emphasised in the introduction, there are major difficulties in making such cross-national comparisons, especially as the nature of the ethnic groups involved are often very different. For example, Turks and Moroccans have tended to migrate to mainland Europe but not in anything like the same numbers to the classic immigration countries of Australia, Canada and the USA. Caribbeans have tended to migrate to North America and to the former colonial powers in Europe, but the Caribbeans who migrated to the

---

[5] In Israel another important factor is the spatial segregation of Israeli Palestinian communities. These communities will have their own elites providing some opportunities for highly educated Palestinians. This links with the concept of 'plural societies' where different ethnic or religious groups are organised into separate pillars.

Netherlands will have come from Surinam and the Antilles while those who migrated to Britain or Canada will have come from Jamaica and other former British possessions. Dominicans have tended to go in large numbers to the USA but not to the other main receiving countries. Strict comparability is not therefore a realistic goal. There are also, of course, the technical and measurement issues that our authors have discussed in detail in their chapters. Any account of the cross-national differences has to be sensitive to these technical issues, which are too often ignored in cross-national research.

However, provided we bear these limitations in mind, it will still be of great interest to see how well groups from different kinds of origin are able to compete with similarly qualified members of the charter populations. We begin with ethnic minorities of European ancestry, who were the classic migrants to North America and Australia in the nineteenth and early twentieth century. We then turn to the new migrant groups of the last few decades coming from less developed, non-European origins and then finally discuss the involuntary minorities—indigenous groups and African Americans. We focus on second and later generations and we look separately at ethnic penalties with respect to avoidance of unemployment and access to the salariat, and at those experienced by men and by women.

While it would be tempting to construct a single index of ethnic disadvantage, a single index can be misleading if the phenomenon under consideration is not uni-dimensional. As we shall see, ethnic disadvantage does prove to be multidimensional: in some countries groups experience disadvantage only with respect to employment, in others they experience disadvantage both with respect to employment and with respect to occupational attainment. To summarise disadvantage in a single index might involve missing the most important aspect of ethnic disadvantage.

Minorities of European ancestry

We begin, then, with the classic migrant groups of European ancestry who made up the bulk of the migration to the new societies of Australia, Canada and the USA in the nineteenth and the twentieth century up until the 1960s when preferences for white settlers began to be removed in Australia, Canada and the USA. These groups have historically been the success story of migration, initially enduring considerable disadvantages but gradually assimilating in most senses of the term until their ethnic identity had largely become symbolic. As Alba has suggested, America has seen the 'twilight' of ethnicity among groups of European ancestry (Alba 1985). It is likely that the same holds true for many of the long-established groups of European ancestry in Australia and Canada too and that they are now largely indistinguishable from the charter populations in their success in the labour market, patterns of intermarriage, and so on.

In Table 15.2 we look at third (or later generation) groups who can be regarded as the descendants of these pre-1960 migrations. The only countries in which we can identify these groups are two of the classic countries of immigration—Australia and Canada—together with South Africa.[6] We should recall that in Australia and Canada these third or later generation groups all have to be identified through self-report measures not through parental and grand-parental origins. There is thus likely to be a selection issue—only individuals who have retained some ethnic identity will be included. Those who have in Gordon's terms experienced 'identificational assimilation' (Gordon 1964) will be invisible in the data and will be merged with the charter population. In the case of South Africa however the white groups are distinguished on the basis of language.

Bearing in mind the methodological caveats, we can immediately see that in Canada and Australia almost all these third-generation groups of European ancestry are at least as successful as their respective charter populations. (And the statistically significant negative signs for Irish men and German women in Canada are not substantively large.) This is no surprise of course. Almost certainly we would find a similar phenomenon in the USA.[7]

In contrast to the situation in Australia and Canada, however, Afrikaners in South Africa have not established parity with white English speakers in access to the professional and managerial jobs of the salariat. Treiman explains some of the reasons for this in his chapter, but perhaps the crucial point in the present context is that Afrikaners' ethnicity cannot be regarded as a largely symbolic one in the way that ethnicity is likely to be largely symbolic for third or later generation Germans, Italians or Irish in Australia or Canada. Among Afrikaners there is a distinct ethnic group built around the Afrikaans language. In contrast we find that in

---

[6] As Model and Fisher explain in their chapter, their US measures for the third generation are based on a racial classification and does not enable them to distinguish between white groups of European ancestry.

[7] See for example Alba (1990) and Perlmann and Waldinger (1999) although a somewhat contradictory argument is presented by Borjas (1994).

Table 15.2. Ethnic penalties (and premiums) in the third or later generations of European ancestry (parameter estimates).

	Avoidance of Unemployment		Access to the Salariat	
	Men	Women	Men	Women
Australia				
Anglo-Celtic	+0.04	+0.07	+0.09	+0.04
German	**+0.58**	−0.10	**+0.37**	−0.22
Italian	**+1.28**	+0.86	−0.14	−0.26
Canada				
French	**−0.19**	**−0.23**	**−0.23***	**−0.14***
Irish	+0.04	0.00	**−0.13**	−0.09
German	**+0.41***	**+0.38***	−0.12	**−0.15**
Ukrainian	**+0.51**	−0.07	+0.08	+0.05
Polish	−0.09	+0.31	+0.08	+0.08
Italian	−0.05	−0.14	+0.04	+0.01
Jewish	+0.24	−0.30	**+1.42**	**+1.62**
South Africa				
Afrikaner	**−0.05***	**−0.14***	**−0.91***	**−0.55***

Source: the chapters in this volume.
Notes: * indicates that there was a significant interaction with education in the relevant model. The parameter estimate thus represents the ethnic penalty (premium) for respondents with full secondary education.
Figures in bold indicate statistically significant estimates.

Canada only 15.9% of third (or later) generation Germans report a knowledge of German and as few as 6.3% report that it is the language they use at home. For Italians, Poles and Ukrainians, the proportions using their ethnic language at home are down to 1 or 2%. These are not distinct ethnic groups in the way that Afrikaners are.

The third (or higher) generation French in Canada also exhibit ethnic penalties relative to the British comparison group (although it should be noted that they are not disadvantaged relative to third-generation Canadians).[8] They too are a distinct ethnic group with high usage of the French language and are of course concentrated in Quebec. Afrikaners and French also have the common history that they were conquered by the British and thus were in a sense involuntary minorities. They share, therefore, a legacy of exclusion from the dominant positions in the economy.

The third-generation Jews in Canada may also represent a distinct ethno-religious community and Table 15.2 suggests that they are if any-

---

[8] It may also be the case that the occupational opportunities in Quebec where the majority of French Canadians live are not quite so favourable as in English-speaking Canada.

thing more successful than the charter population. The argument cannot therefore be that the retention of a distinct ethnic community leads to disadvantage but simply that it may be associated with distinctive patterns of occupational success. The general story of the 'twilight of European ancestry' is not therefore an inevitable feature even in the classic countries of migration, although for most of the European groups it does seem a reasonable characterisation.

We turn next to second-generation minorities of European ancestry. These are the children of more recent migrants. Our question, to which we expect the answer yes, is whether they have in two generations achieved the equality of opportunity with the charter populations that we have already seen for the third and earlier generations in Australia and Canada. For this analysis we can add the US, Israel and a number of European countries. The results are shown in Table 15.3.

We find a pretty clear pattern. In the classic immigration countries of Australia, Canada and the US there are scarcely any significant ethnic penalties for these groups of European origin (the sole exception being Italian women in Australia). In fact there are more positive signs, indicative perhaps of 'ethnic premiums', than negative signs, quite a few of the positive signs being statistically significant. This is clearly in line with the idea of second-generation success that was discussed in both the Canadian and US chapters. These three classic immigration countries are however joined by Britain, where the second-generation Irish (a group that was historically quite disadvantaged in Britain and, as Li and O'Leary show in their chapter, continue to be disadvantaged in Northern Ireland) experience no ethnic penalties. They are also joined by Israel, although here we find the rather puzzling penalty for men of North American ancestry with respect to unemployment.

Within this group of five countries it does not make sense to say that there are any real differences in the success of these groups of European descent.[9] Among the other European countries, on the other hand, we see

---

[9] There are two groups that we can compare across countries—Italians in Australia, Canada and the US and Irish in Britain, Canada and the US—and as we can see both groups are rather successful with a number of significant positive estimates. One might perhaps put forward an argument that Italians and Irish are even more successful in Canada than they are in the other countries to which they have migrated, but given the methodological differences between the studies we do not feel that any strong conclusion is warranted. By far the safest conclusion is that second-generation groups of European ancestry compete on more or less equal terms with the charter populations in these five countries and if anything tend to outperform the charter population.

Table 15.3. Ethnic penalties (and premiums) in the second generation of European ancestry (parameter estimates).

	Avoidance of Unemployment		Access to the Salariat	
	Men	Women	Men	Women
Australia				
Anglo-Celtic	−0.03	−0.12	**+0.20**	+0.17*
German	+0.09	−0.55	−0.06	+0.24
Italian	**+0.68**	+0.17	+0.20	**−0.38**
Dutch	+0.04	+0.27	+0.11	+0.08
Greek	−0.14	−0.14*	**+0.47**	−0.13
Maltese	+0.59	+2.25	−0.04	−0.19
Austria				
Yugoslav	−0.10	**−0.88**	**−0.98**	−0.58
Belgium				
Italian	**−0.45**	**−0.63**	**−0.65***	**−0.53**
Canada				
British	**+0.35***	+0.11	**+0.42**	**+0.32**
French	+0.97	+0.16	+0.32	+0.52
Irish	−0.08	+0.50*	**+0.46***	**+0.81**
German	**+0.60***	+0.47	+0.16	**+0.40**
Ukrainian	−0.30	+0.76	+0.19	+0.32
Polish	−0.34	+0.10	+0.04	+0.08
Italian	**+0.46**	+0.20	**+0.33**	**+0.70**
Jewish	+0.22	+0.31	**+0.96**	**+0.75**
France				
Repatriate	**−0.87**	**−0.65**	+0.32	−0.24
South European	−0.13	**−0.28**	+0.07	**−0.43**
East European	+0.60	+0.35	+0.60	+0.14
Germany				
Italian	−0.30	−0.27	−0.32*	**−0.92**
Iberian	−0.56	−0.15	+0.19	**−0.12**
Yugoslav	−0.24	−0.37	−0.12	**−0.73**
Greek	**−0.87**	−0.23	**−1.22***	−0.54
Israel				
North American	**−0.95**	**+1.36**	0.00	0.00
West European	0.00	0.00	0.00	0.00
East European	0.00	0.00	0.00	0.00
Sweden				
Norwegian/Danish	**−0.32**	−0.15	−0.10	−0.08
German	**−0.44**	−0.22	+0.18	+0.04
Polish	**−0.49**	−0.35*	**+0.31**	−0.17
Finnish	**−0.29**	+0.01*	−0.16	−0.10
Yugoslav	**−0.83**	**−0.39**	+0.01	−0.35*
Greek	**−1.32**	**−0.82**	**−0.53**	−0.14
UK—GB				
Irish	−0.30	+0.11	+0.24	**+0.45**

USA				
German	−0.43	−0.31	+0.11	+0.39
Irish	−0.09	−0.36	**+0.69**	**+1.03**
Italian	−0.01	+0.24	+0.18	+0.44
Polish	+0.36	−0.54	+0.43	−0.26

Source: chapters in this volume.
Notes: * indicates a significant interaction with education. The parameter estimate thus represents the ethnic penalty (premium) for respondents with full secondary education.
Swedish figures are for non-employment and for access to the lower salariat.

quite a number of significant ethnic penalties even for these groups of European ancestry. This applies almost equally to Austria, Belgium, France, Germany and Sweden. This does not appear to be simply a matter of different ethnic groups being present in the two groups of countries. For example, Greeks fare rather badly in Sweden and in Germany, but are relatively successful in Australia; Italians fare rather badly in Belgium, less so in Germany, but even better in Canada, Australia and the USA. Poles fare badly in Sweden (at least with respect to non-employment) but much better in Canada and the US.

It is important to recognise that there are major methodological difficulties in making these comparisons. In the case of Austria and Germany, for example, the figures largely exclude naturalised members of the ethnic minorities.[10] In Australia and Canada the measure of ethnicity is based on self-reported ancestry rather than on parental birthplace. In Sweden, our figures relate to employment and non-employment rather than, as in the other countries, to unemployment. Nor have we attempted to test formally whether these parameter estimates are significantly different across countries (although the standard errors reported in the individual country chapters will give us a pretty good guide).

While differences in the measurement of ethnicity must be taken very seriously, the pattern shown in Table 15.3 seems too clear-cut and too large to be purely an artefact of measurement. Kogan in her chapter for example suggests that citizenship has an effect of 0.35 on male access to the salariat. Given the small numbers who are likely to have naturalised in Austria or Germany, excluding naturalised citizens will not have a very large impact on the overall ethnic penalties found in these countries. Differences in the measurement of ethnicity also seem unlikely to make a

---

[10] It should be recalled however that members of the second generation who were born abroad but migrated to the country of destination before the start of compulsory education can be identified in the German and Austrian datasets without use of the measure of citizenship.

great deal of difference: in Britain we were able to replicate the analyses using both self-report measures of ancestry and parental place of birth measures. We found that the parameter estimates were very similar, although if anything they tended to be rather larger when using the self-report measures. This is not perhaps surprising since parental birth measures may introduce some noise into the measurement thus bringing estimates closer to zero.

Only in the case of Sweden, then, is there a major problem of comparability over the measure of non-employment. To assess consequences of the different Swedish measure, we have reanalysed the data for Canada (choosing Canada as it has a number of ethnic groups in common with Sweden), constructing variables in exactly the same way as was done for Sweden. That is to say we have selected the same age range as for Sweden (26–49) and simply distinguished between employment and non-employment (combining the categories for unemployment, full-time education and other inactivity to form a single category for non-employment). The results were reasonably reassuring. We found that, when applying Swedish procedures to the Canadian data, parameter estimates of interest tended to become closer to zero. This is what we would expect if the Swedish procedure introduces noise into the measure. More specifically, we find no reason to change our conclusion that the second generation of German and Polish ancestry is more likely to gain access to employment in Canada than they are in Sweden.[11]

Our tentative conclusion, then, is that in Austria, Belgium, France and Germany and possibly in Sweden too the experience of second-generation groups of European ancestry is rather different, and rather worse, than that of the same groups in the classic immigration countries of Australia, Canada and the USA. We will consider some possible explanations for this pattern later in this chapter.

Second-generation minorities with non-European ancestry

One of the key questions with which we began this chapter was whether second-generation groups from non-traditional (that is, non-European)

---

[11] However, there is one very important caveat. We did find in Canada that the Swedish procedures gave significant ethnic penalties for Chinese and Indians whereas the original procedure did not find any penalty for these groups. The reason is simple: both these groups (unlike Germans and Poles) had relatively high rates of full-time education even at the age of 26 and above. If high proportions of, say, second generation Greeks or Yugoslavs in Sweden were still in full-time education, this could account for their apparently large ethnic penalties with respect to employment.

origins would make the same transition to equality of opportunity as did the traditional migrant groups. As Model and Fisher argued in their chapter, optimists thought that they could while pessimists thought that ethnic penalties for these non-traditional groups might persist across several generations. Table 15.4 enables us to begin an answer to this question.

Once again comparisons between countries are hindered not only by the methodological problems but also by the presence of different ethnic groups in the different countries, reflecting different histories, geo-political links, and immigration policies. It is notable that Australia, for example, has no major black group while the most disadvantaged minorities in continental Europe, those of Turkish and Moroccan ancestry, are not to be found in sufficient numbers for analysis in any of the classic immigration countries. However, some patterns are perhaps discernible, although they are not quite as clear as in the case of European ancestry.

First of all, at one extreme we find Canada where the optimistic picture looks very broadly to hold true. Most groups have achieved equality of opportunity with the charter population. The only significant ethnic penalties are for women of Lebanese origins and men and women of Caribbean origins, and both are with respect to unemployment only. Lebanese men and women also experience ethnic penalties with respect to unemployment in Australia. It makes sense to group these two countries together—we do not have enough evidence (or confidence in the measurements) to rank one above the other although our suspicion is that these non-traditional groups tend to be more successful in Canada than in Australia as well as being much more numerous.[12]

The US has considerable similarities with Australia and Canada. As with Australia and Canada, the ethnic penalties for groups of non-European ancestry are predominantly with respect to unemployment. Those who are fortunate enough to get jobs tend to get ones commensurate with their qualifications. However, four groups—men and women of Dominican, Caribbean, Mexican and Puerto Rican origins—do experience quite substantial ethnic penalties with respect to unemployment, so the overall picture looks less optimistic than in Canada. There are just

---

[12] We should also note that there is a problem of choice of comparison group in Australia and Canada. In Australia the comparison group are third generation Australians (whose experiences are very like those of third-generation Anglo-Celts). However in Canada the comparison group are third-generation British, who actually do significantly better than third generation Canadians. If Canadians were taken as the reference group, the ethnic penalties for groups like Caribbeans in Canada would be even smaller.

Table 15.4. Ethnic penalties (and premiums) in the second generation of non-European ancestry (parameter estimates).

	Avoidance of Unemployment		Access to the Salariat	
	Men	Women	Men	Women
Australia				
Chinese	+0.35	+0.02	**+1.24**	+0.37
Lebanese	**−0.63**	**−0.67**	**+0.68***	+0.67
Austria				
Turkish	**−0.30***	NA	**−1.62**	NA
Belgium				
Moroccan	**−1.49**	**−1.10**	**−1.56***	**−1.18**
Turkish	**−1.93***	**−1.84***	**−1.44**	**−1.33**
Canada				
Lebanese	+0.11	**−1.02**	+0.64	−0.18
Chinese	+0.14	−0.08	**+0.96**	**+0.57**
Indian	−0.03	−0.03	**+0.32**	**+0.38**
Caribbean	**−0.49**	**−0.48***	+0.12	**+0.32**
African	−0.05	−0.21	+0.15	−0.30
Filipino	+0.77	+0.37	**+0.45**	−0.31
France				
Maghrebin	**−1.67**	**−1.69**	**−1.19**	**−1.13**
Near Eastern	(−1.21)	(−0.93)	(+.38)	(−0.22)
Sub-Saharan African	(−0.33)	(−1.45)	(−1.42)	(−0.52)
East Asian	(−1.46)	(+.02)	(+.09)	(+.69)
Germany				
Turkish	**−0.69***	**−0.61**	**−1.25**	**−0.88***
Israel				
Middle Eastern Jews	**−0.50**	−0.29	**−0.55***	−0.27
North African Jews	**−0.65***	**−0.59**	**−0.46***	−0.09
Netherlands				
Surinamese	**−1.14**	**−0.23***	**−0.40**	−0.40
Antillean	−0.41	**−0.42**	−0.08	−0.23
Turkish	**−0.82**	**−0.56**	**−0.75**	**−0.78**
Moroccan	**−1.11***	**−0.90**	**−0.69**	**−1.11**
Sweden				
African	**−1.13**	**−0.90**	+0.02	+0.22
Latin American	**−0.46**	**−0.55**	+0.31	+0.22
UK—GB				
Indian	**−0.43***	**−0.86**	+0.67	+0.00
Caribbean	**−0.80**	**−0.74**	−0.11	**+0.62**
Pakistani	**−1.11**	**−1.13**	−0.17	−0.15
US				
East Asian	+0.39	+0.87	−0.06	−0.03
Cuban	+0.19	+0.02	**+0.52**	**+0.86**
Filipino	−0.41	−0.03	+0.27	+0.16

Dominican	−0.67	−0.91	+0.29	+0.04
Black	−0.84	−1.11	−0.15*	−0.32*
Mexican	−0.39	−0.65	−0.33	+0.37
Puerto Rican	−1.08	−0.77	−0.19	−0.02

Source: chapters in this volume.
Notes: coefficients for Israel have been adjusted to show contrast between salariat and semi- and unskilled work, as in the case of other countries.
* indicates a significant interaction with education. The parameter estimate thus represents the ethnic penalty (premium) for respondents with full secondary education.
Parameter estimates for France are in brackets because they are based on Ns below 100 and hence have particularly large standard errors.

two groups that we can compare in the two countries—Filipinos and Caribbeans (following Model and Fisher's suggestion that second-generation Blacks in the USA are predominantly of Caribbean ancestry although they will also include people of African ancestry). On the whole both groups seem to have smaller ethnic penalties in Canada.[13] We must remember the measurement issues, but we are inclined to conclude that the USA fits the optimistic scenario slightly less well than does Canada.

Britain and Sweden also appear to come close to the US pattern. Like the USA (and Canada and Australia), the significant ethnic penalties are all with respect to unemployment, not access to the salariat. Both countries also show significant ethnic penalties with respect to unemployment (non-employment in Sweden) for all their minorities from less-developed countries, so the overall picture is somewhat more pessimistic than in the USA. We can more specifically compare Caribbeans in the USA and GB, and here we find that the pattern of ethnic penalties is remarkably similar.[14] We should also note that Indians are clearly more disadvantaged in Britain than in Canada with respect to unemployment, reinforcing our provisional conclusion about the optimistic Canadian picture. However, we must place a caveat against any conclusions about Sweden: it is quite possible that the large apparent ethnic penalty with respect to employment for Africans in Sweden is a result of a high proportion continuing in full-time education after age 25. (See above, n. 11.)

---

[13] Inspecting the standard errors suggests that some of the US parameter estimates for these two groups would be significantly worse than the Canadian estimates, while none would be significantly better.

[14] Our other source for GB, the LFS, which constructs ethnic categories in a somewhat different way from the US, actually shows slightly larger ethnic penalties for Caribbeans in Britain, but the differences between the two countries for this group are unlikely to be statistically significant whichever source we use.

Whereas in this first group of Australia, Canada, Britain, Sweden and the USA the significant ethnic penalties are only with respect to unemployment, in all our other countries we see significant ethnic penalties with respect to access to the salariat; indeed in many countries—Belgium, France, Germany, Israel and the Netherlands—there are ethnic penalties both with respect to unemployment and to the salariat. First impressions suggest that the pessimistic scenario holds for all of these countries, particularly for Belgium where men and women of both Turkish and Moroccan origin experience very substantial ethnic penalties for both outcomes. We can compare the second generation of Turkish origin across a number of European countries. Ethnic penalties for this group are largest in Belgium, somewhat smaller but still very substantial in Germany and the Netherlands, and very large in Austria, although only with respect to access to the salariat. These ethnic penalties are on a scale that we simply do not see in the classic immigration countries.

We cannot directly compare the experience of people of Turkish origin in Europe and North America, but one comparison we can make is of people of Caribbean ancestry in the Netherlands, Britain, Canada and the US. Interestingly, in the Netherlands Caribbeans (that is, people of Antillean and Surinamese ancestry) are much less disadvantaged than Turks or Moroccans. People of Antillean ancestry in the Netherlands appear to be more successful than Caribbeans in Britain or the US, but Surinamese men are rather less successful (although we should remember that Surinamese are a rather diverse group including many Hindustanis and some Chinese, which complicates the comparison). Given the methodological differences between the Dutch study and those in Britain and the US, we have to be very cautious in drawing any conclusions but it would be wise to avoid any simple characterisation of the relative level of ethnic inequalities in Britain and the Netherlands.

Israel is also hard to interpret. We have no groups that we can directly compare across countries. There is also the problem, as Shavit and his colleagues emphasised in their chapter, that the comparison group in Israel—the third generation Jews of European origin—are not really equivalent to the charter populations in our other countries. Nevertheless, Israel does seem to belong to the same pattern as Belgium, Netherlands and Germany with significant and fairly substantial ethnic penalties both with respect to unemployment and with respect to occupation. Israel does not therefore fit the optimistic scenario quite as well as might have been expected.

Involuntary minorities

We finally come to the involuntary minorities, who in some ways provide the toughest examination of contemporary developed countries with respect to their professed ideals of equality of opportunity. Table 15.5 shows the results, and they do tend to call into question the rather optimistic impressions that have been suggested by earlier tables exploring voluntary minorities.

The broad outlines of the picture are clear enough: South Africa stands out at one extreme, as we might expect, with some extraordinarily large ethnic penalties for Blacks, both with respect to unemployment and with respect to the salariat. However, Australia, Canada and the USA all show large ethnic penalties for both outcomes (at least for men). This looks much more like the continental European pattern of ethnic minority disadvantage for people of Turkish and Moroccan origin than it does to the more optimistic pictures that we obtained for non-traditional migrants in the classic immigration countries. Moreover, there is not a great deal of difference between the experience of the involuntary

Table 15.5. Ethnic penalties (and premiums) among involuntary minorities (parameter estimates).

	Avoidance of Unemployment		Access to the Salariat	
	Men	Women	Men	Women
Australia				
Aboriginal	−1.00*	−0.98	−1.13	+0.04
Canada				
Aboriginal	−1.50	−1.28	−0.44*	−0.13*
Israel				
Palestinian	−0.54	−0.21	−0.97*	+0.47*
South Africa				
Asian	−0.98*	−1.04*	−1.09*	−1.00*
Coloured	−1.27*	−1.56*	−2.14*	−1.78*
Black	−2.16*	−3.06*	−2.35*	−1.96*
UK—NI				
Catholics 1985	−1.07	−0.22	−0.25	−0.21
Catholics 2002/3	−0.27	−0.35	−0.36	+0.14*
US				
African American	−0.91*	−0.83	−0.77	−0.67*
American Indian	−1.07	−0.99	−0.35	−0.25

Source: chapters in this volume.
Notes: coefficients for Israel have been adjusted to show contrast between salariat and semi- and unskilled work, as in the case of other countries.
* indicates a significant interaction with education. The parameter estimate thus represents the ethnic penalty (premium) for respondents with full secondary education.

minorities in Australia, Canada or the USA. The optimistic story that we were able to tell about non-traditional migrants in Australia and Canada does not appear to apply to their indigenous minorities.

We must also remember the considerable problems in identifying indigenous groups—these are all based on self-report measures and there could well be considerable variation in how people of mixed ancestry report themselves. Cross-national differences in willingness to report aboriginal ancestry could easily account for some of the differences apparent in Table 15.5. We should not therefore reject the hypothesis that the experiences of aboriginal minorities in Australia, Canada and the US are similar.

The one possible area for optimism comes with the UK's involuntary minority—Catholics in Northern Ireland. Despite the religious terminology, there should be no mistake that Catholics in Northern Ireland are an indigenous ethnic group who were conquered and subordinated by the invading British in much the same way that other indigenous groups were conquered and subordinated in the establishment of the British Empire. However, as Li and O'Leary report in their chapter, the ethnic penalties with respect to unemployment have diminished very considerably over the last two decades, and we suspect that if we had data over a longer time period it would show an even more dramatic decline. We suspect that some of this decline can be attributed to the affirmative action policies introduced in Northern Ireland in 1990 (McCrudden *et al.* 2004). These policies have some unusual features not found in the better-known American affirmative action legislation (or in the lesser known Indian legislation) and seem to have been rather effective. However, it will not have escaped readers' notice that this legislation was only enacted after twenty years of armed conflict, so perhaps we should not paint too optimistic a picture. Still, the Northern Irish case does suggest that ethnic inequalities may be susceptible to remedy through government action.

The picture that has emerged from this detailed examination of the ethnic penalties in the second and later generations therefore is that:

- In the group of classic immigration countries of Australia, Canada and the USA the offspring of traditional migrant groups of European ancestry do not experience any ethnic penalties in the second generation while the more recent groups of non-European ancestry do experience ethnic penalties, although only with respect to unemployment. Ethnic penalties tend to be rather smaller in Canada and distinctly larger in the USA.

- Britain and Sweden are quite similar to the classic immigration countries, showing ethnic penalties for groups of non-European ancestry primarily with respect to unemployment. The magnitudes are rather similar to those found in the USA.
- Israel has a rather ambiguous position with moderate ethnic penalties both with respect to unemployment and access to the salariat for second-generation groups from non-European origins.
- Austria, Belgium, France, Germany and the Netherlands show large ethnic penalties both with respect to unemployment and access to the salariat for groups of non-European ancestry and also in some cases for groups of European ancestry too. Within this group of countries, minorities in the Netherlands appear to be somewhat less disadvantaged while those in Belgium and France are particularly disadvantaged.
- South Africa represents an outlier both in the magnitude of ethnic penalties and the process of stratification, although there are some parallels in Israel with respect to its involuntary minority of Palestinians.
- Even in the classic immigration countries where the optimistic scenario holds reasonably well for minorities of non-European ancestry, involuntary minorities experience substantial ethnic penalties rather akin to those found for voluntary minorities in continental Europe.

We thus have a number of rather distinct patterns to try and explain. One task is to explain the cross-national differences in the general magnitude of the ethnic penalties. Another is to explain why in some countries ethnic penalties are present both for unemployment and for access to the salariat, whereas in others they are restricted by and large to unemployment. And a third is to understand why patterns for involuntary minorities tend to be so different from those for voluntary minorities.

Explaining cross-national differences in ethnic penalties

The small number of countries, the relatively small number of ethnic groups about which we can make cross-national comparisons, and perhaps most importantly the fact that we have only cross-sectional data (other than in Northern Ireland), means we cannot hope to offer anything more than tentative suggestions. To get close to understanding causality in comparative sociology, we need to investigate the consequences of natural experiments, as for example the natural experiment with affirmative action in Northern Ireland. However, in the absence of a larger sample of countries and of over-time data, we can perhaps make some progress by considering the plausibility of the mechanisms and social processes that might potentially generate the observed cross-national patterns. As suggested in the introductory chapter, it may be useful to distinguish between explanations that focus on the general nature of the economy, those that focus on general processes of social reproduction, and those that focus on specifically ethnic-related phenomena such as discrimination and xenophobia, the conception of the nation and access to citizenship.

We shall look at these phenomena one by one and shall carry out exploratory bivariate analyses. With only thirteen countries at most multivariate analysis becomes absurd. We focus particularly on the ethnic penalties experienced by the second-generation of non-European ancestry. We begin with the economy.

The economy

The simplest explanation, at least for ethnic penalties with respect to unemployment, is the actual rate of unemployment in the country as a whole. The rationale here is that, when there is a shortage of labour, employers will be less likely to discriminate against ethnic minorities: they may prefer to hire an ethnic-minority worker rather than having an unfilled vacancy. However, when there is a surplus of labour they may be more likely to indulge any tastes they have for discrimination since there will be more job-seekers from preferred ethnic groups from which to recruit employees. For this kind of reason, ethnic minority unemployment rates are sometimes found to be hypercyclical. That is, they increase more rapidly than does the unemployment rate of the charter population when there is an economic downturn. The same kind of reasoning could also apply cross-nationally.

A second kind of economic explanation focuses on the overall level of competitiveness of the economy. Standard economic theory suggests that discrimination against ethnic minorities is irrational in a perfectly competitive labour market since a firm that does not discriminate will make higher profits than one that does discriminate. Discrimination essentially means hiring (charter population) workers with lower productivity in preference to (minority) workers with higher productivity and hence profit-maximising firms will not discriminate and will drive out discriminatory firms. However, the more the market departs from competitiveness, the less the pressures on discriminatory firms to maximise their profit. A monopolist could indulge his taste for discrimination without endangering his market position (although he will of course pay for his tastes with reduced profits).

In the context of ethnic minority disadvantage, this argument can be linked to the distinction between primary and secondary labour markets, primary labour markets having higher wages and security, greater chances of job advancement and barriers to entry against those such as ethnic minorities employed in the secondary labour market. In essence, then, the barriers between primary and secondary labour markets create market imperfections which protect privileged categories of workers (such as men or members of the charter population) from competition from ethnic minorities.

A related argument focuses on the level of government regulation of the labour market (in contrast to the regulation introduced by firms, perhaps at the instigation of trade unions, which lies at the heart of the primary/secondary labour-market distinction). As Kogan (2005) argues, employment protection legislation increases the costs to firms of firing workers and firms therefore have a greater incentive to screen out seemingly less productive workers. In this case firms may use 'statistical discrimination' (based on assumptions about the productivity of different categories of workers) against ethnic minorities.[15]

It is beyond the scope of this chapter to test the detailed mechanisms underlying these explanations, but we can explore whether general characteristics of the labour market are related to the size of the ethnic penalties. In Table 15.6 we report two key indicators—unemployment rates and OECD measures of employment protection legislation.

In the first two columns of Table 15.6 we give the unemployment rates of men and women from the charter population as reported in the chapters of this volume. In the third column we check this with OECD information on standardised unemployment rates for the year or period in question. In general the chapter measures are quite close to the OECD

---

[15] However, it should be emphasised that, under a strict EPL regime, if ethnic minority workers do gain employment (for example during labour shortages), then they might be expected to have higher chances of remaining employed than would similar workers in more flexible regimes. To test the EPL argument, therefore, we should ideally use panel rather than cross-sectional data.

Table 15.6. Measures of the economy.

	Unemployment rate (chapter estimate) of charter population: men	Unemployment rate (chapter estimate) of charter population: women	Standardized unemployment rate (OECD data)	Employment Protection legislation score 1990	Employment Protection legislation score 1998
Australia (2001)	7.8%	6.0%	6.8%	0.9	0.9
Austria (1995–2001)	3.7%	4.1%	3.6%–4.5%	2.8	2.8
Belgium (1991)	6.4%	17.2%	6.4%	1.6	1.6
Canada (2001)	4.7%	3.9%	7.2%	0.9	0.9
France (2003)	7.6%	10.7%	9.4%	2.5	2.4
Germany (1993–6)	6.2%	7.2%	7.7%–8.7%	3.0	2.9
Israel (1992–2000)	6.0%	6.2%	NA	NA	NA
Netherlands (1988–98)	8.3%	15.2%	7.2%–3.8%	3.2	3.1
South Africa (1996)	4.2% (28.3% overall)	4.4% (42.7% overall)	NA	NA	NA
Sweden (1990)	NA	NA	1.7%	3.0	3.1
UK—GB (1991–2001)	9.1%	5.7%	10.0%–5.0%	0.7	0.7
UK—NI (2002–3)	6.0% (1985–15.3%)	3.4% (1985–10.3%)		0.7	0.7
USA (1995–2001)	3.1%	2.9%	5.6%–4.0%	0.1	0.1

Sources: column three-OECD (2004); columns four and five—Nicoletti et al. (2000).

Notes: where our chapter authors have pooled years, we show in the third column the range for the OECD measures for the period in question, ie the highest and lowest (which are not necessarily the first and last although sometimes they are). Figures in brackets after the name of each country show the year(s) of the data used by our chapter authors. Since in South Africa the unemployment rates of the white 'charter' population and the overall figures for the population as a whole are so different, we show the overall figures as well. The OECD figures for the standardised unemployment rate are for the UK as a whole and not GB.

data (which is not surprising since they will sometimes be based on exactly the same sources). Note, however, that the chapter estimates in Canada and the USA are markedly lower than those in the OECD source while those in the Netherlands are markedly higher. It is not clear what the explanation for the discrepancy is in the Canadian and US cases, but in the Dutch case it is likely to be because the SPVA surveys on which our chapter authors have drawn are not nationally representative but are restricted to municipalities where ethnic minorities are concentrated.

These municipalities may well have generally higher unemployment than the national average.

If we take the chapter estimates of male unemployment rates as our preferred measure, we find a weak relationship, although in the predicted direction, between unemployment and the magnitude of the ethnic penalties experienced by minorities from non-European ancestries. The relationships for men and for women are plotted separately in Figure 15.1.[16] For each country we show the full set of ethnic penalties derived from Table 15.4. Even though we include only minorities of non-European ancestry in Figure 15.1, we must remember that these ethnic penalties will relate to very different ethnic groups. As we can see, there is considerable variation within each country.

What we find is that, for both men and women, there is a modest relationship in the expected direction. At one extreme we find the USA with the lowest unemployment rate and a relatively low median ethnic penalty together with (for men only) Austria, which has the lowest unemployment rate of our European countries and a small ethnic penalty for its one

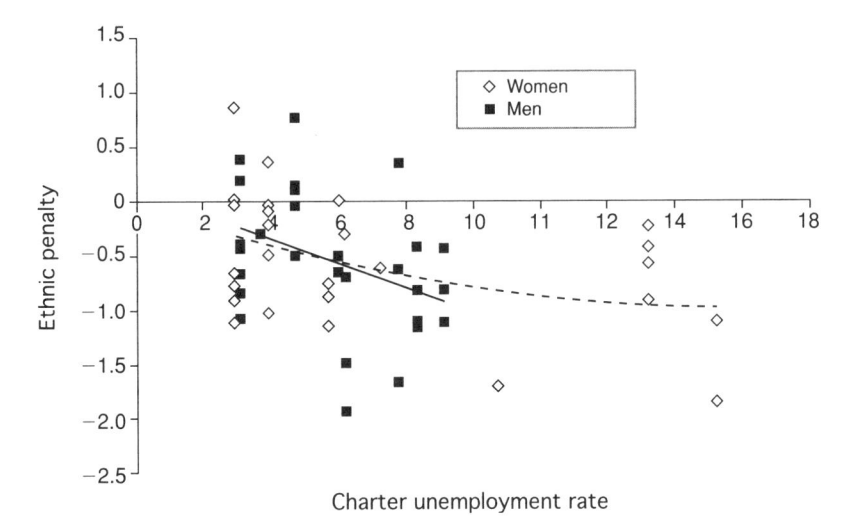

Figure 15.1. Unemployment rates and ethnic penalties (unemployment).

[16] We exclude Sweden from these two figures since we do not have any estimate of male and female unemployment rates from the Swedish chapter data. We fit quadratic trend lines to this and to all subsequent figures. As we shall see, linear trendlines would often be very misleading, and while higher order polynomials or non-parametric smoothers might be better still, we feel that these would run the risk of providing somewhat spurious senses of scientific accuracy given the small numbers of countries involved and the considerable measurement errors in the measurement of the country-level variables.

major second-generation ethnic minority of Turkish ancestry; at the other extreme come Britain and the Netherlands with quite high male unemployment rates and some substantial ethnic penalties. However, other countries do not fit this pattern at all well with Australia for example having one of the highest male unemployment rates but some of the lowest ethnic penalties while countries such as Belgium and Germany with some of the highest ethnic penalties have intermediate levels of unemployment. While we cannot reject the hypothesis, support for it is scarcely overwhelming.

In Figure 15.2 we then look at the relationship between ethnic penalties and the OECD measure of employment protection legislation (EPL). The EPL measure basically sorts countries into two groups—deregulated economies such as the USA, Great Britain, Australia and Canada on the one hand and regulated European countries of Austria, France, Germany, the Netherlands and Sweden on the other with Belgium falling in between.

Much as with the previous exploration of unemployment rates, we find weak relationships in the predicted direction, but the story is not an especially convincing one. In particular Belgium and France do not fit the expected pattern at all well with their large ethnic penalties but intermediate levels of regulation (at least when measured by the EPL score).

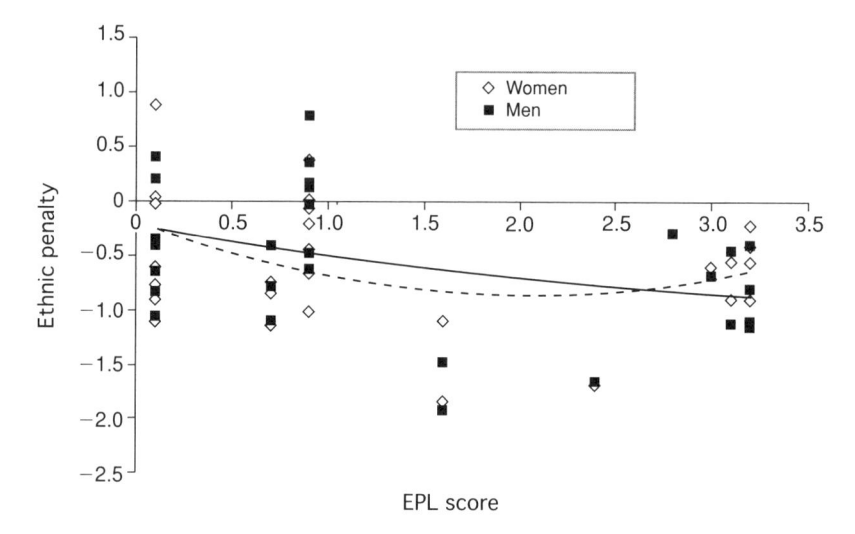

Figure 15.2. EPL and ethnic penalties (unemployment).

Given the measurement error that is involved not only with the ethnic penalties but also with our 'explanatory' variables of unemployment rate and employment protection, even a modest relationship in the predicted direction is not to be despised. We cannot therefore reject these economic arguments out of hand. However, they are not so persuasive as to warrant ending our investigation at this point. We therefore move on next to consider general processes of social reproduction.

Class fluidity

In the introductory chapter we raised the possibility that patterns of ethnic disadvantage might parallel patterns of class fluidity/rigidity. Class reproduction might be one of the mechanisms explaining intergenerational continuity in ethnic disadvantage, and the kinds of processes involved in increasing class fluidity may also tend to assist ethnic minorities' occupational attainment. Moreover on theoretical grounds we might expect class fluidity to be related to ethnic penalties with respect to occupational attainment rather than to the experience of unemployment. After all, mobility studies are precisely concerned with movements between social classes such as the salariat and the semi-skilled and unskilled class which is the basis for our estimates of ethnic penalties in access to the salariat. Typically mobility studies ignore unemployment altogether.

As we explained in the introductory chapter, we might expect processes of class reproduction to be important in explaining the lack of access to the salariat of ethnic minorities from lower working class origins (which fits the case of many groups of non-European ancestry). If class origins have large effects on class destinations (net of educational attainment) in these countries, then class origins will be able in part to explain the large ethnic penalties of these ethnic groups in gaining access to the salariat.

To explore this line of argument we begin, in Table 15.7, by showing the results of some recent studies of social mobility. In all three studies the authors have focused on social fluidity rather than absolute mobility rates and, while they use somewhat different procedures, in all three studies higher estimates indicate greater rigidity. (For an excellent discussion of the distinction between absolute and relative mobility and the statistical measures involved see Breen 2004.) On theoretical grounds, too, we would expect measures of fluidity to be more relevant than absolute rates of mobility to understanding cross-national patterns of ethnic penalty in access to the salariat.

All the usual methodological caveats apply of course. Estimates of class fluidity vary considerably from survey to survey (as Ganzeboom, Luijkx and Treiman 1989 very helpfully make clear) and also according to the precise measure of fluidity that is used. There is also growing evidence that fluidity has been increasing in some countries over time but not in others (Breen and Luijkx 2004a) and hence we must recognise that these are not fixed characteristics of our societies.

While different studies of social fluidity show rather different patterns, perhaps reflecting (as in the Dutch case) real change over time, measurement error or different statistical procedures, a fairly general picture emerges from Table 15.7 with Israel, the USA, Australia and Canada exhibiting the greatest fluidity and Germany, France and Belgium at the other extreme, exhibiting the greatest rigidity. The situation of Sweden, the Netherlands and the USA is more controversial. While Ganzeboom, Luijkx and Treiman's evidence suggested that both Sweden and the

Table 15.7. Cross-national differences in class fluidity (measures of association).

	Ganzeboom, Luijkx and Treiman[a] 1970s–80s	Erikson and Goldthorpe[b] 1970s: men	Breen and Luijkx[c] 1970s: men	Breen and Luijkx[c] 1990s: men
Australia	1.24–1.73	0.79		
Austria	1.73–2.22			
Belgium	2.01–2.40			
Canada	1.39–1.74			
France	2.01–2.10	1.17	1.17	1.06
Germany	1.37–3.21	1.14	1.22	1.14
Israel	1.20		0.65	0.64
Netherlands	1.39–3.22	1.17	1.16	0.82
Sweden	1.68–3.16	0.84	0.88	0.78
UK—GB[d]	1.38–2.46	1.09	0.99	0.94
UK—NI	2.16	1.20		
USA	0.98–1.57	0.82		

Notes:
[a] Ganzeboom, Luijkx and Treiman (1989) measure fluidity with Goodman's association models. We report their measure of association, Ue, taken from their table 2, reporting the range of results obtained from studies conducted in the 1970s and 1980s.
[b] Erikson and Goldthorpe (1992) use the Unidiff parameter to measure social fluidity but they set the overall average to 0. See their table 11.1. We have taken the antilog of their measures, thus centering them around 1 as with the measures used by our other authors.
[c] Breen and Luijkx (2004a, pp. 59–60) measure fluidity with the Unidiff parameter, setting GB in the 1980s to 1. We are very grateful to Richard Breen for providing us with the actual parameter estimates.
[d] The figures in the first two columns refer to England only rather than to GB.

Netherlands were relatively rigid in the 1970s and 1980s, this is not supported by Breen and Luijkx's (2004a) more recent work which suggests that these are two of the most fluid societies. Another contentious case is the USA; while Ganzeboom, Luijkx and Treiman's evidence suggests that the USA is one of the most fluid countries, Erikson and Goldthorpe's specific comparion of the USA and Britain, employing a coding scheme that allows a more precise comparison, suggested that there was little difference in fluidity in the two countries (Erikson and Goldthorpe 1985). The USA should, therefore, perhaps be placed with Britain as a middle-of-the-road society.

In Figure 15.3 we plot the ethnic penalties experienced by groups of non-European ancestry with respect to the salariat against class fluidity. For our measure of fluidity we use the median of the Ganzeboom, Luijkx and Treiman scores for the 1970s and 1980s, largely on the grounds that this gives us a systematic measure that covers all our countries (apart from South Africa) and one that does not seem to be seriously out of line with more recent research.[17] However, in the case of Sweden and the

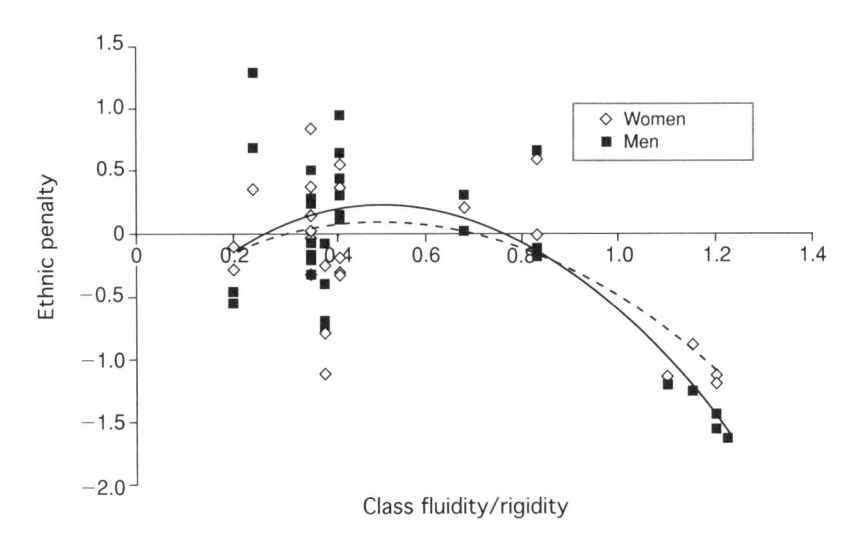

Figure 15.3. Class fluidity and ethnic penalties (salariat).

---

[17] In the cases of Australia, Austria and France, Ganzeboom et al. (1989) report only two survey estimates. In the latter two cases we take the estimate based on the larger of the two samples but in the case of Australia we take the lower estimate as this seems to be more in line with Erikson and Goldthorpe's evidence. We thus have scored countries as follows: Australia 1.24, Austria 2.22, Belgium 2.20, Canada, 1.42, France 2.10, Germany 2.15, Israel 1.20, Netherlands 1.39, Sweden 1.68, GB 1.83, USA 1.36. This rank ordering is identical to that found by Breen and

Netherlands where we think these earlier scores could be misleading because of the trends over time, we take the most recent of their scores (which in both cases are also the lowest of the range shown in Table 15.7). This is admittedly rather arbitrary but we feel this reflects the pattern shown in the more recent evidence.

Figure 15.3 shows a curvilinear relationship between class fluidity generally and both women's and men's ethnic penalties in access to the salariat, which is not what we would have predicted. The most rigid societies of Belgium, France and Germany do indeed have some of the highest ethnic penalties, in line with our expectations, but there are some major anomalies at the more fluid end of the spectrum. On our measure of fluidity, the two fluid societies of Israel and the Netherlands have moderately large ethnic penalties. In the case of the Netherlands it may well be that we have over-adjusted the figures, or possibly that the ethnic penalties in the mid-1990s were more influenced by the more rigid nature of Dutch society twenty years earlier rather than by its current fluidity. Britain also seems to be rather out of line with its above-average level of rigidity but modest ethnic penalties.

Israel is particularly anomalous as it shows the highest level of fluidity according to all the class mobility studies but still exhibits moderate ethnic penalties (although it must be said that these are not nearly as large as those found in the rigid countries). However, one problem that has not been fully addressed in the mobility literature is that migration itself may weaken the relation between origins and destination and that the high level of fluidity observed in Israel may be in part a consequence of the very high proportion (29%) of its population that are first-generation migrants.[18] Possibly, then, Israeli fluidity among the native born is not quite as exceptional as appears at first sight. This might also apply to the USA, and indeed to Australia and Canada to some extent.

We hesitate to draw any strong causal conclusions from the pattern shown in Figure 15.3 therefore. The evidence in this chapter also produces some doubts about the possible mechanisms underlying any hypothetical relationship between fluidity and ethnic penalties. As we noted earlier, one possible explanatory mechanism would be the presence of direct

---

Luijkx, with the exception that the placing of Sweden and the Netherlands is reversed. For presentational reasons, we deduct 1.00 from all these scores in Figure 15.3.

[18] As Breen and Luijkx (2004b, p. 402) point out, while Yaish (2002) and Goldthorpe et al. (1997) dispute the role of migration in accounting for high Israeli fluidity, their analyses are inconclusive because of the small number of non-migrants in their data.

effects of class origins on occupational destinations (net of educational attainment). Ideally, as we noted earlier, we would have included controls for class origins into our models, but our data sources did not in general permit this. In the British case, however, we do have data on father's class and we can add it to our models. When we do so we find that the addition of class origins has a negligible impact on the size of the ethnic penalties with respect to unemployment and a very modest impact on penalties with respect to the salariat.[19] However, it may well be that in other European countries where the ethnic penalties are much larger than in Britain social class origins will have a larger role to play.

Moreover, it is unclear whether the direct effect of class origins (net of educational attainment) on class destinations are larger in the more rigid societies than they are in the more fluid ones. The evidence that we saw in Table 15.1 indicates that the most rigid societies are also ones which have the strongest link between education and class destination. This suggests that it could well be the strength of the ED link, rather than of the OD link, that accounts for cross-national variation in social rigidity. Since the ED link is already included within our models of ethnic penalties, the strength of that link does not provide an independent explanation for the magnitude of the ethnic penalties.[20]

We have to keep an open mind on the nature of the relationship and of any potential explanation. Ideally we would obtain better data on cross-national variations in class fluidity and on the processes involved. We therefore move on to consider other mechanisms more specifically related to ethnicity.

Racism and xenophobia

We turn, then, from these general social processes to more specific processes linked to the treatment of ethnic minorities. As we suggested in the introductory chapter, the extent of racial prejudice may vary across

---

[19] The very small impact of class origins on ethnic penalties with respect to unemployment is not at all surprising since the main effects of class origins on avoidance of unemployment are substantively quite small (although statistically significant). The effects of class origins on access to the salariat are rather stronger, and hence there is more scope for them to account for ethnic penalties in occupational attainment.

[20] Breen and Luijkx (2004b) suggest that more fluid societies are ones where the partial effects of class origins on class destination, controlling for education, are weaker. However, their analysis is based only on four countries, one of which is Britain where as noted above controls for class have very limited impact on the ethnic penalties.

countries and may have an important role in social exclusion through mechanisms such as discrimination or the chill factor. Levels of prejudice and xenophobia may in turn be linked to the prevailing conception of the nation among the host society, ethnic conceptions of the nation being accompanied by higher levels of xenophobia than civic conceptions. (Hjerm 1998 shows that this holds true at the individual level in Australia, Britain, Germany and Sweden alike.)[21] These conceptions may in turn relate to immigration policies, citizenship policies and the existence of anti-discrimination legislation. Again we must emphasise that we do not postulate any precise causal linkages between these different specific elements although we suspect that conceptions of the nation may well be rather long-standing and possibly have some causal priority.

Table 15.8 provides some rudimentary cross-national comparisons. The table reports both some survey-based measures of ethnic conceptions of the nation, attitudes towards immigration (which can be thought of as a measure of xenophobia), attitudes towards race discrimination legislation together with some harder evidence on support for Extreme Right parties (a euphemism for racist parties) and on anti-discrimination legislation.

Cross-national comparisons of subjective concepts have to be treated very cautiously because the same question can often mean very different things in different contexts (King *et al.* 2004). There are indeed some striking inconsistencies between the subjective measures and the harder evidence on Far Right voting that should certainly make us pause for thought about the validity of these subjective measures.

In the first column we show Jones and Smith's 'difference measure' of ethnic versus civic conceptions of the nation based on the 1995 International Social Survey Programme (ISSP) module on national identity (Jones and Smith 2001). Negative scores indicate a tendency for respondents in that country to favour civic conceptions and positive scores indicate a tendency to favour ethnic conceptions of the nation.[22] In

---

[21] However, this process appears to work rather differently in the Israeli context. See Lewin-Epstein and Levanon (2005).

[22] To construct this measure Jones and Smith first constructed separate standardised scales of ethnic and civic conceptions of the nation (standardised on the complete set of countries participating in the 1995 ISSP after a couple of exclusions). They then calculated the difference and then standardised this difference score. We were not able to replicate their scores exactly and report in Table 15.8 our scores rather than the original Jones and Smith ones. The differences between our and their measures are relatively small. For details of the wording of the questions used see the appendix to this chapter.

Table 15.8. Ethnic and civic conceptions of the nation, xenophobia and prejudice.

	Ethnic vs civic conception of the nation 1995	Ethnic vs civic conception of the nation 2003	Attitudes towards immigrants 1995	Attitudes towards immigrants 2003	Immigration and asylum policy preferences 2002–3	% very or quite racist 1997	Attitude towards law against racial discrimination 2002–3	% electoral support for the Extreme Right	Anti-discrimination legislation
Australia	−0.34	−0.35	44.7	42.5				8.4 (1998)	1975 Act
Austria	+0.19	+0.08	55.1	57.1				21.9 (1995)	
Belgium					Flanders 55.3 Wallonia 50.9	42 55	33.5 35.8	Flanders 12.1 Wallonia 5.2 (1995)	2002 Act
Canada	−0.30	−0.08	39.7	42.0				<1.0	1986 Act.
France		−0.82		52.8	45.9	48	31.3	12.4 (1993)	2001 Act
Germany (West)	−0.05	−0.20	55.4	58.6	52.5	34	33.2	2.0 (1994)	
Israel		Jews +0.08 Arabs +0.81		Jews 49.9 Arabs 70.4	49.4		15.9		
Netherlands	−0.34	+0.75	52.3		52.6	31	30.2	2.5 (1994)	1994 Act
South Africa								<1.0 (1994)	
Sweden	−0.63	−0.88	52.5	48.7	39.7	18	26.1	6.7 (1991)	1999 Act
UK—GB	+0.27	−0.05	55.3	59.3	53.8	32	28.7	<1.0 (1992, 1997)	1968, 1976 Acts
USA	+.15	+0.01	52.2	49.6				<1.0 (1992, 1996)	1976 and 1989 Acts

Sources: columns 1 and 3, 1995 ISSP module on national identity. Column 2 and 4, 2003 ISSP module on national identity. Column 5 and 7, 2002–3 ESS. Column 6 Eurobarometer 47.1 Racism and Xenophobia in Europe. Column 8: Lubbers 2001 and national election websites.

the second column we have repeated the measures using the 2003 ISSP data. In general we find that the results are very similar in the two years, suggesting that these are indeed rather stable features of Western societies. The 2003 data enable us to extend the coverage to some additional countries, and while 2003 is of course subsequent to almost all our evidence on ethnic penalties, the overtime stability of the measures suggests that they could in principle have some causal role to play.

At any rate, the results of the difference measure show that France, Sweden, Australia and Canada are the most civic nations while Austria, Britain and South Africa are the most ethnic. Rather surprisingly the USA, which has usually been assumed to be a model civic nation proves to be rather average on this measure, as is Germany which has usually been taken as an exemplar of a country with an ethnic conception of the nation.

We can check this pattern with some other measures more directly linked to xenophobia and racism. In the third and fourth columns we show a measure of attitudes towards immigrants (again derived from the ISSP modules of 1995 and 2003). (With all the measures in Table 15.8 higher scores indicate more xenophobic or racist attitudes.) These results tally fairly well with the cross-national differences in conceptions of the nation and once again the rank ordering of countries on this measure seems to be quite stable over time.[23] Australia and Canada stand out as the most welcoming to immigrants. This makes good theoretical sense as both countries have historically had policies of positively encouraging immigration for nation-building purposes. Next come the USA, Israeli Jews, the Netherlands and Sweden while Austria, Germany and Britain are the most hostile, apart from Israeli Palestinians who, for understandable reasons, are hostile to immigrants (the Palestinians presumably assuming that immigrants will in practice be Jewish). We can extend our coverage to include Belgium using the 2002 European Social Survey (ESS) which included some similar questions (and which obtained a very similar rank-ordering of countries to the 2003 ISSP). Belgium, or more particularly Flanders, proves on this measure to be one of the countries most hostile to immigrants.

---

[23] These results include both members of the charter population and the ethnic minorities, who might be expected to be more favourable to immigration. If we exclude migrants and ethnic minorities from the samples, all the figures do in fact become slightly more hostile to immigration but the rank ordering of countries remains the same.

While hostility towards immigrants is conceptually distinct from racism or hostility towards ethnic minorities, we suspect that they will empirically be quite highly correlated. An explicit measure of racism is shown in the fifth column. This is a straightforward self-report measure in which respondents were asked to say how racist they were. (For details of question wording see the appendix to this chapter.) These data come from the 1996 Eurobarometer and hence are restricted to the Western European countries. Belgium, France and Austria prove to be noticeably racist on this measure while the least racist country by far is Sweden. We also show the results of another question in the European Social Survey which asked about support for anti-discrimination policy. Again, Austria, Belgium and Germany prove to be relatively hostile to such legislation with Israel and Sweden the most supportive of anti-discrimination measures.[24]

There are some strong parallels between all these different measures but also some puzzling anomalies. France in particular is remarkable as, on the difference measure, it is the most civic of all countries in its conception of the nation, while it is fairly average with respect to anti-immigrant attitudes and appears to be quite racist on the Eurobarometer measure. France has also of course displayed rather high levels of electoral support for the racist Front National. We show recent electoral support for such racist parties in the eighth column of Table 15.8.

To be sure, even the hard evidence of Far Right voting is somewhat problematic. Voting for Far Right parties tends to be highly volatile. For example, in Sweden the Ny Demokratie party experienced one good election in 1991 and became for a while a pivotal party in the Swedish parliament, but it shortly thereafter disintegrated and was declared bankrupt in 2000. Similarly Pauline Hanson's xenophobic One Nation party in Australia polled 8.4% of the national vote in the 1997 election but this fell to 4.3% in 2000 and 1.2% in 2004 while in the Netherlands the Far Right only polled 2.5% of the vote in 1994, but under Pim Fortuyn the vote went briefly up to 17% in 2002 before falling back abruptly after his assassination. Still these brief successes of racist parties in apparently civic-minded nations like Australia, Netherlands and Sweden make one suspect that some degree of racism is endemic in Western nations.

---

[24] Somewhat similar results were obtained in the 2000 Eurobarometer which contained a more detailed analysis of attitudes toward minority groups in the European Union. See EUMC (2001).

Nor should the absence of successful racist parties in Britain or the USA lull us into thinking that racism is absent from these societies. Different electoral systems may also have an independent effect on the actual level of Far Right voting. It is much harder for a small new party to break into the first-past-the-post system of the UK, for example, than it is in the case of a proportional system such as the Netherlands.

Finally, some of our countries, notably the USA and Northern Ireland, have had vigorous affirmative action programmes. Several others have long-standing anti-discrimination legislation, whereas many of the European countries have not had such legislation until very recently, or not at all. Again there is some parallel with the immigration and citizenship legislation. Such legislation may perhaps affect the extent to which citizens are able to put into effect any racist attitudes that they have.

The best evidence of all on the actual practice of racial discrimination comes from field experiments. In these field experiments applications for actual jobs are made (sometimes by actors but more often by post) by candidates from different ethnic backgrounds but with the same formal qualifications. The success rates of candidates from different backgrounds in securing an interview or job offer can then be compared. Unfortunately, there have been no systematic cross-national studies using field experiments but perhaps the key finding is that, in every country where such studies have been carried out—Austria, Belgium, Germany, Netherlands, Britain and the USA—substantial discrimination has been discovered.[25] In passing it should be noted that Sweden, on ethical grounds, refused to participate in the ILO field experiments. The ethics of field experiments can certainly be debated since they involve deception, but the Swedish decision has the unfortunate and no doubt unintended side effect that Sweden's reputation for liberal attitudes cannot be put to a strict test. One might indeed want to argue that the members of the Swedish charter population who made this 'ethical' decision themselves had a conflict of interest.

As in the case of class fluidity, then, we find that different studies, concepts and measures give somewhat different results. Given the evidence on

---

[25] See for example the results of the ILO investigations reported in Zegers de Beijl (2000). The economist Heckman has raised some doubts about the validity of these field experiments, and there may indeed be some problems where actors are used, because in these circumstances the experiment cannot be 'double blind'. On the other hand, these field experiments almost certainly have a great deal more validity than any other method that has been suggested and are immeasurably superior to the kind of indirect evidence that economists often use on selection effects and so on.

support for the racist parties of the Far Right and of the results of field experiments, we are in fact rather sceptical of the extent to which racism actually varies across our twelve countries. However, if we trust subjective measures, we would conclude that Australia, Canada and Sweden are the most civic of our societies, the least racist and the most welcoming towards immigrants. Israel and the Netherlands should probably be placed next followed by the USA, Germany and possibly France while Britain, Austria and Belgium are, on these subjective measures, the least friendly towards immigrants. In passing we should note that there are some striking parallels between this pattern and the very different data on class fluidity that we saw in Table 15.7 with the more fluid societies also tending to be more civic and the rigid ones more ethnic and xenophobic.

In Figure 15.4 we plot ethnic penalties with respect to unemployment against the difference measure of ethnic versus civic conceptions of the nation. (We focus on unemployment since our hypothesis is that racial discrimination is particularly important in the decision whether to hire a worker or not.) We use this measure as our base partly because it covers all but one (Belgium) of our countries and also because it can be thought of as a more fundamental property of a society and probably less subject to endogeneity problems.[26] Where available we use the 1995 data, since

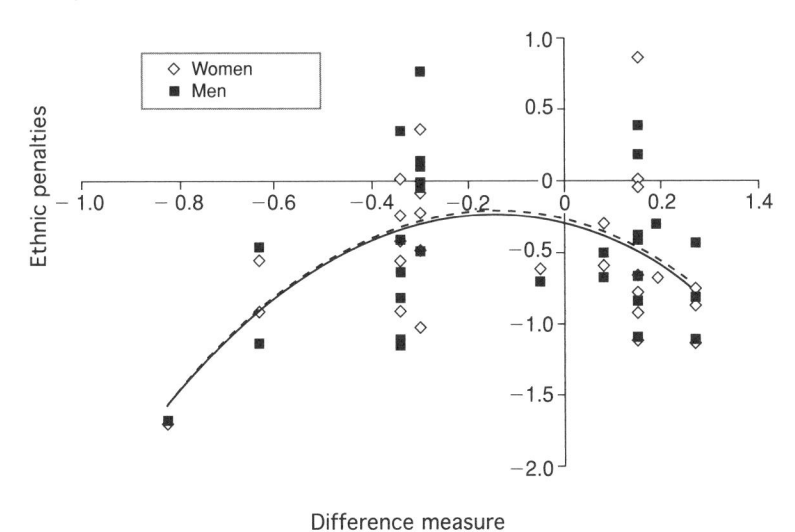

Figure 15.4. Civil/ethnic conceptions and ethnic penalties (unemployment).

[26] It is quite likely that attitudes towards immigration will be a consequence of the numbers of immigrants arriving in a country and the extent to which they are in competition for jobs. See for example the literature on the 'threat' hypothesis such as Quillian (1995) and McLaren (2003).

they correspond better with the date of most of our surveys on ethnic minority disadvantage, but we also use the 2003 data to expand our coverage to France and Israel.

As we can see, there is only a curvilinear relationship between civic conceptions of the nation and ethnic penalties, which is not what we had expected. And if anything the relationship is in the wrong direction with the most civic societies (France and Sweden) tending to have rather high ethnic penalties with respect to unemployment. This is partly driven by the anomalous case of France which is strongly civic in its conception of the nation but where Maghrebins experience major ethnic penalties and where, as we noted above, different subjective measures give very different pictures. The Swedish case is also somewhat problematic as the ethnic penalties related to non-employment rather than unemployment. But even if we delete these two countries, we still fail to see a relationship in the predicted direction. We therefore reject the hypothesis that conceptions of the nation can explain patterns of ethnic disadvantage.

We might well be able to do rather better than this if we used one of our other subjective measures, although questions of causal direction will become rather worrying as we move to subjective measures collected after the major immigration waves had occurred. We suspect, although we cannot prove it from these data, that racial prejudice and discrimination occurs in all the countries in our study and that it is not therefore the main explanation for variations in ethnic penalties.

Immigration and citizenship policies

While the subjective measures have proved rather disappointing, possibly because of methodological problems, government policies have a more robust and 'hard' character. In addition they can be dated accurately and thus potentially may be more convincing explanatory mechanisms than the attitudes of the charter population where major issues of causal direction will arise. To be sure, in a democracy government policy too may well be a consequence of public attitudes and may be generated by public concern over immigration, but the dating means that we can regard these attitudes and policies as prior to the current ethnic penalties measured in our study. There are also important questions about the actual enforcement of government policies, analogous to the questions about the validity of subjective data that we raised in the previous section that unfortunately we cannot address.

There are two main areas of policy that may be relevant. First, immigration policies and second, access to the right of becoming a full citizen. We might well expect immigration policy to be particularly relevant to the first, migrant generation. However, such policies could well have legacies for the second and later generations. This could well be the case if what are sometimes termed 'contextual effects' operate. For example, guest-worker policies of the sort followed in many West European countries may result in large concentrations of relatively unskilled manual workers in the first generation. As well as leading to individual-level effects on educational and occupational attainment of the sort dealt with by mobility researchers, there may also be group-level effects. As Wilson (1987) has compellingly shown in the case of African Americans, the concentration of Blacks in relatively homogeneous lower working-class (or indeed under-class) environments may be highly relevant to their lack of economic success, perhaps as a result of lack of social networks and information, lack of middle-class community leaders and organisations. This is analogous to the economists' notion of human capital externalities (see for example Borjas 1995) although Wilson's conceptualisation perhaps implies processes involving social capital rather than human capital.

Secondly, we might expect access to citizenship to be important for the second generation. Citizenship is important in many societies for gaining jobs in the civil service, and while these jobs will not be numerically large they may well be important avenues of advancement for ethnic minorities. Access to citizenship may also have more general symbolic consequences, lack of citizenship perhaps leading to a feeling of social exclusion, alienation and perhaps a greater readiness to resort to the black economy. It may also be linked to the issues of xenophobia and racial discrimination on the part of the charter population that we explored in the previous section.

Table 15.9 provides a brief summary of the main outlines of government policy in these two areas. The first column provides an overview of government policies on immigration and is based on the detailed accounts given by our chapter authors. We focus in particular on policies for migrant workers: all countries alike had policies for allowing family reunion (although the details vary) and also for accepting refugees under international agreements (although again with some variations in interpretation of the agreements). Members of the EU have also permitted free movement of workers between member states in recent years. However, it is with respect to policies for labour migration from less-developed countries that there has been most controversy and most variation.

Table 15.9. Immigration policy, anti-discrimination legislation and citizenship rules, 1994.

	Immigration policy	Principles underlying nationality legislation	Period of residence required for naturalisation	Whether dual nationality allowed
Australia	White Australia policy formally abolished in 1973 and a non-discriminatory selection policy based on the Canadian point system adopted.	Combination	3 years	
Austria	Guestworker agreements from 1962 onwards with specific sending countries.	*Ius sanguinis*	10 years	No
Belgium	Guestworker agreements from 1946 onwards with specific sending countries. Severely cut back after 1974.	Combination	5 years	
Canada	Point system introduced in 1967 (alongside 'sponsored dependants' and 'nominated' categories.	*Ius soli*	3 years	
France	Unrestricted entry to individuals from French overseas departments and initially free entry from former colonies. Some guestworker agreements (ended after 1973)	*Ius sanguinis*	5 years	
Germany	Free entry to ethnic Germans. Guestworker agreements from 1955 onwards with specific sending countries, ended after 1973.	*Ius sanguinis* (until 2000)	10 years	No
Israel	Freedom of entry for all Jews under 1950 Law of Return.	Open to any resident Jew	0	
Netherlands	Initially unrestricted entry from colonies, in particular from Antilles. Guestworker agreements with specific countries in the 1960s.	*Ius sanguinis*	5 years	
Sweden	Free entry from other Scandinavian countries after 1954. Gradual introduction of individual controls on non-Nordic immigrants. No guestworker policies.	*Ius sanguinis*	5 years	No

UK—GB	Unrestricted entry to Irish and initially to Commonwealth citizens, the latter increasingly restricted after 1962. Work permit system for individual migrants.	Mixed	5 years
USA	Free entry for Puerto Ricans (citizens). New immigration regulations of 1965 opened immigration to more non-Europeans with reduced emphasis on skill criteria.	*Ius soli*	5 years

Sources: column 1: chapters in this volume (see also Reitz 1998 on Australia, Canada and the USA); for columns 2–4 see Guimezanes 1994.

While policies have changed considerably over the years, as the first column of Table 15.9 indicates, Austria, Belgium, France, Germany and the Netherlands all had major guestworker programmes during the late 1950s and 1960s through which the parents of the current second generation would have been recruited. These programmes took the form of agreements with the sending countries and involved less-skilled workers recruited for short stays on the rotation principle. These agreements were primarily with non-European countries such as Turkey and Morocco, but also included Italy and Greece in the case of Germany. None of the other countries in our study had these collective guestworker programmes. Australia, Canada, Israel and the USA all had relatively liberal policies for individual migrants, opening up considerably in the 1960s to increased migration from less-developed countries. In these countries migration was expected to be permanent and to lead to full membership and citizenship of the receiving country. Canada and Australia had somewhat more selective entry requirements with their point systems whereas the USA was less selective and Israel completely non-selective. Sweden and the UK fall somewhere in between.

Immigration policy tends to be closely linked to citizenship policy. Again we must emphasise that citizenship policy is continually evolving and our classification in Table 15.9 (based on the study by Guimezanes 1994) refers primarily to the situation in the 1970s and 1980s which would have been the relevant period for most of our empirical findings. For example Germany changed its citizenship policies and made it easier to acquire citizenship in 2000, but too late to affect our sample and results.

In the table, following Guimezanes, we have made a broad distinction between *ius soli* and *ius sanguinis*. *Ius sanguinis* essentially bases citizenship on descent from a national of the country concerned. *Ius soli*, on the other hand, adopts a territorial viewpoint and grants citizenship to those born in the country, irrespective of their parents' nationality. While there are many complications in the legislation of the individual countries, Guimezanes classifies Canada and the United States as countries where *ius soli* is the underlying principle, Australia, Belgium and the UK as countries where both birthplace and descent are take into account, and Austria, France (perhaps controversially), Germany, the Netherlands and Sweden as countries where descent is the principal criterion. Within these three broad groupings we can make some further sub-divisions. (Guimezanes' study relates only to OECD countries and therefore excludes Israel and South Africa.)[27]

A related set of issues concern the criteria for naturalisation. Again the details vary between countries, but in most cases a period as a legal resident is required. As we can see from the third column of Table 15.9, the qualifying periods vary from three years in Australia and Canada to ten years in Austria and Germany. Austria, Germany and, surprisingly, Sweden require one to give up any previous nationality on acquiring citizenship.

Guimezanes emphasises that there is gradual tendency for countries' policies to converge over time, and so the patterns described in Table 15.9 should be seen as an indication of the historical conditions that would have affected the second generation when they were growing up, not the current state of affairs. Castles and Miller (2003, table 10.2) for example show that there have been considerable increases between 1988 and 1998 in the numbers acquiring citizenship in Belgium, France, Germany, the Netherlands and Sweden. This is not simply because of increases in the numbers eligible but appears also to reflect increases in acquisition rates among those who are eligible.[28]

There are two distinct ways of conceptualising these policies. One way would be in terms of their degree of inclusion and exclusion. Countries such as Austria and Germany where nationality was based in our period on the principle of *ius sanguinis*, where longer periods of residence are

---

[27] On citizenship in South Africa see Klaaren (2000) and for Israel see Shachar (2000).
[28] For example, the acquisition rate increased from 4% to 15% in Germany between 1988 and 1998, from 10% to 27% in Belgium, from 13% to 45% in France, from 43% to 76% in Sweden, and from 14% to 94% in the Netherlands.

required for naturalisation and which prohibit dual nationality can be regarded as the most exclusionary. In contrast a country such as Canada operating under the principle of *ius soli* and offering naturalisation after only three years would be regarded as the most inclusive. Similarly a country such as Israel with easy access to citizenship for Jews can also be regarded as highly inclusive. Inclusivity might have consequences for ethnic disadvantage through encouraging immigrants and their descendants to make greater investments (not only in education but also in learning the language, acquiring knowledge about how the society works, and so on) in the country of destination. As suggested above, inclusivity might also ease access to salaried jobs in the public sector which are often reserved for citizens. Inclusivity might therefore be expected to have some impact on chances of accessing the salariat. It is striking that all the countries that rely on *ius soli* fall into our broad group of countries where ethnic penalties are primarily with respect to unemployment, whereas all those with *ius sanguinis* fall into the category where there are substantial penalties in access to the salariat.

Another way of conceptualising the policies would be in terms of their degree of selectivity. In effect guestworker policies selected negatively for skills, since less-skilled workers were deliberately being recruited in order to fill vacancies at the lower end of the labour market. Point systems, such as Canada's, select positively, whereas the US, Sweden and historically countries such as Britain, France and the Netherlands with former colonies have also been relatively neutral, at least with respect to immigration from the former colonies. (France and the Netherlands have also had guestworker programmes aimed at countries other than their former colonies and so represent mixed cases.)

In Figure 15.5A we plot a rank ordering of countries on their selectivity (ranking countries from positive selection ones on the left to negative selection ones on the right) against ethnic penalties with respect to the salariat.[29] As we can see, this provides the clearest and strongest relationship that we have seen so far. There are no major exceptions or outliers. To be sure, our rank ordering of countries according to the selectivity is not as robust as we would like (although the same could be said of all our

---

[29] Our ranking is Canada, Australia, Britain, Sweden, Israel, the USA, Netherlands, France, Belgium, Austria and Germany. Broadly speaking we have placed countries with point systems first, ranking Canada above Australia since it introduced its point system earlier. We then have countries with more neutral systems, followed by those such as the Netherlands and France with mixed systems, and finally those primarily with guestworker systems in the relevant period, ranking Germany last since it introduced its system first.

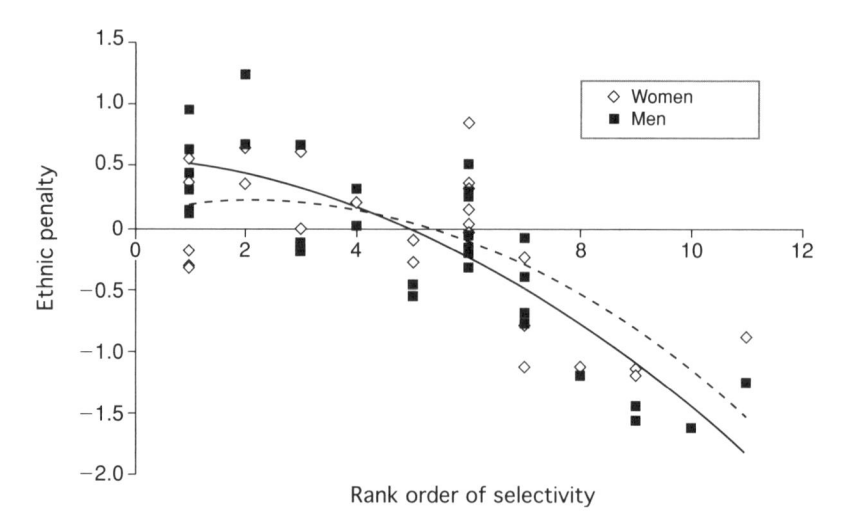

Figure 15.5A. Selectivity and ethnic penalties (salariat).

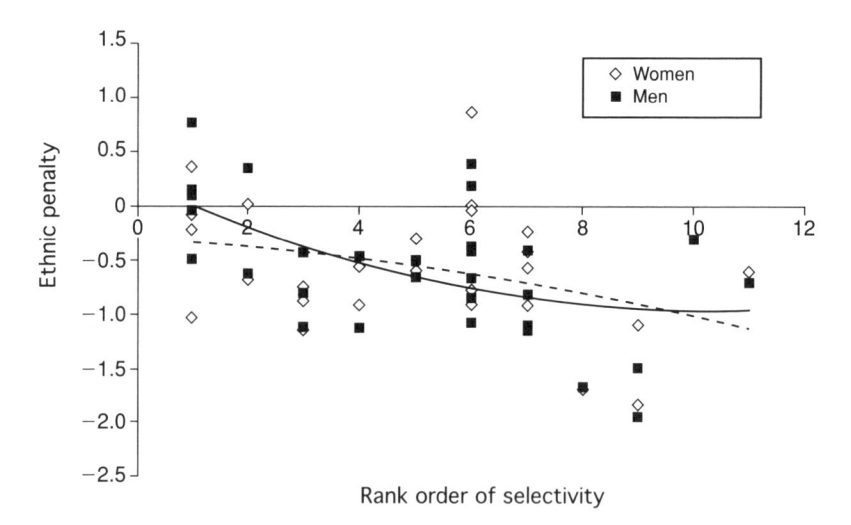

Figure 15.5B. Selectivity and ethnic penalties (unemployment).

other cross-national measures). While there would probably be general agreement about placing Australia and Canada at the 'positive selection' end of the spectrum and the 'negative selection' guestworker countries of Austria, Belgium and Germany at the other extreme, other observers might well place individual countries somewhat differently. However, experiments with alternative rank-orderings suggest that the relationship is a reasonably robust one.

We have also checked whether selectivity is related in the same way to ethnic penalties with respect to unemployment. As we can see from Figure 15B the relationship is not nearly as strong as it was with respect to the salariat. While positive selectivity is associated with some reduction in ethnic penalties in access to employment, the relationship is no stronger than those we found earlier with national unemployment rates or employment protection legislation.

In Figure 15.6 we follow a similar exercise but ranking the countries according to their degree of inclusiveness, based on access to citizenship and the presence of anti-discrimination legislation. We place Israel as the most inclusive country since, while it follows *ius sanguinis*, in the case of Jews (who are the subject of the ethnic penalties in question) this amounts to automatic citizenship on arrival.[30]

Overall we find a relationship in the predicted direction but it is not as strong as that for selectivity and there are some major anomalies. As with class mobility, Israel proves to be an anomaly as the ethnic penalties experienced by second-generation Jews from the Middle East and North Africa are rather larger than would have been expected given Israel's fluid and inclusive character. At the other extreme Sweden is an anomaly with

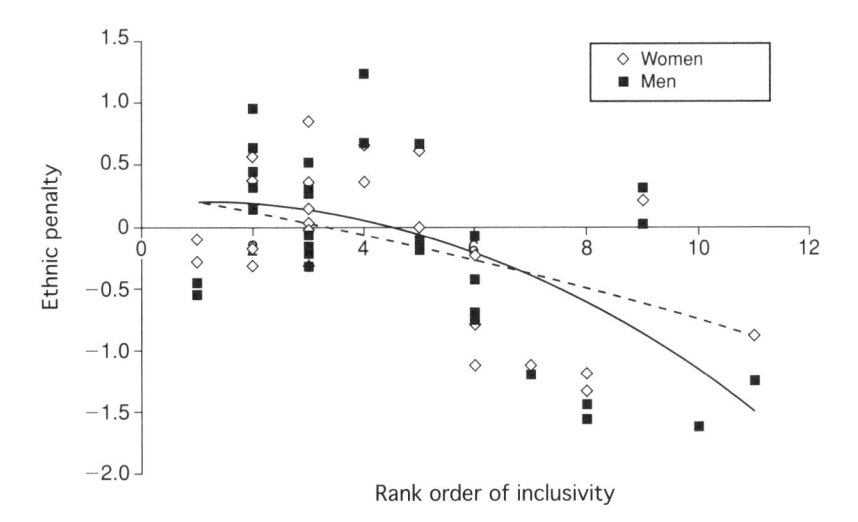

Figure 15.6. Inclusivity and ethnic penalties (salariat).

[30] Our ranking is Israel, Canada, the USA, Australia, Britain, Netherlands, France, Belgium, Sweden, Germany and Austria. Where countries have broadly similar access to citizenship we have ranked them according to the number of years required for naturalisation and whether dual citizenship was allowed.

its rather restrictive citizenship legislation, at least at the time of the OECD report (which is of course the relevant time for the Swedish data).

Broadly speaking then, our measure of selectivity appears to provide the best potential explanation for ethnic penalties among groups of non-European ancestry in access to the salariat. It is also noticeable that some of the groups of European ancestry who experience ethnic penalties in access to the salariat, for example Yugoslavs in Austria or Italians in Germany and Belgium also had guestworker origins in the first generation.[31] This mechanism therefore appears able to explain in principle some of the major anomalies among the European groups.

In contrast, none of our explanations for ethnic penalties with respect to unemployment are all that convincing. We incline to the view that some degree of racism and racial discrimination is widespread in all our countries and that this leads to difficulties for the second generation from non-European ancestries in obtaining jobs. The state of the labour market may well be relevant too, and here we incline towards the simplest explanation, which is that it is simply the overall demand for labour that is crucial for ethnic penalties in gaining employment

Conclusions

On the whole our findings tend towards the pessimistic rather than the optimistic. While the second generation from European origins and a few groups such as Chinese and Indians from non-European origins appear to compete on fairly equal terms with the charter populations, most groups with non-European origins continue to experience major ethnic penalties in the second generation particularly with regard to unemployment. The pessimistic picture is accentuated by the major disadvantages experienced by indigenous populations and by involuntary minorities such as African Americans.

We suspect, although we cannot prove, that racism and prejudice against 'visible' minorities is widespread throughout the charter populations of all our developed countries and that this may well be a major part

---

[31] Note that this argument is quite distinct from Portes and Zhou's theory of segmented assimilation and downwards assimilation. It is the class composition of the ethnic community not of the neighbourhood that we postulate is important whereas for Portes and Zhou it is the composition of the other ethnic groups resident in the same neighbourhood that is central to their account.

of the explanation for the difficulties that the second generation have in obtaining jobs in competition with equally qualified members of the charter population. Possibly there will be some decline in racism over time, particularly among younger generations who have been brought up in multicultural societies. There is anecdotal evidence that, early in the twentieth century, Irish immigrants to Britain or the USA experienced something remarkably similar to racism and this has surely declined over time. There is also some survey evidence suggesting that prejudice against visible minorities might be lower among younger generations (Rothon and Heath 2003). Our pessimism should perhaps, therefore, be somewhat tempered although we suspect that any decline will be of glacial slowness and may well be interrupted by intermittent resurgences of ethnic prejudice.

Another reason for pessimism is the evidence of a continuing legacy of initial disadvantage passed on from generation to generation. This may simply be due to the usual processes of class reproduction, but we suspect that there are additional processes at work. In particular we suspect that 'contextual effects' may play an important role. Thus where, as in much of western Europe, guestworker programmes were introduced in the 1950s and 1960s, large and relatively low-educated and poorly qualified migrant communities were established. While conventional research in social mobility has taken an individualistic approach, our hypothesis is that group processes (of the sort for example documented by Wilson in the case of African Americans) may serve to limit the advance of members of these communities. This may result, for example, from lack of 'bridging' links with the charter population and lack of knowledge about opportunities outside the ethnic community. There may therefore be what could be termed 'social class externalities'.

Social class externalities of this sort could in principle explain why we find major ethnic penalties with respect to access to the salariat in many of the European countries. It could also explain why some groups of European ancestry continue to experience major ethnic penalties in for example Belgium or Germany, whereas similar groups in Australia, Canada and the USA do not. These processes are not, therefore, restricted to groups of non-European ancestry. Moreover, while guestworker programmes were one major source of these less-educated communities, they are not the only source. In the USA, for example, such processes may well be at work in the case of Mexicans (who as we have seen continue to experience major ethnic penalties in access to the salariat) and in Britain with respect to Pakistanis. These processes, we hypothesise, depend not only on the 'negative selection' involved in guestworker programmes but also on the numerical scale of these programmes and the resulting geographical concentration of disadvantaged communities. Scale and concentration will tend to increase the extent to which social class externalities operate.

Our suggestion, then, is that the presence of continued ethnic penalties with respect to the salariat in many European countries (such as Austria, Belgium, France, Germany and the Netherlands) is the legacy of the guestworker programmes of the 1950s and 1960s. Countries such as Australia, Canada, Sweden and Britain where ethnic penalties are largely restricted to employment are ones that have never had guestworker (or equivalent) programmes.

Guestworker programmes were of course largely abandoned after the 1973/4 oil shock although the communities continued to grow through processes of family reunion. It should perhaps be remembered too that in recent decades western countries have tended to outsource much semi- and unskilled labour to less developed countries, which may also have unintended undesirable consequences. It is not our aim, therefore, to make a normative point about guestworker programmes or to suggest that selective systems of immigration such as the point systems of Australia and Canada are normatively to be preferred. Our aim is rather to suggest that class contextual effects arising from previous immigration policies may continue to disadvantage members of those communities in later generations.

In passing it may also be noted that our emphasis on the legacy of immigration policies helps us to make some sense of the continued disadvantage experienced by indigenous groups in countries like Australia and Canada. Our hypothesis is that ethnic penalties are lower among the second generation in these countries not because of general characteristics of those societies which might have been expected to benefit indigenous groups too but because of the specific legacies of immigration policies.

We did not intend this study to lead to specific policy recommendations. But one implication of our broadly pessimistic conclusion is that policy interventions will be needed to bring the reality of our liberal western democracies closer to their professed ideals of equality of opportunity. If the optimistic scenario had held true, we could perhaps simply allow the passage of time to bring about a gradual convergence of the fortunes of ethnic minorities with those of the charter populations. On our more pessimistic reading of the evidence, intervention will be needed.

While we cannot of course undo the guestworker policies of the 1950s, more could perhaps be done to help the descendants of those guestworkers. This could take the form of the affirmative action legislation that has perhaps reduced ethno-religious disadvantage in Northern Ireland. It could take the form of the improved access to citizenship that we have already seen in Germany and some other European countries. But governments should not be complacent.

Appendix 1

Measures of ethnic/civic conceptions of the nation; attitudes towards immigrants and racism

Jones and Smith's difference measure of civic and ethnic conceptions

This is based on the following seven questions included in the 1995 ISSP module on national identity:

> *Some people say the following things are important for being truly [country nationality]. Others say they are not important. How important do you think each of the following is?*
> *To have been born in [country]*
> *To have [country nationality] citizenship*
> *To have lived in [country] for most of one's life.*
> *To be able to speak [country language]*
> *To be a Christian.*
> *To respect [country's] political institutions and laws*
> *To feel [country nationality].*

Response codes were 'very important', 'fairly important', 'not very important', and 'not at all important'. Our understanding is that Jones and Smith (on the basis of factor analysis) first created a scale of ascribed identity from the first three and the fifth questions and a scale of civic identity from the remaining three. Both scales were then standardised (for the whole set of ISSP countries excluding Bulgaria and the Philippines). The difference was then calculated and again was standardised. Jones and Smith do not say how they treated the 'can't choose' response. They are treated as missing in the ISSP file that has been released so we assume that this is the default and have excluded them in our calculations.

Since Jones and Smith excluded Bulgaria and the Philippines when constructing their measure, we have done likewise in making our own calculations for 1995. For 2003 we have based our measures on the same set of countries as in 1995 (where possible) and have simply added France, Israel and South Africa.

Ivarsflaten's measure of immigrant preferences

The European Social Survey conducted in 2002/3 contained many questions on attitudes towards asylum and immigration. The ten questions used by Iversflaten were:

> *Now, using this card, to what extent do you think [country] should allow people of the <u>same race or ethnic group</u> as most [country] people to come and live here?* (D4)
> The response codes were 'allow many to come and live here', 'allow some', 'allow a few', 'allow none'.

> *Using this card, please say how much you agree or disagree with each of the following statements.*
> *If people who have come to live and work here are unemployed for a long period, they should be made to leave.* (D21)
> *People who have come to live here should be given the same rights as everyone else.* (D22)
> *If people who have come to live here commit a serious crime, they should be made to leave.* (D23)
> *If people who have come to live here commit any crime, they should be made to leave.* (D24)

> *Some people come to this country and apply for refugee status on the grounds that they fear persecution in their own country. Using this card, please say how much you agree of disagree with the following statements.*
> *While their applications for refugee status are being considered, people should be allowed to work in [country]* (D50)
> *The government should be generous in judging people's applications for refugee status.* (D51)
> *While their cases are being considered, applicants should be kept in detention centres.* (D53)
> *While their cases are being considered, the [country] government should give financial support to applicants.* (D54)
> *Refugees whose applications are granted should be entitled to bring in their close family members.* (D55)

The response codes for both sets of questions were 'agree strongly', 'agree', 'neither agree nor disagree', 'disagree', 'disagree strongly'. Principal component analysis indicated that there was only one clearly distinct factor. Ivarsflaten therefore combined the questions on asylum and immigration policy to form a single additive scale balanced for question direction. She concluded that 'The analysis, therefore, contains little evidence to suggest that the Western European public distinguished between asylum and immigration policies. In other words, Western Europeans do not generally support liberal immigration policies while insisting on restrictive refugee policies, or vice versa.' (Ivarsflaten 2005, pp. 98–9). A single additive index of all ten items was therefore constructed and rescaled from 0 to 100. Cronbach's alpha for the pooled ESS dataset (excluding Israel) was 0.78.

We followed a similar procedure to construct a measure of attitudes towards immigrants using the 1995 and 2003 ISSP modules. The 2003 ISSP module on national identity asked the following five questions:

Q. 10. There are different opinions about immigrants from other countries living in [COUNTRY]. (By 'immigrants' we mean people who come to settle in [COUNTRY]). How much do you agree or disagree with each of the following statements? (Please tick one box on each line)

Immigrants increase crime rates
Immigrants are generally good for [country's] economy.
Immigrants take jobs away from people who were in [country]
Immigrants improve [country nationality] society by bringing in new ideas and cultures

The response codes were 'agree strongly', 'agree', 'neither agree nor disagree', disagree', 'disagree strongly'.

Q. 11. Do you think the number of immigrants to [country] nowadays should be . . . increased a lot, increased a little, remain the same as it is, reduced a little, reduced a lot? Can't choose.

Only one factor was extracted from these five items. Cronbach's alpha was 0.75 in 1995. An additive scale was constructed from these five items and rescaled from 0 to 100.

Eurobarometer measure of racism

Eurobarometer 47.1 included the following question:
Some people feel they are not at all racist. Others feel they are very racist. Would you look at this card and give me the number that shows your own feelings about this? If you feel you are not at all racist, you give a score of 1. If you feel you are very racist, you give a score of 10. The scores between 1 and 10 allow you to say how close to either side you are.

Scores of 4 to 6 were scored as quite racist and 7 to 10 as very racist.

ESS measure of attitudes towards race discrimination legislation

The 2002/3 ESS also included a question on attitudes to race discrimination legislation. The question read:

How good or bad are each of these things for a country? Please use this card. Firstly . . .
A law against racial or ethnic discrimination in the workplace.

The response codes, shown on the card, were numbered from 0 to 10 where 0 represented extremely bad and 10 represented extremely good. We have reversed the scale and scaled it from 0 to 100 in order to make it more similar to Ivarsflaten's metric.

Appendix 2

Table 15.A1. Returns to education in the second generation (statistically significant interaction terms).

	Avoidance of Unemployment		Access to the Salariat	
	Men	Women	Men	Women
Australia				
AngloCeltic				−0.21
Greek		+0.69		
Lebanese			−0.86	
Aboriginal	−0.98			
Austria				
Turkish	−0.96			
Belgium				
Italian			−0.16	
Moroccan			−0.37	
Turkish	−0.19	−0.28		
Canada				
Irish		−0.76	−0.46	
British	−0.59			
German	+0.52			
Caribbean		+0.11		
Aboriginal			−0.34	−0.18
France				
Germany				
Italian			−0.67	
Turkish	−0.31			−0.81
Greek			−0.59	
Israel				
N. African	+0.17		+0.17	
M. East			+0.16	
E. Europe		−0.26		
W. Europe				
N. America				
Palestinian			+0.75	+0.56
Netherlands				
Surinam		−0.41		
Antillean				
Turkish				
Moroccan	+1.03			
South Africa				
Afrikaner	+0.16	+0.10	+0.12	+0.22
Asian	+0.42	+0.68	+0.58	+1.04
Coloured	+0.18	+1.52	+0.86	+1.82
Black	+0.42	+1.38	+0.82	+1.87

Sweden			
German			
Polish		yes negative	
Finnish		yes negative	
Yugoslav			Yes negative
Greek			
African			
UK—GB			
Irish			
Indian	−0.37		
Caribbean			
Pakistani			
UK—NI			
Catholics			+0.32
USA			
Black		−0.66	
African American	+0.13		+0.19

Source: chapters in this volume.
Notes: the Israeli figures do not distinguish generations as they come from a pooled model. The Swedish results are derived from a somewhat different model.

References

Alba, R. D. (1985), 'The twilight of ethnicity among Americans of European ancestry: the case of Italians', *Ethnic and Racial Studies*, 8, 134–58.

Alba, R. D. (1990), *Ethnic Identity: The transformation of white America* (New Haven: Yale University Press).

Borjas, G. J. (1994), 'Long-run convergence of ethnic skills differentials: the children and grandchildren of the great migration', *Industrial and Labor Relations Review*, 47, 553–73.

Borjas, G. J. (1995), 'Ethnicity, neighbourhoods and human capital externalities', *American Economic Review*, 85, 365–90.

Breen, R. (2004), 'Statistical methods of mobility research'. In R. Breen (ed.), *Social Mobility in Europe* (Oxford: Oxford University Press), pp. 17–35.

Breen, R. and Luijkx, R. (2004*a*), 'Social mobility in Europe between 1970 and 2000'. In R. Breen (ed.), *Social Mobility in Europe* (Oxford: Oxford University Press), pp. 37–75.

Breen, R. and Luijkx, R. (2004*b*), 'Conclusions'. In R. Breen (ed.), *Social Mobility in Europe* (Oxford: Oxford University Press), pp. 383–410.

Castles, S. and Miller, M. J. (2003), *The Age of Migration.* 3rd edn. (Basingstoke: Palgrave).

Erikson, R. and Goldthorpe, J. H. (1985), 'Are American rates of social mobility exceptionally high? New evidence on an old issue', *European Sociological Review*, 1, 1–22.

Erikson, R. and Goldthorpe, J. H. (1992), *The Constant Flux: A Study of Class Mobility in Industrial Societies* (Oxford: Clarendon Press).

EUMC (2001), 'Attitudes towards minority groups in the European Union: A special analysis of the Eurobarometer 2000 survey on behalf of the European Monitoring Centre on Racism and Xenophobia by SORA, Vienna' (Vienna: EUMC).

Ganzeboom, H. B. G., Luijkx, R., and Treiman, D. J. (1989), 'Intergenerational class mobility in comparative perspective', *Research in Social Stratification and Mobility*, 8, 3–84.

Goldthorpe, J. H., Yaish, M., and Kraus, V. (1997), 'Class mobility in Israeli society: a comparative perspective', *Research in Social Stratification and Mobility*, 15, 3–27.

Gordon, M. (1964), *Assimilation in American Life: the role of race, religion and national origins* (New York: Oxford University Press).

Guimezanes, N. (1994), 'Acquisition of nationality in OECD countries'. In OECD, *Trends in International Migration: Annual Report* (Paris: OECD), pp. 157–79.

Hjerm, M. (1998), 'National identities, national pride and xenophobia: a comparison of four Western countries', *Acta Sociologica*, 41, 335–47.

Ivarsflaten, E. (2005), *Immigration Policy and Party Organization: Explaining the Rise of the Populist Right in Western Europe* (D.Phil. Thesis, Oxford University).

Jones, F. L. and Smith, P. (2001), 'Individual and societal bases of national identity: a comparative multi-level analysis', *European Sociological Review*, 17, 103–18.

King, G., Murray, C. J. L., Salomon, J. A., and Tandon, A. (2004), 'Enhancing the validity and cross-cultural comparability of measurement in survey research', *American Political Science Review*, 94, 191–207.

Klaaren, J. (2000), 'Post-apartheid citizenship in South Africa'. In T. A. Aleinikoff and D. Klusmeyer (eds.), *From Migrants to Citizens: Membership in a Changing World* (Washington, D.C.: Brookings Institution Press), pp. 221–52.

Kogan, I. (2005), 'Unemployment among recent immigrants in Europe: the role of host-countries' labor-market characteristics' (Unpublished paper, MZES, Mannheim).

Lewin-Epstein, N. and Levanon, A. (2005), 'National identity and xenophobia in an ethnically divided society', *International Journal on Multicultural Societies*, 7, 90–118.

Lubbers, M. (2001), *Exclusionistic Electorates: Extreme right-wing voting in Western Europe* (Ph.D. thesis, University of Nijmegen. Nijmegen: ICS Dissertation Series).

McLaren, L. M. (2003), 'Anti-immigrant prejudice in Europe: contact, threat perception, and preference for the exclusion of migrants', *Social Forces*, 81, 909–36.

McCrudden, C., Ford, R., and Heath, A. F. (2004), 'Legal Regulation of Affirmative Action in Northern Ireland: An Empirical Assessment', *Oxford Journal of Legal Studies*, 24, 363–415.

Nicoletti, G., Scarpetti, S., and Boyland, O. (2000), 'Summary indicators of Product Market Regulation with an extension to Employment Protection Legislation'. Economic Department Working Papers No. 226. (Paris: OECD).

OECD (2004), 'Economic Outlook'. Volume 2004/2, no 76, December (Paris: OECD).

Perlmann, J. and Waldinger, R. (1999), 'Immigrants, past and present: a reconsideration'. In C. Hirschman, P. Kasinitz and J. DeWing (eds.), *The Handbook of International Migration: The American experience* (New York: Russell Sage Foundation), pp. 223–38.

Quillian, L. (1995), 'Prejudice as a response to perceived group threat: population composition and anti-immigrant and racial prejudice in Europe', *American Sociological Review*, 60, 586–611.

Reitz, J. G. (1998), *Warmth of the Welcome: The Social Causes of Economic Success for Immigrants in Different Nations and Cities* (Boulder: Westview Press).

Rothon, C. and Heath, A. F. (2003), 'Trends in racial prejudice'. In A. Park *et al.* (eds.), *British Social Attitudes the 20th Report: Continuity and change over two decades* (London: Sage), pp. 189–214.

Shachar, A. (2000), 'Citizenship and membership in the Israeli polity'. In T. A. Aleinikoff and D. Klusmeyer (eds.), *From Migrants to Citizens: Membership in a Changing World* (Washington, D.C.: Brookings Institution Press), pp. 386–433.

Wilson, W. J. (1987), *The Truly Disadvantaged: The Inner City, the Underclass and Public Policy* (Chicago: Chicago University Press).

Yaish, M. (2002), 'The consequences of immigration for social mobility: the experience of Israel', *European Sociological Review*, 18, 449–72.

Zegers de Beijl, R. (ed.) (2000), *Documenting discrimination against migrant workers in the labour market: A comparative study of four European countries* (Geneva: ILO). <www.ilo.org/public/english/protection/migrant/publ/imp-list.htm>.

Author Index

Adlakha, A. 635
Adler, I. 346, 355
Aguilar, R. 452, 459
Aigner, D. J. 280
Alba, R. 12, 35, 144, 163, 175, 223, 235, 279, 595, 597, 598, 648, 649
Albrich, T. 104
Al-Haj, M. 322, 327
Allport, G. W. 10
Altman, J. 57
Amit, K. 325
Anderson, E. 597
Anderson, J. 554
Anderson, K. G. 419
Andersson, L. 452
Andersson, R. 483
Angelini, P. U. 182, 184
Arai, M. 452, 459, 494
Armstrong, D. 557
Arrow, K. J. 5, 279, 280
Åslund, O. 483, 495

Bach, R. L. 624
Bade, K. J. 273, 274
Barlow, J. 581
Baubock, R. 108
Baudelot, C. 238
Beaud, S. 238
Becker, G. S. 4, 279
Beishon, S. 521, 542
Belorgey, J. P. 229
Bender, S. 272
Bennich-Björkman, L. 464
Berthoud, R. 25, 521, 524, 542
Bevelander, P. 452, 494
Bew, P. 552, 560, 562
Billiet, J. 144
Black, D. A. 280
Blau, P. M. 16, 367
Blohm, M. 282
Blossfeld, H. P. 4
Bögenhold, D. 483
Bolotin, S. 325

Bonachich, E. 278
Booms, B. 147, 149
Borjas, G. J. 6, 11, 94, 95, 214, 274, 277, 280, 452, 494, 592, 595, 596, 634, 649, 679
Boulot, S. 223
Bourdieu, P. 10
Bousetta, H. 145, 153
Bovenkerk, F. 230
Boyd, M. 189
Boyland, O. 664
Braham, I. 346, 355
Brauns, H. 312
Breebaert, M. 147
Breen, R. 15, 16, 29, 279, 554, 556, 557, 581, 667, 668, 669, 670, 671
Bridges, W. P. 424
Brimelow, P. 596
Brinbaum, Y. 223
Broderick, M. 182, 184
Bronars, S. G. 280
Brooks, C. 55
Brown, C. 542
Brown, R. 10
Brubaker, W. R. 14, 152, 163, 176, 229
Bulder, B. 171
Burstein, P. 7
Butschek, F. 104

Caestecker, F. 145, 151
Caille, J.-P. 159, 223
Cain, G. G. 280
Card, D. 2, 595
Carliner, G. 452, 598
Carmichael, F. 25, 524, 542
Carton, A. 144
Case, A. 419
Castles, S. 3, 7, 508, 533, 682
Cediey, E. 230
Chambers, G. 552, 557, 561, 569
Chan, S. 594
Cheng, Y. 600, 624
Cheung, S. Y. 14, 413, 421, 563, 576, 584
Chiswick, B. R. 5, 278, 452, 508, 598

Christopher, A. J. 411
Cinar, D. 109, 110
Clark, K. 162, 523, 568
Clément, M. 232
Cohen, Y. 322, 358
Compton, P. 554
Constant, A. 272, 311
Cormack, R. 554, 557, 559, 560, 561
Costello, L. 59, 60, 61
Coulter, C. 556, 561
Crul, M. 144
Curle, E. 108
Curry, C. 557, 559, 561

D'Costa, R. 184
Dagevos, J. M. 396
Dale, A. 521
Daley, P. 518
Daniel, W. W. 508, 512, 542
Darity, W. A. 31
Darroch, G. A. 189
Davenport, T. R. H. 405, 407
Dayan, J. L. 223
de Beer, P. T. 365
de Kadt, R. 417
De Schutter, O. 230
Deboosere, P. 143
Deschouwer, K. 154
Dickens, P. 581
Diehl, C. 282
Diekmann, A. 271
DiNardo, J. 595
Doeringer, P. B. 8, 135
Dominitz, Y. 323, 326
Driedger, L. 184
Drinkwater, S. 162, 520, 523, 534, 568
Dryler, H. 502
Duncan, O. D. 10, 16, 367
Dunn, S. 552
Duru-Bellat, M. 237, 238
Dustmann, C. 7, 278, 311, 524

Ebbinghaus, B. 17
Échardour, A. 223
Edin, P.-A. 483, 495
Eggerickx, T. 147, 148, 154, 155, 168, 176
Ekberg, J. 452, 453, 458, 459, 461, 485, 494
Ell, R. 280
Elliott, J. L. 182
Elmelech, Y. 324
Emery, A. L. 408
Engelhardt, H. 271

England, P. 280
Erikson, R. 10, 15, 16, 25, 29, 279, 413, 421, 467, 470, 476, 500, 600, 668, 669
Esping-Andersen, G. 144, 146
Espiritu, Y. L. 597
Esser, H. 279
Establet, R. 238
Estes, E. 595
Evans, M. 55, 95

Fabbri, F. 524
Farley, R. 595
Fassmann, H. 105, 106, 107, 108, 109, 116, 135
Favell, A. 150
Featherman, D. L. 599
Fedderke, J. W. 417
Feliciano, C. 633
Fieldhouse, E. A. 542
Fielding, T. 581
Fisher, G. 2, 9
Fix, M. 635
Flap, H. 164, 171
Flatau, P. 55
Fleras, A. 182
Fodor, E. 404, 405, 408, 414, 432, 446
Ford, R. 556, 583, 660
Foroni, F. 230
Fournier, I. 223, 227, 228, 242, 252
Fradet, D. 223
Fredriksson, P. 483
Friedberg, R. M. 6, 278, 524

Gallagher, A. M. 554
Gans, H. 12, 368
Ganzeboom, H. 15, 421, 668, 669
Garcea, J. 184
Garner-Moyer, H. 230
Garson, J. P. 225
Gay, P. 542
Geschwender, J. A. 189
Geva-May, I. 326
Ghanem, A. 327
Gibson, M. 12
Girard, A. 223
Glaude, M. 223
Glazer, N. 39
Goldthorpe, J. H. 4, 15, 16, 29, 189, 279, 413, 421, 467, 573, 581, 600, 668, 669, 670
Gordon, M. 17, 649
Gould, M. I. 542

Goux, D. 242
Granato, N. 7, 14, 144, 147, 272, 279, 311
Granovetter, M. S. 6, 557
Grosfoguel, R. 593
Grusky, D. 15
Gsir, S. 150
Gudgin, G. 557
Guimezanes, N. 681, 682
Guppy, N. 189
Gustafsson, B. 452, 459

Haberfeld, Y. 322
Hall, P. A. 17
Hammarstedt, M. 483
Handl, J. 279
Hansen, R. 153, 163, 176, 512, 513
Hartmann, P. 271
Hauser, R. M. 15, 599
Heath, A. F. 7, 10, 14, 25, 164, 174, 413, 421, 508, 514, 524, 542, 556, 563, 573, 576, 576, 583, 584, 660, 687
Heckmann, F. 278
Heer, D. M. 592, 593
Hemmings, P. 55
Henry, M. 230
Héran, F. 231, 232
Herberg, E. N. 182, 185
Herzog-Punzenberger, B. 103, 108, 135
Hirschman, C. 2, 598, 599
Hjerm, M. 15, 672
Hodge, R. W. 322
Hoffmann-Nowotny, H.-J. 278
Holdsworth, C. 521
Holton, R. 52, 54
Horowitz, T. 326
Houghton, D. H. 405
Hout, M. 10, 26
Huys, R. 144

Inglis, C. 12, 50, 52, 60, 91, 93, 94
Irwin, G. 552
Isajiw, W. W. 181, 182, 184
Ivarsflaten, E. 690, 691

Jacobs, D. 150, 151, 153
Jacubowicz, A. 53
Janssens, R. 154
Jencks, C. 368
Jones, F. L. 2, 15, 54, 55, 59, 60, 95, 672, 689
Jonsson, J. O. 10, 25, 279, 461, 470, 476, 500, 502
Jupp, J. 46

Kalbach, M. A. 182, 184, 185
Kalbach, W. E. 182, 184, 185
Kalter, F. 7, 14, 144, 147, 272, 279, 311
Karle, W. 279
Karn, V. 522
Kasinitz, P. 161
Kelley, J. 55, 95
Kelley, N. 183, 184
Kemp, A. 326
Kennedy, R. 635
Kesler, C. 2
Kesteloot, C. 147
Khalidi, R. 327
Khazzoom, A. 323, 325
Khoo, S.-E. 55, 56, 57, 59
Kieffer, A. 223, 237, 238
King, G. 672
Kitschelt, H. 13
Klaaren, J. 682
Klinthäll, M. 495, 501
Knowles, V. 181, 182, 184
Kofler, A. 108
Kogan, I. 2, 17, 18, 356, 663
Kohlbacher, J. 135
Konietzka, D. 272, 278, 310
König, K. 108, 111, 279
Kosack, G. 508, 533
Kraly, E. P. 598, 599
Kraus, V. 322, 670
Kreyenfeld, M. 278, 310
Kristen, C. 11, 279, 311
Kumcu, A. 171
Kunz, C. 59, 60, 61
Kurian, G. 183

Lakey, J. 521, 542
LaLonde, R. 495
Lam, D. 419
Landale, N. S. 595
Lapeyronnie, D. 222
Laumann, E. O. 598
Layton-Henry, Z. 513, 514
Le Bras, H. 231
le Grand, C. 453, 460, 461, 494
Lebhart, G. 110
Lee, E. S. 614
Lerenthal, T. 323, 325
Leshem, E. 326
Leslie. D. 520, 534
Lesthaeghe, R. 143, 145, 146, 154, 155, 164, 168, 176
Levanon, A. 672

Levene, G. 598
Lever, H. 409
Lewin-Epstein, N. 322, 323, 324, 327, 346, 347, 355, 356, 672
Li, Y. 22, 554, 576, 581
Lieberson, S. 2, 18
Light, I. 162
Lim, N. 14, 599
Lin, N. 6, 163
Lindbeck, A. 461
Lippi-Green, R. 8, 594
Lischke, U. 109
Llanes, D. 595
Lubbers, M. 144, 673
Lucas, D. 59
Luijkx, R. 15, 668, 669, 670, 671
Luiz, J. M. 417
Lundh, C. 464
Lustick, I. 327
Lüttinger, P. 279, 282
Lutz, A. 598

Ma Mung, E. 226
Maas, I. 164
MacEwen, M. 15
Madden, J. F. 279
Manow P. 17
Marginson, S. 62
Marry, C. 238
Marsden, D. 279
Martens, A. 145, 146, 151
Martin, J. 52, 79
Mason, P. L. 31
Massey, D. S. 147, 272, 311
Maurin, E. 242
Mayer, N. 223
McCrudden, C. 556, 583, 660
McDonald, P. 55, 56, 57
McKeever, M. 404, 405, 408, 414, 432, 446
McLaren, L. M. 677
McLaughlin, E. 561
McLaughlin, J. L. 405
McMahon, D. 10, 25, 164, 524, 542, 576
McNabb, R. 508
Meade, P. 79
Melich, A. 110
Merens, J. G. F. 396
Meurs, D. 223
Miller, M. J. 3, 7, 682
Miller, R. 557, 559, 560, 561
Mincer, J. 4
Mingat, A. 223

Model, S. 2, 9, 12, 93, 163, 534, 599
Modood, T. 521, 542
Mollenkopf, J. H. 161
Moore, R. L. 483
Moore, R. S. 7
Moors, G. 149
Moulier-Boutang, Y. 225
Müller, W. 4, 27, 54, 279, 280, 417, 467, 600
Münz, R. 104, 105, 106, 107, 108, 110, 273, 276, 282
Murphy, A. 557
Murphy, R. 367
Murray, C. J. 672
Murray, R. 560
Musterd, S. 147

Nahon, Y. 324, 325
Nakhaie, M. R. 189
Nazroo, J. 521, 542
Nee, V. 144, 163, 171, 175, 595, 597, 599
Neels, K. 149
Nekby, L. 495
Nelson, R. L. 424
Nicoletti, G. 664
Nielsen, H. S. 452, 494
Noiriel, G. 222, 229
Norris, D. 189

O'Leary, R. 22, 534, 559
Ogbu, J. U. 11, 597
Ohlsson, R. 452, 464
Oosthuizen, G. C. 410
Oropesa, R. S. 595
Osborne, R. 554, 557, 559, 560, 561, 571
Ouali, N. 149

Pachai, B. 410
Pailhé, A. 223
Parkin, F. 367
Parnreiter, C. 107
Passel, J. 635
Patterson, H. 552, 560, 562
Patterson, S. 410
Pedersen, P. J. 464
Perlmann, J. 2, 597, 649
Petersen, T. 281
Phalet, K. 144, 150, 152, 154, 176
Phelps, E. S. 280
Piore, M. J. 8, 135, 161, 173
Platzky, L. 407
Pollak, R. 279
Poole, M. E. 53

Porter, J. 1, 189
Portes, A. 9, 11, 167, 174, 281, 557, 595, 597, 624, 686
Poulain, M. 147
Power, J. 554
Prandy, K. 508
Price, C. 47
Psacharopoulos, G. 508

Quillian, L. 677

Raftery, A. E. 337
Raijman, R. 326
Rawls, J. 3
Rea, A. 149
Reeger, U. 135
Regnér, H. 494
Reitz, J. G. 2, 4, 94, 95, 164, 183, 214, 681
Renan, E. 222
Resnik, J. 326
Rex, J. 7
Rhodes, C. 598
Richard, J.-L. 223
Richardson, P. 410
Richmond, K. 70
Richmond, A. H. 183, 189
Ridge, J. M. 7, 508
Riede, T. 282
Roberts, J. 164
Roberts, L. W. 184
Robertson, B. L. 417
Robertson, N. L. 417
Robinson, J. G. 635
Rogl, H. 109
Roos, P. A. 424
Rooth, D.-O. 452, 453, 461, 464, 485, 494
Rosenfeld, H. 327
Rothon, C. 508, 687
Rouhana, N. 327
Rozenhek, Z. 326
Rumbaut, R. G. 281, 595
Russell, R. 555, 556

Sa'di, A. 322, 327
Salomon, J. A. 672
Sanders, J. M. 171, 599
Santelli, E. 223
Saporta, I. 281
Satzewich, V. 182
Savage, M. 581
Scarpetti, S. 664
Schammah-Gesser, S. 326

Schnapper, D. 222, 229, 230
Schor, R. 222, 231
Schröder, L. 494
Segev, T. 324
Seibert, H. 272
Seifert, W. 272
Semyonov, M. 322, 323, 325, 327, 346, 347, 355, 356, 405
Shachar, A. 682
Shavit, Y. 4, 27, 54, 325, 326, 355, 417, 467, 600
Sheehan, M. 556
Shohat, E. 324
Shuttleworth, I. 554, 560
Shuval, T. T. 326
Silberman, R. 223, 225, 227, 228, 231, 232, 235, 242, 252
Similä, M. 464, 470, 476
Simmons, A. B. 182
Simon, P. 223, 231, 232
Smith, A. 552
Smith, D. 557, 561, 569
Smith, J. P. 594
Smith, P. 15, 521, 542, 672, 689
Smooha, S. 327
Snower, D. 461
Soskice, D. 17
Spencer, I. R. G. 513
Spring, J. 593
Staber, U. 483
Stadler, B. 108, 111
Steinmann, S. 280, 312
Stewart, M. 508
Stier, H. 325
Stoetzel, J. 223
Stoop, R. 147, 149, 155
Stubos, G. 184
Studlar, D. T. 512
Sturman, A. 53
Surkyn, J. 155
Swyngedouw, M. 144, 150, 152, 154, 176
Szulkin, R. 453, 460, 461, 494, 502
Szydlik, M. 272

Tandon, A. 672
Tapinos, G. 222, 224, 225
Tastsoglou, E. 184
Taylor, K. W. 184
Tazi-Preve, I. M. 109, 110
Teague, P. 552, 560, 562
Terrell, K. 434
Tesser, P. 20, 396

Thomas, W. 410
Thompson, L. 404, 405, 406, 409
Tomlinson, M. 556
Trebilcock, M. 182, 183, 184
Treiman, D. 15, 16, 18, 21, 404, 405, 408, 414, 421, 424, 432, 434, 446, 668, 669
Tribalat, M. 222, 226, 231, 232

Vallet, L.-A. 159, 223
Van Praag, C. S. 396
Van Soest, A. 311
Van Tubergen, F. 2, 164, 168, 174
Van Zanten, A. 223
Velling, J. 271, 273, 276
Vermeulen, H. 144
Vessilinov, E. 598
Vilhelmsson, R. 452, 453, 459, 461, 462
Virdee, S. 521, 542

Wadensjö, E. 452, 458, 459, 460
Waldrauch, H. 109, 110
Walker, C. 407
Wanner, R. 356
Waters, M. 161, 633

Weber, M. 34
Welch, F. R. 594
Weil, P. 152, 153, 163, 176, 225, 229
Whelan, C. 556
Wieviorka, M. 222
Williamson, A. 559, 560
Wilson, W. J. 11, 367, 368, 599, 679, 687
Wooden, M. 52, 54
Woods, R. 25, 524, 542
Wrench, J. 542
Wright, E. O. 367
Wu, C.-T. 94
Waldinger, R. 2, 7, 14, 168, 169, 174, 597, 633, 649

Xie, Y. 633

Yaish, M. 670
Yiftachel, O. 327
Yu, S. 189, 508, 514

Zegers de Beijl, R. 676
Zeng, Z. 633
Zeroulou, Z. 223
Zhou, M. 9, 11, 557, 597, 686

Subject Index

Abitur 27
Aboriginals 12, 20, 45, 47, 54, 58, 60, 61, 62, 63, 64, 65, 67, 68, 70, 71, 74, 78, 79, 82, 84, 90, 91, 92, 181, 189, 193, 194, 197, 208, 213, 217, 646, 660
Achievement 16, 367
Acculturation 9, 214, 215, 377
Adversarial subculture 597
Affirmative action 15, 16, 18, 230, 552, 562, 584, 594, 660, 676, 689
Afghanistan 106
Africa 19, 592
African Americans 2, 11, 12, 40, 593, 594, 598, 639, 648, 679, 686, 687
Africanisation 510, 513
Africans 24, 112, 114, 194, 197, 202, 203, 208, 215, 283, 284, 286, 289, 290, 292, 296, 304, 308, 310, 458, 511, 516, 518, 523, 525, 527, 530, 534, 538, 657
  See also North Africans; Sub-Saharan Africans; South Africans
Afrikaans language 416, 649
Afrikaans-speakers 23, 410
Afrikaners 405, 406, 407, 409, 410, 411, 416, 418, 422, 423, 424, 432, 434, 435, 446, 649, 650
Age
  differences 27, 75
  measurement of 98, 137, 543
Age at arrival 37, 38, 39, 187, 233
Aleutian Eskimos 600
Algeria 225, 228, 234, 324, 329
Algerians 226, 229, 259
Aliens Act of 1989 455
American Indians 12, 20, 23, 593, 594, 600, 605, 607, 612, 619, 632, 634, 641
Americans
  Central and South 185
  Latin (South) 330, 338, 345, 354, 453, 455, 458, 465, 470, 472, 473, 484, 488, 491, 494
  North 329, 330, 332, 339, 340, 341, 349
Amerindians 189

Amsterdam 399
Ancestry
  importance of in Israel 322
  measurement: in Australian Census 36, 96; in Austrian microcensus 36, 111–12; in Belgian census 36, 155–7; in British GHS 515; in Canadian Census 36, 187–8; in Dutch SPVA surveys 36, 370–1, 399; in French FPQ 36, 234–5; in German microcensus 36, 282–4; in Israeli labour force surveys 36, 328–9; in South African census 404; in Swedish census 463; in US CPS 599–600
  mixed 46, 60, 93, 329, 511
  multiple 35, 59, 187, 188, 189, 197
  self-report measures of 35, 36, 39, 58, 60, 653
  single 59
Anglo-Celts (in Australia) 45, 52, 53, 55, 59, 65, 71, 75, 78, 80, 85, 90, 655
Anglo-Irish Agreement 555
Anti-discrimination legislation 13, 16, 23, 151, 184, 364, 460, 514
Anti-immigrant vote 144, 150, 512
Anti-immigration legislation 231
Anti-Semitism 323
Antilles 362
Antilleans 23, 363, 370, 371, 376, 377, 380, 381, 382, 384, 385, 390, 391, 392, 395, 396, 398, 399, 400, 658
Apartheid 8, 12, 21, 22, 404, 407–8, 425, 444
Arabs 226
  See also Palestinians
Argentina 106
Arrival
  time of 56, 122, 214, 215, 486
  support 465
  years since 486–96, 614, 619
Aruba 593
Ascription 1, 16, 367
Ashkenazim 324, 325, 328, 331, 332, 338, 346, 353, 355

Asia, South 19, 329, 642
Asians (in South Africa) 20, 23, 404, 408, 409, 410, 411, 414, 416, 417, 418, 419, 420, 423, 424, 425, 429, 432, 434, 435, 436, 441, 444, 446, 646
  East 112, 117, 252, 253, 598, 600, 601, 602, 607, 613, 614, 616, 618, 619, 623, 624, 625, 632, 633
  Middle Eastern 23, 112, 114, 116, 117, 118, 123, 126, 127, 128, 129, 130, 133, 283, 284, 287, 289, 290, 304, 308, 310, 328, 329, 331, 338, 346, 355, 356, 451, 456, 458, 465, 488, 491, 494, 499
  Near Eastern 235, 239, 241, 243, 245, 246, 248, 251, 252, 256
  South Eastern 235, 242, 243, 245, 246, 247, 248, 249, 257, 490
  South 331, 346, 349, 355, 510
Aspirations 223, 328
Assimilation
  economic 277, 499
  identificational 649
  segmented 11, 259, 597, 606, 633
  social 2, 51, 52, 91, 150, 208, 222, 223, 230, 259, 593, 598, 633
  structural 310
Assistance for immigrants 51
Assyrians 463
Asylum 592
Asylum Act of 1954 454
Asylum compromise 277
Asylum seekers 105–107, 225, 276, 363, 366
  See also refugees
Aussiedler 276, 278, 310
Australia 2, 3, 12, 13, 18, 20, 21, 22, 23, 30, 33, 35, 36, 39, 45–99, 181, 228, 465, 509, 592, 640, 641, 643, 644, 646, 647, 648, 649, 651, 653, 654, 655, 657, 658, 659, 660, 666, 668, 669, 670, 672, 674, 675, 677, 681, 682, 683, 684, 685, 687, 688
Australians 59, 73, 45–99, 655
Austria 13, 18, 19, 20, 22, 23, 24, 33, 35, 36, 38, 103–41, 465, 641, 643, 644, 646, 653, 654, 658, 661, 665, 666, 669, 674, 675, 676, 677, 681, 682, 683, 684, 685, 686, 688
Austrians 103–41, 273, 283

Baccalaureat 27, 237, 238
Bangladesh 488, 508, 510
Bangladeshis 516, 519, 521, 522, 523, 525, 530, 533, 534, 535, 538, 541

Bantustans, *see* TVBC states
Barbados 516
Beamte jobs 135
Belgians 143–80, 283
Belgium 13, 18, 19, 20, 23, 33, 36, 110, 143–80, 224, 465, 517, 640, 641, 643, 644, 653, 654, 658, 661, 666, 668, 669, 670, 674, 675, 676, 677, 681, 682, 683, 684, 685, 686, 687, 688
Belize 516
Berbers 226
Berlin Wall 274
BIC statistic 337, 344
Bilateral agreements, *see* guestworker agreements
Bilingualism 184
Blacks
  in France 227
  in South Africa 12, 20, 23, 404, 405, 406, 407, 408, 409, 410, 411, 414, 417, 418, 420, 421, 422, 423, 424, 425, 428, 429, 432, 434, 435, 436, 441, 444, 446, 641, 646, 659
  in USA 23, 368, 405, 598, 600, 602, 604, 605, 606, 607, 608, 609, 610, 612, 616, 618, 622, 623, 626, 627, 633, 634, 657, 679
  See also African Americans; Caribbeans; West Indians
Bophutatswana 407
Bosnia-Herzegovina 106, 112, 114
Bosnians 61, 456
Botswana 516
Boundaries 11
  bright or blurred 35, 39, 175, 353
Britain 13, 15, 17, 18, 19, 20, 24, 30, 47, 184, 465, 507–50, 641, 643, 644, 648, 651, 654, 657, 658, 661, 666, 667, 669, 670, 671, 672, 674, 676, 677, 683, 685, 687, 688
  See also UK
British 23, 182, 190, 193, 197, 202, 215, 283, 518–43, 640, 650, 655
British Commonwealth 508, 509, 510, 511
British Empire 509, 511, 660
British Nationality Act 1948 512
British Nationality Act 1981 513
Brussels 147, 148, 154, 156, 164, 169
Bulgaria 689
Burakamin 19
Burundi 148

Subject Index

Cambodians 226, 235
Cameroon 226, 235
Canada 2, 3, 12, 20, 21, 22, 23, 33, 35, 36, 39, 46, 94, 181–220, 228, 465, 592, 593, 640, 641, 643, 644, 646, 647, 648, 649, 650, 651, 653, 654, 655, 657, 658, 659, 660, 664, 666, 668, 669, 670, 674, 677, 681, 682, 683, 684, 685, 687, 688
Canadian point system 49, 184, 190, 217, 681, 688
Canadian and Canadien 189
Canadians 181–220, 193, 197, 600, 603, 607, 650, 655
Cape Town 411
Caribbean 19, 21, 193, 600
Caribbeans 23, 190, 193, 194, 197, 200, 202, 203, 208, 215, 217, 508, 509, 510, 511, 516, 517, 519, 521, 522, 523, 525, 527, 534, 538, 541, 542, 641, 647, 655, 657, 658
CASMIN schema (of education) 27, 164, 189, 312, 339, 467, 502
Catholics (in Ireland) 12, 20, 22, 516, 552–86, 660
Causation 18, 32, 662, 672, 678
Census
  Australian 33, 51, 55, 57, 91, 96, 97
  Belgian 33, 144, 147, 154, 155
  British 515
  Canadian 33, 186
  German 273
  Northern Ireland 554, 555, 558, 559
  South African 33, 404, 408, 409
  Swedish 34, 453, 462
Central America 594
Centre for Equal Opportunities and against Racism (CGKR) 151
Ceskei 407
Ceylon 48
Charter population
  definition of 1, 36, 37
  size of 20
Children, adopted 455
Chile 106, 465, 488
Chileans 490, 491, 494, 495, 501
Chill factor 557
China 21, 47, 48, 50, 56, 488, 600
Chinese 23, 45, 47, 50, 53, 55, 63, 65, 67, 69, 70, 71, 73, 75, 76, 78, 79, 81, 82, 90, 91, 93, 182, 183, 190, 193, 194, 197, 200, 202, 203, 208, 226, 252, 410, 490, 494, 593, 598, 641, 654, 658, 686

Chinese Exclusion Act 1923 184
Christians 327, 329, 410, 516
Church of Ireland (Anglican) 554
Citizenship
  dual 109
  for Australian indigenes in 1967 51, 92
  in Austria 109, 110, 135, 136
  in Belgium 148, 152
  in Britain 512, 513
  in Canada 680
  in France 229, 235
  in Germany 276, 282
  in Israel 326, 685
  in Netherlands 363–4
  in South Africa 682
  in Sweden 455, 686
  in USA 593
  'local' 231
  policy 681–3, 685
  role of 12, 14, 18, 135, 153, 176, 222, 225, 258, 653, 679, 681, 685, 689
  see also inclusivity
Civil Rights movement 594
Class, see occupational class
coal mining 145
Colonial system 646–7
Colonies
  Australian 46, 47
  British 510
  Dutch 360, 362
  former 19, 148
  French 224, 226, 228
  modern 593, 634
  overseas 22
Colonisation 509
Coloureds (in South Africa) 20, 404, 405, 406, 407, 408, 409, 410, 411, 414, 415, 418, 420, 421, 422, 423, 424, 425, 429, 432, 434, 435, 436, 441, 444, 446, 646
Commission for Racial Equality 514
Communism, fall of 50
Competition 17, 663
Conceptions of the nation
  ethnic 14, 15, 17, 23, 672, 689
  civic 14, 15, 17, 18, 23, 672, 689
Confidential unit record files (CURFs) 57, 58, 96
Conflict
  Arab-Israeli 327
  Northern Irish 553, 555, 660
  Racial 223, 512
Conflict theory 367

Congo 148
Conseil Représentatif des Associations Noires (CRAN) 227
Contact hypothesis 10
Contextual effects 687
Countries of immigration
　classic 2, 3, 4, 23, 181, 592
　new 4
　settler 3, 20, 21, 91
Country of birth 35, 36, 37
Croatians 61, 103, 106, 112
Cubans 600, 607, 608, 610, 612, 616, 618, 619, 622, 623, 624, 626, 627, 632, 634
Culture 10, 245, 398
Cultural capital 542
Cultural distance 499, 500, 596, 599
Cultural preferences 82
Cultural knowledge 281
Cultural values 150
Czech Republic 105, 106
Czechoslovakia 454
Czechs 103, 106, 112

Danes 283
De Champlain, Samuel 182
Decolonisation 235
Democratisation of schooling in France 237
Demographic explanations 558–9
Denmark 456, 460, 517
De-regulation 17, 18, 96
Destinations (in OED diagram) 25
Developed countries 18, 20
Diaspora
　Chinese 60, 511
　Indian 510
　Jewish 325
Differential returns, *see* human capital; education
Disadvantage
　gross 24, 26, 157, 200, 640
　net 24, 25, 157, 200, 640
Discouraged workers 27, 193, 419, 516, 541, 566
Discrimination
　direct 7, 8, 14
　error 280
　ethnic or racial 5, 10, 11, 13, 17, 31, 55, 86, 90, 91, 135, 150, 161, 228, 229, 230, 252, 279, 310, 453, 460, 462, 496, 500, 508, 512, 514, 516, 521, 542, 599, 676, 678, 686
　exclusionary 55, 95
　gender 619
　indirect 7, 514
　institutional 78
　positive 230
　religious 557
　self-reported 135
　statistical 5, 18, 280, 370, 453, 663
　tastes for 17, 279, 280, 662, 663
Dominicans 600, 602, 604, 605, 606, 607, 608, 610, 612, 616, 618, 623, 626, 627, 635, 648, 655
Doukhobors 184
Druse 327, 329
Dual labour market theory 8
Dutch 23, 61, 71, 73, 75, 84, 148, 283, 361–99, 405, 640

Early retirement 157
Earnings
　differentials 30, 535, 538, 544, 576, 581, 627
　measurement: in British GHS 544; in Northern Ireland CHS 585; in USA CPS 600
　See also income
Economic activity
　measurement of 98, 137, 193, 243, 313, 335, 371, 418, 468, 544
　rates of 26, 67–71, 116–18, 158–9, 193–4, 243–5, 286–9, 332–3, 337–43, 374–5, 378–82, 418–20, 458, 459, 519–60, 565–6, 602–6
Economic conditions 17
Economic restructuring 226
Education
　attainment 61–7, 94, 114–16, 157–9, 190–3, 237–42, 284–6, 372–3, 417–18, 469–70, 518–19, 559–61, 563–4, 601–2
　differential returns to 29, 85, 122–3, 129–33, 134, 167, 172, 174, 186, 208–13, 215, 253, 257, 279, 295, 296, 299, 304, 309, 391, 485, 527, 534, 541, 613, 619, 625, 633, 645–6
　in interaction term 29, 30
　in multivariate analysis 27, 75
　in OED diagram 25, 643
　measurement of 27, 34, 98, 137, 190, 250, 312–13, 328, 371, 400, 447, 467, 502–3, 544, 636
　parental 467, 497

relationship with occupational attainment 643–4
selective systems of 644
vocational 470, 643
see also qualifications
Egypt 329
El Salvador 593, 595
Employment
full-time versus part-time 437, 440
protection legislation (EPL) 663–7
status 437
See also non-employment
Enfranchisement 153
English 19, 59, 406, 411
English language fluency 50, 52, 56, 79, 87, 91, 93, 510, 521, 541, 542
See also language fluency
English-speakers
in South Africa 23, 410
in Australia 56, 59
see also Whites, English-speaking
English speaking backgrounds (ESB) 53
Entry rights 228
Equality Commission for Northern Ireland 562
Equality, principle of 225, 230
Equality of opportunity 1, 2, 3, 24, 25, 40, 148, 259, 398, 514, 639, 647, 651, 688
Eritrea 455
Eritreans 488, 490
Ethiopia 488
Ethnic community 173, 226
Ethnic enclave 7, 171, 483, 495, 597
Ethnic penalties 24, 25, 26, 27, 28, 31, 45, 75, 93, 120–9, 135, 136, 164, 200–8, 222, 250–5, 259, 281, 311, 352, 446, 453, 475, 480, 524, 640, 641, 645, 647–61, 686, 688
Ethnic premiums 25, 200, 214, 252, 257, 651
Ethnicity
definition of 34, 552
measurement of 28, 34, 187, 231, 232, 409, 463
symbolic 12, 648
see also ancestry; nationality
Ethno-religious penalty 558, 569
Exclusionary attitudes 13
European Union (EU) 362, 517
EU nationals 110, 227, 228
EU convention on protecting national minorities 463
Eurobarometer 13, 110, 675, 691

Europe
Western 3, 19, 592
Eastern 19, 49, 63
Northern 49
European integration 19
European Social Survey (ESS) 674, 690–1
European Union Labour Force Survey (EULFS) 137
Europeans
Central and Eastern 56, 67, 71, 76, 78, 80, 90, 104, 112
Eastern 23, 106, 112, 114, 116, 118, 120, 126, 127, 128, 129, 130, 235, 240, 241, 243, 245, 246, 249, 252, 253, 255, 259, 283, 285, 289, 296, 299, 304, 308, 309, 310, 330, 338, 345, 354, 458, 469, 470, 473, 480, 483, 484, 486, 496, 497, 640, 641
Jewish 323, 658
Southern 23, 54, 56, 223, 235, 236, 239, 240, 241, 243, 245, 246, 248, 249, 252, 253, 255, 256, 257, 258, 259, 453, 458, 462, 465, 469, 480, 486, 490, 496, 497, 640
South-Eastern 23, 61, 63, 65, 67, 71, 72, 75, 76, 78, 79, 80, 84, 90
Western 23, 56, 112, 114, 236, 283, 284, 285, 286, 287, 289, 292, 295, 296, 299, 304, 308, 309, 345, 354, 465, 469, 470, 473, 484, 488, 490, 491, 497, 500, 509, 517, 525, 527, 530, 534, 541, 542, 640
Experiments
field 31, 32, 230, 512, 542, 676
natural 662
Extreme Right, *see* Far Right

Fair Employment Act 1976 561
Fair Employment Act 1989 555, 562
Fair Employment Commission 562
Fair Employment legislation 552, 561–2, 583
Family dependants 228–9
Family reunion 49, 50, 108, 146, 156, 224, 276, 361, 363, 366, 455, 592, 688
Family workers 440
Far East 21
Far Right political parties 13, 110, 150, 154, 225, 231, 366, 512, 672, 675, 676
Fertility 425, 557
Fiji 510
Filipinos 23, 193, 194, 197, 200, 202, 203, 208, 215, 595, 598, 600, 602, 606, 607, 608, 609, 612, 616, 618, 632, 657

Finland 454, 460
Finns 23, 184, 283, 456, 460, 463, 467, 469, 470, 472, 476, 478, 484, 490, 491, 497, 499, 501
First generation 2, 28, 29, 36
  disadvantages in the labour market 5
  size of 20
Flanders 13, 147, 148, 150, 151, 154, 156, 164, 165, 674
Flemish 19
Fluidity, social 15, 16, 17, 18, 23, 667–9
Fortuyn, Pym 366, 675
Frames of reference 543
France 13, 15, 17, 18, 19, 20, 23, 33, 35, 36, 38, 110, 221–69, 465, 516, 640, 641, 643, 644, 653, 654, 657, 658, 661, 666, 668, 669, 670, 674, 675, 677, 678, 681, 682, 683, 685, 688, 689
Freedom Party (in Austria) 110, 111
French 23, 148, 182, 190, 197, 202, 215, 221–65, 283, 650
French Antilles 227
French Canadian 189
French Huguenots 405
Front National (in France) 675
FRG 274

Gambia 516
GDR 20, 273
Gender differences 30, 45, 53, 62, 65–6, 69, 73–4, 84, 90, 92, 93, 117, 158, 186, 193, 240, 243, 286, 333, 374, 378, 417, 424, 469, 476, 632, 633, 642
Gender inequality 635
Gender roles 159
Generations
  definition 37, 38, 39
  differences 4–12, 39, 55, 118, 120, 126, 127, 129–30, 134, 144, 157, 167, 174, 185, 190, 197, 202, 203, 208, 213–14, 223, 243, 252, 258, 285, 290, 296, 307, 308, 310, 345, 356, 369, 375, 385, 476, 516, 525–6, 534, 598, 614, 616, 627, 633, 639, 640, 642, 651, 655, 687, 688
  measurement 36, 98, 111, 156, 187, 233–4, 284, 329, 400, 464, 516, 594, 599
  parental and filial 29, 223, 233, 239, 248, 642
  see also first generation; second generation; third generation
Geneva Convention 106, 455
Geographical residence 87, 569

German language fluency 135, 311
German Socio-Economic Panel (GSOEP) 310, 311
Germans 23, 61, 70, 71, 73, 76, 79, 105, 106, 184, 202, 215, 271–319, 405, 409, 411, 454, 470, 473, 484, 490, 491, 497, 600, 602, 603, 607, 640, 649, 650, 654
Germany 14, 15, 16, 18, 19, 20, 22, 23, 33, 35, 36, 38, 48, 49, 104, 110, 229, 271–319, 416, 516, 640, 641, 643, 644, 646, 653, 654, 658, 661, 666, 668, 669, 670, 672, 674, 675, 676, 677, 681, 682, 683, 684, 685, 686, 687, 688, 689
  West 20, 23, 312
Ghana 516
Global cities 89
Globalisation 50
Good Friday Agreement 552, 562, 583, 584
Greece 48, 49, 52, 63, 274, 416, 516
Greeks 23, 53, 61, 65, 69, 73, 75, 79, 82, 184, 235, 283, 284, 287, 289, 292, 296, 304, 307, 308, 311, 361, 469, 470, 472, 474, 478, 480, 483, 484, 485, 490, 491, 495, 496, 499, 501, 640, 653
Griquas 410
Guadeloupe 227
Guestworker agreements 145–6, 274, 454, 681, 684, 686, 687, 688
Guest workers 107, 108, 114, 134, 135, 145, 173, 274, 641
Guatemala 593
Guyana 510, 516
Gypsies, *see* Roma

Hague, The 399
Haiti 600
Halakha (Jewish religious law) 326
Harkis 225, 235
Hart-Celler Act 1965 592
Hawaiians 612, 613, 616, 619
Hindus 23, 410, 420, 521
Hindustanis 658
Hispanics 594
Holocaust survivors 323
Hong Kong 185, 511, 600
Human capital
  differential returns to 24, 26, 29, 84, 277
  externalities 11, 13, 164, 679
  portability of 453, 485–6
  role of 4, 5, 6, 8, 277–81, 310, 367, 400, 679
  see also education

Humanitarian entry 49
Hungarians 60, 103, 106, 112, 183, 184
Hungary 105, 106, 454
Hut tax 406
Hutterites 184

Iberians 283, 284, 286, 289, 290, 292, 295, 308
Iceland 460, 465
Immigrant assistance programmes 48
Immigrant status, *see* generations
Immigrants, *see* migrants
Immigration 18
  attitudes towards 672–4, 676, 677, 690
  to Australia 46–51
  to Austria 103–8
  to Belgium 145–8
  to Britain 509–12
  to Canada 181–5
  to France 224–8
  to Germany 273–77
  to Israel 322–5
  to the Netherlands 360–4
  to South Africa 415–17
  to Sweden 454–8
  to USA 592–4
  family 454
  post-colonial 148
  restrictions 47, 184, 224, 362
  selective 407
Immigration policy
  active 182
  effects of 678–86
  liberal 225
  'open door' 325
  'populationist' 224
  'preference system' 592
  selectivity 683–4
  varieties of 679
  reform 592
  restrictive 111, 513
  selective 94
Inclusivity 685–6
Income
  inequality of 596
  levels 86–91, 391–5, 411, 423–5, 437–44
  measurement in Australian census 99
  measurement in Dutch SPVA surveys 372, 392
  measurement in South African census 447–8
  see also earnings

Index of Human Development 18
India 38, 48, 106, 112, 329, 405, 416, 488
Indians 193, 194, 200, 202, 203, 208, 215, 406, 490, 508, 510, 511, 515, 516, 518, 519, 521, 523, 525, 527, 530, 534, 535, 538, 541, 543, 546, 595, 641, 654, 657, 686
Indigenes 45, 57
Indo-Chinese 50
Indonesia 360, 405
Industrial sector 555, 556
Inequality of condition 16
Inheritance laws 224
Integration 93, 364–70
  definition of 150
  measures 106, 108, 109, 150, 151, 326, 460
  policy 460
Interaction effects 29, 85, 202, 295, 307, 338, 339, 343, 347, 352, 356, 374, 378, 380, 381, 385, 392, 426, 427, 430, 441, 485, 491, 534, 560, 572, 576, 612, 613, 614, 618, 619, 625, 626, 645
  see also education, differential returns;
Intermarriage
  conception of 554
  prohibition of 406
  patterns 9, 39, 40, 46, 93, 168, 227, 361, 410, 501, 596
International Social Survey Programme (ISSP) 672–4, 689–90
Iran 106, 112, 323, 324, 329, 453, 456
Iranians 453, 456, 463, 469, 470, 472, 484, 488, 490, 491, 494
Iraq 106, 112, 277, 323, 324, 329, 453, 456, 488
Irish 23, 59, 182, 202, 215, 283, 507, 508, 509, 515, 516, 519, 521, 523, 525, 533, 542, 600, 602, 603, 606, 607, 612, 616, 619, 640, 649, 651
Ireland 47, 465, 509, 511
Islam 153, 231
Islamic schools 364, 366
Israel 12, 15, 18, 20, 21, 22, 23, 33, 37, 321–58, 640, 641, 644, 645, 646, 647, 651, 657, 658, 659, 669, 670, 672, 675, 677, 678, 681, 682, 683, 685, 689, 690
Italians 22, 23, 61, 65, 67, 69, 71, 73, 74, 75, 77, 82, 84, 90, 112, 147, 148, 152, 156, 158–76, 183, 184, 190, 193, 202, 227, 235, 236, 283, 284, 286, 289, 295, 304, 307, 308, 309, 361, 598, 640, 649, 650, 651, 653, 686

Italy 48, 52, 145, 224, 274, 416, 465, 516
Ius sanguinis 14, 152, 282, 682
Ius soli 14, 152, 229, 682
  double *ius soli* 229
Ivory Coast 226, 235

Jamaica 516
Japan 19, 600
Japanese 183, 184, 490, 523, 598
Jerusalem 327
Jews 19, 21, 23, 37, 104, 183, 190, 193, 197, 202, 224, 235, 240, 322–58, 409, 463, 598
Job reservation 406

Kanakas 61
Kenya 510
Khoi 405
Korea 600
Koreans 19
Kosovo 106
Kurds 112, 277, 463

Labour force participation, *see* economic activity
Labour market
  demand 686
  experience 252
  flexible 17, 23
  fluctuations 370
  needs of 228
  regional 87
  regulated 17, 23
  restructuring of 175
  secondary 135
  segmented 161, 173, 279, 311, 597, 663
  structure 461
Language
  as criterion for ethnicity 409, 414
  area 458
  compulsory courses 460
  fluency 3, 5, 8, 10, 31, 78, 134, 155, 208, 278, 281, 391, 397, 453, 460, 485, 496, 508, 633
  retention 176, 650
  spoken at home 235, 650
  see also English language fluency; German language fluency
Laotians 226, 235
Latin America 21, 329, 592
Law of Return 325–6
Lebanon 49, 329, 453, 456, 488

Lebanese 60, 65, 69, 71, 73, 75, 76, 77, 78, 79, 81, 82, 90, 91, 93, 112, 194, 197, 202, 203, 208, 215, 235, 248, 641, 655
Lesotho 417, 516
Less developed countries 20, 21, 592, 593, 688
Libya 329
Life-cycle processes 214, 425
Logistic regression
  binary 29, 120, 200, 334, 372, 425, 476, 524, 569, 643
  multinomial 30, 124, 299, 335, 372, 385, 480, 531, 573
Luxembourg 283, 465, 516

Macedonia 112
Maghrebins 112, 222, 223, 225, 226, 230, 236, 238, 239, 240, 241, 242, 243, 245, 246, 248, 249, 251, 252, 253, 255, 256, 257, 258, 259, 641, 678
Malaysia 56, 405, 511
Mali 226, 235
Malta 49, 52, 63
Maltese 61, 65, 69, 71, 72, 73, 75, 79, 80, 93, 640
Maoris 19, 61, 72
Marcinelle disaster 145
Marginalisation 91
Marital status 27
Market imperfections 8, 279
Marseille 226
Martinique 227, 593
Mauritius 227
Melanesians 61
Melbourne 87, 89, 90
Mennonites 182, 184
Meritocracy 2, 4, 13, 25, 360
Methodists 554
Mexico 21, 593
Mexicans 22, 523, 595, 598, 599, 600, 601, 602, 606, 607, 612, 613, 614, 616, 618, 619, 622, 623, 624, 626, 627, 632, 633, 634, 641, 655, 687
Micronesians 61
Middle Easterners, *see* Asians, Middle Eastern
Microcensus
  Austrian 33, 111, 136
  German 33, 282, 310, 311
Migrants
  'human capital' 597
  humanitarian 50

Subject Index 711

illegal 106, 225, 229, 326, 363, 417
indentured 406
labour 19, 20, 107–8, 271–7, 283, 295, 310, 407, 454
skilled 50, 80, 95
temporary 50, 277
undocumented 148, 593
Migration 3, 6, 20, 21
labour 19, 362, 679
return 276, 495, 501, 509
selection criteria 50
selective nature 243, 519
Military service 328
Minorities
indigenous 12, 39, 641, 686, 688
involuntary 11, 12, 641, 659–61, 686
visible 2, 11, 13, 187, 197, 203, 216, 222, 228, 371, 453, 497, 508, 509, 541, 686
voluntary 12
Missing values 392, 437, 463, 465, 469
Mizrahim 324, 325, 332, 334, 338, 339, 340, 342, 346, 349, 350, 356
Modernisation 16, 17
Modernisation theory 367–9, 391, 397
Montenegro 112
Moravians 182
Mormons 183
Morocco 146, 225, 234, 274, 324, 329, 362
Moroccans 146, 147, 148, 149, 152, 156, 158–76, 226, 259, 361, 364, 365, 370, 371, 373, 374, 375, 376, 377, 380, 381, 382, 383, 384, 390, 395, 396, 398, 399, 400
Mozambique 416, 417
Multiculturalism 52, 96, 184, 217, 222, 230, 514
Multiculturalism Act 1971
Muslims 23, 96, 153, 194, 231, 243, 145, 327, 329, 343, 354, 410, 414, 420, 516, 521

Namibia 416
Natal 406
Nationality 35, 36, 152, 282, 683
See also citizenship
Native Americans, *see* American Indians
Naturalisation 14, 35, 38, 104, 109, 110, 111, 148, 152, 154, 176, 222, 228, 229, 282, 363, 653, 680–2
Near Easterners 23
Netherlands 13, 15, 18, 19, 20, 23, 24, 30, 33, 37, 38, 49, 359–401, 416, 465, 516, 641, 643, 644, 648, 658, 661, 664, 666, 668, 669, 670, 674, 675, 676, 677, 681, 682, 683, 685, 688
New Zealand 19, 48, 465, 509
New Zealand citizenship 72
New Zealanders 60
Niger 235
Nigeria 106, 511, 516
Nigerians 112
Non-employment
measurement of 468
rates of 470, 653
risks of 478
Non-English speaking backgrounds (NESB) 53, 56, 57, 63
Nordic countries 19, 454, 458
Nordic labour market 454, 456
North Africa 224, 324, 325
North Africans 23, 328, 329, 331, 338, 346, 347, 355, 356, 488
North America 329, 509
North America Act 1867 182
Northern Ireland 12, 15, 18, 19, 20, 21, 22, 23, 37, 551–89, 644, 647, 651, 660, 662, 767, 689
Norway 456, 460
Ny Demokratie party (in Sweden) 675

Oceania 61, 329
Oceanians 20, 63, 67, 71, 72, 73, 76, 78, 80, 84
Occupational attainment 71–5, 79–86, 118–19, 124–9, 168–73, 194–200, 203–13, 246–9, 253–7, 289–91, 299–309, 333–4, 375–6, 421–3, 429–37, 471–5, 480, 522–3, 531–5, 568, 573–81, 607–9, 614–27
Occupational class
Erikson/Goldthorpe (EGP) schema 29, 34, 246, 313, 421, 467, 502, 600
measurement of 99, 137, 246, 313, 348, 372, 413, 421, 544, 600
structure 553
Odds ratios 15
OECD 144
Oil crisis of 1973/4 224, 274, 362, 454, 688
OLS regression 372, 538
One Nation party (in Australia) 675
Openness 13, 15, 16
Optimists 2, 3, 595, 596–7, 639, 655, 686, 688
Origins
in OED diagram 25
social class 26, 31
mixed 35, 38
Orientations 9, 278, 543

Pakistan 329, 488, 510, 516
Pakistanis 22, 23, 112, 227, 508, 510, 516, 519, 521, 522, 523, 525, 530, 533, 534, 535, 538, 541, 687
Palestine 323
Palestinians 12, 20, 21, 23, 322, 326, 327, 328, 329, 331, 334, 339, 340, 341, 342, 343, 345, 346, 349, 350, 353, 354, 355, 356, 405, 646, 647, 661, 674
Parenthood, single 467, 497, 521
Permits
  residence 109, 228
  work 109, 153, 228, 276, 465, 681
Pessimists 2, 3, 595, 639, 655, 686, 688
Petty bourgeoisie 29, 30, 71, 73, 82, 84, 85, 87, 124, 128, 132, 161, 203, 246, 248, 307, 309, 349, 376, 390, 422, 431, 435, 522, 538, 615, 618, 619, 623, 624
Philippines 112, 593, 689
Plural society 647
Point system, *see* Canadian point system
Poland 48, 105, 106, 145, 224, 276, 454, 456, 466, 593
Polish 60, 106, 112, 184, 202, 215, 235, 273, 283, 466, 470, 473, 480, 483, 484, 486, 490, 491, 509, 600, 602, 603, 607, 616, 619, 627, 641, 654
Polynesians 61
Population Registration Act 1950 414
Portugal 274, 416, 465, 516
Portuguese 184, 227, 235, 236, 238, 239, 242, 246, 283, 409, 411
  see also Iberians
Post-industrial society 360, 364
Potato famine 182
Powell, Enoch 512
Predicted probabilities 122–4, 129–32, 296–9, 307–9, 349–51, 428–9, 432–7, 527–30, 535–7, 576–8, 622–7
Predicted incomes 441
Prejudice 10, 13, 55, 163, 175, 686
Presbyterian Church in Ireland 554
Protestants (in Ireland) 22, 23, 37, 516, 552–86
Public and private domains 150, 230
Public sector 14, 135, 153, 257–8, 345, 355, 510, 554, 555, 556
Puerto Rico 593
Puerto Ricans 23, 598, 600, 602, 605, 606, 607, 608, 609, 610, 612, 616, 618, 622, 634, 641, 655

Qualifications
  foreign 26, 93, 167, 208, 213, 278, 460, 622, 645
  full secondary 27
  lower secondary 27
  social minimum 27
  tertiary 27
  vocational 238, 242, 280
  see also education
Quebec 217, 650
Quotas 49, 106, 107, 108, 225, 276

Race 10, 58, 409
Race Relations Acts 1965 and 1976 514
Racial group 37, 404
Racism 13, 110, 150, 151, 225, 231, 597, 671–8, 686, 687, 691
Refugees 9, 19, 20, 49, 50, 61, 104, 105–7, 112, 182, 183, 228, 240, 274, 276, 323, 363, 454, 455, 469, 495–6, 509, 690
Registers, Swedish 34, 453, 462
Regression toward the mean 598
Religion 37, 366, 409, 554
Religious non-identifiers 554
Remittances 7, 9, 543
Reparations 324
Repatriates (from North Africa) 225, 226, 234, 235, 236, 240, 242, 247, 249, 251, 252, 255, 257, 258
Republican Model 222, 223, 225, 230, 232, 258, 259
Reservation wages 9, 531, 543
Residence, length of 78, 127, 486
Response rate 32, 136, 311, 543
Retirement 67
Riots 150, 259, 510
Roma 19, 104, 463
Romania 105, 106, 276
Romanians 112, 235, 283
Rotation principle 107–8, 274
Rotterdam 399
Routine non-manual class 29, 124, 127, 132, 161, 203, 246, 249, 255, 290, 307, 309, 349, 350, 376, 390, 434, 484, 532
Royal Commission for Migrant policies (KCM) 150, 151
Ruanda 148
Russia 183
Russians 184

Salariat 8, 24, 26, 29, 30, 71, 80, 85, 118, 124, 130–1, 160, 161, 194, 203, 247, 249,

253, 255, 289, 290, 299, 307, 308, 349, 350, 376, 385, 390, 411, 431, 461, 480, 532, 535, 538, 573, 581, 616, 619, 622, 643, 648, 649–61, 667, 669, 670, 671, 683, 685, 686, 687, 688
Sami 463
Scots 19, 59
Second generation
  defined 8, 187
  new 595
  size of 20
Segregation
  ethnic 147, 163
  geographical 31, 327, 542, 647
  in schooling 560
  indices 148
  residential 13, 147, 176, 406, 483, 502
Selection
  bias 27, 31, 32, 35, 194, 253, 420, 522, 635
  negative 6, 272, 277, 284, 309, 310, 596, 634, 684, 687
  positive 6, 8, 27, 208, 392, 459, 495, 500, 614, 684
  processes 194, 197, 378, 397–8, 432, 683
Selectivity 683–6
Self-employment 73, 149, 161, 197, 200, 226, 228, 248, 249, 447, 483, 568, 615
Semi- and unskilled class 29, 71, 124, 161, 246, 249, 289, 290, 299, 349, 385, 422, 436, 533, 538, 667
Senegal 226, 235
Sephardim 324, 353
Serbians 61, 112, 114
Sierra Leone 516
Signalling theory 280
Sikhs 11, 183, 231, 521
Singapore 56, 511
Sinti 104
Sioux Indians 182
Skilled manual class 29, 128, 161, 203, 255, 290, 307, 308, 349, 422, 431, 435, 484, 533, 538
Slavs 598
Slavery 12
Slovakia 105
Slovaks 103, 106, 112, 283
Slovenes 103
Small N problem 18
Social capital 174, 281, 542, 679
Social class
  externalities 687, 688
  origins 10, 16, 53, 453, 497, 641, 671

Social closure 2, 360, 367–8, 382, 390, 395, 397
Social democratic policies 15, 16
Social exclusion 213
Social mobility
  absolute and relative 15, 667
  role of 10, 15, 16, 279, 667–9
Social networks 6, 7, 9, 135, 281, 311, 453, 557
Social reproduction 642, 667, 687
Social security benefits 370, 371, 393, 396
Social welfare 57
Sojourner orientation 7, 9
SOPEMI 107, 108
South Africa 12, 15, 18, 20, 21, 22, 23, 26, 33, 37, 403–49, 509, 510, 511, 641, 644, 645, 646, 647, 649, 659, 661, 664, 669, 674, 682, 689
South Africans (in Australia) 60
South Sea islanders 61
Soviet Union (former) 276, 283, 323, 338, 343, 345, 347, 354
Spain 224, 274, 465, 516
Spatial mismatch 557
Spanish 227, 235, 236, 283, 361
  see also Iberians
Spanish Civil War 224
Sri Lanka 227, 488
Standard errors, robust 312
Statistical discrimination, see discrimination
Stigma 223, 597
Stratification
  ethnic 1, 24, 160–1, 197, 272, 274, 278, 309, 322, 330, 446, 640, 641
  process of 640, 642–7
  social 25, 367
Students, international 50, 67, 96, 225, 455, 518
Sub-Saharan Africans 23, 225, 235, 236, 240, 242, 243, 245, 246, 247, 249, 251, 252, 253, 255, 257, 259, 488
  see also Africans
Suriname 362, 648
Surinamese 23, 362, 363, 370, 371, 374, 376, 377, 380, 381, 382, 383, 384, 385, 390, 391, 392, 395, 396, 398, 399, 400, 658
Surveys
  Belgian surveys of foreign nationals 154
  British General Household (GHS) 34, 511, 515, 543
  British Fourth National Survey of Ethnic Minorities 521

Surveys (*cont.*)
  British Labour Force Survey (LFS) 515
  European Social Survey (ESS) 674, 690–1
  French Formation Qualification
    Professionel (FQP) 33, 232, 233
  Israeli labour force 33, 326, 328, 333
  Dutch SPVA 33, 370, 399–400, 664
  Northern Irish Continuous Household
    (CHS) 34, 552, 554, 555, 563, 576, 584
  US Current Population (CPS) 34, 594,
    595, 599, 601, 635–6
Sweden 15, 16, 18, 19, 20, 23, 24, 34, 35, 37,
    451–505, 643, 644, 653, 654, 657, 658, 661,
    665, 666, 668, 669, 670, 672, 674, 675, 676,
    677, 678, 681, 682, 683, 685, 688
Swedish 283
Swiss 112, 283
Switzerland 104, 465
Sydney 87, 89, 90

Taiwan 56, 416, 600
Technical and Further Education colleges
    (TAFE) 61
Thatcher, Margaret 18, 513
Third generation
  attainments of 11, 36, 37, 39, 329, 649,
    650, 651, 655, 658
  defined 187
  measurement of 599
  size of 20
Torres Strait Islanders 45, 58, 60, 61, 91
Training programmes 461
Transkei 407, 411
Transnational communities 9
Transportation (of convicts) 12
Trinidad and Tobago 516
Tunisia 274, 324, 329
Tunisians 226, 234, 259
Tunkers 182
Turkey 19, 49, 146, 274, 276, 329, 362, 453,
    456
Turks 22, 23, 24, 38, 94, 95, 104, 105,
    109–36, 146, 147, 148, 149, 152, 156,
    158–76, 235, 236, 240, 242, 248, 283,
    284, 285, 286, 289, 290, 292, 295, 296,
    299, 304, 308, 309, 311, 361, 364, 365,
    370, 371, 373, 374, 375, 376, 377, 380,
    381, 382, 384, 390, 391, 395, 396, 398,
    399, 400, 463, 641, 646, 647, 655, 658,
    659, 666, 681
TVBC states 404, 407

Uganda 106, 510
UK 18, 19, 20, 23, 37, 56, 59, 228, 553
Ukrainians 183, 184, 190, 202, 215, 650
Underclass 360, 367, 368, 599
Unemployment
  avoidance of 27, 75–9, 120–4, 164–8,
    200–3, 250–3, 292, 343–7, 382–4, 425–9,
    524–31, 569–72, 610, 649–61, 648, 671,
    677–8, 683, 685, 686
  benefits 371
  hyper-cyclical 17, 381, 459, 525, 662
  ILO definition 137, 600
  measurement of 99, 137, 245, 313, 343,
    371, 543, 600
  rates 24, 27, 149, 159–60, 197, 245,
    291–9, 354, 375–6, 411, 461, 553, 561,
    567–8, 609–10, 640–1, 643, 646, 663–7,
    685
United Empire Loyalists 182
Unskilled jobs 461
USA 2, 3, 12, 15, 17, 20, 21, 22, 23, 30, 37,
    46, 94, 181, 189, 208, 228, 283, 465,
    591–638, 640, 641, 643, 644, 645, 647,
    648, 649, 651, 653, 654, 655, 657, 658,
    659, 660, 661, 664, 665, 666, 668, 669,
    670, 674, 676, 677, 681, 683, 685, 687
USSR, *see* Soviet Union
Utrecht 399

Variables
  confounding 31
  mediating 31
Venda 407, 414
Vietnam war 50, 185
Vietnamese 60, 94, 185, 226, 235, 455
Visas, temporary entrance 81
Vouchers, entry 513

Wage differentials 406, 452, 459, 461
Wallonia 147, 148, 150, 151, 154, 156, 164
Walloons 19
Welcome, warmth of 3, 21
Welsh 19, 59
West Indians 184, 593, 598
White Australia policy 49, 60
Whites
  English-speaking (in South Africa) 404,
    406, 409, 411, 414, 415, 417, 418, 422,
    423, 424, 430, 431, 432, 434, 435, 441,
    444, 446, 646
  Non-Hispanic 595
Work experience 6

Xenophobia 13, 110, 222, 224, 671, 672, 674
Xhosa 23, 410

Yemen 323, 324
Yeshiva 333, 342, 354
Yugoslavia, former 19, 49, 50, 274, 277, 284, 454, 456, 457, 466
Yugoslavs (Ex) 23, 104, 105, 110, 112, 114, 115, 116, 117, 118, 119, 122, 123, 126, 127, 128, 129, 130, 133, 134, 135, 136, 235, 284, 286, 287, 290, 296, 299, 304, 308, 454, 456, 459, 461, 466, 469, 470, 472, 473, 474, 478, 480, 483, 484, 486, 490, 491, 494, 495, 496, 499, 501, 641, 654, 686

Zimbabwe 415, 516
Zionism 323, 327
Zulus 23, 410